ALSO BY ALAN WALKER

A Study in Musical Analysis
An Anatomy of Musical Criticism
Franz Liszt: Volume One, The Virtuoso Years, 1811–1847

EDITOR OF

Frédéric Chopin:
Profiles of the Man and the Musician

Franz Liszt:
The Man and His Music

Robert Schumann:
The Man and His Music

IN THE GREAT COMPOSER SERIES

Franz Liszt

Robert Schumann

Franz Liszt

THE WEIMAR YEARS

1848–1861

Alan Walker

Franz Liszt

VOLUME TWO

The Weimar Years

1848 · 1861

Cornell University Press

Ithaca, New York

First published 1993, Cornell Paperbacks, by Cornell University Press.

Published by arrangement with Alfred A. Knopf, Inc.

Library of Congress Cataloging-in-Publication Data
(Revised for vol. 2)

Walker, Alan, 1930–
    Franz Liszt.

    Includes index.
    Bibliography: v. 1, pp. 449–462.
    Contents: v. 1. The virtuoso years, 1811–1847—v. 2. The Weimar years, 1848–1861.
    1. Liszt, Franz, 1811–1886.   2. Composers—Biography.
    I. Title.
    ML410.L7W27   1987   780'.92'4 [B]   87-24459
    ISBN 0-8014-9721-3

Printed in the United States of America
Musical examples drawn by Paul Courtenay

To Lisztians across the world,
wherever they may be, these volumes
are affectionately dedicated.

Contents

PROLOGUE

BOOK ONE: NEW BEGINNINGS, 1847–1848

The character of Carolyne Iwanowska ⌐ her childhood in the Ukraine ⌐ her relationship with her mother and father ⌐ her marriage to Prince Nicholas von Sayn-Wittgenstein ⌐ the death of her father, Peter Iwanowsky ⌐ Carolyne inherits a fortune ⌐ the château Woronince ⌐ Liszt meets Carolyne in Kiev, February 1847 ⌐ he visits her in Woronince ⌐ he is introduced to her daughter, Princess Marie, and her husband, Prince Nicholas.

Chronicles of an adventure ⌐ a winter journey ⌐ a sojourn in St. Petersburg ⌐ she hears the music of Berlioz ⌐ growing love for Liszt ⌐ Carolyne and Liszt meet again in Odessa, July 1847 ⌐ Liszt gives his "farewell" concert in Elisabetgrad, September 1847 ⌐ the lovers of Woronince ⌐ *Glanes de Woronince* ⌐ Liszt sets out for Weimar ⌐ Carolyne leaves for Kiev to sell her estates ⌐ farewell to the Ukraine ⌐ Liszt and Carolyne are re-united at Kryzanowicz.

The seeds of the '48 revolutions ⌐ the awakening of Hungarian nationalism ⌐ Széchenyi, Kossuth, and Batthyány ⌐ the Hungarian war of independence ⌐ the evacuation of Pest ⌐ the victories of General Artúr Görgey ⌐ the Hungarian Declaration of Independence ⌐ Pest re-taken ⌐ the Russian intervention, June 1849 ⌐ the surrender at Világos ⌐ Batthyány executed ⌐ Kossuth goes into exile ⌐ Liszt and Carolyne travel to Vienna and Eisenstadt ⌐ a visit to Father Albach ⌐ Liszt's attitude to the war of independence ⌐ Heine's poem against Liszt, *Im Oktober 1849* ⌐ *Funérailles, October 1849* ⌐ Liszt and Carolyne take up residence in Weimar.

BOOK FOUR: GATHERING STORMS, 1857–1861

Illustrations

Acknowledgements

Six years have elapsed since the publication of the first volume of my ongoing life of Liszt. That is a rather long time, but the explanation is simple enough. As was the case with the earlier book, it soon became apparent that I would have to travel to many different parts of the world—Germany, Hungary, Italy, America, and England—in pursuit of original Liszt documents whenever I felt that their inspection was vital to the integrity of my narrative. Such journeys cannot be accomplished in haste. The days have long since gone when it was possible to write the story of Liszt's life from the comfort of one's own fireside. After all, it took Liszt nearly seventy-five years to live out the details of his extraordinary life. Would it not be presumptuous of any biographer to despatch them in one or two? To write a life requires a life. And now it is my pleasant duty to extend my thanks to all those friends and colleagues who helped me along the way.

Among the highlights of my travels were several trips to Rome, where I worked in the Vatican Library and the Vicariato di Roma. One such visit will linger long in the memory. It was the summer of 1985, and my work had come to a temporary halt. One afternoon, and quite without warning, I came across the long-lost file of documents which tell the story of Carolyne's twelve-year struggle for an annulment of her marriage to Prince Nicholas von Sayn-Wittgenstein and of her thwarted attempt to marry Liszt. Every scholar of the topic will appreciate the importance of this find. I myself had been forced to conclude, in the Prologue to Volume One, that "the Vatican remains innocent of all knowledge" of such a file. I had no idea that less than two years after I had penned that despairing phrase the documents would fall into my hands—almost by chance. Since it seems important to me to draw attention to them without delay, a selection has been included in Appendix II, and the story they tell has been woven into the fabric of the final chapters of the present volume. I am now preparing a separate book dealing with Liszt and the Vatican documents. Meanwhile, it is a particular pleasure to acknowledge the help I received from Monsignor John Hanly, former head of the Irish College in Rome, and from Father John Hayes, the parish priest of the church of San Carlo al Corso, where Liszt and Carolyne had planned to marry on October 22, 1861, his fiftieth birthday. Both priests took an active interest in my biographical work, and Monsignor Hanly helped to open many doors in the complex

xv

corridors of the Vatican that might otherwise have remained closed to me—as they had remained closed to other scholars for a century or more. The difficult task of rendering the original Latin and Italian texts (filled as they are with the intricacies of canonical phraseology) into their proper English equivalents was undertaken by my colleague Professor Gabriele Erasmi, of McMaster University, to whom I also extend my grateful thanks.

In Weimar it was my privilege to become acquainted with a number of people who went out of their way to help me with my work. In particular, Dr. Herbert von Hintzenstern, a noted authority on Thuringian history, brought me to a fuller understanding of the central place that Liszt occupied in the artistic life of Thuringia during the years 1848–61. For it was clearly Liszt's intention not only to regenerate the musical life of Weimar but to form cultural bonds among the satellite communities surrounding the royal city—including Erfurt, Jena, Eisenach, the Wartburg, Tiefurt, and Denstedt. I visited these places not once but several times in an attempt to imbibe the atmosphere that Liszt himself had helped to create. It was at such moments as these that I came to appreciate the "geography of biography," the absolutely irreplaceable experience of having visited the various locations that one is called upon to write about. Without it biography is still possible, but there will almost certainly be times when the narrative will lack verisimilitude. I also want to thank Monsignor Karl Schneider, bishop of the Catholic parish in Weimar, for making his church records available to me and for giving me some useful information about the small Catholic community in Weimar during Liszt's tenure there. Acknowledgements are likewise extended to Arnulf Brieger, the Weimar architect in charge of the restoration of Ettersburg Castle, one of the summer homes of the grand dukes of Weimar, who also accompanied me on extensive tours of Belvedere Castle, of the historic Wartburg castle, and of the royal castle in Weimar itself. It was Herr Brieger who arranged for me to make a thorough inspection of the Altenburg, the home to which Liszt was so deeply attached during his Weimar years, and whose rooms have been occupied by a number of East German families since the end of World War Two. There is talk of one day turning the old building into a shrine to Liszt's memory. Meantime, the Liszt tradition is kept alive by Dr. Jutta Hecker (her book *Die Altenburg: Geschichte eines Hauses* draws attention to the many historical figures who visited him there), who, with her sister Irmegard, occupies an apartment on the ground floor. On all my visits to the Altenburg the Hecker sisters received me with courtesy and kindness, and they invariably added to my pleasure by offering their hospitality in the very room in which Liszt gave piano lessons to his pupils—Bülow, Tausig, Klindworth, and others.

To my many friends in Budapest I can say only that this book is almost as much theirs as it is mine. On all my visits to the city of the Magyars they offered me new material and an inexhaustible supply of thought-provoking ideas. Dr.

Dezső Legány spent countless hours conducting me to places in Hungary associated with Liszt; and from the abundance of his knowledge he stimulated afresh those areas of my work that still lay moribund. But it is to Mária Eckhardt, the director of the recently formed Liszt Memorial Museum and Research Centre in Budapest, that this particular volume is most indebted. She read through the entire manuscript in the spring of 1988 and made a number of practical suggestions that I was happy to accept. The assistance I received from both scholars was impeccable.

A book of these dimensions could not have been written at all without the constant support of research libraries across the world. I owe a great debt to the staffs of the Goethe- und Schiller-Archiv in Weimar, the National Széchényi Library in Budapest, the Vatican Library in Rome, the British Library in London, the Library of Congress in Washington, D.C., the Bibliothèque Nationale and the Archives Nationales in Paris, the Municipal Library in Versailles, the Pierpont Morgan Library in New York, and not least to my friends in the Inter-Library Loan Services of McMaster University in Canada, who for years have met my most extravagant demands for esoteric material from depositories across the North American continent with efficiency and despatch. Their unruffled diplomacy is all the more impressive since they know that there are yet more demands to come. Among the many individuals who assisted me with special problems were Anne Troisier de Diaz, Oksana Sokolyk, Audrey Ellison, László Jámbor, Roman Sawycky, Professor Peter Potichnyj, and Professor Gerhart Teuscher. I must also thank Professor Elyse Mach and Roch Serra, secretary general of the Liszt Society of France, who very kindly placed at my disposal some hitherto unpublished Liszt correspondence.

My warmest words of praise must be reserved for my faithful assistant Pauline Pocknell, who has been the recipient of a dazzling array of inquiries across the years, has dealt with a great deal of correspondence on my behalf, and has often burned the midnight oil while preparing synopses, transcriptions, translations, and commentary on foreign-language material of all kinds related to my work. I admire the way she swims so elegantly through the boiling ocean of Liszt research while I am merely buffeted by its waves. Her support has been exemplary, and it is a pleasure to acknowledge it here.

Budapest, Spring 1988   ALAN WALKER

The Wittgenstein-Iwanowsky
Family Tree

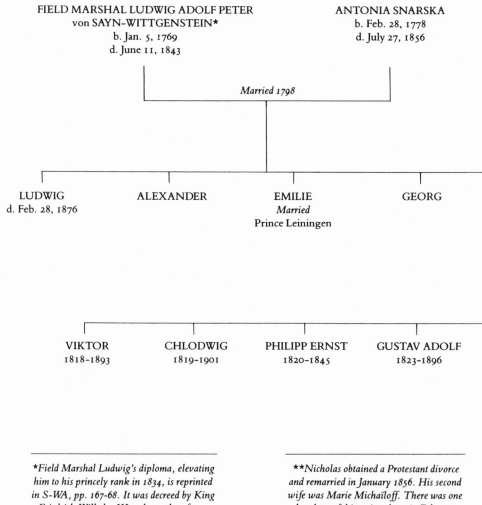

FIELD MARSHAL LUDWIG ADOLF PETER
von SAYN-WITTGENSTEIN★
b. Jan. 5, 1769
d. June 11, 1843

ANTONIA SNARSKA
b. Feb. 28, 1778
d. July 27, 1856

Married 1798

LUDWIG
d. Feb. 28, 1876

ALEXANDER

EMILIE
Married
Prince Leiningen

GEORG

VIKTOR
1818-1893

CHLODWIG
1819-1901

PHILIPP ERNST
1820-1845

GUSTAV ADOLF
1823-1896

★*Field Marshal Ludwig's diploma, elevating him to his princely rank in 1834, is reprinted in S-WA, pp. 167-68. It was decreed by King Friedrich Wilhelm III and was therefore a German, not a Russian title.*

★★*Nicholas obtained a Protestant divorce and remarried in January 1856. His second wife was Marie Michaïloff. There was one daughter of this union, born in February 1857 and baptized Marie.*

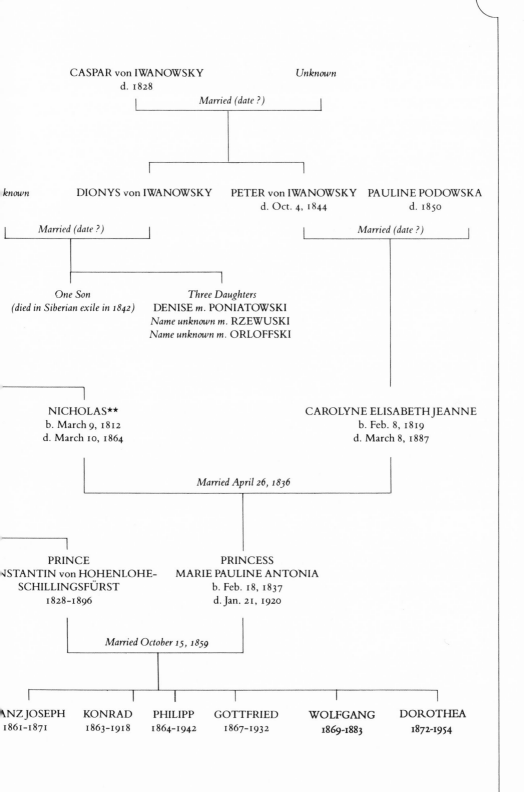

CASPAR von IWANOWSKY
d. 1828

Unknown

Married (date ?)

known

DIONYS von IWANOWSKY

PETER von IWANOWSKY
d. Oct. 4, 1844

PAULINE PODOWSKA
d. 1850

Married (date ?)

Married (date ?)

One Son
(died in Siberian exile in 1842)

Three Daughters
DENISE *m.* PONIATOWSKI
Name unknown m. RZEWUSKI
Name unknown m. ORLOFFSKI

NICHOLAS★★
b. March 9, 1812
d. March 10, 1864

CAROLYNE ELISABETH JEANNE
b. Feb. 8, 1819
d. March 8, 1887

Married April 26, 1836

PRINCE
NSTANTIN von HOHENLOHE-
SCHILLINGSFÜRST
1828-1896

PRINCESS
MARIE PAULINE ANTONIA
b. Feb. 18, 1837
d. Jan. 21, 1920

Married October 15, 1859

ANZ JOSEPH
1861-1871

KONRAD
1863-1918

PHILIPP
1864-1942

GOTTFRIED
1867-1932

WOLFGANG
1869-1883

DOROTHEA
1872-1954

Prologue

A Giant in Lilliput

The time has come for me (Nel mezzo del cammin di nostra vita—thirty-five years old!) to break out of my virtuoso's chrysalis and allow my thought unfettered flight.

LISZT TO CARL ALEXANDER[1]

I

The reader who has followed the story of Liszt's life this far will recall that the narrative of Volume One was broken off at the point where he had achieved his greatest celebrity as a pianist. No other virtuoso in history had travelled so far, had given so many concerts in so brief a period, had enjoyed such fame with the general public. The last and longest of his world tours had ended in September 1847, in Ukraine, in the city of Elisabetgrad, where his long-cherished dream of giving up the life of a wandering minstrel was finally realized. Not yet thirty-six years old, the reforms that he had already introduced into piano playing were so fundamental that had he died at that moment, the title of "the first modern pianist" could not have been withheld from him.[2] He had become, in the memorable phrase of Saint-Saëns, "the incontestable incarnation of the modern piano."[3]

And then Liszt simply walked away from it all. There are few more dramatic contrasts in his long and colourful life than his move to Weimar in February 1848. The decision to abandon his epoch-making career as a pianist in order to pick up a Kapellmeister's baton in one of the smaller German principalities is

---

1. LBLCA, p. 8. Dante's famous line from *The Divine Comedy,* "Midway through the path of our life," has come to mean something for Liszt. He is nearly thirty-five years old and will soon have reached the exact halfway point in life's biblically allotted span of three-score years and ten.
2. For an account of those reforms, see the chapter "Liszt and the Keyboard" in Volume One of the present work.
3. *Portraits et souvenirs* (Paris, 1900), p. 19.

one that the outside world has always found baffling. Yet the signs were already there, as a backward glance at his years of transcendental execution will show.

During his *Glanzzeit* Liszt had lived like a prince. A river of gold had poured in, but a river of gold had also poured out. Nothing better illustrates the lavish life-style in which he indulged than the brief period he spent in Vienna in April 1846. He occupied a luxurious suite of rooms at the Hotel zur Frankfurt and gave a banquet every night in honour of his many friends. Since he declined all invitations to give public concerts,[4] he quickly ran out of ready cash. At the end of his two-week stay he had run up a considerable bill—more than a thousand gulden—and he lacked the means to pay it. Just before he departed, Liszt summoned the landlord, explained his predicament, and asked in the politest way possible if he might postpone payment of the bill. "I am about to set out for Prague," Liszt told him, "where I shall give several concerts. In six weeks' time I will be back in Vienna. Will you give me credit until then?" In consternation the landlord had to explain to his famous guest that he could not afford to lend him such a large sum and that he required immediate payment to keep his business going—whereupon Liszt contacted one of his powerful friends in Vienna, who had the money delivered to the hotel, in cash. Liszt then lined up the entire serving staff in the lobby, paid the landlord in full view of the public, and distributed a further two hundred gulden among the servants as a sign of appreciation for their services to him and his guests.[5] The gesture was flamboyant, but it made a point. It was Liszt's way of demonstrating to the world that money was of little consequence to him; as far as his debts were concerned, his word was his bond.

Such fame carried with it special problems. If there were piano factories in the towns and cities through which Liszt happened to pass, he was put under pressure to sponsor local instruments. His legendary fingers increased the value of any piano they touched. That naturally gave rise to petty squabbles between rival firms. In 1843 a typical dispute broke out in Breslau, when a "Friend of Justice" complained to the local newspaper that Liszt had shown preference for a piano from C.F. Alexander, owner of the Ignatz Leicht piano factory.[6] Liszt felt constrained to reply, and charged Gaëtano Belloni (whom he had appointed as his secretary two years earlier) with the delicate task of issuing a denial.

> I have been commissioned by Herr Hof-Kapellmeister Dr. F.
> Liszt to observe that he used only Bessalie instruments for his first two
> concerts. Afterwards, and out of friendship for the makers, in addition
> to the Bessalie instruments, he also played on instruments from the

---

4. In March 1846, Liszt had given numerous concerts in Vienna. The visit in question occurred shortly afterwards and was of a semi-private nature (GAWZ, pp. 313–14).
5. GAWZ, pp. 313–14.
6. *Privilegierte Schlesische Zeitung,* February 6, 1843, p. 221.

Alexander and Berndt factories (which latter also produces excellent pianos).

For the rest, Dr. Liszt does not intend to consider either the number or the choice of pieces he played on the Alexander piano. It was pure chance if Dr. Liszt executed a greater number of works on this instrument.

GAËTANO BELLONI
Secretary to Herr Dr. F. Liszt[7]

This protestation has a peculiarly modern ring to it. Sponsorship, Liszt seems to say, means everything when it is bestowed, nothing when it is sought. For the rest, if it had ever become known that Liszt had allowed his name to be used for commercial gain, especially in the field of piano manufacture, he would have been buried beneath the avalanche of business propositions that would surely have fallen on him. The only piano that Liszt ever "sponsored" during his years as a touring virtuoso was his beloved seven-octave Erard grand. He genuinely believed it to be a superior instrument, and he was bound to the Erard family by ties of loyalty and affection that went back to his boyhood.[8] The endless round of speeches, banquets, and civic honours that formed the shining backdrop to his early career, and which have been catalogued in detail in Volume One of this study, frequently led to presentation ceremonies that burdened him with scrolls, medals, batons, silverware, goblets, jade, and fine furniture. The most magnificent gift he ever received, of course, was the bejewelled sword of honour presented to him on behalf of the Hungarian nation in January 1840; the most bizarre was a pair of performing bears sent to him by Tsar Nicholas I during Liszt's visit to St. Petersburg in 1843. Had he taken everything on the road with him, Liszt and his entourage would have required a fleet of caravans to move this exotic collection back and forth across Europe. Most of it was despatched to Paris for safekeeping in the home of his mother, Anna Liszt. The performing bears, it seems, were left behind in Russia.

II

As for the number of charitable causes to which Liszt had lent his name and his fame during his *Glanzzeit,* that would make a separate study. His contributions to the victims of the Danube floods (1838) and to the erection of the Beethoven monument (1839–45) are well known, and they are rightly mentioned in all the standard biographies of Liszt. There were dozens of other

---

7. *Privilegierte Schlesische Zeitung,* February 9, p. 241.
8. See Volume One, pp. 92–93 and 315–16.

humanitarian gestures, however, many of which remain unchronicled. He had, for example, given concerts in behalf of the Prague General Hospital (1840), the Leipzig Musicians Pension Fund (1840), the Cologne Cathedral Building Fund (1842), the victims of the Great Fire of Hamburg (1842), the Dortmund Gymnasium Fund (1842), the Moscow Orphans Fund (1843), the Lisbon Orphans Fund (1845), and the Nagyenyed (Aiud) Kindergarten Fund (1846). His donations to private persons in distress are too numerous to mention. There is something deeply affecting about Liszt's desire to share the material benefits of his genius with the underprivileged. No other artist in history had ever given so generously of time and money. Art, for Liszt, was a moral force which functions best when it serves a moral end. He himself put it well when he coined the phrase *Génie oblige!*

The worst aspect of Liszt's *Glanzzeit* was the sheer physical fatigue that it imposed on him. By 1847 his career had reached exponential growth. Every public appearance led to demands for a dozen others. The pressures on his time and his purse were almost insupportable. He knew that the moment had come for him to get out or be destroyed in the process. There was also a deeper artistic imperative at work within him: he wanted more leisure to compose. A number of large-scale orchestral works were already germinating in his mind, but his itinerant life-style prevented him from working them out.

That is why Liszt now turned his gaze towards Weimar, the town that had appointed him its honorary Kapellmeister in 1842. The thought of taking up permanent residence there held many attractions for him. Weimar was one of the cultural centres of Germany; already the city of Goethe and Schiller could boast of a century's unbroken association with the arts. It had a theatre and an orchestra, its own poets and painters, and an academy of scientists. The nearby city of Jena possessed a university. Most important of all, Weimar enjoyed the benign patronage of Grand Duchess Maria Pawlowna, the sister of Tsar Nicholas I of Russia. This triple alliance of court, theatre, and academia was difficult to resist. Moreover, Weimar was small and appeared to offer a quiet harbour from the storms of the outside world. In 1843, two years after Liszt had first glimpsed it, Weimar consisted of a mere 11,823 citizens and 1,011 dwellings; sixteen years later, that number had increased to only 13,154 citizens and 1,055 dwellings. And there were other advantages. The arrival in the city of its first railway line in 1848 gave Liszt ready access to all parts of Germany. He could travel to Erfurt in half an hour, to Leipzig and back in half a day, to Berlin and back in a day. Trips to Düsseldorf and Cologne were simple matters of an overnight stop. What this meant to Liszt in pursuit of his artistic goals cannot be overestimated.

There is evidence that Liszt saw in his Weimar appointment a historic opportunity not merely to revive the music of a flagging court but to regenerate the cultural life of the old domains of Thuringia itself. The towns of Jena, Erfurt, Eisenach, and Sondershausen all fell under the rule of the grand dukes of Weimar. Liszt got to know these places well, made friends with the local musicians there, and through the sheer force of his personality persuaded them to look beyond their narrow confines and unite for the common good. When he put on his great Wagner and Berlioz festivals in the mid-1850s, he summoned up the whole of Thuringia's musical resources to help him and imported players and singers from across the region. And when the "satellite towns" put on special events, Liszt reciprocated by answering all appeals for help.

Nothing better illustrates Liszt's attachment to his overview of Thuringia than his interest in the Wartburg. This centuries-old castle, which stands on a hill overlooking Eisenach, dominates the Thuringian countryside for miles around. Liszt made many a pilgrimage to this historic shrine, within whose walls St. Elisabeth had lived and Martin Luther had been offered sanctuary and had translated the Bible. The Wartburg symbolized Old Germany for Liszt. He knew that if Thuringian culture was to be regenerated, the crumbling edifice of the Wartburg itself must be restored, however long it took and however much it cost. He was delighted when the process of restoration was finally begun in the mid-1840s by the hereditary grand duke, Carl Alexander.[9] When Liszt proposed (in 1850) opening the Great Hall of the Wartburg for musical festivities, he may well have been inspired by Wagner's *Tannhäuser,* whose second act unfolds there; but when he went on to suggest the idea of reviving the medieval singing-contests that used to be held in the Great Hall, he anticipated by seventeen years the plot of *Die Meistersinger.*

Closely related to these historical considerations was Liszt's interest in the old tradition of organ playing in the nearby towns and villages, which went back to Bach. Liszt often visited the small churches in Tiefurt, Denstedt, and Buttelstedt, in the company of such local organists as Gottschalg and Winterberger, and he made it his business to study the instrument and compose for it. It is unthinkable that Liszt would have written his two organ masterpieces "Ad nos, ad salutarem undam" and the Prelude and Fugue on "B-A-C-H" in any other environment than the one now offered him in Weimar. Most telling of all was his determination to revive and promote the musical "sons" of Thuringia, Bach and Handel, both of whom had been born in the old kingdom

---

9. As early as May 1846 Liszt had tried to secure an article from Franz von Schober (his old Viennese acquaintance, who had meanwhile become a political attaché in Weimar), for publication in the French press, which would rouse the conscience of Europe and call on all civilized peoples to help in the restoration of the Wartburg. Liszt suggested that the article should fall into three parts: "I: a short account, historical and legendary, of the Wartburg; II: how it has been allowed to fall into ruins; and III: how it is to be restored." (LLB, vol. 1, p. 63) Schober never wrote this article. A few years later Liszt incorporated some of these ideas into his own brochure *De la fondation-Goethe à Weimar* (1850).

more than a century and a half earlier. Liszt's performance of Handel's *Judas Maccabeus* on May 20, 1859, to commemorate the one hundredth anniversary of Handel's death, may well have been the first in that part of Germany.

III

Had Liszt known of the trials and tribulations that lay in wait for him in Weimar, the chances are that he would have given the place a very wide berth. This may come as a surprise to those whose view of Liszt is formed by popular legend. His Weimar years, after all, are commonly supposed to have crowned a remarkable life with glory. This was the period during which he produced his major orchestral works, embarked on a career as an orchestral conductor, and began his famous masterclasses in piano playing. There is a darker side to the picture, however, and we come to understand it only when we scrutinize his life on a day-to-day basis. Liszt was too great a personality for such a small place as Weimar; he aroused envy and made enemies. The petty squabbles and malicious intrigue to which he was subjected, almost from the first day of his arrival in "the Athens of the North," gradually wore him down and eventually forced his resignation. They produced the sorry spectacle of a giant in Lilliput. The story has never been told in the depth it deserves, and it may well change our perspective on the way in which we view his life as a whole.

Liszt soon discovered that one of the greatest burdens he would be called upon to bear in Weimar was the very thing that made the city unique: its glorious past. By 1848, the year in which he took up his full-time duties, Weimar had become a museum which existed mainly to preserve history. The spirits of Goethe and Schiller still haunted the city. Their family descendants, together with those of Herder and Wieland, were now part of Weimar's treasured establishment. Many disciples of the immortals had also put down roots there. They regarded it as a sacred duty to preserve old memories, to cherish old values, to keep classical Weimar alive. They were proud to be known as "Old Weimar." Typically, they lived in the old part of the city.

"New Weimar" was inseparably identified with the Altenburg, Liszt's home for twelve of the thirteen years he lived in the city. The hill on which it stood, just beyond the city limits, gave it a symbolic importance: it dominated the town, and Old Weimar must often have felt itself to be under siege. During the 1850s Bülow, Cornelius, Raff, Klindworth, Reubke, Draeseke, Bronsart, Winterberger, Pohl, and others all converged on the Altenburg simply to be near Liszt. They rightly guessed that this was where the future lay. Some of them were among the avant-gardists of the day, and under Liszt's leadership they eventually became known as the New German School. They advanced the language of harmony, they developed new orchestral sounds, they threw out

The grand ducal castle and park in Weimar, an etching by C. Müller (c. 1810).

traditional forms and invented new ones. They were mainly young, argumenta-
tive, boisterous, and bent on change. They even formed a club called the
Neu-Weimar-Verein, which held regular meetings, circulated its own journal
(*Die Laterne*), and issued occasional manifestos. All this made them dangerous.
Old Weimar resented them and wanted them to go away.

The River Ilm, which separated Old Weimar from New Weimar, was a
symbolic dividing-line that Liszt had to cross every day on his way to and from
the theatre. There he fought his major artistic battles—against the ignorance
and prejudice of a hidebound management, against the slothfulness of performers, and against the philistine taste of the general public. That the division
between Old and New Weimar was well understood at the time is indicated
by Hoffmann von Fallersleben, the court poet, in his poem "Der Altenburg!,"
which contains the pun: "Es ist nicht eine Burg der Alten!" And he went on:
"Here one does not ask what one has . . . but rather what one *is* and what one
does."[10] Such language was not calculated to win friends and influence people;
the implication was that Old Weimar had long since ceased to *do* or *be*
anything. Liszt himself did not help matters by his withering references to "the
posthumous party."[11] Old Weimar daily smarted beneath such insults, and it
nourished a secret desire to see Liszt toppled. We do well to remember that
the so-called War of the Romantics, which is traditionally depicted as taking
place on a European stage between "progressive" Weimar on the one hand and
"conservative" Leipzig and Vienna on the other, began in Weimar itself among

10. HML, vol. 6, p. 76.
11. LLB, vol. 3, p. 136.

the reactionaries and revolutionaries who happened to live on Liszt's own doorstep.

I V

In all these activities, Liszt was sustained by his mistress and companion, Princess Carolyne von Sayn-Wittgenstein, the woman who, for better or worse, was to dominate his life until they were parted by death. Carolyne, it will be recalled, was already separated from her husband, Prince Nicholas; and within weeks of meeting Liszt during his last tour of Ukraine, in 1847, she had thrown in her lot with his. She joined him in Weimar, both of them believing that her annulment was imminent and that she would be free to marry Liszt. Although they were to live together in Weimar for twelve years, the marriage never took place, in part because of the intransigence of high-ranking clerics, and in part because of the opposition of the Wittgenstein and Hohenlohe families—to both of whose princely households Carolyne was connected, and whose members had a vested interest in keeping her single. The story is long and complex, and forms a substantial part of the narrative that follows. Documents recently brought to light in the Vatican allow us to tell this particular tale in more detail than has hitherto been possible in biographies of Liszt.

As practicing Roman Catholics in what was an overwhelmingly Protestant city, both Liszt and Carolyne were subjected to petty harassment, made all the worse by the fact that they chose to live together as man and wife. The Protestant population was led by a particularly aggressive pastor named Dr. Wilhelm Dittenberger, the *Hofprediger* to the grand dukes of Weimar. Dittenberger soon took a dislike to Liszt and Carolyne and frowned on their *ménage à deux* at the Altenburg. When asked if he would like to be introduced to Carolyne, he declined on the grounds that he did not wish to meet someone against whom he would have to take action if she were a member of his own congregation.[12] What the good shepherd did today, his flock did tomorrow.

---

12. KLF, p. 61. There were good reasons for the mutual dislike that sprang up between Liszt and Pastor Dittenberger. It was well known in Weimar that this Lutheran cleric had made repeated attempts to convert both Liszt and Carolyne to Protestantism, and had been energetically rebuffed (GLW, p. 56). Nor was it particularly easy for Liszt to avoid Dittenberger in the pursuit of his daily affairs in Weimar, for this powerful preacher was also the general superintendant of the Herderhaus, and in this secular capacity he was much in evidence at official functions. In 1861 (the year in which Liszt left Weimar) Dittenberger suffered an apoplectic stroke which rendered him almost completely blind. He died on his sixty-fifth birthday, in 1871.

Incidentally, the number of Catholics in Weimar was always small. In 1819 the total population of those living in Weimar and its environs was about one hundred and thirty. By 1853 this number had risen to about four hundred. Before the present Catholic church was built, towards the end of the nineteenth century, the Catholic community used to worship in a small building on Marienstrasse, which Liszt once described as "a grimy hangar" (LLB, vol. 6, p. 35). Nevertheless, this humble chapel

Many of the indignities to which Carolyne in particular was subjected by the townspeople of Weimar may be laid at Dittenberger's door. Meanwhile, we do well to remember that in the Weimar of the 1850s adultery was punishable by imprisonment. Liszt's close connections with the court ensured that in his case the law was never enforced. Nonetheless, the fact that others who chose to live together without benefit of clergy were sent to jail created a smouldering resentment in the tiny community which was always ready to burst into flame at the slightest provocation.[13] Nor was it forgotten that Goethe had lived with Christiane Vulpius for eighteen years, and had had five children by her, before he had regularized their union in the Hofkirche itself. He was fifty-six, a state minister, and a favourite of the reigning grand duke, Carl August. Such things created a double standard. But that had happened nearly fifty years before, and the passing of time had made it all seem respectable. Yet no one should suppose that the Weimar of 1850 was any less sanctimonious than the Weimar of 1806.

Paradoxically, it was in Protestant Weimar that Liszt experienced a renewal of his Catholic faith. Perhaps it was the very loneliness of his religious position there that daily reminded him of his different background and drove him back to the sources of his faith, won through his childhood prayers in the churches of Raiding, Vienna, and Paris and nourished by his youthful encounters with some remarkable clerics, including his confessor Abbé Bardin and Abbé Félicité de Lamennais. During the 1840s Liszt had become worldly-wise and had stopped going to confession. It was Princess Carolyne who, after 1847, encouraged his return to orthodox Catholicism and a re-discovery of that faith which, in any case, had never been entirely extinguished within him during his prodigal years. Together they set up a prie-dieu and a small altar-piece in the Altenburg, before which they would kneel down, say their daily prayers, and ask God's blessing on their union. Whenever Liszt left Weimar on his more extended journeys, Carolyne spent much time at the prie-dieu invoking heaven's protection and a safe return for the man she loved. Joachim Raff, one of his closest colleagues during the Weimar period, tells us that the religious streak in Liszt was so pronounced that whenever he was overtaken by moods of contrition he would prostrate himself on the flagstones before a *Muttergottesbild* and remain like that for extended periods, oblivious to whatever was going on around him. Anton Rubinstein observed something similar when he accom-

---

was important to both Liszt and Carolyne, but particularly to Carolyne. It was there, for instance, that her daughter Princess Marie was confirmed in 1853, and it was there, too, that Marie was married in 1859. Three priests served the congregation during these years: Johann Gerling (1819–31), Caspar Diesing (1831–52), and Anton Hohmann (1852–86). Hohmann was a good friend to both Liszt and Carolyne. He officiated at the wedding of Princess Marie, and he was also one of Liszt's sponsors when the marriage formalities for Liszt's own wedding to Carolyne started to get under way in Rome. See Appendix II, doc. 3.

13. See pp. 82–83.

panied Liszt from Rotterdam to Cologne in the summer of 1854. They were
walking through Cologne Cathedral, Rubinstein tells us, when Liszt suddenly
disappeared into the shadows. It was already dusk, and Rubinstein had to search
for a considerable time through the many corners of the darkened building
before he finally came upon Liszt kneeling before a prie-dieu. Liszt was so
engrossed in meditation that Rubinstein felt unable to disturb him and quietly
withdrew.[14]

v

When Liszt settled in Weimar, he took it to be his primary mission to continue
to help musical talent, wherever he found it. It is strange, therefore, that so
many of the prominent musicians he supported turned against him. The pattern
of his early years, in which he was abandoned by those whom he supported—
including Mendelssohn, Hiller, and Chopin—has already been touched on in
Volume One, and the phenomenon is about to repeat itself. In venturing to
explain this paradox we do well to remind ourselves of one of Liszt's most
characteristic traits. He had the rare ability to distinguish between genius and
the individual personality in whom that genius happened to reside. The respect
that Liszt felt for genius was totally disinterested, and it carried with it a
corollary: any artist so endowed was duty-bound to express it—that is to say,
he was in the grip of natural forces he might not understand but had no
alternative but to obey. And where such expression was obstructed, it was
nothing less than a cultural evil which Liszt charged himself with the task of
removing—through financial support, through words of encouragement,
through the plotting of friendly stratagems via third parties. Not to do so was
to lend tacit approval to that evil. In thought and word and deed Liszt's chief
concern was that artists should be helped, not for their own sake but for the
sake of Art. His correspondence proves it. He once referred to the artist as "the
Bearer of the Beautiful." The artist, for Liszt, was a sacred vessel through which
the Beautiful passed. An analogy with the priesthood is not far-fetched, since
he himself made it on several occasions.[15]

All this proved to be his undoing, for he naively supposed that his contemporaries shared his disinterested view of Art. He discovered too late that his gods
had feet of clay. Most of the great musicians whom Liszt observed struggling
for recognition—Chopin, Schumann, Wagner, and Berlioz among them—
took the thoroughly mundane view that they had to vie with everyone else
for a place in the sun. At various times and in various places Liszt helped them

14. MMML, pp. 144–45.
15. See p. 390.

all, thinking only to improve the general condition of music. But even as he did so, the others, lacking his detachment, saw him helping a rival, and this was never truer than when he diverted financial and material aid towards artistic goals of which they disapproved. As long as Liszt was throwing the full weight of his resources behind Wagner, Wagner was hardly in a position to complain. But what comfort could this bring to Berlioz? By the same token, when Liszt helped Berlioz, the cause of Wagner was temporarily held in abeyance. Largesse for others always appears to be less just than largesse for oneself. The conclusion may seem bizarre, but it will withstand scrutiny. So many of Liszt's contemporaries turned against his universal beneficence precisely because it *was* universal, and not reserved for their own exclusive use.[16] Genius can tolerate much, but the one thing that it is usually quite incapable of tolerating is the recognition of genius in others. Certainly it is not in the nature of genius to subordinate itself before its own kind. That is why the appearance of a Franz Liszt is such a rare phenomenon in Art.

For the rest, charity sometimes leaves a secret resentment in the heart of the recipient. It is a common enough principle in human nature to bite the hand that feeds one: aggression is the unconscious way par excellence of repaying a debt since it is the best way of obscuring it. Some of Liszt's contemporaries had to protect themselves against his benevolence or be overwhelmed by it, and so they fought to assert their individuality. None of them wanted to end up, as Chopin once put it, as "part of his empire." They preferred to turn their backs on him and rule their own empires, albeit with borrowed orb and sceptre.

The fact that none of these composers—Schumann, Wagner, or Berlioz—happened genuinely to care for Liszt's music, even though he admired theirs and actively promoted it, made the situation more problematic for him. It might be argued that reciprocity in such matters is a poor substitute for a correct judgement, truthfully expressed. Did they not have a perfect right to dislike his music? Of course they did, even though we now know that they were deeply mistaken about much of it. Whether or not they should have continued to accept largesse from him while privately criticizing his music before others is

---

16. The negative proof of all this lies in the fact that not one of these composers offered his fellow artists any material aid or comfort whatsoever. The thought of Wagner or Berlioz sending money to Schumann or Chopin (let alone arranging concerts of their works) is hilarious, and is crowned only by the thought of their sending money to one another. It would be a slur on Schumann's memory, however, not to mention the generous recognition he accorded to rising talent, including Chopin and Brahms, in the columns of the *Neue Zeitschrift für Musik*. But recognition of this sort, offered from the armchair of a study and taking no more time than the half-hour or so required to dash off a five-hundred-word review, involves neither lifelong commitment nor the evangelical fervour that Liszt brought to the task. When Liszt took up a cause, he nailed his colours to the mast in a way that was totally unnerving to his onlookers. The speech he made after the first performance of *Lohengrin,* and to which further allusion will be made in this volume, here takes on the proportions of an obsession. "Hier stehe ich, ich kann nicht anders!" (p. 126) If a cause that he supported fell, Liszt was telling the world, he was willing to fall with it.

an ethical problem with which Liszt refused to concern himself: he continued to hand out largesse anyway. We do well to remember, however, that while dislike of a man ought not to lead to dislike of his music, it frequently does so. In fact, if the psychopathology of music criticism has anything at all to teach us about such matters, it is that one's likes or dislikes are all too often an unconscious rationalization of the total human relationship. Prejudice moves in mysterious ways its wonders to perform.

VI

But Liszt had still wider problems with the world at large. To be known as "the incontestable incarnation of the modern piano" carried a high price. The great public could never quite forgive him for abandoning his life as a touring virtuoso in order to concentrate on composing, and so it punished him by refusing to take his music seriously. Moreover, it spared no effort to bring him out of retirement. During the 1850s rumours were continually sweeping Weimar that Liszt was about to return to his old life of vaga-bondage. They were undoubtedly started by Old Weimar, who wanted nothing better than to see Liszt leave and probably thought that if they wanted it hard enough the will would become father to the deed. But every letter Liszt addressed to this topic shows his inflexible determination not to be seduced back to the concert stage. His communication to Baron Georg von Seydlitz can stand for all the others:

> With regard to the question you ask me about my supposed plans for a trip to Vienna, I can reply with complete assurance that there could be no question at all of me returning to a career which I have pursued and finished with, and which I definitely renounced about five years ago. . . . You know me well enough to realize that I keep my word, both to others and to myself. If cataclysms, improbable to my mind, were to devastate Europe from end to end, I would try to find refuge in the East Indies, since America has become a kind of artistic commonplace which would tempt me only moderately.
>
> Meanwhile, I work as peacefully as I can, with my mind and my pen, for it is only by continuing to toil in this manner for several years that it will be possible for me to reach that level of superior and solid renown that is my serious aim.[17]

17. LLB, vol. 8, p. 95.

Liszt never wavered from this twin resolve. Any request that he return to the concert platform invariably met not only with his refusal but also with his reason: composing was now infinitely more important to him.

The rumour that P. T. Barnum wanted to bring Liszt to America provokes mirth today. Is it true that Barnum offered Liszt $500,000 to visit the United States?[18] The mind boggles at the picture of the King of Pianists playing under the big top. True or false, there is something deeply symptomatic about the idea for those who wish to understand the sort of reputation Liszt still enjoyed with the public at large. To see the lion caged and put on public display is part of the dark pathology of the crowd, and it dates from time immemorial. The impulse to examine both tooth and claw, to stand fearless before the great mane—albeit from a distance—stirs deep in each one of us, even though both man and beast are debased in the process. The mere suggestion that Liszt might be thought of in the context of a circus, and his piano playing compared with the tricks of the high-wire acrobats or the fire-eaters, is sufficient commentary on the world's view of him. In the end this dilemma—pianist versus composer—became too intractable for Liszt to resolve. Disdained by his peers and misunderstood by the great public, he gradually became an isolated figure. That he recognized his fate, and accepted it, is the true meaning of his Weimar years. The thirteen summers that he spent in the city were for him a period of slow martyrdom.

VII

Thirteen summers! The brevity of the period never ceases to astonish us when set beside the great quantity of work that Liszt produced in Weimar. Those fleeting years have been the object of attention before, of course (notably by Peter Raabe, Ernest Newman, and Emile Haraszti), but they have never been treated in the depth that they deserve. This is surprising in the case of Raabe, who spent the last thirty-five years of his life as curator of the Liszt Museum in Weimar and well understood the importance of the city in Liszt's artistic development. How many scholars of distinction were not at first attracted to Liszt, but later became aware of his value and were overcome with a desire to serve him! Raabe's conversion was perhaps the most spectacular of all. He began his professional life as a conductor and directed the municipal opera houses of Königsberg, Zwickau, and Elberfeld between the years 1894 and 1899. It was not until 1907, when he was thirty-five years old, that Raabe arrived in Weimar as principal conductor of the Weimar Court Orchestra. He still knew little

---

18. PGS, vol. 2, pp. 91–93. See also pp. 260–61 of the present volume.

about Liszt, and when, in 1910, he was asked to take on the part-time duties
of the custodian of the Liszt Museum as well, it seemed like the worst possible
appointment. Raabe had had no training as a music historian, and he was
antipathetic to his subject. Moreover, the Liszt Museum contained tens of
thousands of documents, mostly uncatalogued. As Raabe began the herculean
task of sifting through this legacy, he became aware of Liszt's powerful personality and came to recognize his central place in musical history. The sense of
mission he subsequently brought to his task more than compensated for his lack
of experience as a musicologist. Within six years Raabe had submitted a
successful doctoral dissertation to the nearby University of Jena, based on an
original study of Liszt's orchestral manuscripts and entitled *Die Entstehungsgeschichte der ersten Orchesterwerke Franz Liszts* (1916). Fifteen years later this
dissertation was absorbed into Raabe's two-volume study *Liszts Leben und
Schaffen,* a standard work on which his scholarly reputation still rests today.
It is generally conceded that Part Two, the *Schaffen,* is a more important piece
of work than Part One, the *Leben:* Raabe, after all, brought a conductor's ear
to bear on Liszt's orchestral textures, and he could speak with authority about
Liszt's earliest attempts (as a thirty-five-year-old composer, newly arrived in
Weimar) to come to grips with the art of instrumentation. Moreover, the
Schaffen contains a complete catalogue of Liszt's works, which has become the
standard measurement for all subsequent efforts in the field. Other scholars have
been able to modify it, but they have not been able to dispense with it. As for
the *Leben,* this was the first and only time that Raabe ventured into the field
of biography. Not only did he not consult the important archives in France
and Hungary, whose documents would have thrown a flood of light on Liszt's
activities beyond Germany; he unaccountably neglected to consult many of the
thousands of documents in his care in Weimar itself. The result was a missed
opportunity from which Liszt biography is only now beginning to recover.
One or two simple examples will make this point clear.

It is an instructive reflection on Raabe in particular, to say nothing of the
way in which biographical work is done in general, that although he had access
to more than two thousand of the unpublished letters of Carolyne to Liszt, the
only paragraphs that he saw fit to publish place her in the worst possible light.
These portions were soon translated into English by Ernest Newman from the
comfort of his study in Tadworth (Newman would not have dreamed of
venturing beyond Surrey's borders in order to embark on a field-trip to Central
Europe in search of archival material on Liszt) and were joyfully included in
his character-assassination *The Man Liszt* (1934) for the delectation of the
English-speaking world. Here is a sample of the prose in question:

> I kiss your hands and kneel before you, prostrating my forehead to
> your feet, laying, like the Orientals, my fingers on my brow, my

lips, and my heart, to assure you that my whole mind, all the breath of my spirit, all my heart, exist only to bless you, to glorify you, to love you unto death and beyond—beyond even death, for love is stronger than death.[19]

And yet another:

I am at your tiny feet, beloved—I kiss them, I roll myself under the soles of them and place them on the nape of my neck—I sweep with my hair the places where you are to walk and prostrate myself under your footprints. . . . You know that all these things are not Oriental hyperbole but *faits accomplis.* . . . You know how I adore you—O how I long to see you again! O dear masterpiece of God whom I adore, and how could I help adoring the Good Boże [Polish for God] who created you so good, so beautiful, so perfect, so made to be cherished, adored and loved to death and madness![20]

Newman calls this her normal epistolary style. One wonders how he could bring himself to utter such a remark, since they are the only letters of Carolyne to Liszt that he ever saw.[21] It is sufficient commentary on the painful slowness with which biographical work on Liszt has unfolded that even today, fifty years later, these are among the very few examples of her published prose to Liszt available in English. Yet her letters are full of vital information about her family in Ukraine, about her childhood there, and about her complex financial position in Weimar during the 1850s—to say nothing of Liszt's comings and goings—and no modern Liszt biographer can afford to dispense with them.

Another curious sin of omission was the heavily censored letters of Liszt to Agnès Street-Klindworth, which tell of a guarded love-affair begun in Weimar and pursued in various German cities between 1855 and 1861. La Mara had published her expurgated edition of these letters in 1894 under the bland title *Briefe an eine Freundin,* [22] and Raabe cited it many times in the course of his biographical work. In 1927 the unexpurgated *Abschriften* of these letters, prepared for La Mara from the holographs, found their way into the Liszt Museum

---

19. From an unpublished letter dated April 19, 1851. WA, Kasten 33, u. 3.
20. From an unpublished letter dated July 12, 1853. WA, Kasten 34, u. 2.
21. On both occasions, Princess Carolyne was under emotional stress. Throughout April 1851 she was under medical care at Bad Eilsen, and a few days before writing her letter of April 19 she had undergone a minor surgical procedure (see pp. 137–38). As for the letter of July 12, 1853, Liszt and Carolyne had been separated for a month, and she was once again seeking medical therapy, this time in Carlsbad.
22. LLB, vol. 3.

as part of her literary legacy. That was four years before Raabe's book appeared. However, Raabe's cursory treatment of Agnès herself (only two lines in a book of 250 pages) suggests either that he did not examine these censored texts or that he, like La Mara, knew about them and suppressed them.[23] Whatever the case, we remain grateful to Raabe for his devotion to Liszt. His conversion when it came was dramatic, and he brought Liszt scholarship into the twentieth century.

Haraszti's work,[24] too, is indispensable to the modern researcher who wishes to gain a fuller understanding of the minutiae of Liszt's daily life in Weimar. With his usual flair for the esoteric and the arcane, Haraszti introduced some hitherto unknown documents into the literature, which dealt with a number of vexing questions. Carolyne's relations with the tsarist court in St. Petersburg, her subsequent banishment from Russia, and the sequestration of her vast properties there were examined from a fresh perspective. Most important of all, perhaps, was the matter of her daughter's marriage to Prince Konstantin Hohenlohe and the property settlement which thereafter rendered Carolyne dependent upon her daughter for money. Haraszti may well have been the first Liszt scholar to work in the Weimar Staatsarchiv, where he became familiar with the legacy of Baron von Maltitz, the Russian ambassador to the Weimar court. The Staatsarchiv contains hundreds of missives from Carolyne on the question of her marriage annulment. It was while he was sifting through these materials that Haraszti appears to have come across a cache of documents which included the important letter from the twenty-two-year-old Princess Marie Wittgenstein to Baron von Maltitz informing him of her unshakable resolve to help her dispossessed mother secure a Russian annulment by releasing to her, for legal fees, 70,000 silver roubles from her former inheritance. Haraszti, who has often been quoted on this subject, will probably remain the ultimate authority, but for the wrong reasons: the original documents he cites can no longer be found.[25] Fortunately, the unpublished letters of Princess Carolyne to Liszt not only

---

23. The story of how La Mara stumbled across the Liszt–Agnès Street connection in 1892, while she was busy collecting letters for her ongoing edition of the *Gesammelte Schriften,* borrowed the correspondence from George Street (Agnès's eldest son), copied it, and subjected it to censorship, is told on page 210 of this volume. After La Mara had made her *Abschriften* (WA, Kasten 444, no. 1), the originals found their way into the Breitkopf and Härtel archives in Leipzig. In 1951 those archives were auctioned, and the letters were acquired by the Hessische Landes- und Hochschulbibliothek in Darmstadt, where they may be consulted today. It is important to add that La Mara, apart from subjecting the more sensitive letters to censorship, decided for a variety of reasons that there were some letters that she could not even bring herself to copy. The modern scholar would do well to avoid consulting her *Abschriften,* then, and concentrate instead on the Darmstadt holographs. A new, annotated edition of the *Briefe an eine Freundin* is now in preparation under the capable editorship of Pauline Pocknell, who has generously allowed excerpts from her work-in-progress to be published in the present volume (see the chapter entitled "Liebestraum," pp. 209–24).
24. HFL (1967). See also Volume One of the present study, pp. 19–20.
25. After our own attempts to track them down in the Weimar Staatsarchiv during the summer of 1986 had met with no success, the director of the archives, Dr. Günther Michel-Triller, conducted

corroborate the basic situation as presented by Haraszti but even allow us to add more detail to it. We now know that Marie's husband, Prince Konstantin, forced her to renege on this promise to her mother and that Liszt himself had to borrow a part of this vast sum from the Rothschilds' bank in Paris, against some of Carolyne's long-time securities invested through his lawyer-uncle Eduard in Vienna. This particular tangle is just one more illustration of the many frustrations Liszt endured in Weimar as a result of his association with Carolyne.

The Weimar period also forces the biographer to deal with Liszt's complex relationship with his three children by Marie d'Agoult—Blandine, Cosima, and Daniel. This particular tale has been woven before, of course, but usually with too few threads. The resulting tapestry is often patchy, and it constantly calls out for repair. The best account so far was written by Count du Moulin-Eckart,[26] but his narrative was flawed in two important respects. First, although he had access to much of the unpublished correspondence between Liszt and his children, he did not have access to all of it.[27] Second, his book was a virtual deification of Cosima—"the woman of the century," as he called her—and since there were aspects of her difficult childhood and upbringing of which she herself deeply disapproved, it was inevitable that du Moulin-Eckart disapproved of them too. We propose to re-tell this story, and base our text on a somewhat fuller documentation than has hitherto been available. It is through Liszt's relationship with his children, in fact, that we are reminded of one of his strongest character traits: namely, his ability to detach his public from his private life. Few, if any, of his professional colleagues in Weimar had the remotest idea of the intense pressure to which his family obligations subjected him. They saw only a man without personal cares, who drove himself with fanatical energy towards his goals. Yet it is no accident that Liszt reached his peak as an instrumental composer during these very periods of greatest personal agitation. The two factors were causally, not casually, connected. At times of outer stress, Liszt invariably composed his way back to inner calm. Work, as we observe elsewhere, consoled him.

The biographer on the trail of Liszt's daily life in Weimar will find a rich store of explanatory detail in the writings of Adelheid von Schorn (1841–1916). The daughter of the art-historian Ludwig von Schorn and Henriette von Schorn, a lady-in-waiting to Maria Pawlowna, Adelheid lived in Wei-

---

a systematic search through the entire Maltitz legacy and reported that these documents were missing (written communication dated August 8, 1987). Haraszti's solitary visit to the archives was recorded as having taken place in 1938.

26. MCW.

27. His handling of the Bayreuth materials was exemplary, but he appeared to know nothing of the Paris-based documents which are today in the Bibliothèque Nationale and which contrast with and complement the Bayreuth letters along the way.

mar for more than sixty years, and she knew the city and its inhabitants more intimately than almost any other chronicler. Her two books *Zwei Menschen-alter* (1901) and *Das nachklassische Weimar* (1911–12) contain irreplaceable information about Liszt and his Weimar connections. Later on, Schorn became a confidante of Princess Carolyne, who, after her removal to Rome, arranged for Schorn to send her a regular series of reports about Liszt's activities in the town. There is also much useful information of a supplementary kind in Adolf Stahr's *Weimar und Jena* (1852), written by a scholar and historian who lived in both places and had contacts across Germany. He and his wife, Fanny Lewald, were members of Liszt's circle in Weimar, and Fanny's biographical sketch of Liszt (contained in her book *Zwölf Bilder nach dem Leben,* 1888) owes much of its interest and liveliness to the fact that it sprang from her personal links with him.

Nor must we forget to mention one other source frequently neglected by Liszt biographers. Enshrined within the pages of the *Weimarische Zeitung* is the history of the town. At first its publication was erratic, but in January 1852 it was taken over by a new editor, Hans von Mangoldt, who brought out two issues a week and improved the quality of the journalism.[28] Thereafter the *Weimarische Zeitung* often carried reports of Liszt's activities in and around Weimar. Its coverage of the first Berlioz Week, in November 1852, was most detailed, and it published a number of thoughtful accounts of Liszt's place in the musical life of the town. In 1855 the *Zeitung* was taken over by Karl Biedermann, and it began to adopt a more critical stance. Typical was its long article "Liszts Rücktritt und das Publikum" published shortly after Liszt had announced his retirement from the Weimar theatre.[29] Weimar also possessed two other newspapers at this time: the *Weimarisches Sonntagsblatt* (edited by Joseph Rank) and the influential *Deutschland* (edited by Karl Panse). This last journal was by no means favourably disposed towards Liszt, and there are few better ways to savour the turbulent climate of the times than to thumb through its yellowing pages.

Many gaps in our knowledge of this brief thirteen-year period still wait to be filled. The vast collection of more than nine thousand holograph letters belonging to Varnhagen von Ense[30] would throw much light on Liszt's comings and goings during his Weimar years. The archive contained many communications from personalities who were intimately acquainted with Liszt (including twenty-five from Marie d'Agoult) and may also include some Liszt autographs. At the outbreak of World War II, this important collection was

---

28. SNW, vol. 1, p. 300.
29. "Liszt's Retirement and the Weimar Public"; issue of February 6, 1859. See p. 497 of the present volume.
30. Karl August Varnhagen von Ense (1785–1859), the German historian, was dubbed "the Prussian Plutarch" by his contemporaries because of his interest in biography.

removed from Nantes and deposited in Silesia for safe-keeping. It was never returned, and its present whereabouts is unknown.

Tactics may win battles; only strategy wins wars. Not until we survey the field of Liszt scholarship in its vast entirety can we identify the four monumental requirements without whose fulfillment the topic will always rest on shifting foundations.

(a) A thematic catalogue of his works, which will extend proper scholarly attention to each one of his more than thirteen hundred individual compositions. Nothing short of a reference tool comparable to Köchel's Mozart Catalogue or Schmieder's Bach Catalogue will satisfy the demands of modern scholars.

(b) A complete edition of his correspondence, free from editorial censorship. The old Breitkopf and Härtel edition, under the editorship of La Mara, has done yeoman service across the years, but it will not carry Liszt scholarship into the twenty-first century. Its mutilated texts are symptomatic of the grave crisis in which Liszt studies find themselves today.

(c) A complete edition of his music, based on the urtexts, with all the sketches and different versions of the same piece available for comparison. With Liszt this is difficult, since he sometimes worked and re-worked an individual composition three or four different times, but it is not impossible.

(d) A large-scale multi-volume biography, which will encompass the many-sided activities of this most industrious of musicians—pianist, composer, teacher, conductor, administrator—in a narrative which is not only useful to the scholar but enlightening to the general reader.

While the present study is an attempt to remedy this last deficiency, there is a sense in which all four requirements hang together, as any student of the topic will recognize: a discovery in one of these fields is likely to have repercussions in all the others. The beleaguered Liszt scholar is in the unenviable position of Buridan's Ass, a beast reputed to be so intelligent that when it was placed among several equally succulent bundles of hay it starved to death because, it was said, it could find no logical reason for proceeding in one direction rather than another. Nonetheless, there are good arguments for proceeding with the biography. We believe that it is better to light a candle than curse the darkness, and "darkness" is not too strong a word to describe a situation in which today's general musician, however well informed he may be, can scarcely write two pages of prose about Liszt which are not threatened by the archival evidence. For the rest, it is probably true to say that whichever one of our projects were to emerge first, it would be called upon to bear a disproportionate amount of critical scrutiny from experts toiling on the leading edges of the others. And here a note of reason must be sounded. A biography cannot be all things to all men. It is pointless to turn to such a genre in search of detailed information about holograph sources, watermark evidence, or in-depth musical analysis, to say nothing of the history of the epoch against which a man's life unfolds. Such subjects may be both important and compelling, but their enthusiasts must surely exhaust them in their own time, and not expect the biographer to exhaust them in his.

VIII

In few other creators is the mysterious link between life and art so clearly revealed as in Liszt. A Bach, a Mozart, a Michelangelo, or even a Shakespeare is likely to reduce the biographer to despair, for these masters show almost no connection between their high art and their low life, if the phrase be permitted, lived out as it was on a humdrum level of daily existence. It is as if an inscrutable providence had condemned both life and art to unfold along parallel planes, with no prospect of an intersection. In such circumstances, biography can seem to be irrelevant, even intrusive. Liszt's work, by contrast, might almost be described as the fragments of a diary jotted down from life, and they clamour for biographical narrative. Indeed, Liszt himself gave evidence of this when he chose to bestow on his compositions such titles as *Album d'un voyageur, Glanes de Woronince,* and *Hungarian Historical Portraits.* It is a fairly simple matter for the biographer to plunge into the sea of correspondence, diaries, and newspaper accounts surrounding Liszt's composing activity and emerge with a rich supply of explanatory detail. Liszt's biography, in short, forms a vibrant whole, with life and music engaged in constant, creative dialogue. Such considerations, needless to add, determined the structure of the present volumes. Whenever the life results in a body of work, we "stop the clock" and look at that work. The conventional division of Liszt's career into a two-part pattern of "life" and "work," while highly convenient for the control of one's material, hardly does him justice, for that is not how Liszt himself lived. The idea that there are two Liszts, one who dwells in music and one who dwells outside it, is a myth. And this was never truer than during the Weimar years, to which we must now turn.

BOOK ONE

New Beginnings
1847 · 1848

Enter Carolyne von Sayn-Wittgenstein

*A woman of great sympathy and intelligence who
has often sustained me in my darkest hours.*

BERLIOZ[1]

I

It is natural that the figure of Princess Carolyne should loom large in any biography of Liszt. She was, after all, his mistress throughout the thirteen troubled years of his tenure in Weimar, and she was to remain his friend and faithful companion for a quarter of a century after that. No other person understood him so well, and had fate dealt her a different hand Liszt would certainly have married her. He himself wrote in his testament that he had dearly wished to call her his wife, but malice and the deplorable chicanery of others had conspired to prevent it.[2] We shall come to understand that when Liszt penned these bitter lines he was reporting no more than the simple truth. Carolyne's life in Weimar was one long Calvary. She endured much slander because of her irregular association with Liszt; he knew that she suffered, and he loved her all the more for it. Today there are good reasons for devoting more space to Carolyne than ever before. Liszt's biographers, particularly the ones who wrote in an earlier, "romantic" vein, have tended to disapprove of her. Some have even vilified her—usually in inverse ratio to the approval they heaped on Marie d'Agoult, the mother of Liszt's children and a seemingly more attractive alternative. It is almost as if they wanted to punish Carolyne for taking Marie's

---

1. BM, p. 484.
2. LLB, vol. 5, p. 53. In the early published versions of Liszt's will, this sentence was always suppressed. La Mara did not publish the complete text until 1900, fourteen years after Liszt's death, having already issued a severely truncated version in 1892 (LLB, vol. 1, pp. 364–68). See Appendix I.

place.[3] That Liszt himself was in favour of the changes she wrought in his life is brushed aside. Liszt, it seems, should have consulted them before proceeding. Even those among Liszt's chroniclers who prided themselves on their objectivity are not beyond reproach. When Haraszti depicts Carolyne as a Baba Yaga, a witch, a spider even, spinning the intricate web that will hold Liszt prisoner for life, he is saying that he understands better than Liszt himself what was good for him. When Newman depicts her as "a half-cracked blue-stocking" and "a religious bigot," he is saying that he is a better judge of this particular character than Liszt, who knew her and lived on daily intimacy with her. Such all-knowing attitudes, based on highly selective evidence, do not inspire confidence. A biography is not a novel. It attempts to report things as they are, not as the biographer would prefer them to be. The plain fact of the matter is that Carolyne met a genuine need on Liszt's part. She was receptive to his ideas, sympathetic to his aims, and she invariably placed his interests above her own. Moreover, she provided Liszt with a comfortable home for several years, at an important time in his life, when he took immense strides forward in the field of composition. It is doubtful that he could have achieved so much without her help and encouragement. It was at Weimar that he composed his great B-minor Piano Sonata and the *Faust* and *Dante* symphonies, arguably among his finest compositions. In addition, he composed there his unique series of symphonic poems—a form he invented, which was to have far-reaching historical consequences. He developed the orchestra at Weimar to a pitch of excellence that it had never before enjoyed in Germany. He initiated a steady stream of productions at the opera house, giving the first performances of Wagner's *Lohengrin* and Schubert's *Alfonso und Estrella,* among other operas. Pupils and disciples gathered round him—men of the calibre of Hans von Bülow, Klindworth, Raff, Cornelius, Pruckner, Hans von Bronsart—and the work of the Neu-Weimar-Verein, the society they formed under Liszt's leadership for the promotion of new music, became world-famous. All in all, then, Carolyne was far from being the malignant influence that history depicts. This groundless charge is refuted by the evidence of Liszt's creative output at this time.

I I

Carolyne was born on February 8, 1819, in the home of her maternal grandfather at Monasterzyska, the only child of an immensely rich Polish landowner named Peter Iwanowsky and his wife, Pauline Podowska. The Iwanowskys were Roman Catholics, and their estates, which were of unimaginable vastness,

---

3. If so, that would be illogical. Liszt's liaison with Marie d'Agoult ended three years before he met Carolyne Wittgenstein. Carolyne did not usurp Marie's position: she filled the vacuum created by Marie's departure. Marie and Carolyne, needless to add, never met.

lay in the province of Podolia in Polish Ukraine. More than thirty thousand serfs were required to work these domains, whose far-flung borders took several days to traverse on horseback. Brought up in isolation, on the fringe of the civilized world, Carolyne was allowed to roam free by her doting father. La Mara described her as "a child of the steppes."[4] When she was eleven years old, Carolyne's parents separated; thereafter she was brought up by her father, and her education was supervised by a French governess, Madame Patersi de Fossombroni.[5] Peter Iwanowsky was a book-worm by nature, and he attempted to forget his matrimonial troubles by sitting up half the night browsing in his library, smoking large cigars. His daughter would often join him there, and they would read his learned tomes together, the father thinking nothing of offering a cigar to his young charge. As she grew older, her favourite pastime was to debate with her father, and they would talk the night away in his smoke-filled library. Carolyne's later reputation as a blue-stocking, her love of argument, and her addiction to tobacco can all be traced to this early environment. It is typical of her industrious nature that when she was only nine, she had already drawn up for herself a table of laws that rewarded the crime of idleness with capital punishment.

A shadow was cast across her childhood and adolescence from which she never escaped. Carolyne was exceedingly plain, a fact made all the more poignant by the radiant beauty of her talented mother. Pauline Iwanowska had many admirers. In Metternich's salon she had charmed the cream of Viennese society by the purity of her singing voice. Schelling had praised her in his poetry; and both Spontini and Meyerbeer had heaped compliments at her feet. Whenever her daughter accompanied her to the fashionable watering-places of Europe, the contrast between them was so disconcerting as to draw comment. So upset was Pauline at the trick that nature had played on her that the sensitive girl, painfully aware that she was the cause, attempted to console her mother by urging her to wait until the Resurrection, after which Carolyne would be transformed into a great beauty.

Concerned for the welfare of his daughter, who would one day inherit his fortune, Iwanowsky trained her in the daily affairs of his business. Carolyne became a skilled horsewoman, and under her father's tutelage she assumed greater responsibility for the grain transactions on which the family's wealth ultimately rested. But Iwanowsky was also anxious to secure a good marriage

---

4. LSJ, p. 10.

5. Madame Patersi de Fossombroni (c. 1778–1862) was a governess of such repute that she had been attached to some of the most distinguished families in Russia and Poland. She numbered among her pupils the countesses Isaure de Foudras and Ludmilla de Thermes, Princess Zénaïde de Wagram, and of course Princess Carolyne herself. This early connection with Carolyne was to have profound consequences for Madame Patersi, who was brought out of retirement in order to educate Liszt's daughters in Paris. We shall meet her elsewhere in this volume (see pp. 432ff).

for her. She was only seventeen when she received an offer of matrimony from Prince Nicholas, the youngest son of Field Marshal Ludwig Adolf Peter von Sayn-Wittgenstein.[6] Iwanowsky knew full well that the Wittgensteins wished to marry money, but he recognized that his straitlaced daughter would never be wooed by a more eligible suitor. Three times Nicholas proposed, and three times Carolyne rejected him.[7] Eventually she yielded through fear of her father. On the day of the wedding, April 26 (Old Style), Iwanowsky was careful to smack his reluctant daughter across the face in full view of the congregation. This old Polish custom served a practical purpose: a public rebuke could be cited as proof of coercion in any subsequent divorce action. Many young brides had been rescued from a lifetime of servitude, or worse, by this simple blow. In due course, Carolyne herself was to include it in her brief when she petitioned the church of Rome for an annulment.[8]

Prince Nicholas, who was twenty-four at the time of the marriage, was a captain in the Russian cavalry and an aide-de-camp to the governor of Kiev. Immediately after the wedding he took his young bride back to Kiev, but Carolyne found life there so unsettling that after only a few months she returned to Woronince, the country estate that her father had given her as a dowry. There she gave birth to her only daughter, Marie, on February 18, 1837. To please his young wife, Nicholas gave up his cavalry commission and joined her.[9] The marriage soon failed, however, owing to their incompatibility, and within four years they had agreed upon a permanent separation. In 1844, Peter Iwanowsky was struck down while attending mass and died on the floor of the church, because, claimed his daughter, he knew himself to be responsible for her misfortune.[10] Distraught with grief, Carolyne sealed his house and en-

---

6. The field marshal (1769–1843), a veteran Russian soldier, had defended St. Petersburg against Napoleon in 1812. In 1834 he and all his descendants had been made princes of Prussia by King Friedrich Wilhelm III despite the fact that they were Russian subjects (See the letter of congratulation from Tsar Nicholas I, S–WA, p. 177). Neither Nicholas nor Carolyne was born into the upper aristocracy. She acquired the title of Princess almost by accident, as it were, through marriage to a man who only acquired it himself when he was twenty-two years old.

7. LLB, vol. 4, p. vii.

8. See Appendix II, p. 566.

9. LSJ, p. 12.

10. MAL, p. 162 and LAG, p. 29. Peter Iwanowsky was not only a loving father but a devoted grandfather as well. An unpublished letter to his granddaughter, Princess Marie, the only such document known to exist, is dated "3 December 1843, Starosteine." Written in Polish, it indicates the great love that Iwanowsky bore the six-year-old girl.

> My Beloved Granddaughter,
>   Thank you very much for the picture you sent me, and which you sketched in colour. This is a very dear proof that you were thinking about me. Remember, I beg you, to think of me and love me because I love you so very much.
>
>   Your devoted Grandfather,
>   Peter Iwanowsky
>   (M S–W)

tombed within it every book, picture, and piece of furniture exactly as he had left them. Three years elapsed before she mustered the courage to unlock its doors again.

At the moment of Iwanowsky's death, Carolyne inherited fourteen estates and became one of the wealthiest women in Ukraine. That same year the seventy-four-year-old Field Marshal Wittgenstein also died. To his son Nicholas he bequeathed the family property of Petrowka, in Bessarabia, "with all its farm buildings, houses, and enclosures." Unfortunately for Nicholas's spendthrift ways, the testament could not be executed until after the death of his mother, Antonia, and she lived on until 1856. This froze not only Nicholas's inheritance but that of Ludwig's other sons too.[11] Thus, almost from the beginning, Carolyne's superior wealth turned her into a hostage of the Wittgensteins. Under different circumstances Nicholas might well have been glad to be rid of his wife altogether. But he and his family were determined to hang on to the millions of roubles Carolyne had inherited, and later events were to prove them to be tenacious adversaries.

III

Carolyne's large château at Woronince was situated in a park with a wide avenue of trees and a lake.[12] The house was plainly furnished and devoid of taste. According to Princess Marie, who lived there until she was eleven years old, the walls of the dining room were painted with parrots.[13] The ground floor was oblong, containing a library, a music room, and a billiards room. Several busts of philosophers and poets stood like sentinels at the doorway and along the corridors. Carolyne's bedroom, on the first floor, was dominated by a large wooden crucifix hanging on the wall, before a prayer stool. One or two flame-coloured sofas stood out garishly against the dull grey wallpaper. Just outside the château Carolyne had built a "house chapel" for her family, her servants, and passing wayfarers. In the absence of the itinerant priest, she and her daughter frequently read the text of the mass, in Latin, to the motley

---

11. Field Marshal Wittgenstein's testament was published in S-WA, pp. 187ff. According to this document, dated November 29, 1842, the field marshal had five children: Ludwig, Alexander, Georg, Nicholas, and Emilie. The family seat was at Kamenka. While the Wittgensteins may have lacked "cash flow," they were far from impoverished. At his death, the field marshal left each one of his children, with the exception of Emilie, estates and dwellings. No one could have foreseen that his will, drawn up with impeccable attention to detail, would become a bone of contention among the children. They grew old while his widow, Antonia, enjoyed her "prior rights" for fourteen years.
12. Woronince is all but impossible to find on modern maps. It lies 49° 40′ north, and 28° 10′ east. That places it, roughly speaking, about one hundred and fifty miles south-west of Kiev. See map on p. 40.
13. LSJ, p. 13.

Princess Carolyne's château at Woronince, a photograph taken about 1943.

congregation. Liszt himself delivered one such reading while he was a guest at Woronince.

Surrounding the house were the miserable huts in which the serfs led an animal-like existence. Clumps of bushes hid these wretched hovels from the eyes of visitors, as if to deny their very existence. The château itself was overrun with domestic servants who would unroll their mattresses at dusk and lie down in the dark corridors, or spend the night propped against the walls. Over this desperate sea of humanity Carolyne exercised absolute control. The climate of Woronince, which lay on the edge of the Russian steppes, was extreme. In summer there was tropical heat; in winter, cold so intense that the inhabitants had to wear masks with holes for their eyes. It was not uncommon to send a servant for purchases only to discover him the next morning frozen to death in the back of his cart. These serfs knew no other world than Woronince, their prison home. After the Polish insurrection of 1830 their lot became particularly harsh. All travel to nearby provinces was abruptly curtailed, and many families were separated. Simply to visit one's kith and kin without travel documents was to risk summary execution.

After the death of her father, which had followed so hard on the failure of her marriage, Carolyne learned the full meaning of adversity. Scarcely had the body of Peter Iwanowsky been lowered into the grave than her three cousins (the daughters of Iwanowsky's brother) confronted her with a false will purporting to name them as beneficiaries. Because the document bore a watermark postdating his death she was able to expose them.[14] The Wittgensteins were equally hostile. Fearing to lose all control over her fortune, they kept a careful watch on her affairs from their two family homes just beyond her borders. These family squabbles turned Carolyne into a recluse. She escaped to her library, like her father before her, seeking consolation from the philosophers. There she read Kant, Fichte, and Goethe, writing a long commentary on *Faust,* all the while secretly yearning for her liberator. A light always burned at her window as she read or scribbled the night away.[15] She became known locally as "the blue-stocking of Woronince," a title which annoyed her and which she several times denied.

I V

Early each year the grain farmers of Ukraine travelled to Kiev, the administrative capital, in order to sell wheat and exchange contracts. That is why Carolyne arrived there in January 1847 and heard quite by chance from her business associates that Liszt had just given a recital in Contract Hall, where they were presently holding their meetings, and that the city was buzzing with talk about the virtuoso. The swift sequence of events which followed has already been touched on: how, out of curiosity, she attended the two subsequent recitals given by Liszt at Kiev University,[16] heard his *Pater Noster* sung in the cathedral, sent him an anonymous donation of 100 roubles for his charity subscription, met him when he insisted on thanking his unknown benefactress in person, and then invited him to stay with her at Woronince, a hundred and fifty miles away.

It is not difficult to imagine the galvanizing effect that Liszt must have had on Carolyne when she first set eyes on him. Extremely handsome, a sophisticated man of the world, golden-tongued, the toast of kings, above all a magical virtuoso, he was certainly different from anyone else she had ever met. Moreover, unlike the "gentlemen farmers" with whom she had been surrounded for most of her life, Liszt actually paid court to her and offered her compliments. At that moment, she may have sensed that her hour of liberation was at hand. As for Liszt, true connoisseur of the fair sex, he would not have failed to recognize the symptoms of repressed desire lurking behind her plain exterior. And when the invitation came to follow her to Woronince, he willingly made the long detour to her fortress manor, there to await his destiny.

---

14. LSJ, p. 16.

15. Unpublished letter to Liszt, dated March 20, 1847. WA, Kasten 33, p. 14.

16. Carolyne regarded the printed programme of her first Liszt recital (February 2, 1847) as a sacred relic. After her death it was donated to the Weimar Liszt Museum by her daughter (LSJ, p. 21).

Neither of them yet knew that this was to be the great turning-point of their lives; indeed, the ostensible reason for the invitation was to attend the tenth birthday celebration of Princess Marie. But in an unpublished letter to Liszt, Carolyne, who was much given to metaphysical speculation, claimed that she felt that she had known Liszt all her life, and that when she first saw him in Kiev it was like meeting an old companion after a lapse of many years.[17] Princess Carolyne, in fact, was one of those rare women who are destined to love but once. When such spirits do not succeed in fulfilling their destiny, they simply wither on the vine and die. But should they encounter the man who sets both body and mind aflame, be it with a single glance or touch, they come to inhabit an emotional paradise which the adversaries of the outside world can never sully. This is a romantic, not to say outmoded, view of love; but it was one to which Carolyne wholeheartedly subscribed. From the moment that Liszt first entered her life, she knew that she had arrived at her destiny.[18]

The very first letter that Carolyne wrote to Liszt contained directions for reaching Woronince.

Zhitomir, February 3, 1847

From here you go to Werdgezen, and from there through Wanow to Woronince—to the home of the Wittgensteins. That is what I forgot to note down for you, and I am leaving that little bit of information here for you—firstly to prove to you that the idea of seeing you come has preoccupied me, somewhat like awaiting a treat, as one of the sweetest things I have encountered on my road through life. And then, because the thought of unexpected friendship often gives more pleasure than the reality itself. . . . Come, then, we will talk a bit about Kiev whose memory will still be vibrating in

17. Dated September 1847. WA, Kasten 33, p. 63.

18. In a revelatory letter written to Liszt about six years after she had first met him, Carolyne declared the cause of that fatal attraction she had always felt toward him: she had always seen in him the spirit and personality of her dead father. Peter Iwanowsky, she recollected, had great intellectual talents, the energy of an orbiting planet. "My father had a great soul, as noble as a Stoic, as meek as a Christian. . . . My father was of the stuff to edify men and raise up things. He had in him those mysterious atoms which, when they cluster around a life, create the luminous traces of its memory and place it among those human comets, irregular and indefinable, which return from time to time to amaze astounded peoples by their splendour, or frighten them by their strangeness." After eulogizing Iwanowsky's memory for two pages, and informing Liszt that during her youth she had subjected herself entirely to her father's all-encompassing will, she brings herself to the psychological point. "If I had not been the daughter of my father, I would never have been capable of being your wife. . . . Without my father, I would never have been in the least way worthy of you, I would not have been able, would never have been capable, of giving myself to you. . . . It was as clear as daylight, in my mind's eye, that the Lord was sending you to take the place my father had left vacant. . . ." (WA, Kasten 34; from a letter dated July 13, 1853) This piece of self-analysis is so sharp that no biographer can improve upon it. The entire text of this letter was recently published in *Silences: Liszt* (Paris, 1986), pp. 23–25.

you. Come, where you will be welcomed with all the cordiality and eagerness of good friends who take great pleasure in owning a precious guest.[19]

That phrase "the home of the Wittgensteins" was a deceptive touch: Prince Nicholas, as we have seen, had not lived at Woronince for four years. Did Liszt know of the true state of affairs at that moment? We cannot be certain. When Carolyne's letter arrived, Liszt was asleep, but Belloni considered it urgent enough to awaken the pianist from his slumbers.

4 o'clock

I was awakened with your note, which is a hundred times welcome. Thank you, Madam, and I will see you soon. When I returned this evening I told Belloni that we must definitely take the Zhitomir road. Yours with heart and soul.

F.L.[20]

Liszt stayed in Woronince a mere ten days. He made his first acquaintance with Carolyne's ten-year-old daughter, Princess Marie (the "Magnolette" and "Farfadet" of his correspondence),[21] and with Prince Nicholas, who was in attendance for his daughter's birthday. He also met Marie's Scottish governess, Miss Anderson, who was to stay with the family throughout the Weimar years, and whom we still find living in the Altenburg in 1861. We shall probably never discover what transpired between Carolyne and Liszt during this brief eternity. But the force of their encounter was strong enough to produce a lasting consequence. When the moment came for Liszt to resume his concert tour of Ukraine (he had further engagements in Nemirov, Berdichev, and Kremenez ahead of him, as well as a trip to Constantinople), it was already understood that he and Carolyne would rendevous a few months later in Odessa and return to Woronince for an extended sojourn in the autumn.[22]

---

19. Hitherto unpublished. WA, Kasten 33, p. 2.
20. LLB, vol. 4, p. 1.
21. Princess Marie Pauline Antonia died in 1920 at the age of eighty-three. Her last two Christian names came from her maternal and paternal grandmothers, respectively. It was Princess Marie who, more than fifty years later, provided the endowment which paid for the monumental Collected Edition of Liszt's works, in thirty-four volumes—a tribute to his memory with few parallels.
22. During this visit to Ukraine, Liszt was followed by the Russian secret police. A report from Lieutenant Colonel Neuman to Governor General Bibikov runs:

Liszt gave three concerts in Kiev and everyone talked about his return trip to Bucharest. Instead he went on to Zhitomir, Nemirov, Berdichev, and lastly Kremenez. All his concerts were marked not only by enthusiasm for his talent, but by meetings of the nobility. From everywhere messages were sent about his arrival, as a result of which the amount of money collected was unusually high, while tickets for his concerts in the country towns were even

Meanwhile, Carolyne had arranged a journey of her own—to St. Petersburg. On the surface this looked like an innocent extension of her normal business journeys. In reality, it was an elaborate cover to enable her to implement a daring plan: to liquidate the Iwanowsky fortune and transfer it beyond Russia's borders and, ultimately, beyond the reach of the Wittgensteins themselves.

---

more expensive than in Kiev. Because of this, there were various speculations about whether the money was not being designated for other purposes—since Liszt did not stop over in the provinces of Great Russia, and did not give concerts there.

(The original document is preserved in the Central State Historical Archive of Ukraine in Kiev, file no. 442, description no. 497, collection 61.)

The Russian authorities were clearly unnerved by Liszt's presence and suspected him of raising money in behalf of the movement towards Ukrainian national independence. This was not the first time that Liszt had captured the attention of the secret police, and for somewhat similar reasons. Readers of Volume One will recall that police files were also started on Liszt in Milan (1837), Pest (1840), and Warsaw (1843).

The Journeys of the Princess, 1847–1848

Genius is the imprint of divinity.
CAROLYNE VON SAYN-WITTGENSTEIN[1]

I

One of the great untapped sources of Liszt material is the two thousand or more unpublished letters Carolyne wrote to him during the long years of their liaison. The existence of these letters has long been known, but few people have actually read them.[2] This is incomprehensible when we recall that they form the other half of a vast correspondence between the pair covering nearly forty years. While Liszt's half was published by La Mara more than eighty years ago, it remains one-sided, and there are many occasions on which a glance at Carolyne's holographs supplies missing links in the broken chain of communication. There are good reasons for supposing that the letters will never see the light of day, however. For one thing, they are heavy going, calling for dogged persistence from all but the most intrepid reader. Some of them run to twenty or thirty pages of densely packed prose, and there are times when that prose becomes so prolix that it loses touch with reality. The princess appears to have invented "stream of consciousness" writing a hundred years before it became fashionable. She will wax lyrical about a sunset, a flower, or a poem but will leave undescribed the city from which she is writing, the events that have filled her day, and the people with whom she has discoursed—in short, everything of interest to the general reader. Even Liszt despaired when receiving such missives, and more than once he politely begged the princess to curb her

---

1. MAL, p. 164.
2. They may be consulted in the Goethe- und Schiller-Archiv, Weimar.

propensity for long-windedness. But there would be a greater objection to having her letters printed in a curtailed form. The amount of editing required to produce a coherent text would merely create a paradox: the casual reader would not add much to his general fund of knowledge about Carolyne, while the scholar would rightly conclude that a mutilated version of the letters rendered them useless as a biographical tool.

That said, it remains to be observed that these are hardly satisfactory reasons for ignoring Carolyne's epistolary legacy. Scattered throughout her letters are vital nuggets of information of great value to the biographer, if only he is prepared to dig them out of the base material surrounding them; and on those occasions when practical circumstances oblige her to come to the point, she can be both forceful and direct. The first, difficult year of her relationship with Liszt, for example, when she parted with her family estates and fled from Ukraine in order to join him in Germany, a rootless exile for the rest of her life, cannot be fully understood without reference to her letters on the topic. Indeed, it is only from these primary documents that the events immediately following Liszt's departure from Woronince can be properly reconstructed.

II

About the middle of March 1847, the business affairs of the princess demanded that she leave Woronince in order to embark on a difficult journey through Ukraine, Lithuania, and Russia, culminating in a sojourn at St. Petersburg lasting for four weeks. It was her task to sell grain, and the business cartels with which she dealt were widely scattered. In her letters to Liszt (who was meanwhile wending his way south to Turkey), Carolyne discloses some of the rigours she endured. The weather was particularly foul that spring, and the terrain was pelted alternately with rain and snow, turning the rough roads into a quagmire of slush and mud. Fed by the first thaws, the rivers became swollen and overflowed their banks. After only two days on the road, the princess's carriage lurched to a halt, axle-deep in water. Accompanied by a solitary chambermaid, she was forced to seek shelter for the night with a German farmer and his family while a raft was built to negotiate the swirling currents ahead.[3] The next day the weather had worsened and the raft was swept away by the raging torrent. Carolyne had to endure her cramped quarters for another twenty-four hours while a new raft was made. Thinking to make her stay more comfortable, the farmer had the idea that she should occupy the more spacious marital bedroom, but this precipitated a quarrel with his wife.

---

3. WA, Kasten 33, u. 1, p. 7, March 20, 1847 (Old Style).

She is an old, one-eyed fishwife—pregnant with her fifteenth child [wrote the princess], a dozen by her former husband. She looked at me very unpleasantly with her *eye* and seemed to bear me a grudge for not being one-eyed and toothless as well, and for having a black silk coat. He wanted to prevent her sleeping in the same room as me. She was furious about it, claiming that I was not a saint to be given a chapel and a sacristan to guard me. . . . I fell asleep about 8 o'clock on a little wooden settee with my head on some rags, while reading my prayer-book. I was so utterly exhausted I did not know what was happening. . . . My chambermaid did not want to awaken me, not even to make me more comfortable, knowing that my sleep is capricious and once disturbed does not return soon. Finally, as the domestic quarrel kept on, the wife entered the bedroom and he dragged her out. To avoid noise, they made even more. The maid went to tell the husband and persuaded him, after a lot of trouble, that I would rather spend the night on my bench, and that I would be upset if his wife did not occupy her bed. When I got up at 3 or 4 o'clock in the morning, I thought it quite natural to see her sleeping there with my chambermaid in her husband's place, and I did not understand the searching look she gave me when I said good morning to her as she awoke, in the most grateful way for her hospitality.[4]

That same day, the princess crossed the water on a newly constructed raft, harnessed fresh horses at the other side, and, despite warnings of further perils ahead, struck out for Vilnius in Lithuania. Around midnight she spotted the twinkling lights of a church, alighted from her carriage, and joined "fifty peasants and twenty beggars" at worship. It was Good Friday[5] and the princess describes this motley congregation and its singing of the chants of the Resurrection in her letter to Liszt. The next obstacle was the river Niemen, which was in full flood. Once more there was a delay while the rafts were used to ford the torrent, but within hours of resuming her journey the princess was again in difficulties. A fierce blizzard blew up, visibility failed, the horses were reined in, and Carolyne and her chambermaid huddled at the back of the carriage while the snow piled up around them. "Have you ever seen a blizzard?" she asks Liszt. "It's a fine moment of nature's folly. The sun sometimes appears in it like a flash of intelligence promptly blotted out. Then everything is white and dark, yet simple and pure, and wild."[6] Having dug themselves out, Caro-

---

4. WA, Kasten 33, u. 1, March 21, 1847 (Old Style).
5. In 1847 Good Friday fell on March 21 (Old Style). Carolyne's letter suggests that although she had been on the road for three days, she had barely covered a hundred miles.
6. WA, Kasten 33, u. 1, March 21, 1847 (Old Style).

lyne and her maid struggled on to Vilnius. The next day Carolyne fell ill, overcome by the hardships of her trip, and for twenty-four hours she lay helpless on a small wooden couch, her legs buckling under her every time she attempted to stand. By chance she found a good Polish doctor whose treatment enabled her to get to St. Petersburg. By April 5 she was installed in her hotel, where she took to her bed and slept the clock round.

Her journey had taken more than two weeks. When we contemplate the rigours of such trips, which Carolyne endured annually, we are not surprised that she often aroused the admiration of her male competitors in the grain business. "Madame," remarked one of them, "you work more laboriously than any of us. I wish my son were man enough to undertake such a journey in this season."[7]

During her month-long stay in St. Petersburg, much of Carolyne's time during the day was taken up with business meetings. In the evenings she undertook the usual social rounds, but she confessed to Liszt that she grew bored listening to polite conversation and gazing at fixed smiles. When Count Mikhail Vielgorsky called on her one day things changed. Vielgorsky, it will be recalled, had done much to make Liszt's visit to St. Petersburg in 1841 a success, and Carolyne lost no time in pumping him for his reminiscences of the great virtuoso. She also picked up a fair amount of gossip about musicians in St. Petersburg, which was duly reported back to Liszt. A few days later she gave a dinner-party to which Vielgorsky brought the pianist Adolf Henselt, who spent the evening re-living his memories of his earlier meeting with Liszt. Vielgorsky also introduced Carolyne to Döhler and Heinrich Ernst, the violinist, who was in St. Petersburg to play the solo viola part in Berlioz's *Harold in Italy*. The climax came when she met Berlioz himself, who had arrived in Russia the previous month and had just returned from Moscow in order to conduct his *Damnation of Faust, Romeo and Juliet,* and *Harold.* Berlioz neglects to mention this historic encounter in the otherwise full account of the Russian trip he gives in his *Mémoires.* [8] When Carolyne heard *Romeo and Juliet,* she left the theatre convinced that it was a masterpiece. She was furious with St.

---

7. Ibid.
8. "I want to tell you about Berlioz, who has just left my home," wrote Carolyne on April 21 (Old Style). "He has returned from Moscow, where he gave a concert and which he claims is a silly town. He seems furious with Paris and enchanted with St. Petersburg. He says that the musical personnel are among the best he has met, and the public too. Perhaps he was serving up food for fools! . . . Berlioz spoke of you in a way that gave me pleasure. He has great faith in your strength." (WA, Kasten 33, p. 27) See also the letter Berlioz wrote to Liszt from St. Petersburg a few days later, on April 27, the first time he mentioned Carolyne. "A very likable and witty princess, who knows better than any of us where you are going and what you are doing, is very willing to take these few lines into her care to forward them to you. Greetings, dear marvellous pilgrim! Greetings, I think about you a lot, and opportunities to talk about you are frequent here, where everyone admires and loves you almost as much as I do. Do you not think we are terrible vagabonds!" (TBC, vol. 1, p. 178)

Petersburg's "high society," many of whose members she considered block-heads, for not sharing her enthusiasm.

> The beautiful ladies flocked there, but they were bored. The ada-gio—that divine adagio—was absolutely not understood. Every-one remained cold, and all around me they were saying: "Is that all it is?" Oh, the imbeciles! The infinite would not suffice for them. They require several infinities. Or, my God, perhaps they need the *finite?* [9]

Not even the most ardent Berliozan can complain about the princess's lack of musical perception. These were the first notes of the composer she had heard, and on the strength of them she did not hesitate to proclaim their creator a genius. As the years rolled by, her growing friendship with Berlioz produced a significant body of correspondence, much of which proves that without her encouragement, the depressed and ailing composer might never have completed his greatest work, *The Trojans.* That Berlioz would not have quarrelled with this conclusion is borne out by the fact that the mammoth score is dedicated to her.

Aside from her business and social preoccupations, Carolyne had other concerns. She was weighed down with anxiety over the health of her daughter, Marie, who had fallen ill almost as soon as she had departed from Woronince and was now being looked after by the Wittgensteins. Carolyne probably feared that her in-laws would use the opportunity to remove the child from her permanently. She was five hundred miles away, and the absence of regular news upset her. The mail, in fact, was erratic, and two or three weeks had now elapsed since she had last heard from Liszt. "Are you alive," she asked him, "or are you dead? I'm writing to you once more before I leave St. Petersburg, and then I will probably not write again until I reach Odessa. Will I meet you again there?"[10] Carolyne had reason to feel apprehensive. Their last words, exchanged more than a month earlier, had been a re-affirmation of their intention to rendezvous in Odessa that summer. But time and distance can change many things. She had heard a rumour that Liszt had been seen in Vilnius; it was not true (by now he was travelling through Rumania, en route to Constantinople), but it served to raise once more the doubts that had nagged her ever since they had parted. Her letters often reveal a depressed personality riddled with self-doubt and anxiety. Several times in her endless epistles she told him that he need not respond in detail to what she was saying, that it did her good to write, that it was enough for her to be *permitted* to write, and that "I do not bear you

---

9. WA, Kasten 33, u. 1., April 25 (Old Style).
10. WA, Kasten, 33, u. 1., May 10, 1847 (Old Style).

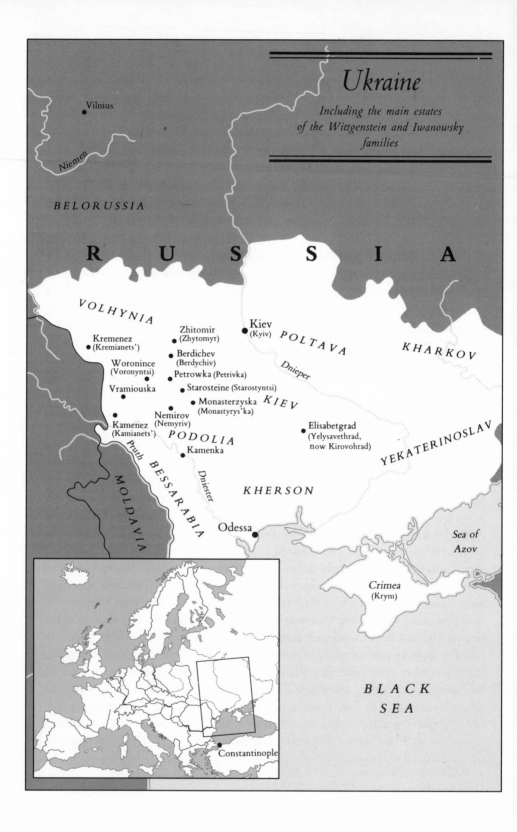

Ukraine

Including the main estates
of the Wittgenstein and Iwanowsky
families

BELORUSSIA

Vilnius

Niemen

R U S S I A

VOLHYNIA

Zhitomir
(Zhytomyr)

Kiev
(Kyiv)

POLTAVA

KHARKOV

Kremenez
(Kremianets')

Berdichev
(Berdychiv)

Woronince
(Voronyntsi)

Petrowka (Petrivka)

Dnieper

Vramiouska

Starosteine (Starostyntsi)

KIEV

Monasterzyska
(Monastyrys'ka)

Nemirov
(Nemyriv)

Kamenez
(Kamianets')

PODOLIA

Elisabetgrad
(Yelysavethrad,
now Kirovohrad)

YEKATERINOSLAV

Kamenka

Pruth

Dniester

MOLDAVIA

BESSARABIA

KHERSON

Odessa

Sea of
Azov

Crimea
(Krym)

Constantinople

BLACK
SEA

a grudge for not writing to me."[11] When Liszt had earlier suggested that he consign her letters to the flame, she begged him not to destroy these "symbols of attachment" to him. It was a golden day for her when Liszt finally wrote from Jassy, explaining that he had been in bed for a week with catarrhal fever, unable to reply, and confirming that he still planned to meet her in Odessa in July.[12]

III

Fresh from his conquest of Constantinople, an account of which will be found in Volume One of this biography, Liszt sailed back to Ukraine across the Black Sea aboard the Russian cruiser *Peter the Great*, which docked in Odessa about mid-July. There he was re-united with Carolyne, who told him for the first time that they would be joined by Prince Nicholas. Why was Nicholas in Odessa at all? It was not to be reconciled with his wife, whom he detested. Nor was it to take part in the tsar's military maneouvres, which were then in full swing, since he had resigned his commission some ten years earlier. The object of his curiosity was Liszt; and far from playing the role of an outraged husband, Nicholas cultivated him in the most cordial manner. The trio were seen together a number of times in Odessa's fashionable society. Carolyne and Nicholas also attended Liszt's recitals in the Hall of the Stock Exchange. And it was with Nicholas's full knowledge that Liszt was invited to spend the winter at Woronince. Is it possible that Nicholas saw in the great pianist the solution to his broken marriage? A letter written by Liszt to his mother shortly afterwards seems to suggest it. Until now, the son had not mentioned a word to her about the princess, who still remained nameless. "A situation offers itself to me with considerable advantages," he wrote. "It is not impossible that at last I shall strike a very good bargain. But I dare not speak of it for fear I shall look ridiculous."[13] This "good bargain" can only refer to a marriage with the princess, although Liszt is careful to avoid using the term. It points to an extraordinary conclusion: that the trio—Carolyne, Nicholas, and Liszt—had met in Odessa for the purpose of making such a marriage possible. Several pieces of evidence corroborate the idea of a "bargain." No sooner had Liszt left Odessa than Nicholas announced that he would not, after all, accompany Carolyne to Woronince but would instead spend the winter in Berlin.[14] After Odessa, also, the tone of

---

11. WA, Kasten 33, u. 1., May 20, 1847 (Old Style).
12. LLB, vol. 4, p. 8.
13. LLBM, p. 81.
14. Some interesting sidelights are thrown on this six-week sojourn in Odessa by Baron Nicholas von Gutmansthal, the Austrian consul to that city, who knew all the concerned parties quite well. Apparently Carolyne and Nicholas stayed at the Odessa home of her mother, Pauline Iwanowska,

Carolyne's letters becomes more intimate. There are open declarations of love. Life, she tells him, would be unthinkable without him. Among the less extravagant epithets for Liszt are "a poem in action" and "my beautiful America."[15] That Liszt was a willing victim cannot be doubted. He looked forward to the winter of isolation he was about to spend with Carolyne—a honeymoon by any other name—even though he must have known that both her mother, Pauline Iwanowska, and the Wittgenstein family occupied neighbouring estates, that they would almost certainly witness the arrangement, and that he would thereafter be hopelessly compromised.

I V

It was now September, and Liszt was journeying towards Elisabetgrad and the final concerts of his tour. He asked his mother to undertake an important commission: namely, to buy a modish hat in Paris for a distinguished lady. She was not to trust her own taste but should consult her friend Madame Seghers and buy it from the fashionable store of Madame Camille. "The price is not important. The more expensive it is, the better it will be . . . This little present comes from my heart."[16] Liszt also asked Anna to send him by the same post her personal copy of the daguerreotype of his birthplace in Raiding which was hanging in her Paris apartment. Almost as a reluctant after-thought, he made his first passing mention of Princess Carolyne, "with whom I am spending two or three months without concerts, without interruptions, without stress. That will be a novelty for me." Anna Liszt's curiosity was now aroused. Her son's letter only confirmed the rumours circulating in Paris: that Liszt was contem-

---

and Liszt frequently socialized with the family there. Gutmansthal tells us that Madame Iwanowska had the habit of turning night into day, and vice versa, and that she rarely descended from her bedroom before dusk, at which point she was ready to engage in intellectual jousting until the small hours of the following morning, leaving everybody else to retire from the field, utterly exhausted. Liszt and Carolyne were often on the sofa, deep in conversation, as Pauline walked into the drawing-room, and Liszt would jump up and exclaim: "Madame, stop your daughter from having *so much* intelligence!" (GSL, pp. 7–8)

After the Odessa episode was ended, and the trio temporarily dispersed, Carolyne wrote to Liszt: "I met my husband at a railway station. He tells me that he has written to you to tell you that he has embarked from Odessa and is having his passport made out to Berlin where he will spend the winter." (WA, Kasten 33, September 7, Old Style) The letter which Carolyne says her husband wrote to Liszt has not survived, but Liszt was too intelligent not to know that he was now part of an "arrangement" between Nicholas and his wife. Indeed, Carolyne's own letter to Liszt seems to prove it. After reminding him of his promise to visit her in Woronince, and assuring him that she would make everything comfortable for him in her "little cottage," she added the significant comment: "Do not be embarrassed at the thought of my husband"—the clearest indication that Nicholas complied with everything.

15. WA, Kasten 33, u. 1., September 14, 1847 (Old Style).
16. LLBM, p. 79.

Princess Carolyne as a young girl aged about ten years.

plating matrimony. The hat and the daguerreotype were despatched, together with some blunt questions, to which Liszt replied:

> How in your wisdom, dear mother, do you attribute to me ideas of marriage without waiting until I vow to you that I am mortally in love? Truly, you are quick at work, dear mother; whereas I advance like a snail. Whatever rumours you hear, believe only what I tell you, and be sure that if I should confide something like this to you, you will have every reason to be happy about it.[17]

Meanwhile, the "distinguished lady" herself had travelled ahead to Woronince in order to prepare her château for Liszt's arrival. She broke her journey at Field Marshal Wittgenstein's property in Vramiouska, "a sterile place situated

---

17. LLBM, p. 82. The crop of unofficial press reports about his forthcoming betrothal to Carolyne led to inquiries from other sources. Liszt replied to Baron von Gutmansthal: "As for the *Journal de Francfort,* it announces the marriage of a famous pianist with a Russian princess, but it is only a rumour that I am not at all in a position to confirm to you." (GSL, p. 30)

in a gorge of dry ravines, into which he sank a fortune," and saw again her mother-in-law, a forlorn widow of seventy, apparently deserted by her sons. She also visited her brother-in-law Georg, who was about to leave with his wife and child on an extended trip abroad.[18] No mention was made of Liszt. What the Wittgensteins did not know would not harm them, she may have thought, though the old adage was never less true than here. After having procured a team of fresh horses from Georg, Carolyne resumed her journey and arrived at Woronince on September 11 (Old Style).[19] Liszt himself reached the château a week later. He and Belloni were given their own quarters.[20] The princess had installed a piano in Liszt's room pending the arrival of his own from Odessa.

Liszt celebrated his thirty-sixth birthday at Woronince. On October 22 the princess gave a large party in his honour, and as a special surprise she invited a group of Gypsies from the surrounding area to visit the château and play for him. "The rays of the waning sun were still strong enough to spread a little warmth," wrote Liszt.[21] Hundreds of serfs joined in the open-air activities. It was turned into a golden day for them, both metaphorical and literal, when Carolyne released them from the payment of a full year's taxes as part of the celebrations. A beautiful Gypsy woman called Agriffina then told fortunes and predicted that the future was about to open its floodgates—an allusion, Liszt thought later on, to the revolutionary events that were to shake Europe the following year.

Princess Marie well remembered Liszt's arrival at Woronince and the enthusiastic manner in which her mother praised the great pianist in front of her. In her childlike way, the ten-year-old girl thought that her mother intended Liszt as a husband for her. When she realized that it was her mother who desired to become his wife, she cried out in astonishment: "But she has a husband already."[22] A natural bond of affection soon sprang up between Marie and Liszt. For the next twelve years she knew no other father, and his many letters to her testify to the love he bore her.

A fresh crop of family nicknames grew up at Woronince, further symbols of growing attachment. Liszt was dubbed "Filzyg-Midas," the pianist with the golden touch (Filzyg was the name of Marie's piano teacher). Marie, in turn, was called "Farfadet" ("sprite" or "little elf"); among the other affectionate

---

18. WA, Kasten 33, u. 1, September 10, 1847 (Old Style).
19. Ibid.
20. Belloni was with Liszt throughout the long stay at Woronince (LLB, vol. 5, p. 62ff). Once Liszt had taken the decision to retire from the concert platform, however, Belloni was effectively removed from active duty. He settled in Paris, where Liszt continued to charge him with delicate family missions from time to time. Many years later, Liszt jokingly referred to Woronince as "Belloni's Austerlitz"! (LLB, vol. 7, p. 377)
21. See Liszt's account of the Woronince Gypsies in RGS, vol. 6, pp. 157–59.
22. LSJ, p. 23.

Princess Carolyne with her daughter Princess Marie,
a lithograph by C. Fischer (1844).

diminutives Liszt applied to her, with ever-extending endings, were "Magne," "Magnet," and "Magnolette." Princess Carolyne was given the oblique title of "Abbé Floup," a label she wore with dogged persistence and insisted on adopting in her correspondence with Liszt over the next ten years. Her favourite nickname for Liszt was "Fainéant" ("lazy-bones" or "loafer"), an ironic reference to his obsession with work. Miss Anderson, Marie's governess, was known universally as "Scotchy." Liszt's lifelong fondness for such epithets has already been observed in Volume One. No one was immune. It helped to remove the barriers of formality that so often kept people apart in the "genteel" society of the nineteenth century.

v

This visit to Woronince was not harmful to his work, although he was at first frustrated because the piano he had sent on from Odessa had not yet arrived. The agent entrusted with this task was one Stieffel, and Liszt wrote to the Austrian consul in Odessa, Baron Gutmansthal, to complain about the delay.

Woronince
October 25, 1847

> Would you believe that my piano from Odessa, sent so they say before my departure from Elisabetgrad (more than two months ago), still has not arrived in Berdichev? Perhaps you could find a way to remedy this, because it is entirely Stieffel's fault, whom I beg you to be good enough to "stieffeln"[23] as thoroughly as he deserves. Which handler did Stieffel choose? What sort of accident can be delaying it? I am angry every morning when I get up, and I am angry again about it when I go to bed. . . .[24]

The piano arrived a week or two later, thanks possibly to Gutmansthal's intervention, and the old house began to ring with the sounds of the instrument as Liszt drew from its keyboard his latest compositions. Soon Liszt could write: "I have worked pretty well these last two months, between two cigars in the morning, at several things which do not displease me."[25] A topical legacy was his piano suite *Glanes de Woronince* (Gleanings from Woronince) whose three movements incorporate melodies he had heard the Ukrainian peasants sing.

---

23. A pun on the German verb *stieffeln,* "to give the boot to."
24. GSL, pp. 17–18.
25. LLB, vol. 1, p. 67.

The titles are

> *Ballade d'Ukraine (Dumka)*
> *Mélodies polonaises*
> *Complainte (Dumka)*

and the complete cycle is dedicated to Princess Marie. The first piece is a set of variations on the old Ukrainian folk-song "Hryts, do not go to the party tonight," attributed to the seventeenth-century Cossack songstress Marusia Churay.[26] Legend has it that Hryts was loved by two women, one of them Marusia herself. Since she refused to share her lover, Marusia resolved to kill him. On Sunday, so the song goes, she gathered poisonous herbs; on Monday she washed them; on Tuesday she cooked them; on Wednesday she served them to Hryts; and on Thursday he was dead. The song begins with a warning to Hryts in which he is cautioned against going to a party to meet Marusia's rival. For her crime Marusia was sentenced to death but was later reprieved by the Cossack chieftain Bohdan Khmelnytsky.

Of more than passing interest is the second piece, *Mélodies polonaises,* which quotes two Polish folk-songs.

The first of these melodies was also used by Liszt in his Duo Sonata for violin and piano, a musical discovery which allows us to post-date the completion of the sonata (usually thought of as a much earlier work) to 1848 or later.[27] As for the second melody, Chopin also borrowed it from folk sources for his song

---

26. "Hryts" is the Ukrainian diminutive for Gregory. For a fuller account of Marusia Churay and the text of her ballad, see SUW.

27. When the manuscript of the Duo Sonata was first discovered in the Weimar Archives in the late 1950s, it was thought by its violinist-editor, Tibor Serly, to belong to a much earlier period, since it is essentially a four-movement paraphrase of Chopin's C-sharp-minor Mazurka (1833), a piece that Liszt used to play during his Paris days. The sonata also contains violin configurations redolent of Paganini, the memory of whose playing (so the argument ran) was still fresh in the young Liszt's imagination. Liszt's letter to his mother, dated "Geneva, 1835," also confirms the existence of this piece (LLBM, p. 21). However, the presence of the Woronince folk-theme within the body of the sonata proves that Liszt could not have completed the work until at least fourteen years later. After

"The Maiden's Wish," a piece that has become widely familiar, paradoxically, because of Liszt's piano arrangement of it.[28]

A charming story surrounds the creation of the last piece, a *dumka,* which is worth preserving here. On the day that Liszt first arrived in Kiev, in January 1847, he wandered over to Contract Hall, where he was to give the first of his recitals, in order to try out the piano. After a brief rehearsal he decided to walk back to his hotel through Kiev's old market-place, which was filled with peasants selling their wares. Although it was a bitterly cold day and there was much snow on the ground, Liszt was wearing a stylish English coat with a top-hat and patent-leather shoes. The Kiev peasants stared at the "man of fashion" as he walked past, but Liszt ignored their prying glances. His eyes were fixed on something else. Sitting by a wall was an old grey-haired man hunched over a bandura, a multi-stringed instrument that Liszt had never seen before. Next to him stood a beautiful girl with jet-black hair, his granddaughter, singing a sad Ukrainian song to the old man's accompaniment. The girl was blind, and her song made a great impact on the onlookers.

> The wind is blowing,
> The trees are swaying,
> How sorrowful I am,
> Yet I cannot weep.

When the song was finished, the old man took off his hat and people threw in their small change. Liszt, however, had had no time to purchase any local currency and had only a banker's draft on his person, so he hurried back to Contract Hall in order to get it changed. When he returned to the market-place, he found that the old man and the girl had left. He inquired as to their whereabouts and was told that they had already returned to their native region

---

all, he himself tells us that he "gleaned" the folk-theme at Woronince. In one of its forms, preserved in the Institute of Folk Music in Warsaw, the melody runs:

The words traditionally sung to the tune are:

> John served at the château
> Near the finest monastery.
> Hey, hey—hop, hop, hop!
> Near the finest monastery.

The tune belongs to the region of Pomerania, although Liszt heard it in Podolia.

28. Liszt arranged six of Chopin's Seventeen Polish Songs for solo piano, including "The Maiden's Wish," in 1857, within weeks of their posthumous publication. Far from being an "arrangement of Chopin," then, Liszt's *Mélodies polonaises* is a fully independent creation which ought never to have become confused with Chopin in the first place. The connection, in short, is casual, not causal.

of Poltava. Liszt was troubled by the image of the blind girl and her sad song, and he spent the next two hours walking along the frozen shore of the river Dnieper reflecting on the music. That night at his recital he improvised on the melody, and thus was born the *dumka* which ends the *Gleanings from Woronince*.[29]

It should be stressed that these folk-songs had been kept alive through an oral tradition stretching back for many generations. Since the discipline of ethnomusicology did not at that time exist, Liszt may well have been the first "educated" musician to notate these melodies for posterity.

A far more important work was resumed at Woronince: the great collection of piano pieces known by the generic title *Harmonies poétiques et religieuses*. The ten compositions which comprise this cycle are listed here, although some of them were not begun until later on.[30]

> *Invocation*
> *Ave Maria*
> *Bénédiction de Dieu dans la solitude*
> *Pensée des morts*
> *Pater Noster*
> *Hymne de l'enfant à son réveil*
> *Funérailles (October 1849)*
> *Miserere, d'après Palestrina*
> *Andante lagrimoso*
> *Cantique d'amour*

Among the numbers Liszt is known to have completed at Woronince are *Invocation, Bénédiction de Dieu*, widely regarded as one of Liszt's pianistic

---

29. LKVL; BSKP. The holograph of *Glanes de Woronince* may be consulted in the Pierpont Morgan Library, New York (Cary Collection). In a marginal note Liszt has jotted down the melody of *Complainte* in the key of G minor, and with slightly different notation. We conjecture that this was the way in which he first heard the melody sung in Kiev. Incidentally, recent research has shown that both the words and the melody of *Complainte* were composed by Ivan Kotliarevsky (1769–1838), founder of modern Ukrainian literature.

30. In a letter to Baron von Gutmansthal, dated Woronince, October 25, Liszt disclosed that "the job which chiefly occupies me is the finishing of my *Harmonies poétiques et religieuses*, which will make a 120–150-page book, which I will give to the printers over the winter" (GSL, p. 22). It will be recalled that Liszt had begun this cycle as early as 1835, in Geneva (see Volume One, p. 219). Interestingly enough, Liszt omitted four pieces from the published cycle, two of which have only recently appeared in NLE 1:9. Their titles are *Hymne de la nuit* and *Hymne de matin*. The other two—*La Lampe du temple* and *Litanies de Marie*—remained unfinished. For more information on the genesis of *Harmonies poétiques*, see C-MCT.

masterworks, and *Cantique d'amour,* behind whose bland title lurks music of haunting beauty which pianists in general have yet to discover. Three of the remaining titles—*Ave Maria, Pater Noster,* and *Hymne de l'enfant*—are transcriptions of choral pieces written in 1846, while *Pensée des morts* is a completely re-worked version of the individual composition called *Harmonies poétiques et religieuses* (1834). When the cycle was finally published in 1852, it was dedicated to "Jeanne Elisabeth Carolyne." Perhaps because of its sentimental origins, it was the work that gave him the greatest pleasure to play to his friends during the Weimar years.

Liszt is also known to have played to Carolyne some fragments of his projected *Dante* Symphony, a work that he had carried in his portfolio since the early 1840s. This work was originally intended to be accompanied by lantern-slides of scenes from *The Divine Comedy* designed by the painter Bonaventura Genelli.[31] Liszt also wanted to introduce an experimental windmachine at the end of the first movement to depict the winds of Hell. To realize this ambitious project 20,000 thalers were needed. Although the princess undertook to provide the necessary capital nothing came of Liszt's plans, and the *Dante* Symphony was shelved until 1856.

VI

By November the first snows had fallen, and the lovers of Woronince were marooned in the icy desolation of a Ukrainian winter. Vows of love were exchanged and the princess gave Liszt a valuable Gordian knot made from pure gold, which symbolized a union that could not be broken. He left her for a few days in order to play in one or two nearby Polish towns for charity. This brief absence merely intensified their feelings. Just before he set out, she gave him a ring. "Keep it on your own finger," he told her, "through the sad and unhappy hours I shall be away from you. Return it to my finger when I come back to you, and restore all the joy to my soul."[32]

The time had now come to lift the veil of silence that Liszt had drawn around his relationship with Carolyne. On December 22 he broke the news to Marie d'Agoult in a letter which is a masterpiece of tact. Ever since their rupture, in 1844, Liszt and Marie had maintained a sporadic correspondence, chiefly because the fate of their three children still bound them together. But the fact that he delayed so long before putting pen to paper (he had been at Woronince for nearly three months) suggests that he spent an unconscionable time reflecting on the consequences of his action. In oblique prose, he told Marie that he felt

---

31. Liszt is known to have been thinking of some such "multi-media" presentation of the *Dante* Symphony since 1845. See ELM, p. 192.
32. LLB, vol. 4, p. 10.

attracted to "a great character united with a great spirit. . . . Attribute the change in my location to a very real change in my life which, at the very least, takes a new direction worthy of it."[33] Liszt understood the volatile nature of Madame d'Agoult's personality too well to risk stirring up trouble unnecessarily; so he must have felt reasonably certain that his union with Carolyne was to be permanent. Sure enough, after a delay of nearly a month, Marie came back with a sarcastic rebuff, calculated to wound, in which she brushed the dust off one of her earlier epithets: "So, a new apparition has seized your imagination and your heart? So much the better. This woman of great character (so you say) will not consent to share your life. She will not want to be *one of your mistresses.*"[34] This last phrase was a reference to a remark Marie had made to Liszt years earlier, when, after a quarrel, she had cried that while she did not object to being his mistress, she objected to being *one* of his mistresses.[35] Marie's response was read by Carolyne, whose amazing rejoinder has never before been published, but deserves to be widely known: "Nélida's reply is scathing, despite all her efforts to disguise it. . . . I would be happy for her to know that, on the contrary, one really wants to be *one of the mistresses . . .* for there are devotions without limits."[36] The princess and Marie d'Agoult never met, of course, nor did they ever correspond. But from the very beginning the smouldering fires of resentment and jealousy that we perceive in these exchanges were a constant threat to Liszt's happiness, and they led to an open conflagration among the parties some six or seven years later which none of them was likely to forget.

Almost insuperable difficulties stood in the way of Carolyne's union with Liszt, but nothing could shake her resolve to link her life with his and follow him to Weimar, there to await her fate. And Liszt? He made only one stipulation: that before leaving Ukraine Carolyne make over to her daughter one half of her fortune so that the child's rightful inheritance would be secured.[37] Neither Carolyne nor Liszt had any inkling of the tribulations that awaited them in Weimar. Both were confident that her marriage annulment would be granted quickly and that they would soon be free to marry. Liszt had a

---

33. ACLA, vol. 2, pp. 390–91.
34. ACLA, vol. 2, p. 417.
35. VFL, p. 152.
36. Letter dated January 27, 1848 (Old Style), WA, Kasten 33. That Carolyne had already read Marie d'Agoult's novel *Nélida* the previous spring, while Liszt was en route to Turkey, is proved by her correspondence with Marie Potocka (LAG, p. 34). The latter, in response to some derogatory remarks that Carolyne appears to have made about the famous *roman à clef,* had told her: "It takes courage to expose oneself in something less than a shirt." Carolyne, then, was well aware of Daniel Stern's depiction of herself as a wronged woman. As for Carolyne's remark that "there are devotions without limits," we can only conjecture what Marie d'Agoult might have said in the unlikely event that Liszt ever heeded Carolyne's wish and passed this advice on to his old lover. It was tantamount to saying that Marie d'Agoult ought to consider herself fortunate to be "one of the mistresses."
37. LSJ, p. 23.

powerful ally in Weimar in the person of Grand Duchess Maria Pawlowna, the sister of the tsar. As the titular head of the Russian Orthodox Church, Tsar Nicholas exercised absolute authority over the dissolution of marriages. Maria Pawlowna would surely intercede with her brother in behalf of her famous Kapellmeister. Thus did the lovers of Woronince dream their dreams and weave their fantasies.

V I I

The enormity of the sacrifice Carolyne was about to make for Liszt emerges from the letters she wrote to him between January and April 1848. A few days after Liszt had left for Weimar, she herself set out from Woronince, on January 29, on another of those nightmare journeys to Kiev. Her primary purposes were to sell off some of her estates, say farewell to her mother,[38] and commence legal proceedings to secure an annulment of her marriage. One of the most painful episodes of the journey was to return to the old property of her father at Starosteine. When she broke the seals on the door, placed there three years earlier, she found everything as it had been on the day of his death. She entered his study and saw again the table covered with his papers, the chair half-turned as his hand had left it, the antique desk he had inherited from his father, and the blond curl he had cut from Carolyne's infant head twenty-five years earlier still hanging from the crucifix on the wall, which bore the inscription: "I am the Way."[39]

It distressed her to part with such lands, for to her it was like breaking faith with her ancestors. "Today I have just sold one of my lands, one of the first that my grandfather bought, one of the cornerstones of that fortune amassed so laboriously and honestly by the hard work and sincere efforts of two generations of men. . . . I burst into tears when it passed into other hands."[40] Word spread like wildfire through the Kiev business community that the

---

38. Since walking out of her marriage with Iwanowsky, Pauline had become a quarrelsome recluse. "I do not know how my mother will end up," wrote Carolyne, on one of the rare occasions she offers any insight at all into the personality of her parent. "She has a talent for getting everybody on her back and making me unhappy as no one else can. I have just received from her a pile of papers, heavy with irritations still to come. She was unable to live in peace with her father, with her husband, with her nephews. Will she finally succeed in turning away from her daughter? That is not impossible." Because Iwanowsky had bequeathed all his wealth to his daughter, it seems that Carolyne may have been responsible for the financial well-being of her mother. This was yet another reason for visiting Pauline, whom she was never to see again. WA, Kasten 33, u. 1, January 6, 1848 (Old Style).

39. WA, Kasten 33, February 13, 1848 (Old Style).

40. WA, Kasten 33, February 6, 1848 (Old Style). It is an indication of the regard in which Carolyne was held by her serfs that when they learned that her lands were being sold, a group of them came to see her "and offered to work double so that I could keep them." (Ibid., March 15, 1848)

princess was selling off her lands, and she found herself besieged by speculators looking for easy pickings. "I am invaded by buyers who think that with a woman one can simply take; since I wish to sell and not give, the deals are sometimes slow." She refused to become their victim, however, and in the same letter she told Liszt: "I have sold a second [property] for a price as high as has ever been paid, which makes people say that I am not stupid." And she added: "Will I be able to bring my frail skiff to port without letting it sink?"[41] That, of course, was Carolyne's euphemistic way of asking: "How shall I get this money into Germany?" We learn that she opened a temporary bank account in Kiev,[42] but she left no direct clues as to how her fortune was transferred to Weimar. What evidence there is, and it is mostly of a circumstantial nature, suggests that she brought much of it with her physically. Russia was about to close its borders as Europe headed towards the bloodbath of 1848. Normal financial transactions had all but ceased, and in any case the princess had no desire to draw attention to her activities by the transfer of huge sums of cash through the tsar's labyrinthine banking system. One of her last acts was to deposit with Archbishop Ignaz Holowinsky, the metropolitan of St. Petersburg, a petition for the annulment of her marriage to Nicholas.[43] Then, the purpose of her two-month journey accomplished, she returned to Woronince in order to pick up Marie and Miss Anderson and flee with them to Germany.

While this traumatic journey was in progress, Princess Marie had been left with old Frau Wittgenstein, and Carolyne now requested that her daughter be returned to her. "No mention was made of the forthcoming voyage," Carolyne told Liszt. Marie was handed back by the unsuspecting grandmother, who little realized that she would never see her granddaughter again. The use of code-words in Carolyne's correspondence suggests a camouflage to keep the Wittgensteins in the dark.[44] By removing their granddaughter to Weimar by stealth, Carolyne lost whatever standing she still possessed in the eyes of that family. As the plot was brewing, and Carolyne was selling off her properties, Nicholas, it will be recalled, was spending a profligate winter in Berlin, blissfully unaware that the source of his income was about to dry up.

---

41. Ibid., January 27, 1848 (Old Style).

42. Ibid., February 6, 1848 (Old Style).

43. LSJ, p. 41. The petition was formally submitted on May 4, 1848, after she had left St. Petersburg, and her plea for annulment was based on the grounds of *vis et metus*—that is, "violence and fear" (ASVR, fol. 142).

44. One of the more intriguing aspects of the princess's correspondence was that as her departure from Russia became imminent, she lapsed into verbal and numerical symbols which are generally impossible for an outsider to decipher, since they were meant for Liszt's eyes only. She was fearful that her letters might be intercepted by the authorities and that the Wittgensteins might learn of her intentions. "Nini" and "Paganini" are thinly disguised references to Nicholas, and their derivation requires no explanation. Phrases such as "I have just learned that one can have a 155.0.a. without anyone suspecting" seem to refer to financial transactions.

On April 2, Carolyne took a last, nostalgic look round the château she was about to leave forever ("the only shelter on this earth where it was granted to me to find peace and to repose in solitude, amidst the bitterest tribulations"), lingered for a few moments in Liszt's old room, where she prayed, and then boarded her travelling coach and headed for the Russian frontier. The thought of the princess's carriage rolling across the Ukrainian wilderness loaded with roubles and precious stones (she had bought Liszt some opals in Kiev) beggars description. The tsar's troops were everywhere, and the journey must have been transformed into high adventure. In troubled times, as the princess well knew, cash is the best passport, and she had more than enough to bribe her way through an army of officials. That Liszt had a hand in the design of her getaway coach seems established beyond doubt by a letter he wrote to "Magnolette" on February 4, 1848, and it only adds to the air of mystery and intrigue surrounding the princess's flight.[45] As the frontiers of Podolia disappeared over the horizon for the last time, she noted bitterly: "I am about to leave the country which has held me in its shrewish bosom for fifteen years, and whose milk has turned to vinegar and bile."[46]

VIII

By the time Carolyne commenced her flight out of Russia, Liszt had already been in Weimar for several weeks. He had set out from Woronince at least a week before the princess had begun her journey to Kiev, travelling via Lemberg and Ratibor on a Russian passport,[47] and had arrived in the city of Goethe and Schiller in early February. He settled into the Erbprinz Hotel in the Marktplatz, not far from the Court Theatre. This was to be Liszt's official residence in Weimar throughout his thirteen-year stay there. Even after he had moved into the Altenburg with Carolyne, his mail was always forwarded to the Erbprinz Hotel, and messages from the court were delivered there as a matter of course.

Within hours of his arrival in Weimar, Liszt had plunged into a busy round of rehearsals for Flotow's *Martha,* which he conducted at the Court Theatre on February 16, in honour of Maria Pawlowna's birthday. He also directed a concert at the castle for the royal household, at which he used a silver baton

---

45. HLSW, p. 23. "Today I am sending the Princess, your mother, the design for the carriage that will have the honour and the good fortune to carry you; I like to think that it will be according to her taste and to all your requirements."
46. WA, Kasten 33, April 3, 1848 (Old Style).
47. This passport was issued to Liszt on December 20, 1847 (Old Style) by the governor of Ukraine in Kamenez (WA, Überformate 136, 1M).

given to him by Carolyne.[48] A few days later he appeared as soloist in a Henselt piano concerto, and between times he had to give four or five singing lessons a week to Duchess Sophie, the wife of Carl Alexander. He had a number of private audiences with Maria Pawlowna, at which he brought her up to date about Carolyne and asked her to intercede with Tsar Nicholas on their behalf.

In the old, unthinking Liszt biographies of yore, it was a commonplace to be told that once Liszt had arrived in Weimar and had picked up the threads of his professional existence there, to say nothing of his social diversions, he started to regret his liaison with the princess and hope that her intention to join him might somehow be thwarted. Such is the view expressed essentially by Haraszti and Newman.[49] It arose from a general prejudice against the princess, rather than from documentary evidence. In fact, the documents force one to the opposite conclusion. Liszt became depressed when the mail from Woronince was delayed, and elated when a batch of Carolyne's letters was unexpectedly delivered to the Erbprinz all at once.[50] "You must count on me at every moment, from the soles of my feet to the roots of my hair," he wrote to her.[51] And a few days later: "Let me be engulfed in you and reside there; it is my sole destiny."[52] This is not the language of a man who wishes to disentangle himself from a relationship with which he has grown bored. The lovers even planned a trip to Venice in order to visit St. Mark's Cathedral during Holy Week, and the journey was only abandoned at the last moment because of growing political unrest across Europe. Carolyne was not sure of her route from Woronince, and the uncertainty in her letters filled Liszt with anxiety. At first she urged him to meet her at Cracow, then at Lemberg. Finally, Liszt travelled to Grätz and waited for Carolyne at Kryzanowicz, the mountain castle of Prince Lichnowsky, just four hours away from the Austro-Russian frontier. "The house is absolutely deserted," wrote Liszt. "I do not see a living soul, except for the servants who wait on me."[53] It was in this

---

48. "The conducting baton has had a stupefying effect," joked Liszt to Carolyne, "but I only gave out the name of the donor with extreme discretion" (LLB, vol. 4, p. 23).

49. "Could he seriously have thought of encumbering himself with an ugly and volcanic wife, rich though she was?" asks Haraszti (HL, p. 139). To which Newman adds: "[Liszt] was a little perturbed when he discovered later that the adoring princess wished the tie to become a permanent one" (NLRW, vol. 2, p. 207).

50. LLB, vol. 4, p. 19.

51. LLB, vol. 4, p. 21.

52. LLB, vol. 4, p. 22. After his arrival in Weimar, Liszt was worried lest Carolyne suffer harassment at the hands of the Wittgenstein family. "When are the bombs and explosions to be expected then?" he asked. This was a reference not to the impending revolution but to the wrath of the Wittgensteins when they discovered that Carolyne had escaped from their control. In the next sentence Liszt wrote: "Try to arrange it so that the heaviest part falls to my share!" (LLB, vol. 4, p. 23)

53. LLB, vol. 4, p. 32. Lichnowsky himself had gone to Berlin to attend an urgent meeting of the Diet. As early as January 26, when Liszt had met his old friend in Ratibor, the possibility of using

romantic setting that Carolyne and Liszt were re-united about the middle of April.

For ten days the lovers of Woronince languished at Kryzanowicz, seemingly oblivious to the fact that Europe was bracing itself for war. All the evidence suggests that events moved too fast for Liszt to comprehend. In France the government of King Louis-Philippe collapsed and was replaced by a national assembly with Lamartine as spokesman for foreign affairs. In Hungary Kossuth began to lay the groundwork for the independence of his country from Austria, a bold act which doomed his patriotic army to defeat and Hungary itself to seventy years more of the stifling embrace of the Habsburgs. Smaller uprisings erupted all over Germany and were repressed. It was a time to stand up and be counted. The question has often been asked: Where was Liszt? Less than a decade earlier he had been hailed by the Hungarian nation as a patriot. And now? While Europe was smouldering, Liszt was cocooned with his mistress in their fortress-haven, planning a nostalgic trip back to Eisenstadt and Raiding in order to show her the humble cottage in which he was born. It is a strange episode in the life of our hero, and one for which he was to be heavily criticized. Meanwhile, the thunderbolts of retribution that the gods should have hurled on the turrets of Kryzanowicz descended, by some inscrutable act of providence, on Lichnowsky instead. He was murdered by revolutionaries in Frankfurt later that year, and Liszt never saw his old companion again.[54]

I X

No account of Liszt's life to appear so far has contained anything like an adequate description of the turbulent political events of 1848. Liszt watched the "Year of Revolution" at first with detachment, then with apprehension as Europe caught fire. Finally, as the unparalleled drama which was the Hungarian

---

Kryzanowicz as a rendezvous may have been discussed. Carolyne arrived at Kryzanowicz in the company of Princess Marie, Miss Anderson, and a maid called Alexandra. The reason for the delay in her arrival (Liszt had expected her on April 3 or 4 at the latest) had to do with Miss Anderson's passport, which was out of order; a few tense days elapsed before new travel documents could be procured. (WA, Kasten 33, u. 1, March 27, 1848 [Old Style])

54. Some details of Prince Lichnowsky's assassination may be found in the *Bayreuther Blätter*, Heft 1–3, p. 25, 1907. See also RLS, vol. 1, p. 83, and EAML, vol. 1, pp. 313–16. Lichnowsky was a delegate at the first German parliament which gathered at Frankfurt in 1848, and the city was in a state of unrest. On September 18, while he was out riding with General von Auerswald during a lull in the fighting, they were ambushed by revolutionaries, pursued, and finally cornered in the cellar of a local gardener's house. General von Auerswald was beaten to death with cudgels, while Lichnowsky's arms and torso were hacked to pieces with blades. Lichnowsky was then held up by two assailants while a third shot him at point-blank range through the body. He was left to die of his wounds.

struggle for national independence began to unfold, he suffered genuine anguish. We propose to trace the main outlines of the Hungarian revolution in somewhat greater detail than is customary in a book about Liszt, and for a fairly obvious reason: he found it impossible to remain immune to the tragedy, which dominated his thoughts and feelings and formed the historical backdrop to the first two years of his tenure in Weimar.

Funérailles, 1848–1849

*It is my solemn wish that should everything be
lost in Hungary, at least this one freedom should
survive: the burden of serfdom should not bend the
people's neck.*

LAJOS KOSSUTH[1]

I

On February 22, 1848, a violent disorder broke out in the streets of Paris.
Troops were called in, and by nightfall forty demonstrators had died in a
fusillade of bullets. The demonstration spread to the National Guard, whose
loyalty to the French throne began to crumble. Within forty-eight hours a
howling mob had surrounded the royal palace. Confronted with the prospect
of civil war, Louis-Philippe (the "Citizen King") abdicated in favour of his
nine-year-old grandson and fled to England.[2] Alphonse de Lamartine was made
head of a provisional government, and after some stormy scenes at the Hotel
de Ville, where the radicals had assembled, a republic was proclaimed. Universal
male suffrage was introduced, and overnight the electorate jumped from two
hundred thousand to nine million. The government also guaranteed that every
citizen would be given a job. By June it had become clear that Lamartine's
radical party had promised more than it could deliver. A brief and bloody civil
war erupted—the so-called "June Days." General Louis Cavaignac was called
in to restore order. A veteran of the Algiers campaigns, Cavaignac understood

---

1. Speech in the Hungarian Houses of Parliament, September 19, 1848.
2. In his memoirs the French composer Massenet, who was six years old at the time, recalled this
violent day as the first memorable experience of his life. "One day I found myself in front of an
old piano, and either to amuse me or to try my talent, my mother gave me my first music lesson.
It was February 24, 1848, a strangely chosen moment, for our lesson was interrupted by the noise
of street-firing that lasted for several hours. The revolution had burst forth and people were killing
one another in the streets." ("Autobiographical Notes of Massenet," *Century Illustrated Monthly*,
October 7, 1892, p. 123)

his trade all too well. He waited until the rebels had entrenched themselves behind their street barricades and then brought up his artillery. Fifteen hundred rebels were killed in the volleys, and twelve thousand were arrested, many of them to be deported to Algiers. The workers' movement had been crushed, and Lamartine's government collapsed.[3]

The revolutionary events in France inspired the workers of Vienna. On March 13, 1848, they took to the streets and clashed with the imperial troops of the Habsburgs. The fighting was fierce and bloody, and the royal guardsmen failed to hold their lines. Thousands of revolutionaries went on the rampage, and the hated Metternich was forced to make an ignominious flight to England, like Louis-Philippe before him. It was the initial success of the popular uprising in Vienna that now led Hungary to loosen the bonds which for centuries had tied her to Austria. Seizing the historic moment, the Hungarian Diet, which was then sitting in its ancient capital of Pozsony (less than thirty miles from a beleaguered Vienna) demanded a series of far-reaching reforms which the Austrian emperor, Ferdinand V, was obliged to accept. On March 15 the people's revolution broke out in Pest itself, and the poet Sándor Petőfi read out the famous "Twelve Points" from the steps of the National Museum. By the end of the day, the ruling circles of Pest had joined the side of the insurgents, and Vienna's hold over the city was broken. Two days later, Ferdinand V agreed to the appointment of Lajos Batthyány as Hungary's first independent prime minister.[4] Thus were the seeds of the 1848–49 conflict sown.

I I

In those days the Habsburg empire consisted of a loose conglomerate of ethnic groups—Hungarians, Rumanians, Croats, Czechs, and Slovaks—each one clamouring for a measure of freedom from Vienna. Had they acted together the House of Habsburg would have collapsed like a house of cards. But their relationship to one another was marred by historical enmities. The empire had lurched from crisis to crisis, with Vienna in cunning alliance with all its incompatible parts. Rumanians quarrelled with Hungarians, Czechs with Slovaks, and the Croats with everybody. They were united only by their distrust

3. The informed reader will not need to be reminded that the *Communist Manifesto* of Karl Marx (1848) drew its inspiration from the revolutionary fervour of these times. Its closing imperative ("The workers have nothing to lose in this Revolution but their chains.... Workers of the world, unite!") was in effect a delayed fuse that did not detonate until 1917, in Russia.

4. It is an indication of the speed with which these events moved forward that the decision to elect Batthyány as Hungary's first prime minister was taken only after the Hungarian delegation had boarded the boat which bore them down the Danube towards Vienna (PHH, p. 257). Batthyány's government included Kossuth (finance), Széchenyi (communications), Deák (justice), and Eötvös (education).

of one another, and this was to be the undoing of the Hungarian uprising. Most of the ethnic groups preferred to remain subject to Vienna rather than to gain liberty under the Hungarian flag. Unlike the vassal states, Hungary was never an Austrian dependency but had been a separate kingdom with its own crown and constitution for more than eight hundred years.[5] It was now linked to Vienna through the historical anomaly that had been the Holy Roman Empire (dissolved forty years earlier by Napoleon). For centuries the emperor of Austria had also been the king of Hungary—as he still was, but with a clear separation of powers. The most telling evidence of all this lay in the oath of allegiance. Hungarians did not swear loyalty to the throne of the Habsburgs but to their own king, whose crown the Habsburgs merely held in trust. That they had betrayed this trust across the generations, ignoring laws passed in Hungary while enforcing ones passed in Vienna, was apparent to all Magyars, who chafed beneath the imperial yoke. During the 1840s, with the awakening of Hungarian nationalism, some sharp political exchanges took place between István Széchenyi and Lajos Kossuth. Both leaders wanted the same thing— independence from Austria. But whereas Széchenyi desired to achieve this goal gradually, through peaceful means, Kossuth desired it at once, through revolution. Kossuth's chief weapon was his newspaper, the *Pesti Hirlap,* through whose columns he waged an unceasing war of words. At the height of the debate he addressed Széchenyi, and the whole class of Hungarian nobles who were urging caution, with the famous words: "With you, by you, if you will; without you, even against you, if it must be."[6] By 1848 Kossuth's radical views prevailed. Even so, Batthyány and his ministers wished to avoid war. In the event, it was thrust upon them by an act of treachery from Ferdinand V. Having signed the March decrees, Ferdinand at once began to regret his act. He entered into a secret understanding with the Croatian general Josip von Jelačić and appointed him military governor of Hungary, with instructions to restore imperial authority in Pest.

On September 11, 1848, Jelačić entered Hungary at the head of a Croatian army of 34,000 men, reinforced by six divisions of Austrian regulars. As he marched towards Pest, his troops committed the most wanton acts of barbarity against the local Magyar peasants. News of Jelačić's carnage swept across Hungary and the nation rushed to take up arms. Jelačić was within a day's march of Pest when, on September 29, he was stopped by General Móga, who defeated him at Pákozd by Lake Velence with an army of less than 15,000 men. The Hungarians captured 12,000 prisoners, twelve field-pieces, and two generals. Had Móga allowed his hussars to carry out reprisals, Hungary might well have

---

5. The coronation of King Stephen I, the greatest of the Árpád kings, took place in A.D. 1000. His crown was conjoined (but never relinquished) with that of foreign powers from 1301, with the death of Andrew III, when the Árpád line expired.
6. *Pesti Hirlap,* February 17, 1841.

won its independence there and then. But Jelačić begged Móga for a three-day truce, which was foolishly granted. Instead of using the time to negotiate a peace treaty, Jelačić fled to Vienna in order to raise an imperial army.

The Austrian battalions hurriedly assembled by the emperor in October 1848 were harassed in Vienna by left-wing insurgents who openly sided with the peasant revolts occurring all over the empire. Street battles ensued, and Vienna was once more drenched in blood. A revolutionary mob hunted down Count Latour, the minister for war, and hanged him from a lamp-post. The emperor fled the city and commanded Prince Windisch-Graetz to muster a fresh army and restore authority.

Batthyány, who had hoped for a peaceful settlement, resigned as prime minister, and Lajos Kossuth now emerged as the undisputed leader of the war of independence. We shall have more to say of Kossuth presently. He was a political leader of the first magnitude, whose golden-tongued oratory did more than anything else to rally the nation to the Hungarian flag. That he was right to view the Habsburgs as mortal enemies, interested only in subordinating the Magyars, was borne out shortly afterwards when Batthyány, who had gone to Vienna at the head of a peace delegation, was arrested and thrown into jail without a hearing.

III

Windisch-Graetz arrived in Vienna in October 1848 with plenipotentiary powers. The city was in disarray, and his energies were spent mainly in restoring order. Móga's victorious army was already poised on the Austrian frontier, ready to seize the imperial capital. At that moment Hungary had a unique opportunity to sweep aside the Habsburgs forever and expand the conflict to European dimensions. As Kossuth put it: "It is a duty of honour to hasten to the aid of the Viennese [people], as they have risen in opposition to the war against Hungary. If we win a battle, it will decide the fate of Austria; if we lose one, it will not discourage the nation, but will spur it to greater sacrifices."[7] Unfortunately, Kossuth delayed too long. By the time he gave the order to cross into Austria, Windisch-Graetz was ready for him. The two armies clashed at Schwechat, just outside Vienna, on October 30, and the badly outnumbered Hungarians suffered great slaughter. Since Windisch-Graetz dared not leave a revolutionary Vienna behind his back simply to pursue the remnants of the Hungarian army, Kossuth was given a brief respite. He relieved Móga of his command and appointed General Artúr Görgey to replace him. This controversial decision was to have far-reaching consequences for the conduct of the war.

---

7. DPKG, p. 168.

Windisch-Graetz entered Hungary on December 16 at the head of an imperial army of 44,000 men. From that moment Kossuth knew that the struggle would be to the death, that it must end with either the overthrow of the Habsburgs or the fall of Hungary. To make matters worse, the feeble-minded Emperor Ferdinand had abdicated the Austrian throne in favour of his eighteen-year-old nephew Franz Joseph I, who was determined to restore Austrian hegemony. During the next few weeks Kossuth's greatness as a national leader stood revealed. He toured the country, making speech after speech to rally the people to the patriotic cause. It was said of him that "wherever he stamped his foot there sprang up a soldier."[8] He had not only to find men, however, but to establish munitions factories to arm them. His eloquence swayed the legislature. He was granted 42 million forints and permission to recruit 200,000 men. A new army was equipped from nothing. Within weeks he had raised 64 infantry battalions, 10 hussar regiments, and 32 artillery units containing 233 cannons.[9]

Since the army was not yet ready to turn the Austrian advance, Kossuth made the courageous decision to transfer the seat of government from Pest to Debrecen, situated in the interior. This move had been made possible by the arrival in Transylvania of the colourful General József Bem, who had been placed in charge of the Transylvanian army towards the end of 1848 and had already cleared the country of imperial forces. Bem was a veteran Polish campaigner who had fought the Russians in 1830. He spoke not a word of Hungarian but nonetheless aroused a fierce loyalty among the rank and file. A man of action, Bem addressed his admiring troops in monosyllabic Polish-German. Major Cretz, who served with Bem throughout the Transylvanian campaign and left some vivid eye-witness accounts of the battles there, well remembered the occasion when the short, stocky general, with a deep scar running across his right cheek (a legacy from a Russian bullet), assembled his officers for their first briefing. "Gentlemen," Bem began, "I require the strictest obedience. Whoever disobeys will be punished. I know how to reward, but I know how to punish too. You may leave." Cretz said that they all stood dumbfounded before this little man. "We felt that we had to do with no ordinary person, but with a tried soldier who was not to be trifled with."[10] Bem was an artillery officer by training and a fanatic about this branch of arms. He not only supervised every gun emplacement himself but insisted on priming and aiming the guns as well. According to legend, his target shooting was so precise that he once shot a cannon-ball straight through the chest of a Russian general who was issuing orders to his troops more than half a mile away.

---

8. DPKG, p. 169.
9. PHH, p. 271.
10. DPKG, p. 175.

The evacuation of Pest was begun on New Year's Eve. A major problem was that the Hungarians had amassed all their ammunition in the capital. For three days and nights Kossuth personally supervised the safe removal of the munitions, and he was one of the last to leave the city. When the Austrians finally entered Pest, they acquired éclat, as a contemporary account puts it, but no solid military advantages.[11] As for the Hungarians, their attitude was summed up in a single sentence: "Pest is not Hungary!" In Debrecen, Kossuth and his staff occupied the old town hall, and it was here that his transcendental abilities as an administrator came to the fore. The large ante-room was always filled with people waiting for an interview. A ceaseless flow of military, civil, and political orders issued from his office. He dictated several letters simultaneously to the clerks and transcribers who surrounded him, chaired committee meetings, signed communiqués. It was nothing for him to work eighteen hours a day without pause. Kossuth became the embodiment of the life-and-death struggle of his people. In his ability to deal with a multitude of problems of the gravest proportions and not break under the strain, he has often been likened to Napoleon.

I V

By the early spring of 1849, the Hungarian army under General Görgey had scored some spectacular victories. These were the days of the classical set-piece battles at Kápolna, Hatvan, Tápióbicske, Isaszeg, Vác, and Komárom, with their cavalry charges, artillery bombardments, and hand-to-hand infantry engagements—sometimes with more than 75,000 men in the field. Within a few weeks the Austrians were in full retreat across the country.

On April 14 Kossuth issued the Declaration of Independence from Austria, one of the most momentous occasions in the history of Hungary. The Protestant church in Debrecen was packed with representatives of the nation, gathered to witness this event. The Declaration is a spectacular piece of literature, designed to arouse the conscience of the nation. In his stunning indictment of the Habsburgs, Kossuth rose to unsurpassed heights of eloquence. He accused the Austrian monarchs of crimes against humanity. "The House of Lorraine-Habsburg is unexampled in the compass of its perjuries. . . . Its determination to extinguish the independence of Hungary has been accompanied by a succession of criminal acts, comprising robbery, destruction of property by fire, murder, maiming. . . . Humanity will shudder when reading this disgraceful page of history."[12] As the last curse fell from Kossuth's lips, a thunderous shout

---

11. DPKG, pp. 193–94.
12. DPKG, p. 206.

The Assault on Buda, May 21, 1849, *a lithograph by August Pettenkofen.*

of exultation broke out in the church. It was caught up by the multitude outside and rolled along the streets like an avalanche. That same day, the Hungarian Diet passed an historic resolution, "that the House of Habsburg had forfeited the throne,"[13] and shortly afterwards Kossuth was elected governor of Hungary. These were heady days, and there was jubilation throughout the land. Nevertheless, there were those who thought that the declaration was premature, that it would have been wiser to issue it not from Debrecen but from Pest, after the Austrians had retreated from the capital and been driven back behind their own borders.

The Hungarians re-entered Pest without difficulty on April 24. In Buda, on the other side of the Danube, however, the Austrians had fortified their hillside defences, and Görgey was forced to lay siege to the town. The Hungarian flag was finally hoisted on the ramparts of Buda Castle on May 21, after a murderous frontal assault directly up the cliff face, in which many Hungarian soldiers died. The Austrians were now in disarray and retreated to their border in disorganized groups.

Franz Joseph, in a desperate attempt to save his crumbling empire, appealed to Tsar Nicholas I for Russian intervention, and it was quickly forthcoming.

13. DPKG p. 227.

About the middle of June a Russian army of 200,000 men broke into Hungary from diverse directions. Along the western borders another 170,000 Austrians were mustered in re-organized divisions. Now began that series of defeats on the battlefield that ended in catastrophe for the Hungarians. General Bem was gradually forced to yield up most of Transylvania. He was defeated at the battle of Segesvár, in which the poet Sándor Petőfi lost his life on July 31. Less than two weeks later Bem engaged the Austrians at Temesvár; his troops were trapped in a Transylvanian gorge and had to scatter in all directions. The Hungarian generals now began to quarrel among themselves and with the politicians as to how the war should be conducted. Meanwhile, the enemy penetrated ever deeper into Hungarian territory. General Görgey broke away from the others and refused to carry out Kossuth's directives. The government ordered Görgey to be relieved of his command, but he ignored the directive. It is today clear that Görgey had already allied himself with the peace party within the Hungarian Diet. There was a classic personal confrontation between Kossuth and Görgey, at which the latter categorically refused to engage the Russians. On the advice of his ministers, Kossuth now made the fatal blunder of the war. He reluctantly gave Görgey absolute authority to negotiate the best possible terms for Hungary. From this position of power Görgey informed General Rüdiger of the tsarist army that he was prepared to surrender unconditionally to him but would not surrender to the Austrians. Two days later, on August 13, the Hungarian army laid down its arms on the plains of Világos, near Arad. The Russian commander gave Görgey an exclusive pardon but handed his officers and men to the Austrians, at whose hands many of them were brutalized. For this act of betrayal, Görgey was branded by Kossuth as a traitor.[14] At the fortress of Komárom, a strong Hungarian force under General

---

14. "Nor could the united Russo-Austrian forces have conquered my heroic countrymen," Kossuth wrote later, "had they not found a traitor to aid them in the man whom, believing in his honesty, and on account of his skill, I raised from obscurity. Enjoying my confidence, the confidence of the nation and the army, I placed him at the head of our forces, giving him the most glorious part to perform ever granted to man. What an immortality was within his reach had he been honest! But he betrayed his country. Cursed be his name for ever!" (ALK, p. 139)

In hindsight it appears that the Russians made oral promises to Görgey that the Austrians were unwilling to fulfil. A few days after the surrender they delivered Görgey to the Austrians. His carriage passed by Tokaj and the people thronged around it, asking: "What will happen now?" All Görgey would say in reply was: "As yet I may not speak; but in a few weeks my story will be told, and the country will bless me!" (PMHL, vol. 2, p. 273) It is Kossuth's curse that has come ringing across the generations, however, and August 13, 1849, is remembered as a day of infamy in the life of the nation.

As rank after rank of Hungarian troops drew up at Világos and laid down their arms before the Russians, Görgey noticed at his side the young violinist Reményi, who was barely eighteen years old. Reményi had been attached to Görgey's headquarters throughout the campaign and had frequently played for the general's staff. He was now wanted by the Austrians as a "dangerous violinist agitator." Görgey asked Reményi what he was going to do and whether he had any money. Reményi replied that he intended to fight his way through the world with his violin but that he had no

Klapka refused to follow Görgey's example and endured a six-week siege of heroic proportions. Klapka's hussars sallied forth at will and created a swathe of death as they charged across the Austrian lines. Only after Klapka had negotiated honourable terms for himself and his men did the defenders of Komárom march out of the fortress, on October 1, with Hungarian flags flying. The conflict was over.

V

Then followed terrible retribution. The Habsburgs appointed the sadistic General Julius Haynau as military governor, and he thirsted for revenge. On October 6, the first anniversary of the uprising in Vienna, thirteen Hungarian generals were executed at Arad.[15] In Pest, that same day, the former prime minister, Lajos Batthyány, was taken to the courtyard of the Neugebäude (the so-called Hungarian Bastille), stood against a wall, and shot. He had earlier stabbed himself in the neck and had made it impossible for the Austrians properly to carry out the order to hang him. Although he had lost much blood, he walked to the place of his execution himself and cried out: "Éljen hazám!" (Long live my country!) as he was pierced by a volley of musket-balls.[16] The

money—whereupon Görgey emptied his pockets and gave all his gold coins to the impoverished youth, including some precious trinkets hanging from his watch-chain. Reményi noticed a small silver key among the latter and refused to accept it on the grounds that it had been given to Görgey by his wife. "Take it," replied Görgey. "After what I have done today my wife will not smile upon me again!" (PMHL, vol. 2, pp. 272–73)

Görgey was interned at Klagenfurt until 1867. He then returned to Hungary, where he lived in complete seclusion until his death in 1916, aged ninety-eight. Most Hungarians had little idea of what became of "the traitor," whose memory they reviled. Shortly before World War I the Austrians and Hungarians were holding military manoeuvres not far from Görgey's home, in which they displayed the impressive power of the latest rapid-fire machine-gun. During a short break in the activities, a group of soldiers was approached by an old man in his late eighties who showed unusual interest in the new weapon. He was asked to identify himself. "My name is Artúr Görgey," he replied, "and with two such guns I could have won a war."

The final casualty figures for the war are hard to come by because neither side kept accurate records. At least 50,000 Hungarian soldiers lost their lives, and about the same number of Austrians. The Russians lost less than 600 men to the fighting but more than 11,000 to an outbreak of cholera in their camps (DLR, p. 329).

15. Four of the generals were shot at dawn—Kiss, Dessewffy, Schweidel, and Lázár. The others were hanged—Aulich, Nagy-Sándor, Lahner, Pöltenberg, Knezich, Leiningen, Vécsey, Damjanich, and Török. The executions lasted from 6:00 a.m. until 10:00 a.m. The last eight generals were condemned to watch their colleagues strangle on the gallows while they themselves waited to die. General Török suffered a fatal heart-attack before mounting the platform. The Austrians continued with the ghastly ritual anyway and hanged his corpse.

16. PMHL, vol. 1, p. 278. The execution of Batthyány aroused revulsion in the outside world and stained the Austrian flag with shame. In an editorial a few days later, The Times of London wrote: "This blood will be a curse on those who shed it; and men who sully their victory by such crimes have conquered in vain" (October 17, 1849). The outcry in England was such that when General

Hungarian officers who had surrendered at Világos were forcibly recruited into the ranks of the Austrian army as privates.

Nor was this the end of Haynau's reign of terror. Wives were forcibly dragged from their homes by Austrian officers, then stripped and flogged before ranks of soldiers simply for harbouring their own sons and husbands. Many government commissioners who had supported Kossuth were summarily court-martialled and led to the gallows. Baron Jeszenák, lord-lieutenant of the county of Nyitra; Szacsvay, the young secretary of the Diet; and Csernus of the treasury board all swung from the end of a rope. Baron Zsigmond Perényi, of the court of justice, listened carefully to the charges against him and replied: "I have to complain that the accusation is incomplete. I request to add that I was the first to press the resolution that the House of Habsburg-Lorraine should be declared to have forfeited the throne of Hungary."[17] István Széchenyi, who had striven all along for a peaceful solution to the conflict, had already suffered a complete mental collapse and was now undergoing treatment in the asylum at Döbling, near Vienna; ten years later he committed suicide, having witnessed his country's utter humiliation at the hands of Austria, whose police had molested him for his brilliant criticisms of the dictatorial government imposed on Hungary.

As for Kossuth, he and his entourage escaped to Turkey, where he began a two-year exile under the protection of the sultan, Abdul-Medjid Khan. Despite threats of reprisals from both Austria and Russia, the sultan refused to extradite the Hungarian leader. Kossuth's wife eventually managed to join him, after being pursued by the Austrians, who had put a price on her head.[18] From Broussa, the place of his banishment, Kossuth issued a series of proclamations against the Austrian emperor—"the beardless Nero," as he called him—and he later embarked on a series of speaking tours of the West, in order to arouse interest in the Hungarian cause.[19] Kossuth's long exile ended only when he died in Turin, in 1894, at the advanced age of ninety-two. His remains were taken back to Hungary and accorded full national honours. It was a poignant scene

---

Haynau visited London not long afterwards, he was dragged from his carriage by the workers of Barclay's Brewery and so savagely beaten that he had to be hospitalized.

17. PMHL, vol. 1, p. 279.

18. ALK, p. 140.

19. See, for example, the speeches Kossuth delivered in England in 1851, in such places as London, Manchester, and Birmingham (ALK). The Americans sent a steamship to Turkey, the *Mississippi,* to bring him to the New World, where he also tried to muster support for Hungarian independence. His eloquence and love of liberty caught the American imagination, and he was dubbed "the Hungarian George Washington." Kossuth's masterly "Address to the People of the United States of America" (March 1850), in which he reviewed the history of the struggle with Austria in depth, not only discloses his passionate commitment to his political ideals but gives further evidence of his mesmeric powers of communication. The document was later deposited in the congressional archives. Despite all his efforts to engage the Western democracies in the Austro-Hungarian dispute, both America and England refused to become politically involved. Lord Palmerston, the British prime minister, would not allow Kossuth to seek permanent exile in England for fear of offending Vienna.

as the hearse passed down the streets lined with mourners. A new generation of Magyars had arisen who had no direct recollection of the revolution at all and had never set eyes on Kossuth. Yet the man was a legend and was already numbered among Hungary's immortals. Although his dream of an independent Hungary was shattered, the spirit of freedom he had ignited in the hearts of the Magyars remained unquenchable.

V I

This was the cataclysmic background which had already started to unfold as Liszt and Carolyne set out on their journey from Kryzanowicz to Weimar in April 1848. As yet, hardly anyone in the small town knew of their liaison. They remained there for only a few days, hardly long enough for Carolyne to unpack her belongings and prepare for the long-awaited pilgrimage to Austria and Liszt's birthplace. By the beginning of May, the pair were en route for Vienna. This was Carolyne's first visit to the city of Beethoven and Schubert, and Liszt took pleasure in showing her the principal districts connected with his boyhood—the house on Krugerstrasse where he had studied with Czerny, the Marienkirche, and the Redoutensaal, where he had given the concert that had marked the official beginning of his career, in April 1823, twenty-five years earlier. The couple stayed at the Hotel zur Stadt London, where on May 6 Liszt was serenaded by a group of medical students. Revolutionary fever filled the air; the Hungarian uprising was popular among the working classes of Vienna, and Liszt was prevailed upon to address the students from his balcony. "When the instruments have taken their places," he said, "it is still necessary to have a capable conductor to harmonize their diverse voices . . . The instruments are in place, but the capable conductor is missing. Hubbub and confusion produce few consequences. The right leader will have to fix bayonets!"[20]

A few days later, the pair travelled to Eisenstadt, where Liszt renewed his acquaintance with Father Stanislaus Albach at the Franciscan monastery, the shrine he had often visited as a child in the company of his father. It was in Eisenstadt that Liszt started work on his Mass for Male Voices, which he later dedicated to Father Albach.[21] The tour reached its nostalgic climax when Liszt

---

20. RLKM, vol. 3, p. 4.

21. LLB, vol. 2, p. 380. Father Albach (1795–1853) was greatly admired by Liszt. The pair may have met for the first time during Liszt's visit to the Eisenstadt monastery in 1823, but we know for sure that they encountered one another in 1840 and again in 1846, so their present meeting was really a reunion of old friends. This Franciscan priest was something of a Renaissance man, for he not only spoke several languages fluently but was a scientist whose interests embraced mathematics, physics, and geography. He also played the organ and composed a number of keyboard works which remain unknown and unpublished. Albach's chief passion, however, was botany, a discipline in which his scientific peers held him in high regard and which culminated in his magnum opus, Botanik (PPSA).

and Carolyne arrived in Raiding and saw the lowly cottage where he was born. A gamekeeper and his family now occupied the main dwellings; the building next door had been turned into an inn for the sale of local brandy. Stirred by his childhood memories, Liszt made a bid to purchase the cottage for himself, as documents in the National Széchényi Library prove.[22] A survey was carried out by the Esterházy directorate, and professional estimates were produced to show that the entire property, together with its attendant income, was worth nearly 18,000 forints. The sale did not take place, probably because the price was too high.[23]

The clouds of war were gathering as Liszt and Carolyne began their journey back to Weimar. Military preparations were already under way for the earliest Austro-Hungarian battles previously described. In Vienna, Liszt inspected the street barricades commanded by Karl Formès, the well-known bass, and distributed cigars and money among the revolutionaries.[24] He aroused great enthusiasm as he walked down the lines, with the Hungarian national colours pinned to his button-hole. Inspired by his contact with the rebels, Liszt even composed an *Arbeiterchor* ("Workers' Chorus") for male voices. The text urges the workers to rally to the spade and shovel, and reminds them that "freedom remains a mighty hammer that will nevermore be allowed to fall from the hand." Liszt thought that it might be inflammatory to publish the work at that moment, and he instructed Carl Haslinger to hold on to the corrected proofs until the revolutionary situation had abated somewhat—a telltale symptom of his unwillingness to become directly involved in the struggle.[25] Despite his

---

The unpublished diaries of Father Albach inform us that Liszt arrived at Eisenstadt on May 21, 1848, "in the company of three ladies," Carolyne among them. During the visit, Liszt confided to Albach that the princess would become his wife "within six months." Liszt left fifty florins with the Franciscans to be distributed among the poor of the city. Did Liszt at one time think of marrying Carolyne in Eisenstadt? An entry in Albach's diary suggests that the question may well have been broached with him. On September 25, Albach received a visit from Eduard Liszt. According to the diary, Liszt's lawyer-uncle reviewed with Albach the entire question of Carolyne's unsatisfactory marriage to Nicholas von Sayn-Wittgenstein, placed before him the theory and practice of canon law, and then inquired how the Church might view a subsequent union between Carolyne and Liszt. Albach's reply was unequivocal: Eduard left Eisenstadt convinced that a marriage was quite impossible so long as Carolyne's husband still lived. The diaries of Albach are in three volumes (I: 1837–39, II: 1840–48, III: 1849–53) and run to more than thirteen hundred handwritten pages, in a unique mixture of Latin, German, French, and Hungarian. Today they are preserved in the Bratislava University Library, ms. 736.

22. Acta Mus., no. 3877.

23. In 1853 Liszt made a second bid, this time for the rooms formerly occupied by his parents. Again, negotiations faltered. Although Liszt kept visiting his birthplace, he never acquired possession of it. In 1911, the centenary of his birth, a thoughtful posterity turned the house into a Liszt museum, a function it still fulfils today.

24. DEM, pp. 20–21.

25. The corrected proofs of the *Arbeiterchor* lay in the Weimar archive (WA, R552, ms. E1) until 1954, at which time the work was published and given its first performance in Hungary. The author of the rabble-rousing words remains anonymous.

support for human rights, Liszt viewed the consequences of military strife with alarm. As later events showed, he wanted no part of the Hungarian uprising, and he saw the warlike utterances of Kossuth as a catastrophe for his country. Like many other Hungarians, Liszt preferred the path of Batthyány and Szé-chenyi, who were even then attempting to achieve a measure of freedom from the Austrian yoke by legislative means.[26] The clarions of conflict sounded less than six weeks later, and Kossuth led the Hungarians into battle, with consequences that have already been described. While Liszt was appalled at the butchery which followed, as his private correspondence shows, he made no public protest about it.[27] This drew from the cantankerous Heine some infamous lines against Liszt in his poem "Im Oktober 1849."

> Franz Liszt lives.
> He is not stretched out
> Bleeding on a field of battle;
> Neither a Russian nor a Croat killed him.
>
> He will live long.
> And while Hungary bleeds to death
> The beknighted Franz remains unscathed;
> His sabre also—it lies in a chest of drawers.
>
> He lives, the noble Franz, and as an old man
> Will relate to his grandchildren
> The great deeds of the Hungarian War.
> "This," he will say, "is how I made the thrust
>   and held the sabre."[28]

---

26. This is proved by a letter Liszt wrote at the time of Széchenyi's death, which sets out his views on the "Hungarian question" so clearly that it is unnecessary for the biographer to embellish them.

[Széchenyi] was a man of great good sense, of prodigious activity, and of practical genius, aware of the requirements of his time and of his country. He gave immense service to Hungary, where he deservedly enjoyed unparalleled popularity until the time when Kossuth gained the upper hand through his *glib talk* and dragged the whole nation on to a false path. Unfortunately, at the present moment, we have still not abandoned it, and I can see hardly any prospect of a favourable outcome from that ardent passion for clannish patriotism, which sows the wind only to reap the whirlwind! If they had followed Széchenyi's example and method consistently and faithfully, Hungary would certainly be strong and prosperous today: I fear that it is too late now to go back. This state of affairs may certainly suit *others*—but those of us who sincerely love their country are grieved over this to the depths of their souls! (LLB, vol. 3, p. 126)

27. Liszt told Raff that he was bowed down with grief at the loss of his best friends in Hungary (RLR, p. 388).

28. HSW, vol. 8, pp. 138–40. The reference to Falstaff's boasting lines in Shakespeare's *Henry IV* is an obvious attempt to depict Liszt as a buffoon. The poem first appeared in the magazine *Deutschen Monatschrift für Politik, Wissenschaft, Kunst und Leben* in September 1850.

Heine, it should be added, was not observed on the field of battle either. The author of "Vergiftet sind meine Lieder" ("My songs are poisoned") poured forth his invective to the end, and Liszt did not rebuke him. But he later told Raff, somewhat wrily, that had he not shunned all political activity in 1848 Heine's poem would have been shorter by several lines.[29] For the rest, would those who criticize Liszt for not rushing to Hungary's defence really have preferred to see him die on the battle-field? In the light of his subsequent career, so much of which was devoted to Hungary, the idea becomes absurd. Liszt's pacifism on this issue was a perfectly legitimate attitude, one shared by large numbers of Hungarians at home.[30]

VII

Liszt, too, left a tribute to the mournful events of October 1849 in the form of his magnificent elegy *Funérailles*. Inspired by the memory of Hungarians who had died in the revolution,[31] this work is not simply the expression of a

---

29. RLR, p. 869.

30. That Liszt supported the humanitarian impulses behind the 1848 Revolution cannot be doubted. Shortly after he arrived in Weimar he gave vent to his feelings against social injustice in an extraordinary diatribe, which was witnessed by Fanny Lewald. Lewald had just finished telling Liszt of the gripping impression made on her by a performance of the "Marseillaise" sung on the Paris stage. Liszt suddenly exploded and cried with an impassioned voice: "How is that possible? How could that have shaken you? How could you have possibly admired it? It is a folly, a criminal act, a sin, to sing the 'Marseillaise' today. What had that revolution [i.e., the Paris revolution of March 1848] to do with the one of the last century? What has this blood-thirsty hymn to do with us, during a social upheaval whose basic principle is love, and whose single solution is only possible through love?" Liszt went on to say that he would be among the first to answer the call to arms, shed his blood, and even face the guillotine if that would bring peace and happiness to the world. But what was required today were ideas to bring about the right social changes. Fanny Lewald remarked that she was utterly astonished to observe the change that came over Liszt's personality as he talked. He spoke with passion and a deep conviction that the Christian ideal of universal charity was the only one that meant anything in those troubled times (SNW, vol. 1, pp. 254–55).

Incidentally, Weimar remained relatively untouched by the revolutionary upheavals that occurred in other parts of Germany. While there were street demonstrations, and while the palace trembled for a few uncertain days in March 1848, the vast majority of Carl Friedrich's subjects remained loyal to him. The worst scenes took place at the beginning of the month, when hundreds of citizens streamed into Weimar from the outlying towns and villages and assembled in front of the Town Hall, demanding the replacement of unpopular ministers by others who were less so. Carl Friedrich simply acceded to the demands, and issued a decree to that effect on March 14. The crowd then swore allegiance to the grand duke and duchess, and Weimar's "revolution" was over. Liszt lived in the city throughout those boisterous days (in fact, his rooms at the Erbprinz Hotel must have afforded him a grandstand view of the demonstrations), but there is not a word about it in his correspondence. The theatre productions carried on as usual, a sure sign that public assemblies were not perceived to be a threat to law and order (GAWZ, pp. 300–07). On March 21 Liszt even conducted a performance of Beethoven's *Fidelio,* whose underlying message concerns the struggle of the individual against the rule of tyranny.

31. In particular the Hungarian prime minister Lajos Batthyány and the thirteen Hungarian generals, whose mass executions on October 6 appear to have been the catalyst for *Funérailles.* The idea that

personal sorrow but a symbol of that universal suffering felt by mankind when great ideals perish and the heroes who espoused them (of whatever nationality) are no more. The opening page of the work evokes funeral bells, which rise in volume to a deafening roar.

The bells culminate in a trumpet-like fanfare

which in turn collapses into a march for the dead, one of Liszt's noblest utterances.

Perhaps it was the climactic central section, with its thunderous left-hand octaves, that originally gave rise to the idea of a "Chopin connection" in this piece.

the work was also an elegy for Felix Lichnowsky and László Teleki is today discounted. By the same token, we can no longer accept *Funérailles* as a memorial to Chopin, who, quite by chance, passed away that same month. Liszt himself tells us that the work was connected with Hungary (LLB, vol. 6, p. 266); as if to clinch the matter, the first sketch for the piece bears the title "Magyar" (WA, ms. N.1).

The above passage does show more than a passing acquaintance with Chopin's Polonaise in A-flat major, op. 53, with its clockwise and anti-clockwise arm rotations; but in light of what we know about the origins of *Funérailles* today, the link with Chopin must be seen as little more than a romantic fabrication.

VIII

Apart from the fact that Liszt had doubts about the revolution (he had, after all, seen the ideals of 1830, for which he had fought, betrayed in France), it is evident that his personal situation with the princess would not allow him to return to Hungary. Carolyne was chronically ill throughout much of 1848 and 1849, and Liszt could not leave her. Even while she was in Kiev, she had complained to him of severe pains in her side. "In the mornings," she wrote, "I must make an incredible effort to get on my feet, and all my nerves vibrate in me like the strings of an instrument." Shortly afterwards she had been obliged to take to her bed "although it is three o'clock in the afternoon. But I'm in a bad way. My side, my nerves, everything hurts."[32] By the end of the year she had developed blood poisoning and had broken out in a painful rash of boils. She was forced to seek a water-cure at Carlsbad, and Liszt stayed with her during her convalescence at Bad Eilsen. To add to their worries, the eleven-year-old Princess Marie went down with typhus, and Liszt spent the fateful month of October 1849 at Bückeburg with her and her mother, seeking treatment for the young girl.

So Liszt and Carolyne returned from Vienna to Weimar, in order to begin a new life, leaving the rest of the world to draw its own conclusions.

---

32. WA, Kasten 33, letter of February 4, 1848 (Old Style).

The Altenburg

Es ist nicht eine Burg der Alten.
                    HOFFMANN VON FALLERSLEBEN[1]

I

It was July 1848, and Liszt and Carolyne were now back in Weimar. In an attempt to keep up appearances, Liszt took up his old quarters at the Erbprinz Hotel, while Carolyne and her daughter moved into a large house called the Altenburg, just outside the city. The lovers of Woronince wished to do nothing to offend St. Petersburg and jeopardize the swift passage of Carolyne's marriage annulment; the finer feelings of the Weimar Court had also to be respected. In the autumn of 1848, however, the situation was to change dramatically when Carolyne received peremptory word that her petition had been rejected by Tsar Nicholas. Only then did Liszt decide to end the comedy and move into the Altenburg. For the next ten years, he and Carolyne lived there as man and wife.

The Altenburg, which still stands today, is located on a hill of the same name overlooking the river Ilm. In those days the old house nestled in six acres of woodland and commanded a splendid view of the city. From its windows one could observe such landmarks as the royal castle, the Rathaus in the market-square, and the Herder church. The house was approached by ascending a formidable series of steps with only an iron railing for support, set into the hillside leading up from the Ilm near the old weir. Visitors to the Altenburg were often breathless by the time they rang the front door-bell. The house lies about a mile from the Weimar theatre; by cutting through the market-square and going along what is today Schillerstrasse, the distance can be walked in

---

1. "It is not a refuge for the *old*." HML, vol. 6, p. 76.

fifteen minutes or so. It was an ideal location; and since there were then no other houses in the vicinity, Liszt could enjoy complete privacy.

The ownership of the Altenburg, and the terms under which it was rented to Liszt, have been the object of unnecessary confusion in the literature for years. The house was originally built in 1811 by Friedrich von Seebach, a cavalry officer and *Oberstallmeister* to the grand duke.[2] In 1817 Seebach was promoted to the rank of major-general, and in keeping with his new status he enlarged the Altenburg to its present dimensions, adding new servants' quarters and a gardener's house. When Seebach died in May 1847, aged eighty, he was survived by his widowed daughter Helene von Rott, who lived there alone for a few more months but found the upkeep of such a large dwelling (which now contained more than thirty rooms) too great a burden to carry. In 1848 the Altenburg was sold to a broker named Ulysses Stock, and that is why the house happened to be vacant when Carolyne arrived in Weimar. Stock agreed to lease the house to the princess, but he proved to be an unpleasant landlord, and Liszt became embroiled in a dispute with him during 1850.[3] Briefly, Stock wanted to chop down a small copse near the house and erect a stand for the sale of beer at which the locals, so he hoped, would slake their thirst during the hot summers after climbing to the top of the Altenburg. He could not understand why Liszt was so vigorously opposed to living in the middle of what, in effect, would have been a beer-garden.[4] Grand Duchess Maria Pawlowna finally bought the house from Stock in 1851 and generously placed it at Liszt's disposal.[5] Thereafter, Liszt became a "grace and favour" tenant of the Weimar Court, and neither he nor Carolyne paid a further penny in rent.

Although the Altenburg was not a particularly distinguished house architecturally, its rooms were spacious, and it offered a comfortable home for Liszt and the princess. Carolyne had set aside one wing of the building as Liszt's personal quarters, consisting of a small bedroom with a linking door to his study, the so-called Blue Room, where he did most of his composing. The Blue Room overlooked the garden and was equipped for work. It contained a Boisselot grand piano,[6] a writing-desk, a table, and some scattered chairs. Two pictures hung on the walls: an engraving of Dürer's *Melancholia* and an artist's impression of *St. Francis de Paule Walking on the Waters,* which later inspired

---

2. HA, p. 29.
3. LLB, vol. 4, p. 121.
4. "This Stock really deserves a *caning,*" punned Liszt (HLSW, p. 33). *Stock* means "stick" in German.
5. HA, p. 101; LLB, vol. 4, p. 121.
6. Liszt did most of his composing on this piano, which had originally been shipped out to him for his Odessa concerts in the summer of 1847. He later wrote to Xavier Boisselot: "You know that for thirteen years I kept in my work-room in Weimar the grand piano that your excellent brother Louis despatched to me in Odessa in 1846 [*sic*]. Although its keys are almost hollow because of all the gambolling by past and present music on them, I will never agree to change it and have decided to keep it, as a favourite associate in my work, until the end of my days." (LLB, vol. 8, p. 153)

The Altenburg, a pencil drawing by Friedrich Preller.

his piano composition of the same name. It was in the Blue Room that Liszt took his breakfast every morning, often to be joined by Carolyne for coffee. Carolyne had her own suite of rooms, which included a master bedroom modelled after the one at Woronince, and its most striking feature was the same large wooden crucifix hanging from the wall above her bed. Next door was Princess Marie's bedroom, which was decorated in white: white furniture, white curtains, white carpets. (So pronounced was Marie's preference for the colour of purity that it also extended to her wardrobe, and it often seemed to those who knew her well that whenever the delicate child emerged from her quarters, wearing her semi-transparent crinolines, she resembled a wraith. Hans von Bülow described her perfectly as "the good fairy of the Altenburg.") By contrast, the rest of the house, which they shared, was a treasure-trove of items that Liszt had collected on his tours—including Beethoven's Broadwood piano, the priceless death-mask of Beethoven, a writing-case that had formerly belonged to Haydn, and jewels and gold medallions received from half the crowned heads of Europe—much of which he had stored with his mother in Paris until a permanent place could be found for it all. The main reception-room on the ground floor was dominated by Liszt's Erard concert grand, while the walls were lined with his music library. A linking room contained all Liszt's souvenirs from his *Glanzzeit*—Oriental rugs, mother-of-pearl tables, Turkish pipes, Russian jade, and a silver breakfast service. Pictures of the great composers adorned the walls, as well as two life-size portraits of Liszt and the well-known canvas by Ary Scheffer called *The Three Magi,* whose central figure bears the unmistakable imprint of the musician's features.[7] On the second floor was the music-room proper. It contained two Viennese grands (by Streicher and Bösendorfer), a spinet that had once belonged to Mozart,[8] and a huge instrument called a "piano-organ," a combination of the two instruments especially designed for him by the firm of Alexandre et fils in Paris. This gigantic instrument had three keyboards, eight registers, a pedal-board, and a set of pipes to reproduce the sounds of all the wind instruments. It was a one-piece orchestra on which Liszt could try out his symphonic works at leisure. When all the stops were out, it must have shaken the Altenburg to its foundations.[9] The library had been placed in an adjoining room, and on its shelves rested many of the books he had acquired in his Paris days, by Hugo, Lamartine, Sainte-Beuve,

---

7. This painting was purchased by Princess Carolyne in 1850 from the estate of the late King Willem II of the Netherlands (see p. 565). According to Bénézit's *Dictionnaire* the sale price was 12,428 francs. Marthe Kolb describes the picture:

> The star which has guided the Magi has stopped above Bethlehem, the goal of their journey. One of them, in the centre, surprised, is contemplating this mysterious, marvellous guide. He seems to be questioning it. His features recall those of Liszt. The beautiful face of a young artist, brightly illuminated, appears in all the fire of holy inspiration. . . . He alone is struck by the sight of wonder. One of the wise men, turned towards him, is observing him as if to read his thoughts. The other, bent with age, keeps his eyes fixed on the ground and meditates. (KS, pp. 370–71)

8. Carolyne bought this spinet for Liszt in 1852, from the Leipzig dealer Barthold Senff. It possessed a compass of about five octaves, and its keys were black. Liszt's letter to Carl Weitzmann dated August 14, 1861, contains an inventory of all the pianos which were housed in the Altenburg during Liszt's tenure (WGC, p. 294). This inventory, drawn up just two days after Liszt had sealed up the Altenburg in readiness for his departure for Rome, consisted of Beethoven's Broadwood, Mozart's spinet, the Alexandre "piano-organ," one Erard, one Bechstein, one Boisselot, one Streicher, one Bösendorfer, and a Hungarian instrument by Beregszászy. The Streicher and the Bösendorfer bore the brunt of Liszt's musical gatherings, and they received regular attention from the Weimar instrument-maker A. Feuerstein (KLP).

9. On July 20, 1854, Carolyne wrote to Liszt informing him that his new piano had arrived at the Altenburg from Alexandre et fils in Paris. She complained that the delivery men had simply left it at the railway station, and had then departed without telling anyone (WA, Kasten 34). Apparently it took three weeks before this monstrous contraption could be hauled through the cobbled streets of Weimar, and up the hill to Liszt's house. The instrument was finally installed in the Altenburg on August 11, 1854. Liszt had already tested the "piano-organ" on a visit to Paris in the autumn of 1853, and joked that the firm of Alexandre wanted to name it the "Piano-Liszt." In a letter to Joachim he disclosed that Berlioz had heard it and was pleased with its well-proportioned sounds. "Now I have to work at and develop the new effects which this instrument can and ought to produce, which will be at least a year's work" (JMBJ, vol. 1, p. 96). An extremely detailed description of the "piano-organ" may be found in PGS, pp. 65–71. See also Liszt's letter to Joseph Hellmesberger in which he praises the qualities of Alexandre's work (LFLW, p. 150). The instrument is today exhibited in the Kunsthistorisches Museum, Vienna.

Lamennais, and others. Also stored there was his unique collection of autographed scores by Chopin, Schumann, Beethoven, Wagner, Mozart, and dozens of composers he had met on his tours across Europe. Even during his lifetime Carolyne turned the Altenburg into a shrine memorializing the career of her hero. Casual visitors to the house could be forgiven for assuming that they were walking through a museum.[10]

A household staff of five lived in the Altenburg and helped to run the house. Alexandra, a young Polish chambermaid, had accompanied Carolyne from Ukraine; shortly after her arrival in Weimar she had married Heinrich, one of the manservants, a factotum who served the meals and dealt with callers at the front door. Another servant who was part of Carolyne's original retinue was the elderly housekeeper Kostenecka, who had been with the princess from the earliest days in Woronince. Liszt's valet, Hermann Becker, often acted as his master's coachman, driving him to and from the Weimar theatre. Hermann also accompanied Liszt on his conducting engagements to various German cities during the 1850s. (This servant appears to have been something of a card. On one occasion, after he and Liszt had been detained at the royal theatre after a late rehearsal, Hermann regaled the duke of Gotha and his circle with an impromptu sequence of conjuring tricks in the duke's private drawing-room— much to Liszt's consternation. Hermann's illusions apparently drew more applause than Liszt's *Künstlerchor*. "I think that the duke is planning to have him do it again," was Liszt's rueful comment.)[11] "Scotchy" Anderson, who was by now almost a member of the family, remained as Princess Marie's governess; she was finally pensioned off when the Altenburg was closed, in 1861, and she returned to live in Britain. And no account of daily life in the Altenburg would be complete without mention of Madame Esmeralda, the family cat, and a guard dog called Rappo, who romped all over the house without constraint and used to bark beneath Liszt's window while he composed.[12]

The domestic routine was simple. Liszt rose early in the morning and usually composed in the Blue Room until midday. Carolyne would often join him there and scribble away silently in a corner at her endless correspondence. Princess Marie, who had free access to the Blue Room, has described how her mother liked to work at a *Stehpult,* at which she also took down from Liszt's dictation a great deal of his literary output, books and polemical articles alike.[13] At lunch, members of Liszt's inner circle (whose acquaintance we shall shortly

10. Further descriptions of the interior of the Altenburg may be found in BB, vol. 1, p. 478, and HFLW, p. 26.

11. LLB, vol. 4, p. 186.

12. There are scattered references to all these servants and household pets in LLB, vol. 4, HLSW, and in WA, Kasten 33 and 34. Joachim Raff was also a valuable eye-witness to the day-to-day running of the Altenburg, particularly for the early period of 1849–50. See RLR, p. 388.

13. PHZ, pp. 289–90. See pp. 372–79 for a fuller account of their joint literary activities.

*The library of the Altenburg, with Liszt's Erard grand piano (left)
and the Broadwood grand that had belonged to Beethoven.*

*The music-room of the Altenburg, with Liszt's three-manual "piano-organ"
and the spinet that had belonged to Mozart.*

be making) would arrive at the house—one day Raff to discuss the copying of orchestral parts, the next day Cornelius to discuss the translation of Liszt's articles or to help with correspondence, and the day after that pupils such as Bülow or Tausig to receive their lessons.[14] Afterwards there might follow a rubber of whist, and Liszt would serve his favourite brandy. In the evenings Liszt and the princess would often hold open house and treat twenty or more guests to a musical soirée. Chamber music was preferred on these occasions, with such Weimar musicians as Karl Klindworth, Ferdinand Laub, and Bernhard Cossmann playing trios by Schubert and Spohr, or Liszt and Joachim playing the *Kreutzer* Sonata.[15] Occasionally Liszt himself might be prevailed upon to play one of his own compositions—the *Bénédiction de Dieu,* for example, which was a great favourite of his in the early 1850s. Afterwards the princess would set up small supper tables in the main salon and serve her guests truffles and ices. An evening in the Altenburg was one to cherish in the memory.[16]

II

Liszt's birthdays were occasions for special celebrations at the Altenburg. It was well known that he had a weakness for anniversaries; and his pupils, friends, and disciples used to turn up in force at the old house in order to make these events as memorable as possible. Two of these birthday parties can typify the others. On October 22, 1855, a festive play was performed which depicted the life and work of Liszt. It was called *Des Meisters Walten* and it was written by Gustav Steinacker, a Hungarian priest.[17] A series of *tableaux vivants* repre-

---

14. It is an indication of the free and easy atmosphere at the Altenburg that Liszt gave his students the run of his home. On September 4, 1852, we find him writing to Cornelius: "The room adjoining that which M. de Bülow occupies is entirely at your disposal, and it will be a pleasure for me if you will settle yourself there without any ceremony, and will come and dine regularly with us like an inhabitant of the Altenburg" (LLB, vol. I, p. 112). Three or four years later he wrote to Anton Rubinstein in a similar vein: "I count on your not letting this year elapse without coming again for a few days to your room at the Altenburg" (LLB, vol. I, p. 235). As for Bülow, he came and went as he pleased throughout the 1850s.

15. The famous Weimar String Quartet was established in the early 1850s, and it, too, became a regular feature of musical life in the Altenburg. The players were Joachim and Carl Stör (first and second violins), Johann Walbrül (viola), and Cossmann (cello). Joachim's place was taken in turn by Laub and by Edmund Singer.

16. The diary extracts of Liszt's American pupil William Mason for April, May, and June 1853 give a good idea of the unceasing flow of entertaining-cum-concertizing that went on at the Altenburg (MMML, pp. 122–26). See also pp. 191–92 of the present volume.

17. SMW. Steinacker (1809–77) was a Protestant priest who had been sheltered in Goethe's *Gartenhaus* by Carl Alexander since 1854. Because of his liberal sympathies it was impossible for him to return to Hungary. He hoped that Liszt might exert his influence to procure for him a parish in the Weimar-Eisenach district. Liszt did, in fact, intercede with the grand duke, who eventually, in 1857, appointed Steinacker to the parish church in Buttelstedt, a small village about ten kilometers outside Weimar.

sented the various aspects of Liszt's career. The "actors" were Liszt's own pupils, and musical interludes from Beethoven, Berlioz, Wagner, and other composers whom Liszt had championed in the course of his life were performed by members of the Weimar theatre orchestra during the scene changes. The lighting effects and the stage-direction were in the hands of Eduard Genast, the manager of the Weimar theatre. The play concluded with a scene in praise of genius, in which Princess Marie advanced towards Liszt's bust and crowned it with a laurel-wreath. According to Liszt, about a hundred guests turned up at the Altenburg to see this play. During the intermission toasts were drunk, one of the wittiest being a panegyric by Peter Cornelius, a word-play on the name "Liszt," which culminated in a dazzling acrostic:[18]

Liszt Ist Sporn Zur Tatentfaltung!	Liszt incites a man to action!
Liszt Ist Seichten Zopftums Töter!	Liszt is death to shallow pedants!
Liszt Ist Seiner Zeiten Träger!	Liszt upholds his era's spirit!
Liszt Ist Seines Zeichens Titan!	Liszt is Titan by profession!
Liszt Ist Süssen Zaubers Trunken!	Liszt is mellow with sweet magic!
Liszt Ist Schöpfer Zarter Töne!	Liszt creates melodious music!
Hebt das Glas, ihr Musensöhne!	Raise your glasses, sons of muses!
L—I—S—Z—T! Das ist	L—I—S—Z—T! That is
Unser Wahlspruch. Vivat Liszt!	Our motto. Viva Liszt!

On October 21, 1857, the eve of Liszt's forty-sixth birthday, a great party was laid on for him in the Town Hall, and members of the orchestra, the theatre company, and the Neu-Weimar-Verein attended in large numbers. Champagne and oysters were consumed in liberal quantities; the wine bill alone came to 136 thalers—more than half a year's salary for the rank-and-file player. (The barrel of oysters was donated by "an anonymous friend of the Verein"—a thinly veiled reference to Carolyne.) The following day, Liszt's birthday was celebrated at the Altenburg with a melodrama called *Des Meisters Bannerschaft,* again by Steinacker.[19] Unlike the first play, which had praised Liszt's art, this one glorified Liszt's circle at Weimar and beyond—a "festival gallery of portraits of the musicians of the future." A large audience gathered at the Altenburg to hear Heinrich Grans, an actor with the Court Theatre, proclaim this long eulogy, during which all those artists present—the Weimar String Quartet, the Weimar Singers, and several local Weimar composers—paid homage to Liszt. The presentation ended with an epilogue in which the disciples swore allegiance to their leader.[20]

---

18. CSB, p. 187.
19. SMB.
20. SANZ, p. 149, and HFLW, pp. 65–68. Hoffmann von Fallersleben also described this evening in his diaries (HML, vol. 6, pp. 232–33). During the banquet which preceded the play, Stein-

III

Behind the glittering façade of life at the Altenburg, with its evening parties, candlelight concerts, and endless round of distinguished callers, the lovers of Woronince were deeply unhappy. At the heart of the problem lay Liszt's irregular union with Carolyne and Carolyne's unceasing tug-of-war with her estranged husband. At first, the Weimar Court turned a blind eye to it, since Liszt was confident that it was only a matter of time before the annulment of Carolyne's marriage was sanctioned by the tsar and she would be free to re-marry. But with the passing years this matter became mired in complexity. Carolyne refused the tsar's eventual directive to return to Russia, and as a result she was exiled.[21] The Weimar Court could not ignore this mark of imperial displeasure, and Carolyne and her daughter were barred from all official court functions. What this meant in a small town like Weimar can hardly be imagined; henceforth no court official could deal with her at all. The ordinary townspeople of Weimar quickly followed suit, and Carolyne found herself treated on all sides like a common outcast. A few simple examples will make her plight clear. We have the word of Adelheid von Schorn, one of Carolyne's few friends in Weimar, that on the day of the ceremony inaugurating the monument to Goethe and Schiller (September 4, 1857), in which Liszt played a leading role, the princess and her daughter entered a room overlooking the Theaterplatz and had barely taken their seats when all the ladies of the court got up and left them alone as a mark of disapproval.[22] Nothing better reflects the hostility that the common folk of Weimar harboured towards Carolyne's *ménage à deux* with Liszt than the interesting court case reported by Frédéric Soret, a former tutor to Carl Alexander, whose diaries are filled with piquant details about life in this small community. The department of justice had forced a man and woman who wanted to live under the same roof without being married to separate or go to prison. As the man was led from the courtroom, he turned towards the magistrate and shouted: "It's just like everywhere else here. Small and helpless people are persecuted; and while you are tormenting us, you let the fine lady up there, who is protected by the court, do whatever she likes!" The usher wanted to have the impertinent fellow arrested, but the magistrate, Baron von Eggloffstein, whispered quietly that it was more expedient to turn a deaf ear.[23] No wonder that the princess was frequently observed

---

acker entertained the Altenburg guests with a toast to Liszt in the form of a thirty-three-line ode.
21. The background to this calamitous development is unfolded on pp. 140–42.
22. SZM, pp. 92–93.
23. SG, p. 210.

to be in tears during the early 1850s. Her nerves were shattered, and she was in a state of constant anxiety, never knowing from one day to the next what fresh tortures she might be called upon to endure.

Had the good citizens of Weimar been content to confine their disapproval of Carolyne to the fact that she and Liszt cohabited without benefit of clergy, the situation would have been intolerable enough. But the plain truth was that the Weimarers took a personal dislike to the princess herself which intensified with the passing years. They objected to her looks, to her dress, to her foreign accent. Above all, they took violent exception to her smoking her strong cigars in public places. She was often insulted as she walked down the street, her only misdemeanour being that she happened to be there. Once, at the Court Theatre, she placed both feet on the ledge of her box in full view of the audience. An attendant tapped her on the shoulder and admonished her with the words: "You musn't do that, Frau Kapellmeisterin!" As Carl Maria Cornelius pointed out, Carolyne may have been a princess in the Altenburg, but to the Weimar townspeople she was simply "the mistress of the honorary Kapellmeister."[24]

From the very first moment of Carolyne's arrival in Weimar, some fantastic rumours swept through the town. The story was put about that she had pursued Liszt there, after he had broken off a passing affair with her, in order to compel him to make an honest woman of her. The Wittgenstein family having cast her aside, so the story continued, she had no one else to whom she could turn. But marriage was the last thing on Liszt's mind, so we are told, especially after he discovered that Carolyne was obliged to leave the bulk of her fortune in Ukraine. One version of this story even has Liszt staying at the Erbprinz Hotel in the spring of 1848 with a woman of ill-repute, from whom he had hastily to detach himself as the princess's coach rolled up to the front door. A more polished variation of the tale comes from Frau von Plötz, a lady-in-waiting at the royal court, who became briefly acquainted with Carolyne not long after she moved into the Altenburg.

> All that was in his mind was a liaison of the usual sort, with the usual vows of love, but with each party knowing from the commencement precisely what it all meant. She, however, took the matter very seriously, though at first he did not notice this. He had probably forgotten the matter, and was living here in Weimar in a hotel with another woman—the ordinary Parisian *femme entretenue;* they said nothing about it here, in order to retain him in the town. Suddenly, to his horror, he receives a letter from Carolyne, telling him that she has made the sacrifice, and that all that remained was for him to meet her at the frontier. He *had* to fetch her, for he could not get out of

---

24. CPC, vol. 1, pp. 157–58.

it—conventional honour forbade that; but he *did* want to get out of it. He did everything in his power to try to persuade her to terminate the relation, for without her millions—and at that time it looked as if she would lose them—Carolyne did not suit him. She never complains, but I have often seen her in tears. Carolyne was also badly treated by Weimar society. Had she merely indulged in an immoral amorous intrigue with Liszt no one would have objected; but they cast the stone at her because her desire has been to be honest in her relations with Liszt.[25]

Even the most cursory glance at Liszt's correspondence with Carolyne during the traumatic spring of 1848 is enough to disprove these fanciful elaborations by Frau von Plötz and others. Carolyne did not arrive in Weimar alone but in the company of Liszt, who then took her almost at once to Vienna. The picture of Carolyne entering the front door of the Erbprinz Hotel while Liszt and his current lady-friend left by the back is too absurd to withstand scrutiny. Moreover, Liszt's letters to Carolyne continually urge her to be precise about where she expects to cross the Russian frontier so that he may meet her. Unless we are to accuse Liszt of covering the paper with lies, we have to assume that he awaited Carolyne's arrival with impatience. As for the notion that Carolyne meant nothing to Liszt without her millions, and that he regarded her love for him as a simple infatuation, indistinguishable from the dozens of others he had attracted during his heyday as a touring virtuoso, it is contradicted by the testimony of Liszt himself, who asserted that he "dearly wished to call [Carolyne] by the sweet name of wife."[26] Among the most harrowing lines in Liszt's

---

25. BLTB, vol. 4, p. 104.

26. LLB, vol. 5, p. 53. For further proof that Liszt desired to marry Carolyne, and that he expressed this desire from the commencement of their liaison in Weimar, see the letter that he wrote to Franz Dingelstedt in June 1850: "The chief obstacle which opposed my marriage up to now has finally been lifted, and before the end of the year I will be able to introduce you to my new wife" (LLB, vol. 8, p. 68). In December 1851 Liszt told his mother: "In a few months . . . I will be able to fix for you the happiest, and the only important and definitive event in my life—my marriage—which will take place despite all the obstacles and hindrances, despite all the hates, calumnies, injustices, and futile discussions!" (VFL, p. 95) In the same envelope Carolyne enclosed a letter of her own to Anna Liszt, which she signed "your daughter." To Baron von Gutmansthal he had written as early as February 1850 that Carolyne was "the woman who will always remain for me the visible blessing of God" (GLS, p. 57). Six months before that, in July 1849, Liszt wrote a letter of congratulation to his old friend Lambert Massart, on the occasion of the latter's marriage to the pianist Aglaé Masson: "So you are married then! No one could congratulate you more sincerely than I, for no one envies you more sincerely! Marriage, family, what sweeter and nobler aims of man! And how I would aspire to them with all the vigorous and harmonious forces in my nature!" (VFL, p. 93) One does not have to be clairvoyant to perceive the sadness and frustration behind these lines. Perhaps the earliest recorded declaration of Liszt's intention to marry Carolyne was the one he made in May 1848 to Father Stanislaus Albach, who noted that fact in his diary (see pp. 68–69, fn. 21).

Incidentally, the alert reader will already have noticed that the story of Carolyne's "chase" of Liszt

testament are the ones devoted to Carolyne. They were written under stress, after the pair had endured thirteen years of purgatory at the hands of Weimar society. Now a testament is the most solemn and binding document a man may ever expect to draw up. When Liszt wrote of Carolyne, "All my joys come from her, and all my sufferings go to her to be appeased," it is not for a cynical posterity to assume that he simply did not know what he was saying.

As for Liszt, the frustrations of daily life in a petty principality also left their mark, and they eventually began to wear him down. During the period 1849–50 a legal action was brought against him by the criminal authorities in Weimar which bore all the trappings of a Lilliputian farce. It seems that Liszt spoke out too freely on the topic of Weimar's small-mindedness and had been incautious enough to make some libellous remarks against the law itself. He was charged with demeaning the high office of Hofkapellmeister by uttering a slander in a public place in front of eleven witnesses. The charge ran as follows:

> The criminal court here [Liszt claimed] is a bad, pitiful authority. He asserted that he has been harassed several times by this same criminal court because of petty and trivial details about which not even a cock would crow anywhere else, and that the authority here—or the authorities—are abominable. And what is more, the ignorant and the philistine are at home here. The Weimarers are all donkeys.[27]

Liszt was found guilty and fined ten thalers. He refused to pay, took his case to the Jena court of appeals, and won.[28] It was a pyrrhic victory nonetheless. For someone of Liszt's cosmopolitan outlook, used as he was to mingling freely with princes and potentates, it was galling to be treated as if he were no better than a small-time miscreant. Nor was this the only time that Liszt had a brush with the law. Gottschalg tells us that Liszt and the princess nearly had their property sequestered because of an unpaid debt of five or six hundred thaler, and it was only because the money was found at the very last moment that the

---

to Weimar is but a weak echo of Marie d'Agoult's "chase" of Liszt to Basel, some thirteen years earlier (see Volume One, p. 210, of the present work). Presumably such fabrications have their origins in the psychopathology of those who start them. There has never been a shortage of observers who wish to re-write Liszt's life according to a script of their own devising.

27. The documents may be found in WA, Kasten 137, under the title *Gerichtsakten über einen Prozess gegen Franz Liszt.*

28. On February 15, 1851, Liszt wrote to Princess Marie: "I have just been told that the Jena court of appeals has completely absolved me, and I will neither have to pay a fine nor submit to prison for my supposed insults against the magistrates of the grand duchy. I confess to you that the result almost surprised me; for no matter how absurd Uzlar's accusations were, I couldn't deny that the official position of my antagonist, with his colleagues and superiors on the bench, gave him a big advantage and a marked superiority over me." (HLSW, pp. 39–40) Uslar (whose name is mis-spelled by Liszt) was the Weimar city magistrate who brought the charge.

charges were dropped. Liszt never forgot this attack on him by the narrow-minded townsfolk of Weimar.[29] He soon learned to adopt outwardly an attitude of polite disdain towards them; and the diplomatic mask he wore whenever his duties compelled him to mingle with those Weimar officials he happened to dislike effectively obscured his true feelings. There were times, however, when the mask slipped and his anger came boiling to the surface. Wagner tells us that in May 1849, after a rehearsal of *Tannhäuser*, Liszt took him and a couple of musical colleagues (the conductor Carl Stör and the tenor Franz Götze) to the Erbprinz Hotel for dinner. In the course of the evening Liszt became extremely agitated, and he almost gnashed his teeth in a passion of fury as he railed against a certain section of Weimar society. Wagner was utterly astonished because he was unable to see the association of ideas which had led up to this violent outburst. He goes on to tell us that Liszt had to recover during the night from an attack of nerves brought on by his uncontrollable anger.[30] The scene was rare, but it was symptomatic. It cost Liszt dear to maintain his outward composure in the face of the humiliations heaped upon him and Carolyne at Weimar. Only when the strain became too great did his self-control snap, as on this occasion, and the outside world would then catch a glimpse of the emotional inferno seething within him.

The bitterness and frustration which formed the backdrop to Liszt's daily life in the Altenburg should never be forgotten. The casual observer saw only the outward pomp and circumstance of a great musician surrounded by an admiring coterie of disciples, in full pursuit of his artistic ideals. This picture is not false, but it is not the whole picture. In reality, Liszt was beset by disappointments at Weimar, which brought him more than once to the brink of resignation. Given all the circumstances, then, it is hardly surprising that the lovers of Woronince spent much time away from Weimar. Carolyne was absent for long periods, taking an endless series of "water-cures" at various spas in central Germany, while Liszt struck out in pursuit of a conducting career which took him to Karlsruhe, Ballenstedt, Berlin, Dresden, Pest, and Vienna, among other cities. It is a fact that during the twelve years that Liszt and Carolyne shared the Altenburg, they lived apart for almost a third of that period. This simple observation explains the vast correspondence between the pair at the very time that the outside world supposed them to be inseparable, living a life of domestic tranquillity.

---

29. Against the idea that Liszt was too prominent a citizen for the Weimar authorities to launch a criminal action leading to imprisonment we must set the cases of Heinrich Marr (the artistic director of the Court Theatre) and Joachim Raff. Both men languished in jail for petty offences which are described elsewhere in this volume (see pp. 201–02 and 268–69).
30. WML, p. 501.

IV

For the next decade, the Altenburg lay at the very heart of the Romantic movement in Germany and fairly teemed with all the new ideas which Liszt and a growing band of disciples discussed there. Raff, Cornelius, Klindworth, Bülow, and Tausig all converged on the Altenburg simply because Liszt beckoned. Moreover, his circle was not confined to musicians. The writers Hoffmann von Fallersleben, Friedrich Hebbel, Gustav Freytag, Fanny Lewald, and Hans Christian Andersen attached themselves to Liszt. Painters, too, came to the old house, and Liszt could count Friedrich Preller and Wilhelm von Kaulbach among his personal friends. Hoffmann von Fallersleben, the court poet, has left many detailed descriptions of artistic gatherings in the Altenburg, and he sketched a charming picture of the young Princess Marie, who liked to dress in Polish national costume for special musical receptions and turn pages for Liszt. This venerable building was often the first to echo to the strains of the latest music of Wagner, Berlioz, and others which, under Liszt's powerful advocacy, the world at large would one day take to its bosom. The story of how all this was brought about, despite hostility abroad and petty intrigue at home, makes compelling reading today and forms the substance of the pages which follow.

BOOK TWO

Court and Kapellmeister
1848 · 1853

Music at the Court of Weimar

*Weimar under the Grand Duke Carl August was
a new Athens. Let us think today of constructing
a new Weimar. . . . Let us allow talent to function
freely in its sphere. . . .*

FRANZ LISZT[1]

I

Every student of European history knows that it was Grand Duke Carl August
(1757–1828) who turned Weimar into the most important cultural centre in
Germany during the late eighteenth and early nineteenth centuries. Under his
benign patronage the city attracted some of the greatest writers, painters, and
thinkers of the day. Goethe, Schiller, Herder, Wieland, and Preller all lived and
worked there, and Liszt was absolutely right when he described the Weimar
of that period as "a new Athens." When Liszt first settled there, the city was
essentially the same as it had been during the time of Goethe and Schiller, half
a century earlier. Its narrow cobbled streets and old gabled houses lent the place
a quaint medieval air. The grand ducal palace, the great park, the bridges over
the river Ilm, the splashing weir, the spired churches, and the outlying summer
castles of Belvedere and Ettersburg all conspired to turn Weimar into one of
the most romantic cities in Central Europe. Weimar had actually boasted a
theatre as early as 1696, but it was not until the eighteen-year-old Carl August
persuaded Goethe to settle there in 1775 that the productions became truly
professional. After Goethe was appointed the first director of the newly formed
Weimar Court Theatre in 1791, one of his first acts was to bring in Schiller
from nearby Jena as his co-director. Then began that great age of German drama
still known as "Weimar classicism," which saw the production of such plays
as *Wallenstein's Camp, Mary Stuart,* and *William Tell,* works which remain in

---

1. ACLA, vol. 2, p. 323.

the classical repertory today. After Schiller's death in 1805, Goethe assumed complete control over the theatre and became a dictator in the training and direction of his actors, laying down those strict principles of pronunciation, staging, and grouping of the actors which other theatres across Germany soon followed. Goethe trained the Weimar audience as autocratically as he trained the actors, forbidding them to express approval except by applause or disapproval except by silence.

It was entirely predictable that shortly before Carl August died, in 1828, he should express the wish to be interred next to the two geniuses he loved most on this earth. In 1827 he commanded that the body of Schiller be exhumed and brought into the royal vault—an unprecedented honour. And when Goethe himself went to meet his maker in 1832, he was laid to his eternal rest at their side. A hundred and fifty years later, the three companions still slumber together in the royal burial chamber—a timeless remembrance of Weimar's past.[2]

After the death of Carl August the artistic splendour of Weimar faded. His son, Carl Friedrich, was a cautious administrator who lacked the vision to follow in his father's footsteps. Moreover, the small city became impoverished, and art came to be regarded as a luxury. Perhaps Carl Friedrich's wisest decision was to marry Maria Pawlowna, the sister of Tsar Nicholas, whose passion for music and drama, to say nothing of her private fortune, kept Weimar's flagging artistic energies from decay.[3] It was left to their son, Carl Alexander, to dream of re-awakening Weimar's past glories, and it was to his everlasting credit that when the twenty-three-year-old duke first set eyes on Liszt, he recognized a man of genius around whom Weimar's artistic regeneration might be accomplished.

Bearing a combination of the names of his two most illustrious forbears (his grandfather Carl August and his maternal uncle Tsar Alexander I of Russia),

---

2. Scholars of this topic will hardly need reminding that when Schiller's remains were disinterred, more than twenty years after his burial, it was discovered that his bones had become mixed with those of ten nonentities. The eleven skulls were placed side by side in a macabre "identity parade" while a number of witnesses who had known Schiller during his lifetime were invited to search their memories and select the cranium which best matched their remembrance of his physical characteristics. All the witnesses made the same identification. Their choice was clinched by evidence provided by Schiller's servant, who insisted that his master had lost no teeth except one, and was able to specify its location. The comparative anatomist Professor Loder, from Jena University, was called in to select the bones which completed the skeleton (SWJ, vol. 1, pp. 51–60).

3. During the day-to-day running of the Weimar Court, Carl Friedrich was strongly influenced by the powerful personality of his wife. It was not uncommon for him to withdraw for a few moments while presiding over some meeting or other in order to confer with the grand duchess, and then return with her words in his mouth (VHW, p. 324). Liszt's complaint against this arrangement was that it left the future of music at Weimar in an ambivalent position. Whatever happened in the opera house did so despite rather than because of Carl Friedrich. With the accession of Carl Alexander in July 1853 Liszt had every reason to hope that the city would receive from its new titular head the artistic leadership that had for so long been lacking.

The Weimar Court, a pencil drawing by Bernhard von Arnwaldt (c. 1836).

Carl Alexander was the only surviving son of Maria Pawlowna.[4] He was born in 1818, the fourteenth year of her marriage to Carl Friedrich, and she bestowed every material advantage on his upbringing. As a child he received a classical education and also became fluent in French. He was a frequent guest in Goethe's house, where he used to play with the poet's grandchildren.[5] His tutors did not fail to impress upon him the shining achievements of his grandfather Carl August, of whom he retained a lively remembrance. By nature Carl Alexander was shy and retiring, and he assumed the burdens of his office with reluctance. He mixed far more readily with the poets and artists who surrounded him from his earliest years than he did with his own officials. Unlike his father, he liked to leave Weimar whenever he could and relax in his country châteaux. His favourite retreat was Ilmenau, because the woods surrounding the manor gave him the feeling of complete isolation. ("Whenever I go alone into the thick wood, with the trees arched over me, I feel truly at peace."[6]) Nonetheless, he worked ceaselessly in behalf of his domains—which included Jena, Erfurt, and

---

4. An elder son, Paul Alexander, had died in 1806, only a few months after his difficult birth. For twelve years Carl Friedrich lacked a male heir.

5. VHW, p. 339.

6. VHW, p. 340.

Eisenach, with its historic showpiece the Wartburg Castle—and he liked to say, "Wer rastet, der röstet" ("Whoever rests, rusts"). It was to be the misfortune of his long reign that he would be constantly preoccupied with the parlous state of the royal coffers, which were almost emptied as a result of the 1848–49 revolutions. A glance at the treasury figures discloses the magnitude of the problem he inherited. From 1844 the duchy of Weimar was already staggering under an annual deficit of 3,800,000 thalers, yet its income from all sources was only 800,000 thalers; the civil list alone ran away with 250,000 thalers in salaries.[7] As Carl Alexander's reign unfolded, it was often remarked that his reach exceeded his grasp.

I I

When Liszt first walked onto the Weimar stage, on November 29, 1841, and gave a public recital there, he had little idea that his destiny would soon be linked with this famous city.[8] Eduard Genast, the stage manager, has left an absorbing account of Liszt's arrival in his memoirs.[9] It was a dark, blustery evening, and a cold north wind was howling through the treetops in the Carlsplatz. Genast had just gone over to the Russischer Hof hotel in order to dine with Robert and Clara Schumann, who were passing through the city. Suddenly the door of the dining-room opened, and a tall, thin man with an expressive face and light brown hair advanced towards them. "Liszt!" cried the Schumanns with one voice. The virtuoso had just arrived in Weimar and quite by chance was staying at the same hotel. After the introductions had been made, Liszt sat next to Clara and chatted to everyone in the friendliest manner. As the conversation unfolded Genast noticed that Clara began to admire the valuable bejewelled brooch that Liszt was wearing suspended from a gold chain around his neck. Liszt must have noticed it too, for he removed the precious adornment and presented it to Clara as a gift. She became embarrassed and at first declined to accept it. But Liszt persisted, and through sheer charm and

---

7. These are the figures provided by Eduard Vehse, who conducted his study in 1854 (VHW). The 250,000 thalers earmarked for wages had to cover everybody who was on the royal payroll, including four marshals, forty-one chamberlains, numberless footmen, coachmen, and ladies-in-waiting, as well as all the actors and musicians engaged at the Court Theatre. After the 1848–49 revolutions the budget was curtailed still further, and in the 1850s (that is to say, at the very time of Liszt's tenure in Weimar) much belt-tightening was in progress.

8. To this, however, should be added the fact that in 1837, just after the death of Hummel, Liszt (who was only twenty-six years old, and staying in Milan) nearly wrote to the grand duke to offer himself as Hummel's replacement. This disclosure was made by Liszt many years later, in 1862, in a letter to his mother (VFL, p. 112). The idea was not pursued, because he embarked shortly afterwards on his European tours; but it shows that Liszt already harboured an unconscious attraction to the ideals of Weimar ten years before he actually settled there, and long before he ever set foot in the city.

9. GAWZ, pp. 308–09.

diplomacy he persuaded her to accept the cluster of stones as a mark of his esteem.

The next day, after the Schumanns had left, the town began to buzz with news of Liszt's presence. "Will he really give a concert?" people asked one another. They did not have long to wait for an answer. Maria Pawlowna had invited Liszt to give a recital on November 26 before the royal family and selected members of the court circle. Such was the success of this concert that she at once arranged for a larger one to take place in the music salon of the castle on November 28. By now the general demand to hear Liszt was uncontainable, and he gave a recital in Weimar's largest auditorium, the Court Theatre, on November 29. The box-office takings of nearly 600 thalers were given to the Weimar Ladies Club, a charitable organization of which Maria Pawlowna was the honorary president.

Liszt still had no inkling that Weimar would one day become his home. In fact it was not until his second visit, the following year, that he was asked by Carl Alexander, the heir apparent, to consider forming an artistic attachment to the Weimar Court. The events surrounding his appointment as Court Kapellmeister in Extraordinary, in November 1842, have already been chronicled and need not be recapitulated here. It is sufficient to recall that Carl Alexander had just taken as his bride the eighteen-year-old Princess Sophie, daughter of Willem II, king of the Netherlands, and that the young couple were still on their honeymoon when Liszt arrived in Weimar. The entire city was decked out for the celebrations, and Carl Alexander had seized on this festive occasion to persuade his father, Carl Friedrich, to bind Liszt to the royal household.[10] More interesting are the terms of Liszt's contract, which, for all its fine-sounding phraseology, would leave him vulnerable to the intrigues of his enemies in the years to come. It was promulgated in the form of a grand ducal decree:

Weimar, November 2, 1842

We, Carl Friedrich, by the grace of God grand duke of Sachsen-Weimar-Eisenach, landgrave in Thuringia, margrave of Meissen, a count exalted to the rank of prince of Henneberg, lord of Blankenheim, Neustadt, and Tautenburg, etc., herewith attest to the following:

---

10. ACLA, vol. 2, pp. 225–26. The reader is directed to Volume One (pp. 370–71) of the present work, where the background is sketched out in greater detail. It is worth noting again, however, that it was the young heir apparent, Carl Alexander, who secured Liszt's services for Weimar, not his father, Carl Friedrich; and it was to Carl Alexander that Liszt always pledged his loyalty. The marriage between Carl Alexander and Princess Sophie took place on October 8, 1842. There were four children of the union: Carl August (1844–94); Marie (1849–1922); Anna (1851–59); and Elisabeth (1854–1908). The duke and duchess were surrounded by their growing family at the very time that Liszt was living in Weimar, and he got to know them all intimately.

We have most graciously reached the decision to appoint the virtuoso Dr. Franz Liszt to be our Kapellmeister, in recognition of his artistic achievements, which are to our particular satisfaction: and accordingly, and in testimony thereof, the present decree, which was signed by our own hand and to which was affixed our official seal, has been drawn up and delivered to the same.

CARL FRIEDRICH
C. W. FR. V. FRITSCH[11]

The harmonious language of this document emits such an agreeable sonic surface that it is impossible for the reader to detect the seeds of dissonance which lurked behind it. Yet already there had been a clue. Four days before Carl Friedrich signed the decree, a separate agreement had been worked out between Liszt and Hyppolyte Chélard, Hummel's successor at Weimar, whose position was clearly threatened by Liszt's presence in the city, and it was issued from the high office of the marshal of the court. It was a far more practical document than a mere grand ducal *Dekret,* and we perceive behind its imperious language a nervous desire to separate the duties of the new Kapellmeister from those of the present director of the theatre, to keep music away from drama—no easy task, since Weimar had only one theatre, whose limited facilities had to be shared. Whether the document was drawn up at Chélard's suggestion or at Liszt's we may never be certain.

Liszt will spend three months here every year, the months of September and October, or October and November, and lastly the month of February.

1. He desires to have, for the concerts he arranges, the direction of the Court Orchestra, without, however, superseding M. Chélard, who will direct the orchestra on all other occasions.

2. Herr Liszt wishes to remain Herr Liszt for life, without accepting any other title.

3. As regards the financial remuneration, Herr Liszt will be satisfied with whatever sum may be thought suitable for his services during these three months.

Written after my conversation with Herr Liszt October 30, 1842.[12]

Liszt's refusal to accept a title, apparently made out of deference to Chélard's feelings, proved to be unacceptable to the grand duke. The following day a codicil was added to the memorandum:

11. RLS, vol. 1, n. 106; RLKM, vol. 2, p. 198.
12. RLKM, vol. 2, p. 197.

October 31, 1842

Herr Liszt has informed me today that he will accept with gratitude and pleasure the title of Kapellmeister in Extraordinary.

In many ways this was a prophetic document, for the inherent rivalry between Chélard and Liszt, which the contract recognized and was supposed to address, was soon to become a source of tension in the theatre. Moreover, the contract made no mention of the biggest potential conflict of all: the one between music and drama, which would one day become Liszt's undoing.[13]

Liszt's appointment to the Weimar Court was everywhere received with disbelief. There were many who thought that the famous pianist was miscast in the role of a minor court official, even a part-time one, and they expected to see him fail. They knew nothing of his aspirations for the small principality, of course; and if they had, they would have laughed aloud at his effrontery. In 1842 Liszt was known to the world only as a pianist. How was it possible, they asked, for a mere "piano hussar" to bring respect and prestige to Weimar, with its all-too-modest resources, when even he admitted that he was a novice as a conductor and had absolutely no experience as a composer of orchestral works? The opposition to Liszt's presence in Weimar itself came from an unexpected quarter. Hummel's family still lived there, and they fought against this appointment for years. Since Hummel's death in 1837, his widow, Elisabeth, and his two granddaughters had lived in the family home at no. 8, Marienstrasse. Elisabeth, who survived her husband by more than forty-five years, refused to leave Weimar and could often be observed tending Hummel's grave in the Stadtfriedhof, where she created a small flower-garden to his memory.[14] Al-

---

13. The merest glance at the theatrical repertory of Weimar in the 1850s is sufficient to reveal the sort of competition that Liszt was up against. Adolf Bartels's *Chronik des Weimarischen Hoftheaters, 1817–1907,* discloses that dozens of second-rate plays were mounted on the Weimar stage, month after dreary month, during Liszt's tenure there. The playwrights included Otto Ludwig, Alfred Meissner, Franz Dingelstedt, Friedrich Halm, Karl von Hotei, Roderich Benedix, Calderon von Lambert, Friedrich Kaiser, and many others of whom the average theatre-goer today has never heard. Of course, the Weimar company regularly mounted as well the masterpieces of Goethe and Schiller, which by the time Liszt arrived in the city were this theatre's chief *raison d'être.* Weimar was, and always remained, a city of the stage. Music was of secondary importance in Carl Alexander's grandiose scheme to revive the cultural life of "the Athens of the North." And even when a Franz Liszt was placed in charge of its development, the literary traditions of the city were too powerful for him to correct the imbalance. Weimar never had a separate concert hall—a plain enough symbol of music's second-class standing there. The practical difficulties arising from that simple fact became the bane of Liszt's existence. Time and again, rehearsals for the purely musical events collided with those for the purely theatrical ones, and the modest resources of the Court Theatre sometimes came perilously close to the breaking point.

14. Elisabeth Hummel (1793–1883) was ninety years old at the time of her death. Above her tomb runs the epitaph "Die Liebe höret nimmer auf!" It is a common enough sentiment in German cemeteries, but it was never truer than here: Elisabeth tended the family grave as if indeed "Love

though Liszt had done much to promote Hummel's piano music (it will be recalled that he had played the concertos many times during his youth), once he took up residence in Weimar the Hummel family wanted nothing to do with him. They accused him of "destroying the true art of piano playing," whose last great representative, they insisted, was Hummel. At bottom, the family feared that the presence of Liszt would obscure the memory of Hummel's own work in Weimar, and as time passed by their fears became reality. Hummel's chief piano student in Weimar had been Ferdinand Hiller, who worked to bring about Liszt's downfall and received much inside information about Liszt's activities direct from the Hummels.[15]

III

Fifteen months elapsed before Liszt passed through Weimar again. He first conducted the Court Orchestra in a performance of Beethoven's Fifth Symphony on January 7, 1844, and was dismayed to find the ensemble in a state of neglect, its morale at a low ebb.[16] It consisted of a mere thirty-five players,

never ceases!" Her daughter by Hummel, Auguste, died in childbirth in 1844 and left two baby girls for the elderly lady to care for: Johanna (1842–1927) and Auguste (1844–1918).

15. Aside from Hiller, Hummel's most notable students were Thalberg, Henselt, and, for a time, Mendelssohn. The claim that he stood at the head of modern piano playing, then, was not without foundation. Hummel's chief pedagogical work was his *Ausführlich theoretisch-practische Anweisung zum Piano-forte Spiel,* in three volumes, which sold thousands of copies within days of its publication in 1828. The fortune that Hummel left at his death was gradually spent by the family, and in the 1880s we find Hummel's granddaughters letting rooms in the large house. (See the interesting memoir left by Bettina Walker, WMME, pp. 102–11.)

The Hummel family's opposition to Liszt sometimes spilled over into the press. In the *Foreign Quarterly Review* of January 1845, for instance, we read: "We mention Hummel, whose solid musical works are before the public of Europe, because his appointment is now possessed by Liszt, a man who has produced nothing. How he will answer to his patrons for this degeneracy, or to the 'inexorable judge within,' is more than we can tell." These libellous comments were published anonymously, of course. The notion that Liszt had somehow acquired Hummel's job by deception is astonishing, and one wonders what the Hummel family thought of the charge. Hummel's appointment was not "now possessed by Liszt"; it was possessed by Chélard.

16. Other works he conducted during the months of January and February 1844 included Beethoven's *Eroica* Symphony (January 21), Beethoven's Seventh Symphony (February 4), and a movement from Schubert's "Great" C-major Symphony (February 18). For the complete programme, see HMW, pp. 196–97. The January engagements, of course, were in violation of the agreement that had so recently been drawn up with Chélard, and undoubtedly contributed towards the ill-will Chélard always bore Liszt. (At the first concert, on January 7, Chélard and Liszt shared the rostrum, and the comparison was hardly flattering to the older man.) Chélard's public outburst against Liszt during the latter's speech at the Beethoven festivities in Bonn in August 1845 can only be understood in this wider context (see Volume One, p. 424). To add insult to Chélard's injury, Liszt disappeared from Weimar for four years after his initial encounter with the orchestra (if one discounts the random concert he conducted there during a lightning visit in February 1846), leaving his aggrieved colleague once more

some of them amateurs drawn from the local community. There was also a chorus of twenty-three singers (ten men and thirteen women), and a ballet of four dancers.[17] Berlioz, who had heard the chorus in 1843 in a production of Marschner's *The Vampire,* described it as "a rabble . . . bawling [its] way through the score with a contempt for the conventions of pitch and rhythm."[18] Part of the trouble was that these ensembles played no real role in the artistic life of Weimar; they were used mainly for entr'acte music in the theatre. Even in Hummel's day there had been only two orchestral concerts a year; for the rest of the season the players were employed on an *ad hoc* basis. The appointment of Hyppolyte Chélard as Hummel's successor in 1840 had not helped matters. Chélard was barely competent, and there were many witnesses to the havoc his baton could create when complex works were being performed. Since Liszt and Chélard now shared the same podium,[19] a comparison between them was inevitable. During much of 1851 Liszt was out of town because of Carolyne's illness, and Eduard Genast wrote to him: *"Robert le diable* was disgraceful. I have neither the courage nor the desire to recount the mistakes and many foolish things perpetrated by that ignoramus Chélard, with the continual smirk on his face."[20] Joachim Raff was even more forceful: "Our theatre gets worse every day! We have just had two performances of *Freischütz* and *Zauberflöte,* and the blunders that occurred were such as to offend the ears of . . . the most unmusical listeners, many of whom left the house before the end of the opera."[21] He added that if Liszt did not return to Weimar soon, he would not find many of his old colleagues left in "this damned village."

Liszt knew that the first thing he had to do was to increase the size of the orchestra and entice better players to Weimar. In the achievement of both these aims he was hampered at every stage by the penny-pinching policies of Carl Alexander. By October 1851 Liszt had only managed to increase his forces to the following thirty-eight positions.[22]

---

in command of the field, only to snatch it back again when he returned to Weimar in February 1848 in order to take up his duties on a full-time basis.

Liszt's attitude towards his Weimar appointment was by no means as cavalier as it may at first have seemed. It will be recalled that he and Marie d'Agoult had still to disentangle their lives; the final rupture did not take place until April 1844, and it caused Liszt endless domestic problems (see Volume One, pp. 402–07). Moreover, Liszt's career as a concert pianist reached its apogee in the mid-1840s and made unprecedented (and unpredictable) demands on his time. But as the months and then the years passed by, Weimar became a fixed star which lent his itinerant life a sense of direction; and when he finally took up permanent residence in the city, it was like coming home.

17. SGSW.
18. BM, p. 289.
19. See the agreement on p. 96, which divided their duties.
20. FLL, pp. 106–07.
21. RLR, p. 864.
22. HMW, p. 152.

5 first violins	Joseph Joachim, Carl Stör, Johann Walbrül, Christian Hart, August Weissenborn
6 second violins	Franke, August Fischer, Müller, Damm, Paul Götze, Weissenborn (Jr.)
3 violas	Gottfried Wintzer, Friedrich Wollweber, August Machts
4 cellos	Bernhard Cossmann, Gustav Apel, Eduard Ulrich, Kessner
3 double-basses	Schwarz, Wilhelm Börner, Friedrich Ahrens
2 flutes	Christian Schöler, Heinrich Kuhnt
2 oboes	Gottfried Abbass, Heinrich Kuhlmann
2 clarinets	Ernst Saul, B. Kohlschmidt
2 bassoons	Hochstein, Gustav Buch
4 horns	Heinrich Klemm, Ernst Sennewald, Julius Wisler, Kiel
2 trumpets	Ernst Sachse, Johann Schorcht
1 trombone	Moritz Nabich
1 tuba	Friedrich Randeckart
timpani	Kallenberg

Later that year Liszt requested two more trombones, a harp, a bass-clarinet, an organ, and extra percussion. During his entire tenure at Weimar the "normal" orchestra rarely exceeded forty-five players, although extras could be brought in from nearby Jena and Erfurt to help out on special occasions.[23]

The appointment of principals was a further cause of frustration. One of Liszt's first moves was to engage Joseph Joachim as leader in 1850, at an annual salary of 500 thalers. After only two years Joachim resigned (for reasons that will be explored elsewhere in this volume); his place was taken in January 1853 by Ferdinand Laub from Prague. The grand duke seized this opportunity to save some money by elevating Laub's title to "chamber virtuoso" while reducing his salary to 400 thalers. This arrangement also lasted a mere two years, and in January 1855 Laub was replaced by Edmund Singer from Pest. These were

---

23. These figures were not unusual for the mid–nineteenth century. According to Dörffel, even the famed Leipzig Gewandhaus Orchestra only had thirty-nine players on its books in 1831. And while the Vienna Court Opera had an establishment of sixty players in 1841, one year before Liszt assumed his Weimar post, they rarely all appeared at the same concert. The Meiningen Orchestra, which Bülow brought to a peak of perfection in the 1880s, consisted throughout his tenure of only forty-eight players. Weimar's orchestra, then, while small by modern standards, was quite a respectable size when compared with others of the time. Liszt's constant badgering for more and better players had to do with his composer's ear, which told him that Romantic music in general, and his own symphonic poems in particular, required more strings and double woodwinds if it was to "speak" effectively. For Classical music, Liszt appears to have been content with smaller forces.

distinguished principals, and they helped Liszt to introduce standards of orchestral excellence hitherto unknown in Weimar.

Other outstanding players whom Liszt brought to Weimar included the harp virtuoso Jeanne Eyth (the wife of the music critic Richard Pohl), the trombonist Eduard Grosse, and the cellist Bernhard Cossmann, who went on to become professor of cello at both the Moscow and Frankfurt conservatories. The Weimar trumpeter Ernst Sachse, one of the best in Europe, was described by Berlioz as "superb."[24] But even he was eclipsed by the virtuoso trombonist Moritz Nabich, whose concerts in England in the 1850s (Nabich appeared in such cities as London, Liverpool, and Manchester) attracted large audiences.

Among the vocal soloists who sang under Liszt's baton during the 1850s, two were of unusual calibre. Rosa Agthe was only twenty-one years old when Liszt engaged her for the Weimar theatre in 1848. This gifted soprano, the daughter of a local orchestral player, created the role of Elsa in *Lohengrin,* and Liszt chose her to be one of his Aachen Festival soloists in 1857. She married the outstanding baritone Feodor von Milde, whom Liszt had invited to Weimar as a guest singer in Donizetti's *Lucia di Lammermoor;* he was so warmly received that he made Weimar his home. The Mildes could have enjoyed more lucrative careers elsewhere; but when asked about that, Feodor gave the unanswerable reply that they stayed in Weimar simply because Liszt was there.[25] Among the other singers who worked with Liszt during these early years, the most prominent was the tenor Franz Götze, who made a speciality of Liszt's songs.[26] From time to time, singers of national stature passed through Weimar. The contralto Johanna Wagner created a sensation when she appeared in two of Gluck's operas, taking the role of Orpheus, and that of Clytemnestra in *lphigenia in Aulis.* [27]

It is one more indication of Carl Alexander's parsimony that he often paid his singers and orchestral players a miserable pittance. Even Bernhard Cossmann's salary as first cellist was a paltry 350 thalers annually, while the rank-and-file members were reduced to levels of grinding poverty, some of them drawing as little as 100 thalers.[28] The plight of some of these musicians is nicely

---

24. BM, p. 289.

25. SZM, p. 29.

26. In 1857 Liszt wrote to Götze: "I very much wish that you would do me the kindness of singing two of my songs [in Leipzig]: "Kling leise, mein Lied," and "Englein du mit blondem Haar," and delight the public with your ardent and beautifully artistic rendering of these little things." (LLB, vol. 1, p. 262).

27. See p. 400. Johanna Wagner was the niece of Richard Wagner, the adopted daughter of his brother Albert.

28. When Johanna Wagner was engaged to sing at the Berlin Opera for a year in May 1851, she received 4,000 thalers, with a bonus of 600 thalers and removal expenses of 100 thalers. This was a fortune in comparison with the salaries given to ordinary musicians. Then, as now, the star system prevailed.

Grand Duke Carl Alexander of Sachsen-Weimar,
an oil portrait by Richard Lauchert (1856).

illustrated by the case of one of them, Friedrich Randeckart, the tuba player who had served for twenty years as a military bandsman in the ducal regiment and had a wife and six children to support. On December 17, 1851, Randeckart petitioned the court for more money, pointing out that his orchestral salary of 200 thalers was insufficient for his domestic needs and that he did not know whether he and his family would be able to survive until the new year. The marshal of the court replied with a handout of 10 thalers, making the unfortunate fellow promise that there would be no repetition of such a request, and adding for good measure that he could always return to the military band if times became hard. He was then made to attach his signature to this document as proof that he had read it.[29]

Liszt was aware of his colleagues' predicament and did all that he could to improve their lot. His petition to the court for extra instruments, dated October 31, 1851, began with two suggestions for raising the morale of the players.

1. to give a retirement pension to seven members of the Kapelle who would otherwise lack an income in their old age
2. to fill these vacant positions by promoting individual players through the ranks or by recruiting new ones from outside

The reply of the marshal of the court, to whom the petition was addressed, requires no embellishment. "To fulfil all these demands now lies beyond the present possibility. The marshal of the court can respond to them only provisionally."[30]

Prevarication, vague promises, dashed hopes were ever Liszt's portion at Weimar. His own salary was even more problematical. He was not paid from the Weimar treasury at all but from the private purse of Maria Pawlowna and her successor, Grand Duchess Sophie. In his contract of 1842 Liszt had stipulated, perhaps unwisely, that he would accept whatever the grand duke wanted to pay him. But after he took up his duties on a full-time basis in 1848, only the vaguest provision seems to have been made to put him on the regular payroll. In the royal account book, which recorded the expenditures from Maria Pawlowna's privy purse, there appears in 1848 an entry of 1,500 thalers, "an honorarium for Kapellmeister Liszt, for helping Her Royal Highness with her advanced musical studies." The following year the same source shows an amount of 330 thalers, "a gift for Court Kapellmeister Liszt for a composition, for instruction, and the like." Between 1850 and 1858 he received annual amounts ranging from 330 thalers (less than the orchestral leaders were paid) to 1,600 thalers, depending on the sort of services rendered. It is perfectly plain

29. RLS, vol. 1, pp. 104–05.
30. RLS, vol. I, pp. 105–06.

that these *ad hoc* payments were regarded by the court as a salary. Liszt called it his "cigar money."[31] In 1850 he was given a "raise" of 1,000 thalers by Carl Alexander, but this money was never paid. Not once did Liszt complain at this shabby treatment. Maria Pawlowna, it is true, had bought the Altenburg in 1851 and placed it at his disposal, and the treasures with which he and Princess Carolyne had filled it had turned this house into a rent-free palace. The lavish way in which Liszt and the princess entertained their guests became the talk of the town, and there is no doubt that the Weimar Court circle regarded Liszt as a rich man who had no need of his modest stipend.[32] For the rest, the bonds of sentiment that always tied Liszt to Carl Alexander prevented him from pressing the grand duke for the money, and so the matter was never mentioned. Liszt turned this unusual situation to good account, however, since the "honorary" nature of the appointment freed him from the constraints that a salary might otherwise have placed on him. In a word, Liszt was not really accountable. A man of his temperament would, in any case, have found it intolerable to think that his artistic labours were "bought and paid for," as if they were no different than a sack of potatoes. Nonetheless, there remained a basic injustice about it all, for once the Weimar Court understood the generous nature of the man who had been placed in charge of their musical affairs, they exploited him to the hilt.

IV

Apart from the royal castle in Weimar, which had long been the administrative centre of the court, the grand dukes owned two summer castles just outside the city, where they and their families often spent the holidays. Belvedere Castle was laid out in the eighteenth century. It stands on elevated ground, with a commanding view of the city, which nestles in a hollow of the Thuringian hills about three miles away. Its lakes and parklands and its close vicinity to Weimar made it an ideal retreat. Carl August had established the custom of putting on plays and musical entertainments there for his guests, and his heirs and successors kept up the practice. Liszt often went out to Belvedere to attend court balls, or concerts in the famous orangerie, or even to perform privately for Carl

---

31. GLW, p. 54. Since Liszt's cigars cost him between 800 and 1,000 thalers annually, his joke was literally true. He and the princess were both heavily addicted to tobacco, and they handed out cigars to their visitors at the Altenburg as a matter of course.

32. More than one cartoon appeared in the press depicting Liszt and the princess holding royal court at the "Altenburg Palace." The model for these caricatures appears to have been the drawing by Sixtus Thon called "Liszt and the Princess Wittgenstein Receiving at the Altenburg," which accompanied a birthday-poem for Princess Marie (February 1855) by Hoffmann von Fallersleben. Seated on raised thrones, Liszt and Carolyne are dressed in ermine and they wear crowns, in which opulent regalia they greet their loyal subjects. (See Dénes Bartha, *Franz Liszt* [Leipzig, 1936], plate 29.)

Alexander and his family. The warm summer evenings at Belvedere were perfect for music-making, and the French windows of the great ballroom were often thrown open to let the audience wander at will through the scented gardens, the music wafting across the still night air. The other summer castle was at Ettersburg, about six miles outside Weimar. Carl Alexander frequently summoned Liszt to Ettersburg for his private dinner-parties, and Liszt used to stay overnight in his own suite of rooms whenever the hour became too late for him to return to the Altenburg.[33]

Despite the distance Liszt always placed between himself and the humdrum duties of Court Kapellmeister, there were times when those duties ensnared him. We have already remarked that he gave private composition lessons to Maria Pawlowna, a chore that he must have found only slightly less irksome than the singing lessons he was subsequently asked to give to Princess Sophie.[34] But there was worse to follow. For formal court functions, as we discover from his correspondence, Liszt was sometimes expected to wear a uniform! The image of Liszt, one of the most independent spirits who walked the earth, and so often described as "the equal of princes," dressed as a court lackey somewhat in the style of "Papa Haydn" a hundred years earlier at Esterháza, fills one with astonishment.[35] One more indication of Liszt's servitude was that he was expected to be on hand for royal birthdays, weddings, and even funerals. In this he was no different from all the other artists whom Carl Alexander brought to his court. Hoffmann von Fallersleben, the poet laureate, filled a volume of verse in praise of practically anything that wore a decoration at Weimar. Likewise, the painter Friedrich Preller produced so many portraits of the royal family and the Weimar en-

---

33. At the grand duke's request, Liszt recommended changes to the design of the ceiling of the chapel at Ettersburg Castle in order to improve the acoustics.
34. Having said that, we have to add that Maria Pawlowna was not without talent as a composer. Liszt's *Consolation* no. 4, in D-flat major, composed in 1850, is based on a melody by his royal benefactress.

Liszt drew attention to the aristocratic lineage of the theme by placing above it a star in the shape of the Order of the White Falcon, the most important decoration within the gift of the grand dukes of Weimar. According to Eduard Genast, Maria Pawlowna had not only taken piano lessons from Hummel but could read and transpose from a full score "like a Kapellmeister" (GAWZ, p. 309).
35. LLB, vol. 4, p. 68.

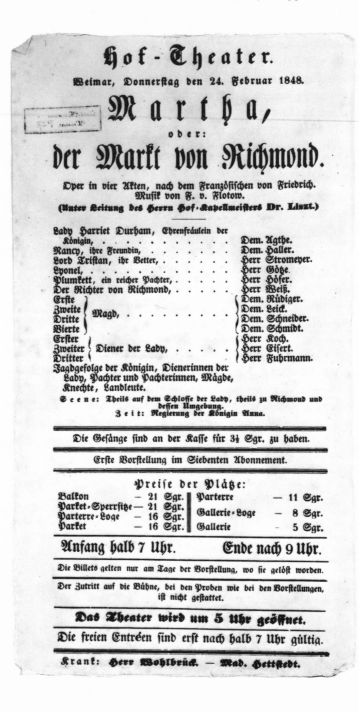

Liszt conducts Martha *in Weimar, a handbill for February 24, 1848.*

virons for the castle galleries that his activities ranked as a branch of light industry. But Liszt, as a "performing artist," had a harder time of it because he was more visible. Whenever he gave a concert at the castle, court etiquette forbade him to mix with the royal family during the intervals and obliged him to remain discreetly in the background until his services were once more requested. A contemporary witness described Liszt on these occasions as "the complete Kapellmeister, without the slightest pretensions to be taken as a man of fashion."[36] Where was the once-proud artist who had publicly admonished Tsar Nicholas for talking during a recital? Where was the *grand seigneur* who declined the snuff-box presented to him by King Willem II of the Netherlands because it was of too little value? Liszt was willing to swallow much pride at Weimar because he needed the continuous support of the court if his ambitious plans for the city were to have any chance of success. At Weimar Liszt became a diplomat, and there is evidence that Carl Alexander, knowing full well the volcanic make-up of the man he had asked to be his Kapellmeister, admired him for it.

V

Whatever its outward show of ostentation, then, the Weimar Court was never well off. It was not until Maria Pawlowna married the Grand Duke Carl Friedrich in 1804 and brought her huge wedding dowry to Weimar that the state coffers were rich enough to build an extension to the royal palace. Carl Alexander, following his father's example, also married into money, and it was his bride, Princess Sophie of the Netherlands, who provided the wherewithal to add yet more wings to the royal castle and to complete the building of their summer palace at Ettersburg. When Liszt saw in Weimar the possibility of renewing its former artistic glory, "as in the days of Goethe and Schiller," he was stating no more than an honourable goal. Yet Carl Alexander, for all his enthusiasm, could not always find the money to support Liszt's plans. A duke who would finish the exterior staircases at Ettersburg in cast-iron and paint them over to look like marble was not about to lavish large sums on the grandiose schemes of his Kapellmeister.

None of this was apparent to Liszt at first. In fact he had every reason to suppose from the friendly correspondence that he and Carl Alexander had already struck up, even before he had established a permanent residence in Weimar, that the royal coffers were full to overflowing and awaited only some worthwhile artistic enterprise on which to be expended. This correspondence, both published and unpublished, throws a flood of light on the special relation-

---

36. BLTB, vol. 2, p. 101.

ship that existed between Liszt and the young duke.[37] Carl Alexander's epistolary style is relaxed: he addresses Liszt as "cher ami" and often signs himself
"your affectionate Carl Alexander." Liszt, for his part, usually confined himself
to the simple "sire" or even "monseigneur." This was unusual in those days of
strict social etiquette, especially in Germany, where the barriers separating
royals and commoners, masters and servants, were more rigidly observed than
elsewhere.

As early as August 1846 the young duke had written a letter to Liszt (who
was about to embark on a long tour of Hungary and Rumania and had paid
only one brief visit to Weimar in two years) in which he expressed the hope
that the day was not far distant when Liszt might include Weimar in the various
occupations to which he intended to consecrate his time.

> Ettersburg
> August 31, 1846
>
> I hope that you will not be annoyed with me if I disturb you for
> a moment in the middle of all your activities. I am picking up the
> pen simply in order to ask you how everything goes, and especially
> how it goes with you yourself. For a long time I have heard nothing
> about you, except for the few words that M. Genast spoke to me
> when he returned from Vienna. He told me that you are working
> a lot, so I regret not seeing you vis-à-vis the task that you have
> imposed on yourself [i.e., building up the musical fortunes of
> Weimar]. . . .
>
> I have been told of the various activities to which you intend
> to consecrate your time. Do not bear me a grudge if I try to slip
> Weimar's name into your plans. . . . Madame the grand duchess and
> I hope that December will see our wishes realized. . . . If the summer
> has already seen my hope of seeing you again die, then make the
> winter keep its promise . . .
>
> Your very affectionate
> CARL ALEXANDER[38]

Alas, the winter did not keep its promise either, and it must have become
clear to Carl Alexander that Liszt did not intend to return to Weimar soon.
By February 1847 the Weimar theatre was experiencing some serious administrative problems caused by the ill-health of the intendant, Baron von Spiegel,
who had held his position since 1828. There was still no sign of Liszt, who,

---

37. LBLCA. The originals may be consulted in WA, Kasten 457, and the Staatsarchiv, Hausarchiv
Carl Alexander, Abt. A, XXVI, 560/a–g.
38. LBLCA, pp. 5–6.

unknown to the duke, was in Kiev and about to go into a ten-day retreat with Princess Carolyne at her Woronince estate. The duke wrote to Liszt, more in sorrow than in anger, telling him that he had been forced to appoint a new intendant, that his choice had fallen on Baron Ferdinand von Ziegesar, and that Liszt's swift return to Weimar would be greatly appreciated.

> Weimar
> February 4, 1847
>
> Although I do not know where you are, and I have not heard from you for a long time, I could not forgo the pleasure of writing to you, all the more so since the business I shall describe to you puts the pen in my hand, so to speak. We have often spoken of the Weimar theatre, asking ourselves what should be done to raise its standards, in order to try to make the present worthy of the past. Your readiness to oblige, of which you have given me so many proofs, allows me to assume that you would not refuse either your advice or your help, if ever the time came for a change of management. That time has come. At my request, Herr von Spiegel has given up his job as intendant. Recalling your recommendation, I proposed Herr von Ziegesar as his replacement, and he was appointed. He takes up his duties from the end of the season, that is, from July 1. Meanwhile, we have to make a lot of arrangements, a lot of preparations, and I am writing to ask you to hasten your return to Weimar and help von Ziegesar with your bright ideas. I say "hasten" because as I am leaving for the Hague in the first few days of April, and since von Ziegesar is supposed to make the trip too, it is absolutely necessary for the arrangements to be completed before then. You will understand that I am forced by circumstance to express this wish to you, which is quite natural in any case. Madame the grand duchess [Maria Pawlowna] shares this wish entirely, as you might well imagine. I shall not tell you about myself, *mon cher,* since you know me well enough to believe in the stability of my feelings. I need your presence all the more because I would like this affair to be taken *au sérieux.* Noble memories demand it of me.
>
> *Adieux* and *au revoir,* God willing. It would crown your achievements if you brought the reply yourself.
>
> Your very affectionate
> CARL ALEXANDER[39]

---

39. LBLCA, pp. 14–15.

This letter did not reach Liszt until June, nearly five months after the duke had written it. It followed him from Kiev across Ukraine and finally caught up with him while he was in quarantine at Galatz, about to take ship for Constantinople. He was in bed, suffering from a violent attack of catarrhal fever, when the duke's letter was handed to him. The sight of an envelope bearing the royal seal of Weimar must have prodded his conscience, for he wrote the duke a ten-page reply from his sickbed. After approving of the duke's decision to appoint Ziegesar, Liszt took the opportunity to tell his royal master some home-truths. He said that he held no illusions about the Weimar theatre as it was presently constituted. They were now in the middle of the seven lean years of Pharoah's dream (which, he added ruefully, did not prevent the prima donnas from growing fat). Everybody wanted to see Jenny Lind, Rachel, and Rubini, but aside from the fact that such artists were rare, they had driven up the price of all other singers by whetting the public's appetite for stars. Somehow, Liszt went on, Weimar must carry out two major reforms: (1) engage new leading singers, and (2) re-organize the chorus, because the present one was unspeakably bad. All things would be possible, he concluded, with a sufficient injection of the sinews of war: money, "for it is money which decides everything nowadays."[40] Alas, Liszt was not yet aware of the painful truth that this was the one commodity which was always in short supply in Weimar.

It is evident from the correspondence that Carl Alexander always followed the fortunes of his itinerant Kapellmeister with pride and enthusiasm. But there were times in the 1840s when he must have despaired of ever seeing Liszt in Weimar again, as the pianist wandered off into the European hinterland for yet another tour through the backwaters of the civilized world. "I am longing to see you again," wrote Carl Alexander, and he assured Liszt, "you are esteemed, loved, and understood among us in Weimar."[41] During one of Liszt's absences the young duke was alarmed to learn that he might be offered Donizetti's post as Kapellmeister to the Imperial Court of Vienna, but he at once brushed aside the thought with the comment "I know you too well . . . ever to doubt that you would not remain one of us."[42] When Liszt was en route to Turkey, Carl Alexander even joked about the pianist's "concerts in the sultan's harem." It was a day of joy for Carl Alexander when Liszt finally turned up in Weimar in

---

40. LBLCA, pp. 15–19.
41. LBLCA, p. 12.
42. LBLCA, p. 14. In 1846 Gaetano Donizetti lay seriously ill, and there was uncertainty about the future of his position. He lingered for two more years, in fact, dying in April 1848. By that time Liszt had taken the decision to settle permanently in Weimar. We know that he found the prospect of Vienna tempting, however, and he tried to reassure the duke that if the job were offered to him, it would not interfere with his duties at Weimar, and would actually allow him to become a closer neighbour (LBLCA, p. 10). These words were not exactly music to Carl Alexander's ears; it was not in his scheme of things to bind Weimar to Vienna in this way.

the early part of 1848. By October he knew that Liszt was there to stay, and he confided to Fanny Lewald-Stahr:

Ettersburg, 4 October 1848

What you tell me about my friend Liszt truly pleases me, because it comes to me from the heart. The world usually judges wrongly what it cannot comprehend. And so it does with him. Most people do not get beyond his personal idiosyncrasies, and fail to realize that his spirit must be still greater to manifest itself in such a way. How many have heard his playing, yet how few have hearkened to his spirit. You call him great; I could not agree with you more! He is one of the rarest apparitions which were and are. I am proud to tell you that I really feel this in my heart.[43]

To students of the Romantic era it has always seemed bizarre that Liszt, one of its greatest representatives, was willing to bind himself to a petty German court, like some minor eighteenth-century drudge, at a time when great musicians had long since broken away from the outmoded system of patronage and were proud to proclaim their independence. A hundred and fifty years have meanwhile elapsed, and the obvious inference has yet to be drawn. Liszt stayed on in Weimar long after whatever illusions he had about the place were shattered because he and Carl Alexander were tied together by bonds of affection and by their ideals. For thirteen years Liszt stubbornly refused to break his pledge to help the young duke build "a new Athens" (even though he came perilously close to throwing in his hand in the spring of 1853, a turning-point in the relationship that will be related in due course). In the end it was Carl Alexander in whom the light failed; and when that happened, Liszt knew that the time had come for him to leave.

---

43. GCAF, vol. 1, p. 33.

The Years of Struggle I,
1849–1852

The day is committed to error and floundering:
success and achievement are matters of long range.
GOETHE[1]

I

If a neglectful posterity today recalls anything at all of Liszt's tenure at Weimar, it is surely his championship of Wagner. That, at any rate, is now safely enshrined in the history books. We can do no better at this juncture than to cast a preliminary glance at the pioneering work he had already achieved for Wagner within a year or two of his arrival in Weimar, since it tells us everything we need to know about the vigour with which he pursued his dreams for the city, despite its modest resources. The story of the Liszt-Wagner friendship, and its consequences for the wider world of nineteenth-century music, will be told elsewhere in this volume. For the moment, it is sufficient to recapitulate the main events in their relationship as it existed at the time of Liszt's first season at Weimar. We recall that Wagner's first encounter with Liszt had taken place in Paris in 1842, at Liszt's hotel. Surrounded by flattering admirers, Liszt (who was then in his heyday as a concert pianist, with most of Europe at his feet) had utterly failed to notice the impoverished twenty-seven-year-old composer and later had no remembrance of the meeting. On February 29, 1844, Liszt heard a performance of *Rienzi* in Dresden, was struck by the force of Wagner's genius, and resolved to mount a Wagner opera at Weimar as soon as he had got the full measure of his duties there. The occasion presented itself during his very first season, when the Dresden production of *Tannhäuser* was successfully transferred to the Weimar stage in celebration of the birthday

---

1. GMR, no. 911, p. 166.

of Maria Pawlowna on February 16, 1849.[2] This was followed by Wagner's precipitous flight to Weimar in May 1849, where, as every student of the subject knows, Liszt harboured him as a political refugee from the Dresden authorities for a few days before seeing him safely on his way to a Swiss exile. While the broad outlines of this story are familiar enough, the details will bear closer inspection, since the full extent of Liszt's intimate involvement in Wagner's cause cannot otherwise be understood.

The Dresden Insurrection had broken out in the early days of May 1849. Street barricades were flung up, and bitter hand-to-hand fighting ensued. The revolutionaries were routed by royalist troops after only a few days. Twenty-six fleeing students found hidden in a single room were taken out one by one and shot. Dozens of people were thrown out of fourth-story windows, their bodies broken on the cobblestones below. More than twelve thousand citizens suspected of supporting the revolution were rounded up by the police for questioning, and many of them received long prison terms.[3] Weimar, which lay only a hundred or so miles from Dresden, looked on uneasily. Would the revolution spread across Thuringia? After some anxious days the answer became clear. The leaders of the insurrection—August Röckel, Mikhail Bakunin, Heubner, Martin, and others—had bungled their escape as badly as they had bungled the revolution. They were captured in their beds at Chemnitz, where they had hoped to set up a provisional government, taken back to Dresden, and sentenced to death.

None of this would be of more than passing interest today were it not for the fact that Richard Wagner played an active role in the insurrection, was forced to flee the city, and was eventually charged with high treason. By a stroke of good fortune he did not proceed to Chemnitz with his companions but travelled there later. Unable to find them, he took lodgings at a different inn from theirs. That night they were dragged from their beds by the police, less than a mile from where Wagner was sleeping, and put into irons. Wagner only learned of his lucky escape the next day. He decided to travel at once to Weimar, there to seek sanctuary with Liszt, and he arrived in the town on

---

2. Liszt had actually conducted the Overture to *Tannhäuser* on November 12, 1848. The performance of the opera itself appears to have been arranged in haste. Eduard Genast, the stage-manager, was obliged to travel to Dresden in order to pick up the full score and the vocal parts because there was insufficient time for Wagner to mail them. During their brief meeting Wagner gave Genast some useful hints on how to produce the opera. At the first rehearsal it was discovered that the tessitura of the title role lay too high for Franz Götze, who became terribly nervous about the entire enterprise. Six days before the performance Götze abruptly announced that he could not do it, whereupon Genast dashed back to Dresden and begged Joseph Tichatschek, in Liszt's name, to fill the breach. With the greatest difficulty Genast brought the man whom Wagner himself had coached for this demanding role back to Weimar, where the great tenor received a standing ovation (GAWZ, pp. 316–18; SNW, vol. 1, p. 257).

3. On June 20, 1853, more than four years later, the *Zeitung für Norddeutschland* reported that one hundred and nine people still languished in Saxon prisons for their part in the uprising.

May 13. When Wagner got to the Erbprinz Hotel, he was told that Liszt was not there and that he was not expected back until the following day. The town was abuzz with rumours of what had happened in Dresden. Röckel, who was well known in Weimar and highly respected there, was said to have personally set fire to a number of public buildings, while Wagner was already being credited with having designed the street barricades. For the first time Wagner understood the gravity of his predicament. Weimar and Dresden were signatories to a joint extradition treaty, and he feared that it was only a matter of time before he was recognized and the Weimar police came looking for him. When Liszt arrived in Weimar on May 14, he hurried down to the Erbprinz to greet his old friend. He knew that if the Dresden authorities issued a warrant for Wagner's arrest, as now seemed imminent, Wagner could not remain on German soil, and some means of escape would have to be planned for him. The first thing was to secure a false identity, and for the next few days Wagner was known locally as "Professor Werder from Berlin." Liszt felt that the only safe course was to arrange an escape to Paris, and from there possibly to London. That same day he wrote a letter to Belloni, his former manager and secretary, who now lived in Paris, enlisting his help in putting these plans into effect.

> Weimar
> May 14, 1849

> Dear Bell,[4]
> Richard Wagner (the Dresden Kapellmeister) has been here since yesterday. He is a man of wonderful genius, a genius he even puts into practice, and he is evidently destined to create for himself a new and glorious path in art. The latest events in Dresden have forced him to an important decision, in the accomplishment of which *I intend to help him with all my might.*
> After talking with him at length about it, here is what we have decided to do and what must be accomplished. First of all, to present a great, heroic musical work, whose score was completed a year ago, *in London and in English.* [5] [Henry] Chorley especially will be very helpful to him in this undertaking. Next, to arrive in Paris the following winter, and with this success in his pocket make the doors of the Opéra open wide for him. . . .
> I do not need to go into long discussions with you. Only understand, and discover whether there is at the moment an English theatre in London (for the Italian opera would be of no use to our friend!),

---

4. A nickname for Belloni.
5. *Lohengrin.* Belloni's efforts to get the opera staged in London came to nothing. It was Liszt who gave the first performance in Weimar the following year.

A facsimile of a letter written by Liszt to Belloni, dated May 14, 1849:
"Richard Wagner . . . has been here since yesterday."

or whether there is any prospect that a great and beautiful work from a master hand could have any success there. *Reply to me on this point as soon as possible.*

Later, that is towards the end of the month, Wagner will pass through Paris. He will see you at once, and will come to an agreement with you in person on the sort of action to adopt for the most complete and earliest realization of his legitimate ambition. Write at once, and help me as you always do. It is a question of a noble end, in which we must not fail.

F. LISZT[6]

Liszt then offered Wagner sanctuary in the Altenburg while they awaited further news from Dresden. Wagner renewed his acquaintance with Princess Carolyne (whom he recalled meeting on her flying visit to Dresden the year before), and he tells us in *Mein Leben* that they held "stimulating conversations on all sorts of artistic topics."[7] By an extraordinary coincidence, Wagner had arrived in Weimar just as Liszt was becoming involved in rehearsals of *Tannhäuser*, a performance of which had been announced for May 20. Although it was not without danger, arrangements were made for the composer to sit at the back of the darkened theatre while Liszt conducted a complete performance of the opera for the benefit of his friend. Writing about this moving experience a year or two later, Wagner observed: "I was astonished to recognize in [Liszt] my second self: what I had felt when I conceived this music, he felt when he performed it; what I had wished to say when I wrote down the notes, he said when he made them sound. Through the love of this rarest of all friends, and at the moment when I had become a homeless man, I won the true . . . habitation of my art."[8]

News of Wagner's flight to Weimar had by now reached the ears of Maria Pawlowna, who expressed the desire to meet him. Liszt and Wagner travelled together to Eisenach, where the grand duchess had taken up her summer residence, and Wagner was given a cordial reception.[9] Liszt was obliged to

6. Ernest Newman suspected that this letter was a forgery (NLRW, vol. 2, p. 104n). He based this claim on the fact that it was first published in a German translation, in an issue of the *Neue Musik-Zeitung* on October 1, 1881, in which the editor, Tappert, admitted that he had not seen the original. And when La Mara included it in her collection of Liszt letters (published in 1893) she was content to reproduce this German translation—a clear indication that she, like Tappert, had not seen the original either. It suited Newman to cast doubt on the authenticity of the letter because he wanted nothing to stand in the way of his general thesis that Liszt's helpfulness towards Wagner during the latter's years of exile had been greatly exaggerated. The holograph, which is undoubtedly authentic, is in the Weimar Archive (WA, Kasten 57, no. 12), and the first folio is reproduced on p. 115 of this volume.

7. WML, p. 500.

8. "A Communication to my Friends" (WGSD, vol. 4, p. 340).

9. Liszt later told Wagner that Maria Pawlowna had already been informed, via the diplomatic

travel on to Karlsruhe, where he had a pressing business engagement, so Wagner took the opportunity to explore the Wartburg. He tells us that he was filled with strange musings as he walked through the old castle, "which was so full of meaning for me."[10]

Matters now moved swiftly towards their *dénouement*. On May 16 the Dresden authorities issued a warrant for Wagner's arrest.[11] Liszt was still in Karlsruhe and did not get back to Weimar until May 18. Among the letters waiting for him at the Erbprinz Hotel was one from Wagner's wife, Minna, telling him that the Dresden police had already searched their house. Liszt waited until nightfall and then secreted Wagner into the home of Eduard Genast, who was hastily despatched to statesminister Bernhard von Watzdorf to seek legal advice. After a moment's reflection von Watzdorf said: "Luckily the warrant has not yet been delivered to us. I know that I would be carrying out the instructions of my noble friend—so hurry! Time is precious." Genast

---

network, that he would be wanted by the Dresden authorities within the next few days, so she had "hastened to make my personal acquaintance at once, knowing that it would compromise her too heavily later on" (WML, pp. 501–02).

10. WML, p. 502. Wagner had composed *Tannhäuser,* whose second act is set in the Wartburg, without ever visiting the castle. He tells us in *Mein Leben* that he had once caught a distant glimpse of the mountain ramparts as he passed by on the Fulda side, during a trip to Dresden in April 1842, and that this "sunlit hour" had made a deep impression on him (WML, p. 265). The image was eventually transformed into the scene for Act Three of *Tannhäuser.* But this visit in 1849 was his first.

11. The *Steckbrief,* or warrant, runs:

> The Royal Kapellmeister Richard Wagner, of this place, who is described in detail below, is wanted for questioning in connection with his active part in the recent uprising here, but has not as yet been found. The police are therefore instructed to look out for him, and if he is found, to arrest him and communicate with me at once.
>
> Dresden, May 16, 1849
> VON OPPELL,
> City Police Deputation

Wagner is 37–38 years old [he was in fact only thirty-five], of medium height, has brown hair, and wears glasses.

When Wagner got to hear of this official description of him, he is said to have remarked: "Well, that applies to a lot of people!" The Dresden *Anzeiger* published this warrant on May 19, and reprinted it on June 14, 20, and 28. The three-day delay between the signing of the warrant on May 16 and its publication on May 19—a delay which was so important in helping Wagner to arrange his escape—has never been satisfactorily accounted for. It has been conjectured that the king of Saxony may have deliberately slowed down the judicial process, since he had a grudging regard for his Royal Kapellmeister. Had Wagner been caught, he, like his colleagues, would have been put on trial and sentenced to death. These death-sentences, by the way, were all later commuted to long prison terms. Röckel, for instance, was given thirteen years—two of them in solitary confinement.

On May 31, 1849, just a week or two after these upheavals, Liszt organized a benefit concert for the family of the condemned Röckel in the Weimar Court Theatre. Röckel's wife, Caroline (née Lortzing), had earlier been a singer there, and after her husband's imprisonment she moved back to Weimar, where she lived until 1861. Given all the circumstances, Liszt's humanitarian gesture demanded political courage.

dashed back to his house, where Liszt and Wagner were waiting, and flung himself on the sofa, gasping for breath. Escape was still possible. Liszt sent a message to the Altenburg asking the princess for an immediate loan of 60 thalers,[12] which he gave to Wagner before sending him to the village of Magdala. It was not a moment too soon: within two hours of Wagner's departure the warrant arrived.[13] Wagner reached Magdala on the morning of May 19 and was sheltered by a local agriculturalist, one Wernsdorf. After five days he moved on to Jena (he walked all the way—a journey that took him six hours), where Liszt had arranged for him to be looked after by Professor Oskar Wolf. In Wolf's home Wagner found Liszt and a Professor Widmann already waiting for him. A hurried conference took place, and it was agreed to adopt Liszt's counsel: in order to avoid capture, Wagner must proceed to Paris indirectly, via Bavaria and Switzerland, and use Widmann's passport to get him across the German frontier. On May 25 Wagner set off for the border with this false document. He travelled through Coburg, Rudolstadt, and Lichtenfels and finally arrived at Lindau. After an anxious delay, during which Wagner felt sure that his identity would be discovered, he was allowed to board a Swiss steamer, and he stepped onto Swiss soil on May 28. A few days later he was in Paris, a city he quickly exchanged for Zürich as his place of permanent exile. He was not to set foot in Germany again for eleven years.

The pioneer work that Liszt did in Wagner's behalf during this long solitude is impossible to overestimate. For five years Liszt was the only conductor in Germany who would have anything to do with Wagner's compositions; the others were either fearful of the political consequences or disdainful of the music. Either way, German opera houses remained closed to Wagner—with the honourable exception of Weimar. Liszt staged *Tannhäuser, Lohengrin,* and *Der fliegende Holländer* many times in Weimar's modest theatre, and he took on tour (to such cities as Berlin, Karlsruhe, Düsseldorf, and Leipzig) the orchestral overtures and preludes to those operas, which ensured that Wagner's name was ever before the public. He made some matchless piano transcriptions of Wagner's scores,[14] sent money and useful artistic contacts his way, visited him several times in exile, and even tried to procure a pardon for him and have

---

12. LLB, vol. 4, p. 35.
13. The details of Wagner's last hours in Weimar, and Liszt's complicity in his escape, may be found in RLR, vol. 1, p. 401, n. 1. It is from Genast himself that the information ultimately derives. This drama, in which Genast was one of the main actors, equals anything he ever produced on the Weimar stage. For a general account of Wagner's brief sanctuary in Weimar, see NLRW, vol. 2, pp. 104–13.
14. Between 1848 and 1854 Liszt transcribed the Overture and the Entry of the Guests into the Wartburg from *Tannhäuser;* and from *Lohengrin,* the Festival and Bridal Song and Elsa's Dream and Lohengrin's Rebuke. Later came the Fantasy on Themes from *Rienzi* (1859) and the Spinning Chorus from *Der fliegende Holländer* (1860). Altogether Liszt completed fourteen arrangements of Wagner for the piano.

him brought to Weimar.[15] The Liszt-Wagner friendship is unique in the annals of musical biography, and we will have occasion to return to it often in the course of our narrative. Quite simply, Liszt recognized in Wagner the greatest musical master of the age, and he took it to be his primary mission to convert others to the same point of view. Such was the zeal with which he pressed Wagner's cause that he appears deliberately to have held back his own career as a composer of "innovative" orchestral compositions until Wagner's reputation was secure. In later years Liszt put it this way:

> Since Wagner had so valiantly broken new ground and created such wonderful masterpieces, my first concern had to be to establish firm roots for these masterpieces in German soil—at a time when he himself was exiled from his homeland and when all the theatres in Germany, both great and small, were afraid to risk his name on the playbill. Four or five years of *obstinacy* on my part, if you want to call it that, were sufficient to achieve this aim, despite the meagreness of the means at my disposal here. As a matter of fact, Vienna, Berlin, Munich, etc. have for five years been doing nothing more than copying what little Weimar (which they had mocked at first) had dictated to them ten years ago.
>
> . . . I am determined to prove the inscription that Wagner wrote for me under his portrait: "Du weisst, wie das werden wird" ["You know where things are heading"].[16]

II

Barely had Wagner left Weimar than Liszt plunged into preparations for the Goethe Festival, which the grand duke decreed would begin on August 28, 1849, the one hundredth anniversary of Goethe's birth. The attention of the whole of Germany was focussed on Weimar for this important event, and many distinguished visitors were expected to attend the plays and concerts mounted in honour of the master's birth. Liszt planned to conduct the closing scene of Part One of Schumann's *Scenes from Faust* and two new orchestral works of his own—the Goethe March and the first version of his symphonic poem *Tasso*. The orchestration of both these pieces was undertaken by Joachim Raff.[17] Some

---

15. See pp. 236–42. The May revolution threw Liszt and Wagner together with unusual violence. Subsequently they exchanged the "Sie" for the "du" form of address in all their correspondence. The turning-point comes in Wagner's first letter from Paris, dated June 5, 1849 (BWL, vol. 1, pp. 20–23).
16. LLB, vol. 3, pp. 136–37.
17. See "The Raff Case" in the present volume.

idea of the immense pressure under which Liszt was placed is indicated by the fact that he did not actually finish *Tasso* until August 12, and even then there were delays in getting the composition rehearsed, since he had to compete with the actors for the use of the Court Theatre.[18] Towards the end of July Liszt fell ill, and his doctor ordered him to take a six-week water-cure at Bad Eilsen. He at once informed the head of the Goethe Committee, Adolf Schöll, and wrote an apologetic note to Schumann in which he explained, "My doctor's orders are most strict that I must not make any break in my cure during the six weeks." He added that the performance of *Faust* was merely postponed, not cancelled.[19] At this point the grand duke appears to have intervened with a request that his Kapellmeister reconsider the decision to vacate Weimar at such a critical time. Liszt heeded the call, and despite his doctor's protests he postponed his treatment until the following October. A second note was swiftly despatched to Schumann, contradicting the first.

> Dear friend,
>
> A summons which cannot be put off obliges me to be present at the Goethe Festival here on August 28 and to undertake the direction of the musical part.
>
> My first step is naturally to beg you to be so good as to send us soon the score of your *Faust*. . . .
>
> Kindly excuse me, dear friend, for the manner in which this letter contradicts the last. I am very seldom guilty in such a way, but in this case it does not lie in me but in the particulars of the matter itself.
>
> Sincerely yours,
> F. LISZT[20]

No later commentator could improve upon the description of the Goethe Festival left to posterity by Adelheid von Schorn in her book *Das nachklassische Weimar*.[21] Warm sunshine and blue skies graced the festivities. The streets were filled with visitors, and the buildings were decorated with bunting. Although the surviving members of the Goethe family declined to play an official role

---

18. GSL, p. 44. As part of the Goethe celebrations the Court Theatre mounted a full-scale production of the master's play *Torquato Tasso* (1790), to which this first version of Liszt's symphonic poem was merely the musical adjunct.

19. LLB, vol. I, pp. 79–80.

20. LLB, vol. I, p. 80. Liszt went ahead with his plan to conduct the *Scenes from Faust* on the second day of the Goethe Festival, August 29. A triple première of this music took place simultaneously in Weimar, Leipzig, and Dresden. "I only wish I could have Faust's mantle for that day," wrote Schumann, "in order to be everywhere and hear everything. How strange, the piece lay five years in my desk. Nobody knew anything about it, and I myself had almost forgotten its existence—and now in this unusual celebration it has come to light!" (JRS, p. 266; edition of 1886 only)

21. SNW, vol. I, pp. 285–89.

in the celebrations, they opened Goethe's house to the public and allowed his manuscripts, his library, and his mineral collections to be exhibited. On the first day of the festival a life-size statue of Goethe, sculpted by Theodor Hütter, was unveiled in the square opposite the house. Not only Weimar but the nearby communities of Tiefurt, Jena, and Erfurt were involved in the festival. Schorn reports that on the morning of August 29 the road to Tiefurt was jammed with people travelling to the royal park in order to attend a performance of Goethe's *Jahrmarkt von Plundersweilern* given on the meadow in front of the tea-house. In the evening Liszt conducted a concert in the Court Theatre which culminated in a performance of Beethoven's "Choral" Symphony; the audience was especially moved by the last movement, whose text, provided by Weimar's other literary giant, Schiller, calls upon all men to be brothers. Afterwards a torchlight procession formed outside the theatre and moved to the Marktplatz. Illuminated by a thousand torches, the assembled crowd joined in a simple ceremony of thanks which marked the end of the festival.

III

Whatever the shortcomings of the ceremonials so hastily mounted for Goethe, their primary goal had been achieved: they had drawn national attention to Weimar. Since nothing succeeds like success, the Goethe Committee now became the Herder Committee, and Adolf Schöll, who was again elected chairman, announced that a Herder Festival would be held in Weimar during the three-day period August 24 to 26, 1850, and that a statue would be unveiled to coincide with the philosopher's one-hundred-and-sixth birthday. No one remarked that this anniversary was unusual. It was as if Weimar had awoken from a long slumber and was intent on recalling its illustrious dead, whenever they were born.[22]

The festival began on the evening of August 24 with a concert in the theatre, directed by Liszt. The programme contained two works that he had composed especially for the occasion: some settings of Herder's *Prometheus Unbound* for mixed chorus and orchestra and, as an overture to them, the earliest known version of his symphonic poem *Prometheus*. Both pieces were orchestrated by Raff. The following day, August 25, was Herder's birthday. At 10:30 a.m. a festival procession assembled in the market-place and, with flags and banners unfurled, made its dignified way along the old cobbled streets towards the newly named Herderplatz.[23] A cluster of town officials were already in place,

---

22. As the decade unfolded celebrations were held not only for Herder and Goethe but for Wieland and Schiller as well. The Weimar cemetery was a constant reminder to the living of the great number of dead who still awaited their monuments.
23. It was previously called Töpferplatz.

seated beneath the veiled statue of Herder, which now stood before the Stadt-kirche, the Church of Saints Peter and Paul, in which Herder had preached for twenty-seven years. Nearby sat the chorus and orchestra, with Liszt at the centre, baton ready. A fanfare, especially composed by Liszt, opened the cere-mony, and there followed a number of declamations and odes in praise of Herder's life and work. Schöll struck a patriotic note: "This noble memorial teaches us that we Germans still have luminaries who, despite the bitter bound-aries that separate us, can bring us together through our oneness of feeling." This was a popular sentiment. Germany was still a conglomerate of small principalities, but the concept of *ein deutsches Volk* which transcended all frontiers was already a vital political force. As the covers of the statue parted, Liszt conducted one of his *Prometheus* choruses. The venerable Dr. Karl Horn then came forward—he was nearly eighty years old and had been a pupil of Herder—and pronounced a benediction. Schöll observed that the scroll held in the statue's right hand bore the words "Light, life, love" (these words are also inscribed on Herder's tomb), and he took them as the theme of his oration. Unfortunately, his frail voice failed to carry, and the royal family, who had been placed on a raised platform at the other side of the square, later complained that not only had they been unable to catch a word of this tribute but they had not heard any of the others, either. At 2:00 p.m. everybody went over to the Town Hall, where a banquet was laid in readiness, during which many toasts were offered—to Herder, to Weimar, to the grand duke. The climax came when Dr. Gottfried Stichling—a Weimar privy councillor and Herder's grand-son—spoke on behalf of the family. The assembly was deeply moved when he reminded them of how small and insignificant they were when they squabbled among themselves, and how mighty they should and *could* become if they would only allow themselves to be penetrated by the spirit of Herder. The oration ended with the rousing sentence: "Give us that which we thirst for: a German Fatherland!"[24] In the evening everybody went

---

24. SNW, vol. I, p. 291. When we pause to consider Liszt's close identification with such overtly "German" causes as the Goethe and Herder memorials, we begin to understand the origin of Peter Raabe's notion that Liszt was a German composer. In those days the question "Was ist Deutsch?" was on everybody's lips. A common language, a common cultural heritage, and a common history were all that then bound the German conglomerates together; so the answer to the question "Wer ist ein Deutscher?" was simply: "Anyone whose mother-tongue is German and who declares himself for German causes." That effectively included millions of German-speaking peoples who lived beyond the borders of the hoped-for confederation of German states—inside Austria, Hungary, Poland, Russia, and the Balkans. As this seductive idea took hold, the desire to "liberate" such peoples and include them in a greater Fatherland became a very powerful one. Everybody knew that Liszt was born in the German-speaking part of western Hungary, that German was therefore his mother-tongue, and that he had chosen to live in Weimar, the cultural capital of Germany. Moreover, as he began to take charge of the great German music festivals at Karlsruhe and Aachen and then became the founder of the so-called New German School, his identification with the then-modern idea of "Germany" seemed complete. We now know that such a diagnosis was false, although at the time

back to the Stadtkirche for a performance of Handel's *Messiah,* conducted by Liszt.

On August 26, the last day of the festival, a grand outing was arranged for the children of Weimar and its environs. More than 1,800 youngsters between the ages of five and thirteen went on a ramble through the Ettersburg woods to Herder's favourite spot—still known as "Herder's repose"—where picnics and games were organized. They were joined by several of Herder's great-grandchildren, and everyone was dressed in white and wore garlands of oak-leaves.

This beautiful day ended in high drama. As the children wended their way across the fields back to town, the local penitentiary caught fire. Just as the procession turned into the Theaterplatz, the children saw flame and smoke billowing across the square, and hundreds of theatre-goers pouring out of the theatre, which stood scarcely a hundred paces from the prison. The prisoners had formed themselves into a human chain, along which buckets of water were passed in a vain attempt to douse the fire. Then the old prison-house collapsed in a roaring inferno, and a wall of heat swept up the street. The children ran screaming in all directions, adding to the general confusion.[25] Inside the deserted theatre stood Franz Liszt, gazing at the empty stalls in disbelief. He had been about to begin the dress-rehearsal of *Lohengrin* when the fire-alarm had sounded.

IV

Ever since Wagner had fled from Weimar, just over a year earlier, the idea of mounting the world première of *Lohengrin* had never been far from Liszt's mind. At first he had hoped that London or Paris might stage this operatic masterpiece; but this aspiration came to nought because Wagner had meanwhile taken up voluntary exile in Zürich, many miles away from these cities. As the Herder Festival drew near, Liszt knew that Weimar would never have a better opportunity. He reasoned that the place would be filled with visitors from all parts of Germany, that the city would still be wearing its festive air, and that the impact of this work, given before a national audience, would make Wagner's name resound across the country. Accordingly Liszt decided that the first performance of *Lohengrin* would take place on August 28, Goethe's birthday, immediately following the Herder celebrations.

---

it seemed attractive enough, and it was still exerting a spell after World War One. Liszt's musical goals were disinterested, a fact that the Germans failed to recognize. To express it bluntly: he was a Hungarian, giving Germany a helping hand. (See Volume One of the present work, pp. 48–49, for a detailed account of Liszt's national origins.)

25. SZM, p. 35.

He faced almost impossible odds. Quite apart from the political consequences of putting into the royal theatre the music of a left-wing revolutionary, the warrant for whose arrest was judicially binding on the Weimar Court, there were artistic problems of the first magnitude to solve. There was also Liszt's work-load in connection with the Herder Festival, which would have been a heavy enough burden for three men to carry. But the evangelical fervour that Liszt brought to his task so inspired his modest forces that a potential defeat was turned into a victory.

That the phrase "potential defeat" is not too bleak to describe the prospect Liszt faced is borne out when we look at the singers with whom he worked. Not one of them had yet emerged from local obscurity. Rosa Agthe, the twenty-three-year-old wife of Feodor von Milde, sang the role of Elsa; von Milde himself sang Telramund. Josephine Fastlinger, who was barely eighteen years old and not yet properly known even in Weimar, appeared as Ortrud; August Höfer and Pätsch, older but equally anonymous, took the parts of the King and the King's Herald, respectively. The first Lohengrin was Karl Beck, who had earlier been a pastry-cook in Weimar and would later return to his profession by becoming a master-baker to the Imperial Court in Vienna.[26] The part of Duke Gottfried was played by Frau Hettstedt, an actress attached to the theatre. On the orchestral side things were not much better. The players were augmented, of course, and the string section especially was strengthened. Liszt wrote to Wagner, "The number of violins will be increased to sixteen or eighteen players."[27] As Raabe points out, Weimar normally could not boast more than eleven violins, so Liszt's expansion of the section to eighteen players represented a considerable achievement. Liszt also reported to Wagner that in order to make this possible, the management had made available a grant of 2,000 thalers—something that had never before happened in Weimar within living memory. Another expense Liszt approved was the purchase of a bass-clarinet, which the Weimar orchestra did not at that time possess.

By the beginning of August 1850, things had started to come together, and rehearsals were proceeding on a daily basis. Liszt's letter to Feodor von Milde written on August 2 indicates the general mood of optimism he brought to his task.

> For five days we have been fully occupied with *Lohengrin,* and while this will tax our forces enormously I am convinced that we will bring it off with honour. For little by little, our people will be inspired by this masterpiece, will be penetrated by its essence, will

---

26. Liszt met him again in Prague in 1856, at which time Beck owned a coffee-shop (LLB, vol. 1, p. 218).
27. BWL, vol. 1, p. 60; KWL, vol. 1, p. 55.

live its life. This is a *conditio sine qua non* for a performance which we can call our own. In order to achieve this we have already had daily rehearsals this week lasting for four hours, and next week we will have two rehearsals every day—mornings and afternoons— because it is necessary to divide the orchestra into strings and brass and to rehearse each group separately.[28]

Altogether Liszt directed forty-six rehearsals of *Lohengrin*—a number without precedent for an opera, and an indication of his determination to succeed.[29] The performance, on August 28, attracted much attention, and Weimar, which was already full of visitors for the Herder Festival, now had to cope with a fresh wave of pilgrims curious to hear this opera. Among the well-known musicians, artists, and critics who converged on the theatre were Jules Janin and Gérard de Nerval[30] from Paris, Joseph Fétis from Brussels, Henry Chorley from London; and Meyerbeer, Robert Franz, Franz von Dingelstedt, Christian Lobe, Bettina von Arnim, Adolf Stahr, Franz Kroll, Joachim, von Bülow, Raff, Theodor Uhlig, Franz Abt, and Karl Ritter, the last of whom lived in the closest contact with Wagner in Zürich and knew every note of the score. By contrast, the ordinary citizens of Weimar were scarcely interested in Wagner and his latest work, and had it not been for the generosity of Maria Pawlowna, who bought up a great many of the unsold tickets at the last moment and distributed them free of charge, the première might have been a flop. Even the dress-rehearsal, which should have taken place on August 26 and for which tickets had already been issued, suffered a major setback. The orchestra was assembled, the audience had taken their places, and Liszt was in the wings waiting for his cue when at about 7:30 p.m., Eduard Genast came from behind the curtain and announced that the fire which had broken out in the nearby prison was now burning furiously.[31] The theatre was evacuated at once, and such was the confusion that the dress-rehearsal had to be put off until the following evening, only twenty-four hours before the performance itself, leaving little room for the incorporation of last-minute changes.

As we now know, *Lohengrin* received a deeply felt interpretation and a

---

28. LLB, vol. 8, p. 70.
29. SGWT, p. 197.
30. Gérard de Nerval later published an exhaustive account of the *Lohengrin* première and of the Herder festivities in Weimar in a series of articles for *La Presse,* which appeared under the title "Souvenir de Thuringe" between September 9 and October 1, 1850 (see NO, vol. 1, pp. 788–803). We now know that Nerval was taken ill en route and that he did not even arrive in Weimar until August 30, two days after the *Lohengrin* performance. Much of the material for his long articles was provided by Liszt and Princess Carolyne. The proof of this may be found in the letter that Nerval wrote to Liszt from Cologne on August 28, in which he declared: "It is impossible for me to arrive in time. Still, prepare, I beg you, the information that I shall require." (NLFL, p. 16)
31. SNW, vol. 1, p. 292; SZM, p. 35.

critical ovation that represented a turning-point in the appreciation of Wagner in Germany. Wagner himself was in Lucerne on a climbing expedition as the performance unfolded, and he sat in the Hotel zum Schwanen and listened to every bar of Liszt's performance in his imagination.[32]

Not all the celebrities who came to Weimar were convinced by Liszt's evangelical fervour, however. Bettina von Arnim disliked *Lohengrin* intensely, and during a small dinner-party that Liszt gave for a group of artists she criticized him for his support of Wagner. Liszt stood up and delivered his reply: "Hier stehe ich, ich kann nicht anders! Mit Wagners Opern stehe und falle ich!"[33] He was as good as his word. By May 11, 1851, Liszt had given the opera five times in Weimar, thus ensuring its place in the repertory.[34] But his work in behalf of Wagner really culminated in the Wagner Festival of 1853, when between February 16 and March 15 he conducted three Wagner operas in a row—*Lohengrin, Tannhäuser,* and *Der fliegende Holländer*—the last-named no fewer than three times. Adelheid von Schorn advanced the notion that without Liszt's support Wagner would have gone to the grave unrecognized, since every other theatre in Germany lacked the political and artistic courage to mount his works.[35] The idea is impossible to prove, because Wagner was a genius, and sooner or later genius shines through, whatever the obstacles. Genius was never harmed by help, however, and Wagner was supremely fortunate in finding Liszt at a time when everyone else had forsaken him, and the alternative might have been a decade of neglect.

v

During the hectic weeks leading up to the Goethe celebrations Liszt became engrossed with the idea of establishing a Goethe Foundation for the distribution of prizes in the arts. Although the idea eventually came to nothing, despite the immense amount of effort that Liszt put into it, it is worth a brief examination

---

32. NLRW, vol. 2, p. 231. Wagner was disconcerted to discover a few days later that the performance had lasted from six o'clock until nearly eleven, for by his own reckoning it should not have lasted beyond a quarter to ten; he thought that Liszt must have dragged the tempi. Wagner had reckoned without the long prologue composed by Dingelstedt and delivered by the actor Jaffé before the opera began (Goethe's birthday traditionally evoked windy orations of this sort in Weimar), and the extended intermissions favoured by the court circle.

33. "Here I stand, I am unable to do anything else! I stand and fall with Wagner's operas!" (HFLW, pp. 37–38) This emotive language was modelled on that of Martin Luther, who, after he had nailed his theses to the door of the Wittenberg church, proclaimed: "Here I stand. I cannot do else. God help me. Amen."

34. Barely a season passed without at least one performance of *Lohengrin* in Weimar. With the passing years, and with the inevitable changes of personnel and theatre directors, Liszt remained ever watchful over the work whose interpretation he had "created."

35. SNW, vol. 2, p. 38.

here because it reveals again his grasp of administrative detail and his flair for organizing artistic matters on a national level. The impetus for the proposal can be traced back to July 5, 1849, about seven weeks before the Goethe anniversary, when an appeal was launched in Berlin by a group of distinguished individuals and published in the leading German newspapers. It urged the nation to cooperate in the creation of an institution whose purpose would be to stimulate and fortify the artistic life of Germany. Weimar, it continued, would be the seat of such an institution by virtue of its illustrious past. Liszt felt that because he lived in Weimar, and because he had special ties to the grand ducal house-hold, he had less excuse than most for not attending to this noble task. The outcome was his seminal brochure *De la fondation-Goethe à Weimar,* which was published in 1851[36] and attracted widespread interest. Liszt did a great deal of research into Thuringian history for this publication. The first seventy pages or so are devoted to a history of Weimar, and they parade the illustrious personalities who lived and worked there. The burden of Liszt's message was simple: Goethe was the greatest of them all; what better gesture than to form a prize in his name? From the start Liszt made it clear that assistance would not be extended to artists in economic need, nor would it be given to gifted children. The sole aim of the foundation was to acknowledge new masterpieces, in Goethe's name, and help to raise artistic standards everywhere.

The constitution of the Goethe Foundation gave Liszt some trouble, and it went through several drafts. His published proposals can be summarized thus:

1. The foundation would be governed by a board consisting of twenty-five members.
2. The grand duke of Weimar would preside over all meetings of the foundation.
3. Two members of the board would be appointed by the grand duke. They must reside in Weimar.
4. Two members of the board would be appointed from among the common citizenry of Weimar.
5. Fifteen of the remaining members of the board would come from other cities in Germany.
6. The members of the board would be appointed for life.

Liszt thought that the day-to-day running of the foundation should be super-vised by a full-time secretary and a treasurer, both of whom must live in Weimar and must be re-appointed every four years, on merit.

But how to select the prize-winning works? And what to do with them after

---

36. By F. A. Brockhaus of Leipzig. The holograph is preserved in WA, Kasten 3, no. 1, and bears the date 1850. See also RGS, vol. 5, pp. 1–109.

each competition was ended? Liszt addressed these questions too, in a resounding sequence of imperatives.

1. The board would be augmented by three artists of national repute, who would share their "special expertise" with its members and so make the task of selection easier.
2. All the arts would be eligible for the contest, on a rotating basis—e.g., one year painting, the next year music, the year after that sculpture, and so on.
3. The winning works would be put on permanent display in Weimar. In the case of music and drama such works would be taken into the permanent repertory of the Weimar theatre.
4. The first prize would be worth a maximum of 3,000 thalers.[37]
5. The prizes would be awarded each year on August 28, Goethe's birthday.

In order to give pomp and circumstance to the prize-giving ceremonies, Liszt urged that "all the musical forces of Thuringia should be mustered" and that the medieval singing-contests be revived. He proposed that the Great Hall of the Wartburg be opened for festivities: "[It] will echo again with poetry and song after so many centuries."[38]

The crucial part of the proposal dealt with its financial cost. Liszt estimated that a capital sum of 100,000 thalers would be required. He suggested that a national subscription fund should be started under the auspices of the grand duke. Once this large sum had been raised, "the names of the subscribers would be engraved in gold letters on a marble tablet in the headquarters of the Goethe Foundation." It would take ten years, Liszt calculated, to raise the required capital. Meanwhile, the grand duke would have to make good the expected deficits.

Liszt's brochure was distributed across Germany and beyond. One of the first recipients was Richard Wagner, to whom Liszt evidently sent the article in proof-sheets.[39] Wagner's response to Liszt's "splendid idea" is worth recalling today because it struck at the artistic heart of the matter. Basically, he told Liszt, the proposals were unworkable. His detailed critique boiled down to two objections.

---

37. The value of this prize is best gauged by the fact that the annual salary of the leader of the Weimar orchestra at this time was only 500 thalers. See p. 100.
38. RGS, vol. 5, pp. 101, 103.
39. See Wagner's acknowledgement, sent on April 18, 1851: "I wanted to write to you about your Goethe Foundation, but must wait for a calmer hour to meet your splendid idea with dignity." (BWL, vol. 1, p. 127; KWL, vol. 1, p. 117)

1. The artist who does not feel within himself an inner urge to create art but waits for pecuniary rewards before doing so will never give birth to genuine works of art.

2. If the main activity of the Goethe Foundation was merely to distribute prize-money for sculpture, painting, poetry, and music, turn and turn about, then it would not further the cause of art at all but simply "make it easier for artists to find a market for their wares."[40]

In short, Wagner argued, the Goethe Foundation would not change artistic reality. The genuine artist did not need the foundation; the others could go to the devil. Wagner's letter is a timeless reminder to all those who plan festivals and competitions, or strike search-committees to uncover "prize-winning" works, that art in its truest sense is a solution without a problem—least of all a bureaucratic one. It says much for Liszt's objectivity towards his own ideas that he suggested to Wagner that his letter be published in order to stimulate further debate.[41] It eventually appeared in the columns of the *Neue Zeitschrift* on March 5, 1852. We do not know Liszt's true opinion of Wagner's reservations. He may well have consoled himself with the thought that, whatever its flaws, the Goethe Foundation would at least succeed in drawing national attention to Weimar, and that surely did not count for nothing.

VI

Whatever the pros and cons of the Goethe Foundation, the ideals which Liszt enshrined within its manifesto prompted a number of luminaries to renew their contact with "the Athens of the North." Alexander von Humboldt, Otto Roquette, Friedrich Hebbel, George Eliot, Bettina von Arnim, and Hans Christian Andersen were all participants in the literary life of Weimar, and one or two of them deserve more than passing mention.

Hans Christian Andersen arrived in Weimar on May 19, 1852, and his diaries and letters contain several entries of interest to the Liszt scholar. Andersen had already recorded his first impressions of Liszt when he heard the pianist play in Hamburg in 1840.[42] Twelve years had meanwhile elapsed, and Andersen,

---

40. WGSD, vol. 5, pp. 5–19.
41. To which Wagner replied on May 22 (his birthday) that his only thought had been to address Liszt alone, and not uselessly to berate the great public with ideas which it would be incapable of understanding, still less of doing anything about. But he added archly: "If you think it useful and appropriate to make a wider use of my communication, you are at liberty to do so" (BWL, vol. 1, p. 131; KWL, vol. 1, p. 122).
42. See Volume One, pp. 289–90.

whose unforgettable *Fairy Tales* had been published in 1849, was now world-famous. "Today I visited Liszt," he wrote:

> [He] resides outside the town and lives with Princess Wittgenstein; their relationship is a great scandal in such a small town as Weimar, but she is well spoken of, however. They would like to be married, but since they are both Roman Catholics and she has left her husband, the pope will not allow this.[43]

A few days later Liszt and Carolyne returned the visit. Andersen observed that they seemed like spirits of fire, burning and flaming wildly. "They can warm you for a moment, but one cannot get near them without being scorched." Andersen was invited to return to the Altenburg and read them his well-known story "The Nightingale," one of Liszt's favourite tales. This charming allegory compares the song of a real nightingale with that of an exquisitely made mechanical one, which is covered in precious stones. The mechanical bird looks beautiful and keeps perfect time ("After all," says the imperial music master, "it belongs to my school of music"), but because it has a cylinder in its chest it can sing only one song, with which people soon become bored. Carolyne interpreted this allegory to mean that Liszt was the real nightingale while Thalberg was the artificial one. Andersen's reaction to this provocative idea is not known.

Andersen was summoned to the grand ducal palace, where he dined with Carl Friedrich and Maria Pawlowna. He had already met the royal pair on several previous occasions, and they held him in affectionate remembrance; but the grand duke was suffering from ill-health and had only a year or so to live. "Many sad days have passed since we last saw one another," observed Maria Pawlowna.[44] Carl Alexander was also present, and as Andersen was about to take his leave, the heir apparent embraced the visitor with the words "Think of this hour as being yesterday. We shall remain friends for the rest of our lives," and they both wept.[45] Carl Alexander would doubtless have liked to attract the Danish story-teller to the Weimar Court. But Andersen stayed for only three weeks in the city, during which time he saw Liszt conduct *Tannhäuser* and *Lohengrin*—productions he claimed that Liszt had mounted especially for him. En route to his home in Copenhagen, he wrote a letter of thanks to Liszt:

---

43. BHCA, p. 228.
44. BHCA, p. 228. Andersen had passed through Weimar several times in 1846 and had read a number of his stories aloud to the theatre company in the home of Eduard Genast (SNW, vol. 1, pp. 252–53).
45. The affection that Carl Alexander felt for Andersen was genuine enough. After their second meeting, in 1846, the young duke had written to Liszt: "Andersen was here for a long time in the autumn. I love him, both as a man and as a writer" (RCAL, p. 18).

Leipzig, June 14, 1852

Dear, admired Dr. Liszt!

My deepest thanks for all the kindness and friendliness you extended to me during the beautiful days in Weimar. Here are my Lieder. Choose the ones that please you best. I would be pleased with whatever musical baptism [*Tönen-Taufe*] they may receive.

Yours most faithfully,
H. C. ANDERSEN[46]

Bettina von Arnim often travelled down from Berlin to Weimar. A fervent admirer of Goethe, she wholeheartedly supported Carl Alexander's plans to foster the city's classical traditions. It was Arnim who suggested to the grand duke the publication of the *Weimarisches Jahrbuch,* a chronicle of the cultural life of Weimar,[47] and she worked unceasingly in behalf of the Goethe Foundation. Liszt had first met Arnim in Berlin in 1842 and had already received some vigorous lectures from her about her literary idol.[48] In the autumn of 1852 she descended on Weimar with her daughters, Armgard and Gisela, and during her two months' sojourn she became a regular visitor to the Altenburg. Arnim was preoccupied with her sketches for a sculpture of Goethe, which depicted him with Psyche, and she commissioned Karl Steinhäuser to execute the work. Steinhäuser was imprudent enough to suggest in front of Carl Alexander that Bettina would be unable to raise the necessary funds for such an important monument, so the heir apparent bought the sculpture himself for 6,000 thalers. In December 1852 it was exhibited in the Tempelherrenhaus, which had been

---

46. LBZL, vol. 3, p. 20. Liszt never set these poems (loosely referred to by Andersen in his letter as "Lieder"), presumably because they were in Danish, a language of which he lacked knowledge.

47. The *Weimarisches Jahrbuch* was eventually edited by Hoffmann von Fallersleben and Oskar Schade, between the years 1854 and 1857.

48. See Volume One, pp. 373–74. What was the basis of Bettina Brentano's special connection to Goethe? Hardly anything at all, as modern scholarship has proved, although at the time of which we are writing she was regarded as an oracle. Her mother, Maximiliane Laroche, had enjoyed a brief but passionate affair with the great poet during his *Werther* period. Bettina herself was twenty-two years old when she first encountered Goethe and, like her mother before her, fell in love with him and pursued him. Goethe kept his distance, however; indeed, when Bettina insulted his wife, Christiane, he forbade her to enter his house. After her marriage to Achim von Arnim, Bettina continued to throw temptation across Goethe's path, with no result. In an attempt to assuage her bruised feelings she busied herself with Goethe's sonnets (inspired by Minna Herzlieb), paraphrased them as prose, and passed them off as letters to herself. Wisely, she waited until after Goethe's death, in 1832, then published the "letters" under the title *Correspondence of Goethe with a Child.* In the eyes of the world this book was proof positive that Bettina herself was the real inspiration for the sonnets, and she came to be regarded as an authority on all things having to do with Goethe. Especially misleading were the facts she fed Goethe's biographers about his childhood (gleaned, so she claimed, from the poet's mother). It was left to a later generation to expose Bettina's fabrications. At the time of her encounters with Liszt and his circle, Bettina's harangues were usually taken at face value and had to be endured in silence.

designed by Goethe himself; but when Bettina saw the sculpture, she was highly critical of Steinhäuser, whom she accused of being unfaithful to her original conception.

In all her encounters with Liszt, this garrulous old lady lost no opportunity to provoke him to argument. She was a fierce opponent of the *Zukunftsmusik*, which appeared to her to destroy the classical traditions of Beethoven, and her one-sided support of Goethe made her an unpleasant adversary. A decisive clash with Liszt was inevitable. The following year Bettina returned to Weimar, bristling for a fight, but this time Liszt and Carolyne were ready for her. Cornelius reported the violent exchange that broke out over the respective merits of Goethe and Schiller, the latter of whom Bettina described as "Jesuitical," whereupon Liszt burst out: "The worst Jesuit is dearer to me than the whole of your Goethe."[49] Bettina left the Altenburg smouldering with animosity, and Cornelius described her unforgettably as "the black-cloaked witch." By November 1854 Bettina was back, and this time Liszt called on her in an attempt to patch up their quarrel. Bettina's first words to him were "Are you still the old Jesuit?" and the argument flared up again. Her parting shot was "I will not see you anymore today, nor tomorrow, nor ever again."[50] When Liszt went to Berlin in 1855, he made no attempt to settle their differences, for he was perturbed by the fact that after his last such effort Bettina had gone the rounds of Weimar planting intrigues against him.

V I I

This review of Liszt's 'prentice years at Weimar has so far dwelt only on the highlights. Important though those highlights were, they give the merest indication to the outside world of what his daily routine at the opera house must really have been like. A glance through the old theatre billings for the period 1849 to 1851 tells a forgotten story. During his first three seasons Liszt presented to the Weimar public a variety of concerts and operas so wide in range and so rich in content that it remained unmatched by any other opera house in Germany. Operas by such well-established masters as Rossini, Donizetti, and

---

49. By quoting this sentence out of context, Peter Raabe placed meaningless words into Liszt's mouth (RLS, vol. 2, p. 83). Commentators without number, content to translate Raabe verbatim instead of looking up his sources, have meanwhile compounded the problem by importing this empty phrase into their prose and having it do duty for Liszt's considered view of Goethe. Liszt's admiration for Goethe was certainly qualified, but when he said that he preferred "the worst Jesuit" to "the whole of . . . Goethe," he was actually telling Bettina von Arnim that he preferred Schiller, whom she had just rashly dismissed as "Jesuitical." The context of their quarrel, reported in detail by Cornelius, makes this conclusion absolutely clear (CLW, vol. 1, p. 147).

50. HFLW, p. 41.

Meyerbeer vied for a place in the repertory alongside those of such nonentities as Johann Hoven,[51] Siegfried Saloman, and the music-loving Duke Ernst of Sachsen-Coburg and Gotha. The last-named was the brother of Prince Albert, Queen Victoria's royal consort. His palace at Gotha contained a 250-seat theatre in which he regularly mounted plays and operas for his own delectation. Liszt had first encountered Duke Ernst in 1842 when he passed through Gotha on a concert tour.[52] He became interested in the duke's musical gifts, and he now undertook to promote them. At the beginning of February 1849 he journeyed to Gotha in order to conduct a performance of the duke's new opera, *Tony, oder die Vergeltung.* Liszt travelled in the company of Ziegesar and Genast, who were curious to hear the royal opera for themselves. So pleased were they with this melodious work, and especially with its tightly knit ensembles, that they were able to overlook its slight plot and decided to produce it at Weimar. When Duke Ernst heard of the decision, he lent them the magnificent set of bells which he had had specially cast in Gotha for use in the finale, and which brought the opera to a ringing conclusion. The Weimar production took place on April 14, 1849. Duke Ernst himself was unable to attend since he was suddenly called away to his military command in Holstein (a reminder of the unsettled political situation in Germany), so he made Genast send him a detailed report instead.[53] The burning question, then as now, is how Liszt could possibly have sustained such a varied repertory with so few resources. We must face the facts that the productions themselves sometimes lacked polish and that the players frequently had to "double up" for missing instruments. In fact, Liszt's constant fear was that the old proverb "The ship will sink for want of a ha'p'eth of tar" must come true. At Weimar, quantity usually existed in inverse ratio to quality. And yet, although singers and players were often hard-pressed to keep up with Liszt, he nonetheless succeeded in establishing a happy atmosphere in the theatre simply because he put the joy of music-making first. A very good illustration of the sense of camaraderie which prevailed at Weimar, at any rate in the early days, occurred when Liszt decided to mount Rossini's *Le Comte Ory* in April 1850. Because of its bubbling melodies he christened it "the champagne opera." When Ziegesar overheard Liszt's jocular reference during one of the final rehearsals, he ordered several dozen bottles of champagne and

---

51. A pen-name for Baron Vesque von Püttlingen (1803–83).

52. In this connection the correspondence between Queen Victoria and her German relatives is interesting. There are frequent mentions of Liszt's visits to the Gotha court in the 1840s (RA [b]).

53. GAW, pp. 314–15. Shortly afterwards, Liszt made a piano transcription of the *Jagdchor und Steyrer* from the opera. In his letter of thanks Duke Ernst wrote: "The greatest triumph for a dilettante is when his humble work wins the high advocacy of the master. . . . While the world bows before the celebrated artist, some glances may fall upon the unknown protégé as well, who thus escapes the danger of falling into total oblivion." (LBZL, vol. 1, p. 122)

had them distributed among the audience at the beginning of the second act. Liszt thoroughly approved of the idea, because, as he punned, it would "rouse the spirits of the chorus."[54] The spectacle of popping champagne corks flying across the auditorium, and people slowly drifting into the arms of Bacchus, had never been witnessed in the Weimar opera house before. It was impossible to float an entire opera season on a sea of champagne, however, as Liszt would soon discover.

---

54. LLB, vol. 1, p. 86.

The Years of Struggle II,
1849–1853

*The theatre is a necessary evil; the concert is a
superfluous one.*

DINGELSTEDT TO LISZT[1]

I

At the beginning of 1852 Liszt took stock of his position. He had now been
in Weimar for four years. The Court Opera had come a long way under his
leadership, but it was apparent to everybody that it was hamstrung by lack of
resources, and Liszt saw no hope of an early improvement. In January 1852
he gave vent to his frustration in a remarkably frank letter to Maria Pawlowna. He told her that she must decide whether Weimar was to have a
Court Theatre worthy of the name, free to mount the best operas without
thought of cost, or whether it was to have a commercial theatre whose sole
purpose was to turn a profit. At present, Liszt remarked bitterly, everybody
had a box-office mentality, and the only thing that meant anything was
ticket-sales. Moreover, plays still took precedence over concerts. He then
went on to catalogue the defects in his recent production of *Lohengrin*: the
choir was deficient by at least a dozen singers; more walk-on parts were
required to avoid the ridiculous effect of a processional march played in the
second act with no procession on stage; the stage-sets were so dilapidated that
they must date from a previous epoch; the costumes were made of materials
that one was accustomed to find only in hotel furnishings; Elsa's seat in the
third act rested on four bare planks; finally, the boat and the swan were so
crude that they failed to harmonize with the splendid illusions created by the
music. And so on and so forth. Liszt concluded: "The moment has come

---

1. LLB, vol. 2, p. 251.

when I can advance no further, nor even continue to occupy the ground that we have gained. *Savoir-faire* can . . . double the worth of material forces; but there are limits, and if it is a question of tripling them . . . it is futile to rely only on *savoir-faire*."[2] Nothing much happened as a result of this plain speaking. Indeed, Maria Pawlowna appears not to have understood what Liszt was complaining about. Was it not because of his *savoir-faire* that Liszt was in Weimar at all? Her Kapellmeister was a genius, and there were no limits to the illusions he could create on the Weimar stage simply through the magic of his personality. For the first time, thoughts of resignation must have crossed Liszt's mind. We see in this letter the model for the much more powerful one he would address to Carl Alexander the following year, which would precipitate a crisis in his relationship with the theatre and the court.

In the early summer of 1852 Liszt received an invitation to conduct at the Ballenstedt-am-Harz music festival. It was the first important out-of-town engagement to come his way since he had arrived in Weimar, four years earlier, and it marked a new stage in a conducting career that would eventually take him across Europe. Liszt directed two concerts at Ballenstedt, on June 22 and 23:[3]

June 22	WAGNER	Overture to *Tannhäuser*
		Duet from *Der fliegende Holländer*
		(soloists: Feodor and Rosa von Milde)
	LISZT	Song "Die Macht der Musik,"
		for soprano and orchestra
		(soloist: Rosa von Milde)
	ALVARS	*Oberon* Fantasy for harp
		(soloist: Rosalie Spohr)
	BEETHOVEN	Choral Fantasy
		(soloist: Hans von Bülow)
	GLUCK	*Orpheus and Euridice* (Act Two)
		(soloist: Franziska Schreck)
	BEETHOVEN	Symphony No. 9 in D minor ("Choral")
June 23	RAFF	Overture to *King Alfred*
	WAGNER	*Das Liebesmahl der Apostel*
		for male chorus and orchestra
	BERLIOZ	*Harold in Italy*
	MENDELSSOHN	*Die erste Walpurgisnacht*

---

2. LBLCA, pp. 33–39.

3. The letters Liszt wrote from Ballenstedt, and the following week from Braunschweig, provide some interesting details about his conducting activities. LLB, vol. 4, pp. 123–29.

The uncompromising nature of these programmes made it necessary for Liszt to take along two of his favourite principals from the Weimar opera, the Mildes. A group of his young disciples was also in attendance—Raff, Pruckner, and Bülow (who was a soloist)—whose acquaintance we shall make in a later chapter.[4] A week later, Liszt moved on to Braunschweig as a distinguished visitor to the "rival" music festival there, an experience which allowed him to compare their efforts with his. He wrote to Carolyne: "The festival here reminded me of M. Talleyrand's quip: 'When I examine myself, I think I'm not worth much. But when I compare myself [to others] I have a better opinion of myself.' " In particular, Liszt was disappointed with a performance of Beethoven's Ninth Symphony, which he claimed was "definitely below ours in Ballenstedt."[5] A few weeks after he had arrived back in Weimar Liszt was delighted to receive a large volume of rare prints of Ballenstedt, bound in dark brown leather and tooled in gold letters: "In deepest gratitude, from the inhabitants of Ballenstedt."[6]

II

Behind this busy round of public activity lurked the troubles of Liszt's private life. Few people in Weimar either knew or cared that almost from the moment of her arrival in the city Carolyne was chronically ill and that her condition gave Liszt cause for concern. She appeared to suffer from a form of blood-poisoning, a diagnosis that will probably always remain circumstantial. The symptoms were plain enough, however. Every few months she would suffer a fresh outbreak of painful boils and abscesses on her body which were treated with hot poultices and lanced. In addition she endured swelling and stiffening of the joints, which she referred to as rheumatism. She was finally driven to seek a lengthy series of water-cures at Bad Eilsen. In the autumn of 1849 both Carolyne and Liszt lived in the Bruns Hotel for several weeks.[7] By October 1850 her condition was so poor that she again left Weimar, in the company of her daughter, and lived in Bad Eilsen for more than nine months. Her physician was a Dr. Moeller, and Carolyne has provided some graphic details of her treatments. On April 9, 1851, she wrote Liszt: "My tumor, which has re-appeared in such a strong way, threatens to become a new abscess."[8] Four

---

4. See p. 167f.

5. LLB, vol. 4, pp. 127 and 129.

6. This volume, inscribed "Ballenstedt, September 2, 1852," is presently exhibited in the Hofgärtnerei, Weimar.

7. WA, Kasten 219, no. 1, contains a series of picture postcards from this hotel, written by Liszt and Carolyne.

8. WA, Kasten 33, no. 3.

days later she wrote him: "My abscess burst several hours ago. I'm suffering a little less from it. It was larger and more painful than the others." Carolyne was dissatisfied with Moeller's treatment of her and called him "negligent." During a physical examination she had "an incredible attack of pain," whereupon Moeller attempted to hypnotize her, but without much success. Both Marie and Carolyne laughed at Moeller's bungled effort, and Carolyne asked: "Why do these imbeciles—Moeller as well as those in my country—claim that I would be such an apt subject for hypnotism, when I am sceptical and make fun of them?"[9]

Carolyne finally left Bad Eilsen at the end of July 1851 and began an extended convalescence. She and Liszt took a leisurely tour along the Rhine, accompanied by Princess Marie and "Scotchy" Anderson. By September 1 the little party had reached Düsseldorf, where they all descended on Clara and Robert Schumann. The Schumanns were somewhat taken aback by this unannounced visit, since they were in the middle of a birthday celebration for their eldest daughter, Marie; and Liszt, Clara noted, proceeded to turn the household arrangements upside down. They had not met Carolyne before and were somewhat surprised to find in the princess of Liszt's dreams a rather plump and matronly figure. Some music-making followed—Schumann's D-minor Symphony on two pianos and his recently composed *Kinderball* for piano duet. Liszt then played two or three numbers from his own *Harmonies poétiques.* Clara later observed in her diary: "He played, as always, with a truly demonic bravura. He lorded it over the piano like a devil (I cannot express it differently) . . . but his compositions, they were too awful!"[10] And she added that while Liszt himself seemed to be affected by his music, she and Schumann were unable to say anything because they could not overcome their inner indignation. The Schumanns, in fact, had reached that most unsatisfactory of all stages in human affairs: they were not yet Liszt's enemies, but they no longer counted him among their friends. Such ambivalent feelings stifle candour, and so it was here. Even as Clara was scribbling her negative impressions of Liszt's music in her diary, he and Robert were discussing plans to perform the latter's overture *The Bride of Messina* in Weimar, a promise that Liszt fulfilled a few weeks later, on November 11.

There were good reasons why Carolyne's convalescence took so long, for she was weighed down with the burden of other problems. About November 1850 she received news of the death of her mother and was devastated by it. Even though Carolyne and Pauline had been separated for much of their lives, the bonds of filial attachment remained strong.[11] Then, not long after their

---

9. Ibid.
10. LCS, vol. 2, p. 263.
11. Within weeks of her arrival in Weimar, Carolyne had already won her mother over to the idea of a marriage with Liszt. In one of the rare letters of Pauline's to have survived, which she wrote

arrival in Bad Eilsen, the thirteen-year-old Princess Marie contracted typhus fever and lay seriously ill for weeks. Liszt travelled back and forth between Weimar and Eilsen and visited the two patients whenever his court duties allowed. It was therefore a time of stress for him as well.[12] On January 22, 1851, for example, he travelled overnight from Bad Eilsen and arrived at Weimar at ten o'clock in the morning. Since there was no one to meet him at the railway station, he walked to the Altenburg. After working all day in the Blue Room he composed a letter to the princess.

> 8 o'clock in the evening
>
> Here I am in this room, at this table, near these windows, where I have seen you many times—suffering so much, weeping so much, loving so much! Everything which surrounds me is known by and steeped in you, and speaks to me in an indescribably sad and eloquent language![13]

Nowhere is Carolyne's emotional dependence on Liszt shown more clearly than in the letter she wrote to him from Eilsen on April 3, 1851. He had just visited her, but within moments of his departure she had picked up her pen to write him a long letter. "It has been less than an hour since your presence illuminated this wretched room. My tears are flowing unchecked, but I need to tell you now that the agony to my soul caused by this separation has not been healed by a single moment's rest."[14] In fact, Carolyne wrote to Liszt every day; her letters are often twenty pages long, and whenever a day or two passed without her receiving some lines from him, she chastised him, even though she knew how busy he was.

---

from Odessa on May 24, 1850, she told Baron von Gutmansthal: "Thank God that matters are working out in a direction which is favourable to them. And soon, perhaps, a solution to my daughter's fate will occur for which we have been waiting for two years with unspeakable anguish." (GSL, p. 66) This sentiment of Pauline's was confirmed by Liszt. Ten years later, when his marriage seemed as distant as ever, he wrote to Carolyne: "I cannot think of the touching kindness your mother showed me during the last years of her life without deep affection" (LLB, vol. 5, p. 20).

12. By April 1851, Liszt's frequent absences from Weimar had started to cause concern. Chélard did much deputizing for Liszt during the six months of Carolyne's illness, an arrangement which revealed Chélard's incompetence to everyone and caused artistic standards at the theatre to plummet (see p. 99). The grand duke finally called for Chélard's resignation and forced him to accept a pension. At the end of April Liszt was "promoted" to the vacant position of Kapellmeister, a title somewhat less resonant than the one of Kapellmeister in Extraordinary he had hitherto enjoyed. Liszt joked to Princess Marie: "Your very humble servant becomes *Kapellmeister* (my! my!) and has the whole crowd under his command . . . with the exception of der Frau Kapellmeisterin [Carolyne] whom Carl Friedrich inadvertently neglected to mention." Liszt also told Marie that the new arrangement would be bound to cause an upheaval when it became generally known (HLSW, p. 45).

13. LLB, vol. 4, p. 42.

14. The princess is of course referring to her six months' separation from what had become her normal life with Liszt in Weimar (WA, Kasten 33, u. 3).

Overshadowing all her other anxieties was the unresolved question of an annulment of her marriage to Nicholas Wittgenstein and the division of property that this entailed. The Wittgenstein family never ceased to pursue Carolyne for her fortune. At the beginning of April 1851 she was contacted by their agents, Messrs Pavleynski and Théodor, who told her that one of her properties in Ukraine had been taken over by Nicholas, and supplied her with false accounts for some of the others. According to Théodor, her tenant farmers had gone bankrupt and had deserted the greenhouses on which they held leases, so that the net revenue for the previous year was nothing.[15] Carolyne also learned that she would inherit nothing from her mother's estate. Théodor seems to have been instructed by the Wittgensteins to find out whether the princess might be willing to bargain for her divorce, and suggested that five-sixths of her daughter's inheritance might be a suitable sum—an offer she found offensive. Théodor sent an emissary to Bad Eilsen, one Bobrowski, to negotiate with her personally. Carolyne was furious that Théodor had the gall to pay for Bobrowski's trip from money that really belonged to her. The only person to whom Carolyne could turn for solace was Liszt, who became the recipient of all her laments. But he was powerless to do much more than listen, and there were times when he must have been frustrated by his helplessness, particularly since he knew himself to be ultimately responsible for her plight.

By the summer of 1852 the annulment proceedings of Prince Nicholas and Carolyne had reached a critical stage. The go-between was the Russian ambassador to Weimar, Baron Apollonius von Maltitz, from whom we gain some unusual insights into the matter. Carolyne had turned her annulment into a crusade, and Maltitz (who by virtue of his official position was her nearest target) had been deluged with letters, briefs, and memoranda, all of which were designed to bring him to a fuller understanding of her woes. When it became clear that the good baron did not in the least resemble the shining god whose distinctive name he bore, if we are to judge from the absence of any illumination he brought to bear on Carolyne's case, she offered him money in an attempt to speed the process along, a ploy that he found objectionable.[16] Through the offices of the governor-general of Kiev it was finally arranged that Nicholas would journey to Weimar in person and bring with him a proposal for a property settlement. Nicholas arrived in Weimar on September 12, 1852, and made his way to the Altenburg the following day. The document was drafted in the presence of the court marshal, Baron von Vitzthum, and it was witnessed by Nicholas, Carolyne, Princess Marie, and Liszt. It was the first time that Nicholas and Carolyne had seen one another since she fled Russia, and the meeting must have been painful. Liszt, we know, had resisted this visit in a vain

---

15. WA, Kasten 33. Unpublished letter of April 1851.
16. BLTB, vol. 2, p. 138.

attempt to spare Carolyne's feelings, and he even threatened to use force to keep Nicholas away from the Altenburg.[17] He felt that Carolyne was being used, and later events were to bear him out.

The essential points embodied in the agreement were these:

1. In the event that Carolyne re-married,
   a. one-seventh of her fortune would pass to Nicholas;
   b. six-sevenths would pass to Princess Marie;
   c. Carolyne would receive 200,000 roubles in cash.[18]
2. Grand Duchess Maria Pawlowna would meanwhile take over the guardianship of Princess Marie and ensure that the morals of the young girl were protected.

This last proposal was a sensitive one, and it was meant to humiliate. Nicholas was determined to register his objection to the fact that his adolescent daughter was growing up under the roof of his wife's paramour. He described the Altenburg, and the atmosphere of sycophantism that surrounded Liszt there, as "a drug." That Carolyne signed the document at all must be regarded as a measure of her desperation to sever the chains that still bound her to the Wittgensteins. Accordingly, the fourteen-year-old Princess Marie, together with Miss Anderson, was removed from the Altenburg and given a room in the royal castle. Liszt joked with Marie about her misfortune in an attempt to revive her flagging spirits, and he nicknamed her spartan quarters "the Bastille." This unhappy arrangement lasted for two years, when it was brought to a sudden and dramatic end. In the summer of 1854 Weimar experienced a series of exceptionally heavy thunderstorms. The castle tower was struck by lightning in the middle of the night, and Princess Marie was discovered senseless on the floor of her room. She suffered intensely from this traumatic event and was brought back to the Altenburg to recover. She never returned to "the Bastille." By this time it was clear that Carolyne had been gulled, that her divorce was no nearer a settlement than it had ever been.

In 1854 the princess was summoned back to Russia in order to explain her non-compliance with the terms of the property settlement. She refused to return, whereupon the Russian minister of justice recommended that the full rigour of the law be applied against her,[19] and Tsar Nicholas sequestered all

---

17. BLTB, vol. 3, pp. 139–40.
18. The properties that Carolyne was expected to yield included Starosteine, Bielaski, Buchny, Iwanki (in the environs of Kiev); Woronince, Tencki, Cetwukowce (in the district of Litin); Wonlowce, Wolfwodowska, Polok (in the district of Berislawl); and Bielany, Szendrowska, Kislicku, and Lozowa (in the districts of Mohilow and Jampol).
19. Extract from the proceedings of the ministerial committee held in St. Petersburg on January 26, 1854 (HFL, p. 175).

her lands and estates. The following year, 1855, his successor, Tsar Alexander II, condemned her to exile. The estates were eventually put into trust for Princess Marie, who received 75,000 roubles a year from the profits. In exchange for this concession, Carolyne was bound to the terms of a marriage contract for Marie which effectively made the young girl the legitimate owner of the Iwanowsky fortune on the day she married or when she reached the age of twenty-one, whichever came first. From this moment Carolyne's means were drastically diminished, and she frequently had to turn to her daughter to settle her debts. Her exile was especially hard for her to bear. This mark of imperial disfavour was at once transmitted to the court at Weimar, with whom Carolyne was already *persona non grata,* and she became a pariah, untouchable by anyone with court connections. It was now increasingly difficult for her to function in Weimar at all, cut off as she was from people in the community with whom she might otherwise have enjoyed a daily discourse.[20]

It is a pity that so few of the documents relating to Prince Nicholas's visit to Weimar during that late summer of 1852 are available to us. The Wittgenstein family archives, for example, would surely allow us to re-construct their side of the case more fully than ever before. Control over Carolyne's fortune was still their primary aim, of course; but there is some circumstantial evidence which leads us to suppose that Nicholas, if not his family, wanted a swift and amicable end to an impasse that caused him almost as much frustration as it caused Carolyne. We know that as early as 1852 he wanted to re-marry and no longer wished Carolyne "to go on bearing my name."[21] Despite the paucity of original sources, however, there are some scattered pieces of information which, when drawn together, help us to reveal the background of tension and mistrust which prevailed at the Altenburg when Nicholas crossed the threshold on September 13. One such source is the diary of Theodor von Bernhardi, politician and military historian, who was in Weimar for much of 1851 and 1852 and was an eye-witness to these extraordinary comings and goings. It appears that Nicholas and Carolyne met by mutual arrangement in the visitors' box at the Court Theatre a few hours before he left Weimar.[22] Their conversation went so smoothly that Carolyne suggested that Baron von Vitzthum and Baron von Maltitz should proceed with detailed negotiations. We do not know what passed between Liszt and Nicholas at this time, but Nicholas later expressed the desire not to meet Liszt again "in order to avoid an encounter that

---

20. It goes without saying that Carolyne's exile was as hard for Liszt to bear as it was for Carolyne, since he knew that whatever sacrifice she bore was for his sake. He later described it as "a decree of civil death! . . . odious and barbaric" (DA, censored fragment from a letter dated November 8, 1860).

21. BLTB, vol. 2, p. 142. The current object of Nicholas's attentions was a widow from Berlin, Frau Kosens. He appears to have tired of her, as of his other amours. When he finally re-married, in January 1856, it was to Marie Michaïloff (see Family Tree, pp. xix–xx).

22. BLTB, vol. 2, pp. 141–42.

might be unfortunate for him rather than for me."[23] Poor Maltitz, who was at his wits' end during the entire period, had the unenviable task of keeping the warring parties apart. We assume that he did this with circumspection and tact; when, a few days later, Nicholas travelled back to Berlin, he told Bernhardi that everything had been worked out to his satisfaction. He had no idea that more than three years would elapse before he himself could procure a Protestant divorce that would enable him to re-marry.

During the period of Princess Marie's exile in "the Bastille" (which was, as we have seen, part of the cynical deal imposed on Carolyne by her husband), a small but significant event took place: Carolyne had her daughter confirmed in the Catholic church in Weimar. So confident was Carolyne, in the summer of 1853, that she and Liszt would soon be free to marry that she wrote to him about the service in the following way:

Sunday, July 3, 1853

We have just returned from the church where "Magne" has been confirmed and henceforth bears your name as a seal of paternity. For six and a half years you have been a good father to her—a father full of affection and wisdom, prudence and solicitude.[24]

". . . Bears your name as a seal of paternity." We may be sure that Liszt and Carolyne had discussed his sponsorship of Marie many times and that he looked forward to becoming the young girl's stepfather. As for Nicholas Wittgenstein, whose name it would never have occurred to Carolyne to use in such a connection, we may be equally sure that he quickly learned of the ceremony from his contacts in the Russian legation. To him, it was one more proof that Liszt and Carolyne were working hand in glove to undermine his paternal position. But Nicholas could take satisfaction from his agreement: if Liszt and Carolyne ever married, the former would never enjoy the benefit of her millions. By the summer of 1854, when it had become clear to all the principals in the little drama that the wedding would have to be postponed, Carolyne allowed herself to utter some telltale lines to Wagner. Liszt, it seems, had felt the strain of the Wittgensteins' enmity as much as anyone. "Another man

---

23. BLTB, vol. 3, pp. 139–40. Were Liszt and Carolyne under threat of physical force during these years? It seems so, to judge from a letter that Carolyne wrote some time later to Baron von Maltitz. In it she complains not only that she was menaced by the police at Nicholas's behest but that these same police, "furnished with imperial orders," attempted a brutal kidnapping of Princess Marie (HFL, p. 180). At the heart of the matter lay the fact that the property settlement between Carolyne and Nicholas carried the authority of the tsar; this was the Russian autocrat's clumsy way of ensuring that the terms of the agreement were enforced. We shall probably never learn the full extent of this human tragedy, but it is clear from these occasional clues that there must have been some appalling scenes at the Altenburg in which Liszt was inextricably involved.

24. WA, Kasten 34, no. 2.

would, during these past six years, have sunk and been drowned eighteen times in the storms which have our poor little barque for a plaything. He alone keeps us calm on the surface."[25]

III

Throughout these traumatic years, Anna Liszt followed the career of her famous son with pride and pleasure, albeit from afar: she continued to live in Paris, where she cared for Liszt's three children. She must have been curious about the character of a woman who signed her letters "your daughter Carolyne" long before they had met, and at a time when the prospects of Carolyne's marriage to Liszt or to anyone else looked hopeless. On January 8, 1850, Anna arrived in Weimar and stayed at the Altenburg for several weeks, accompanied by Liszt's old secretary Gaëtano Belloni. One purpose of the visit was to transport to the Altenburg some of the precious trophies—medals, pictures, scrolls-of-honour—that Liszt had acquired on his concert-tours and had stored in his mother's house. The train journey was a long one—Paris to Frankfurt, then on to Eisenach, with a final connection to Weimar. It was Anna's first reunion with her son for more than five years. Both Carolyne and Liszt were at the railway-station to meet her.[26] What should have been a joyous occasion was shattered not long after her arrival by news from Paris of a crisis in the lives of Liszt's two daughters (a story so full of high intrigue and passion that its telling has been reserved for a later chapter). This led to a tearful confrontation with Liszt and Anna's abrupt return to Paris.[27] She came to Weimar for a second time in June 1852.[28] Again, this was an unlucky visit. Not long after her arrival she fell and broke her foot. Liszt had just set out for the Ballenstedt festival, and he received from Carolyne a series of bulletins concerning his mother's plight. It seems that Anna had insisted on visiting her niece, Madame Louise Girard, who was staying in Erfurt. On June 19 Carolyne accompanied Anna to the Weimar railway station and installed her on the train, with Heinrich, Liszt's servant, as her travelling companion.[29] Having arrived in Erfurt, Anna hurried across to the Hôtel du Kaiser to meet her relative, who failed to turn up. She decided to return to the railway station to wait for

25. BWL, vol. 2, p. 38.
26. VFL, p. 97.
27. The story is told in detail on p. 430.
28. If we discount the trip she made in March 1850, a coda to her first visit, whose only purpose was to tell Liszt what she had found on her return to Paris the month before.
29. Shortly before Anna set out for Erfurt, she and Carolyne exchanged sharp words, which may have had to do with Liszt's plans for the future education of his children. "It is really difficult to bring her round to your point of view," Carolyne told Liszt. "She lives too much with people with narrow ideas." (WA, Kasten 34, unpublished letter of June 19, 1852)

Madame Girard there. According to Heinrich, it was while she was descending the stairs of the hotel that Anna missed the bottom step, fell, and twisted her foot. Within ten minutes an Erfurt doctor had been summoned, who diagnosed a broken bone. Heinrich at once informed Carolyne, who paused just long enough to send a short account of the matter to Liszt and engage the services of two Weimar doctors (Dr. Goullon and Dr. Puch, the chief military surgeon) before setting out for Erfurt and the Hôtel du Kaiser. Anna had already been put to bed; she was in discomfort, and a high fever had set in. "I cannot tell you, my poor angel, how sad it is for me to see your poor mother in this state," wrote Carolyne. For twenty-four hours Carolyne hardly left Anna's room. Both doctors arrived from Weimar to examine the patient. After Dr. Puch had set the broken bone, Carolyne had the Erfurt doctor sleep next door in order to attend to Anna during the night.[30] The medical prognosis was not good. Because of Anna's age (she was sixty-four) and her weight, the doctors correctly foresaw that she would have difficulty in recovering the full use of her leg. She was still convalescing at the Altenburg nearly three months later and could only walk with the help of crutches.[31] As it happened, this was the first of a series of fractures, each more serious than the last, which was to turn Anna into a cripple for the final ten years of her life.

I V

In the midst of all these distractions Liszt still found time to compose. Work restored his tranquillity. The aptly named *Consolations*,[32] a set of six miniatures for the piano, were brought to completion during the period 1849–50, and their reflective, self-communing character reveals a new and much more thoughtful Liszt: this is music tinged with a secret sorrow. It first stirred to life under Liszt's fingers in the Altenburg, when the tragedy of his liaison with Carolyne had begun to penetrate his soul. The *Consolation* in D-flat major has rightly earned a place for itself in the permanent repertory.

---

30. WA, Kasten 34, where this account of Anna's accident appears in Carolyne's unpublished letters to Liszt, dated June 19 and 20, 1852.
31. LLB, vol. 1, p. 113.
32. So called after the *Consolations* of Sainte-Beuve, a set of poems published in 1830.

It has often been observed that this *Consolation* bears more than a passing resemblance to certain works of Chopin—the D-flat-major Nocturne, op. 27, no. 2, in particular. We shall come to understand the phenomenon only if we put it into a larger biographical context. During the anxious days at Bad Eilsen (1850–51) at the time of Princess Carolyne's difficult convalesence, Liszt had become much involved in the life and work of the Polish master. This was the period during which he and Carolyne were working on the text of his Chopin book,[33] an almost unprecedented tribute from one major composer to another, and it is hardly surprising that Liszt soon became engrossed in musical forms that Chopin had made his own—the polonaise, the mazurka, the berceuse, and the ballade. While Chopin was alive, Liszt never touched these genres;[34] but the death of his erstwhile friend in October 1849 seemed to trigger within him a special creative urge: Liszt, that is to say, identifies so closely with Chopin's musical style that he temporarily incorporates some of its leading characteristics into his own works. The result is a body of piano music in which Chopin's personality continues to speak to us, as it were, from beyond the grave:

> Two Polonaises (1851)
> Berceuse (1854)
> Mazurka brillante (1850)
> Two Ballades (1845–48, 1853)

Unconscious imitation is the sincerest form of flattery. The two polonaises, in C minor and E major, contain many a Chopinesque turn of phrase, typical of which is the following:

---

33. It was published in 1852; see p. 379.
34. Although some of the material for the Ballade No. 1 in D-flat major may be traced back to 1845, it was not at that time known by the name "ballade," and the finished piece was not published until 1849.

The melody could easily have flowed from Chopin's pen, a conclusion made all the more authentic when we consider the filigree decorations with which Liszt surrounds it on its subsequent appearance. For the rest, it is strange to think of the two polonaises having their place of origin in the sulphuric waters of a health spa.[35]

Almost from the moment that Liszt settled in Weimar he had begun a profound review of the main pieces of his *Glanzzeit*. Trunkfuls of manuscripts, amassed during his years of travel, had followed him into the Erbprinz Hotel and had later been transferred to his library in the Altenburg. This legacy included the first versions of the *Années de pèlerinage,* the Hungarian Rhapsodies, and the Transcendental and Paganini Studies. The period 1849–53 saw the re-working of most of these old war-horses. Liszt himself was entirely responsible for the virtual disappearance of the early versions of the studies, which even by the mid-1850s had become collectors' items. He bought up all the engraved plates from Tobias Haslinger some time before 1852 and put the firm under contract not to sell any more copies.[36] (Characteristically, Liszt made no money out of this arrangement. He gave the rights in the new versions to Breitkopf and Härtel in exchange for a piano they had lent him and which he now wished to pass on to a friend.[37]) Why should Liszt suppress the earlier versions? The fact is, he wanted to place some distance between himself and their excessive virtuosity; by 1851 there were aspects of his *Glanzzeit* that he was anxious to disown. Moreover, he now wanted to use these studies in his teaching (both von Bülow and Tausig prepared performances of the Transcendentals for Liszt

---

35. LLB, vol. 1, p. 105. Those readers who are interested in pursuing the "Chopin connection" further may wish to compare the Berceuse of Chopin with that of Liszt. The one serves as the unconscious model for the other: both are in D-flat major; both consist of an increasingly elaborate series of variations on a simple four-bar theme; and both pieces unroll across a tonic pedal-point.

36. The strength of his feeling against the earlier versions of these studies came out three years later in a letter to Alfred Dörffel, who had just completed a Catalogue of Liszt's works (based on information provided by the composer himself) and had sent it to him for approval. "I recognize only the Härtel edition of the twelve studies as the *sole legitimate one,"* Liszt wrote, "and I therefore wish that the Catalogue make no mention of the earlier ones. . . . It is the same with the Paganini Etudes and the Rhapsodies hongroises; after settling matters with Haslinger I completely gained the *legal* right to *disavow* the earlier editions of these works, and to protest against the possible piracy of them." (LLB, vol. 1, p. 189) This fear of piracy did not stem from paranoia. The juvenile version of the Transcendentals (1824) had been brought out in a pirated edition by Hofmeister in 1836, with an engraving on the cover of a tiny infant in a cradle bearing the inscription "Travail de la jeunesse." Liszt was then twenty-five!

37. LLB, vol. 1, pp. 114–15.

during the 1850s), and he desired to make them more practical. The piano, too, had undergone some radical transformations, and the heavier actions coming out of Berlin and Vienna had made the 1839 versions even more problematic. Typical of the textures Liszt revised is the following passage from *Wilde Jagd,* the eighth study:

Such measures are virtually unplayable on a modern piano; at any rate, the texture will not speak. In Liszt's revision, the basic melodic shape comes across more vividly, and the stress and strain of "misplaced" accents is removed.

The same process of refinement and clarification was applied to the six Paganini Studies, and for a somewhat similar reason: greater playability. In one of the two early versions (1838) of the fourth study, a glistening arpeggio piece in E major, Paganini's original texture

was transcribed by Liszt in a monstrously overladen way, in which four streams of arpeggios flow up and down the keyboard simultaneously.

The texture was difficult enough on the old Erard piano of the 1830s; on the emerging concert grand of the 1850s it was impossible. By 1851 it was sufficient for Liszt to restore Paganini's simple texture intact and split it between the two hands in this imaginative fashion:

Liszt was by now thirteen years older and a good deal wiser. Whether he was also technically more accomplished remains an open question, but it seems unlikely. Why, then, do we conclude that the eighteen pieces which constitute the revised Transcendental and Paganini Studies are more significant to the history of piano playing than the 1838–39 models on which they are based? Because their greater simplicity stands in inverse proportion to their increased brilliance, and that had never happened before. They are a perfect illustration of the law of economy to which all physical motion strives: "Minimum effort, maximum result." Only the greatest master could conserve more energy than he expends while at the same time achieving a more powerful result. Paradoxically, virtuosity is used here to transcend virtuosity itself.

Word quickly spread throughout the piano-playing fraternity that a definitive edition of Liszt's studies was in preparation. Expectation was tinged with curiosity, for it had long been assumed that Liszt had turned his back on the piano since settling in Weimar. Among the inquiries he received was the following from his old friend and colleague Marie Pleyel, to whose virtuosity he had once paid fulsome tribute in the dedication of his *Norma* Fantasy:[38]

> Brussels, 23 July [1852]
>
> I await with impatience your studies and your fugues [Bach transcriptions]. My classes do not re-assemble until October, but I always practice a lot during the holidays, and the study of your works is the glory and joy of my pupils!
>
> *A revoir,* I hope![39]

V

The crowning achievement of these years was the composition of the Sonata in B minor, arguably one of the greatest keyboard works to come out of the nineteenth century. If Liszt had written nothing else, he would have to be

38. See Volume One, p. 389, n. 21.
39. WA, Kasten 25, no. 9.

ranked as a master on the strength of this work alone. According to Liszt's own inscription on the manuscript, the sonata was finished on February 2, 1853. From the standpoint of the biographer that is a remarkable piece of evidence. Since the work is complex, Liszt must have begun it three or four months earlier, during one of the most turbulent and nerve-wracking periods of his life. Its gestation, that is to say, accompanied such events as the Ballenstedt festival, the first "Berlioz week," and, not least, the unexpected arrival in Weimar of Nicholas Wittgenstein in pursuit of his divorce from Carolyne, which created consternation and uproar at the Altenburg. We can only marvel that the sonata shows no signs of these distractions but moves with somnambulistic certainty towards its goal. It is one more proof that music, for Liszt, was a refuge from the storms and stress of everyday life.

No other work of Liszt has attracted anything like the same amount of scholarly attention as the B-minor sonata. This is not necessarily a blessing for the biographer, who must pick his way across a difficult stretch of territory with care. Not the least fascinating thing about the piece is the number of divergent theories it has provoked from those of its admirers who feel constrained to search for hidden meanings. To confine ourselves to the most prominent:

1. The sonata is a musical portrait of the Faust legend, with "Faust," "Gretchen," and "Mephistopheles" themes symbolizing the main characters.[40]
2. The sonata is autobiographical; its musical contrasts spring from the conflicts within Liszt's own personality.[41]
3. The sonata is about the divine and the diabolical; it is based on the Bible and on Milton's *Paradise Lost.* [42]
4. The sonata is an allegory set in the Garden of Eden; it deals with the Fall of Man and contains "God," "Lucifer," "Serpent," "Adam," and "Eve" themes.[43]
5. The sonata has no programmatic allusions; it is a piece of "expressive form" with no meaning beyond itself—a meaning that probably runs all the deeper because of that fact.[44]

There are other theories, but it would be pointless to enumerate them here. Besides, the case is not yet closed: Liszt studies will surely continue to bring forth new views on this most familiar of structures and make us wonder afresh at the diversity of interpretations it is called upon to sustain. Needless to say,

40. OIL (JALS, vol. 10, pp. 30–38).
41. RLS, vol. 2, pp. 59–62.
42. SLS (JALS, vol. 15, pp. 39–95).
43. MRR, pp. 238–95.
44. WLS, pp. 127–68.

Liszt himself did not sanction any of them. Apart from some scattered references in his correspondence and conversations with friends, he was generally silent about this work and offered no words of any kind on the question of its programme—or lack of it. He was content simply to describe his masterpiece by the generic term "sonata"—an inscrutable title that seems to close the door on further discussion.

One thing about which there is no contradiction is the work's unusual structure. The sonata unfolds about half an hour's unbroken music. Not only are its four contrasting movements rolled into one, but they are themselves composed against a background of a full-scale sonata scheme—exposition, development, and recapitulation—in a masterly fashion. In short, Liszt has composed "a sonata across a sonata,"[45] and that made the work unique. Not until Arnold Schoenberg accomplished something similar in his First Chamber Symphony (1906), more than fifty years later, did the form of Liszt's work have any meaningful succession. This simple chart will make the connection between the two dynamically connected structures clear.

I : Allegro	II : Andante	III : Fugato	IV : Allegro	Prestissimo
Intro.	Exposition	Development	Recapitulation	Coda
m. 32	m. 331	m. 459	m. 533	m. 682

If the term "perfect" still means "thoroughly accomplished," then the B-minor Sonata is a perfect work. Such a claim must be put into perspective, of course. Musical architecture, unlike real architecture, has to be created afresh by each performer. And this has always been Liszt's undoing. We have elsewhere remarked that his music is not pianist-proof; it is easy for an unsympathetic player to obscure the majesty of his larger forms.[46] What the B-minor Sonata requires is a player with the "distant grasp"—someone who even as he deals with the myriad details that clamour for immediate attention is also thinking of events that still lie beyond the horizon. Liszt, that is to say, demands not only a master of tactics but a master of strategy too. When these difficult

---

45. We put the matter like that in order to draw a distinction. Other composers had linked the contrasting movements of their sonatas and symphonies, of course; one thinks immediately of Beethoven's *Appassionata* Sonata and his Fifth Symphony. And Liszt, too, ran the three movements of his Piano Concerto in E-flat major into a seamless join. The B-minor Sonata is different, however. Not only are its movements linked, but they assume an organic function within the greater sonata structure as a whole. The material, that is to say, is constantly making contributions to two sonata forms simultaneously—a local one and a total one. For a fuller discussion of its double structure, see NSB, vol. 3, pp. 373–75, and WLS, pp. 127–68. Incidentally, the "double structure" view of the work is not a modern discovery but has been in circulation for at least seventy years. It was taught by Dohnányi to his pupils in Berlin and at the Liszt Academy in Budapest before World War I.

46. See Volume One, p. 308.

conditions are met, which is rarely, the B-minor Sonata does indeed emerge as a perfect work.

Most of the structure is generated from a tiny group of thematic "tags" first heard in the introduction.

Nowhere is Liszt's "transformation of themes" technique[47] seen to better effect. The first subject proper, which is derived from a skilful combination of themes (b) and (c), may serve as a paradigm of the way in which Liszt handles his material generally: in the foreground all is diversity; in the background all is unity.

A long and highly developmental transition section follows, and theme (a) ushers in the *grandioso* second subject.[48]

---

47. See pp. 309–10.

48. Theme (a) is invariably reserved for marking off the important junctures of the structure: it occurs before the second subject and also before the development, and it separates the slow movement from the fugato. Its most notable appearances, of course, are at the very beginning and the very

It has often been remarked that the outline of this important theme is that of the plainchant "Crux fidelis," which Liszt used in a number of other works—notably *Die Hunnenschlacht* (see page 312), *St. Elisabeth,* the "Gran" Mass, and *Via Crucis.* The "cross motif," as it is sometimes called, occupies a leading place in the theories of those who see in the sonata a depiction of the cosmic struggle between good and evil, between God and the Devil. It is not for biographers to venture where analysts fear to tread. We should note, however, that when the sonata was composed, none of the other works whose verbal associations allow us to recognize this motif as having to do with the Cross had yet been written. The conclusion, in short, is drawn from evidence as yet uncreated.

Two subsequent themes in the long and complex second subject group are likewise derived from (b) and (c). The gentle lyricism of the first of them appears to place it a long way from anything previously heard in the sonata; but on closer inspection we recognize the hammer-blows of (c) in augmentation.

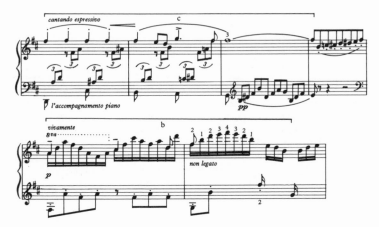

The slow movement, an Andante sostenuto of haunting beauty, is the centrepiece of the sonata. This fully fledged "compound ternary" form passes

---

end of the sonata: it has been likened to the descent of a curtain which serves to separate the acts of a drama.

in review a number of themes heard earlier in the sonata in a tour de force of thematic economy worthy of a Beethoven. Liszt sets the movement in his "beatific" key of F-sharp major[49] and begins with the following new idea.

From the player's point of view, it is the Andante which contains within itself the crucial signals of the success or failure of his performance. If he has lingered too long over the various recitatives and episodes which Liszt has earlier strewn across his path, the error will emerge in the Andante, and the player will never be able to correct it. The work will already begin to sound too long, with another fifteen minutes or so still to unfold. This is but one of many similar spots where Liszt is held responsible for the sins of his interpreters.

After the opening theme of the Andante sostenuto has been recapitulated in apotheosis, the slow movement gives way to a diabolical three-part fugato whose subject is made up of themes (b) and (c):

49. It is an indication of the neglect from which Liszt studies have always suffered that until recent times no serious attempt had ever been made to examine his musical language in terms of its overall stylistic unity—that is, from the standpoint of its thematic and tonal "fingerprints." Bach, Beethoven, Schubert, Brahms, Debussy, Bartók, and Mahler have long since attracted studies of this kind, some of which involved scholarship of a high order. In the case of Liszt, however, the prevailing assumption used to be that he was an unlikely candidate for such treatment, largely because "unity of style" is not the first thing most musicians think of in connection with his music. Yet this has now become a rich field of study. Liszt's choice of keys, for instance, is frequently determined by a higher expressive purpose and is rarely the result of random selection. It cannot be an accident that so much of his "divine" or "beatific" music unfolds in the key of F-sharp major (*Bénédiction de Dieu, St. Francis of Assisi Preaching to the Birds,* the "Paradiso" section of the *Dante* Sonata, and *Les Jeux d'eaux à la Villa d'Este*—this last piece with its quotation from the Gospel According to St. John). Likewise, the key of A-flat major is often associated with love (two of the "Liebesträume," "In Liebeslust," and the "Gretchen" movement from the *Faust* Symphony). Hell is portrayed in D minor (*Totentanz* and the "Purgatorio" sections of both the *Dante* Sonata and the *Dante* Symphony unfold in this key). And so on. Thematic similarities also abound in Liszt's music, and they are worth the same degree of attention as that which Schweitzer lavished on the self-same topic in the musical language of Bach.

Very few works of the nineteenth century attempted to telescope fugues into sonatas, and with the exception of Beethoven's, none does it more successfully. The major difficulty is that the number of places within a sonata structure where one can actually introduce a fugue without harming both forms is strictly limited; one stands a better chance of mixing oil and water. With unerring insight, Liszt has his fugato function as a development section, in which capacity it also serves as a lead-back to the recapitulation. At one point the fugato subject is turned upside down and presented in counterpoint against itself:

Liszt continues to ring the changes on his basic material throughout the sonata. One of the many fascinations for the Liszt aficionado is to observe the myriad ways in which even the recitatives and the linking passages owe their thematic integrity to the *Ursätze* first delineated in the introduction. Even the dreaded octave passages in the coda turn out to be thematically determined—that is, they are variations of theme (b):

From a technical point of view the coda is treacherous: many a fine performance of the sonata has come to grief at this point because of sheer physical fatigue. And this raises an instructive problem connected not only with the B-minor Sonata but with Liszt's keyboard music in general. Time was when only the giants of the keyboard were prepared to tackle the work. Today there are adolescents of sixteen and seventeen who can despatch the piece with ease. Busoni was intrigued by this phenomenon and was convinced that it had "atavistic" roots[50]—that is, it must be a skill acquired by the race across several generations of effort and transmitted genetically. Our model is to be found in today's Olympic champions, who can easily outstrip those of yesteryear (and will in turn be outstripped) in the high dive, the pole vault, and the hundred-meter sprint—and for somewhat similar reasons: physical mastery is always the goal. Piano playing, however, does not work like that. Inside the "keyboard athlete" is a musician, and unless he has been developed along with the technical apparatus which alone makes his expression possible, all else fails. How often do we hear a performance of the sonata in which the notes are all there but the piece is missing! By the same token, technical blemishes will not necessarily harm the piece if the piece is there. The chief problems posed by the sonata, then, are musical ones, and they have remained unchanged since Liszt first penned this work. These include, above all, the necessity to hold its vast structure together. Unless it unrolls as if from a single musical impulse, it cannot succeed; for only when the player himself can hear the Sonata in B minor as a shining whole will his performance become worthy of the work.

Liszt originally intended the sonata to end with a loud flourish; the manuscript[51] reveals that the inspired quiet ending with which the work now concludes came to him as an afterthought. Posterity must be grateful for the unpredictable ways of genius. After a cataclysmic climax, followed by a long silence, Liszt brings back the soft Andante sostenuto, which seems to cast a benediction over all that has gone before, and the sonata expires with the same descending scale with which it began.

The sonata was published in the spring of 1854 with a dedication to Robert Schumann. We know that Liszt meant this as a reciprocal gesture to Schumann in exchange for the dedication of the latter's Fantasy in C major (1839), a work that Liszt described as "sublime and glorious."[52] And what did Schumann think of the sonata? He never knew of its existence. A copy of the newly published work arrived at the Schumanns' home in Düsseldorf on May 25, 1854, by which time Schumann was already incarcerated in the asylum at Endenich. Clara

50. BEM, pp. 82–83.
51. The only known holograph of the B-minor Sonata is on deposit at New York's Pierpont Morgan Library, in the Robert Owen Lehmann Collection. It was published in a facsimile edition by Henle Verlag, in 1973.
52. LLB, vol. 1, p. 256.

Schumann could easily have included the work in her repertory, but she chose not to do so. Her diary entry for that day tells us why: she described the sonata as "merely a blind noise—no healthy ideas anymore, everything confused, one cannot find a single, clear harmonic progression—and yet I must thank him for it [i.e., the dedication to Robert]. It really is too awful."[53] Clara's negative reaction was not untypical. When the work received its première performance, in Berlin, on January 22, 1857,[54] nearly four years after its composition, it provoked a minor scandal among the conservative critics, from which it recovered with difficulty. Rarely did such great music get off to a less promising start.

V I

Especially topical were Liszt's piano transcriptions of the six Preludes and Fugues for organ by Bach. More than a century before Liszt first arrived in Weimar, Bach had lived and worked there. The German master had actually been appointed court organist by a former duke of Weimar, Wilhelm Ernst (a direct ancestor of Carl Alexander), and he had composed many of his greatest organ works in the Stadtkirche, where the organ itself remained intact. Six of Bach's children had been born in Weimar, and the house in which he had lived still stood next to the Erbprinz Hotel. As Liszt walked through the cobbled streets of the city, he became acutely aware of Bach's spiritual presence, and it was natural that he should want to memorialize this musical genius in a form that he understood better than anyone else—the transcription. The six Preludes and Fugues that Liszt chose for this purpose are in the following keys:

A minor	C major (9/8)
C major (4/4)	E minor ("The Wedge")
C minor	B minor[55]

---

53. LCS, vol. 2, p. 317. Brahms was staying with Clara as her house-guest when the B-minor Sonata arrived, and her diary reveals that it was Brahms who played through the work for her—Brahms, who had fallen asleep when he heard Liszt himself play the work from manuscript the previous year! (See p. 229.) Incidentally, there is no evidence that Liszt ever played the work for Schumann, despite the unsubstantiated story that he did, first circulated by Göllerich (GL, p. 45). There is no record that the two composers met between February 1853, when Liszt completed the sonata, and March 1854, when Schumann was admitted to the Endenich asylum.
54. The soloist was Bülow. (See pp. 413–15.)
55. BWV nos. 543–48. Liszt had been preoccupied with the idea of transcribing these organ preludes and fugues ever since he had first set foot in Weimar, in November 1841. He had actually played the early versions of the ones in A minor and E minor in his Berlin concerts during the winter of 1841–42, but the project as a whole lay dormant until he took up his Weimar post on a full-time basis. By 1850 the task was finished. In a letter to his young copyist Joachim Raff, written from Eilsen in October 1850, Liszt urged him, "Apply yourself to Bach's six pedal fugues and please write very clearly and broadly" (RLR, p. 501).

The difference between a transcription and a paraphrase is worth remarking. The paraphrase, as its name implies, is a free variation on the original. Its purpose is metamorphosis. It can concentrate exclusively on one theme, decking it out with ever more complex ornamentation; or it can embrace the entire act of an opera, mixing and mingling the material en route, giving us (so to speak) an aerial view of the composition. Liszt's paraphrases of Verdi, Meyerbeer, and Mozart provide good examples of this process. The transcription, on the other hand, is quite different. It is strict, literal, objective. It seeks to unfold the original work as accurately as possible, down to the smallest detail. In his transcriptions of the Bach fugues, Liszt meets this criterion with conspicuous success; they are widely regarded as models of their kind. In the great Fugue in A minor, whose subject begins

there are times when Bach's original would seem impossible to transfer to the piano in all its glorious detail. Yet Liszt never fails to find a way of keeping Bach's texture intact, however complex it becomes.

Much more than the operatic paraphrases or even the Transcendental Studies, these Bach transcriptions reveal Liszt's total command of the keyboard. This judgement may sound perverse, but it can be substantiated. Transcription is more difficult than paraphrase. In a paraphrase, the arranger is free to vary the original, to weave his own fantasy around it, to go where he wills. This is not so in a transcription. The transcription must be obedient, a true copy of the original; it binds the transcriber to it, making him its slave. And there is the paradox. Only the greatest master is capable of becoming the perfect slave.

Liszt's interest in Bach was sustained by two young organists of merit: Alexander Wilhelm Gottschalg (1827–1908) and Alexander Winterberger (1834–1914). It was the twenty-one-year-old Winterberger who gave the first performance of the "Ad nos" Fantasy for the inauguration of the new four-

---

Liszt's transcription of Bach's Fantasy and Fugue in G minor for organ (BWV no. 542), which logically belongs to the same group, appeared about twenty years later.

manual organ at Merseburg Cathedral in 1855. Gottschalg, who first served as the organist at Tiefurt, later became court organist at Weimar.

Both men were pupils of Johann Gottlob Töpfer (1791–1870), the municipal organist in Weimar. Although Töpfer's credentials as a teacher were impeccable, his real claim to fame was as an organ builder, a field over which he exerted great influence. Liszt got to know Töpfer in Weimar, and he became interested in his forward-looking ideas on registration, a topic on which most German organists held conservative views. Liszt liked to visit various churches in the company of Gottschalg, in order to contrast and compare the various organs scattered across Thuringia. He used to coach his young friend in the interpretation of Bach, and it becomes clear from Gottschalg's account of their sessions together that Liszt enjoyed using the full resources of the instrument and that he had no time for the cautious, colourless renderings of Bach's works which then prevailed in Germany. On one such occasion Gottschalg played Bach's Toccata and Fugue in D minor with the full organ, on one manual, a usual practice at that time. Liszt listened carefully, and then remarked: "In terms of technique, it is totally satisfying . . . but where is the spirit? Without this, Bach is a Book of Seven Seals! Surely Bach did not play his works in such a manner; he, whose registrations were so admired by his contemporaries! When you are playing on a three-manual instrument, why should the other two manuals be ignored?"[56] Gottschalg tells us that he later played the work with the new registrations for Töpfer, who was greatly impressed. "You should always play it like that," Töpfer remarked.

Liszt was not a virtuoso organist (according to Gottschalg he lacked real fluency on the pedals), but that did not prevent him from recommending a number of practical reforms. He was puzzled by the lack of a rational system of pedal notation, and he suggested to Gottschalg that notes for the right foot be indicated with upward-pointing stems, notes for the left foot with downward-pointing ones. Both Gottschalg and his colleague at the Stadtkirche, Bernhard Sulze, adopted the system and found it very practical. Fifty years later, however, Gottschalg reported sadly that it had still not been taken up in Germany.[57]

The first, and greatest, of Liszt's original organ compositions was his Fantasy and Fugue on "Ad nos, ad salutarem undam" from Meyerbeer's opera *Le Prophète*. This gigantic work, which Liszt wrote in the winter of 1850, unrolls about thirty minutes' unbroken music and demands a virtuoso technique. It is based on the chorale sung by the three Anabaptists in the first act of the opera

---

56. NZfM, November 15, 1899, p. 505. This useful memoir of Liszt and the organ was published by Gottschalg under the title "Dr. Franz Liszt als Orgelkomponist und als Orgelspieler." It appeared in NZfM in two instalments, on November 15 and 22.
57. GLW, p. 28.

(whose plot concerns the Anabaptist uprising in Holland in the sixteenth century), who appeal to the people to be re-baptized in the healing water. "Ad nos" falls into three linked sections. We hear first an extended opening fantasy, in which fragments of the Anabaptists' theme are worked out and rise to some grand climaxes. The chorale theme itself then emerges, transposed into Liszt's "divine" key of F-sharp major.[58]

It was widely reported at the time that this was a traditional Jewish melody which Meyerbeer had heard sung as a boy in the private synagogue of his uncle, a wealthy Parisian merchant. Meyerbeer never publicly contradicted the story. But privately he told Liszt that he himself had composed it. Liszt shows great ingenuity in exploring the full potential of this theme. The brilliant fugue with which "Ad nos" closes is based on a metamorphosis of the Anabaptists' chorale. A comparison of the fugue subject with the chorale theme will make the connection clear.

Meyerbeer, to whom the work was dedicated, showed great pleasure when he learned from Maurice Schlesinger that his name was about to be coupled with Liszt's through the publication of "Ad nos" in 1852. He at once wrote a letter of thanks to Liszt, even before he had seen the score, and his flattering remarks contradict the notion that contemporary composers, generally speaking, objected to Liszt "tampering" with their music. Meyerbeer, in fact, saw many advantages to such an association.

Berlin, February 8, 1852

Dear and illustrious colleague:

Monsieur Schlesinger has spoken to me about a letter you wrote to him in which you say that you have composed a large piano composition on the Anabaptists' hymn from *Le Prophète*,[59] and that

---

58. See p. 154, n.59. The words of the chorale, "Ad nos, ad salutarem undam, iterum venite misereri," may be translated as "Come, unhappy ones, come to us, come again to the healing water."
59. Meyerbeer was misinformed; Liszt never composed a solo piano version of "Ad nos." That was

you intend to dedicate this work to me when it is published, but first you wish to write to me directly. I shall not wait for the arrival of that letter to tell you how happy I am that one of my songs impresses you as worthy to be used as a motif for one of your piano compositions, destined to be heard throughout Europe and intoxicate those who have the good fortune to hear them played by your wonderful, poetic fingers. However, I feel even more honoured at the mark of sympathy you offer me in dedicating your work to me, for if it is an honour to see my name linked with yours, it is even more agreeable to me that you make it known in this manner that we are friends.[60]

Liszt himself helped Alexander Winterberger prepare the first performance,[61] and he opened the younger man's ears to the vast range of colour that lay locked up inside the work.[62] With "Ad nos" Liszt led the organ out of the church and into the concert hall.

VII

In September 1852 Liszt opened the Weimar opera season with a performance of Verdi's *Ernani*. It was the first time that the Italian master had been presented on the Weimar stage, and the production was an augury of ever more original things to come. Despite the dissatisfactions with the theatre that Liszt had expressed to Maria Pawlowna at the beginning of the year, his boundless optimism now prompted him to plan an ambitious series of operatic productions. Thus, the 1852–53 season included new productions of Spohr's *Faust,* Auber's *Carlo Broschi,* and Flotow's *Indra.* But the crowning achievements were the two festivals devoted to the music of Berlioz and Wagner, respectively. Liszt raised the banner of Berlioz in Weimar at a time when his old friend had no public following whatever in France. He invited him to Weimar three times during the 1850s, twice for major "Berlioz weeks." During the first of these, November 14–21, 1852, Berlioz shared the podium with Liszt. Among the works featured were *Roméo et Juliette, La Damnation de Faust,* and the revised version of *Benvenuto Cellini,* in the German translation of Peter Cornelius. Liszt had the greatest difficulty in recruiting a sufficient number of orchestral players for *La Damnation,* so he invited some of his pupils to help out: Bülow played

---

left to Busoni, half a century later, whose transcription of Liszt's organ piece represents one of the pinnacles of twentieth-century virtuosity.
60. LBZL, vol. 1, pp. 204–05.
61. See p. 263.
62. HLSW, p. 74.

the bass drum, Dionys Pruckner the triangle, and Klindworth the cymbals. Berlioz declared himself satisfied—as well he might, for they were possibly the most distinguished percussion section ever assembled to perform his music. Moscheles was present and reported that Berlioz's desk "was wreathed in laurels."[63] Berlioz and Liszt were wined and dined at the palace by Maria Pawlowna, and afterwards they all adjourned to the theatre, where Liszt conducted a performance of Cellini, especially staged to compensate Berlioz for having missed the revival of this opera in Weimar a few months earlier (the first performance of Cellini, incidentally, to have been given anywhere since its humiliating failure at the Paris Opéra fifteen years earlier, after which the French had taken to dismissing the work as "Malvenuto Cellini"). Chorley had described the first Weimar production as "nothing short of marvellous."[64] At the conclusion of the festival, Berlioz was invested with the Order of the White Falcon by Carl Friedrich and was given a gala reception at the Town Hall, with more than eighty guests in attendance.[65]

Despite the brilliance of the Berlioz Festival, the stresses and strains of coping with so many new productions had revealed afresh the flaws of the Weimar opera. Rumours of Liszt's impending resignation had already begun to sweep the city in January 1853, and they even reached Berlin. "Is it true that Liszt is going to Paris?" Fanny Lewald asked Carl Alexander. "The rumour is circulating here, but I do not believe it."[66] By mid-February 1853 Liszt had reached the end of his tether. His next major project—the Wagner Festival—had run into difficulties. He had just launched a series of rehearsals for a cycle of Wagner operas (Der fliegende Holländer, Tannhäuser, and Lohengrin), and nothing went right: the chorus was poor, the orchestra was still too small, and, worst of all, the theatre facilities were stretched to their limit for the production of an inane play by Ferdinand Raimund, The Maiden from the World of the Fairies. On February 16, the birthday of Maria Pawlowna, Liszt conducted Der fliegende Holländer (its first performance in Weimar), and he

---

63. MAML, vol. 2, p. 235.

64. It had taken place on March 20, 1852. Berlioz had been unable to be present since he was in England directing concerts of his music. This first "Berlioz week," then, was really a postponement of that earlier invitation. The impending arrival of Berlioz stimulated Liszt into literary activity. According to a letter Liszt wrote to Léon Escudier, the publisher of La France Musicale, he proposed to write a series of articles about Berlioz's works—Harold, Cellini, Roméo, and the Requiem. He also planned to have these articles bound in the form of a book: "After the last article has appeared in La France Musicale I ask, as the author's share, only for my honorarium of 300 copies." (TLMF, vol. 2, pp. 370–72) Only the Harold essay appeared, and then only in time for the second "Berlioz week," held in February 1855. Were the others ever written? See a later chapter of the present volume, "The Scribe of Weimar."

65. PGS, vol. 3, p. 51. A detailed report of the first "Berlioz week" may also be found in the Weimarische Zeitung, November 24, 1852. See also SZM, p. 48.

66. GCAF, vol. 1, p. 108.

knew that he owed it to himself, and to Wagner, to lodge a formal protest. Never again, he resolved, must he allow the poor conditions in the Weimar theatre to threaten his artistic standards. That same evening he wrote a sharp letter to Carl Alexander (who had been present in the theatre but had rushed away before Liszt could approach him) which was, in effect, an offer to resign.

February 16, 1853

My Lord,

The performance of *Der fliegende Holländer,* and the three works of Wagner announced for February 27 to March 5, mark the final stage of that cycle which the conditions in which I found the Weimar opera house permit me to follow . . .

Because of the parsimonious treatment to which music is subjected here, I consider it impossible to continue my activity in a manner worthy of the renown that its sovereigns have bequeathed on Weimar, to say nothing of the character and reputation I aim for on my own behalf. Your Royal Highness may therefore think it natural that I henceforth abstain from regular participation in a situation that remains too far below the efforts made recently to revive the Weimar theatre. . . .

In *Der fliegende Holländer,* the absence of adequate choirs is particularly shocking, and it would be even more so for the works of Meyerbeer, Spontini, etc., the performances of which could be [adversely] compared with those at other theatres. I am not unaware that they praise the orchestra (perhaps excessively so), and I do think that I am not one of the least causes of its present improvement. All the same, I hold to what I said already a long time ago, that it is impossible for it to bear comparison with that of Leipzig and other towns, as long as the seven or eight new appointments which I proposed are not made, and which I am ready to list again, if it please Their Imperial and Royal Highnesses that I should actively continue my duties in the theatre.

I am not in a position to request—still less to demand. I have only to safeguard the honour of the art which, in this case, is blended with your service. The experience of recent years has demonstrated, even in the eyes of those least able to look ahead, how legitimate were my requests. And were I ever to desist, I would be acting in the same way as those ill-considered mediocrities whose easy and convenient acceptance of the situation destroys art. . . .

I have the honour to be, with deepest respect, sire, the very humble and devoted servant of Your Royal Highness.

F. LISZT[67]

The formal language of this letter, which amounts to a rebuke, was intended to force Carl Alexander to a decision: he must either change conditions at the opera or accept Liszt's resignation. In the event, he did neither. His reply was couched in urbane generalities of the sort that mean all things to all men.

February 17, 1853

I have just read your letter, my dear Liszt. Accustomed to find loyalty and frankness in you, ever since I was first acquainted with you, I am delighted to have garnered fresh proof of it on this occasion. You are, I hope, just as much accustomed to finding goodwill in me, guided by sincere friendship. Therein lie the excellent conditions for collaborative work. We set ourselves to it, do we not, and we do not despair if, while we are fighting, all our desires are not realized at once in this life—which is nothing but a combat.

I would have liked to have given you my applause verbally yesterday evening. The whirlwind in which I was spinning carried me away; I am trying to repair my apparent negligence by writing to you today. Yesterday's opera struck me particularly from the psychological aspect. It is like a chrysalis of Wagner's genius. It is like the childhood of his art, a childhood like that of Hercules, who while still in the cradle strangles serpents. The *Wechselchor* in the third act was admirable.

Good-bye, my dear friend, be courageous, and I wish you a good success.

Your very devoted
C.A.[68]

Liszt's mood on receiving this letter is unknown, but he must have been cruelly disappointed. He had put his future at Weimar on the line, and all that Carl Alexander could do in response to his impassioned appeal was to tell him that life "is nothing but a combat" and bid him be courageous. With no options before him, Liszt completed his planned productions and then simply withdrew from the opera house. For the next few months he was in limbo. Between June 1853 and January 1854, he did not conduct in Weimar at all, except for one performance of *Der fliegende Holländer* on October 30, 1853.

---

67. LBLCA, pp. 40–42.
68. LBLCA, p. 42.

VIII

It is impossible to know whether under normal circumstances Liszt would ever have been interested in seeking a *rapprochement* with Carl Alexander. Fate now took a hand in their relationship, however. On the morning of July 8, 1853, the sound of muffled bells drifted across Weimar. People were at first bewildered, then they learned that Grand Duke Carl Friedrich had died during the night at Belvedere Castle. Hundreds of mourners converged on the grounds around the castle to pay their last respects to a monarch who had ruled them well and wisely for twenty-five years. The funeral took place on July 12. Drawn by coal-black horses, the hearse set out from Belvedere at 5:00 a.m. and travelled along Belvedere Allee towards Weimar. It was already light when the funeral procession reached Weimar's narrow streets and moved into the Marktplatz, where it was awaited by the main procession drawn up in formation. The cortège then proceeded through the Frauenplan, past Goethe's house, and arrived at the Stadtfriedhof, where Carl Friedrich was laid to rest with his forbears inside the royal burial chamber. Eduard Genast recalled the sad ceremony in vivid detail and observed the tearful farewells in the cemetery as Maria Pawlowna and Carl Alexander, together with his wife, Sophie, and their two small children, took their last leave of the royal coffin.[69]

Liszt was not in Weimar when these mournful events unfolded. News of the grand duke's illness and death were brought to him in Frankfurt, and he hastened to return to Weimar for the funeral. He did not arrive at the Altenburg until July 13, the day after the grand duke was buried. By July 17 he had secured an audience with Maria Pawlowna and travelled to Belvedere in order to present his condolences in person. That same day he moved on to Ettersburg Castle, where he met Carl Alexander, who told him that the official inauguration of his new reign would take place on August 28, Goethe's birthday— "a significant date," observed Liszt, "if they really wish to keep the meaning." Liszt described this meeting with Carl Alexander in a letter to Carolyne, who at that moment was in Carlsbad seeking yet another water-cure. The young duke was out walking in the woods which surrounded the castle when Liszt

---

69. GAW, pp. 348–53; SNW, vol. 1, p. 307. Carl Friedrich fell ill towards the end of June 1853, less than two weeks after celebrating the silver jubilee of his reign. He had gone to Belvedere Castle in order to spend some quiet days with his family and had no warning that his death was imminent. On Wednesday, June 29, the *Weimarische Zeitung* carried a terse notice which said that "since Sunday the grand duke has been suffering from a rash." The following day the rash spread with alarming rapidity across his face, and he lay mortally sick. Members of the royal family gathered at his bedside. On the night of July 7 Pastor Dittenberger was summoned to the palace to hold a vigil. The last illness of the grand duke was swift, a mere ten days.

arrived at Ettersburg. Liszt went off in pursuit and caught up with him on one of the trails leading away from the castle. After listening to the expressions of sympathy proffered by Liszt, Carl Alexander turned to his Kapellmeister and remarked: "The Word must now become the Deed." They sat down under the shade of an oak tree, and although Liszt does not say so, it seems fairly evident that they talked about the future of music at Weimar under the new reign, since they remained chatting there for two and a half hours. Carl Alexander then invited Liszt to stay for supper, and it was nearly midnight before Liszt was driven back to Weimar. Just as he was about to leave, he was asked by Carl Alexander to compose a *Huldigungsmarsch* ("march of homage") for the ceremonials on August 28. Liszt tells us that the main theme occurred to him that night as he was journeying back to the Altenburg, and he commenced work on the march the very next morning.[70]

Liszt must have been pleased with this meeting. With the accession of Carl Alexander, he thought, the pendulum would surely swing towards music and away from drama. It was on the strength of such remarks as "The Word must now become the Deed," in fact, that Liszt was prevailed upon to remain in Weimar. Once more he had fallen under the spell of a grand illusion; the word would never become the deed in Weimar. Had Liszt understood this deception, and had he only glimpsed the years of tribulation that still lay in wait for him in "the Athens of the North," he would have turned his back on the city for good. The triumphs and tragedies of the mid-1850s form a chapter unto themselves, however, and we will return to them at a later point in the narrative.

---

70. LLB, vol. 4, p. 160. Although the march was composed at breakneck speed, it was not performed during the inauguration ceremony on August 28 for the simple reason that the young grand duke decided to banish all music from the castle that day "for fear of irritating my grieving mother" (LBLCA, p. 44). Four years later, when Carl Alexander invited Liszt to compose a national anthem for Weimar, Liszt rescued the trio section of the march and presented it (with a few modifications) as a new composition. This was the origin of the so-called "Weimars Volkslied," which was performed for the first time on September 3, 1857, to mark the beginning of the centennial celebrations for Carl August (see pp. 480–81).

A Gathering of Eagles

*He offers the spectacle, rare in our day, of a great
personality, who bears and develops within him
the power to become the centre for the artistic aims
of the century.*

PETER CORNELIUS ON LISZT[1]

I

Among the brilliant band of pupils and disciples which formed itself around
Liszt during his Weimar years, passing mention has already been made of some
of the more prominent members—Bülow, Tausig, Raff, Cornelius. As the years
unfolded, however, the group was considerably enlarged by the arrival of Karl
Klindworth, Dionys Pruckner, Alexander Ritter, Julius Reubke, Hans von
Bronsart, Felix Draeseke, and Alexander Winterberger. Such a gathering of
talent remained unmatched by any other city in Germany, Leipzig and Berlin
not excepted; and Weimar itself could boast of a precedent only by going back
to the glorious epoch of Goethe and Schiller. Attracted to Weimar solely by
Liszt's magnetic presence, these young musicians were responsible not only for
the resurgence of artistic activity that swept through the city in the 1850s but
also for the renewal of the Romantic movement in Germany itself.

Liszt's intention to place Weimar in the vanguard of modern music was
motivated by his bleak diagnosis of the times. Vienna, which had dominated
the musical scene for sixty years, had lapsed into arid academicism since the
death of Beethoven. The position in Leipzig was even worse: Mendelssohn had
been cut off in his prime, and the schoolmen had taken over—the "little
Leipzigers," as Liszt called them, Julius Rietz, Moritz Hauptmann, and Ferdinand David—who wanted to place modern music in a straitjacket. As for Paris,
it was dominated by the Opéra; it was virtually impossible for an unknown

---

1. CLW, vol. I, p. 150.

composer to gain a foothold there. The younger generation of composers now looked to Liszt and to Weimar for leadership, which was quickly forthcoming. With characteristic generosity, he placed himself and his resources wholeheartedly at the service of all who sought his help. No cause, however unworthy, was turned away, even where his own preferences failed to correspond to it. Overnight, tiny Weimar became the Mecca of modern music.

With Liszt at its head, this band of musicians became known as "the New Weimar School." It is a curious fact that this school remains generally neglected by historians, for its impact at the time was little short of sensational. To review the life and work of the "Altenburg eagles" is to observe the presence of a powerful avant-garde in music some fifty years before art historians made the term fashionable.

II

Liszt first got to know the Bülow family while giving concerts in Dresden in the early 1840s. Eduard and Franziska von Bülow invited Liszt into their home whenever the flaming meteor flashed through the city, and he spent some agreeable evenings socializing with them and their friends. It was on one such occasion that the conversation must have turned on the pianistic talents of their twelve-year-old son, Hans. Not long afterwards Liszt was invited to play at a soirée in the neighbourhood. Despite the late hour—Hans was already in bed—Liszt insisted that the boy be roused from his slumbers and brought to hear the performance.[2] It was Bülow's first real glimpse of the man whom he came to revere almost as a god, and with whose life his own was soon to become inextricably linked.

As a child Bülow was a weakling. According to his mother he succumbed to "brain fever" five times and was continually in the care of doctors. Bülow himself tells us that in his early youth he showed "neither talent for music nor delight in it." Both gifts put in an abrupt appearance after a serious illness, but then to a phenomenal degree. During his periods of convalescence, the boy lay propped up in bed, silently reading the scores of Beethoven and Bach, engraving every note on his remarkable memory. At nine years of age he began his first music lessons with a local teacher named Henselt, who, unlike his famous namesake, was a cellist. Later he studied at the Leipzig Conservatory with Louis Plaidy, who laid the foundations of his piano technique, and with Moritz Hauptmann, the theorist. He also took some instruction in Dresden from Friedrich Wieck, whose pupil he briefly became in 1845. (Since the fifteen-year-old Bülow's fleeting apprenticeship to Wieck is almost totally forgotten

2. BB, vol. 1, p. 11.

today, we do well to recall the glowing tribute that he paid to his old master many years later: "You were the one who first . . . taught my ear to hear, who impressed upon my hand the rules of correct formation, and who led my talent from the twilight of the unconscious towards the bright light of the conscious."[3]) Music aside, Bülow's adolescence was not a happy one. The deep divisions between the personalities of his parents eventually spilled over into daily quarrels, and Bülow suffered great anguish when their marriage ended in divorce in the autumn of 1849.[4]

Two lifelong legacies of these traumatic times can be noted here. Bülow was ravaged by headaches, a functional symptom which struck him down whenever the problems of life overwhelmed him. He also became self-conscious about his physical appearance; his short stature, high forehead, and slightly bulging eyes caused him youthful embarrassment. Eventually he learned to protect himself from the imagined hostility of the world by his trenchant use of language, which became the scourge of his enemies and the despair of his friends.

Married or divorced, neither Eduard nor Franziska had any intention of allowing their gifted son to pursue a musical career. Frau von Bülow in particular believed that something more stable and secure was required for her delicate "Hänschen" than to go through life as a concert pianist. Bülow's letters tell their own sad story. "I should be very glad," he wrote wistfully to his mother, "if I had a little encouragement in my piano playing. . . . Today I am again not very well, with some giddiness and headache."[5] Such pleas to maternal solicitude were brushed aside, and it was determined that Hans would study jurisprudence, a subject for which his bright intelligence and his industrious

---

3. BB, vol. 3, p. 554. See also, in passing, the informative "curriculum vitae" provided by Bülow to an unknown correspondent in March 1858 (BB, vol. 3, pp. 166–73).

4. Passionate and impulsive by nature, Franziska von Bülow had never reconciled herself to the quiet, reflective character of her husband, a classical scholar who spent most of his adult life studying the dead languages. Eduard re-married almost at once, taking as his second wife Louise Bülow-Dennewitz. The couple bought a castle in Switzerland, where Eduard lived out his remaining days working on a huge biographical lexicon containing entries on all the great personalities of antiquity, a project he did not live to complete.

The Bülows, by the way, were of noble stock—hence the "von"—but unlike other branches of the family, they were impoverished. Their lineage is traced in detail in Heinrich Reimann's *Hans von Bülow: Sein Leben und sein Wirken* (Berlin, 1909). Reimann not only publishes the family tree but reproduces the Bülow coat-of-arms as well.

5. BB, vol. 1, p. 109. Long after Hans had established himself in Germany with his first successful recitals, a feat of which any normal mother would have been proud, we find Franziska still railing against the career of her son. "At last, a letter from Hans! . . . Tonight he is playing to the students at Breslau. On Sunday there is to be a monster-concert, at which he plays, and where he hopes to make some money. God grant it, if one may trouble God about such a thing." A few months later she writes: "To have such a child rushing about the world in all sorts of adventures is truly no sinecure." And she adds gratuitously: "As our shoemaker recently said: 'The Herr Sohn has become a genius.' " (BB, vol. 2, p. 332)

nature seemed to fit him. In 1848 he enrolled as a law student at the University of Leipzig, but he began to chafe under its restrictions. A year later he transferred to the University of Berlin, and it was while he was en route to that city that he stopped off at Weimar in order to renew his acquaintance with Liszt. This encounter proved to be decisive and brought some badly needed direction into his life. Liszt heard Bülow play and also arranged for his young visitor's string quartet to be performed at the Altenburg a few days later. "Very nice," was Liszt's verdict, "but very difficult."

> Liszt gave us immense pleasure that same day [reported Bülow] by his performance of the *Tannhäuser* Overture, which he has paraphrased in the most wonderful manner. . . . The playing of it was such a strain upon him that he was obliged to stop for a moment near the end; he very seldom plays it because it exhausts him so much, so he said to me afterwards: "You can write in your diary that I have played the *Tannhäuser* Overture to you."[6]

Both Hans and his mother attended the Herder Festival at Weimar the following year, in August 1850, and saw Liszt conduct. Afterwards Liszt came up to them, pressed Franziska's hand, told her of his admiration for her son's talent, and added, as he embraced Hans in farewell, "I am very attached to this boy."[7] It was just the sort of healing gesture called for by Hans's difficult family circumstances.

With Liszt's encouragement, Bülow visited Wagner in Zürich, and during the 1850–51 season he undertook some apprentice conducting at the theatres of Zürich and St. Gallen, an experience that was to stand him in good stead in the years ahead. By now, his goals were clear, and in June 1851 he returned to Weimar in order to perfect his piano playing under Liszt.

When Bülow arrived at the Altenburg in early June 1851, he found it deserted. Princess Wittgenstein was ill once more, and Liszt had taken her to Eilsen for a water-cure. "When I arrived here," Bülow wrote, "Liszt was expected back at the beginning of July; but the latest tidings are different, and Liszt has had all his clothes sent on to Eilsen, a proof that we must not expect him back yet awhile."[8] At first Bülow stayed at the Russischer Hof Hotel, since he was unable to find a private room in the city; but Raff, acting in Liszt's name, persuaded him to take up quarters in the Altenburg, where a set of rooms and a piano were placed at his disposal. There, he tells us, he would rise at six o'clock every morning and practice for eight hours a day. Liszt's cook would bring him

---

6. BB, vol. 1, pp. 178–79.
7. BB, vol. 1, p. 240.
8. BB, vol. 1, p. 329.

breakfast, while Liszt's valet cleaned his boots and clothes. Raff called at the house every day to make sure that everything was in order. At one o'clock Bülow went down to the Erbprinz Hotel for lunch, after which he resumed work at the piano. At about nine o'clock in the evening he would venture into the town again in search of supper at some local restaurant. By half-past ten he was climbing the steep steps leading back to the Altenburg. Since he did not have a house-key he used to clamber over the old wall into the courtyard and enter the house through a window which he could open from the outside. He became friendly with both Joachim and Cossmann, and within a week of his taking up residence at the Altenburg, the three young men had formed a piano trio and had performed a difficult work of Raff's before a small audience in Liszt's music-room. "I have never yet had two such capital players to play with," he wrote.[9] The summer of 1851 was a golden time for Bülow, filled with work and the happy anticipation of Liszt's return.

Liszt finally arrived in Weimar on Sunday, October 12. Bülow waited all day for him at the railway station, but as one train after another arrived and departed, and Liszt failed to appear, he went to the theatre to hear a performance of Spontini's *Cortez* under Chélard's baton. Halfway through the opera Liszt suddenly appeared in the stalls a few feet away from where Bülow was sitting, "as though he had sprung from the earth by magic." News of his presence ran through the darkened theatre like wildfire, and the orchestra, which until now had played badly, played even worse through sheer nervousness. Liszt became angry and, as Bülow put it, "would have liked to seize the sceptre from his humdrum deputy," but he restrained himself and silently fumed in his seat for the rest of the evening.[10] Afterwards Bülow and Joachim joined Liszt and the princess for supper, and the conversation lasted for most of the night. Bülow observed that the princess still looked very ill but had lost none of her love of disputation. And in a witty line to his father he prophesied that since he was more accustomed to French than Raff was, he, Bülow, would probably now be promoted to the office of "house disputator."

The next day Liszt and Bülow began their studies together. Bülow reports that they concentrated on the bigger sonatas of Beethoven, the best of Chopin

---

9. BB, vol. 1, p. 330.
10. BB, vol. 1, p. 372. During Liszt's four-month absence from Weimar, the orchestra had fallen into its old, slipshod ways. Genast and Raff had both complained to Liszt about it (see p. 99), and Bülow had also added his voice to the rising clamour of protest. In June, shortly after his arrival in Weimar, Bülow went to hear *Tannhäuser,* an opera that Weimar's players and singers alike had performed several times under Liszt's direction. All that Bülow could find to tell Liszt about the ensemble was: "Oh, how we missed your magic wand, the breath of life, the soul of this inanimate body!" (BB, vol. 1, p. 341) When Liszt went directly from the railway station to the theatre instead of returning straight to the Altenburg after his tiring journey, he was motivated by concern that the bad reports coming out of Weimar all that summer might be true. In the event, his worst fears were realized, and it took him the rest of the year to pull the orchestra back into shape.

and Schumann, and the newer works of Liszt himself, so as to build up a repertoire "that no other pianist could show." Since Liszt was not interested in teaching technique, either then or later, the young man was left to his own devices in this area, and he prescribed for himself Czerny's *School of Velocity* and the studies of Henselt, on which "I crucify, like a good Christ, the flesh of my fingers, in order to make them obedient, submissive machines to the mind."[11] This "crucifixion" of the fingers was no exaggeration. In order to intensify their suffering, the young penitent picked out a piano with a particularly stiff keyboard, had it delivered to the Altenburg, and punished his tired digits on this ungrateful instrument for four or five hours daily. Liszt's admiration for the talent of his young pupil was unbounded, and he came to regard him as his true heir in piano playing. That Bülow was an excellent technician before he ever went to Liszt goes without saying. Indicative of his latent physical prowess was the fact that when he was only fifteen he could already play Bach's two-part Fugue in E major with each hand in octaves—an idea he apparently got from Otto Goldschmidt, who was at that time a pupil of Mendelssohn. He also advocated the art of transposition. In the preface to his edition of the Cramer Studies he observed that the modern virtuoso should be able to play Beethoven's F-minor Sonata (*Appassionata*) in F-sharp minor with ease. Not long after his lessons with Liszt began, Bülow, in a letter to his father, summarized Liszt's opinions with regard to the direction his career should now take.

Weimar, October 25, 1851

... When I had gone through my piano examination with him, in which I very much pleased him by a rather happy performance of one of his most difficult piano pieces, this was pretty much the judgement that he passed upon me: he says he places positive, well-grounded hopes on me—indeed, more than hopes (he wanted me also to write and tell you this), for he says I shall, now that he has once and for all retired from public playing, be able to take up again the position of a virtuoso where he has left it. Eight months with him will be amply sufficient for my preparation—granted, of course, the necessary industry on my side; then I am to make my début, perhaps in Berlin or, better still, in Vienna, and go thence to Paris and London. Within three years I shall have attained my object—that is, an assured independence; I may consider him as surety for this.

I on my side, in my inexperience, not only need to seek the support of an authority like Liszt, to attach myself closely to him and strictly to follow his advice, but I also have such great confidence

11. BB, vol. 1, p. 381.

in his knowledge of the world and mankind that, without being afraid of the *"jurare in verba magistri,"* I have made him unconditionally the arbiter of my fate, and have told him so.[12]

The lessons lasted for two hours a week, and Bülow was never charged a penny for them. Liszt also continued to allow him full board and lodging at the Altenburg and to treat him in every respect like a member of the family. At Liszt's prompting Bülow began that profound study of the late Beethoven sonatas which later turned him into their most notable interpreter. Bülow's edition of these sonatas bears continual witness to the influence of his master, and it is, appropriately, dedicated "to Franz Liszt, as the fruits of his teaching."[13] Especially fascinating to Bülow were Liszt's unexpected solutions to difficult technical problems, some of which he recorded for posterity. Towards the climax of the great fugue from the *Hammerklavier* Sonata, for example, Beethoven demands a violent crescendo followed by a series of awkwardly placed trills:

Liszt's solution, recommended by Bülow, produces a greater climax and makes the trills "speak" more effectively. It is not nearly as difficult as it looks, and it does not harm Beethoven's musical thought:

---

12. Ibid., pp. 380–81.
13. J. G. Cotta, Stuttgart, 1871. See also Liszt's mention of this edition in LLB, vol. 2, p. 306. By this time, incidentally, Liszt had already dedicated to Bülow his piano transcriptions of the nine Beethoven symphonies (1865), a token of his admiration for the way in which Bülow interpreted these masterworks.

In order to repay Liszt for his kindness, Bülow willingly undertook various chores for his "dear and illustrious master," such as making fair copies of his manuscripts and writing articles for various magazines about the work of the Weimar School.[14] Unfortunately, Bülow's taste for polemics got him into trouble almost at once. An article about Henrietta Sontag, who sang on the Weimar stage in January 1852, created a scandal, and the aggrieved prima donna began a whispering campaign against him in Leipzig and Dresden.[15] This merely served to stiffen Bülow's resolve to expose artistic incompetence wherever he found it, and he began to issue a series of sarcasms about music and musicians which are still treasured by the profession today. He once told a trombone-player: "Your tone sounds like roast-beef gravy running through a sewer." Incompetent singers were a favourite target, drawing from him the timeless aphorism "A tenor is not a man but a disease." To a committee which had honoured him with a laurel wreath he replied: "I am not a vegetarian." When he heard of a music critic who regularly handed out favourable notices in return for moderately priced lessons from him, Bülow remarked: "He charges such small fees you might almost call him incorruptible." Bülow once visited the Royal Opera House in Berlin for a performance of Meyerbeer's *Le Prophète;* he was so disgusted at the poor ensemble that he wrote a letter to a Berlin newspaper in which he likened the Royal Opera to a circus. Then, to add insult to injury, he apologized to Herr Renz, the owner of the greatest

---

14. Bülow's literary activity is still a neglected topic, but during the 1850s and '60s he wrote extensively for such journals as the *Berliner Abend-Post,* the *Berliner Feuerspritze, Die Fackel,* the *Neue Berliner Musik-Zeitung, Deutschland,* and *Das Echo.* Initially, his motive for taking up the pen was financial (see his letter to Theodor Uhlig, BB, vol. I, pp. 420–21, in which he says that he is tired of writing for Brendel's *Neue Zeitschrift* for nothing). Soon, however, it became evident that he enjoyed employing his debating skills in public for the prestige this earned him.

15. The article was published in the *Neue Zeitschrift für Musik* on February 13, 1852. In a letter to his father, Bülow sketched in the background to the Sontag affair in great detail (BB, vol. I, pp. 442–43). His attack on Sontag had been published anonymously by Brendel, the editor of the *Zeitschrift,* and it was at first widely believed that Liszt himself was the true author, much to Bülow's chagrin. The *Leipziger Tageblatt* carried an open letter to Liszt saying in effect that his continued silence would be interpreted as complicity in the slanders of "his pupil and protégé" (February 22, 1852). The matter was also aired on the front page of *Deutschland* (February 26, 1852), which described Bülow's article as "an impertinence." Since *Deutschland* was published in Weimar itself, the message was clear: even the town in which Bülow presently lived wanted nothing to do with him. Shortly after Sontag's appearance in Weimar, and before the offending article appeared, Bülow ran into Johann Eckermann, who still lived in the city. Although it was pouring with rain, Eckermann crossed the street with raised umbrella in order to hold an animated conversation with his young acquaintance. Goethe, he told Bülow, had also heard Sontag and had been similarly offended. "When I had understood what kind of creature she was," Goethe was supposed to have told Eckermann, "and had got sufficiently enraged over the bad taste of the public, I took both my grandchildren, in spite of their resistance, and led them, one in each hand, out of the theatre, just as Lot fled with his two daughters from Sodom and Gomorrah when his wife was turned into a pillar of salt." To which Bülow added: "Eckermann has forgotten to publish this [in his *Conversations*], so now boast that you know it" (BB, vol. I, p. 425).

circus in Germany, saying that he meant no insult to him and that he had always admired the Circus Renz.[16] But it would be wrong to remember Bülow only by the destructive comments, since flashes of wisdom abound. He advised budding conductors: "Always conduct with the score in your head, not your head in the score." And to pianists he said: "Bach is the Old Testament and Beethoven the New Testament of music." Biblical language, in fact, informed one of his better ideas: "In the beginning was rhythm."

As the years unfolded, the tragedy of Bülow as man and artist became clearer. This eminently gifted musician, who was to become one of the outstanding interpreters of the century, had fallen too early under the spell of three of the most powerful personalities in musical history—Liszt, Wagner, and, to a lesser extent, Berlioz—and he lacked the creative strength to escape their pull. Bülow occasionally signed his name

$$
\begin{array}{lll}
\text{B ü L o W}[17] & & \\
\text{e} & \text{i} & \text{a} \\
\text{r} & \text{s} & \text{g} \\
\text{l} & \text{z} & \text{n} \\
\text{i} & \text{t} & \text{e} \\
\text{o} & & \text{r} \\
\text{z} & &
\end{array}
$$

and his invention of this symbol, which shows their names supporting his, tells us that he was not unaware of the lesser place in history to which his talent had consigned him. His talent, in fact, existed to serve their genius, and since he was too intelligent not to recognize that fact, he suffered accordingly. As the drama played itself out and Bülow entered the seven years of purgatory that were his marriage to Liszt's daughter, and her subsequent flight with Wagner in the most ignominious of circumstances, his suffering was transformed into exquisite agony. His living hell, or so it must have seemed to him, had been brought about by the very people he loved most on this earth. Was it his destiny to be nothing more than a pawn in the hands of his gods? Seeing him in this light, posterity should not begrudge him the luxury of an abrasive tongue, the sword and shield with which he defended himself against life's adversities. The story of how this tragedy unfolded will be related in its proper place. Meanwhile, Bülow's halcyon days were upon him, and his life with Liszt at Weimar illuminated every waking hour and filled his future with promise.

The friction between Bülow and his mother persisted throughout his stay in Weimar, and Liszt sometimes felt it necessary to intercede in the young man's behalf. A friendly correspondence sprang up between him and Franziska von

---

16. DMML, p. 85.
17. BB, vol. 3, p. 439.

Bülow, in which he kept reassuring her that it was only a matter of time before Hans's talent was recognized and all his material cares were resolved. In March 1853 the twenty-three-year-old Bülow set out for Vienna on the first leg of a concert tour that would then take him on to Pest, Dresden, and Leipzig. Liszt watched his pupil's progress anxiously, for he knew better than anyone else that if the tour failed Bülow would face almost certain ruin, and Frau von Bülow could still compel her wayward son to return to his law studies. From Vienna the news was bad: Bülow lost money on his first two concerts and had to make up the deficit from his own pocket; moreover, the newspaper criticisms were hostile. Predictably, Bülow fell into an acute depression, stayed in bed all the next day with a headache, and felt "forsaken by God and all the world." "Everything I foresaw, when he took that unlucky step in the autumn of 1850," Frau von Bülow wrote despairingly, "has come to pass literally. God forgive those who led him to it."[18] Liszt, recognizing that Bülow may have lost a skirmish but would still win the battle, wrote Franziska von Bülow a worldly-wise letter, full of confidence in her son's future.

Weimar, March 26 [1853]

Madame,

. . . I am far from judging [Hans's] actual position at Vienna to be as bad as he seems to have described it to you. The losses which his first two concerts have occasioned him can easily be made up, and I am going to write to him directly, to recommend him in a friendly spirit not to give way to despondency or ill-humour, which would not be at all in season. The experience I have gained in these matters allows me to pacify you as to the final result of his journey to Vienna, which, I am persuaded, will appear more favourable to the interests of his talent, his career, and even his purse than you imagine possible at this moment. The only thing necessary is that he must not let himself be discouraged, and that he must preserve a little *sangfroid* in order to profit by the means, which will continue to offer themselves to him, of conquering step by step the ground to which he has a right. The bitter and one-sided tone of the newspaper critic ought not to make him in the least uneasy; he must learn to bear his part in these things quietly, like a man of sense and talent:

---

18. BB, vol. 2, pp. 9–10. Bülow did nothing to enhance his reputation with the Viennese critics by billing himself as a *"Pianist aus Weimar."* By appearing in public as a representative of the Liszt School, he aroused partisan feelings at the very start of his career which became a liability to him as time wore on. This Vienna début, by the way, was given in the concert hall of the Gesellschaft der Musikfreunde on March 15 and included two arrangements by Liszt—a waltz from *Soirées de Vienne* (after Schubert) and *Les Patineurs* (from Meyerbeer's *Le Prophète*).

accidents of this sort must not be considered as sinister and have never prevented anybody from taking his rightful place, as our friend Hans will be able to do, be it a little sooner or a little later. I advise him to remain in Vienna during the months of April and May, except for a short journey to Pest at an opportune moment, about which they will be able to advise him at Vienna. It is probable that he will earn some money at Pest, and perhaps at Pressburg; but in order for him to attain this end, I consider it indispensable for him to take a more permanent footing in Vienna than he can do in a fortnight. As he is extremely intelligent and possesses all that he needs to make a good and fine career, it will be best to leave him entirely free in his actions and movements during these two months; and simply to help him to bear calmly the misfortunes which are inevitable in this profession. . . .

Pray believe me, madame, there is really nothing to be anxious about, still less to lament over in regard to Hans's two concerts in Vienna; and I hope you will soon get news to help to make you share the certainty and confidence that I continue to hold.— Pray believe me, madame. With every expression of respectful friendship,

Yours sincerely,
F. LISZT[19]

Liszt then contacted his cousin Eduard Liszt, who now looked after his investments in Vienna, and asked him to advance a hundred florins to Bülow at once and hold a further hundred in reserve. He also sent Hans a talisman ring for good luck, which the superstitious young man wore constantly and from which he drew much comfort and inspiration. In this, as in so much else, Liszt showed himself to be psychologically perceptive and to have a sympathetic understanding of his pupil's need of fatherly support and approval. Unknown to Bülow, he also despatched various letters to his powerful contacts in Pest, asking them to extend a helping hand to the young pianist when he arrived in the Hungarian capital.[20]

---

19. BB, vol. 2, pp. 10–11.
20. Typical of such letters is the one that Liszt wrote to Antal Augusz on May 12, 1853, in which he begs his friend to grant Bülow his protection in Hungary. "Although he has worked with me for eighteen months in Weimar," wrote Liszt, "I do not consider him my pupil but rather my heir and successor." (CLBA, p. 42) For a detailed account of Bülow's stay in Vienna and Pest, and of the concerts he gave there, see the long sequence of letters he wrote to his parents and to Liszt from these cities during the period March–August 1853 (BB, vol. 2, pp. 11–78).

Bülow, by the way, was one of the very few of Liszt's many pupils and disciples whom he ever encouraged to address him with the intimate "du" form. It was extremely difficult for Bülow to make

Bülow lingered in Vienna for two months, on Liszt's advice, establishing all those professional connections which are indispensable to a young artist on the brink of a musical career. His only other public appearance in the city was at a Concert Spirituel on April 3, when he took part in a performance of Bach's Triple Concerto in D minor, with Josef Dachs and Joseph Fischof playing the other two pianos. At the end of May, Bülow moved on to Pest, where the groundwork already laid in advance by Liszt helped to bring about his first major success. On June 1, he appeared on the stage of the Hungarian National Theatre, the scene of Liszt's spectacular triumphs thirteen years earlier, and played Liszt's Fantasia on Motifs from Beethoven's *Ruins of Athens,* with Ferenc Erkel conducting. "The shouts of 'Éljen!' ['Hail!'] are still ringing in my ears," he told his mother in a letter which bubbles over with youthful enthusiasm at his first real public ovation. "It was an unparalleled triumph, according to what everyone says."[21] And he added: "The greatest share of it is due to Liszt's name," an acknowledgement that Bülow was to make time and again, at any rate in the early part of his career, until his debt to Liszt became so large that it threatened to overwhelm him and he felt constrained to cast his master aside in a desperate attempt to preserve his artistic independence.

III

It was well known that Liszt disliked infant prodigies; but when Aloys Tausig brought his thirteen-year-old son, Carl, from Warsaw to Weimar in the summer of 1855, he appears not to have heard the news. Liszt at first refused to hear the *Wunderkind* ("They never amount to much"), and Tausig senior was forced to concoct a simple ruse. While Liszt was enjoying a cigar and drinking wine with a group of friends, young Tausig was smuggled to the piano in an adjoining room, and at a pre-arranged signal he began to play Chopin's A-flat-major Polonaise with such brilliance that after a few bars Liszt looked round and cried: "I take him!"[22] Thus began one of the closest relationships

---

the transition, and Liszt had to chastise him about it. "I enjoyed reading your excellent letter too much this morning to stress the scolding which I must nonetheless give you for having completely forgotten *unser herzliches Baseler Du, was ich Dich bitte, in deutscher Sprache, mit mir immer zu gebrauchen* [our friendly "du" usage in Basel, which I ask you always to use with me in German]" (LBLB, pp. 35–36). This was a reference to the party that Liszt and the "Murls" had given for Wagner at Basel, in the Hotel zu den drei Königen (see pp. 233–34). It seems that there had been a good deal of merrymaking, and formal barriers had been lowered. Bülow dealt with Liszt's request in the only way possible for him, coming as it did from someone whom he venerated as a god: he steadfastly refused to write to his mentor in German at all but preferred to use French, the language of diplomacy, which allows the most intimate forms of expression beneath the formal mode of address.

21. BB, vol. 2, pp. 53–54. The letter, dated June 2, 1853, is headed: "The day after the first victory."
22. FMG, p. 251. In a letter to Agnès Street-Klindworth, dated July 21, 1855, Liszt wrote: "This morning I accepted a new pupil, aged thirteen-and-a-half, named Tausig . . . He already plays

Liszt ever enjoyed with a pupil. Tausig moved into the Altenburg and lived there as a member of the family for two years.

On July 21, 1855, a few days after their first encounter, Liszt held a soirée at the Altenburg at which the Tausigs were presented to Bülow and various members of the Weimar School. Liszt had the lad brought to the keyboard to play half-a-dozen pieces, which confirmed his earlier impression. "He is an amazingly gifted boy whom you will enjoy hearing. He plays everything by heart, composes (fairly well), and seems destined to make a brilliant reputation for himself very quickly."[23] Then Bülow played three of his own works— *Fantasy Reverie,* a mazurka, and *Invitation to the Polka.* The session was concluded by Liszt, who played his Scherzo and his Sonata in B minor. Afterwards the whole crowd went down to the Erbprinz for dinner and did not disperse until midnight.

Aloys Tausig had once been a pupil of Thalberg and was now a respected piano teacher and the composer of some virtuoso pieces. His young son had already acquired through him something of Thalberg's aristocratic bearing at the keyboard; and Thalberg's leading principle—the greater the technical difficulty, the greater the physical repose—eventually found its chief representative in Carl. "Never did such a talent come under my hands," Liszt used to say.[24] The lessons were irregular, since Liszt was obliged to spend several weeks away from Weimar in 1856 and 1857, but the fact that he had taken Tausig under his wing gave the boy a chance to develop his gifts without exploitation and lay the foundations of a mighty piano-playing career. What life in the Altenburg was like for this thirteen-year-old can hardly be imagined. Hardly a day went by without a group of distinguished visitors coming to the house, and Tausig was petted and fussed over until he became quite spoiled. Sometimes, holding a reception at the house after a concert, Liszt was understandably tired and did not feel like playing to his guests; so Tausig would be summoned

---

everything in an astonishing fashion, and composes pieces which are altogether striking." Liszt then made a witty pun on the name Carl Tausig: "Er ist ein ganz tausiger Kerl"—"He is a phenomenal fellow." (LLB, vol. 3, pp. 35–36) Cornelius, who also was present on this occasion, vouches for the impact made by Tausig's playing. "He dashed into Chopin's A-flat-major Polonaise and knocked us clean over with the octaves." (BFA, p. 131)

Incidentally, if further evidence of Liszt's general dislike of infant prodigies be sought, he himself had already provided it in an article he had written about eighteen months before Tausig arrived in Weimar. His words contain much food for thought. "Nowadays we all too often see parents who, alas, pointing to certain shining examples [in history] and prompted by motives that have nothing to do with the love of the beautiful, wear out their children and exhaust them on mechanical studies whenever they show the slightest spark of talent and the smallest hope of material gain. They waste all on the attainment of a fruitless virtuosity . . . on a soulless, senseless delivery of masterworks, which for sheer thumping and thrashing cannot be comprehended. The fledglings remain strangers to all other intellectual development and are in danger (unless they are outstandingly gifted) of running wild into a purely material sleight-of-hand." (RGS, vol. 4, pp. 197–98)

23. HLSW, p. 68.
24. FMG, p. 250.

to the keyboard instead, and, putting on the airs of his master, often "did not feel like it either," much to Liszt's annoyance and his guests' amusement.[25] Tausig was frequently left to his own devices, and his escapades taxed Liszt's patience. Once, the lad's father bought him a new grand piano from Leipzig. The first thing young Tausig did was to saw off the corners of the keys in order to make them more difficult to strike, and his father had to settle a large repair bill before the instrument was even paid for. Tausig always seemed to be short of money, and Liszt often paid his debts. Once, Tausig sold a pile of music, including the manuscript of Liszt's *Faust* Symphony, for five thalers, to a servant who in turn disposed of it to a waste-paper man. The world might have lost Liszt's orchestral masterpiece had not Gottschalg, his suspicions aroused, traced the man, bought the pile of music back again, and returned to the Altenburg with the precious score. Quite by chance, the publishers had requested the score that very day, and when Gottschalg arrived at the house, he found Liszt searching frantically: "A whole year's labour lost!" he cried. When Gottschalg produced the missing manuscript, Liszt's joy was boundless. He rushed to the stairs and shouted: "Carolyne! Carolyne! We're saved!" The entire household had been in an upheaval because of Tausig's action. Liszt soon forgot the episode, as he always did with Tausig. When, a few days later, the boy celebrated his birthday, Liszt embraced him and remarked with a twinkle in his eye: "Cärlchen, you'll either become a great blockhead or a great master!"[26]

Whenever Liszt was out of Weimar, Tausig was left in the care of the princess. She often took him along with Marie, her daughter, for short trips to nearby cities simply to see the sights and to keep herself occupied during Liszt's absence. After one such outing to Erfurt, the princess reported to Liszt that "Tausig was a charming boy, and *very well behaved"*—a clear enough hint that his boisterous conduct had been a topic of conversation between them in the past.[27]

It is an indication of Tausig's rapid strides in piano playing that by the late summer of 1856, little more than a year after his first encounter with Liszt, the fourteen-year-old boy was already working on his master's Transcendental Studies. The princess wrote to Liszt: "Yesterday Tausig dined with us and played us your two studies *Eroica* and *Mazeppa*. . . . He is not yet the master

---

25. In later life Tausig's artistic "temperament" could easily be mistaken for arrogance. He was once asked by the Epsteins (a rich family of baptized Jews, who lived in Berlin) to play at one of their private receptions, for the large fee of four hundred roubles. His hand-delivered reply was not likely to be forgotten by them soon. "I only play on three occasions: (1) when the king of Prussia commands it; (2) in public; and (3) in the homes of people I know well." (LMM-K, p. 213)

26. FMG, pp. 250 and 278–79.

27. WA, Kasten 35, August 16, 1856.

of *Mazeppa,* but he played the admirable *Eroica* with fire."[28] And she added this revealing sentence a few days later: "Tausig played *Prometheus* [Liszt's symphonic poem] in his own arrangement for two hands quite passably."[29] Such a talent was far too precious to remain buried in Weimar indefinitely. For the next sixteen months Tausig worked with Liszt towards his public début, which took place in Berlin in January 1858, with Bülow conducting. Liszt observed of his young charge at this time: *"There* is a real 'iron-eater,' as Hummel said of me when he heard me in Paris in the twenties."[30] Liszt saw his second self in Tausig, and the subsequent career of this gifted youth proved that he was not mistaken. It was entirely in keeping with Liszt's character that he did much good by stealth for Tausig, who in the early days of his career encountered some unexpected setbacks from the critics. By throwing the weight of his immense prestige behind the young pianist, and writing various letters of recommendation in behalf of his protégé, Liszt opened many doors for him which might otherwise have remained shut.[31]

In the summer of 1858 Tausig travelled to Zürich in order to see Wagner, who, at Liszt's insistence, rashly accepted the "iron-eater" into his home.[32] Almost at once Wagner regretted it; he complained that Tausig drank huge quantities of tea and devoured all his cheese and biscuits. Tausig's strong cigars, smoked as an accompaniment to his incessant piano playing, drove Wagner to distraction ("Already he puts on the airs of a Liszt," Wagner remarked slyly), and he finally banished the young man to an old piano in a nearby tavern. Nonetheless, Wagner was shrewd enough to recognize a talent when he saw one. "As a musician he is enormously gifted," he wrote to Liszt, "and his furious piano playing makes me tremble."[33]

After giving various recitals in Germany, Tausig settled in Vienna, where he attempted to emulate Bülow's efforts in Berlin by putting on programmes of modern orchestral music, which he himself directed. These events, which also featured his own unpublished symphonic poems, were not successful, and he lost money. For a time he went into seclusion in order to come to terms with himself and his career. He embarked on a deep study of philosophy, reading the works of Kant and Hegel. It was in Vienna that he got to know Brahms and that he and Peter Cornelius helped to arrange the only known meeting

---

28. WA, Kasten 35, September 18, 1856.

29. WA, Kasten 35, September 23, 1856.

30. LLB, vol. 1, p. 287.

31. See, for example, LLB, vol. 1, pp. 288 and 305–06; also LLB, vol. 4, p. 440.

32. "I send you today a *wonderful fellow,* dearest Richard," wrote Liszt, "receive him kindly. Tausig is to work your Erard thoroughly and to play all manner of things to you. Introduce him to our mutual friends at Zürich—Herwegh, Wille, Semper, Moleschott, Köchly—and take good care of him. Weimar, May 18, 1858." (BWL, vol. 2, p. 197; KWL, vol. 2, p. 200)

33. BWL, vol. 2, p. 119; KWL, vol. 2, p. 204.

between Brahms and Wagner.[34] While the meeting itself was cordial enough, there were unfortunate consequences for which Tausig must be held responsible. Knowing that Brahms was a collector of autograph scores, Tausig presented him with the manuscript of Wagner's *Tannhäuser* revisions for Paris, which he had somehow acquired from the composer in Zürich. Brahms was taken aback when he received a letter from Cornelius in 1865 asking him to return the score to Wagner, since "Tausig was undoubtedly in error when he declared that the score was his property."[35] For ten years Brahms stubbornly refused to yield the manuscript, and it was only after Wagner himself intervened and initiated an unpleasant correspondence with him that it was reluctantly returned.

In 1864 Tausig married the pianist Serafina Vrabély (from whom he was later divorced), and the following year he settled in Berlin, where he opened a school for advanced pianists. His name and his fame really date from this time. All were agreed that his playing was transformed. Critics talked of the deadly accuracy of his leaps, the diamond brilliance of his scales, and the cold fire that burned at the heart of his wonderful tone. His Chopin interpretations were generally conceded to be models of their kind. Liszt heard him again in 1869 and declared that his technique was "infallible" and that he had "fingers of steel." No one who has heard Tausig's remarkable transcription of Wagner's "Ride of the Valkyries" would disagree with this description. It was an irreparable loss to the world of music when Tausig contracted typhoid fever in Leipzig and died in the summer of 1871; he was not yet thirty years old.

Compelling evidence of Tausig's important place in the history of the piano may be found in his *Tägliche Studien,* a set of ingenious finger-exercises strangely neglected by pianists today.[36] Two examples from this large collection will serve to give us an insight into Tausig's particular obsession with finger-

---

34. This meeting took place on February 6, 1864. Brahms played for Wagner his "Handel" Variations, and Wagner could not help being impressed. "One sees what can still be done with the old forms in the hands of one who knows how to deal with them."

35. Unpublished letter, dated August 18, 1865. See GB, pp. 84–85.

36. Tausig's *Tägliche Studien* were first published in 1873, in Magdeburg, from manuscripts assembled and edited after his death by his teaching colleague Heinrich Ehrlich. Six years later they were published in Berlin with a useful introduction by Ehrlich (EK). From this source we learn that Tausig had small hands but compensated for this drawback by his ability to leap.

One of the characteristic features of Tausig's piano playing was his calmness under stress. Nothing seemed to fluster him. This quality of detachment extended to his daily life and was sometimes the source of amusement to his friends. Whenever Tausig played in Breslau, he stayed in the home of Leopold Damrosch. Once, in the middle of the night, the bed in which he was sleeping collapsed and he fell to the ground with a resounding crash. Undaunted, he re-arranged the mattress on the floor and continued his slumbers as soundly as before. For Tausig, the unexpected had to be dealt with as routinely as the expected. Tausig's favourite dish at the Damrosch home, incidentally, was apple-pudding, which Frau Damrosch always prepared for him herself, adding some special spices which appealed to him; it became known to everybody as "Tausigsche Apfel-Speise" (DMML, p. 3).

dexterity. The first study must be played at speed, *without* the use of the third finger:

The second study must be played with the thumb and fifth finger firmly anchored to the keyboard, while the others scramble to position themselves on the keys in readiness for their headlong sweep across the chromatic scale:

Within a week of Tausig's death La Mara had written to Liszt, asking him to furnish her with details about the pianist for a biographical sketch she proposed to write. Liszt's reply contains much that would interest students of Tausig today. "The intellectual claws and pinions were already giving signs of mighty power in the youth who was scarcely fourteen years of age," he wrote. About three months later, La Mara submitted her sketch to Liszt for scrutiny. His response was typical. "To your sketch of Tausig only a single objection could be raised: namely, that you bestow too high praise on me. Pardon me if I cannot argue about it. . . ."[37]

I V

Other students who worked with Liszt in Weimar during the mid-1850s, as we have seen, included Karl Klindworth, Hans von Bronsart, Dionys Pruckner, and the American pianist William Mason. None of them equalled Bülow or Tausig in pianistic stature, but all of them went on to pursue brilliant careers and to carry

37. LLB, vol. 2, pp. 166 and 171. See the useful memoir of Tausig in WMME, pp. 42–50. Since biographical information about the Polish pianist is somewhat scarce, the interested reader cannot afford to overlook the scattered references to him in the correspondence of his compatriot Marie Mouchanoff-Kalergis, who knew him well. She was at Tausig's bedside when he died. "The doctors, with their usual blindness, were sending off reassuring telegrammes and administering the usual remedies to him. I proposed some radically different ones, but they laughed in my face. During the night of Sunday and Monday, Tausig expired between the two people who knew and loved him best. [The other was Countess Krockow.] Death throes of a quarter of an hour, a look of deep sorrow, and everything was over." (LLM-K, pp. 270–71) See also the letter from Emilie Genast to Eduard Lassen in which she describes Liszt's reaction to Tausig's death (SNW, vol. 2, p. 295).

the ideals of their master to far-flung corners of the globe. Liszt regarded these young men as members of his family and referred to them affectionately as "the boys." Whenever he was out of town, he would allow "the boys" to use the guest-rooms in the Altenburg or, alternatively, to go up to the house every day and practice on one of his pianos if they had difficulty in finding a proper studio of their own. "Bring the boys to the Erbprinz for supper tomorrow evening," he would sometimes say to Klindworth. Or to Mason: "Tell the boys to prepare a musical get-together at the Altenburg next Sunday." Occasionally their number would be augmented by Cornelius or Raff, slightly older disciples, to whom the newcomers looked up in awe and who would add yet more colour and vigour to the party. During these musical sessions Liszt would serve cognac and pass around cigars. A lighted candle generally stood on a table near the piano so that anyone could wander across at will and puff his dying cigar back to life. Since Liszt knew that one or two of "the boys" were impoverished (Klindworth, for example, had to borrow money to make the journey to Weimar), he happily passed on to them whatever local students he himself was disinclined to teach. He also gave them money if he suspected that pecuniary hardship was preventing them from carrying out their artistic plans. He once took Cornelius aside and told him: "You know that I am no banker, nor anything like it. But if you ever need a hundred thalers to carry out some project (for example, to set out for Breslau), I am at your service. . . ."[38] In such a warm and caring atmosphere all formal barriers were swept aside, and it was not long before these young men became *Dutzenbrüder*, in Mason's happy phrase, forming friendships with one another that lasted a lifetime.

Although Karl Klindworth was only twenty-one years old when he joined Liszt in Weimar in the summer of 1852, he was already an experienced operatic conductor of four years' standing: he had been appointed music director of a touring opera company in Silesia when he was a mere youth of seventeen, and he knew all the major operatic scores by heart. Born in Hanover on September 5, 1830, Klindworth was the son of a gifted engineer and optician who played a wide variety of musical instruments. His first love was the violin, an instrument on which he might have become a virtuoso, for even during his boyhood he was playing the concertos of Rode, Molique, and Vieuxtemps. He was entirely self-taught as a pianist, however, and he had no particular ambition to excel in this direction until he encountered Liszt, who happened to be staying near Hanover, at Eilsen. "Liszt was very charming," recalled Klindworth, "and was quite the *grand seigneur*. He asked me to play something, adding 'Play this to me,' which proved to be his Concert Study in D-flat major, in manuscript."[39] Fortunately, Klindworth's youthful love of sight-reading from full scores came

---

38. CSB, p. 115.
39. These recollections of Klindworth are preserved in an interview he gave to *The Musical Times*, published on August 1, 1898, during a brief sojourn in London.

to his rescue, and Liszt was pleased with his impromptu rendering of this difficult work. Liszt himself then sat down and played the piece to Klindworth, and from that moment the young man was seized with a desire to study with him. Not long afterwards a letter arrived from Raff, inviting him to go to Weimar and present himself to Liszt. Klindworth remained with Liszt for eighteen months. "My companions at Weimar were Bülow, Joachim, Peter Cornelius, Ferdinand Laub, and Bernhard Cossmann," said Klindworth. More than forty-five years later he still had the clearest recollection of meeting Berlioz during the first Berlioz festival at Weimar, in 1852.[40]

In 1854 Klindworth settled in London, where he remained for fourteen years. His début took place in Willis's Rooms, on March 30, 1854, but it was not a success.[41] Thereafter, he had a difficult time in making ends meet and was compelled to accept a job as a piano teacher at a school in Hendon. The following year Wagner arrived in London as conductor of the Philharmonic Society concerts for that season. He carried with him a letter from Liszt, which ran:

January 25, 1855 Weimar

I commend to you Klindworth, a Wagnerian *de la veille*. He is an excellent musician, who formerly acted as conductor at Hanover, and there gave a performance of *Le Prophète* at the Tivoli Theatre, of which the newspapers were full some years ago. He is also a splendid pianist, who studied eighteen months with me at Weimar, and you must allow me to send Klindworth a few lines of introduction to you. As far as I know, there is in London no pianist like him; but on account of his determined and open sympathy with the so-called "Music of the Future," he has placed himself in a somewhat awkward position towards the philistines and handicraftsmen there.
Your F.L.[42]

A few weeks later Wagner and Klindworth had become acquainted. The younger man went over to Wagner's rooms at 22 Portland Terrace, Regent's Park, and dined with him. Afterwards Klindworth played Liszt's B-minor Piano Sonata, which he had studied in Weimar the year before. Wagner wrote to Liszt:

---

40. Ibid.
41. Klindworth's programme (in which he was billed as "a pupil of Liszt") included Beethoven's Sonata in C major, op. 2, no. 3, and Liszt's arrangement of the Wedding March from Mendelssohn's *A Midsummer Night's Dream*. J. W. Davison gave him a poor review in the *Musical World,* telling his readers that Klindworth exhibited "the faults of his master with none of his beauties. He thumps the instrument with right good will, and is by no means exact in his execution."
42. BWL, vol. 2, pp. 51–52; KWL, vol. 2, p. 48.

April 5, 1855
London 8:30 evening.

Klindworth has just played your great sonata to me. We passed the day alone together; he dined with me, and after dinner I made him play. Dearest Franz! you were with me; the sonata is beautiful beyond compare; great, sweet, deep and noble, sublime as you are yourself. It moved me most deeply, and the London misery was forgotten at once. More I cannot say, not just after having heard it, but of what I say I am as full as a man can be. Once more, you were with me! Ah, could you only be with me, body and soul, how beautiful we could make life!!

Klindworth astonished me by his playing; no lesser man could have ventured to play your work to me for the first time. He is worthy of you. Surely, surely, it was beautiful![43]

What particularly impressed Wagner about Klindworth was his ability to play full operatic scores at the keyboard while singing the main vocal parts as he went along. Wagner remarked that "if the fellow had a tenor voice, I should most certainly kidnap him, because, apart from that, he meets every requirement for my Siegfried, especially in regard to physique." From this time, Klindworth became closely involved in arranging Wagner's operatic scores for the piano. He eventually completed the entire *Ring* cycle, and Wagner used to refer to him as the best of "meine Klavierauszügler"—"my piano extractors." By the time Klindworth had finished this marathon task, he had moved to Moscow, where he taught at the Imperial Conservatory. His arrangement of the second act of *Götterdämmerung* caused him many problems, but he was finally able to despatch the finished manuscript to Wagner in Bayreuth. Unfortunately, the Bavarian town was unknown to the Russian post-office, and the parcel was sent to Beirut in the Middle East instead! It remained there for a year, and when it was eventually re-directed, Wagner had to pay substantial postal charges. Meanwhile, poor Klindworth was obliged to undertake a fresh piano arrangement in time for the Bayreuth rehearsals.

Klindworth's edition of the complete works of Chopin, published in 1878, won universal acclaim. Hans von Bülow used to say that there were only two ways to learn Chopin's works properly: the first was to hear Liszt play them, and the second was to study them in Klindworth's edition. Liszt himself paid a fine tribute to the scholarly activities of his former pupil when he inscribed a presentation-copy of one of his own pieces with the following sentence: "To

---

43. BWL, vol. 2, p. 69; KWL, vol. 2, p. 65. According to Klindworth himself, he had learned the sonata in six days, shortly after it was composed, and had then played it to Liszt from memory—a remarkable tribute to his powers of musicianship.

Karl Klindworth, the very conscientious expert and intelligent annotator of the best edition which has yet appeared of the works of Chopin."

V

Bülow's namesake Hans von Bronsart—whom Liszt dubbed "Hans II"—arrived at the Altenburg in 1853. Like Bülow, he was descended from an old family of the lesser nobility. All his brothers were military officers, and Bronsart himself would abandon his artistic career for a time in order to fight in the Franco-Prussian war of 1870. Liszt paid many compliments to Bronsart's gifts. He once told Draeseke: "I value him both as a character and as a musician."[44] And he wrote to Agnès Street-Klindworth: "I have become very attached to [Bronsart], who has developed a real performing talent and has composed a trio that I consider to be among the best in that genre, and much superior to the trios of Rubinstein."[45] Liszt entrusted to Bronsart the first performance of his A-major Piano Concerto, which he dedicated to his young pupil. In return Bronsart gave Liszt his unswerving allegiance, a fact that was very well illustrated by his forthright denunciation of Hiller during the "paper war" that erupted after Liszt's appearance on the podium at the Aachen Festival in 1857 and by his general defence of the Weimar School in his brochure *Musikalische Pflichten* (1858).

In 1861 Bronsart married Ingeborg Starck, a Swedish pupil of Liszt, who was also a prolific composer.[46] After leaving Weimar, he went on to enjoy a notable career as a theatre director, first at Leipzig and then at Hanover. Eventually he returned to the city of Goethe and Schiller in order to take up the vacant post of intendant at the Weimar theatre.

VI

No one has captured the atmosphere of the Altenburg times more perfectly than William Mason, whose *Memories of a Musical Life* contains some of the very

---

44. LLB, vol. 1, p. 295.
45. LLB, vol. 3, p. 84.
46. The beautiful Ingeborg Starck (1840–1913) used to turn all heads in Weimar. Wagner talked of her "bewitching elegance" in *Mein Leben*. Eduard Lassen fell in love with her, prompting Liszt to remark: "She will go a long way, but it is doubtful that it will be in Lassen's company. . . . That makes poor Lassen quite melancholy" (DA, August 20, 1859). The rivalry among Liszt's students for her attentions only ceased on the day of her marriage to Bronsart. She was the composer of operas, a piano concerto, and fugues. When Liszt, thinking only to compliment her beauty, remarked that she did not look like a composer of fugues, Ingeborg replied: "I am happy not to have a fugal face" (LLB, vol. 1, p. 330).

best descriptions of Liszt in Weimar and has become an irreplaceable source document for historians of the period.[47] Mason arrived in Weimar in April 1853 and, after booking a room at the Erbprinz Hotel, walked up the hill to the Altenburg. He was twenty-four years old and apprehensive at the prospect of meeting Liszt. He had come to Weimar on impulse, or rather on the vaguest of invitations thrown out by Liszt four years earlier, and no one was expecting him. The servant who opened the door mistook him for a local wine-merchant. There was a delay before he was ushered into the dining-room, where Liszt sat at the table, drinking his afternoon coffee and cognac. As Mason advanced on him, he said, "Well, Mason, you keep people waiting a long time." Mason paused and looked bewildered; until five minutes ago Liszt had not even known that he was in the house. Then Liszt added: "I've been expecting you for four years." Nothing could have been better calculated to put the young man at ease. Liszt invited him to try a new Erard grand he had just received from Paris. Mason, who thought that this was too good an opportunity to miss, sat down and played one of his own pieces, *Amitié pour Amitié,* which had just been published by Hofmeister in Leipzig. During the performance Liszt moved about the room, gathering together some papers for a meeting with the grand duke already arranged for later that afternoon. As Mason finished, Liszt commented: "That's one of your own? Well, it's a charming little piece." Mason suspected that Liszt was merely being polite, that he had heard the piece with only half an ear. Nothing was mentioned about him being accepted as a pupil. As they left the Altenburg together, Mason accompanied Liszt down the hill until they reached the grand ducal palace. Liszt then turned and said casually: "You say that you are going to Leipzig for a few days on business? While you are there you had better select your piano and have it sent here. Meanwhile, I will tell Klindworth to look up rooms for you. Indeed, there is a vacant room in the house in which he lives, which is pleasantly situated just outside the limits of the ducal park." Fifty years later, Mason wrote that he could still recall the thrill of joy that passed through him as he heard those words. He was now a pupil of Liszt.[48]

Mason then went on to describe his lessons with Liszt. "He never taught in the ordinary sense of the word. During the entire time that I was with him I did not see him give a regular lesson in the pedagogical sense." At his first session Mason played Chopin's A-flat-major Ballade. As the music progressed, Liszt became increasingly excited. Eventually, he pushed Mason off the piano-stool: "Don't play it that way. Play it like this." Liszt then sat down at the keyboard and repeated the same passage, but with different accentuation, letting in a flood of light on the music. "From that one experience," reported Mason,

---

47. MMML, pp. 86–182.
48. MMML, pp. 88–89.

"I learned to bring out the same effect, where it was appropriate, in almost every piece that I played. It eradicated much that was mechanical, stilted, and unmusical in my playing."[49] Mason played for two or three hours at this first lesson, with Klindworth and Pruckner looking on. It was an unnerving experience, he tells us; they lounged on the sofa and smoked, and Mason silently reflected that they were having a nice time at his expense. A few days later, however, it was his turn to light a cigar and lounge while Liszt criticized their playing. These group lessons with "the boys" marked the true beginning of Liszt's master classes, an idea which is usually associated with his work in Weimar in the 1870s and '80s, and which has been widely adopted by the teaching profession in our own century. Liszt's belief was that young masters found one another artistically stimulating, that it helped them to play well in front of their peers. This process of learning from one another as well as from Liszt was a true baptism of fire, as more than one student testified. And the plain fact is that no other teacher of the nineteenth century produced so many distinguished pianists as Liszt. After Bülow and Tausig left the Altenburg, in fact, Liszt never gave "private" lessons to anyone. And there was one more thing about those friendly get-togethers with "the boys." Since Liszt wanted to give his pupils the best possible education, he always tried to introduce them to distinguished visitors who happened to pass through Weimar. In this way, these young men were frequently brought into touch with poets, painters, dramatists, scientists, and politicians, as well as musicians, whom they would never have met under normal circumstances. No other teacher of the day would have done that. It was all part of Liszt's well-known view that piano playing must never be confused with finger-dexterity, that piano playing involved the whole person, and to improve the one you must improve the other.

Mason heard Liszt play the piano many times during his sojourn in Weimar and declared that although the master no longer practiced, he was beyond question the greatest pianist he had ever heard. Liszt, he said, was what the Germans call an *Erscheinung*—an epoch-making genius. "His genius flashed through every pianistic phrase, it illuminated a composition to its innermost recesses, and yet," Mason added, "his wonderful effects, strange as it must seem, were produced without the advantage of a genuinely musical touch." In illustration of this point, Mason recalled an occasion when the pianist Julius Schulhoff came to Weimar and played in the drawing-room of the Altenburg immediately after Liszt, and on the same piano. Liszt played his *Bénédiction de Dieu,* and the strains of this mighty conception had scarcely dissolved into silence when Schulhoff followed with some small salon piece of his own. He "produced a quality of tone far more beautiful than Liszt's; but about the latter's performance there was intellectuality and the indescribable impressiveness of

---

49. MMML, p. 99.

genius, which made Schulhoff's playing, with all its beauty, seem tame by contrast."[50] Mason is also very interesting on the subject of Liszt's technique. Because Liszt had neglected the purely physical aspects of piano playing for the past four or five years, there was less pliancy in his muscles; his tone had become somewhat harder, and there was a lack of economy in some of his movements. Liszt himself was well aware of this and told "the boys" that they were to learn all they could from his musical interpretations but not to copy his touch, since it was not a good model to follow. He blamed this on the fact that he was largely self-taught as a youth. "In early years," he said, "I was impatient for immediate results . . . and jumped through sheer force of will to the goal of my ambition. . . . I do not advise you to follow my way, for you lack my personality." Mason made the perspicacious point that it was vital for a student to have acquired an absolutely sure foundation before he studied with Liszt; given this basic preparation, Liszt could develop the best that was in him. Liszt's last great contribution to keyboard technique was made in 1851, when he published the final versions of the Transcendental Studies. Thereafter, his interest in technical problems waned, and he was content to leave further progress in this direction to others. It even became a form of praise with him to underplay the technical excellence of other pianists. "What I like about So-and-So," Mason reports Liszt saying about a pupil in 1858, "is that he is not a mere 'finger virtuoso'; he does not worship the keyboard of the pianoforte; it is not his patron saint, but simply the altar before which he pays homage to the idea of the tone-composer."[51]

Musicianship and artistic truth, then, were the twin ideals towards which Liszt encouraged his pupils to strive. He constantly reminded them that the artist was "the bearer of the beautiful." He could not abide chicanery, and whenever he detected it in a prospective student the consequences could be unpleasant. This was very well illustrated shortly after Mason arrived in Weimar. One evening while Liszt and his pupils were chatting, he announced that the following day a young Hungarian pianist would be arriving at the Altenburg, who claimed to be able to play Beethoven's *Hammerklavier* Sonata. This piece, which had been one of Liszt's war-horses in earlier years, was still regarded as so challenging that Liszt wanted "the boys" to hear it for themselves. Everybody turned up at the appointed hour, and the young pianist began to play. It became clear at once that he had not the vaguest notion about the correct tempo of the first movement, which he played at half the speed in order to simplify the difficulties. He had not progressed very far before Liszt stopped him, seated himself at the piano, and played the first page at the correct tempo in order to show him the proper interpretation. "It's nonsense for you to go

---

50. MMML, p. 113.
51. MMML, p. 116.

through the sonata in that fashion," said Liszt, and abruptly left the room. The poor pianist was mortified. Mason felt sorry for him and accompanied him out of the house. As they were walking down the street, the young man turned to Mason and said: "I'm out of money; won't you lend me three louis d'or?" A few days later Mason happened to tell Liszt that the hero of the *Hammerklavier* had tried to borrow money from him. Liszt became very angry, stamped up and down the room, seized a long pipe from his pipe-rack on the wall, and brandished it like a stick, exclaiming: "Drei louis d'or! Drei louis d'or!" Liszt's outrage was absolutely genuine. He saw the young man as an imposter: not only had he deceived Liszt by telling him that he could play Beethoven's most difficult sonata when he could not, but he had added insult to injury by attempting to borrow money from someone he had met under Liszt's roof. Had the wretched fellow simply announced himself to Liszt and his circle as a beggar, who did not know where his next meal was coming from, they would doubtless have showered him with hospitality. But because the miscreant had attempted to impress them with an incompetent performance of Beethoven, Liszt felt that he and "the boys" had been insulted, and he reacted accordingly. Such a spirited defence of artistic integrity was not lost on Liszt's students.[52]

During his sixteen-month stay in Weimar, Mason kept a diary. Simply to skim through the entries for May and June 1853 is to bring the period vividly to life.

May 1. Quartet at the Altenburg at eleven o'clock, after which Wieniawski played with Liszt the violin and pianoforte "Sonata in A" by Beethoven.

May 3. Liszt called at my rooms last evening in company with Laub and Wieniawski. Liszt played several pieces, among them my *Amitié pour Amitié*.

May 6. The boys were all at the Hotel Erbprinz this evening. Liszt came in and added to the liveliness of the occasion.

May 7. At Liszt's, this evening, Klindworth, Laub, and Cossmann played a piano trio by Spohr, after which Liszt played his recently composed Sonata, and one of his concertos. In the afternoon I had played during my lesson with Liszt the C sharp minor Sonata of Beethoven and the E minor Fugue of Handel.

May 20. Attended a court concert this evening which Liszt conducted. Joachim played a violin solo by Ernst.

May 22. Went to the Altenburg at eleven o'clock this forenoon. There were about fifteen persons present—quite an un-

---

52. MMML, pp. 103–06.

usual thing. Among other things, a string quartet of Beethoven was played, Joachim taking the first violin.

May 27. Joachim Raff's birthday. Klindworth and I presented ourselves to him early in the day and stopped his composing, insisting on having a holiday. Our celebration of this event included a ride to Tiefurt and attendance at a garden concert.

May 30. Attended a ball of the Erholung Gesellschaft this evening. At our supper-table were Liszt, Raff, Wieniawski, Pruckner, and Klindworth. Got home at four o'clock in the morning.

June 4. Dined with Liszt at the Erbprinz. Liszt called at my rooms later in the afternoon, bringing with him Dr. Marx and a lady from Berlin, also Raff and Winterberger. Liszt played three Chopin nocturnes and a scherzo of his own. In the evening we were all invited to the Altenburg. He played *Harmonies du Soir* (no. 2) and his own Sonata. He was at his best and played divinely.

June 10. Went to Liszt's this evening to a bock-beer soirée. The beer was a present to Liszt from Pruckner's father, who has a large brewery in Munich.[53]

No wonder that Mason, in later life, used to look back on this musical paradise and call it *Die goldene Zeit*—"the golden time." In July 1854 he left Weimar and never saw Liszt again. The memory of those days remained undimmed, however. Mason and his young friends had rubbed shoulders with genius, and the experience transformed them all.

VII

Peter Cornelius well remembered the day he arrived at the Altenburg. It was Saturday afternoon, March 20, 1852; he was nervous, and he did not have an appointment.[54] "As I was walking up the steps to Liszt's rooms in the Alten-

53. MMML, pp. 122–25.
54. Cornelius had recently reviewed Liszt's book on Chopin for the Berlin journal *Das Echo* (February 29, 1852; CLW, vol. 3, pp. 25–28). The previous year there also had been a sporadic correspondence between the pair. Anxious to make Liszt's personal acquaintance, Cornelius had journeyed to Weimar on March 5, 1852, but when he got there Liszt was out of town. He lingered for two weeks until Liszt returned, by which time he was in a state of high tension. Finally, he plucked up courage, advanced on the seemingly impenetrable front door of the Altenburg, and sent a couple

burg," he wrote, "the superstitious idea came over me: an even number of steps is lucky; uneven, unlucky. And, alas! there were twenty-one steps."[55] Was this a portent of the future? Neither Liszt nor Cornelius could have known at the time that the young visitor would become the unwitting cause of Liszt's downfall at Weimar, six years later. A housemaid appeared on the landing and addressed Cornelius in broken German. She in turn passed word of his arrival to a manservant, who spent a long time feeding him with false hopes. Dejectedly Cornelius descended the twenty-one steps and hovered uncertainly outside the front door. Suddenly a window was flung open and the manservant called out: "He can't see anybody else today." In the face of one last plea, the servant relented and signalled him to go up. Back he went, up the twenty-one steps, and at last he entered Liszt's room, unannounced. Although Liszt had been besieged by visitors, he showed no sign of irritation with his unexpected guest.[56] "He shook hands with me in a friendly manner," Cornelius noted in his diary. "To portray him now would be difficult; perhaps I may be able to do so when he has 'sat for me' in different moods."[57] Two days later Cornelius met the other members of the Altenburg circle and heard Liszt, Joachim, and Cossmann render a performance of César Franck's Piano Trio, a work of which Liszt thought highly.[58] Cornelius stayed on in Weimar for a fortnight, returned sporadically during the autumn of 1852, and took up full-time residence there the following year.

Cornelius was born in 1824, in Mainz. When he first came into contact with Liszt, he was already in his twenty-eighth year and almost formed as an artist. His parents, both actors, spotted his talent early, and by the time he was sixteen years old he was playing the violin in the Mainz theatre orchestra. Two years later he was acting in a touring theatre troupe in Wiesbaden, an invaluable experience which he turned to advantage after his interest in opera was aroused. He had composed from the age of thirteen and already had an impressive number of chamber pieces in his portfolio. After the untimely death of his father, he moved to Berlin, where he lived from 1844 to 1852 in the care of an uncle, the famous painter Peter von Cornelius. There he came into contact with some outstanding literary figures, including Humboldt, Eichendorff, and Paul Heyse, and his own talents as a poet began to stir within him. It was because Berlin contained no great musical personality from whom Cornelius

---

of hammer-blows echoing through the old house. With that simple summons Cornelius bound his fate to that of the New Weimar School.

55. CLW, vol. I, p. 119. That same staircase is still in the Altenburg today—twenty-one steps.
56. That same evening Liszt conducted a performance of Berlioz's *Benvenuto Cellini* in the Weimar theatre. When Cornelius blundered into the Altenburg, Liszt had already rehearsed the opera that morning and was just then in the middle of pre-performance discussions with the theatre personnel.
57. CLW, vol. I, p. 119.
58. CLW, vol. I, p. 120.

could receive stimulation that he looked to Liszt and Weimar. He felt much at home there among the actors, poets, and musicians who formed the golden circle of talent that Carl Alexander had drawn around the court. Cornelius became one of the protagonists of the New Weimar School, helped to develop its ideas, and published many articles about its activities in the national press.

Liszt took a lively interest in the compositions of his protégé and often had them performed in Weimar. Because Cornelius was a committed Catholic, convinced of the moral value of art, Liszt at first advised him to devote himself to church music. "You have but to assimilate Palestrina and Bach," Liszt told him in September 1852; "then you can let your heart speak, and can say with the prophet: 'I speak because I believe—and I know that our God lives forever!' "[59] He helped Cornelius with several masses and a setting of "Domine salvum fac regem," which were despatched to Vienna, Liegnitz, and London in the hope that they might win prizes there, but they met with no success. Their failure was necessary to Cornelius, however, because it helped him to find his true direction. Shortly afterwards he turned to the Lied and composed his set of nine songs *Vater unser* (op. 2) and the cycle *Trauer und Trost* (op. 3), which, by common consent, reveal a mature hand. A stream of songs poured from his pen during the Weimar years. Many of them were first performed in the Altenburg by Rosa von Milde, the gifted young soprano from the Weimar theatre, accompanied by Liszt.

In 1853 Cornelius moved into the Altenburg as a permanent resident. This solved a serious financial problem, for he had no money. In view of his gifts as a linguist, Liszt employed him not only as a secretary but also as a transcriber and translator of his articles, and it was useful to have him under the same roof. Many of the essays that appeared over Liszt's signature in the 1850s (on Wagner, Schumann, Chopin, and others) were translated by Cornelius from French into German. Cornelius also provided German translations of a number of Liszt's song texts, perhaps his most sensitive work in this area. Of Liszt he wrote: "From the moment I first got to know him, he has never ceased to be the most lovable and helpful of friends."[60]

Nevertheless, Cornelius soon began to find the atmosphere at the Altenburg stifling, and he feared that his close proximity to Liszt might harm his originality. He retired during the summer of 1854 to a small cottage in the Thuringian Forest, owned by relatives, in an attempt "to find myself again." Here, in isolation, he composed several sets of songs and translated the libretti of Berlioz's *Benvenuto Cellini* and *L'Enfance du Christ*. This desire for creative independence was one of Cornelius's strongest traits. He showed himself capable

---

59. LLB, vol. 1, p. 112.
60. CLW, vol. 1, p. 150.

of resisting that paralysis of the brain which seems to afflict so many second-rate talents when they find themselves in the presence of genius, and Liszt respected him for it. When Cornelius returned to Weimar in October 1854, he moved back into the Altenburg,[61] where he was occasionally invited to dine with Princess Carolyne and the other guests. Once, the post-prandial conversation turned to orchestration. Carolyne informed her guests that Liszt was a better orchestrator than Berlioz, an idea with which everybody nodded in vigorous assent, in order to please her. Carolyne turned to Cornelius and asked: "Don't you agree?" Without hesitation Cornelius replied "No." He later confessed that he blushed all over because he had "dared to contradict the dear, great lady in the silk dress. Yet my 'No' was more precious to me than all the treasures of the world."[62]

VIII

The names of Julius Reubke (1834–58) and Alexander Ritter (1833–96) are all but forgotten today. But when they joined Liszt's growing band of disciples in the mid-1850s, they were acknowledged at the Altenburg as two of its brightest stars. Reubke arrived in Weimar in 1856, when he was twenty-two years old, and quickly became a favourite pupil of Liszt, who regarded him as a composer of great promise. His Organ Sonata is a brilliant example of his early genius and happens to be the only work by which he is remembered today. The sonata, which is of importance in the history of organ music, is a programmatic description of Psalm 94 ("O Lord God, to whom vengeance belongeth, shew thyself"). It reveals the influence of Liszt's "Ad nos"; but since "Ad nos" remained largely unknown until modern times, Reubke's daring harmonic procedures were wrongly attributed to Wagner. Reubke gave the first performance of his sonata on the organ of Merseburg Cathedral in 1857, and it created a stir at the Altenburg. When the history of the New Weimar School comes to be written, one other work of Reubke will surely receive its due. Although

---

61. Cornelius later lived at Geleitstrasse 10, about a hundred yards from the Court Theatre.

62. CLW, vol. 1, p. 196. This exchange took place in February 1855, at the end of the second "Berlioz week," and only two days after Liszt had conducted a performance of the *Fantastic* Symphony in the Weimar theatre. The question of Berlioz's orchestration, then, was on everybody's lips, and the princess was doing no more than her duty as a good hostess in keeping the conversation topical. It was doubtless as tactless of Carolyne to invite this comparison between Liszt and his guest-of-honour as it was courageous of Cornelius to disagree with her; but it must be remembered that the pair were in almost daily conflict by this time over the translations of Liszt's articles, and some sort of altercation was to be expected. It is also worth bearing in mind that Liszt's symphonic poems, to say nothing of the *Faust* and *Dante* symphonies, had not yet been published. Liszt, in fact, was still experimenting with some of these pieces, which Cornelius could not yet have heard in their final form.

his Piano Sonata in B-flat minor (1857) was begun only after he got to know Liszt's own Sonata in B minor, it remains a work of formidable originality. Reubke openly acknowledges the connection between the two pieces by quoting from his master's work. This sonata aroused the admiration of the Altenburg circle, particularly when Reubke himself played it. Richard Pohl recalled the scene well:

> Playing us his sonata, seated in his characteristically bowed form at the piano, sunk in his creation, Reubke forgot everything about him; and we then looked at his pale appearance, at the unnatural shine of his gleaming eyes, heard his heavy breath, and were aware of how wordless fatigue overwhelmed him after such hours of excitement— we suspected then that he would not be with us long.[63]

Reubke had already contracted tuberculosis and was staring death in the face. When he went to meet his Maker in 1858, his immense potential unfulfilled, Liszt wrote a letter of condolence to the young man's father, Adolf Reubke, the well-known organ builder:

Weimar, June 10, 1858

Dear Sir:

Allow me to add these few lines of deepest sympathy to the poem by Cornelius[64] which lends such fitting words to our feelings of sorrow. Truly no one could feel more deeply the loss which Art has suffered in your Julius, than the one who has followed with admiring sympathy his noble, constant, and successful strivings in these latter years, and who will ever remain true to the memory of his friendship—the one who signs himself with great esteem

Yours most truly
F. LISZT[65]

The letter is a model of its kind. Liszt's pupils were ever referred to as his "friends" or his "colleagues": all were united in the service of art.

Alexander Ritter was eleven years old when he was taken to hear Liszt play in Dresden in 1844. Afterwards he went round to the artists' room and asked Liszt for one of his gloves as a keepsake for his sister Emilie.[66] The Ritters lived

---

63. Richard Pohl, "Nachruf Julius Reubke," NZfM 48 (1858), Supplement.
64. Within a few days of Reubke's demise, Peter Cornelius had written a memorial poem, "On the Death of Julius Reubke," which Liszt enclosed with his letter.
65. LLB, vol. 1, p. 307.
66. HAR, p. 27.

fairly close to the Bülows in Dresden, and it was through Hans von Bülow that Alexander was later re-introduced to Liszt.[67] In 1854 Liszt offered Alexander an appointment among the first violins in the Weimar Court Orchestra. The offer was timely, since it coincided with the impecunious Ritter's marriage to the actress Franziska Wagner, a niece of the composer.[68] Two years later, when Ritter was twenty-three, Liszt helped him to secure the conductorship of the Stettin orchestra. Ritter kept this position for only two years, since his championship of modern music made him enemies. He performed Liszt's *Tasso* at one of his last concerts, and it was the incomprehension aroused by this work that led Ritter to collaborate with Károly Kossmaly on a brochure entitled *Eine Vorlesung über Programmusik* (1858). In October 1860 Ritter settled in Schwerin, where his wife was engaged; later he moved to Würzburg, where he began to compose an important series of chamber and orchestral works. These compositions were utterly neglected by his contemporaries, and it was not until Richard Strauss took them up in Munich nearly thirty years later that their true worth began to be recognized.[69] One month before Ritter died, in the spring of 1896, Strauss conducted his *Sursum corda*. Such was the response that Ritter was prevailed upon to mount the platform and acknowledge the applause. "The audience gasped with surprise," reported one eye-witness, "when they saw the bearded, elderly gentleman bow to the ovation. They had expected a much younger man."[70]

I X

One other important figure from the Altenburg years remains to be considered. In many respects he was closer to Liszt than any of the others (with the exception of Bülow), if only because he was not merely a pupil but an assistant.

---

67. The Ritter family also got to know Richard Wagner during his tenure as Kapellmeister in Dresden. In later years Ritter's mother, Julie, began a long correspondence with Wagner and provided him with material support (WJR). His older brother, Karl, became a protégé of Wagner in Zürich and launched a modest career there as a conductor.

68. See Liszt's letter to Ritter on the topic (LLB, vol. 1, pp. 168–69), from which we learn that Liszt offered to find quarters for the honeymoon couple in Weimar.

69. One of the most sensitive accounts of Ritter's life will be found in Siegmund von Hausegger (HAR), who also provides a complete catalogue of Ritter's works. A revival of the tone-poems, in particular, is long overdue, since they represent a bridge between Liszt and Richard Strauss. Incidentally, Strauss always maintained that it was Ritter who introduced him to the music of the New German School and helped him to break out of the conservative mould of his youth. It was Ritter who wrote the poem *Tod und Verklärung* after getting to know Strauss's tone-poem of that name. The poem and the orchestral work were published together, leading many people to the erroneous conclusion that the music is based on the text.

70. HAR, p. 122.

Liszt entrusted a great deal of literary and musical work to Joachim Raff, and he sought his views on a wide variety of topics. Indeed, unlike the other acolytes, Raff had the distinction of having been specially imported to Weimar as Liszt's amanuensis. Because the case of Raff is so unusual, and because the full extent of his collaboration with Liszt still causes controversy today, a full account of his Weimar connection will be given in the following chapter.

The Raff Case

I am determined to have a little influence . . .
on Liszt's latest works.

JOACHIM RAFF[1]

I

When Liszt took up his duties at Weimar he had very little experience in handling an orchestra. Although he had appeared as a conductor from time to time (notably at Pest, Bonn, and Breslau, where he had directed a performance of Mozart's *Die Zauberflöte*), his knowledge of the technique of instrumentation was defective and he had as yet composed hardly anything for the orchestra. At first he sought help from August Conradi, a well-known composer of operettas and musical farces, who resided in Weimar for about eighteen months, from February 1848 until the summer of 1849.[2] It was Liszt's practice to submit to Conradi a short score, on two to six staves, with instrumental cues. From these sketches Conradi produced a full score, which Liszt then revised after rehearsing it with the Court Orchestra; the process might be repeated two or three times, until Liszt was satisfied that all his wishes had been incorporated. The arrangement was terminated when Conradi left Weimar to take up the post of Kapellmeister in Stettin. It was not until Joachim Raff came to Weimar, a few months later, that Liszt found a collaborator worthy of his genius. Raff was a gifted composer with an imaginative grasp of the orchestra, who was of great practical assistance in helping Liszt to find his "orchestral voice" during these 'prentice years. Since the relationship was a problematic one, and since the precise nature of Raff's help

---

1. RLR, p. 390.
2. Liszt had actually used Conradi as a copyist since 1844 (see RLS, vol. 2, pp. 69 and 224–25).

became the object of a dispute at the turn of the century, we shall have to consider its history in detail.

Born in 1822 in Lachen, Switzerland, Raff was a self-made character who had originally been destined by his parents for the career of schoolmaster or clergyman. His musical talent directed him along a different path, however, despite some formidable obstacles along the way, which included sharp parental opposition and an adolescence marred by abject poverty. Raff was a child prodigy who not only played the violin, piano, and organ without any formal instruction but was so advanced in his linguistic studies that he was able to translate fluently from German into Latin by the time he was eight years old.[3] Entirely self-taught as a composer, he received early encouragement from Mendelssohn, who, impressed by a group of piano pieces the twenty-one-year-old youth had sent him, persuaded Breitkopf and Härtel to publish them and then invited Raff to study with him in Leipzig. Mendelssohn's premature death in 1847 dashed these plans, and for a time Raff, who had a ready pen, earned an uncertain living writing musical criticism in Cologne and Stuttgart.

Liszt had befriended Raff as early as 1845, and the story of how this came about makes lively reading. Hearing that the great pianist was about to give a recital in Basel, the impoverished young man walked all the way from Zürich through downpours of rain to hear him. By the time he had battled his way to the box office, soaked to the skin, all the seats were sold. Amazed by the crumpled appearance of this dripping disciple, Gaëtano Belloni, Liszt's secretary and factotum, who happened to be standing nearby keeping an eye on the concert-receipts, reported the matter to Liszt, who was about to walk onto the platform to play his Reminiscences of *Robert le diable*. Liszt paused in midflight. "Bring him forward! He can sit near me on the stage."[4] The bewildered Raff was at once propelled by Belloni onto the stage, where he found himself sitting in full view of the audience, surrounded by a bevy of elegant ladies. A large pool of water slowly formed itself around Raff's chair as Liszt played. "I sat there like a running fountain," he said later, "oblivious to everything except my good fortune in seeing and hearing Liszt." After the concert he and Liszt had their first long chat, and Raff told him of the many hardships he had endured in order to pursue a career in music. With that characteristic generosity Liszt always showed towards rising talent, he offered to take Raff with him on a concert tour through the Rhineland. Raff was with Liszt throughout the Beethoven Festival in Bonn; and thanks to the older man's magnanimity, he made many connections of use to him in his struggling career. Before resuming his world tours Liszt secured a position for Raff with the piano warehouse of Eck and Lefèbre in Cologne. For two years Raff corresponded with the man

---

3. RR, p. 18.
4. RR, p. 38.

whom he now regarded as his friend and benefactor. When he once more fell on hard times, it was to Liszt that he turned, and again Liszt helped him to secure employment, this time with the publisher Schuberth in Hamburg. He also suggested that Raff should seriously think of joining him in Weimar, where he could be more helpful to the young composer, "and you could repay me with a few hours' work now and then in sorting out manuscripts, copying, orchestrating, taking dictation, etc."[5]

This was the background to Raff's arrival in Weimar, in Liszt's company, in January 1850.[6] Raff soon proved himself to be one of the staunchest supporters of the Weimar School. He absorbed Liszt's views about programme music, became an advocate of Wagner, and gave the world ample evidence of his own gifts as a composer by producing a series of works that reveal an exemplary command of the orchestra and a thorough grasp of counterpoint. Liszt's production of Raff's youthful opera *König Alfred* at Weimar in 1851 brought Raff to prominence. His eleven symphonies bear impressionistic titles such as *Im Walde, Zur Herbstzeit,* and *In den Alpen,* a clear enough indication of where his musical sympathies lay. Nor were his merits as a writer neglected: his influential book *Die Wagnerfrage,* which was published in 1854, was much discussed at the time and focussed attention on the Weimar School.[7] None of this publicity resolved his pressing financial cares, however. The grinding poverty he endured in Weimar eventually led to his arrest for an old debt incurred in Switzerland, and which he could not repay. According to William Mason, the room in which he was confined was more comfortable than the one he was forced to vacate. An anonymous benefactor sent in a piano, a table, music-paper, and ink so that he might compose. No one knows how this was

---

5. RLR, p. 121.

6. Raff actually entered Liszt's service in December 1849. He travelled to Bad Eilsen, where Liszt was taking the waters, and was briefed on his duties almost at once. From Eilsen he wrote: "Every morning about ten o'clock Liszt comes into my room, where we chat about work for the day" (RLR, p. 389, December 1849; see also LBZL, vol. 1, p. 126)

7. What Liszt thought of this widely read book was never made public at the time, but he expressed some private reservations in a letter to Franz Brendel. He feared—not without reason—that the book's polemical tone might place fresh obstacles in the path of the Weimar School. In particular, he was upset at Raff's long-winded analysis of *Lohengrin.*

> [Raff] is perpetually getting on scientific stilts, which are by no means of very solid wood. Philosophic formulas are sometimes the envelope, the outer shell, as it were, of knowledge; but it may also happen that they only show empty ideas and contain no other substance than their own harsh terminology. . . . Do not repeat this to *anybody,* for I could not go against Raff in any but the most extreme case . . . Against the many charges to which he has exposed himself I even intend to shield him. . . . (LLB, vol. 1, pp. 165–66)

This was not the first time that Liszt indicated his willingness to come to the defence of a member of his school who had worked himself into an intellectual cul-de-sac. On the whole Liszt was philosophical about such difficulties: he knew that it was the price one pays for having a school at all.

accomplished, or who paid off Raff's creditors, since he had no relatives and few friends in Weimar. Mason is convinced that it was Liszt, who was probably outraged at the rough justice meted out to his colleague by the petty bureaucrats.[8]

Raff was by nature a controversialist. He liked nothing better than to persuade his antagonists to take up certain propositions and then attack them for having done so. His blunt manner probably made as many enemies for Liszt as friends; but once one had penetrated the rough exterior and won his heart, Raff usually remained a friend for life. In 1856 Raff's association with Liszt ended, but there was never any suggestion of a formal break between them. Raff had meanwhile become engaged to Doris Genast, eldest daughter of Eduard Genast, and he followed her to Wiesbaden after she had secured some acting engagements there. They were married in 1859, and for some years Raff enjoyed a successful career as a piano teacher in Wiesbaden. He became director of the Frankfurt Conservatory in 1877, a post he served with distinction until his death in 1882. Such a brief survey of Raff's achievements cannot obscure the tenacity of his character and the size of his talent. And if it be asked why Raff consented to live in Weimar under Liszt's benevolent shadow and undertake routine chores of a kind that even the dullest hack would not envy, the answer lies in his gratitude to Liszt, without whom his career might well have foundered on the shoals of the world's indifference.

I I

From the start there appears to have been a basic misunderstanding as to why Raff was in Weimar at all. Liszt himself was in no doubt: he simply wanted to learn more about instrumentation, a field in which he readily acknowledged his younger colleague's greater experience, and to this end he submitted piano sketches of his works to Raff to orchestrate (after the fashion of those that he

---

8. MMML, p. 162. Liszt may well have made Raff's prison cell more comfortable for him, but he appears not to have paid off the latter's debts. In a letter to Princess Carolyne dated September 17, 1853, he told her:

> I have been to see Raff, who has been in prison for eight days for an old debt of eight years ago; but if anyone speaks to you about it, I beg you to say that you are completely ignorant of it. Although it is only a question of 80 ecus, I will not pay it on principle! I therefore have advised him to stay in his new lodgings for as long a time as it suits his creditors to keep him there. (LLB, vol. 4, p. 170)

It seems that Raff may have languished in prison for at least two months. At the beginning of December 1853 Liszt wrote to Bülow: "According to my advice, R. left his temporary lodging as he had entered it, without paying a cent of his debt, as his creditor (on the instigation of his lawyer) had wished. If the thing had gone on for a year, I would not have advised him otherwise. . . . (LBLB, p. 50)

had earlier given to Conradi) so that he might rehearse them, reflect on them, and then, as his confidence in the orchestra grew, change them. As Liszt himself put it to Raff: "Anyone could perform this service for me."[9] Raff saw the situation differently. He formed the erroneous impression that Liszt had brought him to Weimar as an associate and that it was his pre-ordained task to colour the black-and-white sketches Liszt handed to him so that the world might then admire them in all their glory in the orchestra. At a rehearsal of Liszt's *Prometheus* in 1850, Raff turned to Bernhard Cossmann, who happened to be sitting next to him in the theatre, and whispered: "Listen to the instrumentation. It is by me."[10] To compound the problem, Joachim was the leader of the Weimar orchestra during the very period when Raff was most in evidence, and he later recalled to the latter's widow that he had seen Raff "produce full orchestral scores from piano sketches,"[11] a comment that requires a lot of qualification, and to his biographer Moser that "the E-flat-major Piano Concerto was orchestrated from beginning to end by Raff," a totally bogus assertion which is easy to refute.[12] Now Raff was an intelligent and sensitive man. As Liszt handed back his heavily corrected orchestrations, together with a request for a fair copy of the full score and a fresh set of band parts (Raff was a meticulous calligrapher, and Liszt often used him as a copyist), the mundane role that Liszt envisaged for him must have struck him with force. He was to create the negative models against which Liszt would react; he, like Conradi before him, was to become a mere springboard from which Liszt would propel himself towards his artistic goal. This realization, when it finally came, brought sorrow and disillusion into Raff's life. And since he was at Weimar when the full scores of the first six symphonic poems were published in 1856, he must have observed at once that they did not contain a note that Liszt himself had not written. Liszt, in fact, mastered the orchestra very quickly; after 1853 he dispensed with Raff's services altogether. From Raff's point of view it was as if four years of work had vanished into thin air, as if four years of residency in Weimar had left no trace of a visitation.

None of this would matter today were it not for the fact that Raff's insistence on the importance of his role came out in a series of letters written to a former lady-friend whom he had known before his arrival in Weimar, one Frau Kunigunde Heinrich, which made a stir when they were published at the turn of the century. Raff was justly proud of his special relationship with Liszt, and the charitable assumption to make after reading these letters is that he liked to indulge in some quiet boasting about it—a perfectly natural human weakness

9. RLR, p. 394 (February 1850).

10. MRL, p. 268.

11. MRL, p. 267.

12. MJ, p. 82. Raff merely copied the 1849 version of the concerto, the later revisions of 1856 being entirely by Liszt and made after Raff had left Weimar.

in a rising young composer. In fact, the arrogant tone exhibited by the twenty-eight-year-old Raff in the correspondence, unexpected from one who was employed as a humble amanuensis, is not out of keeping with the rest of his character. We have it on the authority of his daughter, Helene, that he was so confident of his ultimate artistic destiny, so convinced that he would one day be placed among Germany's greatest composers, that he failed to make any provision for his family in his will, believing that after his death they would live comfortably off his royalties.[13] But by then Raff's music had fallen into that oblivion from which it had neither the strength nor the originality to emerge.

> Last week [writes Raff to Frau Heinrich] I cleaned up Liszt's first concert-symphonique. . . . Then follows the instrumentation and fair copy of an overture, *Ce qu'on entend sur la montagne.* [14]

> Now I am busy with the re-modelling of the *Tasso* overture, out of which I intend to make him [Liszt] a symphony in two movements.[15]

> My labours for Liszt, it is true, are endless. But, as you know, I am not afraid of a heap of paper.[16]

> I was just occupied with the instrumentation of Liszt's *Héroïde funèbre,* and the broad, gloomy motives, to which I was yet to give the sombre instrumental tints which summon up thoughts of the last events in us all, penetrated my soul. . . . My melancholy had reached a high degree, and to this circumstance I owed some technical inspirations which drew from my friend exclamations of joy and surprise.[17]

---

13. RR, pp. 264–65. "He was too proud," observes Helene Raff, and cites in evidence the motto adorning the head of her father's Sixth Symphony: "Gelebt, Gestrebt, Gelitten, Gestritten, Gestorben, Umworben," which might be translated as "Lived, Struggled, Suffered, Fought, Died, and was Glorified," and which might be described not as pride but more accurately as arrogance.

14. RLR, p. 388 (December 1849). The jaunty phrase "cleaned up" *(bereinigen)* was often used by Raff to describe the process of making a fair copy of Liszt's scores—admittedly not always a simple task, as anyone who has examined a typical *Urschrift* of Liszt will appreciate. The mistranslation of Raff's verb *bereinigen* into "expurgated" (by Niecks among others; NPM, p. 485) conveys the false impression of creative intervention—a process that never occurred.

15. RLR, p. 397 (February 1850). This plan was never executed, and we have no evidence that Liszt even knew anything about it.

16. RLR, p. 389.

17. RLR, pp. 393–94. There is a fourteen-page holograph of *Héroïde funèbre* in the Bibliothèque Nationale (R. 28,596, ms. 158) which proves that Liszt had started to orchestrate this work long before he arrived in Weimar and long before Raff had even become his assistant. Many of the orchestral details with which we are so familiar today can be traced directly to Liszt's autograph.

I am determined to have a little influence—this I must have—on Liszt's latest works; and thanks to his intelligence, he has already perceived that this is as it should be—because four eyes can see better than two—and he accepts readily observations which he used to repugn.[18]

When Raff's damaging observations appeared in print they clamoured for an answer which was not at first forthcoming, for if taken at face-value they could only mean that all those orchestral works Liszt composed at Weimar between 1849 and 1856 (including the first six symphonic poems, the First Piano Concerto, the *Faust* and *Dante* symphonies—in short, those very works on whose originality of orchestration, texture, and form Liszt's claim to lead the New German School largely rested) were at least in part by Raff himself—an absurd and false conclusion. The main participants, Liszt and Raff, were by now dead. Moreover, all those musicians grouped around Liszt in Weimar during the 1850s—Cornelius, Bülow, Ritter—who might have been in a position to refute Raff's extravagant claims had they been published a mere ten years earlier, had likewise passed on. The truth lay in the Liszt Museum in Weimar, where, thanks largely to the collector's instinct in the composer, which rarely allowed him to discard a manuscript, however trivial, many of the original sketches were still preserved. When Peter Raabe was appointed director of the museum in 1910, he began the long process of sifting through this legacy and addressed himself with particular care to the question of Liszt's "collaborators." His summary of the problem is still one of the best available.[19] Through the conscientious comparison of all known manuscript sources, Raabe's inquiry led to the conclusion that the real business of scoring did not begin until after Conradi and Raff had finished their work, that every note in the final versions of Liszt's orchestral compositions emanated from Liszt's own pen. Liszt did not learn to orchestrate from Conradi or Raff but from daily contact with the Weimar orchestra itself. If Conradi and Raff never had come to Weimar, Liszt would still have emerged as an orchestrator of the front rank.

All of this leaves untouched the question of whether Liszt should have invited collaborators to Weimar at all. Friend and foe alike may regret the fact that he did, and they may even choose to censure him for it; but ultimately only Liszt himself could have known just how vital and necessary to him was the stimulation brought about by working with other composers. In any event, the legend that he dressed in borrowed plumage has today been demolished.

---

18. RLR, p. 390.

19. RLS, vol. 2, pp. 71–79. Raabe reproduces five facsimile sketches of the same passage from *Tasso* in the calligraphy of Conradi, Raff, and Liszt. His long involvement with the "Liszt-Raff question" is shown by the fact that it occupied most of his doctoral dissertation (REOL) submitted to the University of Jena in 1916, long sections of which turned up fifteen years later in his book on Liszt.

If further evidence be sought, it lies readily to hand. William Mason, who studied with Liszt in 1853, reports that his teacher was in the habit of inviting the best orchestral players to the Altenburg in order to grill them about their instruments and to discover whether certain passages were idiomatic. Liszt was at that time revising *Tasso,* and before putting the finishing touches to the score he decided to have a last-minute rehearsal. Everyone went down to the theatre, but since the main auditorium was unavailable, Liszt crammed the players into a room only just large enough to contain them. "Imagine the din in that room!" wrote Mason. "To everybody else the effect was a terrible noise, but to Liszt it was the clue to the polyphonic effect that he was seeking."[20] By itself the story is trivial, but it serves to remind us that Liszt went to endless pains to get his orchestrations right, and that he held himself responsible for the results.

                                    I I I

One person in Weimar saw with absolute clarity the host of troubles that Liszt was laying up for himself by his early reliance on Raff. Princess von Sayn-Wittgenstein at first looked on with concern while Liszt appeared to mortgage his artistic independence to someone she regarded as little better than a "hanger-on," and whom she had no hesitation in describing as "an unfeeling man who cultivates art only as a science."[21] Whether, with her penetrating intuition and sharp intelligence (qualities that even her worst enemies never denied her), she sniffed the makings of some future plot against Liszt or whether, on a more mundane level, she simply hated him to share the success of his works with someone whom she openly called "an apprentice," she wrote him a letter that is probably without parallel in their entire correspondence. We describe it so because in the two thousand or so unpublished letters from Carolyne to Liszt, there are hardly any which refer to his musical activities, and fewer still which criticize his artistic judgement.

> Why do you entrust Raff with the task of orchestrating the [Goethe] march? What painter would content himself with handing over his drawing and leaving the colouring of it to his apprentice? You will say that Raff is not an apprentice: but he is not you! Instrumentation demands individuality, and his is heavy-going. I think that you do not put enough emphasis on giving colour to musical thoughts. You content yourself with re-touching. It seems to me that this is not entirely enough, and if I compare it with a literary style: correction

---

20. MMML, pp. 121–22.
21. RLR, p. 390.

Liszt in Weimar, a photograph by Louis Frisch (1849).

is never as good as original writing. One can only invent by giving one's thought its first form and first method of expression—a predetermined outline chains the imagination; to a certain extent it sees the road marked out for it, but it discovers no new paths, no new turnings to round out the new forms of thought which one wishes to express.

I may be stupid, but it seems to me that this style, this dress, this clothing of the thought to which you rightly attach such importance, always suffers if it is first indicated or suggested by someone other than the genius who created the work. I at least, if I had this genius (though even here I would be impatient), would much sooner leave the filing, the varnishing, the pruning, and the polishing to others, rather than have my first model sketched out by them. It would be impossible for me to follow other lines than my own. In order to animate them with the sacred fire, these lines must have originated in my spirit and have been dictated by it.[22]

Every line of this letter rings true. So sharp is its tone, so direct its message, that we could almost believe that there had been a number of earlier discussions between the pair on the same topic, of which this letter was but a hard-hitting summary. The date of the missive suggests that its influence may have been decisive, since it was followed by the termination of Raff's services later that year.

---

22. RLS, vol. 2, pp. 78–79. The princess wrote this letter on July 25, 1853. It is certainly a response to the one Liszt wrote to her on July 22, 1853, in which he said: "Yesterday I finished my march for August 28 [Goethe's birthday]. It contains more than two hundred measures, in 4/4 time, and it seems quite successful. The conductor of the military band will take it for his group, and Raff will make another orchestration of it for the theatre orchestra. I wrote it only for the piano, merely cueing in a few entries of the other instruments." (LLB, vol. 4, p. 164)

Liebestraum

The smallest hair casts its shadows.

GOETHE[1]

I

In the autumn of 1853 the latest of Liszt's pupils, the beautiful Agnès Street-Klindworth, arrived in Weimar. Mystery and intrigue already surrounded this twenty-eight-year-old woman.[2] She was the daughter of Georg Klindworth, Metternich's master spy, who had the ear of Emperor Franz Joseph and Tsar Nicholas I and who in the 1840s controlled an espionage network which stretched across Europe. Not without musical gifts, Agnès, we are usually told, was attracted to Weimar because her cousin Karl Klindworth was already in residence there, and she found the prospect of higher piano studies with Liszt appealing. The facts point to a radically different conclusion, however. Until modern times the world knew nothing of the double life that Agnès led as her father's emissary, knew nothing of the child that she bore Ferdinand Lassalle, the left-wing revolutionary and friend of Karl Marx. Indeed, had Agnès been just another pupil in the long line of aspiring pianists to present themselves at Weimar (and one, moreover, whose modest talent paled when set beside that of a Bülow or a Tausig), it would hardly be necessary for us to do much more than acknowledge her presence and move on to more compelling topics. But there is evidence that Liszt soon fell under Agnès's spell, that he knew she was a political agent, and that within months of their first meeting he had fallen

---

1. GMR, no. 82, p. 35.
2. Agnès was born on October 19, 1825, in Bremen, according to her birth certificate (Bremen Standesamt, cert. no. 1090/1825).

in love with her. Their subsequent affair was one of the best-kept secrets of the Weimar years. Even as late as the 1870s and '80s only a small handful of people suspected the truth. The situation is not very different today. Agnès Street-Klindworth remains a shadowy figure for most Lisztians; yet she was central to his life in the mid-1850s, and for that reason we propose to bring her into the mainstream of Liszt scholarship.

The official account of Agnès stems from La Mara's book *Liszt und die Frauen* (1911). This version was written more than fifty years after the events it was meant to portray, and we know it to be defective. La Mara paints a touching picture of Agnès as a single mother, trailing two small boys in her wake. It was widely assumed that she was a widow. But we have no evidence that Agnès was a widow in 1853; in fact, we have evidence that she was not. She was briefly married to Captain Ernest Denis-Street, an Englishman who was brought up in Vienna as the adopted son of a South German envoy; and in 1856 they were described as divorced.[3] As for the four children to whom Agnès actually gave birth, all of them appeared later, and three of them were illegitimate. La Mara seems to have stumbled across Agnès almost by accident, in 1892, while preparing her ongoing edition of Liszt's *Briefe*. She tracked Agnès down in Paris and inquired whether she had in her possession any letters suitable for inclusion in the series. On July 25, 1892, Agnès (who was now sixty-six years old) sent a terse reply[4] in which she said that she had given all Liszt's letters to her son George for safe-keeping. That was the first indication the world had that one of the most significant collections of Liszt letters still existed; indeed, it was the first indication that Liszt and Agnès had even corresponded. Agnès added that her son would probably publish them himself one day but that the right moment had not yet presented itself. What that meant, as La Mara soon discovered, was that these letters told of a clandestine love-affair conducted between the years 1854–61, and they were so sensitive that they would expose Agnès to scandal (even one that was rooted in events now nearly forty years old), to say nothing of damaging the memory of Liszt. With dogged persistence La Mara pursued the matter further and finally persuaded George to allow her to make copies.

The discovery of these letters seems to have shaken La Mara and led her into unusual reticence. She published a heavily censored version of the text in 1894 under the anonymous title *Briefe an eine Freundin*[5]—"[the] name does not matter," she added archly. Posterity nonetheless must be grateful to La

---

3. From a secret police report prepared in Düsseldorf, dated October 24, 1856, and sent to the Prussian minister of the interior. Cited in HLLA.
4. WA, Kasten 416, no. 11.
5. "Letters to a Lady-Friend." LLB, vol. 3. The holographs may be inspected in the Hessische Landes-und Hochschulbibliothek in Darmstadt. See the Prologue, n. 23.

Mara for her prompt initiative; Agnès died in 1906[6] and took many secrets to the grave. It was now possible for La Mara to lift the veil of anonymity and disclose Agnès's identity, though she waited for five more years before doing so. As for the mutilated text, that was something she could not or would not restore.

From a glance at the bland surface of the censored letters, no one could suspect anything more than a warm friendship. Yet an inspection of the holographs indicates an ardent love-affair which began and was pursued for a time in Agnès's apartment on the Carlsplatz, a stone's throw from the Weimar theatre.[7] Not the least remarkable thing about the correspondence is that it commenced only after Agnès had left Weimar, in the spring of 1855. Had Agnès destroyed Liszt's letters to her (as he destroyed most of hers to him), or had he behaved still more prudently by not writing to her at all, the world would surely have remained in ignorance of their attachment to one another. But Liszt evidently missed Agnès after she had departed from Weimar, was determined to see her again, and arranged various trysts with her in Berlin, Cologne, and Düsseldorf whenever his work took him to those cities.

II

When Agnès arrived in Weimar she was pregnant. In December 1853 her mother, Brigitta Klindworth, accompanied her to Hamburg, where the two ladies took up temporary residence at the Waterloo Hotel, there to await the confinement. On January 21, 1854, Agnès gave birth to a boy and named him Ernst August Georg.[8] (Thereafter this son was always known as George Street, and it was rumoured that he was an offspring of Liszt. We shall have more to say about that presently.) After the birth Agnès was detained in Hamburg until at least mid-April 1854.[9] She was forced to pawn most of her possessions in order to procure a passport, issued to her at exorbitant expense by the independent Hanse police.[10] The child was not baptized until the following

---

6. Correct. Agnès died on December 25, 1906, aged eighty-one. Her death certificate, which wrongly describes her as "aged eighty-three," is filed under "Klindworth 1562," in the town hall of the ninth arrondissement of Paris.

7. In today's Weimar the Carlsplatz has been re-named the Goetheplatz.

8. This is shown by the baptismal certificate in the Catholic Church records of the Hamburg Staatsarchiv (no. 80/1854), where the child is described as "unehelich geboren"—that is, illegitimate. The father's name is not indicated.

9. According to the police register for foreign nationals, Agnès applied for an extension of her residency permit in Hamburg on April 6, 1854, and continued to live with her mother at the Waterloo Hotel (Hamburg Staatsarchiv, A1, vol. 22, p. 201).

10. HLLA.

September.[11] Given all these difficult circumstances, why did Agnès come to Weimar at all? Before we can answer this question it is necessary to know something of the complex career of her father, Georg Klindworth, from whom she inherited many qualities.

Georg Klindworth was a political exile from the 1848 upheavals, who had been variously a theatre director, a lawyer, and a statesman. He was well described as "one of the most influential secret diplomats of his time. The secret papers of every cabinet in Europe, from the Congress of Vienna to the time of Bismarck, were filled with his polished and detailed reports."[12] For a time he was a fugitive in London, where he edited a political newspaper, *Le Spectateur de Londres,* and gathered intelligence for the Habsburgs from the many exiles there. Disraeli knew him, and in August 1848 wrote: "The mysterious Klindworth showed me on Saturday a letter from Paris in cipher from the highest authority."[13] Later he became a member of the secret cabinet of the Stuttgart Court and was elevated to the rank of state minister. Klindworth's activities as an intelligence agent were so highly respected that he featured in at least one *roman à clef.* In the novel *Um Szepter und Kronen* ("For Sceptre and Crown") by Gregor Samarow,[14] the author does not even bother to disguise the identity of Klindworth, whose dialogue with Emperor Franz Joseph about the dangers of German expansionism in the 1860s was probably taken from real life. His daughter, Agnès, was often seen in his company; the pair travelled extensively through Europe, and both were known to counter-intelligence. In a secret report prepared by the director of police in Düsseldorf in August 1856, Agnès is described as "well versed in court etiquette, and familiar with the high nobility of all countries." A second report, submitted in October of that year, refers to her as a linguist, at home in Italian, French, Spanish, German, and Latin.[15]

The answer to our earlier question "Why did Agnès come to Weimar at all?" can now be attempted. Deeper reasons than mere piano study with Liszt had brought her to the city. Her arrival in the autumn of 1853 was well timed. Grand Duke Carl Friedrich had recently died and had been succeeded by Carl

---

11. The baptism took place on September 12, 1854, in Hamburg. Agnès and her mother were the only family members present, and they returned to Hamburg especially for the ceremony.

12. HLLA.

13. LBD, p. 55. The best account of Klindworth's clandestine operations (which brought him into contact with such diverse personalities as Bismarck, King Georg V of Hanover, Lord Palmerston, and Emperor Franz Joseph) comes from Alfred Stern's foundation-study *Georg Klindworth: Ein politischer Geheimagent des neunzehnten Jahrhunderts.* From this source we learn that Klindworth was involved in banking deals worth hundreds of thousands of guilders, which financed his intelligence activities.

14. A pseudonym for Oskar Meding, minister to Georg V of Hanover.

15. SGK, p. 450.

Alexander. The house of Sachsen-Weimar had treaties with Prussia, Hanover, and St. Petersburg. What would its policies be under the new ruler? Agnès was sent there by Georg Klindworth to find out. In brief, she was what she had never ceased to be: a part of her father's intelligence-gathering network.[16] The Altenburg made a perfect cover for such activity; it was a proven haven for fugitives on the run, such as Wagner, Ede Reményi, Gustav Steinacker, Hoffmann von Fallersleben, and Ede Szerdahelyi.[17] It even had its own "exile-in-residence" in the person of Princess Carolyne, who was always giving parties at which revolutionary personalities were present and politics was constantly in the air. Liszt himself knew everyone in the court circle, had friends in both the French and Russian legations in Weimar, and was on terms of intimacy with the royal family. It was shrewd of Georg Klindworth to recognize all this and tempt Liszt with the beautiful face of his only daughter.

I I I

Agnès returned to Weimar in the autumn of 1854 in the company of the infant George, and it was from this time that her relationship with Liszt intensified. She also got to know Princess Carolyne, was cordially received by her at the Altenburg, and afterwards corresponded with her. We cannot be sure when Agnès and Liszt became lovers. The very first surviving letter dates from early January 1855 and shows that Liszt was already in the habit of visiting Agnès in her apartment.[18] It was the departure of Agnès for Brussels on April 5, 1855, however, which threw Liszt into despair. He was haunted by her memory and by the thought that he might never see her again. After only six days came this

---

16. Liszt knew all along of the double life that Agnès led, and it may well have been one of the reasons why he became intrigued by her in the first place. In a letter he wrote to her shortly after she had left Weimar for good, he appealed specifically to the "element of improvization in your father's organization," which he hoped would be flexible enough to allow her to leave Brussels (where she now resided) for a few days in order to meet him in Düsseldorf a few weeks later (DA, censored fragment from a letter dated May 4, 1855). Did Agnès carry out covert missions for her father during her tenure in Weimar, over and above those of a mere eavesdropper? To judge from a letter written to Liszt by Anton Rubinstein on October 6, 1854, it certainly seems so. Rubinstein, who was at that moment in Leipzig, had observed Agnès there a day or two earlier disguised as a man. His chagrin at being taken in by the deception had turned to amusement when he learned that a local music-dealer, one Klemm, "had also mistaken Madame Denis-Street for *un monsieur*" (LBZL, vol. 1, p. 351). We gather from various accounts of Georg Klindworth's own covert activities that he was a master of disguise, a legacy of his years as a theatre director. In this, as in so much else, Agnès was her father's daughter.

17. Ede Szerdahelyi was a Hungarian pianist who had served a prison sentence for his part in the Hungarian uprising of 1848–49. Between January and July of 1851 he was a guest of Liszt in Weimar. For information on the fugitive priest Gustav Steinacker, see p. 80, n.17.

18. DA, suppressed letter, dated January 3, 1855.

cri de coeur: "What affliction and what dark shadows reach me now from those two windows at which I used to see you so often!"[19] And a few days later he added: "I still cannot pass by those windows without an ineffable thrill."[20] The dominant idea in the early run of letters is that of a tryst in Cologne or Düsseldorf. He uses the excuse of the thirty-third Lower Rhine Music Festival to get away from Weimar for a few days at the end of May, and he pleads with Agnès to join him. She agrees, and the plan is finalized in a letter Liszt writes on May 20, 1855, in which he instructs her:

> Leave on Saturday morning, the 26th of this month, by the first train to Cologne. Stay *in Cologne* at the Hotel Royal (Diezmann's). I will probably get there before you (as early as Friday evening). Let me know of your arrival at once, and should mine be delayed by a few hours, leave a note with the maître d'hôtel, telling him to let me have it as soon as I arrive. I will probably write to you again before I leave here [Weimar]. In any case, send someone to the Brussels post-office on *Friday,* both morning and evening. You yourself will no longer have time to write to me again here. All the same, I shall tell C[ornelius] to forward your letter to me in Cologne.
>
> It is better that we should meet each other again in *Cologne,* so as to avoid the bustle of the festival and make our arrangements a little more peacefully. So, then, it will be at the Hotel Royal (Diezmann's) that we will see one another again. I will leave here probably on Thursday the 24th, and will remain for a day in Brunswick, where I need to see Litolff.[21]

Liszt knew that a flood of international visitors was about to converge on Düsseldorf for the festival and that the chances of someone observing him with Agnès were great. He went on to ask her to exercise discretion.

> Madame Kalergi[s] has just written to me to ask me if I will be coming to Düsseldorf. She intends to go there and I will answer her tomorrow. If by chance you were to travel with her, do not tell her that I will be in Cologne.
>
> I am writing to you very hastily (so as not to miss today's post), surrounded by people who create a solitude for me. I still have a mass of things to see to before I set off.

---

19. DA, censored fragment from a letter dated April 11, 1855.
20. DA, censored fragment from a letter dated April 22, 1855.
21. DA, suppressed letter.

I will see you soon . . . till Saturday, May 26th.

They have just brought me your letter (no. 7). I embrace and bless you.

Tomorrow: concert for the king of Saxony at the castle. Wednesday: *Der fliegende Holländer* at the theatre, and afterwards
our club at the Hotel de Russie.

No more light at your windows, but I will bring our candlestick
to Cologne.[22]

The pair appear to have spent several days together, first in Cologne and then in Düsseldorf. After Agnès returned to Brussels, Liszt wrote to her on June 10, 1855: "Keep the memory of our *cabin*. Tell me it remains sweet and radiant in your heart."[23]

I V

Liszt was now in the middle of an affair that was potentially ruinous for him. He had already instructed Agnès to direct her letters through Peter Cornelius in order to avoid their interception by Carolyne at the Altenburg. (Later, when Cornelius was out of town, this delicate task was taken over by Ferdinand Schreiber, the secretary of the Neu-Weimar-Verein, and later still by Eduard Grosse, the Weimar trombonist and Liszt's trusted orchestral librarian.) He kept each letter just long enough to reply to it and then threw it on the fire. "This time it will cost me even more to burn your letter, but it must be done," he told her.[24] But what of his letters to her? She evidently agreed to destroy them in batches of a dozen at a time. Liszt was nervous about the arrangement, and he kept reminding her: "*Burn all my letters* before you leave, like a faithful slave.*"[25] As we now know, Agnès reneged on this promise. We should surely not begrudge her the deception. She appears to have regarded her literary legacy

---

22. Ibid. It seems that Agnès had kept a candlestick burning in the window of her apartment, perhaps as a signal to him that she was at home to receive him. After her departure from Weimar she had either forgotten it or had given it to Liszt, for whom it had come to symbolize the flame of their love. Incidentally, her letters to him appear to have contained codes and ciphers (a legacy, no doubt, of her work with Georg Klindworth). She got into the habit of using musical symbols to express extra-musical thoughts. Liszt was at first perplexed and asked her to explain. "Imagine how stupid I am not to guess the three *f*'s. In music it means *fortiss*[*iss*]*imo*, of course, but I suppose that you have some other idea in mind. Please explain it to me, for I am anxious to know." (DA, censored fragment from a letter dated April 22, 1855)
23. DA, censored fragment from a letter dated June 10, 1855.
24. Ibid.
25. DA, censored fragment from a letter dated July 28, 1855.

of 157 letters,[26] received across a period of thirty-one years, as a sacred remembrance of her union with Liszt. This young woman must have been at first flattered, then overwhelmed, by Liszt's attentions. She was not about to destroy the only evidence she had that she was loved by one of the major musical geniuses of the century. She numbered his letters and lovingly inscribed on them the dates on which they were received. In every other respect, however, she appears to have been a model of discretion. She knew from the start that Liszt would never openly acknowledge the relationship. But because she loved him, she neither threatened nor cajoled him, although she could easily have done both.

During the separation that followed their Cologne encounter, Liszt became concerned for Agnès's material welfare, and with good reason. It used to be thought that she left Weimar in order to teach piano in Brussels, but the evidence suggests that this source of livelihood occurred to her only as an afterthought, when her father's organization had begun to falter and she herself had fallen on hard times. Liszt knew that she was "surrounded by bad luck," and he told her that he suffered because he was unable to lighten her "heavy burden."[27] But even he was surprised when she informed him that she intended to set up as a piano teacher. "I never imagined that circumstances would oblige you to have a career as a piano teacher," he replied, "and even now I can hardly take it in."[28] We have remarked that Agnès's talent was modest. Nonetheless, she played Beethoven sonatas and certain works of Chopin in a manner that pleased him.[29] Agnès had also taken harmony lessons from Cornelius during her brief stay in Weimar,[30] possibly at Liszt's prompting, and this background would have been helpful to her as a teacher. Liszt urged her to contact Marie Pleyel, the *doyenne* of pianists in Brussels. "She could be useful to you, and recommend you to Fétis—and if you like, I will write you a few lines for the latter as well as for Mme Pleyel."[31] He also promised to ask Litolff to intercede with the Belgian aristocracy—a useful source of wealthy students. Despite Liszt's backing, Agnès made no mark on the profession she had entered by default, and in the Brussels census of 1856 she described herself simply as "a housewife."[32]

Other trysts followed the one in Cologne. On November 25, 1855, Liszt travelled to Berlin in order to conduct a programme of his own works (includ-

26. From this legacy we can infer that the total number of letters written by Liszt to Agnès actually exceeded two hundred, of which more than forty have gone astray. La Mara published 133 letters in LLB, vol. 3, and three more in LLF, pp. 224–35.
27. LLB, vol. 3, p. 44.
28. LLB, vol. 3, p. 47.
29. LLB, vol. 3, pp. 176–77.
30. LLB, vol. 3, p. 178.
31. LLB, vol. 3, p. 45.
32. Census of 1856, Register "T," folio 1008, city archives, Brussels.

ing the first performance of his Thirteenth Psalm),[33] and Agnès joined him there, at the Brandenburg Hotel. Liszt returned to Weimar on December 14 and remained there for Christmas. Early in the new year he went back to Berlin, only to find that Agnès had departed. Liszt unburdened himself:

Berlin, Hotel Brandenburg
Jan[uary] 8, [1856]

Here even the snow and ice are *burning* with memories for me, and since I no longer see you at the B[randenburg] H[otel]—I am in a hurry to leave, with a goad in my side and a burning coal in my breast! My thoughts and my desire swell up and boil over. Agnès, I cannot write to you, and I cannot manage to go on living like this![34]

The extent of Liszt's involvement with Agnès here stands revealed, as does his deception of Princess Carolyne. Soon he was referring to his longing for Agnès as "an incurable sickness" and to himself as "the patient."[35] But archival material that has recently come to light discloses a still more complex state of affairs. On July 18, 1855, Agnès had given birth to her second child, Charles. This explains why she left Weimar in April of that year: she was six months pregnant. According to the birth certificate, the father was her husband, Ernest Denis-Street, with whom, we surmise, she must have been briefly re-united in the autumn of 1854.[36]

V

We do not know under what conditions Agnès and her elusive husband went their separate ways; but at the beginning of 1856 Agnès began an extended love-affair with Ferdinand Lassalle—writer, left-wing philosopher, friend of Karl Marx, and founder of the revolutionary Workers' Party of Germany. In June 1856 she accompanied Lassalle to Bonn as his secretary, to help him do research in the university library for his magnum opus *Heraklitus*. While his

---

33. The concert took place on December 6, 1855.
34. La Mara censored this paragraph, together with a sensitive passage about the problems Liszt was having at that moment with Marie d'Agoult concerning the welfare of their two daughters, who were now living in Berlin with the von Bülow family. No better impression of the full extent of La Mara's editorial interventions can be formed than by comparing the text of this letter with the mutilated version that she finally allowed herself to publish in LLB, vol. 3, pp. 55–57.
35. DA, censored fragment from a letter dated January 18, 1856.
36. The birth certificate is preserved in the records of the parish of Saint-Josse-ten-Noode, in Brussels (no. 272, 1855). Ernest Denis-Street is described as "a soldier, born in Paris, department of the Seine, France," one of the few direct references to the husband of Agnès that we have so far encountered.

erstwhile mistress, travelling companion, and benefactress, Countess Sophie von Hatzfeldt, obligingly departed on a short tour of the nearby watering-spas, Lassalle and Agnès moved into the Hotel Kley in Bonn, where they spent several days together.[37] On December 19, 1856, Agnès bore Lassalle a daughter, named Fernande, who died in infancy.[38] Georg Klindworth bears some blame for this tragedy in Agnès's life. It was entirely at his bidding that she pursued Lassalle in order to extract from him the latest news about political exiles in London.[39] But the wily Lassalle did not give out such information for nothing, and Agnès may have received more than she bargained for when she conceived his child.

Liszt appears to have known little of this complex background when he arranged to meet Agnès again, this time in Aachen, in the summer of 1857. Once more he had good professional reasons for absenting himself from Weimar. During the third week of May he set out for Aachen in order to direct the

---

37. Lassalle and Agnès were evidently unaware that they were under surveillance by the secret police. It seems that Georg Klindworth was at that moment in the pay of the Russians and was attempting to ship arms into Russia as a preliminary to establishing modern armament factories there. The Crimean War, in fact, offered Klindworth some lucrative opportunities as a gun-runner (for an account of his "Russian connection," see ADGR, pp. 40–45). When Agnès turned up in the company of Lassalle in 1856, the pair were trailed by police on their peregrinations through the Rhineland. The episode was described in detail by police-director Wilhelm Stieber, whose comprehensive report (dated October 1856) makes passing mention of Agnès's private life:

> La Denis-Street professes to be a good Catholic. However, under Lassalle's influence she has dispensed with going to church, and with other devotional practices, which do not suit his rational ideas. . . . While the Countess Hatzfeldt took herself off to Wildbad for a cure, she [Agnès] went to the Hotel Kley in Bonn, where Lassalle spent several days with her (HLLA).

It is from Countess von Hatzfeldt (who had actively encouraged the flirtation between Lassalle and Agnès) that we have one of the rare character sketches of Agnès to come down to us. Shrewdly perceiving the way in which Agnès was insinuating herself into Lassalle's life, she warned her old friend:

> From all that I have seen and heard, I feel that we may have made a mistake about Agnès. She has a pleasant personality, and, I believe, a nice disposition; but she has little character and takes on the colour of whomsoever she happens to be with. She lacks a firm foundation, and, as I have noticed in certain small matters, she is not always sincere. . . . Do be careful. I have felt for some time that you are being exploited. . . ." (FPP, p. 89)

Lassalle evidently came to the same conclusion. At any rate, he did not marry Agnès but moved on almost at once to the conquest of two other mistresses: Frau von Dohm and Lina Duncker, the wife of his publisher.

38. Birth certificate no. 5354, city archieves, Brussels. Lassalle acknowledged paternity. On September 12, 1857, he wrote: "My little Fernande is dead. A few days ago I received a despairing letter from her mother. I am very sad about the child. I wanted to do wonders for her education." (MLB, vol. 4, p. 182) Apparently this baby girl died of teething convulsions ("Es starb am Zahnen"), and Agnès had written to Lassalle with a request for help with the burial expenses.

39. SLMI, p. 179.

Lower Rhine Festival. While he was there he arranged to take a water-cure to try to rid himself of the painful rash of boils which had appeared on both legs. In July he moved into the Hotel Nuellens, where he could sample the waters of the famed "Rose Baths," and he invited Agnès to join him.[40] He well understood the risks he was taking, for he wrote:

> . . . There is no apartment available at the moment. If I were a bit less in the limelight here I would gladly spare you the hotel negotiations (but I could not promise not to make some gaffe); and I would prefer you, for these few days, to make your own arrangements as completely as you see fit. Send me a note to the Rose Baths when you get here (unless you alert me in advance as to the date of your arrival), and come in your own good time, which will always be mine![41]

At the time of this encounter Agnès and Ernest Denis-Street were divorced.[42] It was not until January of the following year, 1858, that Liszt picked up rumours that Agnès was planning to marry Lassalle, and he seems to have taken it philosophically. He thought that it might even be feasible for them to meet more frequently (and possibly more openly) if she were married. As he put it:

> At the risk of appearing very strange to you, I will tell you that I would welcome it if it meant that I would see you more often! Do not misunderstand this remark and do not talk to me about it. If ever this change in your life were to happen, I would not misunderstand you, believe me, and would certainly not cause you either embarrassment or bother of any kind.[43]

---

40. Liszt's name figured in the weekly bulletin *Aachener Kur- und Bade-Liste* for May 24 and 31 and June 4, 1857, along with those of hundreds of fellow sufferers come to enjoy the spa's healing springs. Each summer the halt, the lame, and the blind converged on Aachen in vast numbers in an attempt to purge away whatever it was that ailed them. Liszt's boils, which at one time covered the lower part of his body, had plagued him for the better part of a year.

41. DA, suppressed letter, dated "Saturday morning, July 25." To this La Mara has added in pencil the year "1861," which is incorrect. July 25 fell on a Saturday not in 1861 but in 1857.

42. This was the belief of the Düsseldorf police, who, in one of their aforementioned reports (October 24, 1856), observed: "Mme Denis-Street is divorced from her husband. . . . His nationality is extremely difficult to classify. His father was English, his mother French, and he himself was supposed to be the adopted son of a South German envoy."

43. DA, censored fragment from a letter dated June 26, 1858.

V I

During the years of his involvement with Agnès, Liszt had grown used to exercising caution whenever they appeared in public places together, because (as he once told her) of a propensity he shared with Metternich—that of making a *Spektakel* of himself without ever knowing that he did so. Even so, and despite his best efforts to conceal it, Carolyne discovered the truth. That she suffered in consequence is undeniable. It seems that in July 1858 one or two of Agnès's letters had been intercepted. "Do not write to me *at all,*" Liszt urged. "As a result of I do not know what inquisitiveness your letters would risk not reaching me before they had passed through other hands."[44] He also told her: "Do not write at all to the princess for the moment." It was not until the following Easter, 1859, that he was able to explain more fully.

> Do not worry about the silence that I have had to keep in recent months and whose reason I will tell you. As for the Pr[incess], various *rumours* had made her a little upset, especially certain light-hearted remarks which were charged with meaning and which had been spread in Berlin by someone I like well enough personally (although I have only met him casually at my daughter's) and who was extremely close to Mme de Hatz[feldt], at whose home you saw him a lot.[45]

Liszt could only have been thinking of Lassalle. We are left to infer that Agnès, assuming her marriage to Lassalle to be imminent, had told him about her liaison with Liszt, and that Lassalle in turn had spread gossip among his friends in Berlin which had reached the ears of Princess Carolyne. Subsequently there was a break of several months in the correspondence. Eventually Liszt instructed Agnès to resume writing to him "care of Herr Gross[e], Hofmusikus, Schlossgasse 99, Weimar." Whatever passed between Liszt and Carolyne on the

---

44. DA, suppressed letter, dated July 16, 1858. This was not the first exposure of their "secret" correspondence. Three years earlier, in July 1855, Liszt had received an anonymous note in an envelope addressed to Cornelius. "Good old Cornelius was extremely surprised," wrote Liszt to Agnès, "when he received [. . .] the enclosed scrap of paper, which I opened indiscreetly before I sent it to you." (DA, censored fragment from a letter dated July 15, 1855) A week later Liszt wrote to her again: "This morning, the second edition of the note with the mysterious initials B.A. reached me. This time it was addressed to me, and I am sending it to you as proof of my veracity, urging you, however, to request the person in question not to return to the attack, because that could have fairly serious consequences. You can guess why." (DA, censored fragment from a letter dated July 21, 1855)
45. DA, censored fragment from a letter dated simply "Easter Sunday," which fell on April 24 in 1859.

topic of his infidelity remained locked in their hearts, and they took it with them to the grave. Carolyne knew that Liszt would never abandon her; they had come too far and suffered too much for that. And so she forgave him, for she saw that Agnès was a temporary aberration.

Thereafter Agnès and Liszt met but fleetingly. In the early summer of 1861 he called on her at her house in Brussels. He had already informed her that the princess had secured an annulment of her marriage to Nicholas Wittgenstein,[46] and she knew that he was shortly to set out for Italy to join Carolyne at the altar. By October 1861 Liszt had taken up residence in Rome, and although he and Agnès continued to meet from time to time, their correspondence suggests that they succeeded in transforming their romance into a cordial and lasting friendship—the sort of metamorphosis that is all too rare in human affairs.

VII

One question remains. Why did Liszt allow himself to become involved with Agnès at all? When she first crossed his path, he was vulnerable. After four years' tug-of-war with the Wittgensteins his marriage to Princess Carolyne seemed as distant as ever. Moreover, he was at the end of his tether with the Weimar Court and stood on the brink of resignation.[47] By the autumn of 1853, as we know, his work with the Weimar theatre was almost at a standstill, and he had come to regard his years at Weimar with despondency. Into this gloom Agnès had brought a little light. Not only was she a charming and beautiful companion, but she lent an intelligent ear to his ideas and was receptive to his music. Indeed, in the published portions of his letters to Agnès he disclosed a wider range of information about his professional activities—including his works-in-progress—than to any other single correspondent except Princess Carolyne. Agnès had one other quality, too, which we have already touched on: her whole life long she was surrounded by intrigue, which was for her a natural part of existence. A fatal source of attraction must have been that she was unobtainable as a wife. When Liszt first met her, she was estranged from Captain Denis-Street. Later, after her divorce, he made a revealing disclosure when he told her that he would welcome her marriage to Lassalle. He seems to have had much more in mind than the social convention that made it possible for married women to mingle more freely in society than their unmarried counterparts. We recall that both Marie d'Agoult and Carolyne were estranged from their husbands when Liszt first met them. It is difficult to resist the

---

46. DA, censored fragment from a letter dated November 8, 1860.
47. See Liszt's letter to Carl Alexander dated February 16, 1853, quoted on pp. 163–64.

conclusion that with all three women Liszt created a *Liebestraum,* an ineffable longing for the female ideal, placed ever and always just beyond his reach. Agnès, for her part, knew that there could never be any question of an open relationship with him, and he never misled her about his prior responsibilities towards Carolyne. Her acceptance of these conditions suggests that she, too, may have seen in Liszt a diversion. Her subsequent career shows her to have been an experienced woman of the world, well able to cope with the exigencies of life.

And how does Liszt emerge from these disclosures? One of the thorniest problems facing the biographer is to account for the love Liszt undoubtedly felt for both Agnès and Carolyne simultaneously. Society still deems it to be a dishonourable thing for a man to be enamoured of two women at the same time. Yet there is nothing in human nature to prevent it from happening, and Liszt is by no means the only figure in musical history to find himself in such a predicament. To condemn or to condone is not the question. Princess Carolyne (who understood him better than anyone else) did neither, thus making it difficult for the modern observer to arrogate such powers unto himself. The affair probably brought Liszt as much pain as pleasure. He was not the kind of man who liked human relationships to rest on a foundation of deceit, and he must have suffered accordingly. We stand by our earlier assertion that Liszt was no Don Juan.[48] That he loved female companionship, was susceptible to female charm, and respected female intuition goes without saying. These are the very attributes which are so notably lacking in the true Don Juan, who sees in the female form only his sexual prey, there to be dominated and destroyed by him. Liszt never destroyed anyone, least of all the women who were admitted to the inner circle of his friends and intimates.

VIII

The story of Agnès Street-Klindworth is not quite finished. On August 2, 1862, she gave birth to her fourth child, an illegitimate son named Henri, whose birth certificate is preserved in the Brussels city archives.[49] Since nothing further is known about this offspring, we surmise that he was either brought up by foster parents or, like his sister Fernande, died in infancy. We gather from the birth certificate that Agnès had returned to her domicile in Brussels, that she was now a property-owner, and that she lived at no. 5, rue Belliard. Further light is thrown on Agnès by the Brussels census records, which show that she continued to live in the city with her ageing father, Georg (her mother had died there

---

48. Volume One, pp. 389–91.
49. Birth certificate no. 3332, August 1862.

in 1864), until February 1868, when the family—Georg, Agnès, and her sons George and Charles—moved to Paris and took up residence at no. 66, boulevard Haussmann. Now in her mid-forties, Agnès became a lady-in-waiting to the exiled Queen Cristina of Spain, an appointment that probably owed something to the older Klindworth's royal connections. She also concentrated on the education of her boys. George Street was highly musical, took violin lessons from Léonard, and became a well-known composer of operettas. For a time he was a disciple of Bizet, and he collaborated with André Messager on the score of the ballet *Scaramouche*.[50] Later he became a music critic for the newspapers *L'Eclair* and *Le Matin*. He died in Paris on February 6, 1908, aged fifty-four. His younger brother Charles was given a scientific training. As a nineteen-year-old student, he enrolled in the Ecole Centrale des Arts et Manufactures in 1874 and graduated in 1877 with a diploma in metallurgy. He rose to become a manager of the Carbone company and was awarded the Legion of Honour in 1900 for inventions in industrial engineering. He died at Enghien-les-Bains in 1922.

Agnès does not appear to have hidden her relationship with Liszt from her sons. Indeed, by entrusting her legacy of Liszt letters to George for safe-keeping she may quite unwittingly have fuelled some gossip, for George was a bar-fly, and alcohol sometimes loosened his tongue. It became common talk in Paris in the 1880s and '90s that George was the natural son of Liszt—a rumour that persisted until modern times.[51] But the baptismal records prove that he was conceived before Agnès met Liszt. Like all such tales, this one will not bear scrutiny, but it added mystery and romance to an otherwise modest career, and it did Liszt no harm. Similarly, the birthdates of Charles and Henri offer little hope to those who would add to the long roll-call of illegitimate children that Liszt is supposed to have fathered.[52]

Agnès lived to see published all three volumes of Lina Ramann's official life of Liszt (1881–94). Not once does her name appear in the parade of personalities which troops through its pages and forms the backdrop to his career. What were her feelings? Perhaps hurt pride suggested that she publish Liszt's letters under George's editorship; but that was pre-empted by the unexpected arrival on the scene of La Mara in 1892, with consequences that have already been related.

---

50. *Scaramouche* received its première in 1891. Another work of George Street that attracted attention was his operetta *Mignonette* (1896), a parody of Ambroise Thomas's *Mignon*. Apart from Messager, George Street's circle included Maurice Lefèvre and Raoul Pugno. In 1882 the four men got into the habit of meeting every afternoon in George's apartment to play through the score of Bizet's *Carmen*, which they regarded, in their youthful enthusiasm, as the opera of the century. It was due in part to the advocacy of Street and Messager that *Carmen* was taken up by the Paris Opéra as a standard repertory work.
51. See, for example, Michel Augé-Laribé's *André Messager: Musicien de théâtre* (1951), p. 82; and Florian Bruyas's *Histoire de l'opérette en France (1855–1965)* (1974), p. 285.
52. See Volume One, pp. 23–27, where this diverting topic is treated at greater length.

What Agnès thought of La Mara's mutilated edition remains unknown, but she approved of the mantle of anonymity with which La Mara temporarily cloaked her.[53] When Agnès went to the grave in 1906, aged eighty-one, she probably thought that posterity had been given as much of her story as it wanted to hear. She could not possibly have guessed that the call would one day go out for a fresh examination of her case.

---

53. La Mara tells us that Agnès herself wanted her name to remain secret (LLF, p. 222) but that by 1911 La Mara no longer felt bound by this undertaking because her identity had meanwhile been disclosed in Glasenapp's biography of Wagner (Leipzig, 1899, vol. 3, p. 252).

BOOK THREE

The Years of Maturity
1853 · 1857

Growing Achievements, 1853–1855

The eagle flies to the sun.

I

Liszt's voluntary withdrawal from the Weimar theatre for much of the 1853–54 season released a great deal of his energy for other purposes. It is no coincidence that he now brought to completion four of his symphonic poems—*Festklänge, Orpheus, Les Préludes,* and *Tasso*—and composed his Sonata in B minor as well. His career as a guest conductor in important centres outside Weimar also received a new impetus at this time and led him eventually to such cities as Karlsruhe, Pest, Vienna, Berlin, and Aachen.[2] But it was his pupils and disciples in Weimar who were among the immediate beneficiaries. Their Sunday matinées at the Altenburg took on greater significance because of Liszt's participation in them. He liked nothing better than to join the various members of the Weimar String Quartet (Laub, Stör, Walbrül, and Cossmann) in performances of the classical chamber-music repertory. In fact, these concerts soon outgrew the Altenburg, so Liszt had them moved into the main hall of the Rathaus, where they became a regular feature of the musical life of the city. It was there, in the autumn of 1853, that Klindworth, Pruckner, and William Mason performed Bach's Triple Concerto in D minor. Liszt himself coached the three young players, and Mason recalled the care Liszt took to secure a correct interpretation of the ornaments.[3] Such was the success of the concerto, which

---

1. BWL, vol. 2, p. 76; KWL, vol. 2, p. 71.
2. See the chapter "Liszt the Conductor," pp. 270–99.
3. MMML, pp. 107 and 229–30.

was barely known at the time, that the "mighty handful" was asked to repeat it at an evening concert in the grand ducal palace shortly afterwards.

The circle of Liszt's followers was also enlarged. Although Klindworth left for London not long after the performance of the Bach concerto, and Bülow had already moved to Berlin, Pruckner, Cornelius, Mason, and Raff remained in residence, and their numbers were swollen by the arrival of Richard Pohl, Hans von Bronsart, Alexander Winterberger, and Martha von Sabinin (the daughter of the Russian provost in Weimar). The powerful sense of camaraderie that grew up within this talented group has already been remarked, and it prompted Liszt to come forward with one of his more colourful notions. Towards the end of 1853 he formed the so-called "Society of Murls," in which Liszt was known as "Padischa" ("king" or "president") while his adherents were the "Murls." The name "Murl" was an improbable combination of two German nouns, "Mohr" ("Moor") and "Kerl" ("fellow"), whose inner meaning emerges from the familiar German saying "Einen Mohren kann man nicht weisswaschen" ("You can't wash a blackamoor white")—to attempt to do so is to attempt the impossible. So a "Murl" was one whom the Philistines could never whitewash to their colorless ways. By dubbing his followers with this affectionate epithet, Liszt was telling them that the road ahead was not easy, that the new in music had always provoked opposition, and that the artistic Camelot he envisaged for Weimar would only be possible provided that they all remained true to their "Murlship." (Such evangelism was not new, of course. Robert Schumann, too, had formed his *Davidsbund* some twenty years earlier, with a view to fighting the Philistines. But whereas Schumann's society had existed only in his imagination and had had no life beyond the columns of the *Neue Zeitschrift,* [4] Liszt's Society of Murls included some of the more prominent musical personalities of the day.) Liszt's pupils often addressed one another as "lieber Murl"[5] as an expression of the kinship they felt for one another. "Murlship," in its broadest sense, then, meant adherence to the ideals of the New Weimar School. Liszt himself left several indications of what he understood the term to mean. After observing the powerful streak of conservatism running through the personality and works of Anton Rubinstein, he remarked, "*Murlship* alone is *wanting* in him still"[6]—and this despite the personal regard in which Liszt held the younger man. And on the manuscript of Liszt's B-minor Sonata, arguably the most radical composition he had so far written for the piano, he wrote the words "Für die Murlbibliothek"— "For the Murls' library."[7]

---

4. As Schumann himself put it, just two years before his death: "In order to express contrasting points of view about art, it seemed not unfitting to invent antithetical artistic characters, of which 'Florestan' and 'Eusebius' were the most important, with 'Master Raro' as intermediary." (GSK, Preface)
5. See, for example, RR, p. 130, and BB, vol. 3, p. 99.
6. LLB, vol. 1, pp. 160–61.
7. MMML, p. 159.

I I

No account of the Altenburg matinées of 1853 would be complete without passing mention of the most memorable of them all. It was in June 1853 that the twenty-year-old Brahms arrived in Weimar bearing a letter of introduction from Joachim. Brahms, who was at that time virtually unknown, was in the middle of a concert tour with the violinist Reményi (now an exile from the Hungarian revolution, and himself not yet acquainted with his great compatriot), and the two young men were cordially invited to attend a musical session at the Altenburg the following morning. A small group of Liszt's friends and pupils were assembled to greet them, including Klindworth, Pruckner, Raff, and William Mason—who left an eye-witness account of the occasion.[8] Mason recalls seeing a pile of Brahms's unpublished compositions on the table as he walked into the room, including the manuscript of the Scherzo in E-flat minor, op. 4, which, he says, was practically illegible. Liszt himself finally came in, and after engaging in some good-humoured banter, he turned to Brahms and said: "We are interested in your compositions whenever you are ready and feel inclined to play them." At that, Brahms became very nervous, and neither Liszt nor Reményi could persuade him to go to the keyboard. Seeing that further persuasion was useless, Liszt went over to the table, picked up the nearly illegible scherzo, placed it on the music desk, and said: "Well, I shall have to play." Liszt's remarkable powers of sight-reading had been witnessed many times by the Weimar circle, but both Raff and Mason had a lurking dread that this time he was inviting disaster by attempting to read such an untidy manuscript. Not only did he perform the scherzo in a masterly fashion, however, but he also kept up a running commentary on the music—much to Brahms's amazement and delight. After further conversation someone asked Liszt to play his own B-minor Sonata, a work he had recently composed.[9] Liszt at once returned to the piano and began to play. It was well known within the Weimar circle that Liszt was especially fond of this work, and he used to charge his interpretation of it with great feeling. Having reached a particularly expressive moment, Liszt cast a glance at his listeners, only to observe Brahms dozing in his chair. Liszt played the sonata to the end, got up, and silently left the room. No playwright could have improved upon this scene, which symbolized to perfection the indifference that Brahms experienced whenever he was in the presence of Liszt's music.[10] (All his life Brahms was to remain metaphorically

---

8. MMML, pp. 127–32.
9. The holograph of the first version of the sonata bears the date February 2, 1853.
10. Since several biographers of Brahms (influenced by Max Kalbeck in his massive four-volume life of the composer) have cast doubt on this story, it might be well to try to sort out fact from fiction.

asleep to Liszt.) Brahms and Reményi spent nearly three weeks in Weimar, as house-guests in the Altenburg, occupying the rooms that had formerly been used by Bülow.[11] After that they parted, because Reményi (who actually abandoned Brahms in Weimar) did not wish to be associated with the hostility that Brahms had already begun to harbour against Liszt and his circle, which he felt was incompatible with the generosity they had enjoyed while staying under Liszt's roof.[12]

III

On June 28, 1853, while Brahms was still languishing at the Altenburg, Liszt journeyed to Karlsruhe to hold some preliminary talks about the music festival he had been invited to direct there in the autumn. From Karlsruhe he proceeded directly to Zürich, where he was re-united with Wagner on July 2. The two composers had not met for four years, and Wagner has described the emotion he felt on seeing his friend and benefactor once more. Liszt was now the only musician in Germany who performed Wagner's works. Moreover, he never ceased trying to persuade the grand duke of Weimar to intercede in the question of Wagner's pardon. A few weeks before the Zürich reunion, in fact, Liszt had

---

Kalbeck's main contention was that Liszt and Brahms could not possibly have parted on bad terms, since after he left Weimar and arrived in Düsseldorf Brahms showed his friend Louise Japha a cigar-box that Liszt had given him, erroneously inscribed with the name "Brams" (KJB, vol. 1, p. 86). Liszt's habit of giving small keepsakes to new acquaintances, however, did not depend on whether or not they liked his music. Kalbeck further surmised that Brahms had not slept the night of his arrival in Weimar, and that he may have fallen asleep the following morning through sheer physical exhaustion. This statement is basically unprovable: Brahms never attempted to defend himself against the charge of "dozing while bored," and there was no suggestion that he slept while Liszt was playing his (Brahms's) scherzo! Because Mason wanted to be absolutely sure that his account of the incident was accurate (apparently Brahms was hidden from his view while Liszt played, although he knew that something untoward had taken place), he wrote to Karl Klindworth, who by then was the only other living witness, and asked him to corroborate the description given above. Klindworth replied that Mason's recollection was basically correct, but it becomes clear from a careful reading of Mason that the ultimate source of the story was Reményi, who sat next to Brahms throughout Liszt's performance. Karl Geiringer and others have called Reményi an "absolutely unreliable" witness and have dismissed the story on that account. But Mason accepted it, and no one disputes that something occurred to upset Liszt. Reményi's account, incidentally, may be found in RKU, pp. 79–95. It is based on an interview he gave to the *New York Herald* in January 1879, the very first time that this famous story found its way into print. The violinist provides some interesting details about his tour with Brahms, long since forgotten, and the first meetings with Joachim, Liszt, and, later, Schumann.

In one important respect Kalbeck's summary of the affair is correct. Brahms and Reményi stayed in Weimar for nearly three weeks and did not, as both Mason and Klindworth have it, "leave without explanation" the following day.

11. JMBJ, vol. 1, p. 63.

12. See the letter that Brahms wrote to Joachim from Weimar on June 29, 1853, in which he remarked that his friend Reményi had left Weimar without him (JMBJ, vol. 1, p. 65).

been introduced to the king and queen of Saxony at a small concert given in the Goethe Gallery of the royal castle at Weimar, and he had broken all the rules of etiquette by raising the topic of Wagner's exile with the king himself. "Alas," Liszt wrote, "there is little hope of obtaining a pardon soon."[13] In fact, the authorities seemed more determined than ever to prevent Wagner from re-entering Germany. The old *Steckbrief* of 1849 had just been reprinted in the *Freimüthige Sachsen-Zeitung,* with a reminder to the police that should Wagner attempt to cross the border, he was to be apprehended and delivered at once to Dresden. Liszt himself had sent a copy of the article to Wagner in order to alert him to the danger.[14]

Although Liszt's sojourn in Zürich lasted a mere three or four days, there was an abundance of conversation and of music-making. Wagner tells us that Liszt played him several of his "celebrated pianoforte pieces" and then treated Wagner to performances of some of the newly composed symphonic poems. This was the very first occasion on which Wagner had heard any of Liszt's orchestral music, and he became so enthusiastic that he later recorded his impressions in the form of his famous letter to Marie von Sayn-Wittgenstein, which was subsequently published.[15] The visit was a tonic to Wagner, who after four years of exile constantly yearned for the sort of artistic stimulation that only Liszt could give him, and he even felt the urge to compose again after a long lapse of time. Liszt described the experience as their "Valhalla days"[16] and added: "I praise God for having created such a man." Wagner, for his part, was filled with gloom after Liszt's departure. He wrote: "Silently I returned home; silence reigned everywhere. Thus we celebrated your leave-taking, you dear man; all the splendour had departed! Oh, come back soon, and stay with us for a long time!"[17] In fact, they had already arranged to meet again after the Karlsruhe festival, in a few weeks' time.

IV

That festival occupied much of Liszt's attention during the summer of 1853. By the time he got back to the Altenburg, in mid-July, Princess Carolyne and Marie had already departed for the watering-spa of Carlsbad, where they spent most of July and August taking the cure. Liszt's busy itinerary that summer

---

13. LBLB, p. 24.
14. BWL, vol. 1, p. 251.
15. The letter was sent to Princess Marie on February 15, 1857, from Zürich, and was published in the *Neue Zeitschrift für Musik* on April 10 of that year under the title "Liszts symphonische Dichtung-en." See also WGSD, vol. 5, pp. 182ff.
16. LLB, vol. 1, p. 141.
17. BWL, vol. 1, p. 256; KWL, vol. 1, pp. 248–49.

included trips to Frankfurt, Wiesbaden, and Teplitz as well as to Darmstadt and
Mannheim, two cities that had promised to muster additional support for the
Karlsruhe festival. Between times he also travelled to Carlsbad to visit the two
"patients" and check on the progress of their regimen. Both Carolyne and Marie
were in high spirits, delighted to be away from Weimar,[18] and were planning
occasional trips into the environs of one of the most picturesque regions of
Bohemia. It was on one of their forays into nearby Dresden that an amusing
incident took place. As they passed Meser's music shop, Carolyne glanced
through the window at the sheet-music displayed there and was surprised
to see nothing by Liszt. She went in, marched up to the shop-keeper, and
demanded:

> "How is it, sir, that you do not have anything by Liszt there?"
> According to Magne, his face was a picture. Wavering between
> shame and offendedness, seeing himself berated thus, he did not know
> whether to excuse himself or be annoyed. But I looked so resolute,
> asking him "What do you have of his in the shop?," that he chose
> the former and brought me a big pile of your things, which con-
> tained more or less all the new publications—the Etudes and the
> Konzertsolo were not there. I asked him what sold the best, and he
> showed me the Rhapsodies, the Soirées de Vienne, and the Harmonies.
> . . . I found something of yours which I did not know, an opus 3,
> [Impromptu brilliant, Raabe 29] on themes from Rossini and from
> Spontini's Olympie, which I bought. Magne claims that he must have
> racked his brains trying to guess which hurricane had passed through
> his place.[19]

Liszt himself must have been briefly in Dresden, for it was there, in September
1853, that he renewed his acquaintance with a twenty-seven-year-old music
critic named Richard Pohl and invited him to Karlsruhe to cover the festival.[20]
Liszt also offered Pohl's wife, the harp virtuoso Jeanne Eyth, a place in the
festival orchestra. (The following year, when she became a permanent member
of the Weimar orchestra, Pohl settled there and became one of Liszt's staunchest
supporters.)
    When Liszt finally arrived in Karlsruhe, during the last week of September,

---

18. Between the autumn of 1852 and the summer of 1854, we recall, Marie and her governess, Miss
Anderson, were quartered in the royal castle, and Princess Carolyne saw correspondingly less of her
daughter as long as they remained in Weimar.
19. WA, Kasten 34, no. 2. Letter dated Dresden, July 6, 1853.
20. Pohl's brochure Das Karlsruher Musikfest, published under the pseudonym "Hoplit," quickly
became a classic (HKM). Pohl tells us that he was first introduced to Liszt in 1852 by Brendel, in
whose Leipzig home the members of Liszt's group often assembled (PA, p. 17).

it was at the head of a contingent of Murls which included Cornelius, Joachim, Bülow, and Pruckner. The old city had been decked out with bunting and was in a festive mood. The music festival itself was combined with a *Volksfest* displaying an abundance of attractions for the visitors. The programme of events included a fireworks display, a torchlight procession, and a spectacular release of air-balloons which filled the sky with colour. Inside the castle square and the Marktplatz, pavilions and booths had been set up to contain the various exhibitions, and the town band played for the crowds of people who thronged the enclosures. The residents of Karlsruhe received free admission to all the displays, which were consequently immensely popular. For the wealthy out-of-towners, come to take the spa's waters, a series of balls and dinners was arranged throughout the three-day festival. Liszt conducted two concerts in Karlsruhe, on October 3 and October 5. The main work of the opening concert was Beethoven's "Choral" Symphony. According to Richard Pohl, the massed orchestras and choirs gathered on the stage of the Karlsruhe theatre behind closed curtains. It created a grand spectacle when the house lights were lowered and the curtains were raised to reveal all the performers in position, with Liszt already on the podium, baton at the ready.[21] Joachim was a soloist in this concert and delivered a brilliant account of his "Hungarian" Concerto; in the second concert, Bülow played Liszt's Fantasy on Motifs from Beethoven's *Ruins of Athens*. Wagner was given a prominent place in these celebrations. At Liszt's insistence the *Tannhäuser* Overture opened the festival and some excerpts from *Lohengrin* closed it. Such was the impression created by the *Tannhäuser* that Liszt decided to repeat it at the end of the closing concert "by public demand." As far as the general public was concerned, then, these concerts were an unmitigated success. The brouhaha created by the critics, however, was another matter. They accused Liszt of lacking baton technique, which wrung from him his "manifesto" on the art of conducting—a *pièce de résistance* which deserves to be better known.[22]

v

From Karlsruhe Liszt journeyed to Basel for his pre-arranged meeting with Wagner. The city was chosen because it was close to the Swiss border with the duchy of Baden and did not put Wagner at risk. Wagner tells us that he arrived at the rendezvous first. He was sitting alone in the dining-room of the Hotel zu den drei Königen when he suddenly heard the trumpet fanfare from *Lohen-*

---

21. HKM, p. 24. The Karlsruhe orchestra was combined with the ones from Mannheim and Darmstadt for the festival. Liszt faced a sea of 260 instrumentalists and singers in the "Choral" Symphony (see HKM, pp. 17–19, for a breakdown of the forces involved).
22. It is reproduced, in part, on pp. 281–82.

grin, which announces the king's arrival, sung by a group of male voices in the adjoining vestibule. It was Liszt and the Murls—Cornelius, Pruckner, Bülow, Joachim, and Pohl, whom he had brought from Karlsruhe so that they might pay their respects in person to the exiled master. A night of merrymaking followed. The next day Princess Carolyne and Marie descended on them from Carlsbad. This was only the second time that Wagner had met Carolyne, and he enthused about the sharpness of her intellect. "It was impossible," he wrote, "for anyone coming into contact with Princess Carolyne not to be fascinated by her bright manner and the charming way in which she entered into all our little plans."[23] (Wagner later got to know her better. He once told the voluble Carolyne that four weeks of uninterrupted companionship with her would have been the death of him.)[24] By contrast, Wagner found Princess Marie quiet and unusually pensive. "She had a rather dreamy look on her young face," Wagner recalled, "and was at the stage where 'childhood and womanhood meet.'" This allowed him to pay her the compliment of calling her "the Child," a nickname that was taken up in his correspondence with Liszt.[25] Surrounded by such convivial companions, Wagner needed little encouragement to talk about himself and his work, and he began a series of readings from his newly completed poem *Der Ring des Nibelungen.* These readings, delivered by Wagner in his most compelling and incisive tone of voice, fired Liszt with enthusiasm for the great saga, and he resolved to mount *Der Ring* at Weimar—an ambitious idea that was to be quashed by the grand duke.[26] After a few days the

---

23. WML, p. 605.

24. WML, p. 652.

25. Princess Marie's own recollections of the Karlsruhe episode, and of this meeting with Wagner, may be found in HERW, pp. 12–13.

26. Both Liszt and the princess had already read the *Nibelungen* poem in Weimar earlier that year. Wagner had had fifty copies printed at his own expense for private circulation, and Liszt had been one of the first recipients. Liszt wrote to Wagner on February 20, 1853: "The princess read your *Ring des Nibelungen* . . . from beginning to end, and is full of enthusiasm for it." (BWL, vol. 1, p. 224) Liszt also gave a copy of the poem to Maria Pawlowna, for he hoped to arouse her interest in Wagner's tetralogy. In April he arranged a private reading of the *Nibelungen* for a small group of Wagner admirers in the Altenburg, narrated by Counsellor Adolf Schöll, director of the Weimar art collections. By the time that Liszt met Wagner in Zürich, then, he was well acquainted with the poem (BWL, vol. 1, p. 235; KWL, vol. 1, p. 229). Liszt's dream, then as later, was to secure for Weimar the first staged performance of the as yet uncompleted *Ring* cycle. It is no coincidence that in January 1854 he mounted the première of Heinrich Dorn's opera *Die Nibelungen,* which treats of the same saga. While Liszt respected Dorn's work, it is unlikely that he would have gone to the trouble of staging his opera (which by one of those strange accidents of history had been composed without reference to, and apparently with no knowledge of, Wagner's own work) had he not perceived in it the possibility of drawing attention to Wagner's immeasurably superior treatment of the same material. That this plan came to nought was due to Carl Alexander's unwillingness to find the resources to make it possible, and there is evidence that he later regretted it. In this connection one would like to know more than Wagner discloses in *Mein Leben* about the meeting between him and Carl Alexander at Lucerne in 1859, arranged at the latter's request. They talked among other

party dispersed. Since Wagner's readings had only got as far as the *Siegfried* poem, it was decided that Carolyne and Marie would accompany Wagner and Liszt to Paris, where the readings would continue with *Götterdämmerung*, instead of pursuing their original itinerary and proceeding to Strassburg. The Murls, in the meantime, began their trek back into Germany. They entered Baden singing the same fanfare which had heralded their arrival in Basel a week or so earlier and got into difficulties with the local police, who regarded them as undesirables.[27]

In Paris Liszt combined a number of public activities with some purely private ones. Among the former was a visit to the Opéra, to which he took Wagner and the two ladies for a performance of Meyerbeer's *Robert le diable*. Liszt had rented a box for the evening, and Wagner observed that he appeared to be seized with nostalgia as he gazed around the familiar building, absorbed in reflections on times past. No wonder that Liszt was nostalgic. This was his first visit to the city of his youth since his break with Marie d'Agoult in 1844, and the venerable building must have echoed with memories of his musical past: the "duel" with Thalberg; the first glimpse of Paganini; performances of operas by Auber, Donizetti, and Bellini which he had later paraphrased. And there may have been deeper reasons still for his nostalgia. While Liszt was in Paris, his thoughts cannot have been far from Caroline d'Artigaux, his first love. She was about to journey from her home in Pau near the Spanish border (where she and Liszt had last met, in 1844) in order to attend a medical consultation in the French capital for her sick daughter, Berthe; and she wrote to Liszt to tell him that she hoped to see him there. Alas, Caroline arrived in Paris a few days after Liszt had left, and so the two were never re-united.[28] Liszt also gave a dinner-party in the Palais Royale for some of his old acquaintances, and he played at a *soirée* in the home of the Erard family. Berlioz joined the

---

things of mounting the *Nibelungen* tetralogy at Weimar. Baron von Beaulieu-Marconnay, formerly the Weimar theatre intendant and now the grand duke's chamberlain, was present; and since Wagner had every reason to suppose that the pair were serious in their intentions, he readily agreed in principle to this grandiose plan. He would later reflect on the meeting with amusement, for after he left he never heard another word about it and never saw Carl Alexander again (WML, p. 683). It has to be acknowledged that the mere thought of Wagner's *Ring* cycle being performed in Weimar's small theatre was impractical. Of course, no one could have foreseen, least of all Wagner himself, the enormous dimensions his work would eventually encompass.

27. WML, p. 607. This visit to Basel is also described in the diary of Dionys Pruckner, who adds some detail to the night of merrymaking in the Drei Königen. Pruckner also tells us that after the Wagner readings Liszt sat down and played Beethoven's *Hammerklavier* Sonata to the assembled company, a performance which does not appear to be documented elsewhere, and which Wagner (untypically) fails to mention in his own account of the episode preserved in *Mein Leben*. (See "Aus Dionys Pruckners Tagebüchern," *Schwäbische Kronik*, no. 562, December 1, 1906.)

28. LAG, p. 57. Their correspondence continued, however, and it later resulted in a genuine friendship between the princess and Caroline. See the run of thirteen letters from Caroline to Liszt and/or the princess, covering the period 1853 to 1859, in LAG.

company during this period, and Wagner had an opportunity to re-assess his ambivalent relationship with the Frenchman.

Liszt's chief reason for being in Paris, however, was to visit his three children, whom he had not seen for eight years. Blandine, Cosima, and Daniel had lived in Paris since their infancy, where, it will be recalled, they had at first been brought up in the home of Anna Liszt. Liszt had meanwhile transferred his daughters first to a boarding-school and then to the care of a private governess, Madame Patersi de Fossombroni, who, apart from being their teacher, was in effect their guardian as well. It would take us too far afield were we now to embark on a lengthy account of Liszt's complex dealings with his family across the years; that tale has been reserved for a later stage of our narrative. Suffice it to say that this reunion with his children, which gave him an opportunity to observe their welfare at first hand, represented a new chapter in all their lives. Thereafter, Liszt saw them at least once a year, sometimes for extended holidays in Weimar.

After Liszt and the princess left the city, Wagner stayed on for two or three days before returning to Zürich. As on the previous occasion of their parting, Wagner experienced an aching void: "Here I stand and stare after you; my whole being is silence; let me not seek words, even for you. Speech seems to exist only to do violence to feeling. Therefore no violence, only silence."[29] As for Liszt, he returned to Weimar more determined than ever to promote Wagner's cause. On October 30, 1853, after an absence of several months, he picked up the baton once more in Weimar and directed a performance of *Der fliegende Holländer*. "The 'pale mariner' has once more gone across the stage here," Liszt told Wagner. "With *Der fliegende Holländer* I left the orchestra for a time at the beginning of last March, and with the same work I resume my connection with the theatre for this season."[30]

V I

At the risk of getting a little ahead of our story, we must give some account of the deepening relationship between Liszt and Wagner. Theirs, after all, was one of the great friendships in musical history. While the topic has never lacked for discussion, there are still aspects of it that will bear fresh scrutiny. It is widely recognized today that Liszt sustained Wagner's flagging morale through their correspondence and through his personal visits to Wagner beyond Germany's borders. They exchanged more than three hundred letters during the twelve

---

29. BWL, vol. 1, p. 283; KWL, vol. 1, p. 274.
30. BWL, vol. 1., p. 285; KWL, vol. 2, p. 276.

years of Wagner's exile; and Liszt's visits to Switzerland (often made in the company of Wagner's friends and admirers) were intended to bring comfort and succour to the composer in his artistic isolation. Wagner's constant cry is for money. Only a month after his flight from Dresden and the issuing of the warrant for his arrest, we find him writing to Liszt: "Make it possible to let me have some money soon."[31] The money arrives, and Wagner picks up his pen to ask for more, this time for his wife who is still living in Dresden, lacks the means to pay her debts, and is unable even to buy a ticket for the railway journey to Zürich. Again Liszt obliges, telling Wagner that the money comes from "an admirer of *Tannhäuser*, who has especially asked me not to name him to you."[32] By October 1849 Wagner is telling Liszt that at the end of the month "our last florins will be gone."[33] Liszt now feels it necessary to draw Wagner's attention to his own precarious financial state. "My purse is completely dry at this moment; and you are aware that the fortune of the princess has been for a year without an administrator and may be confiscated at any day."[34] He also points out that he must provide for his mother and children in Paris and continue to pay Belloni a small salary for services rendered. In reply to Wagner's continued pleas for help, however, Liszt sends him a note for five hundred francs, drawn on his account at Rothschild's bank in Paris.[35] That Wagner regarded Liszt as an immensely rich man, and that he did not understand the difficulties his friend had in discharging his own financial responsibilities, goes without saying, for he continued to ply Liszt with requests for money, not only for necessities but for luxuries as well. In June 1852, for example, he writes that he wants to take a holiday near the Italian frontier but is deterred from this extravagance by "my ordinary income" (the implication being, of course, that while his own income is merely ordinary, Liszt's is extraordinary). Once more he is successful in pumping Liszt for money, this time as an advance on funds he hopes to receive from the forthcoming performance of *Der fliegende Holländer*, to be conducted by Liszt himself[36]—"I herewith send you a bank-note for one hundred thalers and cordially wish you good luck and a good mood . . . for your Alpine trip."[37] By 1856 Wagner's pleas have become arrogant imperatives. "Franz, I have an inspired idea! You must get an Erard grand piano for me. Write to the widow . . . Tell her a hundred thousand fibs, and make

31. BWL, vol. 1, p. 25; KWL, vol. 1, p. 20.
32. BWL, vol. 1, p. 36; KWL, vol. 1, p. 30. The anonymous "admirer of *Tannhäuser*" is generally thought to have been Carl Alexander.
33. BWL, vol. 1, p. 43; KWL, vol. 1, p. 37.
34. BWL, vol. 1, p. 45; KWL, vol. 1, pp. 39–40.
35. BWL, vol. 1, p. 52; KWL, vol. 1, p. 46.
36. BWL, vol. 1, p. 180; KWL, vol. 1, p. 169. This first performance of *Der fliegende Holländer* in Weimar was the one that Liszt gave on February 16, 1853, in honour of Maria Pawlowna's birthday.
37. BWL, vol. 1, p. 181; KWL, vol. 1, p. 170.

her believe that it is a point of honour for her that an Erard should stand in my house."[38] And so on and so forth throughout the correspondence. It would be tedious to document this aspect of the relationship any further, since everyone agrees that Wagner's egotistical demands on Liszt's time and his purse are among the more unsavoury aspects of their letters, and that they place Wagner in a poor light. We ought to observe in passing, however, that Liszt himself viewed matters differently. Quite simply, if he helped Wagner more than he helped others, this was because Wagner's genius was greater than theirs, and his needs were correspondingly more acute. Liszt's help, in short, was disinterested. It was the *artist* in Wagner who had to be helped, and to that end Liszt was prepared to move heaven and earth. It would likewise be tedious to document all the good by stealth that Liszt did in promoting Wagner's operas across Germany at a time when they might otherwise have been neglected. During the 1850s he had a hand in the productions of Wagner's works in Hanover, Leipzig, and Gotha; and the long-delayed performance of *Tannhäuser* at Berlin on January 7, 1856, was due entirely to his persistence with the theatre intendant there, Botho von Hülsen. In fact, Liszt took over some of the rehearsals when they threatened to overwhelm the conductor, Heinrich Dorn. Well might Wagner exclaim, "Without you I should have been entirely forgotten"[39] and "I call you openly the creator of my present position."[40]

Nothing better illustrates the depths of the Liszt-Wagner relationship than the question of Wagner's amnesty. Wagner knew that his best hope lay in obtaining a free pardon from the king of Saxony, so that he might once more return to Germany and allow his genius to flourish on its native soil. Thanks mainly to Liszt's advocacy, *Der fliegende Holländer, Tannhäuser,* and *Lohengrin* were now being taken up across Germany and were gaining for their composer a national reputation. However gratifying this was to Wagner, he was nonetheless frustrated in being unable to conduct such performances himself, have a say in their production, and generally reap whatever material benefits they might bring his way. Then there was the pressing matter of the *Nibelungen* drama. Wagner had finished *Rheingold* very quickly, between November 1853 and September 1854; *Die Walküre* had followed eighteen months later. However, *Siegfried* was broken off in the summer of 1857 and, together with *Götterdämmerung,* was not completed until after the exile was ended. Wagner knew that only his safe and swift return to Germany would bring about the right emotional and artistic conditions to enable him to complete his mighty tetralogy.

His chief representative in this delicate matter was Liszt. We shall never know the full extent to which Liszt entered into negotiations, first with Saxony

---

38. BWL, vol. 2, p. 137; KWL, vol. 2, p. 133.
39. BWL, vol. 1, p. 151; KWL, vol. 1, p. 141.
40. Ibid.

and then with the smaller German principalities, in an attempt to bring Wagner home; the unpublished German archives have more to tell us about this matter than they have hitherto revealed. But even if we do not go beyond the published correspondence we can see that Liszt's efforts to secure Wagner's amnesty were considerable and merit attention. He interceded directly with the kings of Saxony and Hanover, the duke of Gotha, Prince Wilhelm of Prussia, and the grand duke of Weimar—initiatives that were not without risk to his own reputation. As early as the summer of 1849 we find him cautioning Wagner against making any political allusions in the press, so as not to undermine still further his reputation in Germany.[41] By the summer of 1850, after Wagner learned that Liszt definitely planned to produce *Lohengrin* at Weimar, he asked Liszt to procure for him a safe-conduct from Maria Pawlowna and so enable him to hear the performance incognito "and dupe the united police forces of Germany."[42] To such a request Liszt could only reply: "Your return to Germany and visit to Weimar for the performance of *Lohengrin* is an *absolute impossibility*. When we meet again, I can give you verbally the details, which it would be too long and useless to write."[43] Still Wagner persisted, and in January 1853 he demanded that Liszt find out whether anything had yet been done in Weimar by way of securing a passport for him, and to inquire whether, were he to make his way secretly to the city for a mere four weeks or so (in order to hear a revival of *Lohengrin,* which Liszt planned to present on March 5), his extradition might yet be forced by Saxony. In short, would the *Steckbrief* be suspended for that brief period? "See what can be done about this," Wagner demands. "I must hear *Lohengrin.* "[44] For the first time Liszt's reply was optimistic, and we learn that he was having direct talks with Carl Alexander about Wagner's future. "A few days ago I spoke about it again to our hereditary grand duke, who positively assured me that he will actively intercede for you. This you must not mention anywhere."[45]

---

41. BWL, vol. 1, p. 37; KWL, vol. 1, p. 31.

42. BWL, vol. 1, p. 58; KWL, vol. 1, p. 52.

43. BWL, vol. 1, p. 62; KWL, vol. 1, p. 56. Among the "details" Liszt had in mind must have been the little matter of the extradition treaties which bound the German principalities to one another in the case of political offenders. Still, Liszt was in a unique position to bend the ears of the German aristocracy when it came to pleading Wagner's cause. To give but one example: on February 16, 1853, he conducted *Der fliegende Holländer* in honour of Maria Pawlowna's birthday. Among the dignitaries present were the duke of Coburg, the duke of Mecklenburg-Schwerin, Prince Charles and Princess Charlotte of Prussia, the prince of Sondershausen, and various foreign ambassadors based in Dresden, the city in which the *Steckbrief* for Wagner's arrest had been issued (BWL, vol. 1, p. 221; KWL, vol. 1, p. 210). Liszt's difficulty in dealing with these people was always the same: individually they were more than ready to offer sympathetic consideration to Wagner's case; collectively, however, they presented a stone wall which Liszt could never breach. The solution lay with the king of Saxony, who had signed the original *Steckbrief,* and for the time being he was to prove unyielding.

44. BWL, vol. 1, pp. 217–18; KWL, vol. 1, p. 207.

45. BWL, vol. 1, p. 234; KWL, vol. 1, p. 227. This promise of Carl Alexander, like so many others the young duke made to Liszt, turned out to be worthless. He had no real authority, since he did

By January 1854 Wagner's desire to gain free access to Germany has become almost unbearable. He declares that he is on the point of rushing to Leipzig without a passport in order to repair the damage to his reputation brought about by a disastrous performance of *Lohengrin* there at the end of 1853. Not long afterwards he sees his plight more calmly and asks Liszt: "Would it be of any use if I sent you a letter to the king of Saxony, which the grand duke of Weimar might forward to him through a confidant—perhaps his ambassador?"[46] Liszt reminds Wagner that he has already approached the king, and after such an experience ("of which I told you only the smaller part"), he does not believe the monarch is inclined to decree an amnesty soon. "I will try again, however."[47]

That same summer finds Wagner vacillating when he discloses that his brother-in-law, Eduard Avenarius, the Leipzig publisher, has written to say that there is a possibility of Germany being opened up to him for the special purpose of a short journey, but "I do not believe it and at this moment do not care much about it."[48] Eighteen months elapse, and by April 1856 it is once again evident that Wagner's desire to re-enter Germany is about to lead him into folly. He confides to Liszt:

> From Prague, the director of police there, Baron von Peimann, sent me the advice that I should become a Swiss citizen. In that case the Austrian minister would give his *visé* to my passport for all the imperial states, and I might then reside there without being disturbed, for if Saxony should claim me, the reply would be that no Saxon subject of the name of R.W. was known.

He goes on to tell Liszt that he is determined not to allow Berlin or Munich to press ahead with planned performances of *Lohengrin* without him, and says that he is ready to apply to the king of Saxony for his amnesty in a letter in which he will confess his rashness and promise never to meddle in politics again. This long epistle finally reaches its true goal, and he asks Liszt: "Will you undertake to demand an audience of the king of Saxony on the strength of a letter from the grand duke of Weimar? What you should say to the king at such an audience I need not indicate, but we surely agree that in asking for my

---

not succeed to his title until August 1853. In fairness, however, we must record that Carl Alexander later interceded several times with the king of Saxony, both by word and by letter, but to no avail (BWL, vol. 2, p. 275; KWL, vol. 2, p. 291). He undoubtedly faced grave difficulties; but it is abundantly clear that while Weimar and Dresden had mutual extradition treaties, Carl Alexander had it within his absolute discretion to shelter Wagner in Weimar for a few days, but chose not to do so.

46. BWL, vol. 2, p. 20; KWL, vol. 2, pp. 21–22.
47. BWL, vol. 2, p. 21; KWL, vol. 2, p. 23.
48. BWL, vol. 2, p. 36; KWL, vol. 2, p. 34.

amnesty, stress should be laid on my *artistic nature.*"[49] To all this Liszt has only one reply: he has never neglected to take all the necessary steps to secure Wagner's return to Germany, despite formidable obstacles, and he tells Wagner plainly that the advice from Prague (i.e., to avoid arrest by becoming a Swiss citizen) is an illusion that he should not cherish. He counsels Wagner:

> You should, in the first instance, ask for an amnesty to the extent only *that you might be permitted to hear your works in Weimar,* because this would be necessary for your intellectual development, and because you felt sure that the grand duke of Weimar would receive you in a kindly spirit. It breaks my heart to have to prescribe such tedious methods, but believe me, in that direction lies your only way into Germany.[50]

Not content with such practical advice, Wagner now begins to talk of the possibility of a position at the Court of Weimar. He proposes to live at the Altenburg incognito or, alternatively, to appear at the court, reading his poems. He also raises with Liszt the possibility of receiving a pension from the grand duke.[51] Had Carl Alexander acceded to Liszt's request and brought Wagner to Weimar, the entire history of nineteenth-century music would, of course, have unfolded along different lines. Then would Liszt have realized his long-cherished dream of raising Weimar to the glory it had enjoyed in Carl August's day—"a city in which Wagner and I would have been the leading spirits, just as Goethe and Schiller were formerly."[52] Cosima Wagner expressed it more succinctly when she observed that had Wagner settled there, the Bayreuth theatre would today stand in Weimar, and the *Ring* cycle would have been heard at least fifteen years earlier than the Bayreuth première.[53] By January 1857, however, it was clear that the grand duke dared not risk Wagner's presence in his city, and Liszt wrote: "Our grand duke here said that for the present nothing could be done for you, and that I must have patience. How sick I am of this patience you may easily imagine."[54] Three more years were

---

49. BWL, vol. 2, pp. 120–22; KWL, vol. 2, pp. 115–17.
50. BWL, vol. 2, pp. 124–25; KWL, vol. 2, pp. 119–20.
51. BWL, vol. 2, p. 147; KWL, vol. 2, p. 142.
52. LLB, vol. 1, p. 366.
53. WZL, p. 483.
54. BWL, vol. 2, p. 150; KWL, vol. 2, p. 146. There are few more telling documents dealing with the question of Wagner's amnesty than the letter Liszt wrote to Prince Wilhelm of Prussia on December 31, 1856. Prussia was on the verge of sending an army of occupation into Zürich in order to resolve its conflict with the Swiss canton of Neuchâtel. Liszt knew that if that happened, Wagner, as a German fugitive, could well be expatriated forcibly to Saxony. After reminding Prince Wilhelm of Wagner's genius, and of the various moves that already had been made behind the scenes to secure Wagner's amnesty, Liszt went on: "Would it not be dreadful if, as a result of the military occupation of Zürich, where Wagner is now living, he became a victim of a fate that posterity might perhaps

to elapse before Wagner received a partial amnesty, in 1860, thanks not to Carl Alexander but to his sister Princess Augusta of Prussia.[55] From the summer of that year Wagner was free to enter all parts of Germany with the exception of the kingdom of Saxony. Two years later, in 1862, Saxony followed suit with a full pardon. The first time that Wagner set foot in Weimar again was in August 1861, when he attended the festival of the newly formed Allgemeiner Deutscher Musikverein and was reunited with Liszt and many of the leading personalities of the New German School.

V I I

Meanwhile, to return to our main story, the spring of 1854 was further enlivened for Liszt by the arrival in Weimar of the poet Hoffmann von Fallersleben. Exiled from Breslau in 1849 for his revolutionary activities (he had been a professor of German poetry there), Hoffmann was much pursued by police before he arrived in Weimar. It was Carl Alexander who brought him to the city, at the suggestion of Bettina von Arnim, because he wanted someone to edit the new *Weimarisches Jahrbuch,* which was intended to become a chronicle of the cultural life of Weimar.[56] Even after Hoffmann had settled in the city with his wife and family and had become a "poet-in-residence," the petty officials there never ceased to intrigue against him. Liszt befriended the poet early on, and Hoffmann not only became a regular member of the Altenburg group but left some vivid accounts of the various events that took place in the old house. Hoffmann's first encounter with the composer took place on May 26, when Liszt arranged an audience with Carl Alexander at which the idea of a *Jahrbuch* was discussed. By June 20 the friendship had developed, and Liszt took the poet and his attractive wife, Ida (who was forty years

---

think too long a punishment for a second's folly? Since Your Royal Highness has been assigned as the army leader to enter Switzerland . . . I am taking the liberty of asking you to be kind enough to inform me if there are any moves that Wagner could still make to avoid the danger that would threaten him, or if it is advisable for him to leave Zürich." (hitherto unpublished; from the *Abschrift* in the Prussian State Archive, Berlin)

Such a letter could easily have incurred royal displeasure and entangled Liszt in diplomatic complexities unhelpful to his career. It appears that Wagner had requested that Carl Alexander write this letter. Based on his frustrating experiences with the grand duke in the past, to say nothing of the political uncertainties of the present, Liszt decided to write it himself. We can only marvel at his readiness to stand in harm's way whenever Wagner's welfare was at stake (BWL, vol. 2, pp. 149–50; KWL, vol. 2, p. 145).

55. The full story of the pardon is told in NLRW, vol. 3, pp. 46–51, and p. 180.

56. Carl Alexander was at first deeply committed to this project, for which he set aside the annual sum of 1,000 thalers. In 1857, however, after the first six numbers were published, he removed his subvention, and the *Weimarisches Jahrbuch für deutsche Sprache, Litteratur und Kunst* collapsed (SNW, vol. 2, p. 27).

younger than her husband), on a detailed tour of the royal castle. Afterwards they all went back to the Altenburg, where, Hoffmann relates, he met Anton Rubinstein, newly arrived from Russia, and there followed much music-making.[57] Three days later, Liszt invited Hoffmann to lunch, during which the poet turned to Carolyne and remarked: "Tomorrow there will be a surprise." On June 24 Liszt and Carolyne gave a lunch-party at the Altenburg, to which Hoffmann, Rubinstein, Cornelius, and Brendel were all invited. "The table shone with silver and decorative floral arrangements; fine dishes were followed by still finer ones, noble wines by still nobler ones." Champagne was served and toasts were called for. It was, in fact, the thirty-sixth birthday of Carl Alexander. But where was the surprise? Suddenly Hoffmann rose to his feet and delivered an ode, which he then presented to Princess Carolyne, who was so overcome that she wept. Two more odes followed and were presented to Princess Marie and to Liszt.[58] From that day forth, Hoffmann von Fallersleben and his wife were treated as members of the family. There was hardly an event of any significance at the Altenburg to which Hoffmann was not invited; and his many odes, declamations, speeches, and toasts became an essential element in the proceedings. Hoffmann even wrote a poem in praise of the Altenburg itself, which contains the word-play "Es ist nicht eine Burg der Alten" ("It is not a refuge for the old") in deference to all those who congregated there and were still young at heart. It was Hoffmann, incidentally, who wrote the words of the German national anthem, "Deutschland, Deutschland über alles," one of the most misunderstood texts in German poetry.[59] It is sufficient evidence of

---

57. Rubinstein arrived in Weimar on or about June 1, 1854. Liszt himself confirmed this in a letter to Hans von Bülow written on June 7: "Rubinstein has been installed in the Altenburg for a week now, and although he expresses consistent prejudice against *Zukunftsmusik* I esteem him as a talent and as a person." (LBLB, p. 89.) This was not their first meeting. Liszt had heard Rubinstein play in Paris in 1840, while the latter was still a ten-year-old child prodigy, and he had predicted a brilliant career for him. Rubinstein, in turn, had been taken to a recital by Liszt and was so overcome by the latter's playing that he had a nervous seizure. Liszt himself is said to have cradled the boy in his arms until he recovered. (BFA, pp. 31–33.) In reporting this incident, which at first sight looks like yet another manifestation of Romantic theatricality, Rubinstein's biographer Catherine Drinker Bowen reminds us that even Liszt suffered seizures in his youth, and that Mozart had fainted away at the sound of a trumpet. Incidentally, when Rubinstein arrived in Weimar, it was not as Liszt's pupil but as a fully formed artist in search of the master's blessing. This he received, but he never allied himself with the Weimar School. In fact, his prejudice against the "Music of the Future," of which Liszt was already aware, erupted into open rebellion during the second "Berlioz week," held in Weimar the following year (pp. 257–58).

58. HML, vol. 6, pp. 10–12. These poems came from Hoffmann's well-known collection *Lieder aus Weimar,* which the poet published in 1854 and dedicated to Liszt (HLW). Incidentally, this June 24 must have been a particularly busy day, even for Liszt. That evening he conducted the first performance of Schubert's *Alfonso und Estrella* in honour of Carl Alexander's birthday. See also Liszt's essay on *Alfonso,* written to coincide with this event (RGS, vol. 3 [part 1], pp. 68–78).

59. The words, needless to add, have nothing to do with German superiority, or even with German militancy, but rather with the idea of German unity, which was much discussed in these pre-Bismarckian days.

the affection Liszt felt for Hoffmann to know of his interest in the latter's children. He was the godfather of the Hoffmanns' elder child, who bore the name Franz in his honour. Princess Marie herself carried the Hoffmanns' second child to the font. A few days later it died in its crib. Liszt went round to his friend's house to console him, and the following day Carolyne invited the Hoffmanns to the Altenburg so that she too could share in their mourning.[60]

VIII

In the summer of 1854 Liszt accepted an invitation to attend the Rotterdam music festival, which was directed by the Dutch royal kapellmeister, Johannes Verhulst. This international event, held on July 13, 14, and 15, attracted an international body of artists and critics, including Hiller, Berlioz, William Sterndale Bennett, Reinecke, Schlesinger, and Karl Formès. Even though Liszt was not directly involved in the festival, he wanted to attend in a "supernumerary" capacity (as he put it) because it featured two works in which he was interested: Handel's *Israel in Egypt* and Haydn's *The Creation*. More than nine hundred choristers and orchestral players had been amassed for the performances. Liszt attended the rehearsals on July 10 and 11, and he was also present at the opening concert on July 13.[61] Despite the presence of so many friends and colleagues in Rotterdam, Liszt feared that he might nonetheless become bored by the generally conservative atmosphere of the festival; he therefore wrote to Klindworth in London and urged him and Reményi to come and help him introduce a more progressive note into the proceedings.[62] They failed to turn up, but their absence was compensated for by the unexpected arrival of Anton Rubinstein, who, having stayed with Liszt in Weimar the previous month, had pursued him to Rotterdam. The Russian pianist was excellent company for Liszt, who took to calling the younger man "Van II" because of his uncanny resemblance to Beethoven. It was in Rotterdam that the two men had a somewhat comical experience. One day they shared a carriage down to the quayside in order to do some shopping. When they completed their purchases, they were disconcerted to discover that the carriage had left without

60. HML, vol. 6, pp. 237–38.
61. The Rotterdam festival was organized to celebrate the twenty-fifth anniversary of the Association for the Advancement of Music (Maatschappij ter Bevordering der Toonkunst) and was reported in the columns of the *Rotterdamsche Courant* between July 9 and 17. Throughout his stay in Rotterdam, Liszt was a private guest in the home of Mr. van der Hoop, a wealthy banker. The festival celebrations, which were presided over by Prince Henry of Nassau and Orange, included such extra-curricular activities as yacht-racing and fireworks displays, both of which attracted Liszt's interest. See his letter to Princess Marie Wittgenstein dated July 15, 1854, in which the social side of the festival is described in faithful detail (HLSW, pp. 58–61).
62. LLB, vol. 1, p. 159.

them, and they had no alternative but to walk home. On "fashionable" occasions such as this, Liszt liked to wear kid gloves, carry a silver-topped cane, and sport a top-hat and a morning coat. With his long hair streaming in the wind he made an unforgettable sight. Rubinstein, with his leonine head and his Beethoven-ish cast of features, looked equally grand. Their route home took them along the roughest part of the quayside, past a group of fisherwomen standing amid their baskets of fish. The sight of the approaching dandies filled the fisherwomen with mirth, and they taunted the two artists as they passed by. Liszt remained aloof and tried to retain his aristocratic poise. This seemed to annoy the fisherwomen, "brawny, red-armed Amazons," who started to pluck at his clothes. Their progress barred, the pair stood there while the burly women formed a circle around them and danced derisively, tugging at their coat-tails. Suddenly, Rubinstein's nerve broke, and he forced his way out of the ring and took to his heels. Liszt followed suit, and the two men fled from the scene with the insults of the jeering mob ringing in their ears. It was an ignominious end for the gentlemen of fashion.[63]

Rubinstein and Liszt were travelling companions on the journey back to Germany. The first stop was Brussels, where Liszt had arranged to spend a few days' holiday with his two daughters, whom he had not seen for almost a year.[64] There were two marvellous evenings of music-making in the home of the Belgian composer Kufferath (a former pupil of Mendelssohn), which culminated in a four-handed performance of Beethoven's Ninth Symphony, played by Liszt and Rubinstein.[65] Their leisurely journey took them as far as Cologne, where they put up at the Hotel Royal;[66] then "Van II" broke away and went off to spend the rest of the summer at the watering-spa of Biebrich, enjoying a tryst with an unknown lady-friend to whom Liszt refers only as "Madame S." Before Liszt and Rubinstein parted, Liszt extracted a promise from the Russian to return to the Altenburg later in the year; Rubinstein had recently completed a new opera, *The Siberian Hunters,* which Liszt wanted to put into production during the coming season in the composer's presence. Shortly after Liszt got back to Weimar, in the last week of July, he asked

---

63. MAR, pp. 32–33; BFA, p. 118.
64. For an account of this family reunion, see p. 440.
65. About the first of the two evenings at Kufferath's (July 20, 1854), at which Schott, the music publisher, was also present, Liszt remarked: "After dinner I sat at the piano and . . . played the Konzertsolo, my invariable etude, and *Les Patineurs.* " (LLB, vol. 4, p. 206) During this stopover Liszt spent an hour with Fétis and Marie Pleyel, and he also called on the Hungarian novelist Baron Miklós Jósika and his wife, who told him that the "learned Diotyma" (an ironical reference to Marie d'Agoult) had recently been in Brussels to consult General Bedeau for her forthcoming history of the 1848 revolution (LLB, vol. 4, p. 208). Thereafter the nickname "Diotyma" stuck to Marie d'Agoult (Diotyma was the name of the legendary priestess who appears in Plato's *Symposium* and voices his metaphysics of love) and was even picked up by Liszt's children and used in their letters to one another.
66. LLB, vol. 4, p. 208.

Cornelius to translate the libretto and arranged with Beaulieu, the theatre intendant, to set aside a date for the first performance. Liszt then wrote to Rubinstein, tongue-in-cheek, that duty now compelled him to snatch the young musician from his Rhine-side leisure and set him to work with fresh determination on the banks of the Ilm.

[August 1854]

My dear Van II,

... The only thing wanting is for you to come at once, and spend a fortnight at Weimar to finish everything. I will rendezvous with you at the Altenburg, where your former quarters await you. No one will bother you there, and you can give yourself up to cultivating *murrendos* to your heart's content whenever the fancy takes you. Try, therefore, not to be too long over your farewells to the Tann-häusers of the banks of the Rhine (and if by chance Madame S. is there, pack yourself off secretly so as to avoid ardent scenes), and get to Weimar between the 1st and 3rd of September, for your score must be given to the copyist between the 15th and the 20th. I will keep your three librettos until you come and will give them back to you at the Altenburg, and I take great pleasure in advance in your success on our stage.

Au revoir then, my dear Rubinstein, in a week's time.

Yours ever in friendship,
F. Liszt[67]

The first performance of *The Siberian Hunters* was given under Liszt's baton on November 9, 1854, in celebration of the fiftieth anniversary of Maria Pawlowna's arrival in Weimar from the Court of St. Petersburg. It was an auspicious event in the young man's career, yet Liszt failed to win him for Weimar and the New Music; the conservative streak in Rubinstein's musical character was too strong for that. Less than three months later, as we shall see, Liszt and Rubinstein quarrelled over the music of Berlioz, and Rubinstein drifted away from Weimar.

IX

Among the distinguished visitors to the Altenburg during that summer of 1854 was Mary Ann Evans, better known to the world as the novelist George Eliot.

---

67. LLB, vol. I, p. 167. Rubinstein's side of the correspondence surrounding the first performance of *The Siberian Hunters* may be found in LBZL, vol. I, pp. 343, 347–48, and 351–52.

She arrived in Weimar in August 1854, in the company of George Henry Lewes, who was collecting material for his biography of Goethe, and her journal contains some lively impressions of her various meetings with Liszt.[68] When Lewes called on Liszt, on August 9, he explained that his irregular union with George Eliot did not permit him to introduce her formally. Liszt, who was the last person in the world to concern himself with what Weimar society thought of such matters, brushed Lewes's excuses aside. The following morning he marched down to the Erbprinz Hotel in person to deliver an invitation to join him and Princess Carolyne for breakfast later in the day.[69]

> On arriving at the Altenburg [wrote Eliot], we were shewn into a garden, where in a saloon formed by overarching trees, the *déjeuner* was set out. We found Hoffmann von Fallersleben, the lyric poet, Dr. Schade, a *Gelehrter* who has distinguished himself by a critical work on the 11,000 virgins (!) and a Herr Cornelius, an agreeable looking artist. Presently came in a Herr or Doctor Raff, a musician who has recently published a volume called *Wagnerfrage*. Soon after we were joined by Liszt and the Princess Marie, an elegant, gentle looking girl of 17, and last by Princess Wittgenstein with her nephew Prince Eugène, a young French (or Swiss?) artist, a pupil of Scheffer.[70]

Eliot was at first disconcerted by the appearance of the princess. She had expected to see a tall, distinguished-looking woman, possibly even a beautiful one. Instead she found the princess to be surprisingly short of stature, somewhat plump, the face "not pleasing," and her profile "harsh and barbarian." Her teeth were "blackish," stained by too much tobacco. During breakfast Eliot sat between Liszt and Miss Anderson, the governess, "an amiable but insignificant person." The conversation turned on Goethe and was dominated by Carolyne, who wished to give Lewes the benefit of her erudition. Eliot was content to sit back in silence and observe Liszt. "Genius, benevolence, and tenderness beam from his whole countenance, and his manners are in perfect harmony with it," she wrote. Cigars were passed around, and Hoffmann von Fallersleben was prevailed upon to read some of his poetry aloud. During the oration a shower

---

68. After her return to England, Eliot published her recollections in *Fraser's Magazine* under the title "Three Months in Weimar" (EE, pp. 83–95). The essay makes mandatory reading today, since Eliot had the good fortune to meet many people in the Altenburg circle; and she also wrote about Weimar society, as well as the town itself, with the eye of a trained observer.

69. Then, as now, the Germans enjoyed the civilized custom of *ein zweites Frühstück*—a second breakfast, often more elaborate and convivial than the first, starting about 11:00 a.m. According to Eliot's journal, she and Lewes arrived at the Altenburg about 10:30 a.m.

70. EGEL, vol. 2, pp. 169–70.

of rain sent the party indoors. Then came the thing for which Eliot had longed—Liszt's playing.

> I sat near him so that I could see both his hands and face. For the first time in my life I beheld real inspiration—for the first time I heard the true tones of the piano. He played one of his own compositions—one of a series of religious *fantaisies*. There was nothing strange or excessive about his manner. His manipulation of the instrument was quiet and easy, and his face was simply grand—the lips compressed and the head thrown a little backward. When the music expressed quiet rapture or devotion a sweet smile flitted over his features; when it was triumphant the nostrils dilated. There was nothing petty or egoistic to mar the picture. Why did not Scheffer paint him thus instead of representing him as one of the three Magi?[71]

It was at this same breakfast that the subject of *Nélida* was broached, the novel in which Marie d'Agoult had sought to humiliate Liszt by depicting him as an impotent painter. George Eliot had read the novel and was anxious to hear what Liszt had to say about it. "I asked her why she had been so hard on poor Lehmann," Liszt replied. The joke was not lost on Eliot, who recorded it in her journal.[72] By casting the "hero" of her novel in the role of a painter, Marie d'Agoult had only herself to blame if, as we observed in the first volume of this biography, "Liszt jestingly insisted that she had pilloried her admirer Lehmann instead."[73]

A few days later Eliot met Liszt again. He joined her and Lewes for dinner

---

71. EGEL, vol. 2, p. 170. Scheffer's painting *The Three Magi* had hung in the annex to the music-room of the Altenburg since 1849 (see p. 77, n.7). George Eliot could only have seen it for the first time that very morning, yet her curiosity was at once aroused by the problem of reconciling the central figure in that canvas (a figure, we recall, that bears Liszt's physiognomy, albeit in transfigured form) with the musical genius, all fire and flame, sitting before her. Her answer is perceptive, and it comes in the continuation of the above passage, a continuation that has been suppressed in many of the most respectable editions of her prose works: "But it just occurs to me that Scheffer's idea was a sublime one. There are the two aged men who have spent their lives in trying to unravel the destinies of the world, and who are looking for the Deliverer—for the light from on high. Their young fellow-seeker, having the fresh inspiration of early life, is the first to discern the herald star, and his ecstasy reveals it to his companions." (EG, vol. 9, p. 257.) Eliot's observations raise a deeper subject. Anyone who is familiar with even a small portion of the many hundreds of paintings, drawings, and photographs which make up the Liszt iconography will appreciate that he had one of the most mobile of faces, and there is consequently an immense diversity among the many likenesses, leading us to ask of two quite different portraits: "Can these be one and the same man?" Moreover, dozens of people who got to know Liszt only after they had seen a likeness of him testified to the fact that his real face was much more interesting than anything an artist might try to capture for posterity.
72. EGEL, vol. 2, p. 169.
73. Volume One, p. 401, n. 46.

*Liszt's certificate of nomination to the Order of the White Falcon,
second class, dated Weimar, February 13, 1854.*

at the Erbprinz Hotel on August 16, and the post-prandial conversation sparkled as usual. Eliot confided in her letters that Liszt was "the first really inspired man I ever saw." Many years earlier she had read George Sand's famous letter to Liszt in the *Lettres d'un voyageur,* and she confessed that at that time she never thought that she would one day "be seated *tête-à-tête* with him for an hour, as I was yesterday, and telling him my ideas and feelings."[74] As for the city of Weimar itself, Eliot had mixed views. Her initial impression was not favourable ("How could Goethe live here in this dull, lifeless village?"). She also became frustrated with the local shopkeepers, who not only failed to display any signs indicating what they sold but were utterly indifferent to the

---

74. EGEL, vol. 2, p. 171. It has often been suggested that Liszt may have been the real-life model for Klesmer, the concert pianist, in Eliot's novel *Daniel Deronda.* Eliot formed many first-hand impressions about music and musicians while mingling with Liszt's circle in Weimar, and they transformed her bourgeois notions of the art. In the novel there is a classic confrontation between a philistine English politician, Mr. Bult ("who had no idea that his insensibility to counterpoint could ever be reckoned against him"), and Klesmer, whom he has unwittingly insulted by telling him that he has too much talent to be "a mere musician." Klesmer's response is withering: "No man has too much talent to be a musician. Most men have too little. A creative artist is no more a mere musician than a great statesman is a mere politician. We are not ingenious puppets, sir, who live in a box and look out on the world only when it is gaping for amusement. We help to rule the nations and make the age as much as any other public men. We count ourselves on level benches with legislators. And a man who speaks effectively through music is compelled to something more difficult than parliamentary eloquence." Bult, like many of his ilk in England at that time, was stunned by such ideas. And in the famous scene between Gwendolen and Klesmer, when the pianist makes it plain to her that her aspirations to succeed as a performer will come to nought because she lacks real talent, the great British public learned for the first time what sacrifices are involved if one is to succeed in music. The potential musician must submit his mind and his body to rigorous discipline and push them to breaking-point if necessary. Moreover, he must commence the process in childhood. After listening to Gwendolen chatter about her "talent" and her unrealistic hopes for the future, Klesmer is more convinced than ever that he must speak plainly:

> "I will tell you the steps, not that I recommend, but that will be forced upon you.
> . . . You must put yourself under training—musical, dramatic, theatrical; whatever you
> desire to do you have to learn. . . . You have not yet conceived what excellence is. You
> must unlearn your mistaken admirations. You must know what you have to strive for,
> and then you must subdue your mind and body to unbroken discipline. . . . Your muscles,
> your whole frame, must go like a watch, true, true, true, to a hair. That is the work of
> springtime, before habits have been determined." (EDD, pp. 99–101)

Daniel Deronda may well have done more than anything else to convince Britain's large reading public that the man who took up music as his life's work had not necessarily sold his soul to the Devil. Incidentally, one of the themes running throughout the novel is anti-Semitism, and the character of Klesmer is, of course, a Jew. This has led some recent authorities to speculate that Klesmer was based not on Liszt but on Anton Rubinstein, to whom Eliot was introduced by Liszt in the summer of 1854. The matter cannot be decided with certainty since Eliot left no conclusive evidence. But simply to read the words that Eliot puts into the mouth of Klesmer is surely enough. His ideas on talent, genius, musicality, and priest-like devotion to work are basically the ideas of Liszt, and Eliot had opportunity enough to hear them expounded many times by him during her nine-week stay in Weimar. Klesmer's lofty dismissal of Bult's stupid views on the nature of musical talent could not have been better phrased by Liszt himself; indeed, it is not impossible that George Eliot took them down from Liszt *verbatim.*

needs of their customers ("With peculiar Weimarian logic, we bought our lemons at a ropemaker's, and should not have felt ourselves very unreasonable if we had asked for shoes at a stationer's").[75] But she was impressed with the broad, tree-lined avenue leading up to Belvedere Castle and with the grand ducal park, which she compared to the best parks in England. It was not an uncommon sight to see large flocks of sheep grazing in this park, with two or three sheepdogs racing along the distant horizon to round up the strays. These pastoral scenes, with Goethe's *Gartenhaus* in the background, lingered long in Eliot's memory. One hot day in August they rambled all the way to Ettersburg Castle (a sixteen-mile return journey), and on another occasion to Tiefurt, an even further excursion, whose park was "a little paradise."

On August 28 Liszt and Carolyne gave a great banquet at the Altenburg in celebration of Goethe's birthday. Eliot and Lewes were invited, and it gave them a chance to savour the full brilliance of Liszt's circle of acquaintances. The French diplomats were there in force, and so were Raff, Oskar Schade, Hoffmann von Fallersleben, the Prellers, and many others. The occasion also marked the launching of the first issue of the *Weimarisches Jahrbuch* under the joint editorship of Schade and Hoffmann. It was Hoffmann who brought the festivities to a rousing conclusion by delivering an ode to Carl Alexander, one year to the day after his accession, which expressed the hope that Weimar might shake off its image as a "city of the dead" and be praised instead as a city of the living, as it had been in Goethe's day. This timely reproof was endorsed by Liszt, who sent the grand duke a copy of Fallersleben's lines so that he might reflect on them at leisure.[76]

Before leaving Weimar, Eliot and Lewes visited the theatre and saw Liszt conduct *Martha, Der Freischütz,* and *Ernani:* "Liszt looked splendid as he conducted [*Ernani*]. The grand outline of his face and floating hair were seen to advantage as they were thrown into dark relief by the stage lamps." On October 22 they heard *Lohengrin* but walked out before the third act because they were bored. After several attempts to come to terms with Wagner's music, Lewes later wrote, "we came to the conclusion that [it] is not for us."[77] George Eliot and Lewes departed from Weimar on November 3, 1854. Although she never saw Liszt again (she was dead when he visited England in 1886), the memory of this trip to "the Athens of the North" never left her. Her journal is filled with references to the many personalities she encountered during her three months' residence in the city and has secured for England's great novelist an unexpected niche in the Liszt literature.

---

75. EE, p. 93.
76. LBLCA, p. 48. See also Liszt's letter to Rubinstein dated July 31, 1854, in which he writes: "Schade is . . . radiant, for he has already got a heap of subscribers to his *Weimar' sche Jahrbücher,* the first number of which is half printed and will definitely appear on August 28."
77. HGE, p. 424.

X

Ever since the creation of his irreverent Society of Murls the previous year, Liszt had felt the need for the establishment of a formal academy of arts and sciences in Weimar, an organization that would carry the fight against the Philistines across Germany. Despite five years of ceaseless propaganda, the music of Wagner, Berlioz, and Liszt himself still aroused opposition. As for the music of their young cohorts—Bülow, Raff, Cornelius—it remained largely unknown and unplayed outside Weimar. From these considerations emerged one of Liszt's more fruitful creations: the Neu-Weimar-Verein (the "New Weimar Association"). This was a mutual defence-pact, so to speak, whose primary purpose was to form a united front at home in the face of mounting hostility abroad. In October 1854 Hoffmann von Fallersleben, acting in Liszt's name, sent out a call for members and was overwhelmed by the response. Cornelius suggested the name "Liszt Club" to describe the new academy; but such was the general opposition to this idea that he withdrew it in favour of Fallersleben's proposal that the group name itself the Neu-Weimar-Verein. According to the business papers of the Verein, the first meeting was held in the Russischer Hof on November 20, 1854,[78] at which the following members were registered:

I : LOCAL MEMBERS

Bronsart, Hans von
Cornelius, Peter
Cossmann, Bernhard
Genast, Eduard
Grans, Heinrich
Fallersleben, Hoffmann von
Liszt, Franz
Montag, Carl
Pohl, Richard
Preller, Friedrich
Pruckner, Dionys

Raff, Joachim
Rank, Josef
Ritter, Alexander
Schade, Oskar
Schreiber, Ferdinand
Singer, Edmund
Soupper, Eugen von
Stör, Carl
Thon, Sixtus
Walbrül, Johann

II : OUT-OF-TOWN MEMBERS

Berlioz, Hector (Paris)
Bülow, Hans von (Berlin)
Joachim, Joseph (Hanover)

Klindworth, Karl (London)
Viole, Rudolph (Berlin)
Wagner, Richard (Zürich)

---

78. WA, Kasten 228, nos. 1 and 2. The foundation of the Verein is described by Hoffmann in HML, vol. 6, pp. 32–33; and by Cornelius in his *Tagebuchblatt* for 1854–55.

The Verein was not confined to musicians; painters, poets, and dramatists were also included.[79] One wonders how many of the "out-of-towners" had actually been consulted before their recruitment to the ranks. Joachim, as we have seen, had already left Weimar for Hanover, but since he had not yet expressed his dissatisfaction to Liszt, the latter probably felt that he still had a claim on his loyalty. As for Wagner and Berlioz, they were in sympathy with Liszt's aims throughout the Weimar period. Needless to add, all the Murls were incorporated without question into the Verein, which was bound together by a formal constitution, by democratically elected officers, and by regular meetings, first in the Russischer Hof and later in the Rathaus. A handwritten newsletter was circulated among the membership, each member signing it before passing it on to the next. The first newsletters were written by Richard Pohl, the later ones by Cornelius. In December 1854 the association began to circulate its own house-journal, called *Die Laterne* ("The Lantern"), by whose light the members were presumably supposed to find their way. Its subtitle—"eine Witzzeitung," or "joke-magazine"—is a sufficient commentary on its weight; but the contents throw much light on the aims and aspirations of the association, especially in its early years.[80]

Adelheid von Schorn has left an account of the first full meeting, called on November 27, 1854, in the Russischer Hof Hotel.[81] Liszt presided at the head of a large conference-table which ran the full length of the windows overlooking the Carlsplatz. Next to him sat three members of the Weimar orchestra—Stör, Singer, and Walbrül. At the opposite end of the table sat Hoffmann von Fallersleben, Carl Montag, Bronsart, Pruckner, and Pohl. Nearby, grouped around a smaller table, were Cornelius, Raff, Schade, and Joseph Rank, the newly arrived editor of the Weimar *Sonntagsblatt*. A lively discussion ensued, during which the aims of the Verein were established and the officers elected. Liszt was named president and Hoffmann von Fallersleben, vice-president. The member elected to take the minutes and keep in touch with the others rejoiced in the name of Ferdinand Schreiber (i.e., "clerk" or "secretary"); he certainly lived up to his appellation during the first year or two of the association's existence.

Not long after the first meeting Fallersleben, in a fit of evangelical fervour, formulated a set of Twelve Commandments for the Verein, which culminated in the following:

---

79. The painters Bonaventura Genelli, Hermann Wislicenus, and Karl Hummel and the librarian Reinhold Köhler were all inducted into the association, as was the famous scientist Alexander von Humboldt.
80. The full title of the magazine was *Die Laterne: Witzzeitung des Neu-Weimar-Vereins*. The holographs are preserved in WA, Kasten 232–39. An informative account of *Die Laterne* and of its place in the chequered history of the Verein will be found in Guido Schnaubert's "Aus Weimars nachklassischer Zeit" (SANZ).
81. SNW, vol. 2, p. 40.

11. Enough of the old; we hope for something new in Weimar.
    That is why we have named ourselves the Neu-Weimar-Verein.
12. If we find the new within ourselves, it will be found in Weimar.
    Long will we then endure—fresh, happy, and free.[82]

It was Fallersleben who designed the membership certificate of the Verein—a scrolled diploma decorated with vine- and oak-leaves, symbols of tenacity and strength. In the bottom corner was a panorama of Weimar; in the middle, a space for the official stamp of the association. (Less than a hundred of these certificates were ever issued, and they are collectors' items today.) Not a single member of the Old Weimar establishment was invited to join. The surviving members of the Goethe, Herder, Hummel, and Chélard families were all ignored; the gulf that separated Old Weimar from New Weimar was now unbridgeable. Old Weimar could afford to smile at the antics of the Murls and their preposterous Padischa; but a formal organization with international contacts, whose avowed aim was to revolutionize the traditional city of Goethe and Schiller, was a different matter, and it could be dangerous. Fallersleben's poetical lines to the grand duke, delivered to the young ruler on Goethe's birthday and reminding him that Weimar was a "city of the dead," were tantamount to a declaration of war; at the very least they were an insult, and Old Weimar rallied. In the newspaper *Deutschland,* under its conservative editor Karl Panse, Old Weimar found the perfect organ for registering its opposition. Whenever Liszt and his colleagues struck out across Germany in pursuit of their ideals, they in turn were pursued from the rear by their critics at home. Henceforth, Liszt had enemies on his own doorstep, and the Verein was obliged to fight its battles on two fronts simultaneously.

It would be pleasant to report that the Verein survived the hostilities. The organization soon showed signs of collapsing, however. Beleaguered from without, it was also sundered by dissent from within; after 1855 the association experienced some stormy sessions. Raff and Schade especially objected to the membership having to follow every decision blindly, and they finally dropped out. Richard Pohl soon followed. New members were recruited—Milde, Lassen, Dingelstedt—but to little avail. By 1857 Fallersleben was complaining that "the participation of the members leaves much to be desired; many seldom turn up, some not at all."[83] The last important meeting of the Verein took place

---

82. HML, vol. 6, pp. 53–54. Fallersleben appears to have been by far the most zealous member of the Verein. Apart from the Twelve Commandments and a fair sprinkling of poems written in praise of his fellow members, he also wrote the words of the Verein's "fraternity song," which Liszt set to music and which was first performed at a meeting of the Association on July 2, 1855. The spectacle of Liszt, Fallersleben, Raff, Genast, and others standing up and singing the club song beggars description and is best passed over in silence.
83. HML, vol. 6, p. 232.

in June 1859 to commemorate the recent death of Maria Pawlowna, at which Liszt delivered a eulogy.[84] Fallersleben left Weimar in 1860; Liszt and several of his pupils, the following year. Dingelstedt then assumed the presidency, but the organization had by this time lost its vitality. On November 3, 1863, the Verein met to celebrate the end of its first ten years of activity and to pay tribute to its founder, Liszt, who was by then living in Rome and did not attend the meeting. That is the last record of the Neu-Weimar-Verein, on which so many hopes had rested and which today is merely a historical curiosity in the field of Liszt studies.

X I

Between February 16 and 21, 1855, Liszt held a second "Berlioz week" at Weimar. More than two years had elapsed since his old friend was last honoured in this way, and Liszt was anxious to arrange a festival that would reflect the great Frenchman's latest advances as a composer. A formal letter of invitation was secured from Carl Alexander, and Liszt had it forwarded to Berlioz at the end of 1854. Berlioz replied:

January 1, 1855

Dear friend:

I accept with pleasure the invitation from His Honour the grand duke which you have passed on to me. Thank His Highness on my behalf. I have a musical performance-in-progress with the Théâtre des Italiens for January 28; perhaps there will be a fourth concert on the following Sunday, February 5th. In any event, I will leave here for Weimar on the 10th at the latest; I will arrive on the 12th, and we will have four days for the rehearsals.[85]

Liszt left the choice of works to Berlioz, who suggested that Weimar should mount his newly completed trilogy *L'Enfance du Christ.* The Weimar musicians already knew one of the three oratorios that make up this work, "La Fuite en Egypte,"[86] but the other two had only recently been added: "Le Songe d'Hérode" and "L'Arrivée à Saïs." In addition, Berlioz requested a complete performance of the *Fantastic* Symphony, with the rarely heard part two, "Le Mélologue, le Retour à la vie." By mid-January all the parts had been despatched to Liszt,[87] and towards the end of the month the Weimar chorus began

---

84. HML, vol. 6, p. 290.
85. LBZL, vol. 2, p. 3.
86. They had performed it under Liszt's baton as recently as January 1854.
87. LBZL, vol. 2, pp. 5–6.

rehearsals. The orchestra was augmented with players brought in from Jena, Gotha, and Erfurt. The choice of soprano for *L'Enfance* posed a problem, since Rosa von Milde was pregnant and had to withdraw from the theatre for the 1854–55 season. Berlioz joked: "Mme Milde in an interesting condition for six months! What a misfortune! Such a pretty woman!" But he consoled himself with the thought that "we are sure to find at the theatre a Virgin Mary of some sort."[88] Liszt's choice fell on Emilie Genast, who acquitted herself with honours.

Altogether Berlioz spent ten days in Weimar which were filled with rehearsals, concerts, and general festivities. Liszt opened the festival on February 16 (the birthday of Maria Pawlowna) with a performance of *Benvenuto Cellini*. [89] On February 17 Liszt gave the first performance of his newly completed Concerto in E-flat major at a court concert, with Berlioz conducting. Since Berlioz did not arrive in Weimar until February 12, he had a mere five days in which to learn the unfamiliar score. The following day, February 18, was Princess Marie Wittgenstein's eighteenth birthday, and a great party was organized at the Altenburg. Berlioz, Cornelius, the Prellers, and Hoffmann von Fallersleben were invited to lunch, during which the last-named regaled everyone with an ode. At 8:00 p.m. there was a concert to which crowds of people had been invited. Liszt crowned the evening when he sat down at the piano and played his Transcendental Study *Mazeppa* in Princess Marie's honour.[90] Berlioz himself brought the festival to a climax on February 21 with a gigantic concert in the Court Theatre, consisting of complete performances of *L'Enfance du Christ* (in a German translation by Peter Cornelius) and the *Fantastic* Symphony. Because of the frantic activity in Weimar itself, Berlioz had to put off an invitation to visit Gotha, where Duke Ernst waited in vain to hear a second performance of *L'Enfance* for his personal delectation.

A highlight of the festival came on February 20 when Berlioz was made an honorary member of the Neu-Weimar-Verein—the first "out-of-towner" to be elected. A banquet was arranged in his honour at which more than a hundred guests were assembled in the Stadthaus, including the grand duke, Franz Brendel, Hoffmann von Fallersleben, Cornelius, and various musical directors from

---

88. LBZL, vol. 2, p. 3. The Mildes asked Liszt to be the godfather of their son, who was baptized Franz (SNW, vol. 2, p. 39).

89. As in November 1852, this was the revised version in the German translation of Peter Cornelius. Maria Pawlowna not only relished the opera but clearly enjoyed the company of Berlioz. The following September she received from him a letter, sent via Liszt, in which all the usual formalities were swept aside as he begged permission to dedicate the score to her. "My *Benvenuto Cellini*, assassinated in France several years ago, has somewhat regained a spark of life due to the care of a famous doctor, your Weimar Kapellmeister. . . . I am taking the liberty of begging Your Highness to continue your patronage of the convalescent by allowing the dedication of the work. . . ." (HLSW, p. 73)

90. HML, vol. 6, p. 64.

nearby cities—for instance, David Engel from Merseburg and Friedrich Stade from Jena. During the banquet Raff greeted Berlioz with a Latin ode; the Frenchman was then toasted by one Professor Hoffmann. Various speeches followed, including one by Liszt, which was punctuated with toasts "To youth!," "To art!," "To truth!" Peter Cornelius rounded off the evening with an amusing poem to Berlioz in which every strophe ended with the rousing imperative: "Vor Berlioz nimm ab Mütze!" ("Take off your caps in front of Berlioz!") This banquet, in the words of Hoffmann von Fallersleben, honoured not only Berlioz but the Neu-Weimar-Verein itself.[91]

No account of the second "Berlioz week" would be complete without passing reference to the little *contretemps* that Liszt had with Anton Rubinstein, since Liszt's championship of Berlioz was its cause. Throughout the festival Rubinstein had been a house-guest at the Altenburg, where he had mingled with all the other dignitaries, including Berlioz. It soon became apparent that Rubinstein did not like Berlioz's music. Liszt, with his boundless faith in the power of good music to win converts for itself, not only took Rubinstein to all the concerts but insisted that he attend the rehearsals as well. Rubinstein took as much as he could stomach and simply decided to leave. Since he was not a member of the Neu-Weimar-Verein and was therefore not present at the banquet given in Berlioz's honour on February 20, he appears to have waited until the Altenburg was deserted, packed his bags, and escaped. When Liszt went to Rubinstein's room the following morning to fetch him for the rehearsals, it was empty. Liszt dashed off an angry letter:

> Weimar,
> February 21, 1855
>
> Your *fugue* ["flight"] of this morning, my dear Rubinstein, was very little to my taste. . . . Is it a fact that Berlioz's music works on your nerves? And, after the specimen you had of it the other time at the court, did the resolution to hear more of it seem to you too hard to take? . . . Whatever it may be, I do not want any explanations in writing, and only send you these few lines to intimate to you that your nocturnal flight was not a very agreeable surprise to me, and that you would have done better in every way to have heard "Fuite en Egypte" and the Fantasy on Shakespeare's *Tempest*.
>
> . . . Please do not harm the sentiments of a sincere esteem and cordial friendship invariably maintained towards you by
>
> F. Liszt[92]

---

91. For some eye-witness accounts of the second "Berlioz week," see HML, vol. 6, pp. 64–66; HFLW, p. 73; and the issues of the *Weimarische Zeitung* and the *Weimarisches Sonntagsblatt* for February 21, 1855.
92. LLB, vol. 1, pp, 191–92.

Liszt, it is clear, was upset not because Rubinstein disliked Berlioz's music but rather because of what he perceived to be the latter's *determination* not to like it. And his abrupt departure struck Liszt as churlish, coming as it did only a few weeks after Liszt had mounted the first performance of Rubinstein's opera *The Siberian Hunters,* at which the Russian had been the object of the same sort of flattering attention that was now being showered on Berlioz. There was also talk of a performance of Rubinstein's *Oceanic* Symphony under Liszt's baton. In the circumstances, Liszt felt, not unjustly, that he and the other members of the Weimar School had a claim on Rubinstein's loyalties, and he felt slighted. It is one more example of the way in which Liszt's wholehearted enthusiasm for whatever project he undertook led him to interpret an attack on it as an attack on himself.

This was a turning point in their relationship—until their famous reunion in Pressburg on April 13, 1885, when they played together in a concert to raise funds for a statue of Hummel. Rubinstein did return to Weimar in 1856, only to find that Liszt had already left on an extended trip to Hungary. "Van II" arrived at four o'clock in the morning, tired and dishevelled, and rang the front doorbell of the Altenburg after struggling across Weimar in the dark. The princess took him in as her house-guest, but he appears to have left after only a day or two.[93]

X I I

It was now the late spring of 1855, and much of musical Germany was gearing itself for the thirty-third Lower Rhine Music Festival, one of the most celebrated events in the calendar. This year the festival was to be held in Düsseldorf,[94] and Ferdinand Hiller had been appointed its artistic director. At the beginning of May, Liszt received an invitation from Hiller to attend the festival in an honorary capacity. As with the Rotterdam festival a year earlier, he accepted because he was curious to see what other festival organizations could do and to compare them with his own efforts in Weimar and elsewhere. Mendelssohn had been the festival's most distinguished director in the 1830s and '40s; Hiller and Schumann had shared the podium in 1853, the latter with disastrous consequences.[95] Already, then, the Lower Rhine Festival had a "con-

---

93. WA, Kasten 35, August 10, 1856.
94. The Lower Rhine Music Festival was held every three years. It involved the cities of Aachen, Düsseldorf, and Cologne, which took turns hosting it.
95. Schumann was on the brink of a mental breakdown, and because of the paralysis in his right hand he had taken to conducting the Düsseldorf orchestra with the baton tied to his wrist (NRS, p. 299). By the time of Liszt's visit to Düsseldorf in May 1855, Schumann was already incarcerated at Endenich.

servative" image, which Liszt's impressions merely confirmed. He wrote to Wagner:

> I got back yesterday [June 1] from the Düsseldorf music festival tired and dull. Hiller, who conducted the whole, had invited me, and it interested me to go through the whole thing for once, to hear [Schumann's] *Paradise and the Peri,* and to applaud Jenny Lind. I need not tell *you* anything about it, and I am not much the wiser myself. Although the whole festival may be called a great success, it wanted something which, indeed, could not have been expected from it. In the world of art there are very different kinds of laurels and thistles, but you need care very little about them. "The eagle flies to the sun."[96]

With Hiller's conducting Liszt was especially disappointed; he found it the perfect accompaniment to the festival itself—correct, conventional, and ultimately boring.[97] Even negative models can bring forth positive results, however. When, two years later, Liszt himself was invited to direct the Lower Rhine Festival in Aachen, he resolved to do things differently, and he succeeded in standing the festival on its head. This trip to Düsseldorf was scarcely redeemed by a social visit to the home of Clara Schumann, where were gathered Joachim, Wasielewski (Schumann's biographer), and Brahms, whom Liszt had not seen since their rude encounter in the Altenburg the previous summer. Liszt was reluctantly drawn into an impromptu Schumann matinée at which Clara and Joachim played the Sonata in D minor and Clara played the Etudes Symphoniques. Liszt crowned the occasion with a performance of Bach's Chromatic Fantasy. Afterwards they all went to a local pastry shop for lunch.[98] The strain Liszt felt at this gathering was not entirely imaginary; there was a good deal of "background" to the occasion, which is explored elsewhere in this volume. Meanwhile, the others instinctively knew that Liszt was not flesh of their flesh, blood of their blood. The lines of battle were not yet drawn, but "the War of the Romantics" was not far distant.

It must have been a relief to Liszt to take his leave of Düsseldorf, especially since his route back to Weimar took him through Cassel, where he had dinner with his old friend Louis Spohr. "Spohr is a fine and worthy man," Liszt wrote, "decent and diligent. He must be about seventy-five now, and of all the musicians of his time I reckon him to be the most competent and best by far."[99] One of the things that Liszt most admired about Spohr was the interest that

---

96. BWL, vol. 2, p. 76; KWL, vol. 2, p. 71.
97. For Liszt's devastating view of Hiller as a conductor, and for Hiller's of him, see p. 419, n.82.
98. LLB, vol. 3, p. 21.
99. LLB, vol. 3, p. 22.

the older musician had taken in Wagner, whose *Der fliegende Holländer* he had staged in Cassel as early as 1843. For all the esteem in which he held Spohr, however, Liszt knew that he could hardly count on him in the ongoing struggle for recognition of his own music. He described him perfectly when he called Spohr "a patriarch of the art—but neither a prophet nor an apostle."[100]

X I I I

Liszt resolved to spend the summer of 1855 in Weimar, composing. In June he resumed work on the *Dante* Symphony, a task that was to occupy him for at least a year. He also composed his Thirteenth Psalm and the *Prometheus* choruses at this time. As if this were not enough to absorb his creative energies, he completed most of the Prelude and Fugue on the name B-A-C-H for organ, which was required by Alexander Winterberger for the inauguration of the Merseburg Cathedral organ later that year. His social life in Weimar was as active as ever. On June 14 he acted as godfather to Hoffmann von Fallersleben's new-born son. A week later, he and Carolyne hosted a large party at the Altenburg for Prince Eugène von Sayn-Wittgenstein, her nephew, who was on a visit from France. Meanwhile, he was surrounded by the usual crowd of disciples—Bülow, Ritter, Bronsart, Tausig, and Cornelius—and he chaired one or two meetings of the Neu-Weimar-Verein.

During the summer of 1855 rumours began to circulate that Liszt was about to leave Weimar and settle in America. Although he denied them, they were taken up by the *Weimarische Zeitung, Deutschland,* and other German newspapers, and the city buzzed with speculation. Some townspeople said that the Old Weimarers were sending Liszt to America in order to be rid of him; others, that he was disillusioned with Europe and needed to make money. One of the more colourful embellishments was that Liszt had had a gigantic piano built which he proposed to ship to the New World to make his fortune. Some reports said that P. T. Barnum was behind it all and wanted to bring Liszt to New York as a "main attraction." It was common talk in Weimar that Barnum would have offered Liszt $500,000 to visit the States and let him count out the money "on the table."[101] Such stories, in fact, were to pursue Liszt for many

---

100. Ibid.
101. PGS, vol. 2, pp. 91–93. When Richard Pohl stepped in with his witty "Letter from Weimar, August 1856," in which he attempted a rebuttal of all these stories, the rumour of Liszt's departure for America had been in circulation for at least a year. In June 1855 Liszt told Brendel: "If you should by chance have read that I am going to America (!—there are many people here who would be glad to have me out of sight!) . . . you can simply laugh, as I have done, at this old *canard.*" (LLB, vol. 1, p. 202) And on June 10, 1855, he wrote to Agnès Street-Klindworth: "The rumour of Wagner's hasty departure from London, printed by several newspapers, has about as much substance as their announcement of my departure for America . . . It goes without saying that I am not leaving Weimar."

years.[102] Allied to these concoctions were the rumours that Liszt had stopped playing the piano altogether, even in private. "Whoever believes that is mistaken," wrote Pohl. "Liszt can even understand the nature of a keyboard which has lost its creative power, and he can control it so completely that under his hands it recovers its soul. Liszt is unable to disown or forget such an instrument."[103] One wonders what Pohl had in mind when he jotted down these words. The presence in Weimar of so many fine pianists, however, to say nothing of the "King of Pianists" himself, did nothing to guarantee the existence of fine pianos among the citizenry of the old town. Adelheid von Schorn

---

(LLB, vol. 3, pp. 26–27) One pianist who did tour North America shortly after Pohl's rebuttal was Liszt's old rival Sigismond Thalberg, who, between November 10, 1856, and mid-June 1858, gave over three hundred concerts in the United States and Canada—a gruelling itinerary made all the more astonishing by the fact that it was preceded by a tour of Brazil. But Liszt himself was never tempted by the blandishments of the New World.

102. At the back of everyone's mind was the sensational American debut of Jenny Lind, and P. T. Barnum's role in it. In his autobiography, Barnum has bequeathed to posterity a colourful account of his dealings with the "Swedish Nightingale." He describes their first meeting, provides his readers with details of their contract, and publishes the balance sheets, which reveal the spectacular profits they both made from her tour of the United States. Between September 1850 and June 1851, Lind appeared in ninety-five concerts, for which she received a net fee of $176,675.09. The master showman himself grossed $535,486.25 (BST, p. 354); this amounts to several million dollars in present-day currency. In order to make these mind-boggling figures come true, Barnum had generated a whirlwind of advance publicity in the daily press, had brought into mass circulation potted biographies of the singer, and had even aroused the interest (and the ire) of Wall Street financiers whom he had invited to underwrite the tour. In the event, Barnum was forced to mortgage practically everything he owned in order to bring Lind to America—and all this without having heard her sing a note. One of his more idiosyncratic enterprises was the "Jenny Lind Song Contest," the winner of which (one Bayard Taylor, whose ode was entitled "Greetings to America") was to receive $200 in cash and have his lines sung by Lind at her first concert in New York, on September 11, 1850. The unseemly scramble for immortality which this contest engendered across the United States provided Barnum with a rich crop of anecdotes, which were duly published in his "Confidential Disclosures of the Prize Committee on the Jenny Lind Song, with Specimens of the Leading American Poets in the Happiest Effulgence of Their Genius" (New York, 1850)—yet another money-spinner. One of the best of them concerned the poet from Cincinnati who, having almost missed the deadline, attempted to telegraph his lines to the prize committee at the closing hour, only to be interrupted during the transmission of the tenth stanza by the unexpected rise in the value of pork, which required that the telegraph wires be commandeered for the communication of this infinitely more important piece of information.

By the time Jenny Lind stepped off the steamship *Atlantic* at New York's Canal Street wharf, thousands of people lined the streets to catch a glimpse of her. She gave thirty-five concerts in New York, twelve in New Orleans, eight in Philadelphia, seven in Boston, and others scattered in more than a dozen cities, including Memphis, Cincinnati, St. Louis, and Baltimore. She even appeared in Havana. Not since Barnum had presented General Tom Thumb to Queen Victoria at Buckingham Palace had he had such a runaway success on his hands. Perhaps it was the series of financial setbacks he suffered in the mid-1850s, notably the collapse of the Jerome Clock Company, in which he had invested a fortune, which prompted him to hope that the "Lind Enterprise" might be repeated. All eyes were now turned on Liszt. It is against the background of the Lind episode—that curious admixture of circus romance, seedy commerce, and pure New World razzmatazz—that rumours of Liszt's departure for America, and his refusal to have anything to do with them, must be interpreted.

103. PGS, vol. 2, pp. 74–75.

tells us that Liszt attended a party in the home of Frau von Schwendler (the former widow of Prince Schlabrendorf), and since he was fond of her, he allowed himself to be seated at her piano—a derelict, out-of-tune instrument—on which he began to play. "What make of instrument is this?" he asked, smiling, while continuing to play. "A Wallenstein!" replied the lady, bridling at the suggestion that it was a less-than-perfect specimen. "Ah, a Wallenstein!" remarked Liszt, as if there were nothing more to be said[104]—whereupon he launched into a rhapsody that shook the piano and the floorboards on which it was standing to their foundations. The next evening he and a small group of friends, including some who had been present on the earlier occasion, gathered in the home of the Schorn family, who possessed an equally bad piano. Once again Liszt began to play. He paused in mid-phrase and announced with a straight face: "And this one here is probably a Piccolomini!" Peals of laughter broke out. From that day forth the Schorn family piano was never called by any other name than "a Piccolomini"![105]

In July Carolyne and Princess Marie set out on extended travels of their own; they went first to Berlin, where they toured the various art galleries, and then to Paris, where Marie had her portrait painted by Ary Scheffer.[106] During their absence Liszt's three children spent the summer holidays with him in the Altenburg, an unexpected complication in all their lives which is dealt with elsewhere.[107] On August 15 he conducted the first performance of Cornelius's Mass in Weimar's small Catholic church. And on August 28 he attended a commemoration service for Goethe, held "beneath cloudless skies" in the grounds of the poet's *Gartenhaus*. The grand duke and his retinue were present, together with Gustav Steinacker and his family, who, thanks to Liszt, were now living in the venerable house.

---

104. The Wallenstein factory was located in nearby Eisenach.

105. SZM, p. 69. Liszt's joke, which was well understood by his Weimar entourage, may require some explanation for the modern reader. General Piccolomini (1583–1634) had served on the field of battle under Wallenstein, whom he later betrayed. The drama formed the substance of Schiller's historical play *Wallensteins Tod*. To contrast a Wallenstein and a Piccolomini was to produce a comparison so base as to be unspeakable.

106. LLB, vol. 4, p. 250; SZM, pp. 79–80.

107. See p. 450. Carolyne and Marie were away from Weimar for more than two months, a trip Liszt actively encouraged them to make. The stresses and strains of the private affairs of the princess had brought her once more to the brink of despair. Tsar Alexander II, we recall, had just sequestered her properties in Ukraine, and she was henceforth homeless. This cruel act robbed her of much hope. "Weimar holds few charms for them at the moment," wrote Liszt in a masterpiece of understatement. "It is simply a question of waiting patiently and persevering, but that is no fun at all. Fortunately, the princess's searching and passionate interest in works of art (painting, sculpture, architecture) has revived quite a lot recently, and since she has not visited Berlin for about twenty years, she will easily find ways of spending her time pleasantly and instructively along these lines. . . . That will be better for her than walks through our park or fruitless correspondence with Monsieur de M[altitz]." (LLB, vol. 3, p. 33) The reference to Maltitz, Carolyne's old sparring partner on the question of her Russian annulment, was censored from the published version of the letter.

Carolyne and Marie were still abroad when Liszt travelled to Merseburg Cathedral for the inaugural concert of the new organ on September 26. This magnificent instrument had been constructed between 1853 and 1855 by the North German organ-builder Friedrich Ladegast, who provided its four manuals with 81 stops, 5,686 pipes, and 37 chimes.[108] It was by far the largest organ in Germany. Since his Prelude and Fugue on the name B-A-C-H was not yet ready, Liszt asked Alexander Winterberger to prepare the "Ad nos" Fantasy instead, a work composed five years earlier but still awaiting its first performance. Liszt travelled to Merseburg on at least two occasions before the festivities in order to help Winterberger with the complex registrations. He wrote to Princess Marie:

> The inauguration of the Merseburg organ will take place on Wednesday, September 26. Perhaps things will arrange themselves so that you can get to Merseburg on that date; as for me, I will have to be there from the evening of the 25th on, in order to try out some of the new registrations. Sacha Winterberger will play the *Prophète* Fantasy, which is now taking on quite a different character after the work I had him do.[109]

That Liszt ran past his deadline is proved by the printed programme, which carries no title for his composition.

Fantasy and Fugue in G minor, op. 16	DAVID HERMANN ENGEL
(Played by Herr Engel, organist of the Cathedral)	
Two Sacred Songs	J. W. FRANK
(Sung by Emilie Genast of Weimar)	
Aria from the *Saint Matthew Passion*	J. S. BACH
(Sung by Emilie Genast; violin obbligato played by Edmund Singer)	
Organ Work	FRANZ LISZT
(Played by Alexander Winterberger)	
Aria from *Saint Paul*	MENDELSSOHN
(Sung by Feodor von Milde)	
Fantasy on "Ein' feste Burg," op. 3	H. SCHELLENBERG
(Played by Herr Schellenberg of Leipzig)	

And what of the Prelude and Fugue on B-A-C-H? It was finished a few weeks later, and Winterberger (to whom the work is dedicated) returned to Mer-

---

108. CJR, p. 96.
109. HLSW, p. 74.

seburg the following year and gave the first performance on May 13, 1856. The work vies with "Ad nos" for a place in the modern organ virtuoso's repertory. Never before had the letters of Bach's name yielded such a rich treasury of harmonic and melodic resource. From this simple motif:

Liszt produced hundreds of permutations, including the following:

while the forward-looking fugue hovers on the brink of atonality.

Liszt was deeply impressed by Winterberger's performance of the work and wrote:

> Alexander Winterberger is showing real promise of becoming a matchless organist. He operates with his feet in a way that others cannot manage with their hands, and that sureness in the handling of the pedal-board gives his playing an amplitude and magnificence which I have never before encountered, although I have heard the most renowned organists.[110]

After these inaugural performances, the young virtuoso took both works on a concert tour of Holland. "Winterberger is scoring an extraordinary triumph

110. LLB, vol. 3, p. 71.

with his organ playing in Holland," wrote Liszt. "He played the *Prophète* [Fantasy] and the B-A-C-H Fugue before an audience of two thousand people with immense success."[111]

X I V

Two concerts in the latter half of 1855 call for special mention, since they were devoted in their entirety to Liszt's own music. On October 15, 1855, he journeyed to Brunswick and conducted two of his symphonic poems, *Orpheus* and *Prometheus*. Since *Prometheus* was being given its first performance, and since both scores contained unheard-of "modernities," Liszt called for sectional rehearsals, and he was visibly pleased with the results. "The players seemed excellently disposed towards me," he told Carolyne after the first performance, "and it was easy for me to preserve the most perfect politeness and suavity"[112] —a phrase which betrays the fact that he may not always have been diplomatic when faced with orchestras less able to cope with his music. The performance itself he described as "a solid success," and he added, "with two or three years' patience I think I will manage to achieve what I want"[113]—an indication of the distance that still separated his ideal performances of these symphonic poems from the mundane musical realities of the day.

There was the usual round of socializing in Brunswick. A big banquet was laid on for Liszt after the concert, and since Henri Litolff, Franz Abt, and Kamienski were all in attendance, there were several small dinner-parties on the side as well. It was a particular joy for Liszt to renew his acquaintance with Litolff (who after an outstanding career as a pianist had settled in Brunswick, where he ran a music-publishing business) and to hear him give a private performance of Liszt's own E-flat-major Piano Concerto, an interpretation which Liszt described as admirable.[114] Liszt's days in Brunswick were so busy, in fact, that they reminded him of his period of vagabondage, ten years earlier, and he joked, "As this is my old way of life, I am adapting to it quite naturally."[115] Throughout Liszt's brief stay in Brunswick, however, Carolyne fretted over his health; just before his arrival cholera had struck the town, and she urged him to take all the usual precautions. Again he brushed aside her concerns with humour. "Do not worry about cholera in Brunswick. Everyone

---

111. LLB, vol. 1, p. 233.
112. LLB, vol. 4, p. 272.
113. LLB, vol. 4, p. 275.
114. LLB, vol. 4, p. 272. This performance, which was given before a select group of admirers and with a handful of instruments, took place on October 16, 1855. When the concerto was published, in 1857, it bore a dedication to Henri Litolff.
115. LLB, vol. 4, p. 274.

here is eating raw fruit, and Kamienski declared that he would give at least a dozen cases of cholera for one bunch of grapes."[116]

The other concert was much more ambitious. It took place in Berlin on December 6[117] and consisted of the following works:

> Symphonic Poem *Les Préludes*
> Ave Maria (for mixed chorus and orchestra)
> Piano Concerto No. 1, in E-flat major
>   (soloist: Hans von Bülow)
> Symphonic Poem *Tasso*
> Thirteenth Psalm (for tenor solo, chorus, and orchestra)
>   (soloist: Theodor Formès) (first performance)

Liszt took a sizeable band of his followers and supporters to Berlin, including Singer, Pohl, and Tausig. The party travelled by train from Weimar and was greeted at the station by an even larger group of friends and admirers, including Bülow, Julius Stern, Franz Kroll, Alfred Jaëll, Ludwig Ehlert, and Laub. Liszt jestingly called the group "the basis of my audience"[118] and took everybody on to his hotel, where they were joined by Marx and Heinrich Dorn. The party broke up at about 11:00 p.m., but not before they had been diverted (at Liszt's insistence) by the fourteen-year-old Tausig's performance of a Chopin polonaise.[119] During Liszt's fifteen-day stay in Berlin he attended a variety of functions in his honour, saw productions of Meyerbeer's *Les Huguenots* and Dorn's *Die Nibelungen* at the opera house, and directed a number of rehearsals for his forthcoming concert. On the evening of December 6, the hall of the Berlin Singakademie was filled to capacity. King Friedrich Wilhelm IV and Queen Elisabeth were present, together with several other members of the royal family. Afterwards Liszt was taken back to the Arnim Hotel, where more than three hundred guests were assembled in a brilliantly illuminated banquet hall. A toast was drunk to the king, and then Marx made an eloquent speech in praise of Liszt, to which the composer replied, taking as his text a line from Goethe, "If you want to understand me, you will have to grasp me." Despite the presence of so many Liszt supporters at the concert, the general climate was hostile; Berlin, it seems, was not yet ready for "the music of the future." The

---

116. LLB, vol. 4, p. 274.
117. The concert was given under the aegis of Julius Stern, director of the Stern Conservatory of Music, who was also the founder and conductor of the Berlin Gesangverein. The Stern concerts were progressive affairs, designed to introduce to the conservative Berlin public the latest developments in music.
118. LLB, vol. 4, p. 276.
119. LLB, vol. 4, p. 276.

opposition was led by the critics Kossak and Lindner, who could find hardly anything good to say about what they heard.[120] Although Liszt had had six or seven rehearsals, it was still not enough to overcome the difficulties inherent in such a programme. The presence of his Thirteenth Psalm (composed in the summer of 1855, but the première of which he had reserved especially for Berlin) indicates the importance that he had attached to the concert. "I broke off from the score of my *Prometheus* choruses to write this psalm," he remarked, "which came to me out of abundance of the heart."[121] He must have been disappointed at the critical reception of his best choral composition to date[122] and he might well have exclaimed with the psalmist: "How long wilt thou forget me, O Lord?"

Andante maestoso

Herr, — wie lan - ge willst du mei - ner — so gar ver - ges - sen?

"The tenor part is very important," wrote Liszt. "I allowed *myself* to sing along with it, and King David's feelings poured out of me in flesh and blood!"[123]

The failure of the concert (particularly galling in view of the successful pioneer work he had carried out for others) was a foretaste of the uphill struggle he would always have where critics and orchestras were concerned. Not long after his return to Weimar the grand duchess gave a party at which one of the guests remarked that Liszt had returned from Berlin covered in laurels. "In a salad tossed with thistles,"[124] Liszt replied. Inwardly he remained philosophical, however. As he expressed it a day or two later: "Neither the brilliant departure of which I was the hero a dozen years ago[125] nor the less flattering dismissal

120. See Lindner's article in the *Vossische Zeitung* for December 8, 1855.

121. LLB, vol. 3, p. 37. A reference to Matthew 12:34: ". . . for out of the abundance of the heart the mouth speaketh."

122. According to a letter Liszt wrote on the day after the concert (December 7), there was some hissing in the hall. "After the psalm, which went perfectly, there were several *st*'s or *szt*'s (the last letters of my name), and these occasioned a roar of bravos, amid whose noise I climbed down once more the steps of this hall which I had previously known so well." (HLSW, p. 77)

123. LLB, vol. 2, p. 25. The powerful words of Psalm 13 are addressed by King David "to the Chief Musician":

> How long wilt thou forget me, O Lord? for ever?
> how long wilt thou hide thy face from me?
> How long shall I take counsel in my soul, having sorrow in my heart daily?
> how long shall mine enemy be exalted over me?

124. LLB, vol. 3, p. 54.

125. An allusion to March 1842, when Liszt, in his heyday as a touring virtuoso, had been driven in procession along the Unter den Linden in a coach drawn by six white horses, with crowds lining the pavements.

with which the infallible criticism of your capital has gratified me this time
will prevent me from returning [to Berlin] now and again . . ."[126] In fact he
returned to Berlin on January 7 in order to attend the first performance in that
city of Wagner's *Tannhäuser,* under Heinrich Dorn. This was in every respect
a superior performance to any that Liszt himself had been able to mount at
Weimar, as he himself readily acknowledged. He was particularly impressed
with Gropius's design for the Great Hall of the Wartburg, with its territorial
banners and coats-of-arms, which had been copied with absolute fidelity by
order of the king of Prussia. The seats alone in the Hall of Song scene cost 800
crowns, and Johanna Wagner had been brought in to sing the part of Elisabeth.
"I have never seen anything like this noble splendour," Liszt wrote.[127] Even
the dissenters seemed to be muted. As Liszt put it, their presence in the theatre
actually had the positive effect of adding a zero to the box-office receipts.
Before he left Berlin, he cabled Wagner in Zürich: "Yesterday *Tannhäuser.*
Excellent performance. Marvellous staging. Decisive applause. Good luck!"[128]

Such lavish attention to detail only served to remind Liszt of the impoverish-
ment of the Weimar theatre, where dreams had never yet been turned into
reality. The year 1855 had ended on a bleak note with the firing of Heinrich
Marr, the artistic director of the Weimar theatre. Shortly after Liszt got back
from Berlin, he learned that Marr had been arrested by the Weimar constabu-
lary for insulting the new intendant, Baron von Beaulieu-Marconnay; he was

---

126. LLB, vol. 1, p. 211. See also the interesting run of letters that Liszt wrote to Alfred Jaëll (*La
Revue Musicale,* January 15, 1904). Jaëll had expressed some interest in performing the E-flat-major
Piano Concerto after its Berlin performance by Bülow and wanted to take it on tour with him to
St. Petersburg. Liszt had no objection to this plan, but he warned the young pianist about the dangers
inherent in the woodwind and percussion writing. His remarks are worth reproducing here, for they
are filled with good advice about performance practice.

> . . . I venture to advise you not to perform this concerto until you have had two or perhaps
> three thorough rehearsals. In particular, I would like the entry of the Allegro marziale for
> the theme on the oboes and clarinets

> to be very strongly accented and rhythmically defined. In Berlin there was still a little
> hesitancy in the attack of the woodwind instruments, which must function like trumpets
> at this moment, *in a military style,* and not like the national guard, helter-skelter! Generally
> speaking, I cannot make *rhythm* and *accent* too simple, for they are the very sinews of
> music, which, unfortunately, in many orchestras are peculiarly loose and half *chloroformed.*

127. LLB, vol. 3, p. 56. It is an indication of the extraordinary interest aroused by this production
of *Tannhäuser* that no fewer than 10,172 applications were received for seats for the first performance.
The king and queen of Prussia were present, and two days after the last performance they put on
a glittering concert-reception in the White Room of the royal castle (which Liszt attended in a private
capacity), "with more than 2,000 candles and between 1,200 and 1,500 guests" (LLB, vol. 3, p. 57).
128. BWL, vol. 2, p. 109; KWL, vol. 2, p. 104.

sentenced to four weeks in prison and fined 84 thalers.[129] (Marr was formally dismissed from his post on April 1, 1856.) This little drama sent shock-waves through Weimar's artistic community and at once placed a heavier burden on Liszt's shoulders: he was consulted not only about musical but about theatrical problems as well. And since the royal budget benefitted from a salary saved, the court lacked any incentive to find a replacement. In an attempt to shed some of the work-load, Liszt suggested to Carl Alexander that Franz von Dingelstedt be brought to Weimar. Dingelstedt was no stranger to the city, for he had appeared on stage there several times, both as an actor and as a playwright. Nonetheless, it was to take Liszt almost two years to persuade the court to his point of view. Meanwhile, the Weimar theatre entered the 1856–57 season in disarray, and Liszt began to accept more engagements away from home—in Vienna, Aachen, Prague, Pest, and Gran. The Lilliputian atmosphere of the once-proud city of Goethe and Schiller was beginning to stifle him, and travel abroad helped him to breathe more freely.

---

129. BCWH, p. 112; GAWZ, p. 347. Marr's sharp tongue had already provoked several crises with the theatre management, and in particular with the intendant Baron von Ziegesar, who had appointed him in 1852. After Ziegesar's death in 1855 the position of intendant was taken over by Beaulieu-Marconnay, who met Marr's vitriolic criticisms head-on with a writ for libel. A useful summary of the affair will be found in SGWT, pp. 203–05, and HMW, p. 140. When we consider the ongoing squabbles that were part and parcel of everyday life in the theatre administration at Weimar, we see how wise Liszt was to have had himself appointed Kapellmeister in Extraordinary, with no fixed duties and no fixed income (see again the conditions of his appointment on pp. 95–96). These unusual circumstances made him virtually untouchable—that is to say, his contributions to the cultural life of Weimar were all within *his* gift to the administration, and not within theirs to him.

That Liszt himself was exasperated at Marr's fate goes without saying. He had no time for the petty laws that protected the self-importance of local officials. Indeed, Liszt himself was not above indulging in some verbal target-practice at Beaulieu-Marconnay's expense, but he was careful not to let him hear about it. One need do no more than read the letter Liszt wrote to Bernhard Cossmann on September 8, 1854 (a full year before the Marr episode), in which he descended to some nonsense punning by referring to the intendant as a *"Beau lieu,* with or without *marque au nez,"* but quickly added: "I implore you to keep this execrable improvisation to yourself, for in my position as Kapellmeister I should run the risk of being fined by the Hofamt [Court Office]." (LLB, vol. 1, p. 169)

Liszt the Conductor

We are helmsmen, not oarsmen.

FRANZ LISZT[1]

There is without doubt nothing better than to respect, admire, and study the illustrious dead; but why not also sometimes live with the living?

FRANZ LISZT[2]

I

Liszt had no compunction about turning his privileged position at Weimar to his own advantage. Behind the official concerts he directed for the Court Theatre lay a subterranean series he directed for himself—the closed "workshop rehearsals" of his symphonic poems. Experimental sessions were held to test new effects, sectional rehearsals were called to master them, and full orchestral "concerts" were given to an empty theatre, to ensure that everything came together to produce the desired result. Just how right Liszt was to insist on sectional practice is borne out by the originality of his music, which was always difficult for orchestras to handle. Works like *Tasso, Les Préludes,* and the *Dante* Symphony contained many technical innovations: in these compositions can be found storm and wind effects, advanced harmonies, unusual key- and time-signatures, constantly fluctuating tempi, and new forms which could sound disjointed until repetition had clarified them. Above all, there was the constant use of chamber-music textures, in which small groups of soloists periodically emerged from the orchestral mass, forming contrasts among themselves; for this the players had to be of superior calibre, possessed of keen ears, perfect intonation, and an "overview" of the other players' parts. No wonder that Liszt, in his preface to the symphonic poems, urged prospective conductors of these problematic works to "hold aloof" from them unless they were prepared to

---

1. LLB, vol. 1, p. 145.
2. LLB, vol. 1, p. 199.

do them well.[3] That Liszt was not being paranoid when he attached this nervous preamble to his compositions should be obvious to anyone familiar with the poor state of musical performance that then obtained across Europe generally. Most orchestras in the smaller towns, and not a few in the cities, simply could not cope with the newer music placed before them. It is sufficient to recall that in 1826 Habeneck had doggedly rehearsed Beethoven's *Eroica* Symphony with the Paris Conservatoire Orchestra for fifteen months, after first pronouncing it unplayable. When Liszt himself conducted Beethoven's Ninth Symphony at the Karlsruhe festival in 1853, the ensemble started to break up in the finale, and Liszt stopped the performance and started the movement again.[4] Matters had scarcely improved a quarter of a century later when Wagner conducted the Overture to *Der fliegende Holländer* at the Royal Albert Hall in London in 1877: the orchestra of two hundred players broke down three times, and Wagner left the rostrum in despair.[5] Wagner's music, like Liszt's, was technically in advance of its time. It is well known that the Vienna Opera abandoned its production of *Tristan* after seventy-seven rehearsals. Felix Weingartner, who came to maturity as a conductor during this epoch, tells us of the dreadful conditions that greeted him in such cities as Königsberg and Danzig, whose orchestras played not only out of tune but out of time as well. When Weingartner conducted his opera *Sakuntala* in Weimar in 1885, it ended in a shambles, with the singers going one way and the orchestra another.[6] Liszt was in the audience, and it can hardly have pleased him to hear the ensemble that he had

---

3. CE, vol. 1, part 1. Liszt was being absolutely consistent here, for he gave similar advice to prospective conductors of Berlioz and Wagner as well. The fact is, he was one of the first to understand that the technique of orchestral performance itself would have to be advanced if the modern music of his time was ever to make headway. When Liszt heard that Gustav Schmidt, Kapellmeister at Frankfurt-am-Main, was interested in putting on a Berlioz concert, he offered him some cautionary advice.

> It will be necessary for you to have several rehearsals—*and indeed separate rehearsals* for the quartet [of *Roméo et Juliette*] and separate rehearsals for the *wind* instruments. The effect of Berlioz's works can be uncommonly good only when the performance of them is satisfactory. They are equally unsuited to the ordinary worthy *theatre and concert maker* [*Theater- und Concert-Macherei*] because they require a higher artistic standpoint from the musician's side. (February 27, 1853. LLB, vol. 1, pp. 131–32)

These words of warning, born of Liszt's long practical acquaintance with Berlioz and his music, seem so obvious to the modern reader as to be hardly worth uttering. But it is worth reflecting that there are some composers and some works which depend far less than others on a perfect performance for their full effect. Bad performances, after all, did not prevent Beethoven's genius from declaring itself, but they held back the full recognition of Berlioz for half a century. His music, like Liszt's, is not performer-proof. This distinction between good music whose goodness reveals bad players, and bad players whose badness obscures good music, was recognized early by Liszt—perhaps because the reputation of his own music suffered when the distinction was blurred.
4. See pp. 280–81 for a fuller account of this débâcle.
5. KTYM, pp. 74–75.
6. WLE, vol. 2, p. 190.

raised to national prominence thirty-five years earlier deliver a performance ending so ignominiously. During his own tenure with the orchestra, in fact, Liszt had earned a reputation for tyrannizing the players, for he would let them get away with nothing. If the mood took him, he would even treat performances as if they were rehearsals, and if serious mistakes occurred he would spring up from the podium and shout to the players to return to such and such a place. Far from being disturbed, the audience would applaud this sign of his vigilance.[7]

The uncaring, uncritical approach to musical performance was frequently symbolized by the absence of a full score on the conductor's desk. Most conductors simply led the band from the first violin part; later came the "piano reduction." In his performance of the Beethoven symphonies, Habeneck, for example, always used a violin part and consequently had only the vaguest idea of what the rest of the orchestra was supposed to be doing. In Italy it was quite usual for an entire opera to be conducted from two staves. Not surprisingly, the ensemble was often ragged, and it sometimes disintegrated. In 1846 the leader of the orchestra of the Teatro San Carlo in Naples was observed to tap his bow all night against a tin candlestick on his music desk, just to keep the performance going.[8] Even when Bülow conducted in Italy more than forty years later, he found little improvement among the rank-and-file players. A rehearsal of Beethoven's Ninth Symphony almost foundered because the timpanist simply could not play one of the basic rhythms of the scherzo. Bülow gradually worked himself into a frenzy; but the more he roared at the unfortunate fellow, the worse matters became. At last Bülow hit upon the perfect solution. *"Timp-a-ni! Timp-a-ni! Timp-a-ni!* he kept yelling, all the time banging the music desk with his baton. A smile of comprehension slowly dawned across the player's face as he caught the rhythm of the one word with which he was most familiar, and in no time at all he was playing the passage in the correct manner.[9]

In the more sophisticated centres like Dresden or Leipzig the role of the conductor rarely rose above that of a simple time-beater. When Weber conducted his *Freischütz* Overture at Dresden, he would beat the first four bars of the allegro and then stand back with folded arms, his task done, while the orchestra continued playing up to the pauses. Mendelssohn adopted a similar

7. SBBI, p. 147.
8. GSI, p. 45.
9. DMML, pp. 83–84.

practice with the Leipzig Gewandhaus Orchestra; he would frequently stand back, putting his baton down on the desk, and let the orchestra play without further guidance.[10] Such casual behavior must have represented nothing less than a sweeping reform to the Leipzigers, however. Wagner, who grew up in Leipzig, tells us that until Mendelssohn's advent at the Gewandhaus in 1835, orchestral works were not conducted at all but were simply played through under the leadership of the concertmaster. He also reports that this same orchestra bravely attempted to play Beethoven's Ninth Symphony under such conditions, and that the results were so chaotic that he "lost courage and gave up the study of Beethoven for a time."[11] In Vienna, the so-called "home of the classics," symphonies and concertos were frequently chopped up and served piecemeal in order to make them more palatable to the general public. At the first performance of Beethoven's Violin Concerto, the soloist, Franz Clement, regaled the audience with a show-piece of his own, which he played between the first and second movements with the violin held upside down. Schubert's C-major Symphony ("The Great") was despatched with equal lack of respect: during a performance given under the auspices of Vienna's Gesellschaft der Musikfreunde in 1839, a singer interpolated a bravura aria from Donizetti's *Lucia di Lammermoor* lest the attention of the audience start to flag. Some conductors were not above making creative contributions of their own to the classical repertory. When Louis Jullien conducted Beethoven's *Pastoral* Symphony at London's Drury Lane Theatre in 1840, he had dry peas rattled in a box to enhance the storm effects.[12] But this was the least of Jullien's sins. This intrepid showman regularly conducted Beethoven with a bejewelled baton, an act of mock piety for which he publicly donned a pair of white kid gloves brought to him on a silver salver. At times he would have himself shot out of a trap-door, baton in hand, giving the signal to the orchestra to begin at the same moment. It is a sufficient commentary on London's musical life that Jullien remained its brightest attraction until 1859. He died the following year in a lunatic asylum in Paris.[13]

Beyond London's borders the musical conditions that prevailed across Albion can only be described as lamentable. Although there were a number of orches-

---

10. DGG, p. 85.

11. WGSD, vol. 8, pp. 270–71.

12. CLJ, pp. 39–40.

13. In 1857 Joachim turned down a lucrative offer to appear with Jullien, whose "promenade concerts" dominated the London scene for twenty years and attracted audiences of thousands. He was deeply suspicious of Jullien's policy of "democratizing" classical music by sandwiching it between the tritest pieces of the day—quadrilles, waltzes, polkas, etc.—to say nothing of his vulgar, eye-catching mannerisms on the podium. He called Jullien "an undisguised charlatan" and remarked shrewdly: "A jackdaw cannot help stealing, and Jullien could not leave off being a humbug, even if he intended to do so" (JMBJ, vol. 1, p. 408). Joachim's stand is an object-lesson to all those musicians across the generations, be they performers or teachers, who have pursued the illusion that the best way to raise the taste of the general public is to lower themselves to its level.

tras in such provincial towns as Bath, Liverpool, Manchester, and Edinburgh, these ensembles were riddled with incompetence. Moscheles undertook a tour of the country in 1825, and when he arrived in Liverpool, he found that the orchestra consisted of "a double quartet and four halting wind instruments," whose sound he described as "wretched."[14] The following year he played in Dublin, where he suffered "martyrdom at the rehearsal, chiefly from the wind instruments."[15] Things were no better in Scotland. In 1838 the organizers of the Professional Society's Concerts in Edinburgh mounted a performance of Mendelssohn's oratorio St. Paul in which the trombones missed their cues in the introduction, the basses made a false entry and ruined the tenor aria, and the brass instruments "were frequently found wanting"—a humiliating catalogue of errors which was dutifully reported by The Musical World a few days later.[16] One of the things that for many years held back the prospect of any real improvement in orchestral playing in England was the mindless practice of the "deputy system," which allowed individuals to send substitute players to rehearsals provided that they themselves took part in the concert. The privilege was easily abused, and in extreme cases it created an Alice-in-Wonderland world in which two quite separate orchestras were assembled, the first for the rehearsal and the second for the concert. Reform was difficult so long as orchestral players were kept on the poverty-line and sometimes not even paid at all. In 1886, during the second act of a performance of Gounod's Faust at Her Majesty's Theatre, the orchestra simply stopped playing and refused to continue until the management had paid them in cash. The audience was also invited to contribute, and coins rained down from the boxes into the orchestra pit.[17]

The casual attitude of the rank-and-file player even infected the soloists, whose platform deportment sometimes left much to be desired. When Lowell Mason attended the Birmingham Festival in 1852, he was dismayed to observe that during a performance of Handel's Messiah the soloists left the hall during the singing of the chorus "Glory to God in the highest," as if their interest in the proceedings did not extend beyond their own parts.[18] A week or two later Mason heard Messiah performed at the Norwich Festival and wrote that there was "a general whispering and talking over the room" during the playing of the Pastoral Symphony.[19] He was also struck by the fact that Madame Viardot-Garcia transposed the aria "I know that my Redeemer liveth" in order to accommodate her voice.[20] And all this in connection with a work that was

---

14. MAML, vol. 1, p. 112.
15. MAML, vol. 1, p. 119.
16. February 16, 1838, p. 106.
17. KTYM, p. 185.
18. MMLA, p. 235. The distinguished soloists included Karl Formès and Clara Novello.
19. MMLA, p. 282.
20. MMLA, p. 284.

The Weimar Court Theatre in the 1840s, an anonymous lithograph.

known and revered throughout the length and breadth of the land. One hardly dare inquire what shabby treatment was meted out to works of lesser calibre.

II

Until well after the middle of the nineteenth century music was held in such low esteem by European society that it came to be regarded as a profession of last resort. To belong to the middle classes and to have a friend (or worse, a relative) who actually earned his daily bread by scraping, banging, or blowing a musical instrument was a matter for deep regret. One simply did not mention it in social circles—as if the miscreant had cheated at cards or contracted some unmentionable disease. There can be no better illustration of how those with "social status" protected themselves against the siren song of St. Cecilia than the fate of music at Harrow School, one of the bulwarks of the British establishment. Music was simply not allowed to be a regular part of the curriculum, for the authorities refused to acknowledge that music could be of the slightest possible relevance in the grooming of an English gentleman. Eventually the boys hired their own teacher, John Farmer, who visited the school unofficially and gave lessons surreptitiously, as if dispensing poison, but for ten years he was excluded from the regular faculty.

In France and Germany the taste of the great public, while not so philistine as in England, was hardly calculated to make music an attractive profession. Berlioz, Schumann, Bülow, Raff, and many others had to overcome parental opposition in order to pursue a musical career—opposition that was based, in every case, on a real concern that social prejudice could break the strongest talent. It was better to devote one's life to a safer calling—medicine, the law, or even the clergy—than to have one's services bought and sold like a harlot's. As long as music was regarded as a mere trade, and musicians were encouraged to view themselves, at best, as simple minstrels who provided the same sort of basic service to society as that offered by the butcher, the baker, or the candle-stick-maker, conditions could hardly improve. Even in Germany, drinking and duelling were considered to be more "romantic" pastimes, especially among students, than the practice of music. Consequently the talents that were recruited into the ranks of the lesser orchestras rarely rose to the level of incompetence, and musical illiteracy abounded. The rostrum itself, alas, was not always immune from takeover by individuals who were not yet good enough to be bad.

III

A large part of the malaise infecting German orchestras, in fact, had to do with the fixed mentalities of the old-fashioned Prussian Kapellmeisters. These worthies were indistinguishable from military bandmasters, standing at the head of their forces like robots, their batons swishing the air with the unremitting regularity of a metronome. Their job was done if the band started and finished together, with no major mishaps in between. Liszt would have nothing to do with them; he dismissed them as "windmills." He saw conducting as perhaps the greatest interpretative art of the future, and the many reforms he introduced to the podium bear witness to the fact that he was the first modern conductor. If we wish to understand where Liszt's genius lay, we can do no better than recall a phrase of Lina Ramann: "Liszt, at the head of an orchestra, is the continuation of Liszt at the piano."[21] Eduard Genast made a similar remark when he first observed Liszt conduct in Weimar in 1844: "No mere metronome stood on the conductor's podium, but a leader full of fire and energy, who knew how to discover all the musical refinements and display them effectively."[22] Liszt was interested in purely musical considerations—in nuances, phrasing,

---

21. FLL, p. 108; see also RLKM, vol. 3, p. 92.
22. GAWZ, p. 314. A decade later, Richard Pohl was still echoing this idea. "When he conducts Beethoven, Berlioz, and Wagner, he is the composer himself; he enters completely into the world of ideas of those spirits who are kindred to him. He *plays* on the orchestra as he plays on the piano."

Liszt conducts Handel's Messiah, *a playbill for October 1, 1850.*

shading of colours, a proper balance among the parts, and, above all, in the expressive device of rubato, an unheard-of phenomenon in orchestral music. In short, he treated the orchestra as if it were a solo instrument, obedient to his every impulse. In order to achieve these effects, Liszt developed a new repertory of body signals, for he recognized that conducting involves the whole man and not just the right arm. He frequently abandoned a regular square-cut beat in favour of an "arc" in which the baton described the actual shape of a phrase (a technique Furtwängler developed many years later). Sometimes he put the baton down and conducted with his hands (as Stokowski was later to do exclusively) if he felt that this would draw more expression from the players.[23] He would shush the musicians, forefinger to lips, if they played too loud, or growl threateningly if they played too soft (about seventy years before Beecham made these characteristics his own). Sometimes, when he required a pianissimo, he would crouch low over the podium, his body apparently sunk in on itself; at others, when he demanded a fortissimo, he would raise himself to his full stature, hands outstretched above his head.[24] His constant search was for colour. He once turned to the string section during the Amoroso theme from the first movement of the *Dante* Symphony and urged them: "Mehr blau, meine Herren!" ("Bluer, gentlemen!").[25] But the most telling of Liszt's reforms was his facial expression, which registered every inflexion of the music and cast a spell over the orchestra, compelling them to play from the heart. Not surprisingly, he was said to lack technique, particularly by those who thought that they themselves possessed it. Liszt might well have observed about this, as he observed about piano playing: "Technique should create itself out of spirit, not out of mechanics."[26] He conducted a great deal from memory, a practice that had an electrifying effect on his peers, and which became the model for the new generation of virtuoso conductors, with Hans von Bülow at their head. Liszt was particularly sensitive to acoustics, recognizing that the very hall in which he conducted was an instrument whose reverberations could make or break the performance, and he would modify his interpretation accordingly.[27] No two Liszt performances were ever the same. The only predictable thing about him was his unpredictability.

No wonder that Liszt drew criticism from his conservative opponents, who not only objected to his choreography but denounced him as an im-

---

23. On May 8, 1853, for example, he conducted a performance of Flotow's *Martha* without using a baton at all.
24. See RLKM, vol. 3, pp. 93–95, and RLS, vol. 1, pp. 254–55, for further descriptions of Liszt on the podium.
25. János Végh, "Liszt Ferencröl," *Muzsika* (Budapest) 1929/1–2, p. 75.
26. "Aus dem Geist schaffe sich die Technik, nicht aus der Mechanik" (RLP, p. 6, series 1).
27. Liszt, as we have seen, advised Carl Alexander on the acoustics of the church at Ettersburg Castle, the grand duke's summer residence. The ceiling of the Great Hall in the Wartburg was actually re-designed at Liszt's instigation for the performance of his oratorio *St. Elisabeth* in 1867.

poster. Sir George Smart, who had observed Liszt wield the baton at the Beethoven Festival in 1845, remarked drily that there was "plenty of twisting of the person."[28] But the worst comments came from musicians who played under Liszt's baton, like Joachim, who later wrote: "At the conductor's desk Liszt makes a parade of moods of despair and the stirrings of contrition ... and mingles them with the most sickly sentimentality and such a martyr-like air that one can hear the lies in every note and see them in every motion. ... I have suddenly realized that he is a cunning contriver of effects who has miscalculated."[29] These comments were written a year after Joachim had broken with Liszt, and they bear the marks of enmity, but they doubtless represented the feelings of many musicians in Germany, who, failing to recognize that conducting had reached a transitional stage in its development, regarded Liszt's unusual gestures on the podium as a threat to their snug profession.

As long as Liszt stayed in Weimar and conducted his well-rehearsed orchestra on home ground, the criticism remained muted. But word soon spread that unusual things were afoot in the city of Goethe and Schiller, and during the mid-1850s Liszt was invited to direct the great music festivals at Karlsruhe and Aachen. This caused some jealousy among his rivals and led to an outbreak of hostility against him at the Karlsruhe festival of 1853, the first of several such demonstrations. He had planned some modern programmes containing Wagner, Berlioz, Schumann, late Beethoven, and, of course, himself. This represented a break with tradition and displeased the reactionaries. Liszt's pioneering programmes are barely remembered today, but in the context of 1853, when six of the featured composers were still alive, they command our respect.

Monday, October 3, 1853

Overture to *Tannhäuser*	WAGNER
Concert aria "Ah, perfido!"	BEETHOVEN
(soloist: Frau Howitz-Steinau)	
Violin Concerto ("Hungarian")	JOACHIM
(soloist: Joachim)	
Finale from *Die Loreley*	MENDELSSOHN

---

28. SLJ, p. 301.

29. JMBJ, vol. 1, p. 299. Liszt did not always conduct like this, however. There is evidence that after Joachim left Weimar, Liszt began to develop more economical gestures. He once told Gustav Schmidt that he liked to conduct the Scherzo from Mendelssohn's *A Midsummer Night's Dream* as if it were in 4/4 time (i.e., four measures as four beats), "as in the Scherzo of the [Beethoven] Ninth Symphony *ritmo di 4 battuti*. Try it sometime, and I think you will agree that I am right." (MQ, 1946, p. 283) Nowadays this advice is so obvious that it makes us wonder yet again what the general level of conducting must have been like in the 1850s.

Interval

Overture to *Manfred*	SCHUMANN
Festival chorus "An die Künstler"	LISZT
(men's chorus and soloists; words by Schiller)	
Symphony No. 9 in D minor ("Choral")	BEETHOVEN

Wednesday, October 5, 1853

Overture to *Struensee*	MEYERBEER
Aria from *La clemenza di Tito*	MOZART
(soloist: Katinka Heinefetter)	
Aria from *Le Prophète*	MEYERBEER
(soloist: Heinefetter)	
Chaconne, for unaccompanied violin	BACH
(soloist: Joachim)	
Fantasy on Motifs from *The Ruins*	BEETHOVEN–LISZT
of Athens, for piano and orchestra	
(soloist: Bülow)	

Interval

Roméo et Juliette (Part Two)	BERLIOZ
Excerpts from *Lohengrin*	WAGNER
Overture to *Tannhäuser*	WAGNER
(repeated "by public demand")	

The critics attempted to divide and rule. While they praised the musical excellence of the combined orchestras (the Mannheim and Darmstadt orchestras had joined forces with the Karlsruhe orchestra for the festival, producing a total ensemble of 130 players), they argued that this happened despite, rather than because of, Liszt's conducting.[30] But when the orchestras got into difficulties in the finale of Beethoven's Ninth, and Liszt wisely started the movement again, they blamed him for the breakdown. One way he was redundant, the other way he was incompetent; either way he failed. Although it was well known that Liszt had been given only three rehearsals for the entire festival,[31] the *Niederrheinische Musikzeitung* published an article in which his faults as a conductor were catalogued in detail. What particularly incensed the reporter was that

---

30. HKM, p. 24.

31. This unfortunate situation had nothing to do with conditions at Karlsruhe. Liszt was delayed en route to the city and was obliged to hand over two of the preliminary rehearsals, already called for Saturday, September 24, to the local Kapellmeister, Wilhelm Kalliwoda. See Liszt's letter to Hans von Bülow, dated September 23, 1853, which was posted either from Mannheim or from Darmstadt, the other cities participating in the festival (LBLB, p. 32).

"Liszt told his players *not to play too strictly in time* (his actual words during a rehearsal). Is it surprising that not a single work went really smoothly and well?"[32] In a remarkable letter to Richard Pohl, written shortly after the Karlsruhe episode, Liszt made this penetrating diagnosis of his problems with the critics.

Weimar, November 5, 1853

In various accounts that I have read of the festival at Karlsruhe, there is one point on which people seem pretty much agreed—namely, the *insufficiency* of my conducting. . . . It remains to be seen what reasons there can be for crying down a conductor when the execution was satisfactory, especially if, as is just, one bears in mind the novelty of the programme for almost the entire audience. . . . For, as everyone acknowledged at Karlsruhe, the Ninth Symphony, as well as the works of Wagner, Berlioz, Schumann, etc., were not well known to anyone except myself, since they had never been given before in this locality (with the exception of the Berlioz, which a *section* only of the Karlsruhe orchestra had played under the direction of the composer).

. . . The works for which I openly confess my admiration and predilection belong mostly to that category which *capable* Kapell-meisters have honoured but little with their personal sympathies, or not at all, so that they have rarely performed them. These works, starting with those which are commonly described nowadays as belonging to Beethoven's *last style* (and which were, not long ago, with lack of reverence, put down to Beethoven's deafness and mental derangement)—these works, to my mind, demand from soloists and orchestras alike . . . a *progress* in the style of execution itself, in accentuation, in rhythm, in the manner of phrasing and declaiming certain passages, and of distributing light and shade. This establishes between the rank-and-file players and the *musician-in-chief* who directs them a natural link which is quite different from the one

---

32. Issue of 1853, p. 139. The article was signed "H." The general view today is that this was Ferdinand Hiller. See p. 419 for Hiller's reactions to Liszt's handling of the Lower Rhine Festival in 1857.

This was not the first time that Liszt had publicly addressed an orchestra on the need to avoid a rigid adherence to the bar-lines. As early as 1846 he had told the orchestra of the Concerts Spirituels in Vienna that "it is not necessary for me to conduct but merely to indicate the rhythm, the phrasing, and to cue in the entries. Of course," he continued, "such behaviour could very easily confuse a lesser orchestra." To which comment Eduard Hanslick later added the rejoinder that the group in question must indeed have been a lesser orchestra (HGC, vol. 1, p. 310). Astonishingly, Hanslick did not hear this concert, at which Liszt conducted Beethoven's Fifth Symphony. He based his criticism on contemporary newspaper reports alone.

"Forte and Piano": *Liszt at the podium, an anonymous caricature (c. 1851).*

cemented into position by an imperturbable beating of time. In many cases, even the rough, literal maintenance of time and of each continuous bar |1,2,3,4,| 1,2,3,4,| clashes with the sense and expression. There, as elsewhere, *the letter killeth the spirit,* a thing to which I will never subscribe, however specious in their critical impartiality may be the attacks to which I am exposed.

For the works of Beethoven, Berlioz, Wagner, etc., I see less than elsewhere what advantage there could be . . . in a conductor trying to go through his work like a sort of *windmill,* and to get into a great perspiration in order to give warmth to the others. . . . In my opinion, the real task of a conductor consists in making himself seem superfluous. We are helmsmen, not oarsmen.[33]

This manifesto, with its pointed references to Kapellmeisters who understood nothing of modern music, and whose fixed batons could only go |1,2,3,4,| 1,2,3,4,| was published by Richard Pohl in his brochure *Das Karlsruher Musikfest im Oktober, 1853.* [34] The document provoked enmity at the time, although the

---

33. LLB, vol. 1, pp. 142–45.

34. HKM, pp. 83ff. Liszt's letter was later included by Lina Ramann in her edition of the *Gesammelte Schriften* under the title "Ein Brief über das Dirigieren: Ein Abwehr" (RGS, vol. 5, pp. 229–32). The influence of this essay, whose symptomatic title can be rendered into English as "A Letter on Conducting: A Defence," can clearly be felt in Richard Wagner's booklet *Über das Dirigieren,*

ideas it contained would be universally endorsed today. Of particular interest is Liszt's refusal to call himself a conductor, but rather a "musician-in-chief."

IV

By now a mantle of notoriety had spread itself over Liszt, yet that very fact made him attractive to festival committees with an eye on the box-office, and he received invitations to conduct in Ballenstedt, Berlin, Vienna, and Aachen. In January 1856 he directed the Mozart Centenary Festival in Vienna and received a silver baton from the organizers as a mark of their appreciation; but again the event was marred for him when Clara Schumann declined to appear on the same platform. Hanslick also stirred up controversy in the Viennese press by asking why Liszt had been invited to direct the festival at all, since there were others in Vienna better qualified to represent Mozart's music. He reminded his readers that Liszt was a champion of Wagner, who had once dismissed Mozart as "the first among the mediocre composers." What this sentiment had to do with Liszt was not made clear; but in the absence of anything better, guilt by association was a useful enough weapon with which to warn the representatives of the Weimar School to stay out of Vienna.[35] The one stipulation that Liszt usually made before accepting these prestigious invitations was that he be allowed to introduce new, or at any rate unfamiliar, works to his audiences. He was less than enthusiastic about conducting such well-worn pieces as Handel's *Messiah,* a work which had already become something of an institution. "Let the windmills do it" was his attitude. He did compromise when invited to direct this oratorio at the Aachen festival in 1857; but the price that the organizing committee had to pay in order to get Liszt to direct it at all was to accept performances of Berlioz's "Flight into Egypt," Wagner's *Tannhäuser* Overture, his own *Festklänge,* and Beethoven's little-known Mass in C major. His conducting of Beethoven was always a revelation. He directed the symphonies (particularly numbers three, five, and

---

published in 1869, some sixteen years after Liszt's pioneering effort appeared. About the many difficulties Liszt experienced at Karlsruhe, see HKM, pp. 78–82.

This was not the only occasion on which Liszt railed against the "windmills." In the score to his oratorio *St. Elisabeth* Liszt requested that conductors should "scarcely mark the beat." and added that the usual sort of time-beating amounted to little more than a brutal habit, which he would gladly banish from all his works. "Music is a succession of tones which cleave to one another, self-contained . . . and they are not to be joined by thrashing out the beats."

35. HGC, vol. 2, pp. 108–10. See also Liszt's memorial essay "Mozart: On the Occasion of His Centenary Festival in Vienna" (RGS, vol. 3, pp. 151–66). If Hanslick read this essay, he showed no sign of it. Nor does he appear to have known that Liszt was scarcely a novice with Mozart's music, having earlier conducted both *Die Zauberflöte* and *Don Giovanni* in their entirety as well as excerpts from *La clemenza di Tito.* For the complete programme directed by Liszt on January 27, 1856, Mozart's birthday, see p. 398.

nine) with frequency, and it is an interesting fact that he favoured slower tempi than was usual in his day. Mendelssohn had established the habit of fast perfor-mances of the classical repertory at Leipzig as early as the 1830s, an insight that comes to us from Wagner,[36] and the practice had caught on across Germany. The old German Kapellmeisters with no ideas of their own were doubtless grateful to him for establishing the trend, since it helped them to paper over the cracks in their orchestras. Liszt's practice of unfolding these mighty structures in a leisurely way commanded attention (although it was certainly harder on the players), since textural details were disclosed which were generally lost in the murk of a routine performance.

The following chronological table gives an overview of Liszt's activity as a conductor between the years 1840 and 1884. It is not complete, but it serves to draw attention to a neglected aspect of his career. The breadth of his repertory was surprisingly large, ranging from Handel and Gluck to Flotow and Nicolai. No other conductor of the day was responsible for so many first performances. Indeed, during the twelve short years in which he directed the Weimar opera house, he is known to have presented forty-four different operas to the public, twenty-five of them by living composers. That feat remained unmatched by any other opera house in the world.[37]

Although the table offers impressive evidence of Liszt's activity on the podium, it has to be stressed that it represents little more than a preliminary attempt to document his work in this area. In order to keep Liszt's achievements as a conductor intact, we have allowed the table to go beyond the confines of the Weimar years, through to his last engagements in the 1880s. The symbol (*) indicates a first performance. All concerts took place in Weimar unless otherwise specified.

This catalogue is noteworthy not for the amount of music it contains, although that is quite considerable. A casual glance will show that Liszt featured

---

36. WGSD, vol. 8, pp. 276–77. Schindler confirmed Wagner's observation. In 1852 he told Lowell Mason that Mendelssohn had injured Beethoven "by lending his great influence in favour of the quicker tempi, especially the allegros." It was not fast tempi as such to which Schindler objected, however, but the fact that "the inner parts lose their effectiveness" thereby. According to Schindler, three of the most experienced ear-witnesses of the time—Hummel, Hiller, and Czerny—all agreed that Beethoven himself directed his compositions more slowly than later became the fashion (MMLA, p. 147). It was Liszt's slow tempi in the Beethoven symphonies that attracted the attention of the critic of the *Allgemeine Musikalische Zeitung*, J. C. Lobe, when he first heard Liszt conduct three of these works in Weimar: "[Liszt] took the Beethoven symphonies mostly in a slower tempo than we heard them previously, and with surprising profit for their realization." (March 6, 1844)

37. The details of this chronological table have been culled from a variety of sources: e.g., the archives of the Weimar theatre; the contemporary press; Liszt's correspondence; and the diaries and journals of friends, pupils, and acquaintances such as Richard Pohl (PGS), William Mason (MMML), George Eliot (EGEL), and Adelheid von Schorn (SNW). The *Chronik* of Adolf Bartels (BCWH), and Wolfram Huschke's *Musik im klassischen und nachklassischen Weimar, 1756–1861* (HMW), are also indispensable guides. For Liszt's concerts in Hungary, the best information comes from Dezső Legány (LLC and LLFM).

1 8 4 0			
January 11	MOZART	Overture to *Die Zauberflöte*	Pest
	BEETHOVEN	Choral Fantasy	
	WEBER	Overture to *Oberon*	
	DONIZETTI	Duet from *Marino Faliero*	
	BEETHOVEN	Andante from Symphony No. 7 in A major	
	HAYDN	Chorus from *The Seasons*	
January 26	WEBER	Overture to *Oberon*	Pressburg
	ROSSINI	Overture to *William Tell*	
	ROSSINI	Two Choruses from *Semiramide*	

1 8 4 2			
February 28	BEETHOVEN	Symphony No. 5 in C minor	Berlin
	SPONTINI	Overture to *Olympie*	

1 8 4 3			
February 1	MOZART	Opera *Die Zauberflöte*	Breslau
February 16	BEETHOVEN	Overture to *Coriolan*	Berlin
	WEBER	Overture to *Oberon*	

1 8 4 4			
January 7	BEETHOVEN	Symphony No. 5 in C minor	Weimar
January 17	BEETHOVEN	Symphony No. 6 in F major *(Pastoral)*	Gotha
January 21	BEETHOVEN	Symphony No. 3 in E-flat major *(Eroica)*	
		Incidental Music to *Egmont*	
February 4	BEETHOVEN	Symphony No. 7 in A major	
	WEBER	"Jubel" Overture	
February 18	SCHUBERT	Symphony No. 9 in C major (the "Great") (one movement only)	
	BERLIOZ	Overture *King Lear*	

1 8 4 5			
August 12	BEETHOVEN	Symphony No. 5 in C minor	Bonn
	BEETHOVEN	Finale from *Fidelio*	

1 8 4 6			
February 22	BERLIOZ	Overture *Waverley*	
	WEBER	Overture to *Oberon*	
March 19	BEETHOVEN	Symphony No. 5 in C minor	Vienna
May 17	ERKEL	Overture to *Hunyadi László*	Vienna

1 8 4 8			
February 16	FLOTOW	Opera *Martha*	
March 5	BEETHOVEN	Symphony (unidentified)	
	NICOLAI	"Kirchliche" Overture	
March 21	BEETHOVEN	Opera *Fidelio*	
May 25	DONIZETTI	Opera *Lucia di Lammermoor*	
November 12	WAGNER	Overture to *Tannhäuser*	
	MEYERBEER	Opera *Les Huguenots*, Act Four	

1849

January 6	MOZART	Opera *Don Giovanni*
February 16	WAGNER	Opera *Tannhäuser*
February 27	GUSTAV SCHMIDT	Opera *Prince Eugen**
April 14	DUKE ERNST OF SACHSEN–COBURG	Opera *Toni, oder Die Vergeltung*
May 9	MOZART	Opera *Don Giovanni*
May 20	WAGNER	Opera *Tannhäuser*
June 2	BEETHOVEN	Opera *Fidelio*
June 12	MOZART	Opera *Don Giovanni*

Goethe Centennial Festival, August 28–29

August 28	LISZT	Symphonic Poem *Tasso**
	LISZT	*Goethe* March*
	BEETHOVEN	March from *The Ruins of Athens*
August 29	MENDELSSOHN	Overture *Calm Sea and Prosperous Voyage*
	SCHUMANN	*Scenes from Faust* (closing scene)
	BEETHOVEN	Symphony No. 9 in D minor ("Choral")

1850

January 16	BEETHOVEN	Opera *Fidelio*
February 16	GLUCK	Opera *Iphigenia in Aulis* (in Wagner's adaptation)
February 19	LISZT	Symphonic Poem *Tasso*
February 24	BEETHOVEN	Symphony No. 9 in D minor ("Choral")
end of February	LISZT	Symphonic Poem *Ce qu'on entend sur la montagne**
March 13	GLUCK	Opera *Iphigenia in Aulis*
April 1	ROSSINI	Opera *Le Comte Ory*
April 7	VAN HOVEN	Opera *Ein Abenteuer Karls II*
May 10	MENDELSSOHN	Oratorio *Elijah*
June 12	SIEGFRIED SALOMAN	Opera *Das Korps der Rache*

Herder Festival, August 24–26

August 24	LISZT	Overture (first version of the symphonic poem *Prometheus*) and Choruses to *Prometheus Unbound**
	BEETHOVEN	Symphony No. 9 in D minor ("Choral")
August 25	HANDEL	Oratorio *Messiah*
	GLUCK	Opera *Iphigenia in Aulis*
August 28	WAGNER	Opera *Lohengrin** (for Goethe's birthday celebration)
September 14	WAGNER	Opera *Lohengrin*
September 28	DONIZETTI	Opera *La Favorite*
October 1	HANDEL	Oratorio *Messiah*
October 9	WAGNER	Opera *Lohengrin*
October 19	BEETHOVEN	Violin Concerto in D major
	JOACHIM	Hungarian Concerto (soloist: Joachim)

1851

February 1	LORTZING	Opera *Zar und Zimmermann*
March 9	RAFF	Opera *König Alfred**

April 12	WAGNER	Opera *Lohengrin*
April 13	BERLIOZ	Symphony *Harold in Italy*
	CHERUBINI	Finale from *Die Wasserträger* (*Les Deux Journées*)
April 22	MOZART	Opera *Don Giovanni*
May 7	BEETHOVEN	Opera *Fidelio*
	MEYERBEER	Opera *Robert le diable*
	DONIZETTI	Opera *La Favorite*
May 11	WAGNER	Opera *Lohengrin*
June 21	MOZART	Opera *Don Giovanni*
July	LISZT	Symphonic Poem *Tasso*
	LISZT	Symphonic Poem *Ce qu'on entend sur la montagne*
October 3	HANDEL	Oratorio *Messiah*
October 26	MOZART	Opera *Don Giovanni*
November 11	SCHUMANN	Overture *The Bride of Messina*
December 13	BÜLOW	Overture *Julius Caesar* *
December 29	MOZART	Opera *Don Giovanni*

1852

January 14	HILLER	Symphony ("Es muss doch Frühling werden")
March 19	RAFF	Opera *King Alfred*
March 20	BERLIOZ	Opera *Benvenuto Cellini* *
April 11	HASLINGER	Symphonic cantata *Napoleon*
April 17	RAFF	Opera *König Alfred*
May 11	WAGNER	Overture *Faust*
May 31	WAGNER	Opera *Tannhäuser*
June 13	SCHUMANN	Overture and incidental music to *Manfred* *
June	WAGNER	Opera *Lohengrin*

Ballenstedt Music Festival, June 22–23

June 22	WAGNER	Overture to *Tannhäuser*	Ballenstedt-am-Harz
		Duet from *Der fliegende Holländer* (soloists: Feodor and Rosa von Milde)	
	LISZT	Song *Die Macht der Musik,* for soprano and orchestra (soloist: Rosa von Milde)	
	ALVARS	*Oberon* Fantasy for harp (soloist: Rosalie Spohr)	
	BEETHOVEN	Choral Fantasy (soloist: Hans von Bülow)	
	GLUCK	*Orpheus and Eurydice* (Act Two) (soloist: Franziska Schreck)	
	BEETHOVEN	Symphony No. 9 in D minor ("Choral")	
June 23	RAFF	Overture to *King Alfred*	
	WAGNER	*Das Liebesmahl der Apostel,* for male chorus and orchestra	
	BERLIOZ	Symphony *Harold in Italy*	
	MENDELSSOHN	Cantata *Die erste Walpurgisnacht*	
September 12	VERDI	Opera *Ernani*	
October 24	SPOHR	Opera *Faust*	

First Berlioz Week, November 14–21

November 18	BERLIOZ	Opera *Benvenuto Cellini* (revised version)
November 20		*Benvenuto Cellini*
November 21		Symphony *Roméo et Juliette*
		Cantata *La Damnation de Faust*
November 27	WAGNER	Opera *Lohengrin*

1853

February 6	VERDI	Opera *Ernani*
February 16	WAGNER	Opera *Der fliegende Holländer*
February 19	WAGNER	Opera *Der fliegende Holländer*
February 27	WAGNER	Opera *Tannhäuser*
March 2	WAGNER	Opera *Der fliegende Holländer*
March 5	WAGNER	Opera *Lohengrin*
March 13	LORTZING	Opera *Zar und Zimmerman*
March 19	RAFF	Opera *König Alfred*
March 29	MOZART	Opera *Don Giovanni*
April 3	MOZART	Opera *Die Zauberflöte*
April 21	SOBOLEWSKI	Opera *Vinvela*
May 8	FLOTOW	Opera *Martha*
May 21	FLOTOW	Opera *Indra*
May 22	MARX	Oratorio *Moses*
June 15	AUBER	Opera *Carlo Broschi* (to celebrate the silver jubilee of the reign of Grand Duke Carl Friedrich)

Karlsruhe Music Festival, October 3–5

October 3	WAGNER	Overture to *Tannhäuser*	Karlsruhe
	BEETHOVEN	Concert aria "No, perfido!" (soloist: Frau Howitz-Steinau)	
	JOACHIM	Violin Concerto ("Hungarian") (soloist: Joachim)	
	MENDELSSOHN	Finale from *Die Loreley*	
	SCHUMANN	Overture to *Manfred*	
	LISZT	Festival Chorus "An die Künstler"	
	BEETHOVEN	Symphony No. 9 in D minor ("Choral")	
October 5	MEYERBEER	Overture to *Struensee*	
	MOZART	Aria from *La clemenza di Tito* (soloist: Katinka Heinefetter)	
	MEYERBEER	Aria from *Le Prophète* (soloist: Heinefetter)	
	BEETHOVEN–LISZT	Fantasy on Motifs from *The Ruins of Athens,* for piano and orchestra (soloist: Bülow)	
	BERLIOZ	*Roméo et Juliette* (Part Two)	
	WAGNER	Fragments from *Lohengrin*	
	WAGNER	Overture *Tannhäuser* (repeated "by request")	
October 30	WAGNER	Opera *Der fliegende Holländer*	

1854

January 7	MOZART	Opera *Don Giovanni*	
January 22	DORN	Opera *Die Nibelungen*	
January 27	BERLIOZ	Oratorio *L'Enfance du Christ* (Part Two: "La fuite en Egypte")	
February 16	LISZT	Symphonic Poem *Orpheus**	
	GLUCK	Opera *Orpheus and Eurydice*	
February 19	BEETHOVEN	Opera *Fidelio*	
February 23	LISZT	Symphonic Poem *Les Préludes**	
	SCHUMANN	Symphony No. 4 in D minor	
	SCHUMANN	Concerto for four horns	
March 19	WEBER	Opera *Euryanthe*	
March 22	BEETHOVEN	Incidental Music to *Egmont*	
end of March	DUKE ERNST OF GOTHA	Opera *Santa Chiara*	Gotha
April 8	WAGNER	Opera *Lohengrin* (birthday of Grand Duchess Sophie)	
April 16	LISZT	Symphonic Poem *Mazeppa**	
	BERLIOZ	Overture *King Lear*	
April 19	LISZT	Symphonic Poem *Tasso*	
April 30	MEYERBEER	Opera *Robert le diable*	
June 5	DONIZETTI	Opera *Lucia di Lammermoor*	
June 24	SCHUBERT	Opera *Alphonso und Estrella**	
September 16	VERDI	Opera *Ernani*	
September 23	MOZART	Opera *Don Giovanni*	
October 11	MOZART	Opera *Don Giovanni*	
October 22	WAGNER	Opera *Lohengrin*	
October 25	DONIZETTI	Opera *Lucrezia Borgia*	
October 27	SCHUMANN	Overture *Manfred*	
		Symphony No. 4 in D minor	
		Piano Concerto in A minor (soloist: Clara Schumann)	
November 9	RUBINSTEIN	Opera *The Siberian Hunters**	
	LISZT	Symphonic Poem *Festklänge**	
November 22	RUBINSTEIN	Opera *The Siberian Hunters*	
December 10	WAGNER	Opera *Tannhäuser*	

1855

Second Berlioz Week, February 16–21

February 16	BERLIOZ	Opera *Benvenuto Cellini* (revised version)	
April 1	KÜHMSTEDT	Oratorio *Die Verklärung des Herrn*	
April 8	VERDI	Opera *I due Foscari*	
April 9	SCHUMANN	Opera *Genoveva*	
June 4	WAGNER	Opera *Tannhäuser*	
June 24	NICOLAI	Opera *The Merry Wives of Windsor*	
August 15	CORNELIUS	Mass	
October 18	LISZT	Symphonic Poem *Orpheus*	Braunschweig
		Symphonic Poem *Prometheus**	
November 10	BELLINI	Opera *I Puritani*	
November 18	MEYERBEER	Opera *Les Huguenots*	
December 6	LISZT	Symphonic Poem *Les Préludes*	Berlin

Ave Maria, for mixed chorus and
    orchestra
Piano Concerto No. 1 in E-flat major
    (soloist: Bülow)
Symphonic Poem *Tasso*
Thirteenth Psalm, for tenor solo,
    chorus, and orchestra*

1856

January 12	BELLINI	Opera *La sonnambula*	

Mozart Centennial Concerts, January 27–28

January 27	MOZART	Overture to *Die Zauberflöte*	Vienna
		Chorus "O Isis und Osiris" from	
		Die Zauberflöte	
		Piano Concerto in C minor, K. 491	
		(soloist: Josef Dachs)	
		Dies irae (Requiem)	
		Interval	
		Symphony No. 40 in G minor, K. 550	
		Aria from *Don Giovanni*	
		Finale from Act One, *Don Giovanni*	
January 28		Above concert repeated	
February 3	MOZART	Opera *Don Giovanni*	
February 16	BERLIOZ	Opera *Benvenuto Cellini* (revised edition)	
February 24	WAGNER	Opera *Lohengrin*	
March 19	BEETHOVEN	Opera *Fidelio*	
April 8	VERDI	Opera *I due Foscari*	
April 30	GLUCK	Opera *Orpheus and Eurydice*	
May 6	DONIZETTI	Opera *Lucrezia Borgia*	
May 8	GLUCK	Opera *Iphigenia in Aulis*	

Congress of the Music Festival of the Elbe, June 14

June 14	BEETHOVEN	Symphony No. 9 in D minor ("Choral")	Magdeburg
	WAGNER	Duet from *Der fliegende Holländer*	
August 24	MOSONYI	Offertory and Gradual (Mass)	Pest
August 31	LISZT	"Gran" Mass*	Gran
September 4	LISZT	"Gran" Mass	Pest
September 8	LISZT	Symphonic Poem *Hungaria**	Pest
a.m.	LISZT	Mass for Male Voices	
p.m.		Symphonic Poem *Les Préludes*	
	ERKEL	Hymn	
September 28	LISZT	"Gran" Mass	Prague
October 19	BEETHOVEN	Opera *Fidelio*	
November 12	BEETHOVEN	Symphony No. 3 in E-flat major *(Eroica)*	
November 23	LISZT	Symphonic Poem *Les Préludes*	St. Gallen
		Symphonic Poem *Orpheus*	
December 7	MOZART	Opera *Don Giovanni*	
December 26	WAGNER	Opera *Tannhäuser*	

1857

January 7	LISZT	Symphonic Poem *Ce qu'on entend sur la montagne* (final version)*	
	LISZT	Piano Concerto No. 2 in A major* (soloist: Hans von Bronsart)	
February 16	GLUCK	Opera *Armide*	
February 26	LISZT	Symphonic Poem *Les Préludes*	Leipzig
	WAGNER	Duet from *Der fliegende Holländer*	
	LISZT	Piano Concerto No. 1 in E-flat major (soloist: Bülow) Symphonic Poem *Mazeppa*	
March 13	GLUCK	Opera *Orpheus and Eurydice*	
March 15	LISZT	Psalm Thirteen	Jena
April 19	WAGNER	Opera *Lohengrin*	
May 2	WAGNER	Opera *Lohengrin*	

Lower Rhine Music Festival, May 31–June 2

May 31	BEETHOVEN	Overture *Consecration of the House*	Aachen
	HANDEL	*Messiah*	
June 1	BACH	Cantata No. 7, "Christ der Herr zum Jordan kam" (with the final chorus of Cantata No. 21)	
	SCHUBERT	Symphony No. 9 in C major ("The Great")	
	SCHUMANN	*Des Sängers Fluch* (Ballade nach Uhland)	
	LISZT	Symphonic Poem *Festklänge*	
	BERLIOZ	Oratorio *L'Enfance du Christ* (Part Two: "La Fuite en Egypte")	
June 2	MENDELSSOHN	Overture *Ruy Blas*	
	BEETHOVEN	Violin Concerto in D major (soloist: Edmund Singer)	
	WAGNER	Overture to *Tannhäuser*	
	LISZT	Piano Concerto No. 1 in E-flat major (soloist: Bülow)	
June 20	SCHUMANN	Oratorio *Paradise and the Peri*	

For the Unveiling of the Goethe-Schiller Monument in Weimar

| September 5 | LISZT | "An die Künstler," for male chorus and soloists (poem by Schiller) Symphonic Poem *Die Ideale* (after Schiller)* "Gruppe aus dem Tartarus" (Schiller) "Über allen Gipfeln ist Ruh" (Goethe), for male quartet "Schwager Kronos" (Goethe), for male chorus | |

Interval

A Faust Symphony, in three character sketches* (after Goethe)

		Faust	
		Gretchen	
		Mephistopheles, and the Finale, Chorus	
		Mysticus from *Faust* (Part Two)	
		"Weimars Volkslied," for male chorus	
September 6	WAGNER	Opera *Tannhäuser*	
September 27	BEETHOVEN	Opera *Fidelio*	
October 11	MOZART	Opera *The Marriage of Figaro*	
November 7	LISZT	*Dante* Symphony*	Dresden
December 13	LASSEN	Opera *Landgrave Ludwig's Bridal Journey*	
December 26	GLUCK	Opera *Alceste*	
December 29	BRONSART	*Frühlingsfantasie* for orchestra	
	PAGANINI	Adagio and Rondo from Violin Concerto No. 2 in B minor ("La campanella") (soloist: Sivori)	
	SCHUBERT–LISZT	"Die Allmacht" (soloist: Helene von Heimburg)	
		Interval	
	LASSEN	Lied (poem by Cornelius)	
	SCHUBERT	"Widmung" (soloist: Heimburg)	
	SIVORI	Hommage à Paganini (soloist: Sivori)	
	LISZT	Symphonic Poem *Hunnenschlacht**	
December 30	BEETHOVEN	Opera *Fidelio*	

1858

A Mozart Commemorative Concert, January 27

January 27	MOZART	Overture *Il re pastore*	
		Finale from Act Two of *Idomeneo*	
		Symphony No. 40 in G minor	
		Requiem (excerpts)	
February 18	GLUCK	Opera *Alceste*	
March 11	LISZT	Piano Concerto No. 2 in A major (soloist: Carl Tausig)	Prague
		Dante Symphony	
		Symphonic Poem *Die Ideale*	
March 14	LISZT	Symphonic Poem *Tasso*	Prague
		Piano Concerto No. 1 in E-flat major (soloist: Robert Pflughaupt)	
March 22	LISZT	"Gran" Mass	Vienna
March 23	LISZT	"Gran" Mass	Vienna
March 28	MENDELSSOHN	Oratorio *St. Paul*	
April 10	LISZT	"Gran" Mass	Pest
April 11	LISZT	"Gran" Mass	Pest
June 25	LISZT	Symphonic Poem *Hamlet*	
September 30	SOBOLEWSKI	Opera *Comala**	
October 2	GLUCK	Opera *Alceste*	
October 30	SOBOLEWSKI	Opera *Comala*	
November 4	ROSSINI	Opera *The Barber of Seville*	
December 5	MOZART	Opera *Die Zauberflöte*	
December 15	CORNELIUS	Opera *Der Barbier von Bagdad**	

A Beethoven Commemorative Concert

December 17	BEETHOVEN	Overture *The Consecration of the House*	
		Cantata *Calm Sea and Prosperous Voyage*	
		Romance in F major, for violin and orchestra (soloist: Singer)	
		Piano Concerto No. 5 in E-flat major (soloist: Martha von Sabinin)	
		Symphony No. 7 in A major	

1859

| February 27 | LISZT | Symphonic Poem *Die Ideale* | Berlin |
| April 9 | LISZT | *Huldigungsmarsch* | |

To Commemorate the Centenary of Handel's Death

| May 20 | HANDEL | Oratorio *Judas Maccabeus* | |
| May 21 | HANDEL | Oratorio *Messiah* | Erfurt |

The Tonkünstler-Versammlung in Leipzig

May 31	SCHUMANN	Opera *Genoveva*	Leipzig
June 1	WAGNER	Prelude to *Tristan und Isolde*	Leipzig
	LISZT	Symphonic Poem *Tasso*	
June 2	LISZT	"Gran" Mass	Leipzig
November 15	LISZT	Choruses from *Prometheus*	Zwickau

1861

| March 8 | LISZT | "The Dance at the Village Inn"* (First "Mephisto" Waltz) | |

1865

August 15	LISZT	Oratorio *St. Elisabeth**	Pest
August 17	LISZT	*Dante* Symphony ("Inferno") *Rákóczy* March	
August 23	LISZT	Oratorio *St. Elisabeth*	

1866

| January 3 | LISZT | Cantata "Stabat mater speciosa" from *Christus* (Part One) | Rome |
| March 11 | LISZT | *Dante* Symphony | Rome |

1867

| August 28 | LISZT | Oratorio *St. Elisabeth* | Wartburg Castle (Eisenach) |

1869

| April 26 | LISZT | "Coronation" Mass | Pest |
| April 30 | LISZT | "Coronation" Mass | Pest |

1 8 7 0

May 29	BEETHOVEN	Symphony No. 9 in D minor ("Choral")	
		Piano Concerto No. 5 in E-flat major	
		(Emperor) (soloist: Tausig)	

Beethoven Centennial Festival

December 16	BEETHOVEN– LISZT	Cantata No. 2 (soloists: Ilka Pauli, Emma Kvassay, Ferenc Schmidt)	Budapest

	BEETHOVEN	Violin Concerto in D major
		    (soloist: Reményi)
		Symphony No. 9 in D minor ("Choral")
		    (soloists: Ilka Pauli, Emma Kvassay,
		    Richard Pauli, Károly Kőszeghi)	

1 8 7 1

March 26	LISZT	Hungarian Rhapsody No. 6	Pest
March 29	SCHUBERT–LISZT	*Die Allmacht* (soloist: Mihály Bogisich)	Pest
April 5	ERKEL	Overture to *Csobánc*	Pest
	LISZT	Piano Concerto No. 2 in A major (soloist: Olga Janina)	
	ORCZY	Overture to *The Traitor*	
	BERTHA	Wedding March	
	MIHALOVICH	Symphony *The Ghost Ship*	
June	LISZT	Requiem	Jena

1 8 7 2

February 4	LISZT	Missa Choralis "Ave Maria" "O salutaris hostia"	Pest
March 19	HASSLER	Mass	Pest
	PALESTRINA	"O bone Jesu"	
	BERNABEI	"Salve regina"	
March 25	LISZT	Missa Choralis "Ave Maria"	Pest
	PALESTRINA	"Panis angelicus"	

1 8 7 3

March 19	LISZT	Szózat und ungarischer Hymnus*	Budapest
March 25	F. WITT	St. Cecilia Mass	Budapest
	LISZT	"Ave Maria"	
	LISZT	"Pater noster"	
May 29	LISZT	Oratorio *Christus* *	
September 8	BEETHOVEN	Symphony No. 9 in D minor ("Choral")	

1 8 7 4

January 5	LISZT	Psalm 137	Budapest
March 19	PALESTRINA	Mass "Iste confessor"	Budapest
March 25	LISZT	"Coronation" Mass (revised)	Budapest

1875			
March 10	LISZT	Cantata *Die Glocken des Strassburger Münsters* *	Budapest

1877			
March 5	LISZT	Oratorio *St. Elisabeth*	Budapest

1878			
June 19	BRONSART	Piano Concerto (soloist: Bülow)	

1879			
April 8	LISZT	"Gran" Mass	Vienna

1880			
March 23	LISZT	Cantata *Die Glocken des Strassburger Münsters*	Vienna

1882			
March 25	LISZT	"Coronation" Mass	Budapest

1883			
		Wagner Memorial Concert	
May 22	WAGNER	Prelude and Good Friday Music from *Parsifal*	

1884			
February 25	LISZT	"Coronation" Mass	Pressburg
May 25	BÜLOW	Symphonic Poem *Nirvana*	
	LISZT	Oratorio *St. Stanislas* (fragment)	

the works of friend and foe alike, without fear or favour. The compositions of Hiller, Schumann, Mendelssohn, and Joachim (historically regarded as his artistic rivals) are found side by side with those of his closest colleagues, Berlioz and Wagner. In music Liszt was never partisan; he tried to abolish boundaries, not create them. It was his conservative opponents who usually drew a line on the ground and dared him to cross it. Again, we must draw attention to the impressive number of operas that were staged. While Liszt was at the helm, Weimar's modest resources were kept at full stretch.

Why has Liszt's importance to the history of conducting gone unrecognized for so long? There are three possible reasons, although they are hardly valid today. First, his career was relatively short-lived, most of his activity being compressed into the decade between 1848 and 1858. Personalities such as Spohr, Smart, Michael Costa, and August Manns all enjoyed longer careers; one or two of them were there before Liszt took up the baton, and they were still there after he had put it down. Second, Liszt's insistence on championing the cause of contemporary music made it difficult for his peers to judge the musical results objectively, since they were still grappling with the difficulties of the works themselves. Moreover, as Berlioz and Wagner came forward to conduct their own music with increasing success, Liszt's pioneer work in their behalf tended to be forgotten. Finally, there was his reputation as a pianist, which overshadowed everything else that he did and robbed him of recognition in other fields. The great public, then as now, is an irrational judge: it has never been able to accept that a person may do more than one thing supremely well.

There is some evidence to suggest that Liszt hoped to place his disciples in key posts across Germany, so that by the 1860s the battle for the new music would be won. Owing entirely to Liszt's insistence, Bülow procured conducting engagements in Berlin while still in his early twenties; Ritter followed suit in Stettin. Tausig then took up the baton in Vienna, when he was barely out of his teens. Leopold Damrosch in Breslau and Karl Klindworth in London completed this impressive line-up. Each one of these young men featured modern music in his programmes; and some of them (Ritter and Tausig, for example) met with much opposition for so doing. It was to take longer than the ten years that Liszt envisaged for the task; but whatever headway new music made in the 1860s and '70s was made somewhat faster because of the advocacy of Liszt and the "Altenburg eagles."

The year 1857 was a low-point in Liszt's career as a conductor, producing one setback after another. The first occurred in February at Leipzig, when his symphonic poem *Mazeppa* was almost brought to a standstill by hisses from the audience. Shortly afterwards he conducted at the Lower Rhine Festival in Aachen, and after a performance of his E-flat-major Piano Concerto, with Bülow as soloist, there were some disgraceful scenes created by his old rival Ferdinand Hiller and a hired claque. But it was in Dresden in November 1857 that Liszt drank his cup of bitterness to the full, when his *Dante* Symphony was given its first, humiliating performance. This complex work was ruined by the players, who after only one rehearsal were still virtually sight-reading their parts, and the orchestra staggered from one crisis to another. Such incidents, to which we propose to add some detail later in the narrative, must have had a profound effect on Liszt's view of himself as a conductor. The Dresden fiasco, in fact, highlights a problem which Liszt always had to face whenever he took his orchestral works on tour with him: namely, that they had to be played from manuscript parts. Some of these parts may still be inspected in Weimar, and they are so heavily corrected that one wonders how the players ever deciphered them. We know from Liszt's correspondence that he frequently called for fresh copies, but his calligraphers sometimes cut corners and failed to indicate entry-cues despite his vigilance.[38] This must have had an unsettling effect on the players, particularly when the rehearsal amounted, as it did on the Dresden occasion, to little more than a run-through. It is a fact that the symphonic poems were considered to be such a poor commercial risk that the orchestral parts of most of them were not published until the 1880s.

After Liszt left Weimar, he had fewer opportunities to wield the baton in public. He returned to the podium to conduct important first performances of such works as his oratorios *St. Elisabeth* and *Christus* (given in Budapest and Weimar, respectively), but these occasions were exceptions. He had already started to delegate more of his engagements to Hans von Bülow (whose conducting career he had always promoted),[39] although on one or two occasions this may have harmed his cause. After Bülow conducted Liszt's *Die Ideale* in Berlin in 1859 and there were hisses in the hall, Bülow rounded on the audience and delivered the first of those many stage speeches for which he was to become famous, ordering the demonstrators to leave, "as it is not customary to hiss in this hall." His mercurial temperament aside, Bülow was Liszt's true heir as a conductor, carrying on his master's propaganda in behalf of modern music. And when he reached his definitive position with the Meiningen Court Orchestra, he set new standards of technical excellence, the best-known of which was having the entire orchestra play its repertory from memory.[40] But

---

38. There is a rueful hint of autobiography in the following comments of Liszt:

> Principles of economy are *utterly worthless* in copying; and, if you will trust my experience, always choose the best, and consequently the most expensive, copyists for transcribing the parts that you want. Recommend, into the bargain, that they do them with great care, and add the *cues* (which are a great help towards a good performance . . .). Look them over carefully with the copyist before the rehearsal—a work which I have often done in earlier years, and in which I generally make a rule of not sparing myself." (LLB, vol. 1, p. 220)

39. "Bülow should, before anything else, mount the conductor's podium a lot. He has the mind, enthusiasm, talent and vocation for it." (LLB, vol. 1, p. 327)

40. Bülow's work with the Meiningen Court Orchestra, over which he exercised dictatorial control, represents a refreshing exception to the dreary catalogue of misdemeanours that generally passed for music-making in the second half of the nineteenth century. His place in the history of conducting can hardly be overestimated. He became one of the great disciplinarians of the podium and was regarded by some as the best orchestral trainer in Europe. Most of the rank-and-file players had never before encountered a conductor like him, and they lived in fear and trembling of his autocratic manner and cowered before his imperious baton. On one occasion, however, it seems that he may have met his match. Franz Strauss, the leading hornist of the Munich Court Orchestra (and the father of Richard Strauss) played for a time under Bülow's direction. Strauss was given to blunt speech, and during a particularly gruelling rehearsal of *Tristan* he declared that he was tired and could play no more. "Then collect your pension," barked an irate Bülow from the rostrum. Whereupon Strauss picked up his horn, walked off the platform, and went straight to the office of the theatre intendant, Baron Karl von Perfall. "Herr von Bülow has ordered me to collect my pension," he said to the bemused official. It took all Perfall's skill as a diplomat to sort out the tangle, for both he and the crestfallen Bülow (who so admired Strauss that he used to call him "the Joachim of the horn") knew

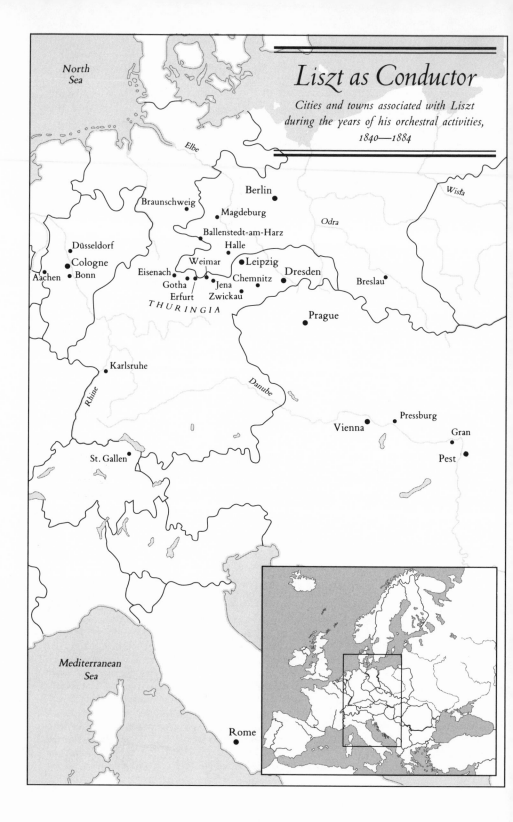

Liszt as Conductor

Cities and towns associated with Liszt
during the years of his orchestral activities,
1840—1884

North
Sea

Elbe

Wisła

Berlin

Braunschweig

Magdeburg

Odra

Ballenstedt-am-Harz

Düsseldorf

Halle

Cologne

Weimar

Leipzig

Aachen

Bonn

Eisenach

Chemnitz

Dresden

Breslau

Gotha

Jena

Erfurt

Zwickau

THURINGIA

Prague

Karlsruhe

Rhine

Danube

Pressburg

Vienna

Gran

St. Gallen

Pest

Mediterranean
Sea

Rome

there were others whose work on the podium also stemmed from Liszt and who were much admired by him, including Damrosch in Breslau, Eduard Stein in Sondershausen, and Max Seifriz in Löwenberg. During the 1860s and '70s, it was not unknown for Liszt to journey to these towns in order to hear his music played under their direction.

The two composers to whom Liszt had devoted most of his time and resources, Berlioz and Wagner, were both active as conductors after Liszt left Weimar—particularly Wagner, who gave many concerts across the years in Vienna, Berlin, Budapest, London, Prague, and St. Petersburg. Neither of them included a single composition by Liszt in their programmes. Lacking his artistic magnanimity, they were not really interested in modern music as such, only in that part of it represented by Berlioz or Wagner respectively. After 1878, when Liszt was often overtaken by physical fatigue, he rarely mounted the podium. On May 22, 1883, however, he was persuaded to conduct the Prelude and Good Friday Music from *Parsifal* at the Wagner Memorial Concert in Weimar. The other noteworthy exception was in 1884, when he conducted Bülow's orchestral work *Nirvana* for the festival of the Allgemeiner Deutscher Musikverein, held in Weimar. (The title *Nirvana*, which means "extinction," was one whose symbolism would not have been lost on Liszt.) At the same concert he directed a fragment of his unfinished oratorio *St. Stanislas,* at the conclusion of which he lay down his baton for good.

---

that the hornist was indispensable. They also knew that Strauss was married to a daughter of Pschorr, one of the wealthiest brewers in Munich, and that he needed neither his pension nor his salary. It is one more example of the way in which Bülow's sharp tongue could get him into difficulties with friend and foe alike.

Liszt and the Orchestra

The world persisted to the end in calling him the greatest pianist in order to avoid the trouble of considering his claims as one of the most remarkable of composers.

CAMILLE SAINT-SAËNS[1]

I

When Liszt put the finishing touches to his first set of symphonic poems in the spring of 1854, he was under no illusions as to how the wider world of music would receive them. In a letter to Antal Augusz dated March 1854, he wrote that a hail of criticism was already falling on his compositions in Vienna, Leipzig, Berlin, St. Petersburg, and even New York. "To approve of my works, or even to hear them without condemning them in advance, is a crime,"[2] he remarked ironically. And he added prophetically that he was prepared for the opposition to last for several years. In the event, it was to last a lifetime. One of the problems, as Liszt saw it, was that modern music in general, and his own music in particular, was made to suffer needlessly because it was so often badly positioned within the programme as a whole. In those days it was not unusual to unfold entire programmes chronologically—that is, according to the historical position of the works in question, beginning with the most remote and ending with the most recent. Liszt once took Erkel to task for not only placing the newly composed *Les Préludes* at the end of the programme but preceding it with a performance of Beethoven's *Pastoral* Symphony, thus forcing an unhappy comparison. "Unless one intends to sacrifice new works, which demand greater attention from audience and players alike," wrote Liszt, "the

---

1. *Harmonie et Mélodie* (Paris, 1885), p. 155.
2. CLBA, p. 43.

300

natural order is to place the symphonies of Beethoven, Mozart, or Haydn at the *end of the concert.* "[3] Even this wise precaution was not always enough to ensure a respectful hearing for his music. Hanslick tells us that when Liszt's *Prometheus* was performed in Vienna in 1860, it was followed immediately by Mozart's G-minor Symphony—according to Liszt's own ideal prescription. Scarcely had the orchestra got beyond the first four bars of the Mozart than the audience broke into spontaneous applause, an expression of its unbounded relief. It was as if a window had suddenly been flung open, wrote Hanslick, and fragrant spring air had wafted through the stale concert hall.[4]

In fact, the problems facing Liszt's orchestral works were of an entirely different order, unresolvable by a mere shift of position within the programme as a whole. The pieces represented a quantum leap forward in their use of musical materials, as we shall presently discover, and it was only to be expected that contemporary audiences would find them puzzling. Some of them had to wait until the twentieth century to find their definitive interpretations. Moreover, they poured out of Liszt's workshop at an alarming rate, or so it must have seemed to his detractors, who even as they successfully dodged one work were hit by another. Liszt composed very quickly, and he liked to work on several compositions simultaneously, even though they differed widely in character—as if each work were stimulated by the presence of all the others. He also had the rather rare gift of composing works in his head, down to the last detail, and holding them there until he had the opportunity to capture them on paper. He once told Agnès Street-Klindworth that although he had worked feverishly for three days on the Credo of his "Gran" Mass, he had at the same time four of the later numbers of this complex work "almost done in my head."[5] Even a cursory glance at Liszt's orchestral output during his Weimar years gives us pause for thought:

Work	Composition	Performance
SYMPHONIC POEMS		
Ce qu'on entend sur la montagne (after Victor Hugo)	(1) 1848–49, scored by Raff	Weimar, Feb. 1850, under Liszt
	(2) 1850, scored by Raff	Weimar, 1853, under Liszt
	(3) 1854, scored by Liszt	Weimar, Jan. 7, 1857, under Liszt
Tasso: Lamento e trionfo (after Byron)	(1) 1841–45, Liszt's sketch	

3. CLBA, p. 45.
4. HGC, vol. 2, p. 200. "I wish I had been there," wrote Clara Schumann. "I should have wanted to join in their rejoicings." (JMBJ, vol. 2, p. 75)
5. LLB, vol. 3, p. 7.

Work	Composition	Performance
	(2) scored by Conradi, later corrected by Liszt	Weimar, Aug. 28, 1849, as overture to Goethe's *Torquato Tasso*
	(3) 1850–51, scored by Raff	
	(4) 1854, revised by Liszt (central section appears for first time)	Weimar, April 19, 1854, under Liszt
Les Préludes (after Lamartine)	(1) 1848, as an introduction to the choral work *Les Quatre Elémens*	
	(2) early 1850s, revised by Liszt	Weimar, Feb. 23, 1854, under Liszt
Orpheus	1853–54	Weimar, Feb. 16, 1854, as introduction to Gluck's *Orpheus and Eurydice,* under Liszt
Prometheus	(1) 1850, as overture to the choruses from Herder's *Prometheus,* scored by Raff	Weimar, August 24, 1850, under Liszt
	(2) 1855, revised by Liszt	Braunschweig, Oct. 18, 1855, under Liszt
Mazeppa (after Victor Hugo, expanded from the piano study)	(1) 1851, scored by Raff	
	(2) 1854, revised by Liszt	Weimar, April 16, 1854, under Liszt
Festklänge (intended for Liszt's forthcoming nuptials with Princess Carolyne)	1853	Weimar, Nov. 9, 1854, under Liszt
Héroïde funèbre (based on first movement of early "Revolutionary" Symphony)	(1) 1849–50, scored by Raff	
	(2) 1854, revised by Liszt	Breslau, Nov. 10, 1857
Hungaria	1854	Pest National Theatre, Sept. 8, 1856, under Liszt
Hamlet	1858, as prelude to Shakespeare's play	Sondershausen, July 2, 1876, under Max Erdmannsdörfer
Hunnenschlacht (after Kaulbach)	1857	Weimar, Dec. 29, 1857, under Liszt
Die Ideale (after Schiller)	1857	Weimar, Sept. 5, 1857, under Liszt

SYMPHONIES

Work	Composition	Performance
Faust Symphony, in three character sketches (after Goethe)	1854 1857 (addition of final chorus)	Weimar, Sept. 5, 1857, under Liszt
Dante Symphony	1855–56	Dresden, Nov. 7, 1857, under Liszt

Work	Composition	Performance
WORKS FOR PIANO AND ORCHESTRA		
Fantasia on Motifs from Beethoven's *The Ruins of Athens*	(1) c. 1837 (2) 1849, revised by Liszt	Pest, June 1, 1853, under Erkel (soloist: Bülow)
Fantasia on Hungarian Folk-Tunes (based on Hungarian Rhapsody No. 14)	1852 (?)	Pest, June 1, 1853, under Erkel (soloist: Bülow)
Piano Concerto No. 1 in E-flat major	(1) 1830–49, scored by Raff (2) 1853, revised by Liszt (3) 1856, revised again by Liszt	Weimar, Feb. 17, 1855, under Berlioz (soloist: Liszt)
Piano Concerto No. 2 in A major	(1) 1839 (2) 1849 (3) 1853 ⎫ revised by Liszt (4) (4) 1857 ⎬ (5) 1861 ⎭	Weimar, Jan. 7, 1857, under Liszt (soloist: Hans von Bronsart)
Totentanz (paraphrase on "Dies irae")	(1) 1838–49 (2) 1853 revised by Liszt (3) 1859 revised by Liszt (3)	The Hague, April 15, 1865, under Johann Verhulst (soloist: Bülow)
CHORAL WORKS		
Missa solennis (for inauguration of the basilica at Gran)	(1) 1855 (2) 1857–58 revised by Liszt	Gran, Aug. 31, 1856, under Liszt
Psalm Thirteen ("Herr, wie lange")	(1) 1855 (2) 1859 revised by Liszt (3) 1862 revised by Liszt	Berlin, Dec. 6, 1855, under Liszt
Psalm Eighteen ("Die Himmel erzählen die Ehre Gottes")	1860	Weimar, June 25, 1861
Psalm Twenty-three ("Mein Gott, der ist mein Hirt")	(1) 1859 (2) 1861 revised by Liszt	

The above table is based on the catalogues of Raabe, Searle, and Winklhofer. Much work is presently going on in the field of Liszt manuscript studies, however, which keeps the dates of his compositions in a state of flux. The purpose of this table is merely to draw attention to the enormous diversity of Liszt's output during the Weimar years, not to raise afresh the old spectre of chronology. The newly begun Complete Thematic Catalogue of Liszt's works, which is now being compiled by an international team of experts centred in Hungary, will attempt to lay this particular ghost to rest, and it promises to become the most authoritative source for the next generation of scholars.

This is an extremely large body of work for so brief a period. With the passing years some of these pieces have assumed historical importance—that is to say, they have changed the way in which subsequent composers have handled musical form, to say nothing of the orchestra. Their stunning originality, both as soundscapes and as structures, cannot be denied: many of Liszt's newer orchestral effects have even found their way into textbooks on instrumentation, where they continue to absorb and influence all serious students of the topic. Liszt, in short, treated the orchestra as he treated the piano, as an instrument of virtuosity, there to be conquered and turned into a tool of musical expressiveness. He learned to orchestrate as he went along. Scholars may wrangle over the question of exactly how much help he received from his assistants Conradi and Raff in the early days of their collaboration, but the argument is rendered academic the moment we recall one single fact: every note of the published scores was penned by him. Many years later, when Liszt reflected on his years in Weimar, he spoke of how important it had been for his development as a composer to secure performances of his works. "I needed to hear them in order to get an idea of them."[6] And he added that it was much more for that reason than for any mundane desire to secure a public for his music that he concerned himself with their promotion in Weimar and elsewhere. Liszt, in short, was a perfect illustration of Schoenberg's aphorism that a genius learns not only from others but also from himself.

Twelve of the orchestral compositions of the Weimar years were eventually offered to the world under the name "symphonic poems." There is evidence that this unique title, which describes a unique genre, dawned on Liszt only slowly. It was used in public for the first time at a concert in Weimar, on April 19, 1854, to identify Liszt's *Tasso,* and the title evidently pleased him. It is, in fact, one of Liszt's happiest terms, meant to describe a one-movement composition, connected in some way with the other arts (particularly poetry and painting), and whose internal musical contrasts are held together by thematic metamorphosis. Five days after the *Tasso* performance we find him writing a letter to Hans von Bülow in which he refers to *Les Préludes* and *Orpheus* also as "poèmes symphoniques."[7] In June, Wagner writes to Liszt and urges him to bring "deine symphonischen Poesien mit"—an indication that the title was not yet properly established even among Liszt's friends. In fact, Liszt himself continued to talk loosely of his "freely composed" pieces as late as the summer of 1854, as his correspondence with the publisher Raimund Härtel shows. Härtel eventually brought out six of the full scores in April 1856, under the title "Symphonischen Dichtungen," and on May 9 he sent fifty copies of each work to Liszt in Weimar—the only "fee" that Liszt ever received for these path-

---

6. LLB, vol. 3, p. 189.
7. LBLB, p. 75.

breaking compositions.[8] Performances of the symphonic poems under other conductors were rare, and Härtel made very little money out of them. Liszt, as we know, was not entirely unhappy about this, since he feared their distortion in careless hands. Nonetheless, it is symptomatic of a general neglect that the orchestral parts were not published until much later, between the years 1864 and 1884. Manuscript parts were used whenever there happened to be a demand for these works, and since they were often re-copied, the Weimar orchestra's library soon filled up with alternative (not to say contradictory) versions of the same piece. In a letter to Härtel dated October 28, 1864 (that is, just before the work of engraving the parts was about to begin), Liszt told him, "Sei es autographiert, sei es gestochen"—"If it is signed by me, it may be published."[9]

Together with the *Faust* and *Dante* symphonies, the twelve symphonic poems represent Liszt's chief contribution to "programme music." Each one of these fourteen works, that is to say, was inspired by the literary or pictorial model which adorns its title-page. It will not escape attention that most of them deal with exceptional heroes—*Hamlet, Mazeppa, Prometheus, Faust, Tasso,* and *Orpheus,* characters who confront overwhelming odds or find themselves in an impossible dilemma. Liszt readily identified with their struggle and did some of his best work in their company, so to speak. To call these compositions "programme music" at all raises many difficulties, but we accept the term because Liszt himself used it and went out of his way to defend it.[10] The essential point is that these pieces are not "representational" in the strict sense of being about specific things or events. For Liszt, the music is always more important than the literary or pictorial ideas behind it, and it will always unfold according to its own laws. By giving his works these titles, he is really disclosing the source of his inspiration, which we may accept or lay aside. But what, it may be asked, of Liszt's written programmes which were published as frontispieces to the scores? Do they not suggest that the music which follows is about something quite literal and tangible? It is here that we find unexpected support for our view. They are not so much programmes as prefaces, and even to call them by this latter term tends to obscure their true nature. Some of them are best described as letters to the general public. One or two of them contain charming autobiographical disclosures in which Liszt tells us how he came to write that particular work, or perhaps draws our attention to the philosophical idea that the music attempts to enshrine. Take the preface to *Orpheus,* for example, which begins with a disarming confession:

---

8. They were *Tasso, Les Préludes, Orpheus, Prometheus, Mazeppa,* and *Festklänge.*
9. WA, Kasten 571/1, p. 10.
10. See, for example, his letter to Walter Bache, written in 1878, in which he quotes with approval Niecks's comment that "Programm-Music is *a legitimate genre of the art*" (Liszt's English, his italics; LLB, vol. 2, p. 265).

I once had to conduct a performance of Gluck's *Orpheus*. During
the rehearsals, I could not prevent my mind wandering . . . to that
other Orpheus whose name hovers so majestically and harmoniously
over one of the most poetic myths of Greece. I recalled an Etruscan
vase in the Louvre collection, which represents the first poet-musi-
cian, clothed in a starry robe, his forehead bound with the mystically
royal fillet, his lips open for the utterance of divine words and songs,
and his lyre resounding under the touch of his long and graceful
fingers.

Within the space of a few simple sentences, Liszt gives his listeners all the
information he thinks they will need about the "programmatic" connotations
of the piece. To be sure, it is both useful and interesting to be provided with
these and other autobiographical asides. But will it help us to pictorialize the
music that follows? Not long after the first few prefaces were ready, Liszt told
Louis Köhler that their purpose was simply "to render the perception of the
[symphonic poems] more plain."[11] Elsewhere he said that he wished only "to
guard the listener against a false interpretation." This was a reflection of the
historical position in which he found himself. During the previous fifty years,
music had been democratized beyond all recognition, and there was now a vast
new public for instrumental music, which previously had commanded the
attention of just a handful of connoisseurs. Liszt was well aware of the general
public's fondness for attaching stories to instrumental music, from Bach to
Chopin, in an attempt to explain the inexplicable, and he wanted to prevent
that from happening to his own. The prefaces, in short, were there to provide
some context before "context" was provided by others.[12] Consider, again, the
preface to *Prometheus*. Liszt reminds us that it was the unveiling of the Herder

---

11. LLB, vol. 1, p. 154.

12. Liszt must have been well aware of the abysmal attempts to subject Beethoven's music to such
treatment. The Fifth Symphony (with its "fate knocking at the door" motif), the Eighth Symphony
(with its supposed tongue-in-cheek references to Maelzel's metronome), and the finale of the F-major
String Quartet, op. 135 (whose motto, "Must it be—it must be!," according to Schindler, depicts
nothing more than the master's cook asking for housekeeping money) show what can happen when
the man-in-the-street becomes too curious about the mysterious workings of a genius's mind. But
these cases, bad though they are, pale into insignificance when set beside the farrago of nonsense which
was already starting to accumulate around the works of Chopin. Thus, the opening figure of his
"Minute" Waltz was supposed to represent the wagging tail of George Sand's dog, while the great
Barcarolle was reduced to a picture of two lovers in a gondola, with a kiss at bar 78! As for the
F-minor Fantasy, its first two bars, so we learn, illustrate a knock at Chopin's door; the next two,
his reply ("Entrez, entrez!"); and the door opens to admit George Sand, Camille Pleyel, Liszt, and
others, who arrange themselves around Chopin to the solemn tread of the march. Eventually Sand,
with whom he has quarrelled, falls on her knees and begs forgiveness. Vladimir de Pachmann used
to tell this particular story on the concert stage, before delivering his "interpretation" of the fantasy,
and after cheerfully informing the audience that he "got it straight from Liszt." Thus is musical
history made.

monument in Weimar in 1850 which was the starting-point for this work. The music originated as an overture to his so-called *Prometheus* Choruses, settings of texts drawn from Herder's *Prometheus Unbound,* which were performed during the ceremonials. Later, Liszt worked it up into a symphonic poem. After acknowledging that there are conflicting versions of the myth, Liszt goes on:

> It was sufficient to translate into music those phases of feeling which, under repeatedly varied forms of the myth, together constitute its entirety, its soul: namely, boldness, suffering, endurance, and redemption. . . .
>
> Suffering and apotheosis! Thus compressed, the fundamental idea of this too-truthful fable demanded a sultry, stormy, and tempestuous mode of expression. A desolating grief, triumphing at last by energy and perseverance, constitutes the musical character of the piece now offered to notice.

Again, Liszt is providing a very general context for the work that follows. The pictorialization of a detailed programme is simply not an issue. And there are two further points to observe. First, the prefaces were written after the music was composed, an unusual sequence of events for genuine programme music: in such circumstances, one might with equal logic talk of "programmes about music." Secondly, there is evidence that Princess Carolyne had a hand in their formulation.[13] The conclusion seems clear enough. Posterity may have over-estimated the importance of extra-musical thought in Liszt's symphonic poems.

---

13. The final proof of that fact is to be found in an unpublished letter from Carolyne to Liszt, dated March 31, 1854. Liszt had left Weimar for a few days in order to conduct the first performance of the opera *Santa Chiara,* by the duke of Gotha, and in the absence of anything better to do, Carolyne had begun to sketch out some of the prefaces while he was away.

> Dearly beloved!
> I have finished the five prefaces—*Montagne, Préludes, Mazeppa, Orpheus,* and *Prometheus.* They are short, and they bring together some quotations that please me! But it's nothing! I won't send them to you, so as to help you bear another expense—for *ein Körbchen* [i.e., "a little basket"—Carolyne had asked Liszt to buy her such a gift in Gotha]. We'll read them together, and we'll argue! Ah! I'm wedded enough to my opinion to defend them blow by blow, word by word. (WA, Kasten 34, u. 3)

This letter was written after all five of these symphonic poems had been composed. Three of them—*Ce qu'on entend sur la montagne, Les Préludes,* and *Orpheus*—had already received their first performances in Weimar, even though the title "symphonic poem" had not yet been extended to them.

Two points of interest to us here emerge from Carolyne's letter. She tells us that she herself "finished" the prefaces—a not entirely helpful comment, since it leaves open the question of who started them. Also she informs us that they "bring together some quotations," but the published prefaces to *Orpheus* and *Prometheus* do not contain any quotations at all. We are therefore left to conclude that when Liszt returned from Gotha he and the princess *did* argue—as she confidently predicted they would—and Liszt's views prevailed.

We would not be without his prefaces, of course, nor any other comments that he made about the origins of his music; but we should not follow them slavishly, for the simple reason that the symphonic poems do not follow them slavishly either. Perhaps the most enlightened gesture that posterity could now make towards Liszt is to attend to his orchestral works as it attends to those of Beethoven or Brahms. In the final analysis, Liszt's "programme music" must stand or fall as music. Indeed, he himself said as much, in one of those thought-provoking aphorisms that jump from the page as if propelled by the interior springs of their own logic. After reminding us that a Slavic poet had once proclaimed, "The word lies to the thought;/The deed lies to the word." Liszt added: "But music does not lie to the feelings."[14]

II

The discovery in modern times of the prophetic music of Liszt's old age has, paradoxically, obscured for us the originality of these pieces of the earlier Weimar period, which in their way contain music as bold and uncompromising as anything he wrote in later life. Particularly striking is Liszt's new approach to form. Judged purely as musical structures, the twelve symphonic poems and the *Faust* and *Dante* symphonies show some stunning departures from those conventional uses of sonata form still employed by his contemporaries. Recapitulations are foreshortened; codas assume developmental proportions; themes are re-shuffled into new and unexpected sequences; three- or four-

---

14. RGS, vol. 4, pp. 31–32. The thought may be found in Liszt's absorbing essay "Berlioz and his *Harold* Symphony" (1855); it occurs in the middle of the section dealing with instrumental programme music, the very genre that was at that moment in the forefront of Liszt's own mind and occupying his own creative thoughts. In this seminal brochure, Liszt goes to great lengths to explain to his readers (who had already been treated to a performance of the Berlioz work in Weimar in 1851) what are the aesthetic foundations and historical precedents for instrumental programme music. He points to Kuhnau's "Biblical" Sonatas, Bach's *Capriccio on the Departure of His Dearly Beloved Brother,* and certain works of Beethoven—notably the *Eroica* and *Pastoral* symphonies, and the *Les Adieux* Piano Sonata—as representative of a whole repertory of pieces that lends the genre both dignity and distinction.

To put Liszt's view of the matter at its simplest, no composer of programme music expects his programme to be divined from the notes of the score alone. The programme merely invites us into the composer's workshop; and once we are there, it may disclose to us the source of his inspiration, explain to us why the music happens to display those manifold characteristics that attracted us to it in the first place. But we cannot be compelled to enter. In which case, what becomes of those who remain outside? It is here that the division between "absolute" and "programme" music melts away. A good programme can never save a bad piece; a good piece can never be harmed by a bad programme. Music remains music, whatever its origin. This truism had already been well expressed by Robert Schumann, who, long before the topic had become divisive, wrote: "I always say, 'First of all let me hear that you have made beautiful music; after that I will like your programme too.' " (NZfM 18 [1843])

movement structures are rolled into one; kaleidoscopic contrasts are integrated by means of the metamorphosis of themes. "New wine demands new bottles,"[15] was how Liszt justified himself before the bar of history. He could be critical of those musicians who continued to use the same stale formulas, and he once accused the youthful Anton Rubinstein of "fishing in Mendelssohnian waters."[16] He would have agreed with Hugo Wolf, who once invited those who still yearned for symphonies in the style of Beethoven to "raise the master from the dead."[17] Liszt's radical treatment of form did not go undetected by Arnold Schoenberg, who selected it for special comment in his little-read commemorative essay on the composer.[18] Bartók, too, was well aware of Liszt's inventiveness in this area. Did he not pay Liszt the greatest compliment by modelling the structure of his B-minor Violin Concerto on the "blue-print" left behind by Liszt in his *Faust* Symphony? In both cases, the last movement is a vast metamorphosis of the first—an audacious solution to the problem of the symphonic finale.

Liszt's "metamorphosis of themes" technique, in fact, represents a lasting contribution to the history of musical form. A simple illustration occurs in the A-major Piano Concerto. Its opening lyrical melody

is later transformed into the march-theme of the finale

which in turn is metamorphosed into the impassioned theme near the end of the concerto.

15. SE, p. 76.
16. LLB, vol. 1, p. 180.
17. *Wiener Salonblatt*, April 27, 1884.
18. SSI, pp. 442–47.

The technique of thematic transformation is essentially that of variation. At its best, we hear a constantly shifting, kaleidoscopic surface, ever changing but ever the same. Basic ideas are plunged into the creative fire and emerge transfigured, donning and doffing their disguises along the way. This kind of procedure placed the whole question of structural integrity into a new context and led to compositional trends which are still being worked out in our century.

Liszt was not the first composer to "metamorphose" his themes, of course; Beethoven had already pointed the way in such works as his Ninth Symphony, where the sublime "Ode to Joy" theme is at one point transformed into a bizarre Turkish march, complete with cymbals and drums. Weber and Berlioz, too, had both employed the technique. But if we wish to identify one work that had a greater influence on Liszt than all the others, we shall find it in Schubert's *Wanderer* Fantasy, whose several movements are all bound together by metamorphosis, and whose original form Liszt so much admired that he arranged the work for piano and orchestra.

These were distinguished precedents, but it was left to Liszt to perfect the technique by creating entire structures from metamorphosis alone. Again the A-major Piano Concerto provides a good example of just how far he was prepared to carry the method. The scherzo begins with the following theme, in B-flat minor:

It re-appears at the end of this section disguised as a totally different melody, in E major. So complete is the transformation, in fact, that we can remain on terms of intimacy with this concerto for years and still fail to recognize the true nature of the connection. Key, mode, time-signature, pace, and colour have all been changed to bring about a radically "new" theme. To alter so much of the notation while remaining true to the essential idea behind it is a tribute to Liszt's ingenuity.

III

Liszt's quest for orchestral colour is endlessly fascinating. Occasionally it leads him to cover the manuscript with imperatives, addressed to players and conductors alike, which are meant to prompt them towards his acoustical goal. What were contemporary players to make of such comments as this, found in the development section of the *Dante* Symphony?

This entire passage is intended to be a blasphemous mocking laughter, very sharply accentuated in the two clarinets and violas.

A similar example of Liszt's pursuit of unusual orchestral colours occurs at the beginning of *Hunnenschlacht* ("Battle of the Huns"). He writes in the score:

Conductors: The entire colour should be kept very dark, and all instruments must sound like ghosts.

And against this background of suppressed fury, Liszt introduces a striking figure on the horns, which he describes in the score as a *Schlachtruf*—a "battle-cry."

This was a new experience for orchestral players. To be told at one moment to "sound like ghosts" and at another to produce a "battle-cry" must have created bewilderment in the rank and file. Nowhere, in fact, is the distance that separated Liszt from the standard orchestral music of the 1850s more clearly revealed than in *Hunnenschlacht.* Inspired by Kaulbach's painting of the same name, this symphonic poem depicts the battle of the Catalanian Fields in A.D. 451, in which the pagan hordes of Attila the Hun clashed with the Christian armies of Emperor Theodoric for the capture of Rome.[19] So fierce was the slaughter that, according to legend, the souls of dead warriors rose into the air and continued the battle in the sky. This image gave rise to one of Liszt's most striking effects. At one point, the music divides into two seemingly different compositions: one unfolds the "battle" itself, while the other unfolds the ancient plainchant theme "Crux fidelis," which rides serenely above the din of conflict.[20] It is difficult to imagine what the average orchestral player of the mid–nineteenth century would have made of such a texture.

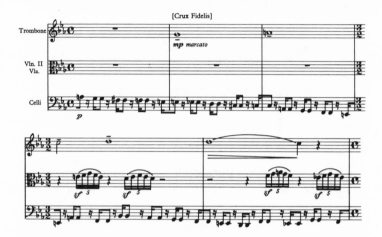

Hunnenschlacht also contains an important part for organ, which in a performance in the concert hall should, according to Liszt's wishes, "be placed out of sight, behind curtains." Under these ideal conditions, the phrases of "Crux fidelis" given to the organ appear to float disembodied above the auditorium. The sonic image is unusual, and it is rarely achieved, because Liszt's instructions are usually ignored. It was Liszt's interest in such "stereophonic contrasts" that led him to experiment with the unusual seating arrangement required in the Magnificat of the *Dante* Symphony. He wanted the female choir not only to be physically separated from the orchestra but to be invisible as well.

> The women's or boys' choir is not to be placed in front of the
> orchestra but is to remain invisible together with the harmonium,

---

19. This information, which comes from Liszt's preface, is historically inaccurate. Theodoric was not yet born in A.D. 451. Moreover, Attila's bid for Rome was in A.D. 452, and it was repulsed by Leo I. As if to forestall such faultfinding, Liszt tells us charmingly that he got the tale from Kaulbach, who in turn got it from "a young savant" in Rome. None of this makes any difference to the music, of course, or to Kaulbach's painting, the topic of which simply moves from the category of history to that of myth.

20. Liszt himself described the dual nature of this music rather well as "two opposing streams of light in which the Huns and the Cross are moving" (LLB, vol. 1, p. 281).

or in the case of an amphitheatrical arrangement of the orchestra, is to be placed right at the top. In places having a gallery above the orchestra, it would be suitable to have the choir and harmonium positioned there. In any case, the harmonium must remain near the choir.[21]

This last injunction, that the choir and harmonium remain together, was born of rueful experience. Liszt had learned much about the limitations of choirs from the first performance of the *Dante* Symphony, in Dresden in 1857, which had come close to breaking down. The harmonium represented a solid support against those renegade players and singers whom Liszt used to call "tone-smearers."[22] He knew that his music often posed problems of intonation, but he felt that half the blame should be shouldered by those performers who all too often ruined it. His withering epithet suggests that he had a demanding ear when it came to orchestral intonation. This is borne out by the occasional direction to individual players, who, possibly for the first time, realized that they were actually expected to listen critically to the sounds that they produced. The hapless double-bass player, faced with such an imperative as the following, would surely rub his eyes in astonishment:

Eis hoch nehmen
[Take the E sharp high]

"Take the E-sharp high" was indeed a sophisticated demand when most double-bass players of the day would have been hard-pressed merely to play the E-sharp in tune.[23]

Nowhere is Liszt's interest in orchestral sound seen more clearly than in his

---

21. Footnote to the Magnificat section of the score of the *Dante* Symphony.

22. LLB, vol. 3, p. 18.

23. To this must be added the fact that the passage in question, from *La notte* (the second of the Three Funeral Odes), did not pose a problem in Liszt's lifetime, because the work had to wait until 1916 before it was even published.

individualistic use of the percussion instruments—the *canaille,* or "rabble," as he humourously called the triangle, cymbal, and drums. Already in 1857, we find him defending the regular use of these instruments in a symphony orchestra and asserting, "I shall yet win for them some effects little known."[24] Liszt was the first to raise the triangle to the rank of a solo instrument in the scherzo of his E-flat-major Piano Concerto.

The effect provoked much criticism from conservative critics, and Liszt concluded (as he often did in such circumstances) that the fault lay with the players. After much thought he proposed a solution: "In the E-flat-major Concerto I have now hit on the expedient of striking the triangle (which aroused such anger and gave such offence) quite lightly with a *tuning-fork.*"[25] And he once told the pianist Alfred Jaëll to "take care that the triangle is not of too base extraction and has not too vulgar a vibration, [and] see that the triangle player does his job delicately, precisely, and intelligently."[26] Liszt also explored the character of the bass-drum, from which he drew some unusual effects. He may well have been the first to call for a bass-drum-roll, which occurs at the beginning of *Ce qu'on entend sur la montagne.* His recommendation to the player is to use timpani sticks.

At the beginning of the Hungarian Fantasy, Liszt employs a muffled kettle-drum, an effect that had captured his imagination when he first heard it in Berlioz's "March to the Scaffold." He returned to the sound at the beginning of the Second Funeral Ode, where he instructs the player to cover the kettle-drum's membrane with cloth and also to employ sponge-headed sticks.

24. LLB, vol. 1, p. 275.
25. LLB, vol. 1, p. 302. In this same letter, to his pupil Dionys Pruckner, Liszt also reveals that he removed the triangle altogether from a number of places in the finale, because the ordinary triangle-virtuosi, as he dubbed them, "usually come in wrong and strike it too hard."
26. *La Revue Musicale,* January 15, 1904.

An equally eerie sound is conjured up in the introduction to the *Dante* Symphony, where a double timpani-roll is crowned by a muffled gong—akin to the ominous rumble of a stifled volcano in Dante's Hell.

One little-known effect that Liszt won for the timpani was that of producing harmony from them. In the closing measures of *Die Ideale* three timpani, tuned to F, A, and C, yield the chord of F major:

In an untranslatable pun, Hans von Bülow called these sounds "Ohrfeigen für feige Ohren" ("cuffs for cowardly ears").[27] Although he considered the effect "a new and bold invention," he begged Liszt to re-write these bars, since the work was hissed after Bülow conducted it in Berlin (January 14, 1859). Liszt quite rightly resisted the idea and refused to allow Bülow to make the change when he repeated the performance in Prague a few weeks later.

It is in the symphonic poem *Héroïde funèbre* that Liszt's fascination with the percussion section comes into its own. He employs four timpani, two bells, military side-drum, gong, cymbals, and bass-drum. From this large battery of instruments he draws a wonderful variety of sonic effects rarely heard in the orchestral music of the nineteenth century.

---

27. LBLB, p. 262.

I V

The presence in the Weimar orchestra of individual virtuosi—the trombonist Moritz Nabich, the harpist Jeanne Pohl, and the violinists Joachim and Edmund Singer—made it possible for Liszt to call for effects which were unobtainable elsewhere. He mixed daily with these musicians, and their discourse must have been filled with "shop talk." At the beginning of *Héroïde funèbre,* for instance, Liszt writes a menacing low B-flat for the bass trombone, a note that lies outside the instrument's official compass, and which was a legacy from the "Nabich years."

Some of the most imaginative harp writing of the nineteenth century may be found in Liszt's orchestral scores. The source of his inspiration was Jeanne Pohl. He was the first to write a true harp glissando (in the harp cadenza near the conclusion of the orchestral version of the First "Mephisto" Waltz), and there are many telling effects in such works as *Orpheus* (where Liszt actually uses two harps) and the *Faust* Symphony (in which he employs some seductive harmonics in his ravishing tone-picture of Gretchen). But it is in the *Dante* Symphony that we find Liszt's use of the harp at its striking best. Apart from summoning up the swirling winds of Hell, it is also used as the sensitive accompanist to the mournful strains of the cor anglais—an unusual colour combination inspired by the famous lines of Dante: "Nessun maggior dolore / Che ricordarsi del tempo felice / Nella miseria." ("There is no greater pain than the remembrance of past joys in times of misery.")[28]

28. *Inferno,* canto 5.

Perhaps it was the experience of conducting *Lohengrin* and *Les Huguenots* in the early 1850s that first brought Liszt into contact with the bass-clarinet. At any rate, he quickly developed a fondness for this rarely used instrument, and brought it into prominence in the *Dante* Symphony. In the "Purgatorio" movement of this work, Liszt writes a recitativo solo for the bass-clarinet in which he calls for the very lowest note of its compass.

Both Edmund Singer and Bernhard Cossmann were widely experienced orchestral players with a good grasp of what, for want of a better phrase, we may term "the art of the possible" in instrumental effects. Liszt must have had many discussions with both players about the resources of the string section. We know from his correspondence that his constant cry was for more strings. Shortly before a performance of *Die Ideale* and the *Dante* Symphony in Prague he wrote to Jan Musil that he would like as many strings to the part as possible and that "five double-basses would not be too many."[29] Nonetheless, he was undoubtedly taking a risk when he asked the strings in *Mazeppa* to divide into no fewer than eleven distinct parts, in which *divisi, pizzicato, arco,* and *col legno* effects all conspire to produce this unique texture:

---

29. BLB, p. 117. The concert took place on March 11, 1858.

V

Liszt was not the first mid-nineteenth-century composer to want to break away from "the tyranny of the bar-line," but he had no peer in the extremes to which he was prepared to go. In the first version of the *Faust* Symphony (1854) the impassioned first subject was originally written in 7/8 time.[30]

He soon discovered that the rank-and-file orchestral player was not yet ready for such complexities, and he modified this notation before the symphony was published, seven years later (compare with the final version, page 331). The "Francesca" theme of the *Dante* Symphony, however, was published with its audacious 7/4 time-signature intact.

With Liszt, experiments in metrical structure went much deeper than the mere choice of unusual time-signatures. In the early 1850s he became absorbed with the idea of combining two or more self-contained structures simultaneously. In a letter to Salvatore Marchesi, dated August 12, 1853, we find Liszt waxing enthusiastic about the work of the Italian composer Pietro Raimondi, whose contrapuntal ingenuity was such that he had written three oratorios— *Joseph, Potiphar,* and *Jacob*—which can not only be performed separately but combined and played together. "Can you imagine what that must be like?" asked Liszt. "As for me, I am astonished and ready to talk of miracles."[31] He expressed the wish to meet Raimondi, but the Italian composer died later that year. Having failed to find a copy of the "pyramids of counterpoint which Raimondi raised single-handedly," Liszt embarked on a study of his four fugues, which can be played separately or in any combination.[32] We have already seen one attempt by Liszt (in *Hunnenschlacht*) to divide the orchestra into two separate groups, each one unfolding a self-contained idea. Something similar goes on inside the minuet from *Tasso*. In a marginal comment, Liszt informs the conductor that the orchestra "assumes a dual function," the strings

---

30. See Liszt's letter to William Mason dated December 14, 1854, in which he jokes about his newly composed *Faust* Symphony, "in which horrible measures of 7/8, 7/4, and 5/4 alternate with common time and 3/4 time" (LLB, vol. 1, p. 186).
31. LLB, vol. 8, p. 105. The complete text of this letter, which was heavily edited by La Mara, will be found in *The Chesterian,* December 1919.
32. This was not the end of Raimondi's ingenuity. Apparently the maestro had composed two operas, one *seria* and the other *buffa,* which could also be performed separately or in combination. "I cannot get over the wonderment that this idea and its realization arouses in me," observed Liszt (LLB, vol. 8, p. 106).

A facsimile page of Liszt's foreword to the symphonic poems,
dated March 1856: "In order to secure a performance of my orchestral
works which accords with their intentions . . ."

providing one self-contained piece and the woodwinds another. (It would be perfectly possible for the conductor, in rehearsal, to exercise a Raimondi-like option and have the strings and woodwinds perform their individual compositions separately!)

V I

A perennial problem for Liszt was how to get the wooden ensembles of his time to respond to "tempo rubato." Until he came along, no one had seriously attempted to find a symbol for rubato, that most elusive of all the dimensions of musical performance, and one which is so important for a correct interpretation of his works. All the other dimensions—pitch, duration, dynamics, tone-quality—had developed their symbols in a very clear way within the traditional system of staff notation. But rubato was too esoteric to be captured. Liszt had been engrossed by this problem for twenty years before his arrival in Weimar: we have already seen that he had attempted to solve it in his solo piano music of the 1830s and '40s by means of some special notational devices.[33] But solo piano music was one thing, orchestral music another. How does one get sixty or seventy players to follow the same fluctuations of tempo with the fidelity of a single player? Liszt frequently used the symbols *R. . . . . . .:* and *A. . . . . . .:* to enclose individual motifs, or even entire phrases, and thus indicate to his players a slight give-and-take in the flow of the tempo. He defined these subtle shifts of pace as "gentle crescendos and diminuendos of rhythm"—a telling description which merits thought.[34] Examples may be found in the symphonic poems *Tasso, Hunnenschlacht,* and *Orpheus.* One such "crescendo of rhythm" occurs near the beginning of *Festklänge:*

---

33. See Volume One, p. 310.
34. See the orchestral scores of the works in question.

The opening motif is treated as a gigantic agogic accent, which brakes against a background tempo whose pulse must remain constant. In the end, it has to be admitted that these symbols are no more successful than the ones that Liszt had developed in his pianistic heyday, only to abandon. But they are of interest today because they offer us an insight into the way in which Liszt himself may have interpreted his music.

VII

One of the charges regularly levelled against Liszt's works in general, and against the symphonic poems in particular, is that they are repetitious. So frequent has this criticism become, in fact, that the charge itself is guilty of the very crime it attaches to the music. Liszt is very interesting on the subject of repetition, about which he had obviously thought a lot. He once wrote: "It is a mistake to regard repetition as poverty of invention. From the standpoint of the public it is indispensable for the understanding of the thought, while from the standpoint of Art it is almost identical with the demands of clarity, structure, and effectiveness."[35] Not all musicians would accept such views, of course. Liszt had an answer to their sentiments which has come down to us from his pupil Felix Weingartner. He once attended a performance of Weingartner's opera *Sakuntala* in the company of the young composer. In the temple scene there occurs a long climax during which the king makes his entrance. Liszt suddenly seized Weingartner's arm and exclaimed: "Splendid, splendid! This climax must be played twice." Weingartner believed that he must have misheard Liszt and retorted: "But, master, I can't have the king enter twice." "It doesn't matter," replied Liszt. "Beautiful things must be repeated."[36]

Closely related to the problem of repeats is the problem of cuts. As if it were not bad enough to be censured for doing things twice, Liszt is also censured for not even doing them once. To the modern mind, steeped as it is in the inviolability of the art-work, whose every phrase is sacred, the whole question

35. RGS, vol. 2, p. 103. Liszt goes on to point out that Beethoven, whom nobody could accuse of poverty of invention, relies heavily on repetition. The scherzo of the Seventh Symphony, Liszt reminds us, is heard three times.
36. WLE, vol. 1, p. 165.

of cuts is very mysterious. How is it possible for a composer to take infinite pains over the creation of a piece of music, parts of which he then proceeds to jettison for the sake of expediency? Does not this cast doubt on the value of whatever remains? Such a notion must be put into historical perspective. We must not forget that the art of abridgement (for it is an art) was a common practice of the times; authorized cuts may be found in the music of Bruckner, Strauss, Rachmaninov, and Wagner. It was symptomatic of a practical, down-to-earth approach to music-making, born of the fact that composers were often performers or conductors as well; and whenever a clash of artistic interests arose, the exigencies of the performance usually took precedence over the exigencies of the work. In all this, Liszt was a child of his time, and the performer in him was happy to build cuts into the very fabric of his works. Sometimes the abridgements are so clever that they amount to the creation of an alternative version of the same piece. Thus, in his symphonic poem *Festklänge*, Liszt authorized cuts totalling more than three hundred measures—about a third of the entire work.[37] (Unless one is intimately acquainted with the longer version, one accepts the shorter as authentic.) On one occasion he told his orchestral leader, Edmund Singer, "Yesterday I hunted out a couple of cuts [in the "Gran" Mass] which could be made if necessary, without any essential harm to the work. You know, dear Singer, that I am a special virtuoso in the matter of making cuts, in which no one else can easily approach me!"[38] For Liszt, then, the cut was a creative thing, a carefully selected choice, which was part and parcel of the composing process.[39]

---

37. Liszt was also willing to detach the whole of *Mazeppa* from its March-finale so that the latter might be performed as a separate piece. On the general question of cuts, it is true to say that wherever Liszt recommended them he tended to lose conventional development and preserve metamorphosis.
38. LLB, vol. 1, p. 231. The performance in question was for the inauguration of the Gran Basilica on August 31, 1856. See page 404f.
39. The reader who wishes to pursue the topic still further will find some interesting examples in the oratorio *Christus*. For the first performance of this vast work, in Weimar in 1873, Liszt sanctioned a number of abridgements. The list was published as a supplement to the score in 1874.

Pastorale	229	measures
Hirtengesang	96	measures
Marsch der heiligen drei Könige	74	measures
Wunder	68	measures
Tristis ist anima mea	66	measures
Stabat mater dolorosa	273	measures
Total	806	measures

In other words, the combined cuts in *Christus* amount to more music than is found in some entire symphonic poems.

VIII

Even those musicians who find little to engage their interest in Liszt's symphonic poems will readily admit that these works represent a compendium of harmonic inventiveness unmatched by his contemporaries—Berlioz and Wagner notwithstanding. Here, if anywhere, Liszt's claim to be "the father of modern music" can easily be sustained. The harmonic deviations at the beginning of *Prometheus* cannot be explained according to academic theory:

Prometheus stole fire from the gods in Heaven and brought it down to mankind; Liszt stole fire from Heaven, too, and we remain grateful for the gift. But it is in his use of the keyless whole-tone scale that Liszt is at his forward-looking best. At the conclusion of the Magnificat of the *Dante* Symphony, he produces the following sequence of harmonies, half a century before Debussy appropriated them in the name of French impressionism:

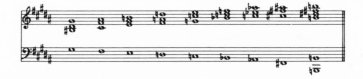

Liszt himself was aware that he had done something new, for in a letter to Julius Schäffer, music director of the Schwerin orchestra, he drew attention to his "modal" harmonies and in particular to the whole-tone scale which supports them, "which until now was unusual in its complete form."[40]

In the symphonic poem *Héroïde funèbre* Liszt delivers some sovereign contributions to harmonic thought. This vast funeral march, of Mahlerian dimensions, with its gongs and bells, is characterized by advanced harmonic progressions in which unrelated chords are juxtaposed and "foreign" keys slip into and out of one another's abode as if they were friendly next-door neighbours.

---

40. LLB, vol. 8, p. 148.

Héroïde funèbre started life in 1830 as a "Revolutionary" Symphony, which was intended to be Liszt's response to the political upheavals of the "July Revolution" of that year.[41] Apart from some scattered sketches, however, nothing appears to have survived of this youthful work except the material from the first movement.[42] Liszt now returned to the detailed sketches of this youthful work and proceeded to revise them as a direct result of the European uprisings of 1848–49. He was now twenty years older and a good deal wiser. In his preface to this magisterial work he makes it clear that it was not his intention to memorialize particular heroes or particular revolutions but rather to erect a musical monument for heroes and revolutions in general, throughout the whole spectrum of human carnage. He regarded war as a "funeral banner [that] floats above all times and places," and he concluded:

> In these successive wars and massacres—sinister sports—whatever
> may be the colour of the flags which rise proudly and boldly one
> against the other, on both sides they float steeped in heroic blood and
> inexhaustible tears. It is for Art to throw its transfiguring veil on the
> tomb of the brave, to encircle the dead and dying with its golden
> halo, so that they may be the envy of the living.

These timeless sentiments drew from Liszt some prophetic harmonies. As the funeral dirge nears its end, and the composer throws his own "transfiguring veil" across the tomb of the brave, the music collapses in a remarkable series of grief-laden chords, on brass, lower woodwinds, and strings.

---

41. See Volume One, p. 144.
42. WA, M.S.A., 21, a file which contains about forty sketch-sheets. Consider also the tantalizing remark that Liszt made in the preface to the work: "People have often spoken of a symphony which I composed in 1830. Various reasons have caused me to keep it in my portfolio. However, while publishing this series of symphonic poems, I wanted to include part of this work, its first movement." The comment implies that the symphony was worked out in much greater detail than anyone has hitherto supposed.

In an unusually candid letter to Princess Carolyne, Bülow admitted that he was "deaf-blind with regard to the sublime beauties of detail contained in this poem." And he freely confessed that he would recommend performances of the work only after the popularity of the others had been assured. He was shrewd enough to recognize that such works as *Héroïde* and *Ce qu'on entend sur la montagne* are compositions "which absolutely require that they be conducted the first time by the composer himself. Frankly, I do not regard myself as sufficiently capable of interpreting them as they require."[43] This was not the only occasion on which Bülow expressed reservations about the uncompromising nature of some of Liszt's orchestral works. After a careful study of the score, he came to the conclusion that the symphonic poem *Hamlet* was "unperformable."[44] When even the staunchest of Liszt's allies held such views, it is not hard to imagine what his detractors thought.

I X

By common consent, the orchestral work which towers above all the others from Liszt's Weimar period is the *Faust* Symphony. Although the structure and historical background of this composition have been discussed many times,[45] there are yet new observations to be made.

Liszt was first introduced to Goethe's *Faust* by Berlioz in 1830, in the French translation of Gérard de Nerval.[46] Thereafter, he long nourished a desire to produce a musical response to it. During the 1840s he actually produced some sporadic sketches for a *Faust* symphony, but his incessant concert tours ensured that nothing came of them. It was Weimar, imbued as it was with the spirit of the dead poet, that gave Liszt the impetus to reach his goal. Indeed, no sooner had he arrived in the city than he seemed to be confronted with Goethe and

43. BB, vol. 3, pp. 215–16. Bülow appears to have been suffering from a typical bout of pre-concert nerves. On March 12, 1859, just a few days after this letter was written, he conducted two of the symphonic poems—*Festklänge* and *Mazeppa*—before an audience in Prague with great success.

44. BB, vol. 3, p. 418. Bülow does not appear to have been alone in this bleak assessment of the work, which did not receive its first performance until 1876 (about eighteen years after Liszt composed it), under the baton of Max Erdmannsdörfer in Sondershausen.

45. Once or twice with distinction. See László Somfai's *Die Metamorphose der "Faust-Symphonie" von Liszt* (SMS, pp. 283–93), which contains an account of Liszt's sketches and their relationship to the finished work.

46. BM, pp. 125 and 139.

the Faust legend at every touch and turn, and a glance at the evidence suggests that the *Faust* Symphony gathered force within him, like some natural phenomenon, at first without his knowledge and then against his will. The compelling sequence of events that now began to unfold has already been remarked, but it is worth bringing into sharper focus here because it demonstrates yet again how vital are the biographical foundations on which the work of musical genius happens to rest. Liszt had barely served out his first season as Kapellmeister before the grand duke decreed that Weimar would celebrate the centenary of Goethe's birth on August 28, 1849. Liszt conducted, among other things, excerpts from Schumann's Scenes from *Faust,* an experience which must have turned his thoughts to the abandoned sketches in his portfolio. Then, as we have seen, followed his work on the creation of the Goethe Foundation, which culminated in the publication of his brochure *De la fondation-Goethe à Weimar.* In the summer of 1850 Gérard de Nerval himself came to Weimar in order to report on the Herder Festival and stayed as Liszt's guest in the Altenburg. There was much talk about *Faust,* a topic which spilled over into their subsequent correspondence.[47] Liszt then invited Berlioz to Weimar in 1852 and witnessed the fiery Frenchman conduct his *Damnation of Faust.* The music pleased Liszt, as always, but still he delayed working on his own score. He wrote to Princess Carolyne: "Anything connected with Goethe is dangerous for me to handle."[48] Perhaps Liszt feared being overwhelmed by the poet.

If we wish to discover a single event that stimulated his recalcitrant pen into activity, we shall find it in the celebrated visit to Weimar of George Eliot in August 1854.[49] It will be recalled that Eliot had accompanied George Henry Lewes, who was in the city to gather information for his life of Goethe. The pair had spent nine weeks visiting Goethe's old haunts, browsing through his library, and interviewing his friends and family. During their visits to the Altenburg, Eliot and Lewes had had a number of conversations with Liszt and the princess about Goethe and his place in German literature. (Even at their first meeting, on August 10, 1854, Eliot reported that Lewes had seated himself next to the princess and pumped her for information about Weimar's literary hero, whom Carolyne dismissed as "an egotist."[50]) It was at this moment that Liszt picked up his pen and commenced serious work on his *magnum opus.* Once the project took possession of him it was all-consuming. Liszt composed his *Faust* Symphony, in a white heat of inspiration, in the remarkably short space of two months, between August and October 1854—that is, during the very period of Lewes's sojourn in Weimar.[51]

---

47. NO, vol. 1, pp. 778–84 and 1,463.
48. LLB, vol. 4, pp. 182–83.
49. See pp. 246–51 of the present volume.
50. EGEL, p. 170.
51. Liszt wrote several letters in the summer of 1854 which allow us to plot the rapid progress of

Although he revised the work three years later, adding the Chorus Mysticus as a finale, much of the original score remained unchanged. The "Gretchen" movement, for example, was composed straight into full score and remained virtually untouched. Appropriately, the symphony is dedicated to Berlioz.

Let us note the full title of Liszt's orchestral masterpiece: "A *Faust* Symphony in Three Character Sketches after Goethe: (1) Faust, (2) Gretchen, (3) Mephistopheles." By subtitling the work "Three Character Sketches" Liszt is telling us that this is not a piece of conventional programme music which contains a plot or tells a story; rather it is an attempt to convey in purely musical terms the varied personalities of the three protagonists in Goethe's drama. Even if one knows nothing of *Faust,* it is still possible to enjoy this symphony as music. (That, after all, is how the vast majority of its admirers get to know it.) But insofar as the Faust legend is what inspired Liszt, a reference to the literary background cannot but be helpful.

The Faust legend goes back to the early sixteenth century. It is based on the exploits of a real-life character named Johann Faustus—magician, astrologer, and charlatan—who wandered across Thuringia casting horoscopes and amazing the local population with his magical illusions. In 1509 he was given a degree by Heidelberg University and thereafter became known as "Dr. Faustus." Faust was known to have stayed at an inn in nearby Erfurt (a town Liszt knew well), where he bragged of his supernatural powers and called the Devil his *Schwager,* or companion. Shortly after his death, in 1540, the stories of his sorcery began to circulate throughout Germany. It was rumoured that he had entered into a compact with Mephistopheles which had lasted for twenty-four years, during which period the Devil had satisfied all Faust's desires but at the end had claimed his soul. This diabolic contract captured the imagination of the world, and a Faust literature soon followed. The best-known of these early efforts was Christopher Marlowe's *Doctor Faustus* (1601), which confirmed the traditional view of Faust as a satanic figure whose black art had cost him his soul.

---

this work. He first announced that he would begin the composition after he got back from the Rotterdam festival, towards the end of July. By the end of August the first movement was finished. On September 8, he reported that he was "working like a being possessed" on the *Faust* Symphony. Finally, on October 19 he declared, "My *Faust* is finished." (See BWL, vol. 2, p. 39, and LLB, vol. 1, pp. 160, 168, 170, and 174)

Meanwhile, Gérard de Nerval had turned up again in July 1854 and had caused consternation at the Altenburg because of his eccentric behaviour. He had just been released from the clinic of Dr. Emile Blanche in Paris, having suffered the latest in a series of "nervous breakdowns," had had a relapse in Leipzig, and had arrived on Liszt's doorstep on July 8. Liszt was still in Rotterdam, so Nerval hovered around the Altenburg for two weeks, waiting for him to return. *Faust* preoccupied his inflamed imagination, for like his hero, Gérard de Nerval was cursed: he was suffering from tertiary syphilis and had only a few more months to live. He apologized to Liszt for his anti-social behaviour: "Forgive me for a number of peculiarities in my personal conduct that you will not have been able to comprehend." (NLFL, p. 37) On January 26, 1855, Nerval hanged himself in the rue de la Vieille-Lanterne in Paris.

Goethe's version of the old legend is different in several important respects. It begins with a prologue in Heaven in which Mephistopheles seeks permission from the Lord to corrupt Faust's soul. So confident is the Lord that Mephistopheles must fail, He allows him to proceed. From the start, then, Goethe's drama assumes cosmic dimensions, for it is directed according to the command of God. Goethe's Faust is a thinker and philosopher who has become disillusioned with the limits of knowledge. He enters into the contract not so much to extend the boundaries of his learning but rather to taste the pleasures of the flesh. Moreover, the danger to his soul seems minimal. If at any moment of procured delight Faust should utter the words "Stay, thou art so fair!" Mephistopheles can claim him as his own. Time passes, and Faust becomes sated with pleasures, none of which has brought him lasting satisfaction. He meets the beautiful Gretchen, and seduces and destroys her. The introduction of "love interest" into the Faust legend was new, and it becomes a crucial element in the way Goethe handles the drama. Remorseful and wearied with sensual enjoyment, Faust turns his magical talents to doing good works, all with the help of Mephistopheles. Finally, at the end of a long life, and conscious that he is leaving the world a better place, he cries out impulsively as his life ebbs away: "Stay, thou art so fair!" As Mephistopheles tries to seize his soul, it is borne away by angels. From the start, Goethe has been interested in Faust's salvation. No matter how much evil a man may commit, Goethe argues, his striving for truth and knowledge are positive things which must help redeem him. And there is something else that the old legend, with its fire-and-brimstone ending, lacked: the love that Gretchen bore Faust becomes a redemptive force that saves his soul. This is the colossal drama, involving Heaven, Earth, and Hell, which Goethe enshrines in literature and which Liszt attempts to encompass in music.

The symphony begins with a slow introduction which contains two of Faust's principal themes, revealing him as magician and thinker, respectively. Appropriately, the first theme offers us a magical glimpse into the future of music, one of the first conscious twelve-note rows in musical history:[52]

---

52. A brief inspection of the "tone-row" shows that it consists of three augmented triads. It has been conjectured that Liszt was attracted to the tonal ambiguities of augmented chords by the theories of C. F. Weitzmann, a Berlin musician whose book *Der übermässige Dreiklang* was published in 1853. In September of that year Weitzmann sent Liszt an unsolicited copy of his book and at the same time sought Liszt's permission to dedicate to him his next book, on the diminished seventh chord. The two men became friends and used to play whist whenever Liszt's travels took him to Berlin. The pair often discussed the theoretical basis of the harmonic system.

The second theme, with its falling seventh, shows Faust in a pondering mood. The entire introduction, by the way, is keyless, a striving after some repose which is never reached, and is symbolic of Faust's own personality:

Motif of "Doubt"

We note that from the purely structural point of view this introduction is an integral part of a vast sonata design, and in due course it will be called upon to bear the brunt of the recapitulation. Is this the first time in the history of sonata form that a slow introduction has ushered in the beginning of the reprise? In any event, it is perceptive of Liszt to attempt a reconciliation of Faust's themes at this later point by telescoping them—as if to tell us that they are but opposite sides of a single personality:

The very first essay ever written on the *Faust* Symphony, by Richard Pohl in 1862, also happens to be one of the best.[53] Not only does it trace the history of the composition with unusual care, but it also analyzes the music in detail and proffers insights not generally available elsewhere. Pohl's identification of the various motifs of "Passion," "Pride," "Longing," "Triumph," and "Love" are useful, for their disclosure could only have come from Liszt himself. Pohl confesses that for him, even Beethoven's last and greatest works contain no more worthy and noble music than the *Faust* Symphony[54]—and although we may take leave to disagree with him, the comment is an indication of the importance he attached to the piece.

The "sonata allegro" proper gets under way with the third of Faust's themes, the so-called motif of "Passion," marked "allegro agitato ed appassionato." Stormy moods, as well as indecision, mark Faust's complex personality. The aficionado of harmony will not fail to observe the texture of the first chord (*). We would be tempted to dub it the *Faust* chord were it not for

53. PGS, vol. 2, pp. 247–320.
54. PGS, vol. 2, p. 320.

the fact that this highly original combination was appropriated by Wagner, albeit seven years later, and made famous as the *Tristan* chord, under which name it has held the musical intelligentsia in thrall for a hundred and twenty years. This is not the first time that Liszt cheated history by stealing from the future of music.[55]

Motif of "Passion"

Two further themes, which form a second subject group in the highly unorthodox key of E major, are worthy of note. One shows Faust as a lover; it is derived through the skilful metamorphosis of Faust's "theme of disillusion," first heard in the introduction.

Motif of "Love"

A series of trumpet calls heralds the other theme, which shows Faust as a hero and is a musical counterpart to Faust's words "Im Anfang war die Tat" ("In the beginning was the deed"):

---

55. Wagner notates the chord enharmonically, thus:

Liszt's effect is the more extreme, however, since he takes the chord in C minor, approaching it from the implied dominant of E minor.

Motif of "Pride"

It has already been remarked that Liszt regarded the full symphony orchestra as the sum total of many different chamber ensembles—a notion later pursued by Richard Strauss and Mahler. The "Gretchen" movement provides a perfect illustration of the idea. Across its sonic surface Liszt unfurls a kaleidoscopic array of chamber-musical textures in which every player is a soloist. Gretchen's main theme, for example, is introduced as a duet for oboe and viola. Later it is heard on a woodwind quartet and then on a quartet of four solo violins.

The theme gives way to a charming illustration of the famous scene in which Gretchen plucks off the petals of a flower, saying, "He loves me, he loves me not, he loves me!"

This passage comes as close to onomatopoeia as anything Liszt ever wrote. The chromatically inflected A-sharp at the end is surely the musical equivalent of a parenthetical question-mark: *"Does* he love me?" The exit from F-sharp minor to A-flat major, as Liszt ushers in the first "Gretchen" theme once more, reminds us of his lifelong fondness for plunging back and forth between remote keys. In a letter that Tausig wrote to Liszt from Warsaw on November 24, 1856, he told his master that he had recently made a musician of the older school "sick with fear" by showing him how to get from F-sharp minor to C major in one bar.[56] Evidently such matters caused considerable amusement at the Altenburg.

---

56. LBZL, vol. 2, pp. 92–93.

A second "love theme" associated with Gretchen now makes its ethereal appearance, on strings alone:

The gentle simplicity of both Gretchen's themes belies the fact that they will later become transformed into the great "Redemption" motifs in the Chorus Mysticus (see page 335).

From the standpoint of its orchestration alone the "Gretchen" movement is flawless and has a strong claim to being one of the best things of its kind to come out of the nineteenth century. The connection may be fortuitous, but it is worth noting that while Liszt was in the middle of this composition, his Alexandre "piano-organ" arrived at the Altenburg. Liszt told Bernhard Cossmann: "My monster instrument with three keyboards arrived a fortnight ago and seems to me to be a great success—and on your return I shall pretty nearly have finished my *Faust* Symphony, at which I am working like a being possessed."[57] This instrument, which had been specially designed to help Liszt with his orchestration, appears to have had a stimulating effect on his aural imagination, if this first contact is anything to go by.

The finale—"Mephistopheles"—is one of the most ingenious movements Liszt ever penned. Mephistopheles is the spirit of negation—in Goethe's words, "der Geist, der stets verneint." He cannot create; he can only destroy. How to portray him in music? Liszt's solution is brilliant. He gives Mephistopheles no themes of his own, but allows him instead to penetrate those of Faust, which become distorted and cruelly mutated. The symbolism is too obvious to require further comment. Invaded by evil, Faust's themes struggle to retain their identity but are torn to tatters. Mephisto's main allegro theme turns out to be a mocking echo of Faust's motif of "Passion":

---

57. LLB, vol. 1, p. 170. See p. 77 and n.9 of the present volume.

All Faust's themes—different aspects of his character—are gradually drawn into the circle of Hell. His motif of "Pride" is the last to yield:

There is an outbreak of jubilation from the orchestra. In Pohl's telling phrase, "Hell celebrates a feast-day."[58] The entire "Mephistopheles" movement, in fact, is a huge parody of the "Faust" movement, and in it Liszt dazzles us with a brilliant display of thematic transformations. Is this the first time in musical history that one movement has been unrolled across another? The evil spell under which Faust labours is reinforced by a self-quotation from one of Liszt's earlier works—the *Malédiction,* or "curse":

Only Gretchen remains immune from mutilation, and her opening theme is recalled intact. As Faust becomes aware of what is happening to him, a titanic struggle ensues for his soul. This is depicted in the form of a fugue, a word whose original meaning denoted "flight." It is no accident that the fugue subject is a metamorphosis of Faust's "theme of disillusion":

The symphony was originally planned as a purely instrumental work, ending with Faust's soul being borne aloft to the strains of the first of Gretchen's melodies. Within three years of its completion, however, Liszt had added his

---

58. PGS, vol. 2, p. 314.

setting of the Chorus Mysticus, for tenor solo and male chorus. Although it
was an afterthought, the choral ending is absolutely right for this work.
Goethe's words in praise of the "Eternal Feminine" provide a powerful epilogue to this remarkable composition:

Alles Vergängliche	All things transitory
Ist nur ein Gleichnis;	But as symbols are sent;
Das Unzulängliche	Earth's insufficiency
Hier wird's Ereignis;	Here grows to Event;
Das Unbeschreibliche	The Indescribable,
Hier ist's getan;	Here it is done;
Das Ewig-Weibliche	The Woman-soul leadeth us
Zieht uns hinan.	Upward and on.

The music given to the tenor soloist is based on a metamorphosis of the two
Gretchen themes, which reappear here as if in heavenly transfiguration. Compare these motifs of "Redemption" with their instrumental counterparts in the
second movement:

The first performance of the *Faust* Symphony took place under Liszt's baton
on September 5, 1857, on the occasion of the unveiling of the Goethe-Schiller
monument in Weimar.[59] A second performance was given there by Hans von
Bülow in 1861, the year of the symphony's publication.[60] Thereafter, apart from

---

59. See pp. 482–83.
60. It was one of the works featured in the festival of the Allgemeiner Deutscher Musikverein (an
organization of which Liszt was the first president) held in Weimar on August 5–7, 1861 (see p. 511).
On July 23 Bülow, who had just received a copy of the full score, wrote an interesting letter to Liszt
in which he discussed a number of the symphony's details. "I almost know it by heart," he said, "and
the conductor's podium could be moved out of the way [for the performance]. . . . I am possessed

one or two sporadic appearances, the symphony endured half a century's neglect. Such was the lack of interest that the orchestral parts were not even published until 1874. The symphony's first modern interpreter was Felix Weingartner, but he stood almost alone in his championship of the work until modern times. Today the *Faust* Symphony stands before us as a monument of the Romantic movement. The further it recedes in time, the greater its stature seems to become. And when it is properly played, it enhances the reputation of its composer wherever it is heard.

x

By the mid-1850s Liszt had emerged as the undisputed leader of the musical avant-garde. The important place of Wagner and Berlioz notwithstanding, it was Liszt who was making all the noise and attracting all the attention. Through his composing, conducting, and teaching, and not least through his polemical articles and pamphlets, the world had been made to sit up and listen. And what the world heard (at least the conservative part of it, which constituted by far the largest majority) aroused its disapproval and then its hostility. The opposition was particularly incensed by Liszt's use of the terms *Zukunftsmusik* to describe his forward-looking compositions and *Zukunftsmusiker* to describe himself and his companions-in-arms. According to Wagner, the term was originally one of denigration, which even as it was levelled against Liszt by his enemies was snatched from their grasp by him and carried aloft like a banner into the fray. Wagner may have been mistaken in this belief, however.[61] It seems that the term may have been coined by Princess Carolyne, in 1850, shortly after a performance of *Lohengrin* in Weimar. In an animated conversation that took place in the Altenburg, Brendel had expressed the view that *Lohengrin* was too advanced for the present. "Very well," was Carolyne's rejoinder, "we are creating the music of the future."[62] The term stuck, and thereafter it

---

with a real passion to enjoy it at last with my ears, and want to ask you the favour of allowing me to conduct the special rehearsal as well." It was Bülow who persuaded Liszt to alter the declamation of the words "Das Ewig-Weibliche," which originally ran:

a setting which jarred on Bülow's linguistic sensibilities (LBLB, pp. 307–09).

61. WGSD, vol. 8, p. 245. Wagner later erroneously claimed to have suggested the term through the title of his book *Kunstwerk der Zukunft* (1850) (ML, pp. 565–66).

62. RLKM, vol. 3, p. 69, n. 2. Carolyne herself claimed this term as her own in a letter to Lina Ramann dated December 29, 1875 (RL, p. 63).

appeared regularly in the correspondence of Liszt and his circle in the 1850s, even to describing concerts of new music as *Zukunftskoncerte*. But where did this leave the concerts of Liszt's conservative opponents? The implication was that they gave "concerts of the past." The damage that the term did to Liszt's image with the general public dawned on him but slowly. Eventually it was abandoned, and in 1859, at the first meeting of the Tonkünstler-Versammlung, the title "New German School" was adopted as a substitute.[63]

The general opposition to Liszt's pioneering work was centred in Leipzig and Vienna. The Leipzig Conservatory, in particular, was a hotbed of conservatism, and a number of its faculty were vocal in their condemnation of Liszt. They were joined by the Viennese critic Eduard Hanslick, who began to mete out death and destruction in the columns of Vienna's *Neue Freie Presse* to all who did not pay lip-service to the ideals of the Viennese classics. It is hardly an exaggeration to say that both cities were closed to Liszt as far as building up sympathetic audiences was concerned. There were smaller pockets of resistance to the Music of the Future in Berlin, Paris, and London. A glance at the map of Europe is sufficient to show that by 1856, the year in which the first batch of symphonic poems were published, Liszt was surrounded literally as well as metaphorically by his artistic enemies. Just a few weeks before that landmark event he had made a wry forecast: "The barometer is hardly set on praise for me at the moment. I expect quite a hard downpour of rain when the symphonic poems appear."[64] Behind the meteorological joke lay a deadly observation. He knew that an epic struggle was about to commence, and that his very existence as a composer was in jeopardy.

---

63. See p. 511, where the background is sketched out more fully.
64. LLB, vol. 3, p. 72.

The War of the Romantics

Unfortunately, musical history is full to over-
flowing with unresolved dissonances.

FRANZ LISZT[1]

I

The stage was now set for one of the chief cultural struggles of the nineteenth century. Historians still refer to that conflict as "the War of the Romantics," when a number of great ideas vied with one another for the allegiance of musicians everywhere: programme music versus absolute music, form versus content, the oneness versus the separateness of the arts, newness versus oldness, revolution versus reaction. These issues had often been debated before, of course, but never all at the same time, never with such passion, and never with the firm conviction that the very fate of music depended on their correct resolution. As with all such struggles, the seeds of this one went back at least a generation. They were to be found in the differing attitudes of musicians who had graced the scene in the 1840s, and even earlier. In the halcyon days of early Romanticism, in fact, Mendelssohn, Schumann, Hiller, Berlioz, Chopin, and Liszt had appeared united in their aims. With all the ardour of impetuous youth they had seemed bent on brushing aside the stale and decaying Establishment, with its worship of things past, and replacing it with a New Establishment for the promotion and development of things present. "Let the dead bury the dead" was their motto. Whatever differences existed among them were at that time no larger than the shadow of a man's hand, and they remained unnoticed by all but the closest of observers. But with the passing years that shadow lengthened, and some of these Young Turks lost their reforming zeal. By 1843,

---

1. LLB, vol. 2, p. 334.

Mendelssohn occupied the twin positions of conductor of the Leipzig Gewand-haus Orchestra and director of the Leipzig Conservatory of Music.[2] The following year Schumann stepped down from the editorship of the *Neue Zeitschrift für Musik* and so discarded the pioneering mantle he had worn with distinction for ten years. Hiller became ever more cautious and reached his "definitive" position when he settled in Cologne and became conductor of the Cologne orchestra and, in 1850, the first director of its conservatory—a double appointment modelled after that of Mendelssohn.[3] Chopin died in 1849, his wonderful genius fulfilled, no longer able to serve the cause. As for Berlioz, he continued to create those unique compositions which placed him at the leading edge of artistic discovery, but the ebullient personality of his youth had been eroded by irony and bitterness against the world for its neglect of him, and he now showed little interest in anyone's music but his own. By the mid-1850s it must have seemed to Liszt that the revolution had been betrayed, that he must carry on the fight alone. It is a fact that he never lost his revolutionary fervour, even into his old age; indeed, the older Liszt got, the more stubbornly attached he became to the new, the original, the young in heart. During the Weimar years he developed a warrior spirit, and his embattled character showed seams of courage that always gleamed most brightly in the face of adversity. If Liszt's place in the history of music were to be marked by a single word, that word would surely be "crusader."

That Liszt understood the historical importance of the ideas he espoused, to say nothing of the opposition they aroused among his conservative adversaries (some of whom were so old-fashioned that their attempts at composition, he thought, amounted to a form of hypocrisy), is borne out by a letter he wrote in 1860, shortly before he left Weimar. Looking back on the War of the Romantics, he reflected that for the past twelve years he had been inspired by a great idea, "the renewal of music through its more intimate connection with poetry." He had found unparalleled creative freedom in this idea, he said, which had kept him going despite all the opposition. Then came this credo:

> If, when I had settled here [in Weimar] in '48, I had wanted to ally myself with the *posthumous* party in music, to share in its hypocrisy, to embrace its prejudices, etc., nothing would have been easier for

---

2. The Leipzig Conservatory had been founded in 1843, thanks to the private wealth of the linen merchants of the Gewandhaus. Mendelssohn was its first director and was therefore responsible not only for drawing up the curriculum but also for appointing the first faculty members, who included Moritz Hauptmann (theory), Ferdinand David (violin), Ignaz Moscheles (piano), Robert Schumann (composition), and Julius Rietz (composition).

3. Hiller retained these posts until a grave illness forced him to retire in 1884. During all these years he never once conducted a programme of the "music of the future." It was left to his successor, Franz Wüllner, to initiate the 1884–85 season with a programme of works by Liszt, Wagner, and Richard Strauss.

me because of my previous ties with the chief bigwigs of that school. I should certainly have won more consideration and courtesy from the outside world. The same newspapers that have taken it upon themselves to heap on me a mass of stupidities and insults would have outdone each other in praising and fêting me to the hilt, without my having to go to much trouble [to deserve it]. They would gladly have whitewashed a few misdeeds of my youth, in order to praise and raise up in every possible way the *preacher* of the good, healthy traditions from Palestrina to Mendelssohn. But such was not to be my fate; my conviction was too sincere, my faith in the present and future of art too fervent and firm, for me to be able to put up with the empty formulae of the objurgations of our pseudo-classicists, who do their utmost to proclaim that art is being ruined. . . .[4]

The exegesis of the War of the Romantics is made more complex for us by the personalities of those who took part in it. Perhaps all wars, ultimately, are extensions of autobiography: the need to have one's own ideas prevail over those of a rival drives one to extreme measures. This particular conflict was no exception. There is no better way for us to start, therefore, than by taking a closer look at Liszt's declining relations with his contemporaries—the outward symbol of inner discord.

II

In order to understand the difficulties between Liszt and Schumann, we have to go back to 1834, the year in which Schumann had founded the *Neue Zeitschrift für Musik,* a progressive journal that supported the cause of the young romantics against the old reactionaries—the "Band of David" against the "Philistines," as Schumann put it. With the passing years Schumann's ideas as to who was a Philistine changed. Though he was never an admirer of Liszt, Schumann's relations with him were nonetheless at first cordial, as his reviews of Liszt's Leipzig concerts in 1840 show,[5] and he found much to praise in Liszt's piano playing at that time. However, Liszt's subsequent pianistic career was viewed by both Robert and Clara Schumann with disfavour. They could not stomach the "Lisztomania" that swept across Europe after 1842—the swooning audiences, the endless supply of medals and decorations, the hobnobbing with royalty, and the tawdry music with which Liszt appeared to fill his recitals and satisfy his public. It seemed to them that Liszt had betrayed his genius, that he

4. LLB, vol. 3, p. 136.
5. See Volume One, pp. 349–51.

was dazzled by his own myth. They came to agree with Mendelssohn's diagnosis of his character as "a continual alternation between scandal and apotheosis."[6] In 1844 Schumann resigned the editorship of the *Neue Zeitschrift für Musik;* the following year he was succeeded by Franz Brendel. The magazine later became a mouthpiece for Liszt and his disciples and began to pour forth a river of propaganda on behalf of the Weimar School. At the same time, it played down the "little Leipzigers" (as Liszt dubbed them) whom Mendelssohn had appointed to the staff of the conservatory, and dismissed them as reactionaries. Schumann was dismayed to see his old magazine used against his friends but was powerless to prevent it. Soon history had been stood on its head. The average reader of the *Neue Zeitschrift* could be forgiven for assuming that Schumann and his colleagues were the Philistines while Liszt and his followers were the Band of David. This takeover of the *Zeitschrift* was a cruel twist of fate, for which neither Schumann nor Liszt were directly responsible, but it coloured all their later discourse.

The outcome was a dreadful scene which took place in Schumann's home in Dresden in June 1848. Liszt, who once more was passing through the city, paid the Schumanns a surprise visit. Clara went to considerable pains to arrange a musical dinner in his honour. A time was set, the musicians assembled, but Liszt failed to appear. The exasperated players had almost finished a performance of Beethoven's D-major Trio in the guest-of-honour's absence when Liszt, in Clara's words, "burst in at the door," two hours late, accompanied by Wagner. A performance of Schumann's Piano Quintet followed, which Liszt tactlessly described as "Leipzigerisch." The atmosphere was tense throughout dinner. Schumann was ready to boil over; Liszt obliged him by providing more heat. He started to praise Meyerbeer at Mendelssohn's expense. At this, Schumann broke into a violent rage. He sprang up, rushed towards Liszt, seized him by both shoulders, and shouted angrily: "Who are you that you dare to speak in such a way of a musician like Mendelssohn?" He then stalked out of the room, leaving the other dinner-guests staring angrily at Liszt. Liszt rose to the occasion superbly, turned to Clara and said: "Tell your husband that he is the only man in the world from whom I would take so calmly the words just offered to me." Liszt then left the house. Clara declared: "I have done with him forever."[7]

---

6. LCS, vol. 2, p. 120.

7. LCS, vol. 2, pp. 121–22; JRS, p. 523. Clara's diary gives a milder version of the story, but Jansen declared in 1879 that he had shown his account to Clara, who had confirmed "everything." The essential correctness of the description was corroborated at about the same time by Liszt himself in the course of responding to one of Lina Ramann's biographical questionnaires. After telling her about his first encounters with Wagner in the early 1840s, he went on: "A few years later we met again in Dresden, where we suffered a very agitated evening at Robert Schumann's house, for which I was blamed." (RL, p. 399; WA, Kasten 351, no. 1) In considering Schumann's extraordinary outburst it has to be remembered that Mendelssohn, who was revered by the Leipzig-Dresden circle, had died

The Schumanns' open hostility towards Liszt contrasted sharply with his own generosity towards them. In 1849, shortly after he had settled in Weimar, and less than a year after Schumann's assault on him, he conducted Part Three of Schumann's Scenes from *Faust*. [8] Three years later he gave the first performance of the incidental music to Schumann's *Manfred*. [9] All he got on that occasion was a note from Clara asking him to return the autograph score of the work, which he had hoped to keep as a token of friendship.[10] Liszt then dedicated to Schumann, in 1854, his B-minor Piano Sonata, a reciprocal gesture for the dedication of Schumann's C-major Fantasy to him some fifteen years earlier. And he followed through, in 1855, with a full-scale production of Schumann's opera *Genoveva* in the Weimar theatre.[11] During all these years, in fact, the Schumanns accepted everything and gave Liszt nothing. Symptomatic of Clara's cold attitude towards Liszt was her response to his Grosses Konzertsolo, a copy of which he sent her in the spring of 1852 in the apparent belief that she might be persuaded to play it in public. Clara looked through it and was appalled at what she considered to be its empty virtuosity. But what to tell Liszt, who was about to begin rehearsals of Robert's *Manfred?* Not for the first time she fell back on feminine guile. "Where can a woman find the strength to play it?" she wrote, and added disarmingly: "Definitely no one can play it like you."[12] This was her euphemistic way of telling Liszt that if he wanted any public performances of his work, he had better give them himself. Despite her resolve to "have done with [Liszt] forever," Clara swallowed her pride in October 1854 and asked him for a concert in Weimar, suggesting either the castle or the theatre as a suitable auditorium. By then Schumann was incarcerated in the asylum at Endenich after attempting to drown himself in the Rhine, and Clara had numerous children to care for. "Advise me, I beg you," she pleaded with Liszt from her family home in Düsseldorf. "I know that you have my welfare at heart."[13] At short notice Liszt gallantly arranged an all-Schumann

---

only a few months previously. More important, Schumann was now irreversibly ill and was already presenting symptoms of tertiary syphilis affecting both his physical and mental behaviour (SMRS, p. 87). More than a year elapsed before Liszt contacted Schumann again, by letter. "When the opportunity occurs," he wrote, "we can surely have a friendly discussion on the importance of a work, a man, and even a town." (LLB, vol. 2, p. 78) This was a direct reference to the topic of their quarrel and indicates that Liszt wanted to make amends. Alas, he was not given the chance to do so. Despite an invitation for Schumann to visit the Altenburg ("a very good grand piano and two or three intelligent people who cling to you with true sympathy and esteem await you here") and a brief encounter in Düsseldorf in August 1851 (their last meeting, as it happened [LCS, vol. 2, pp. 263–64]), the hand of friendship was permanently withdrawn from Liszt.

8. April 14, 1849.
9. June 13, 1852.
10. LLB, vol. 1, p. 113.
11. April 9, 1855.
12. LBZL, vol. 1, p. 210. The Grosses Konzertsolo was composed for the piano competition at the Paris Conservatoire held in 1850. It was published the following year and dedicated to Adolf Henselt.
13. LBZL, vol. 1, pp. 352–53.

concert in which Clara played the A-minor Piano Concerto and he conducted the *Manfred* Overture and the D-minor Symphony. Again, Liszt got little thanks for his trouble, for the best thing that Clara could find to note in her diary was that the piano was "abominable."[14] Two months later Liszt published a glowing article about Clara in the columns of the *Neue Zeitschrift*. [15] This article was meant to draw national attention to her as she picked up the pieces of her shattered life and launched herself afresh into her old career of concert pianist. Clara simply ignored Liszt's gesture. In May 1855, when Liszt attended the Lower Rhine Festival, which was held that year in Düsseldorf, he naturally called on her. "She received me in friendly fashion," he wrote to Princess Carolyne, "but did not mention a single word about the article in the *Neue Zeitschrift*."[16] Less than a year later, in January 1856, Liszt was invited to conduct the Mozart Centenary Festival in Vienna, and Clara Schumann was chosen as the soloist. By declining to participate she proffered Liszt a deliberate snub. Thereafter the pair never saw one another again, although Clara's correspondence is studded with hostile references to Liszt, typical of which is this disclosure made to Joachim: "I despise Liszt from the depths of my soul."[17] In July 1856 Schumann died. Liszt was now approached by Wasielewski, Schumann's first biographer, for help in sketching in some of the details of their relationship. He left his sickbed in order to write to Wasielewski an extremely long letter covering their fifteen-year friendship in affectionate terms, even comparing *Carnaval* with Beethoven's *Diabelli* Variations, and making no mention of their personal quarrel.[18] Nearly thirty years rolled by, and Clara wrote to Liszt, then an elderly man of seventy-two, asking him to return to her any letters in his possession that had been written to him in earlier years by Robert, in order to have copies made. "I need hardly say," she added, "that

---

14. LCS, vol. 2, pp. 350–51. From the handbill preserved in the Court Theatre we learn that Clara played some additional solo items at this concert (October 27, 1854), including Mendelssohn's *Variations sérieuses* and a Chopin nocturne. While Clara was in Weimar, Liszt invited her to a party in the Altenburg, where one of her fellow guests was George Eliot. Under different circumstances this might have proved to be a stimulating encounter, but Clara's depression cast a pall over the occasion. "A melancholy, interesting creature," noted Eliot in her journal for October 28, 1854. "Her husband went mad a year ago, and she has to support eight children."

15. NZfM, December 1, 1854 (RGS, vol. 4, pp. 189–206). The article was widely quoted and was translated into English for publication in *Dwight's Musical Journal* (issues of April 7 and 14, 1855). It observed the physical change that the burden of grief had wrought on Clara and compared the "moist lustre" of the youthful Clara's eyes with her present "fixed and anxious look." The wreath of flowers that once was so freely woven into her hair, wrote Liszt, had become a crown of thorns which scarcely hid the stigmata which had been so deeply impressed on her brow.

16. LLB, vol. 4, p. 220.

17. JMBJ, vol. 2, p. 85.

18. LLB, vol. 1, pp. 253–59. Liszt was confined to his bed for several weeks with abscesses on his feet (see p. 412ff.). He asked Wasielewski to have patience with the length of his letter, which, he added charmingly, "I do not have the time to make shorter"—an unconscious allusion to Pascal, who had expressed the same paradox in his *Lettres provinciales*.

you will receive the letters back safely." Liszt sketched out his cautious reply on the back of Clara's letter.

Weimar, June 22, 1884

> To my regret, I cannot help you with the letters from Robert Schumann which you mention. My long life of wandering, which is not entirely ended, prevented me from collecting. Consequently, many worthy items were lost.[19]

Clara may have felt that Liszt was being uncooperative. It did not matter; her view of him had long since been formed. What that view was she compressed into a few poisoned lines of a diary entry written the day after Liszt's death: "He was an eminent keyboard virtuoso but a dangerous example for the young. . . . As a composer he was terrible."[20] That was about all she could find to say in remembrance of the man who had extended the hand of friendship to her and to her husband across the years. Posterity has reversed Clara's verdict on the music. But what of her verdict on Liszt's "dangerous" virtuosity? It hardly bears scrutiny. Since Liszt produced more pianists of international stature than anyone else in musical history, we can only ask where Clara spent the last twenty-five years of her life, and marvel at her bigotry.

III

There can be no better illustration of the chasm which now separated Liszt from his conservative opponents than the case of Joachim, who was just nineteen years old when Liszt summoned him from Leipzig and made him leader of the Weimar orchestra in 1850. Joachim had been a child prodigy whose performance of the Beethoven Violin Concerto in London, shortly before his thirteenth birthday, had created a sensation.[21] At seventeen he had been appointed

---

19. WA, Kasten 29, no. 1.
20. LCS, vol. 3, p. 479.
21. The performance took place on May 27, 1844, with Mendelssohn conducting. The following day *The Times* wrote: "[The concerto] was played by young Joachim in a manner which caused astonishment in the oldest musicians and professors of that instrument, who discover in a boy of only thirteen years of age, all the mastery of the art which it has cost most of them the labour of a life to attain, if indeed any of them have reached to the same excellence by which he is in all respects distinguished." In November of that year, Joachim crowned this triumph with another when he appeared at a Gewandhaus concert and played Ernst's difficult *Othello* Fantasy, again with Mendelssohn conducting. According to Moser, Joachim's biographer, Mendelssohn was particularly impressed with the bold manner in which the boy attacked the high C-sharp on the E string, and he subsequently made use of this effect in the finale of his Violin Concerto, which had not yet been published (MJ, p. 50).

professor of violin at the Leipzig Conservatory and had already forged close bonds with Mendelssohn, Ferdinand David (his teacher), and the Schumanns. By temperament and by training this wonderful violinist was hardly equipped to remain a *Konzertmeister* for long, and it would have been unthinkable for him to waste his talents by scraping away at his fiddle in a court orchestra for the rest of his life. He accepted Liszt's offer because the short season at Weimar gave him time to travel and develop his solo career; he was, in any case, overwhelmed by Liszt's personality and by his sense of artistic mission. All this comes out in a letter he wrote to his brother Heinrich shortly before taking up his new position.

> In a fortnight's time I migrate to Weimar. Through the influence of my friend and patron, Liszt, the grand duchess [Maria Pawlowna] has made a post for me there as *Konzertmeister* which is for the present no better financially than the Leipzig one, but where I shall, firstly, have a more honorable position, and secondly, extraordinarily little to do (perhaps to play once a week at the opera under Liszt's direction), and thirdly, the prospect of *five months* annual leave. . . . But the chief thing which attracts me to Weimar is the life and cooperation with Liszt, for every time I see him I like him better and I feel sure that he is a true friend to me. . . .[22]

At first there was no reason to suppose that Joachim had not made a wise and sensible decision. We know that he found the artistic climate of Weimar invigorating, for the friendships he formed with Hans von Bülow and Bernhard Cossmann ensured regular opportunities for playing chamber music at a high professional level. But as the weeks and then the months wore on, it became evident to him that simply "to play once a week at the opera under Liszt's direction" hardly began to describe the true nature of his duties. Liszt by then had begun his closed workshop rehearsals, in which the rough sketches of his symphonic poems were tried out and continually corrected, and Joachim found the experience wearing. During his three brief seasons at Weimar he came to detest Liszt's music and to form a poor impression of him as a conductor. Had he said so and left, Liszt would have been the first to applaud his integrity. But it was seven years before he could bring himself to declare his true feelings, during which time he continued to enjoy Liszt's patronage. Liszt engaged him as the featured soloist in the Karlsruhe Festival of 1853, rehearsed Joachim's *Hamlet* Overture with the Weimar orchestra that same year,[23] and opened

---

22. JMBJ, vol. 1, pp. 22–23.
23. The manuscript of this overture bears the dedication: "To the members of the Weimar orchestra." It was not published until after Joachim's death.

various doors for him when the young virtuoso left Weimar in order to embark on his concert tours. Joachim repaid him by storing up a wealth of negative observations, which he later communicated privately to his friends and musical associates across Germany, an action that can only be described as disloyal. We have elsewhere noted his indictment of Liszt as "a cunning contriver of effects who has miscalculated." Through his constant discourse with Brahms and Clara Schumann in the mid-1850s he became convinced that the "new music" was an aberration and that Liszt was little more than a poseur. He also began disparaging Liszt's disciples by calling them "the Weimar lot." In 1856, Liszt, who was blissfully unaware of Joachim's true feelings, sent him the scores of his newly published symphonic poems, and Joachim was dismayed at what he considered to be their poverty of invention. Still he kept silence. The following year Liszt invited him back to Weimar to give a court concert, an offer he declined. Joachim forwarded the letter of invitation to his friend Gisela von Arnim with the gratuitous comment: "Look at this letter from Liszt; such perseverance is odd! I feel that in both art and in life our paths become ever more divergent."[24] A few months later Liszt pressed Joachim once more, this time to take part in the musical festivities surrounding the jubilee celebrations of Carl August. "The new musical Weimar is still so much *yours*," Liszt wrote engagingly, "by virtue of the many delightful memories that it would give us all, and me especially, that it would be a real pleasure to see you again at our festival."[25] And he added that the orchestra would be especially strengthened for a performance of his *Faust* Symphony and his symphonic poem *Die Ideale*. It was at this point that Joachim decided to make a formal break with Liszt by disclosing his real feelings. For candour and frankness, his letter to Liszt has few parallels in the annals of nineteenth-century music, and it is reproduced here in full:

Göttingen, August 27, 1857

The continued goodness and confidence which you show me, great and courageous spirit, in including me in that community of friends who are dominated by your power, gives me a sense of shame for the lack of candour I have shown up to the present—a feeling which I am not now experiencing for the first time, and which would deeply humiliate me in my own eyes if I were not at the same time consoled by the knowledge that this lack of candour, which contrasts so badly with my life at Weimar and your unchanging kindness, is not cowardice, but has its root rather in what I feel—my

---

24. JMBJ, vol. 1, p. 406. Gisela von Arnim was the daughter of Bettina and the wife of Joachim's friend Herman Grimm.
25. JMBJ, vol. 1, p. 439.

passive attitude towards your work would surely reveal it, thinly veiled, to you who are accustomed to meet with enthusiasm, and who know me to be capable of a genuine and active friendship. So I shall remain silent no longer on a subject which, I confess to you, your manly spirit had the right to demand to know long before. Your music is entirely antagonistic to me; it contradicts everything with which the spirits of our great ones have nourished my mind from my earliest youth. If it were thinkable that I could ever be deprived of, that I should ever have to renounce, all that I learned to love and honour in their creations, all that I feel music to be, your strains would not fill one corner of the vast waste of nothingness. How, then, can I feel myself to be united in aim with those who, under the banner of your name and in the belief (I am speaking of the noblest among them) that they must join forces against the artists for the justification of their contemporaries, make it their life task to propagate your works by every means in their power? I must rather make up my mind to strive for that which I have marked out for myself, to separate myself more and more from them, and to work on my own responsibility, though it were never so quietly, for that which I know to be good, and which I consider to be my mission. I can be of no assistance to you, and I can no longer allow you to think that the aims for which you and your pupils are working are mine. I must therefore refuse your last kind invitation to take part in the festival at Weimar in honour of Carl August; I respect your character too highly to act hypocritically, and I revere the memory of the prince, who lived with Goethe and Schiller and wished to rest with them, too much to be present out of curiosity.

Forgive me if I have given you a moment of sadness during your preparations for the festival; I had to do it. Your awe-inspiring industry, the number of your followers, will soon console you, but when you think of this letter believe one thing of me: that I shall never cease to carry in my heart a grateful pupil's deep and faithful memory of all that you were to me, of the often undeserved praise you bestowed on me at Weimar, of all your divine gifts by which I strove to profit.

JOSEPH JOACHIM[26]

What Liszt had utterly failed to grasp about Joachim, as a reading of this letter makes abundantly plain, was not his devotion to the ideals of the Viennese classics but the exclusive nature of that devotion, which left little or no room

---

26. JMBJ, vol. 1, pp. 441–43.

for anything else. It seems never to have occurred to Joachim that Liszt's own devotion to the music of Beethoven, Schubert, and Mozart could not be challenged, and that by exploring new territory Liszt was only following Beethoven's example. Again we are struck by the magnanimity of Liszt's response. After receiving Joachim's letter, he remarked: "Joachim remains a great artist and a noble spirit," a comment that was duly passed on to Joachim by Hans von Bronsart.[27] If Bronsart's ploy was meant to induce remorse in Liszt's erstwhile disciple, it can only be regarded as a lamentable failure. Not long afterwards Joachim arrived at his definitive view of Liszt's compositions, calling them "those stunted weeds," an opinion from which he never wavered.[28]

Now that matters were out in the open, the rift between Weimar and Leipzig began to widen. Joachim's comments, although made privately, were evidently discussed in both cities, and they became the catalyst for new enmities. When Bülow was invited to give a recital in Leipzig in 1857, he offered the committee Beethoven's *Diabelli* Variations and Liszt's Sonata in B minor. In a devious reply Ferdinand David asked him to drop the sonata on the grounds that the low fee of six louis d'or did not give the organizers the right to ask for Liszt, only for Bach and Beethoven. "People have heard that you play the things of your master in public," wrote David. "Show them that you understand no less the works of the older masters."[29] Bülow saw through the deception at once and waxed indignant that his programme was being dictated to him by "these bigots," who did not even have the courage to call Liszt's sonata by its name but instead referred to it obliquely as one of "his things." "How Jewish that is!" remarked Bülow.[30] Later that same year Liszt travelled to Dresden in order to conduct the first performance of his *Dante* Symphony. A large claque from Leipzig was present, and his work was greeted with catcalls and whistles. Liszt's supporters were appalled. In 1859 Franz Brendel, the editor of the *Neue Zeitschrift für Musik* and an ardent Lisztian, exacted a suitable revenge when he celebrated the twenty-fifth anniversary of the magazine in Zwickau, the birthplace of Schumann, its founder, and excluded from the festivities not only Joachim and Brahms but Clara Schumann as well. It was now the turn of the Leipzigers to be appalled.

Despite the deep divisions which separated Liszt from his artistic opponents, the War of the Romantics might never have captured the attention of the world at large had not Joachim, rather against his better judgement, allowed himself to be persuaded by Brahms to take the quarrel into the German press. We shall shortly have to consider the important role played by Brahms in the ongoing

---

27. JMBJ, vol. 1, p. 473.
28. JMBJ, vol. 2, p. 81.
29. BB, vol. 3, pp. 86–87.
30. BB, vol. 3, p. 87. See p. 356, n. 48.

struggle against Weimar, but for the moment it is enough to know only the following. Incensed by the continuous stream of Liszt-Wagner propaganda poured out by the *Neue Zeitschrift,* and angered by the apparent arrogance of its views concerning the Music of the Future, a concept both Brahms and Joachim found offensive, they drew up their famous "Manifesto," which Joachim used as an attempt to clear himself publicly of the suspicion of cowardice.[31] The whole of Germany was canvassed for signatures. Many were promised, but only four signatories had actually attached their names to the document when a copy inexplicably found its way into the editorial offices of the *Berliner Musik-Zeitung Echo.* It ran:

> The undersigned have long followed with regret the pursuits of a certain party, whose organ is Brendel's *Zeitschrift für Musik.*
>
> The above journal continually spreads the view that musicians of more serious endeavour are fundamentally in accord with the tendencies it represents, that they recognize in the compositions of the leaders of this group works of artistic value, and that altogether, and especially in northern Germany, the contentions for and against the so-called Music of the Future are concluded, and the dispute settled in its favour.
>
> To protest against such a misrepresentation of facts is regarded as their duty by the undersigned, and they declare that, so far at least as they are concerned, the principles stated by Brendel's journal are not recognized, and that they regard the productions of the leaders and pupils of the so-called New German School, which in part simply reinforce these principles in practice and in part again enforce new and unheard-of theories, as contrary to the innermost spirit of music, strongly to be deplored and condemned.
>
>
>
> JOHANNES BRAHMS
> JOSEPH JOACHIM
> JULIUS OTTO GRIMM
> BERNHARD SCHOLZ[32]
>
>

---

31. JMBJ, vol. 2, p. 80.

32. KJB, vol. 1 (part 2), pp. 403–04; and MBJ, vol. 1, pp. 278–79. It is generally conceded that the wording of the "Manifesto," with its sweeping condemnation of the New German School, was the work of the twenty-seven-year-old Brahms. (Brahms's Hamburg address was used as the collection-point for the signatories [MBJ, vol. 1, p. 279]) Joachim owed so much to Liszt that he was torn, and he put his hand to the document with difficulty. See the soul-searching letter he wrote to Robert Franz a few days later, in which he poured out his true feelings about Liszt and the pain that his opposition to Liszt's music had caused him. *"Amicus Liszt, magis amica Musica,"* cried Joachim, adapting a phrase that Aristotle had once used about his teacher Plato: "Liszt is my friend, but music is even more my friend."(JMBJ, vol. 2, p. 80)

The delay in collecting additional signatories for the "Manifesto" proved to be its undoing. Before it could be published it was "leaked" to the *Neue Zeitschrift für Musik* (possibly by Carl Weitzmann), and Brendel came out with a parody of it on May 4, 1860. Two days later the "Manifesto" itself made its belated appearance in the *Berliner Musik-Zeitung Echo*. Although the document had meanwhile attracted more than twenty supporters, including Bargiel, Dietrich, Hiller, Kirchner, and Reinecke, the element of surprise was lost.[33]

The lines of battle had been formed, the war declared. Brahms and Joachim began to draw some heavy fire from the other side because the peremptory disclosure of their protest exposed them as its instigators. When Wagner came out with his polemical essay "On Conducting," he did not hesitate to aim some shafts at both men. He described them as members of a "musical temperance society"—a witty description of their conservative position if one thinks about it—awaiting a new Messiah. Brahms's piano playing he dismissed as inflexible and wooden. "I should have liked see Herr Brahms's technique anointed with a little of the oil of Liszt's school,"[34] he declared, maintaining the religious analogy. For Joachim, however, who had meanwhile been appointed head of the newly formed Hochschule für Musik in Berlin, he reserved his cruellest thrust. "I am told that . . . Herr Joachim expects a *new Messiah* for music in general. Ought he not to leave such expectations to those who have chosen him to be a high-school master? I, for my part, say to him: 'Go to it!' And if it should come to pass that he himself is the Messiah, he may, at all events, rest assured that the Jews will not crucify him."[35] After reading such slurs on his character as this, it causes no surprise to learn that Joachim steadfastly refused to allow the works of the New German School in general, and the compositions

---

33. The background to the débâcle has been dealt with in authoritative detail in FBNS. One musician whom Joachim failed to win over was Robert Franz. Two days after inviting him to sign the "Manifesto" (in a letter ostentatiously dated "March 21, Bach's birthday"—as if to say that Bach, too, was a protester) Joachim received Franz's reply. He wished to stand aside from the protest, Franz said, not because he approved of the Music of the Future, still less of Young Weimar, but because "I hear that for some time past, in consequence of many bitter experiences, Liszt is as though crushed, and a fresh blow would surely render his condition yet more unhappy" (JMBJ, vol. 2, p. 82). This was not the only time that Franz proved himself to be a staunch ally of Liszt the man. He could only have been referring to Liszt's resignation from the Court Theatre, which had now rendered him almost superfluous in Weimar, to the myriad complexities of Carolyne's annulment proceedings in St. Petersburg, which were about to force her to seek a solution in Rome, and to his son Daniel's death, which had occurred three months earlier.

34. WGSD, vol. 8, pp. 320-21. Wagner, it will be recalled, had been introduced to Brahms in Vienna in 1864, thanks to the joint efforts of Tausig and Cornelius, and had heard him play his "Handel" Variations. At that time his reaction to the work was favourable (see p. 182, n.34), but with the passing years his dislike of Brahms and all his works had reached such a pitch that he used his solitary encounter with the younger musician as a club with which to beat him. By 1869 Wagner was describing the piece he had earlier liked as "very serious—from which I gathered that [Brahms] was impervious to a joke."

35. WGSD, vol. 8 (1898 ed.), p. 337.

of Liszt in particular, to be used for instruction at the Berlin Hochschule lest the students be contaminated by them.[36]

Liszt never once participated in the debate, preferring to let his music speak for itself. It made no difference to the outcome, however. While Wagner's polemics were directed against Wagner's enemies, they visited almost as much misfortune upon his friends. Wagner's mischievous pen must be held at least partly responsible for the fact that Joachim and Liszt did not speak to one another for nearly twenty-five years after their formal break in 1857. Yet there was a touching postscript to this unhappy story which deserves to be better known. The two men were briefly re-united in 1880, in Budapest, and again in 1884, when they both travelled to Eisenach for the unveiling of the Bach monument there; on the latter occasion Liszt is said to have embraced Joachim like a long-lost son.[37] Eighteen months later they met once more, in London. It was April 1886; Liszt was in the British capital for a performance of his oratorio *St. Elisabeth.* Numerous banquets were arranged in his honour, including a gala reception at the Grosvenor Gallery which was attended by the whole of musical London. Joachim happened to be in the city, giving some concerts of his own, and he unexpectedly turned up at the gallery in order to pay homage to his erstwhile friend. "In the artists' room the king of pianists congratulated the king of violinists, and a complete reconciliation was effected," reported *The Graphic.* [38] As if to emphasize the fact, the same magazine published as a centre-fold a large photograph of the two men shaking hands, with various other dignitaries—Sir George Macfarren, Sir Arthur Sullivan, Charles Hallé—gathered round. It was an illusion, however. The camera could not take the picture behind the picture, which had not really changed in any of its essential details.

I V

In weaving their complex web of intrigue against Liszt and his supporters, Clara Schumann, Joachim, and the Leipzig School in general received the powerful backing of Brahms. From the early 1850s these musicians enjoyed a rare, three-way friendship, which survived for more than forty years and derived a good part of its nourishment from their united opposition to Weimar. The story of Brahms's first, unfortunate encounter with Liszt in the summer of 1853 has already been related; few things better symbolize the War of the Romantics than Brahms sleeping while Liszt played his B-minor Sonata. Within weeks of

36. SE, p. 14.
37. MJ, p. 270.
38. April 17, 1886, p. 415.

his departure from Weimar, in fact, Brahms had sought out the Schumanns. He arrived in Düsseldorf in September 1853, and it was in the warm and friendly atmosphere of their home that he played to them some of the pieces he had been too inhibited to play to Liszt. This visit, which lasted for a whole month, was a turning-point in Brahms's career. Schumann was deeply impressed with Brahms's compositions and dubbed him "the young eagle." He broke a ten-year silence as a critic by writing an article called "Neue Bahnen" ("New Paths") in which he hailed Brahms as a master "sprung fully armed from the head of Zeus."[39] It was published in Schumann's old magazine, the *Neue Zeitschrift für Musik,* on October 28, less than four months after Brahms's visit to Weimar, and it caused a stir there. This recognition by Schumann, which overnight turned Brahms into a celebrity, reinforced the young composer in his determination to have nothing to do with Weimar and the so-called Music of the Future. In 1860 came the "Manifesto" against the New Germans, whose ideas, as he put it, "were contrary to the innermost spirit of music, strongly to be deplored and condemned." This was the stern language of the Old Testament, and it was not surprising that Brahms's supporters came to regard him as a musical Messiah (with whose imminent arrival Wagner had already taunted Joachim), destined to lead new music back to that Promised Land from which it had wandered, and which it should never have left in the first place. It was with a sense of biblical mission that Brahms wrote his symphonies, sonatas, and concertos, which are a noble and entirely successful attempt to keep alive the traditions of a glorious past.[40] When Brahms's First Symphony was nicknamed "Beethoven's Tenth," Brahms took it as a compliment: he knew that there could be no more effective reply to Weimar than to be called Beethoven's successor. As for Liszt, he never acknowledged the succession. He once described Brahms's B-flat-major Piano Concerto as "grey."[41] Brahms in turn called Liszt's music "ein Schwindel," perhaps the most blistering criticism it was ever called upon to endure. By this time, the War of the Romantics was raging in Vienna, where Brahms had acquired a champion in the form of the redoubtable critic

---

39. NZfM, no. 18, October 28, 1853.

40. The notion of Brahms as a musical Messiah, which caused such bewilderment in the Weimar camp, was begun by Schumann. In a letter to Joachim written in October 1853, shortly after his first meeting with Brahms, Schumann had written: "Johannes is the true Apostle. Only the other Apostles understand him, including perhaps Judas Iscariot, who likes to preach with such confidence on the banks of the Ilm. All this is for the Apostle Joseph alone." (JMBJ, vol. 1, p. 84) This astonishing reference to Liszt as a Judas Iscariot—a traitor to art—came sixteen months after Liszt had given the first performance of Schumann's *Manfred* music in Weimar. (The sentence was suppressed by Karl Storck when he brought out his English edition of Schumann's letters in 1907.) The Messianic image was again used by Schumann when he wrote of Brahms: "This is he that should come"—the first time in history that a Messiah had been his own true Apostle (LCS, vol. 2, p. 282). It is only in this wider context that Wagner's tongue-in-cheek reference to "heiligen Johannes"—"saintly Johannes"—can be fully appreciated (WGSD, vol. 8, p. 322).

41. LLB, vol. 8, p. 394.

Eduard Hanslick, who frequently rode out to do battle for his composer-friend in the columns of the *Neue Freie Presse*. Later the young Hugo Wolf, an enthusiastic admirer of Liszt, would ride out to meet him and would strike some powerful blows for the New Music from the sanctuary of the *Wiener Salonblatt*. It was Wolf who delivered the *coup de grâce* to Brahms by informing the world that there was "more intelligence and sensitivity in a single cymbal-crash of Liszt's than in all three of Brahms's symphonies,"[42] perhaps the most mind-boggling assertion ever preserved in the annals of music criticism. In such a poisoned atmosphere Brahms and Liszt were wise to keep one another at a respectful distance during their declining years. It is significant, however, that Liszt never played a single work of Brahms in public, an important omission when we recall the immense range of his repertory and his readiness to promote the music of other contemporaries with whom he happened to find himself in disagreement.

V

No one who is remotely interested in the constant stream of innuendo, nuance, gossip, and downright insult that formed the backdrop to the War of the Romantics can afford to overlook Wagner's *Mein Leben*. The book runs to nearly a thousand pages, but so vivid and gripping is the narrative that it reads like a novel. Many people insisted that it *was* a novel, so extraordinary is the tale it recounts. Yet Wagner is precise about names, dates, and events, most of which can easily be corroborated. Some of the material was libellous, which is why Wagner had the book privately circulated during his lifetime. It was not published until 1911, long after the main participants and their families were dead. The story of how Wagner came to dictate his massive autobiography to Cosima Liszt-Wagner during the years 1865–70 will be unfolded in a later volume. All that the reader needs to recall here is that Wagner devoted nearly five hundred pages of his text to the years 1842–61—that is, to the very period under discussion—and his book provides some startling insights into the personal animosities which helped to keep the "war" going. Wagner had one of the sharpest pens in nineteenth-century criticism. Mendelssohn, Meyerbeer, the Schumanns, Joachim, and Hanslick are all paraded before the reader and are then pierced through with a rapier thrust, often with no more ceremony than if they had been bales of straw. Mendelssohn is depicted as a cunning manipulator of fame and finance.[43] Hanslick is called "uncompromisingly hostile."[44] As for

---

42. *Wiener Salonblatt,* April 27, 1884. Brahms had not yet written his Fourth Symphony.
43. WML, pp. 383–84.
44. WML, p. 846.

Joachim, Wagner calmly reports that the violinist "could not forget my tre-
mendous article on Judaism," and that he subsequently "felt shy and awkward
in my presence." As a bonus Joachim is made to ask Bülow whether there was
"anything Jewish" in his, Joachim's, compositions.[45] We shall shortly have to
consider Wagner's anti-Semitism and its unfortunate consequences for the New
German School.

The fires of acrimony were now burning brightly. True, *Mein Leben* was
read by comparatively few people during Wagner's lifetime, and then only
after 1870. But the malice it bore towards Wagner's adversaries was symptomatic. Even if there had been a genuine desire on the part of those directly
involved to dowse the flames, Wagner would have insisted on fanning the
dying embers back to life. When he published his anti-Semitic tract *Das
Judenthum in der Musik,* it had the effect of someone directing a stream of
gasoline towards a naked flame. The resulting conflagration was such that the
heat and blast are still felt today, nearly a century and a half later.

That *Das Judenthum* is an anti-Semitic document has been demonstrated so
often that it would be a pity to waste another word on the issue. Of far greater
interest is the artistic theory which lies at the heart of the article and is usually
overlooked in the hullabaloo surrounding the "Jewish question." Basically,
Wagner said three things:

> 1. The true composer speaks not for himself alone but for the
>   whole of his society. He is bound to that society through his
>   cultural heritage—language, education, history, race. Because
>   his personality is unconsciously woven into the fabric of society
>   at a thousand different points, his music utters the hopes, aspira-
>   tions, frustrations, and despairs of his fellows. Indeed, they will-
>   ingly turn to it for solace and comfort.

For its time, this was a far-sighted theory of artistic communication, based as
it was on the idea of common backgrounds. But Wagner carried the argument
further:

> 2. The Jew can never become a great composer, and for much the
>   same reasons as given above. He is an outsider. He does not share
>   the education, history, or racial background of the "host" soci-
>   ety. Even his language (Yiddish) is different, and he forever
>   speaks the tongue of whatever land he adopts with an accent.
>   He owes a prior allegiance to his Hebrew forefathers, and that

---

45. WML, p. 606.

simple fact prevents him from empathizing with society as a whole. His Jewishness, in short, is a cultural handicap.

We now know that none of this second argument is true. It is, in fact, utterly false and also offensive. But in Wagner's day everything looked different. The Jew was literally a displaced person. The Napoleonic wars in Central Europe, and a succession of rigorous pogroms in Russia, had encouraged large numbers of Orthodox Jews to migrate into Germany. When Wagner was a boy, growing up in Leipzig, he witnessed their strange customs, their unusual dress, their high-pitched, nasal accents, and, above all, their resolute refusal to integrate, to become a genuine part of society through inter-marriage. It was an indisputable fact that up to 1850 the Jews had produced no great composer other than Mendelssohn (who was born into a converted Christian family anyway). Wagner thought that this phenomenon called for an explanation. His notion of races which are incompatible simply because their members "speak a different culture" and therefore remain blind, deaf, and dumb to one another's art, even while living side by side with it, was an original insight. Nobody else at that time had come anywhere near to offering what is still, in effect, a respectable ethno-musicological theory. But Wagner pressed his argument forward once more, this time with terrible consequences:

3. It is not merely that the members of these incompatible groups "speak a different culture." They are born that way: their culture is a product of them; they are not a product of their culture. Place a dozen sparrow's eggs beneath an eagle, and she will be unable to hatch a single eaglet.

Wagner had now wandered into the field of genetics, which was to have such a devastating effect on our own century. He did not live to see the cultural emancipation of the Jews and the arrival of Mahler and Schoenberg (to say nothing of Milhaud, Bloch, Copland, and Gershwin), the existence of whose works demolished his theory. He was the victim of his time, and he paid a terrible price for his outspokenness when his ideas were incorporated into the ramshackle political philosophy of the Nazi party, fifty years after his death. *Das Judenthum* was regarded by Goebbels as a key document in the Final Solution. Wagner himself provides the damning evidence in his last sentence. Addressing the Jews, he writes: "Remember, there is but one redemption from the curse laid upon you [i.e., being born Jewish], and that is the redemption of Ahasuerus—downfall!" The Jews, in short, were invited to annihilate themselves.

Das Judenthum was published in the *Neue Zeitschrift für Musik* in two instalments, on September 3 and 6, 1850, and it caused an immediate outcry. A letter of protest was delivered to the directors of the Leipzig Conservatory, whose signatories included Joachim and Ferdinand David, insisting that Brendel be dismissed from his post at that institution.[46] Since Wagner had used the pseudonym "K. Freigedank," at Brendel's suggestion, no one could at first be sure from where the attack came.[47] They had little trouble in finding out, however, since the Dresden revolutionary (now living in exile in Zürich) made no secret of his authorship. It is a measure of the pride that Wagner took in this article, and of the scandal that it provoked, that when he expanded it in 1869, he insisted on attaching his name to it.

What, it may be asked, has all this to do with Liszt and Weimar? Five of the most prominent personalities opposing the New German School were Jews: Mendelssohn, Joachim, Hiller, Ferdinand David, and Hanslick. By his unstinting support of the exiled Wagner, Liszt placed himself in the paradoxical position of offering his protection to an anti-Semite. Whenever Wagner shouted to the whole world that Jews made poor composers (and shouted it in the columns of the *Neue Zeitschrift* to boot, which was widely perceived to be the official mouthpiece for Weimar and the New German School), Liszt, his champion, appeared to be saying it too. It was a classic example of guilt by association. With Wagner as a friend, as we have remarked, Liszt did not need enemies. The charge that Liszt himself harboured anti-Semitic feelings will not withstand scrutiny.[48] There is not a single recorded comment from Liszt

---

46. Brendel had held the position of professor of music history and aesthetics at the Leipzig Conservatory since 1846. The signatories who now wished to remove him from office were Becker, Böhme, David, Hauptmann, Joachim, Klengel, Moscheles, Plaidy, Rietz, and Wenzel. The effort failed because Brendel's work as a teacher was outstanding and had nothing to do with the editorial policies of the *Zeitschrift*. Although Brendel was placed under severe pressure by his colleagues, he kept a cool head and allowed the "Jewish question" to be aired in several subsequent issues of the magazine. He himself then summed up the various viewpoints in an able editorial, published on July 4, 1851. "I only wished for calm discussion," he wrote, "and not for the voice of passion." In the event, it was the voice of passion that he got, and the scandal of *Das Judenthum* pursued him across the years, even menacing his private life.

Wagner genuinely admired Brendel for not breaking before the storm. Shortly after Brendel's death, in 1868, Wagner said of him: "He was courageous enough to steadfastly allow the tempest to rage around himself, instead of conducting it across to me," a course of action which would have freed Brendel from all the pother (Appendix to *Das Judenthum*).

47. "Freigedank" means "free thought." In an editorial footnote Brendel told his readers that Germany was renowned for its intellectual freedom and that "to this freedom we now lay claim."

48. That has not prevented the charge from being made, however. Liszt was accused publicly of being an anti-Semite by the Hungarian critic Sagittarius in his pamphlet *Franz Liszt über die Juden*. The source of the charge went back to certain passages in Liszt's book *Des Bohémiens,* some of which are worthy of Wagner's pen. We know today that these pages were actually written by Princess Carolyne. (The background is traced on p. 388.) It remains to be added that Liszt was extremely unfortunate in this matter. A number of people to whom he felt closest on this earth were demonstrable racists. To the name of Wagner we must add those of Princess Carolyne, Cosima Liszt, and Hans von Bülow, whose anti-Semitic ravings come tumbling from the pages of his published correspon-

that would allow us to brand him as a racist. All his life he was surrounded by Jewish pupils and disciples, who have provided us with eloquent testimony to the unfailing generosity and courtesy with which he treated them. These included Moriz Rosenthal, Arthur Friedheim, Carl Tausig, Raphael Joseffy, Eduard Lassen, Emil Sauer, Eduard Reményi, Leopold Damrosch, and Hermann Cohen. For Liszt, music was a branch of the great tree of humanity, a universal language that cut across all racial barriers.

V I

Had the War of the Romantics been generated solely by the personal quarrels of those who participated in it, the struggle would have expired the moment those personalities disappeared from the scene. Mendelssohn, after all, had gone to the grave in 1847; Schumann had followed him in 1856, after lingering for two years in the asylum at Endenich. But the war went on, and even increased in intensity, because the philosophical positions taken by the two sides had by then become so fascinating that it engendered a dispute about the very nature of musical language which is still alive today.

The central problem agitating the world of music in the 1850s was the fate of sonata form. There were only two alternatives open to composers: either they could go on repeating the basic formula handed down to them by the Viennese classics, or they could attempt to modify or develop it. Broadly speaking, Mendelssohn and Brahms chose the former alternative; Liszt chose the latter. His declaration "New wine demands new bottles" was his way of saying that form and content go together, that change in the one necessitates change in the other, that the language of Romantic music was by now so advanced that it could no longer be contained within the outmoded forms of a bygone age, which common sense dictated were never intended to hold that language in the first place. Liszt's "reply" to the classical symphony, as we have seen, was the symphonic poem, a form he invented. Briefly, his work showed three departures:

1. He invented the single-movement "cyclic" structure which rolled the separate movements of the sonata into one. In this, Liszt was only carrying on a procedure established by Beethoven, in whose works—the Fifth Symphony, for example—certain movements are not only linked but actually reflect one another's content.

---

dence, even when opened at random, and make one wonder why he has never been brought before the bar of history to answer for his views.

2. He perfected the "transformation of themes" technique, in which the contrasting ideas of a work are developed from a single musical idea.

3. He believed that the language of music could be fertilized by the other arts, poetry and painting in particular. He popularized the concept of "programme music," and so began a controversy that still goes on today.

No other article of Liszt's faith has been so badly misrepresented as this last one. There are still musicians who think that he fostered the notion that music is a "representational" art, that it can depict a poem, a picture, a flower, or a storm. Of course, it can do no such thing, and Liszt never said that it could. He is quite plain on the matter:

> It is obvious that things which can appear only objectively to perception can in no way furnish connecting points to music; the poorest of apprentice landscape painters could give with a few chalk strokes a much more faithful picture than a musician operating with all the resources of the best orchestras. But if these same things are subjectivated to dreaming, to contemplation, to emotional uplift, have they not a kinship with music, and should not music be able to translate them into its mysterious language?[49]

In other words, music cannot portray a poem, a picture, or a storm. What it does is more subtle. It expresses the mood that such a poem or picture evokes in the heart of the recipient, and transmutes it into musical experience, an experience to be perceived on a purely musical level. Of all the places where it is possible for a composer to seek stimulation, Liszt seems to be saying, the other arts are the best place for him to be, for they inhabit a similar emotional world, even though they may express that world in very different ways. Liszt here comes close to espousing the idea of the unity of the arts. One of the few musicians to grasp that fact was Richard Wagner, whose "Open Letter on

---

49. From the general preface to the symphonic poems, CE, vol. 1. Liszt's admission that he was stimulated by external impressions will surprise no one who has read his introduction to the earliest edition of the "Suisse" volume of the *Années de pèlerinage*.

> I have latterly travelled through many new countries, have seen many different places, and visited many a spot hallowed by history and poetry; I have felt that the varied aspects of nature, and the different incidents associated with them, did not pass before my eyes like meaningless pictures, but that they evoked profound emotions within my soul; that a vague but direct affinity was established between them and myself, a real though indefinable, a sure but inexplicable means of communication, and I have tried to give musical utterance to some of my strongest sensations, some of my liveliest impressions. (CE, part II, vol. 4)

Liszt's Symphonic Poems" (1857) makes mandatory reading, since it was a seminal document in the ongoing War of the Romantics. It is filled with penetrating observations about the true nature of "programme music," about the mysterious relationship between "form" and "content," and about the historical links that bind the symphonic poem to the classical symphony—the very topics that needs must concern any musician who embarks on a serious study of Liszt's music today. And in reply to those purists who accused Liszt of demeaning music by bringing it into association with the other arts, Wagner proclaimed them to be fainthearts who failed to understand that music was the most powerful of the arts. Indeed, Wagner went on, it possessed the magical capacity to rescue the tawdriest of paintings, the most vulgar of verse, the moment it cast its redeeming mantle over them. "Hear my creed," Wagner asserted: *"Music can never, and in no possible alliance, cease to be the highest, the redeeming art. It is of her nature, that what all the other arts but hint at, through her and in her becomes the most undoubtable of certainties, the most direct and definite of truths."*[50] The symphonic poems, Wagner assured his readers, were first and foremost music. Their importance for history, he went on, lay in the fact that Liszt had discovered a way of creating his material from the poetical essence of the other arts; and that, Wagner concluded, amounted to the most significant development in the evolution of instrumental music since Beethoven. Leaving aside the flattering comparison with the Viennese master, Wagner's central observations are so accurate, and they chime so well with Liszt's creative intentions, that we can only assume that there had been a number of discussions between the two men as to what, exactly, a "symphonic poem" really was. For the rest, Liszt's attitude to programme music was certainly derived from Beethoven, the Beethoven of the *Pastoral* Symphony. And if questioned about it, Liszt might well have replied with Beethoven that his music, like the *Pastoral,* was "more the expression of feeling than painting."

Such were the passions aroused by the War of the Romantics in general, and by Liszt's theory of programme music in particular, that in the dust and din of battle it was forgotten that Brahms and Mendelssohn wrote programme

---

50. NZfM, April 10, 1857. In this remarkable essay, Wagner contrasted the realistic programme music of Berlioz with Liszt's efforts to sublimate the emotional content of his poetical models. Sublimation was in fact the key, and it was shrewd of Wagner to observe it. Liszt, as we have stressed repeatedly, would never have dreamed of regarding his symphonic poems as mere musical copies of painting, poetry, or drama. Wagner's paper originally took the form of a letter written to the twenty-year-old Princess Marie von Sayn-Wittgenstein, dated February 15, 1857, from Zürich; Marie had earlier asked Wagner to "explain" Liszt's symphonic poems to her. The "explanation" grew into a rather substantial article, which was first published in the *Neue Zeitschrift* on April 10, 1857. Wagner waxes lyrical about the symphonic poems, and it is clear that whatever his later view of their musical worth, they at first held him in thrall. "Do you know a musician more musical than Liszt? Do you know of one who holds within his breast the powers of music in richer, deeper store than he?"

music too. What is Mendelssohn's *Hebrides* Overture but a musical seascape, based on autobiographical experience, indistinguishable in its musical intentions from the symphonic poems of Liszt? As for Brahms, did he not give the title "Edward" to the first of his Ballades, op. 10, thus informing the world that he had composed a musical counterpart to the old Scottish saga of that name?[51] Nor was this a solitary lapse on the part of the master of "absolute music." The slow movement of Brahms's F-minor Piano Sonata bears the following quotation from Sternau:

> Der Abend dämmert, das Mondlicht scheint,
> Da sind zwei Herzen in Liebe vereint,
> Und halten sich selig umfangen.[52]

If this inscription had appeared at the head of a work by Liszt, much would have been made of it by both pro- and anti-Lisztians. But because it appears at the head of a movement by Brahms, it is generally passed over in silence.

Much of the confusion surrounding the difficult question of what, exactly, music portrays could be dispelled if we jettisoned the widely held definition of programme music as "music which attempts to excite a mental image by means of an auditory impression."[53] This definition was introduced long after Liszt had written his symphonic poems and cannot really be applied to them. He himself would surely have disapproved of such a simplistic formula, which his own writings on the topic contradict. His symphonic poems have nothing to do with this magic-lantern show of the mind, which would attempt to reduce a remarkable series of compositions to baby talk.

VII

The seal of intellectual respectability was placed on these deliberations by the arrival of a musical thinker who took the debate out of the local arena in which

---

51. The version of the "Edward" saga used by Brahms was taken from his well-thumbed copy of Herder's folk-anthology *Stimmen der Völker in Liedern*. It unfolds a dark tale of patricide; and the mother's anguished question "Why is your sword so red with blood, Edward, Edward?" is mirrored exactly in the opening melody. Is there not an unconscious irony in the fact that Herder, who provided the inspiration for this ballade, was one of Weimar's greatest sons?
52. The twilight glimmers, the moonlight glows,
    Two hearts are here in love united,
    And locked in blest embrace.
53. WSPM, p. 140. Liszt's own forays into onomatopoeia are few and far between. The bird-song in "St. Francis of Assisi preaching to the birds" is one such example; another is the famous scene from *Faust* where Gretchen plucks off the petals of a flower to the words "He loves me, he loves me not" (see p. 332). Liszt is far less interested in this kind of thing than any of his successors in the field of programme music, including Richard Strauss, Sibelius, and Respighi.

it was floundering and placed it on a firmer philosophical footing. Eduard Hanslick published the first edition of his influential book *Vom Musikalisch-Schönen* in September 1854.[54] Its central talking-point was the nature of musical language. In answer to the question "What, exactly, does music express?" Hanslick came back with the chilling reply, "Nothing; music is its own meaning." With these few words Hanslick ensured that the debate would rage for another fifty years. His "closed world" view of music was not new. Leibniz had once tellingly referred to music as "an unconscious exercise in arithmetic in which the mind does not know that it is counting." What was new about Hanslick was that he was a musician addressing musicians, and he found a large audience. His famous aphorism "Music is form moving in sound" tells us everything that we need to know about his theoretical picture of music. Overnight he became the philosopher-in-chief of the autonomist school, the champion of Brahms, and the arch-opponent of Wagner, Liszt, Berlioz, and, later, Bruckner. His book went through nine editions and was translated into five languages. It is significant that the first edition of *Vom Musikalisch-Schönen* contained no mention of Liszt. The trouble began with the second edition, which appeared in 1858. In its preface, Hanslick went out of his way to attack Liszt's concept of programme music in general and his *Faust* Symphony in particular.[55] What had happened in between? Two years earlier Liszt had published his first six symphonic poems, together with their defensive introduction; and in September 1857 he had conducted the first performance of the *Faust* Symphony, a work which upset Hanslick's fixed notions of music. Hanslick's preface is dated November 9, 1857. It was, in short, a polemical response to what he perceived to be an attack against his theoretical position.[56] Henceforth he adjusted the text of *Vom Musikalisch-Schönen* whenever he thought that Liszt and his disciples posed new dangers.

One of the most devastating messages contained in the book was that not only can music *not* represent the phenomena of the natural world, but it cannot even express the *feelings* aroused in us by that world. Here is the great agnostic at his best:

> Play the theme of a symphony by Mozart or Haydn, an adagio by Beethoven, a scherzo by Mendelssohn, one of Schumann's or Chopin's compositions for the piano. . . . Who would be bold enough

54. HMS.
55. HMS, 2nd ed., p. ix.
56. Hanslick himself admits as much. "Just as I was busy preparing the second edition," he wrote, "along came Liszt's programme symphonies, which denied to music more completely than ever before its independent sphere, and dosed the listener with a sort of vision-promoting medicine" (HMS, 2nd ed., p. ix). Hanslick may also have been angered by Felix Draeseke's article "Liszts symphonische Dichtungen," which had appeared earlier that year (in the periodical *Anregungen für Kunst und Wissenschaft*) and which had lauded these new compositions.

to point out a definite feeling as the subject of any of these themes? One will say "love." He may be right. Another thinks it is "longing." Perhaps so. A third feels it to be "religious fervour." Who can contradict him? How can we talk of a definite feeling being represented when nobody really knows what is being represented? To "represent" something is to exhibit it clearly, to set it before us distinctly. But how can we call that the subject of an art, when it is really its vaguest and most indefinite element, and which must therefore remain forever on highly debatable ground?[57]

This was thin gruel, and Hanslick's opponents had a hard time swallowing it. Nonetheless, he went on to offer them a second helping. He informed them that one of their most cherished notions, the unity of the arts—to which both Liszt and Wagner at that time subscribed—was based on a fallacy. The arts, Hanslick argued, were not really connected at all.[58] He insisted on detaching music from literature, painting, and sculpture, and he showed that these last arts are modelled after objects, scenes, people, and places in the outside world. Shakespeare, Rembrandt, and Michelangelo, in short, all draw upon real life for their works. But where does music come from? Where in the outside world do we find the model for Mozart's *Jupiter* Symphony? Perhaps it is to be found in bird-song or in the voices of the beasts, remarked Hanslick cynically. And he immediately added the forthright rejoinder: "It is the gut, not the voices, of animals which is important. And the animal to which music is most indebted is not the nightingale but the sheep."[59]

It is easy to see why such arguments caused consternation in Weimar. If Hanslick was correct, Liszt's music was little better than an acoustical perfume which drifted aimlessly around a programme, and it was meaningless without reference to that programme. Hanslick wrote:

> The composer of instrumental music never thinks of representing a definite subject; otherwise he would be placed in a false position: he would be placed outside rather than inside the domain of music. His composition in such a case would be programme music, unintelligible without the programme. If this brings the name of Berlioz to mind, we do not thereby call into question or underrate his brilliant

57. HMS, pp. 36–37.
58. In an aggressive footnote, Hanslick chastised Schumann for having fostered the unity-of-the-arts theory in his critical writings. "Robert Schumann has done a great deal of mischief by his proposition: 'The aesthetic principles of one art are those of the others, the material alone being different' " (HMS, p. 3).
59. HMS, p. 170.

talent.[60] In his steps followed Liszt, with his much weaker "symphonic poems."[61]

When Hanslick declared war on the symphonic poems, in 1858, he had heard only one of them, *Les Préludes*. [62] From the start he chose to fight Liszt on theoretical rather than on practical grounds, and that made him dangerous. The very term "symphonic poem" was offensive to him, for he perceived it to be a contradiction in terms. As for Liszt's general preface, he persistently scorned its central message: that if the other arts be subjected to contemplation, the composer can translate the experience into "the mysterious language of music." Since, according to Hanslick, music was not a language at all and was therefore incapable of expressing anything, Liszt's arguments collapsed through their own internal inconsistency.

As the years rolled by, Hanslick developed into an ever more formidable adversary. In 1855 he had been appointed music critic to the *Neue Freie Presse* in Vienna, and he later became professor of aesthetics in that city's university, where he taught courses in music history and aesthetics for forty years. His brilliant pen and his forthright views earned for him the reputation of a scourge among musical journalists. Vienna became a closed city for Liszt and his disciples, and he often advised his younger pupils who were thinking of making their debut in the city not to appear there, lest their association with him should harm their careers. Nor were they able to wait it out and hope to achieve success by attrition, as it were. Hanslick ruled Vienna until his death in 1904, by which time all the other characters in the drama were dead as well.

VIII

It would be a mistake to assume that Weimar was incapable of producing anyone to deal with the intellectual challenge of a Hanslick. Both Brendel and Bronsart were seasoned writers who had access to the national press, and they readily took up the cudgels on Liszt's behalf. Brendel's contribution as the editor of the *Neue Zeitschrift für Musik* was unremitting, lasting for more than

---

60. Why not? Hanslick's arguments against programme music, if they are sound, must apply to all of it, not just to that part of it of which he personally disapproves.

61. HMS, p. 81.

62. The performance took place in Vienna in March 1857, and Hanslick came out with a polemic against Liszt. In a letter to his cousin Eduard written a few days later, Liszt observed: "The *doctrinaire* Hanslick could not be favourable to me; his article is perfidious." He then went on to inveigh against the unhealthy growth of criticism generally, and marvelled that people were actually paid to deliver their views on artists (LLB, vol. 1, p. 271).

fifteen years. As for Bronsart, his *Musikalische Pflichten*[63] is a forthright defence
of the Weimar school, and his polemic against Hiller brought him to the
forefront of the battle.[64] Spirited articles were also contributed across the years
by Cornelius and Bülow, who emerged early on as crusaders in Weimar's cause.
One of the very first "differential diagnoses" of the issues separating the two
camps, in fact, came from the pen of Cornelius, who had dealt publicly with
the respective merits of "absolute" and "programme" music as early as December 1854.[65] But Hanslick's true counterpart was none of these men. He was a
writer whose contribution to the "war" has been largely forgotten, his name
known only to specialists of the period. That is a pity, because his work suggests
that he, if anyone, had the right to be regarded as Liszt's "bulldog." The
collected articles of Richard Pohl cover a span of thirty years and contain a
faithful record of the activities of the Weimar School. That Pohl saw himself
in the role of a fighter is proved by his aggressive pseudonym, "Hoplit" (a
heavily armed infantry soldier of ancient Greece, equipped with helmet, breast-
plate, sword, and shield). We are not wrong to describe him as Weimar's
"critic-in-residence," for Liszt brought him to Weimar for that purpose. Pohl
attended Liszt on many of the latter's excursions across Germany, was present
at most of the major festivals in Weimar itself, and took a highly professional
interest in Liszt's activities as a composer.[66] He himself tells us that he knew

---

63. *Musikalische Pflichten* (Leipzig, 1858) was Bronsart's answer to a series of negative articles called
Musikalische Leiden which had appeared in the *Augsburger Allgemeine Zeitung* the previous year. In
a brief but pointed preface, Bronsart explained that he had originally sent his answer to the editor
of that same newspaper, but it had failed to appear, whereupon he published it himself. In this
thirty-two-page brochure, Bronsart accused Liszt's opponents of ill-will, unfairness, and spreading
lies.

64. *Das Echo* (no. 27, 1857).

65. NZfM, December 8, 1854. Although Cornelius does not say so, his piece was almost certainly
written in response to Hanslick's *Vom Musikalisch-Schönen*, which had appeared earlier that same year.

66. Some account of Pohl and his wife, the harp virtuoso Jeanne Eyth, is called for, since they
remained at the centre of Liszt's Weimar activities for a period of seven years, and the literature about
them is sparse. Our main sources are Pohl's *Autobiographisches* (1881) and his *Meiner theuren Gattin,
Frau Jéanne Pohl (geb. Eyth) zum Gedächtniss* (1870).

Pohl was born on September 12, 1826, in Leipzig. As a child he was taken to all the Gewandhaus
concerts. He later recalled the conducting of Mendelssohn and the playing of the young Clara Wieck,
who once "rendered Thalberg's *Moses* Fantasy in a white dress with a camellia in her hair." When
Pohl was twelve, he began to take piano lessons from Ernst Wenzel, who aroused the musician in
him; it was Wenzel who advised him to specialize in music theory, a decision for which he was always
grateful. His early years were marked by privation, and he was obliged to work in a machine factory.
He then moved to Chemnitz, where he spent six of "the saddest years of my life." It was a chance
encounter with Berlioz in the 1840s which galvanized him into action. Pohl tells us that he seized
his pen and, with the overture *Les Francs-Juges* still ringing in his ears, dashed off his first article,
"Nothsignale aus Chemnitz." Thus was born his long career as a journalist and critic. Pohl married
Jeanne Eyth on September 22, 1852. Two years older than he, she already stood on the threshold
of a brilliant career. In his touching memoir of his wife, written shortly after her premature death
in 1870, Pohl tells us that she received her first lessons from her mother, on a full-sized pedal
harp by Erard, when she was twelve years old. She created a sensation when she performed Parish-

the symphonic poems intimately, long before they were published in 1856, since he was privileged to hear Liszt "work them up" at rehearsals, at the piano, and even at public concerts.[67] As early as 1854 Pohl was sending detailed reports about Liszt's activities to Franz Brendel, who published them in the *Neue Zeitschrift* under such titles as "Confidential Letters from Weimar" and "Travelogues from Thuringia." Their chief function was to inform the rest of Germany about Liszt's movements, and they were written with Liszt's full knowledge and approval. Pohl must have been privy to Liszt's innermost artistic thoughts at this time, for in these essays he tells us that Liszt was working on a thematic catalogue of his own compositions as well as a book on Gypsy music—perhaps the earliest known reference to that controversial publication.[68] The very first detailed analyses of the symphonic poems and of the *Faust* and *Dante* symphonies were undertaken by Pohl, and they remain among the best ever attempted.[69] While Pohl was a champion of both Wagner and Berlioz, and wrote many pioneering articles in defence of both composers, it is for the warfare that he waged on Liszt's behalf that he deserves to be recognized. He launched a number of direct attacks on Hanslick in the 1850s. A typical blast occurred in his essay "Modern Programme Music," in which he subjected to a *reductio ad absurdum* Hanslick's theoretical picture of music as a thing-in-itself. If music is merely a game of forms and colours, he argued, then the time will come when it can all be done by a "composing machine" with whose help any

---

Alvars's *Feentanz* at a Gewandhaus concert in October 1849. From that time her career was assured.

Pohl was introduced to Liszt in 1852, by Franz Brendel, in whose Leipzig home the members of Liszt's circle would often assemble. From the start Liszt saw in Pohl (who was already an enthusiastic Wagnerian) a potential crusader in the cause of new music, and invited him to settle in Weimar. The invitation was renewed the following year at the time of their Dresden encounter (see p. 232), and this time Pohl leaped at the opportunity, since Liszt also offered Jeanne the position of harpist in the Weimar orchestra. The Pohls moved to Weimar in April 1854. Shortly afterwards Jeanne suffered a serious illness which incapacitated her for three months and caused Pohl much anxiety. The ten years she and Pohl spent in Weimar, however, devoted as they were to the pursuit of artistic ideals, were among the happiest of their lives. The Pohls (like the Mildes and other artists attracted to Liszt's circle) remained in Weimar simply because Liszt made it pleasant for them to do so. In 1864, three years after Liszt himself had left Weimar, the Pohls moved to Baden-Baden, where after a long illness Jeanne died, in the arms of her husband (PMG, p. 59).

Liszt always remained grateful to Pohl for his period of loyal service during the most turbulent years of the War of the Romantics, and later thanked him for the "faithful, noble devotion which you always so courageously and emphatically showed to Weimar's Progressive Period . . ." (LLB, vol. 2, pp. 365–66) Pohl's three volumes of collected works are devoted largely to Wagner, Liszt, and Berlioz, and he could count all three composers as his personal friends. Despite Wagner's later coolness towards him (brought on by Pohl's public disclosures of Wagner's harmonic indebtedness to Liszt; see p. 545), Wagner paid him a high compliment when he called him "Der älteste Wagnerianer" (PA, p. 32). Pohl died in Baden-Baden in 1896.

67. PA, p. 22.

68. The catalogue was published the following year, 1855, and became a foundation document for all subsequent Liszt catalogues. The book on Gypsy music did not materialize until 1859.

69. PGS, vol. 2, pp. 238–320.

child could compose a march or a polka. Pohl drove this point home by asking whether any child could create pictures by shaking a kaleidoscope.[70] With this simple analogy he raised a rather profound issue, one in advance of its time. What is the difference between a visual pattern created by a kaleidoscope and one created by a Leonardo? What is the difference between a sequence of notes created by a calculating machine and one created by a Mozart? Hanslick's theory failed to explain such mysteries, yet they were what his book purported to address.

The trouble with Pohl was not his content but his style. He was a polemicist at heart, and his writing possessed evangelical overtones. He saw it to be his mission to gain converts for Weimar; but as so often happens in such cases, many people disliked being badgered for their souls, and resisted. The opposition to Weimar might not have been so profound had it not been for Pohl's polemics, which did not avoid stooping to a description of Mendelssohn's work as "the Music of the Past," a blow he struck against Liszt's opponents in Leipzig for attacking the Music of the Future.[71] After presenting his readers with a summary list of all the modern composers one could hear in Weimar in 1854, Pohl asked: "Where is there another court in the whole of Germany that can boast of such activity?" Once, when Liszt was away on a conducting tour, Pohl proclaimed that "musical life in Weimar without Liszt is what Rome is without the Pope—although the similarity is weak. For the cardinals in Rome can make a new Pope at any time, but the assembled Kapellmeisters of Europe cannot make a Liszt."[72] Such comments were doubtless meant to be helpful. But to

---

70. PGS, vol. 3, p. 75.

71. There can be no better illustration of Pohl's pugnacity than the squabble he contrived between himself and Karl August Krebs (1804–80), Wagner's successor as Kapellmeister at the Dresden theatre. Poor Krebs was quite out of his depth in this important job, and it was well known that his work was marred by ineptitude. Bülow was convinced that Krebs could not read the simplest score without difficulty, and Wagner consistently refused to entrust his work to him. For two years "Hoplit" subjected the unfortunate Krebs to some heavy blows in the columns of the Neue Zeitschrift, until, goaded beyond endurance, the older man replied—not in a musical journal but in two of the most influential political newspapers in Germany (the Deutsche Allgemeine Zeitung and the Constitutionelle Zeitung), and in terms that were so personally insulting to Pohl that he had to consider challenging Krebs to a duel. Liszt followed the confrontation with keen interest, and at one point wrote to Pohl: "Such a coarse public insult absolutely calls for pistols. . . . Your judgement of his Kapellmeister accomplishments in the Neue Zeitschrift and even the slight allusions to his name ["Krebs" means "crab" in German] have remained entirely within the limits of public and private decorum—while only a drunken stableboy could approve Krebs's behaviour towards you. Police intervention in the matter must be carefully avoided, but you certainly cannot dispense with the satisfaction due to you." (WLP, p. 196) Liszt then went on to promise that if Krebs did not issue a public apology, he would travel to Dresden himself in order to help Pohl sort things out. Fortunately, the matter was settled without resort to violence. Pohl submitted his grievance to an Ehrengericht (a citizens' court set up for the purpose of looking into disputes involving affairs of honour), which ruled in his favour. The War of the Romantics never actually killed anyone, as far as we know, but the Krebs-Pohl incident came close to drawing blood.

72. PGS, vol. 2, p. 97.

Liszt's adversaries in Vienna and Leipzig, they came like a red rag to a bull.

Liszt knew that he and his supporters could never prevail over Hanslick through debate; the man was too powerful for that. Yet, like the humble cuttlefish when attacked, all that Hanslick could really do was eject a cloud of ink. Art, as Liszt understood it, could not be intimidated forever by such a personality, to say nothing of such a weapon. History showed that when art and criticism clashed, criticism must yield. In short, the language of music contains within itself the seeds of its own future development. And so it was here. Neither Liszt's "bulldogs" nor the slings and arrows of a Hanslick had the remotest influence on the outcome of the War of the Romantics. Music soon began to unfold in so many directions simultaneously as to make the divisions of the mid-1850s look like expressions of cultural unity. In our own time, in fact, "music" has become all things to all men; the term itself defies rational definition. The Romantics were at least members of one family, and their "war" need never have been fought. Nonetheless, we remain grateful that it was. It was an epic struggle, and the arguments which were engendered proffer us an insight into the Romantic mentality which we would not readily forgo. Unforgettable light is thrown on the conflicting positions of the protagonists, the very nature of music is called into question, and one more proof is offered that the nineteenth century was a true "golden age" of music, with few if any parallels in the history of art.

The Scribe of Weimar

*Every word a man utters provokes the
opposite opinion.*

GOETHE[1]

I

Liszt's literary output is important. In both size and scope it may be ranked with
that of Wagner or Berlioz. While Liszt may lack the intellectual fascination of
the one and the rapier-like wit of the other, his prose may still be read with
pleasure and profit. It is true that some of his writings are apt to strike the modern
reader as impenetrable. The more problematic of them (the books on Chopin and
Gypsy music, for example) sometimes hide their thoughts behind a smoke-screen
of convoluted prose, and more than one reader has been tempted to cast them
aside in exasperation. That would be an error, however. Liszt's articles and books
have an autobiographical significance; that is to say, they illuminate his interior
life. They reveal his attitude towards such topics as the nature of art, the role of
the artist in society, the function of criticism, and the music of the future—the
very subjects which still exercise the minds of thinking musicians today. Moreover, they are not all difficult to comprehend. The articles on conducting[2] and on
criticism[3] are forthright statements which leave us in no doubt as to the sensible
and highly practical views he held on these topics.

Time was when the subject of Liszt as author lay under a dark cloud of
suspicion. It was charged that the bulk of his writings were not by him. Those
of the pre-Weimar years, so it was argued, were largely the work of Marie
d'Agoult, while the writings of the Weimar period itself came from the pen
of Princess Carolyne. A number of experts came forward between the two

---

1. GMR, no. 9, p. 24.
2. "Ein Brief über das Dirigiren" (RGS, vol. 5, pp. 227–32).
3. "Kritik der Kritik. Ulibischeff und Seroff" (Ibid., pp. 219–26).

world wars in pursuit of this thesis: Haraszti,[4] Raabe,[5] and Newman[6] all cast doubt on Liszt's literary credentials. Their position was made all the stronger by the fact that no one seemed to know where the holographs were. Moreover, the two ladies themselves had been less than helpful when asked about their roles in Liszt's activities. Liszt, in short, was found guilty of a literary fraud (on the basis of little but hearsay), in which he contrived to have his two mistresses publish their own work under his name. Today all that has changed. It is no longer tenable to maintain that Liszt was not the author of his own prose. Holograph fragments are turning up in ever-growing numbers, and they have forced Liszt's critics onto the defensive.

II

At the time of writing, nine holograph documents are known to exist.[7] They are:

1. A 143-page holograph of the brochure *De la fondation-Goethe à Weimar,* with corrections and emendations in Carolyne's hand. It bears the date 1850.[8]

2. A 28-page holograph sketch, dated September 1849, which forms the preliminary draft of the above brochure.[9]

3. A 3-page holograph of the introduction to Liszt's symphonic poems, signed by him, and dated Weimar, March 1856.[10]

4. A comprehensive 12-page holograph draft of a part of his early article "On the Position of Artists" (1835), signed by him.[11]

5. A 3-page holograph of part of Liszt's obituary notice of Paganini (1840).[12]

6. A 23-page holograph of the second chapter of Liszt's book on Chopin, with emendations in the hand of Princess Carolyne.[13]

7. A holograph page of the article "Criticism of Criticism."[14]

---

4. HPL and HFLA.
5. RLS, vol. 2, pp. 175–76.
6. NLRW, vol. 2, p. 315.
7. Four of them (nos. 5–8) have been authoritatively dealt with by Mária Eckhardt in END. See also Volume One of the present study, pp. 15–17 and 20–23, for the general background to this complex topic.
8. WA, Kasten 3/1; RGS, vol. 5, pp. 1–109.
9. Ibid.; GFL.
10. WA, Kasten 5/1; CE, vol. 1.
11. Brit. Lib. MS. Add. 33965, fol. 237–42.
12. WA, Kasten 1/1; RGS, vol. 2, pp. 108–12.
13. RGS, vol. 1. The manuscript was sold at auction in Tutzing in 1976 and is now in the hands of a private collector in Germany. A part of this holograph is reproduced on p. 373.
14. Liszt Museum, Sopron. See also END.

8. A 7-page manuscript entitled "Publications pour le piano (Kroll, Reinecke)," in the hand of Princess Carolyne but with corrections by Liszt. The document, dated Weimar, June 10, 1849, is signed by Liszt.[15]

9. A 2-page holograph of the preface to the piano transcriptions of the Beethoven symphonies, signed by Liszt.[16]

10. An 8-page holograph of the "Letter on Conducting: a Defence."[17]

Now this is a significant body of evidence: some 240 pages of prose in Liszt's hand (or containing his autograph corrections) cannot be lightly dismissed. True, it is small when set beside the six volumes of his published prose, but it is enough to shift the burden of proof. It is no longer up to Liszt to prove that he was an author; it is up to his critics to prove that he was not.

III

When Volume One of this biography was first published, we took the view that as far as authorship was concerned each one of Liszt's books and articles poses a separate problem and demands a separate solution.[18] In view of the existence of so much holographic material which has meanwhile come to light, we are emboldened to put this proposition more forcefully: each piece of writing must be regarded as authentic unless there is evidence to dispute it. Such evidence, in fact, is rare. But where it exists (as, for example, in the "La Scala" article, which was finished for Liszt by Marie d'Agoult,[19] or in the revised and enlarged edition of the book on the Gypsies, which suffered mutilation at the hands of Princess Carolyne), we must remember that this taints only the text in question, not Liszt's entire literary output. Yet that is what has happened, in defiance of all the rules of evidence, and we can only describe the process as a conspiracy to rob Liszt of a part of his intellectual legacy.

---

15. BN Paris. Doc. R. 607. See also END.

16. BN NAF 25180, f. 17 (see the reproduction on p. 377). While the holograph bears no date, the format of the pale blue-green paper is identical to that which Liszt used in Milan around February 1838. We therefore conclude that this preface was originally written for the first batch of these Beethoven transcriptions (nos. 5, 6, and 7), which Liszt had already completed in 1837. It was later revised by Liszt to introduce all nine transcriptions when they were eventually issued by Breitkopf & Härtel in 1865. In a covering note to Lambert Massart (who acted as Liszt's go-between in the late 1830s), Liszt explained that he also intended to send him a preface for the *Album d'un voyageur* a little later on. The holograph of this latter preface, which certainly once existed, has not so far been found.

17. Library of Congress, Music Division. Rosenthal Liszt Collection. Letters of Liszt to Richard Pohl, no. 6.

18. See Volume One, p. 23.

19. See Volume One, p. 264.

Perhaps the most damaging observations were made by the great sceptic Haraszti, who, after announcing in 1937 that Liszt was not the author of his own prose,[20] began to amass evidence in support of that thesis—a strange reversal of the scientific method. Haraszti was struck by a point that had been made much earlier by Daniel Ollivier in the latter's edition of Marie d'Agoult's *Mémoires*: namely, that passages from Liszt's *Bachelor of Music* essays (published in *La Revue et Gazette Musicale* between 1837 and 1839) occasionally turn up in the *Mémoires*. The most famous of these "plagiarisms" will be found in the letter to Louis de Ronchaud, which appeared on March 25, 1838.

Mémoires	*Letter to Ronchaud*
We climb up to the Grande Chartreuse over a gentle slope, on the edge of a torrent, always in the shade of firs, beeches, and chestnut trees. As one penetrates into that solitary gorge, it gets narrower and shadier all the time. The noise of the torrent is followed by silence; it seems as though the vegetation, which is of ever-increasing beauty, wanted to attract and hold man in the peace of the Lord. I have climbed many a mountain in the Alps, yet nowhere have I seen a similar effect of continuity. The Alps are divided into three distinct and contrasting regions. First, there is vegetation, tilled soil; then the region of firs and pastures, which gradually dwindles away, turning bare, until we reach rocks and eternal snow. No such thing here. There is always a carpet of greenery under our feet, always a dome of foliage over our heads, always a hidden voice that says to us: *"Venite ad me, omnes qui laboratis."*[21]	We climb over a gentle slope on the edge of a torrent, always in the shade of firs, beeches, and chestnut trees. As we penetrate into the gorge, it gets narrower and shadier all the time. The noise of the torrent is followed by silence; it seems as though the vegetation, which is of striking beauty, wanted to attract and hold man in the peace of the Lord. I have climbed a great number of mountains in the Alps, yet nowhere have I seen a similar effect of continuity. The Alps are divided into three distinct and contrasting regions: first that of tilled soil and vegetation, then the region of firs and pastures, which gradually dwindles away, turning bare, until we reach rocks and eternal snow. Here there are no interruptions, no sharp cuts; there is always a carpet of greenery under our feet, always a dome of foliage over our heads, always a hidden voice that says: *"Venite ad me, omnes qui laboratis."*[22]

---

20. HPL, p. 130.
21. AM, pp. 102–03.
22. CPR, pp. 153–54. "Come unto me, all ye that labour [and are heavy laden, and I will give you rest]." Matthew 11:28.

The conclusion invited by Haraszti was that Marie d'Agoult was the author of both passages. It is a compelling argument in the absence of anything to contradict it. We submit, however, that the opposite conclusion may just as easily be drawn: namely, that Liszt was the author of both passages. The reason that this conclusion makes sense has to do with the history of the *Mémoires* themselves. In the 1860s Marie began to sift through some of the old papers that might one day serve as a basis for the account she wanted to give the world of her life with Liszt. "I think often about my *Mémoires*," she wrote in 1861. "But what form, what order?" she mused.[23] These questions were never answered by her; the process of selection and rejection was left unfinished at her death. The edition of her *Mémoires* that Daniel Ollivier finally offered the public in 1927 was nothing but a loose assembly of papers and jottings from which few biographical deductions can safely be drawn. And how do we account for the presence of plagiarisms? The most likely explanation has to do with the very human situation in which Marie found herself during her declining years. She wanted to reconstruct her early life with Liszt, particularly the tours through Switzerland and Italy, which had an emotional significance for her. What better way than to refer to the old *Bachelor* letters, published twenty-five years earlier? These articles, in short, served as an *aide-mémoire*. Some of them were certainly the product of their joint efforts (a fact never denied by Liszt), so Marie may have felt reasonably secure when she incorporated this "travelogue" material into her narrative; she may well have intended to paraphrase it at a later stage. In the event, it never became a moral, let alone a legal, issue, since Marie died before she could produce a definitive text.

When Liszt arrived in Weimar in 1848, the desire to write prose was still strong within him. The thirteen years that he spent in the city of Goethe and Schiller, in fact, saw the publication of two-thirds of his entire literary output. It occurred to very few people at that time to question its authenticity. But with the publication of Marie d'Agoult's *Mémoires* the role of Princess Carolyne in the literary output from the Weimar years suddenly became a matter of compelling interest. If Marie had penned the earlier articles, so the argument ran, could not Carolyne have penned the later ones? In an ironic turn of fate, Liszt's two mistresses (who in real life never met but who held one another in near-contempt) were brought before the bar of history to testify against the man who was central to both their lives. Liszt has been fighting a battle on two fronts ever since. But with the discovery of increasing numbers of holographs, and a correct understanding of how, precisely, Marie and Carolyne assisted him in his writing, hostilities must surely cease because of the absence of anything worthwhile to keep them going.

Perhaps the first witness to call in Liszt's defence should be Liszt himself. In

A facsimile page of Liszt's book on Chopin, c. 1851:
"The primitive nature of the polonaise dance . . ."

the general rush to accuse him of deception, it seems never to have occurred to his inquisitors to ask themselves whether he had anything worthwhile to tell them about the authorship of his writings-in-progress. When Haraszti informed the world that "Liszt wrote nothing but his personal correspondence,"[24] he unwittingly delivered himself into Liszt's hands, for it is precisely in his correspondence that Liszt reveals how fully he was implicated in the production of his literary works.[25] The following extracts have been culled at random from his letters:

> In the middle of February I shall send you the complete manuscript of my little volume on Chopin.[26]

> The proofs of the first two articles of my biographical study of Chopin ought to have reached you some days ago. . . . Any alterations, corrections, and additions must be made entirely in accordance with my directions.[27]

> By today's post I send you my *Lohengrin* article, which in the first instance will appear in German in the *Illustrierte Zeitung*. Be kind enough to read the proof *quickly* and return it direct to Weber, Leipzig . . . The *Lohengrin* article must be signed thus: "From the French of F. Liszt." Request the printer's reader kindly not to omit this and to call the editor's special attention to it.[28]

> I am writing a longish article about *Der fliegende Holländer;* I hope it will amuse you.[29]

> Two articles are ready for your paper: *Die weisse Frau* and *Alfonso und Estrella*. As soon as the *Montecchi* and *Favorita* [articles] appear, you shall receive them. The *Fliegende Holländer* is also ready, but must be copied. This article is a very long one, and will take up several of your numbers.[30]

> Tyszkiewicz's letter gave me the idea of asking you to make him a proposal in my name, which cannot be any inconvenience to him. In one number of *Europe Artiste* he translated the article on *Fidelio*.

---

24. HPL, p. 130.
25. It is in his correspondence, too, that Liszt provides us with an excellent yardstick against which to test the authenticity of his prose works. There is a unity of style and a consistency of ideas which flow across his writings, both public and private, which makes the idea that all of it came from the same mind very difficult to resist.
26. Letter to Breitkopf & Härtel, January 14, 1850; LLB, vol. 1, p. 84.
27. Letter to Léon Escudier, February 4, 1851; LLB, vol. 1, p. 92.
28. Letter to Wagner, April 9, 1851; BWL, vol. 1, pp. 122–23; KWL, vol. 1, pp. 112–13.
29. Letter to Wagner, May 20, 1854; BWL, vol. 2, p. 28; KWL, vol. 2, p. 27.
30. Letter to Brendel, July 7, 1854; LLB, vol. 1, p. 162.

Should he be disposed to publish several of my articles in the same paper, I am perfectly ready to let him have the French originals, whereby he would save time and trouble. He has only to write to me about it.[31]

[Robert] Franz, with whom I spent two hours yesterday on the train, is delighted with my promise that [my article on him] would be ready in about two weeks. Naturally he will be glad to fill in the reference numbers which were left blank on the little handwritten manuscript I left in his hands.[32]

Unless we are to accuse Liszt of covering the paper with lies, he is here presenting himself to some of his closest friends and colleagues as an author. He refers several times to "my articles." And he insists that they should not only bear his signature but that he should check the proofs. Liszt never denied that he received help in preparing his manuscripts for publication. Indeed, during the Weimar years that would have been very difficult for him to do, since he was surrounded by secretaries, transcribers, translators, and researchers, all of whom were well aware of the humdrum nature of their tasks. Cornelius, Raff, and Bülow were pressed into Liszt's service at various times, as well as the princess herself. During the year 1854, while work was proceeding on the articles on *Der fliegende Holländer* and *Alfonso und Estrella* as well as on parts of *Des Bohémiens,* Carolyne often signed her letters to Liszt as "Ton Sclavi-chon"—"Thy Slave." It was an apt title that could well have been applied to all four of them.[33]

But what sort of help was it, and why was it needed? On the answers to such questions hangs the definition of authorship. Many of Liszt's articles had to meet urgent deadlines. Some were written in order to shed light on those works and composers Liszt was about to present on the Weimar stage. The *Lohengrin, Orpheus, Alfonso,* and *Weisse Dame* articles were all born in this way. The Mozart and Berlioz articles marked a European-wide centennial celebration on the one hand and a week-long Weimar festival on the other. Either way, the purpose was to focus the attention of the musical world on things topical. Any modern writer placed in such a position would not hesitate to use the research services of a large library. Likewise, a journalist about to publish

---

31. Letter to Brendel, April 1, 1855; LLB, vol. 1, pp. 194–95.
32. Letter to Princess Carolyne, October 15, 1855; LLB, vol. 4, p. 273.
33. The question "Why were such services so willingly rendered?" is rarely asked, but the answer is not hard to find. These students all received their lessons, and sometimes their accommodation, free of charge. It was a way of repaying Liszt for his many kindnesses to them. Although Cornelius (who was at first paid a small honorarium) sometimes rebelled against the heavy demands on his time, it was never Liszt about whom he complained but rather about Carolyne, who was forever prodding him to correct work already corrected on previous occasions (See Volume One, p. 21).

a "think piece" of four or five thousand words would consider it perfectly natural, even necessary, to have his work subjected to editorial scrutiny. The world would not dream of attributing the work of the first to the library or the work of the second to the newspaper. Yet because Liszt put together a team of assistants to copy, translate, and research his articles for him, he has had to face charges of deception.

IV

What, exactly, went on in the Altenburg during those years in which Liszt's writing poured forth in such abundance? It so happens that we can call on a witness who was there, someone who observed everything at first hand, and whose credibility is difficult to deny. For more than ten years Princess Marie von Sayn-Wittgenstein lived on terms of daily intimacy with Liszt. She was eleven years old when she went to live in the Altenburg, and she was twenty-two when she left. She herself tells us that she had total access to the so-called Blue Room, where Liszt and her mother used to do most of their work. According to Marie, Liszt dictated much of his writing to her mother, who used to take down his words with pencil on quarto-sized sheets.[34] When his thoughts concerned musical matters, he insisted on his exact wording; but in the case of more general topics he was content to suggest an outline and let her sketch it in her own way. The next day, however, he would insist that these passages be read aloud to him, and at that point much would be disputed and changed. The corrected pages were then distributed to the pupils—Cornelius, Raff, Bülow—for copying and sometimes for translation into German as well. After a clean copy was made, the original pages, with all their corrections, were usually destroyed. That is why the students assumed that Carolyne wrote much of the prose: they saw only her handwriting. And Princess Marie concludes: "I can certainly testify how carefully Liszt weighed every word my mother wanted to smuggle in, simply because she was intoxicated by its beautiful sound."[35]

In one respect only is Princess Marie's testimony less than helpful to Liszt. From her vantage-point in the Blue Room all she could see was Liszt dictating

---

34. This first-hand account of the literary collaboration between Liszt and Carolyne was given by Princess Marie to Count Géza Zichy in 1911. It remained unpublished until 1932. See *Akadémiai Értesítö* 42, fasc. 451, October–November 1932.

35. Ibid., p. 291. The fact that Liszt was used to dictating his prose would be sufficient to explain the absence of so many holographs. Without wishing to draw any comparisons whatsoever, we cannot help observing in passing that Churchill, Napoleon, Kossuth, Marco Polo, and Henry James all liked to dictate their prose and correct it (where necessary) after reading the preliminary drafts. No one, to our knowledge, has disputed the authorship of their prose on the basis of their working habits.

A facsimile page of Liszt's introduction to his piano transcriptions of the Beethoven symphonies, c. 1838: "The name of Beethoven is today sacred in Art . . ."

and her mother writing, followed by argument, counter-argument, and final agreement. She concluded that the result was a joint effort; in some areas, as she put it, "they came to terms through mutual concessions." It is evident from all the other circumstances with which we are familiar that this phrase "mutual concessions" is by no means the same thing as "joint authorship," although many people unfamiliar with the writing process might think otherwise. The crux of the matter is surely this: expository prose requires two stages, which we can call "background" and "foreground." At the background stage, everything is done that falls into the category of research, and rough drafts are prepared. It is quite usual to do this sort of work with one or more assistants. (When Liszt was preparing his brochure *De la fondation-Goethe à Weimar* he must have had considerable help of this kind, since the text shows an unusually close acquaintance with the history of Thuringia and the fate of the Wartburg.) Then comes the foreground stage, at which the text itself will be worked up. This material, too, may be offered to others for critical scrutiny (even the best of authors are routinely subjected to this kind of editorial control). That Liszt had to exercise both discretion and diplomacy when attempting to curb the excess of zeal that Princess Carolyne sometimes brought to her task goes without saying. The letter that he wrote to her from Gotha, in March 1854, in which he voiced his concern about the forthcoming article on Beethoven's *Egmont,* is a case in point.[36] Apparently the princess had inserted material that went far beyond the scope of the essay, and Liszt was determined that she take it out. After telling her, somewhat mockingly, that it was quite unnecessary for her to broach the subject of the "intellectual and moral progress of musicians from the coming of Jesus Christ," and that he had in any case things of a musical nature that he would prefer to include, he made it plain that he intended to postpone publication of the article by a few days in order to get it right. "Be tolerant of my harshness," he added tactfully—a phrase that sounds symbolic of their general working relationship at this time.

The situation with which we are confronted may be summarized thus:

1. Liszt himself chose the topics of his books and articles. The latter usually arose out of his daily work at the Weimar opera house.
2. He employed assistants to help him with his research.
3. He dictated much of his prose.
4. He revised all manuscript texts taken down from his dictation (including those portions provisionally sketched out by Carolyne) before they were copied out afresh for the printer.
5. Liszt himself checked the proofs.

36. LLB, vol. 4, pp. 182–83. The article on *Egmont* may be found in RGS, vol. 3, part 1, pp. 29–36.

6. He signed the finished articles, often referred to them as "mine," and held himself responsible for the results.

None of this violates the concept of authorship. If it did, a very great deal of literature which is presently deemed to be authentic, not to say masterly, would at once fall into discredit, since it was written in exactly the same way. Nonetheless, the matter cannot be allowed to rest there, as Liszt's critics are quick to point out. There were two works in which we know for sure that Carolyne far exceeded her duties as an editorial assistant. They brought Liszt's name into disrepute, and they are invariably used as a rod with which to beat him whenever the authenticity of his writings is called into question.

v

The impulse to write a book about Chopin arose from Liszt's desire to memorialize the composer after his death in October 1849. In an attempt to furnish himself with some "hard" information about the Polish master, Liszt sent a questionnaire to Chopin's sister Louise, who refused to cooperate.[37] Nothing daunted, Liszt set to work on the book in collaboration with Carolyne, who, since she herself was of Polish extraction, was able to help him reconstruct some of the nationalistic background. The type of work in which she engaged was at first modest, if we are to judge from the rare 23-page holograph which has come down to us and which shows a number of minor changes, added in pencil between the lines of Liszt's own prose. The text first appeared in serial form in the French press[38] and was published as a book by Escudier in 1852. In 1874 Breitkopf & Härtel suggested a new edition, and Liszt drew Carolyne into the work of revision. In hindsight this was a fatal blunder, but Liszt was probably motivated by misplaced chivalry. Carolyne was by now living as a recluse in Rome, immersed in her own literary activities. She had helped him with this book during the difficult times in Weimar, and he doubtless wanted her to know that he still placed value on her opinions. After a few brief consultations, however, the princess herself took on the task of revising the text. A serious conflict arose between the pair which is reflected in their unpublished corre-

---

37. The twelve-point questionnaire was filled out by Chopin's pupil Jane Stirling instead. See Volume One, p. 186.

38. It was published in seventeen instalments in *La France Musicale* during 1851. Liszt had submitted the text to Sainte-Beuve in hopes of getting his erstwhile friend to edit the manuscript, but Sainte-Beuve took one look at the material and decided not to become involved. See his tactful letter to Liszt dated March 1850 (LBZL, vol. 1, p. 129).

spondence.[39] It is clear that Liszt, thanks in part to his itinerant life, lost control of the project, and when the new edition finally appeared, in 1879, it bore little resemblance to the book that he knew, and it is, by common consent, inferior. The text is marred by long-winded digressions and pretentious attempts to be learned which render it virtually useless as biography.

V I

And what of the other work? The origin of Liszt's book *Des Bohémiens et de leur musique en Hongrie* was autobiographical. It was his return visit to his native Hungary in the winter of 1839–40, after an absence of sixteen years, which had revived in him a feeling of intense patriotism. He had visited his birthplace in Raiding, re-lived many of his childhood memories, and been exposed once more to the music of the *Zigeuner*. The first fruits of these experiences were the collections of Magyar Dallok ("Hungarian National Melodies"), which were gradually transformed into the Hungarian Rhapsodies.[40] Liszt attached

---

39. WA, Kasten 91. When La Mara published Liszt's letter to Carolyne dated April 25, 1877, she deleted the following paragraph:

> You give me excellent instructions regarding the new edition; nevertheless, it will be necessary for me to copy all your changes, despite Gregorovius's assurance on the expertise and skill of the Leipzig type-setters. As to my author's sensitivity, this is entirely your invention; I never made a secret of your extensive help at the time in this *Chopin;* on the contrary. And "to act openly" (sometimes exaggeratedly so) is a real habit with me. Consequently, it is not fear of the insinuations of the setters which holds me back, much rather of a blunder in printing—your manuscript being extremely embroiled. Before publication, I shall send you the final proofs.

The published letter, from which the above paragraph was omitted, may be found in LLB, vol. 7, pp. 188–91. Incidentally, Liszt himself told Frederick Niecks that the second edition of *Chopin* was Carolyne's work (NPM, p. 315). One critic who took the book on trust was Eduard Hanslick. In his review (*Die Presse,* September 1879; republished in *Dwight's Musical Journal,* September 22) he, like everybody else, was struck by the digressive nature of the prose, and wrote: "Liszt so loses himself at times in poetic description and reflections, and strays so far from his theme, Chopin, that we almost grow alarmed lest he should not find his way back."

40. By 1846 Liszt had collected hundreds of these Magyar Dallok. On October 8 he wrote to Marie d'Agoult from Dáka:

> During my sojourn in Hungary I have collected a number of fragments with the help of which one might fairly well recompose the musical epic of this strange country, whose rhapsode I want to become. The six new volumes, about a hundred pages in all, which I have just published in Vienna under the collective title Hungarian Melodies—there was enough material on hand for four books six years ago—form an almost complete cycle of this fantastic *epopoeia:* half Ossianic (for there pulses in these songs the feeling of a vanished race of heroes) and half Gypsy. As I go along, I shall write two or three such books, to complete the whole thing. (ACLA, vol. 2, p. 368)

great importance to these pieces. He regarded them as part of a national epic, expressing the soul of a people. In order to explain their unusual origin, he planned to publish them with a preface. From Galatz in July 1847 he wrote to Marie d'Agoult asking whether she would be willing to help him write it, based on notes and indications supplied by him.[41] Their rupture was now three years old, and he received no reply. Time passed, Liszt moved to Weimar, and by 1854 the preface had grown into a book-in-progress. Meanwhile, the rhapsodies were published, between the years 1848 and 1853, and they provoked neither more nor less interest than much of Liszt's other piano music of the Weimar period. It was the delayed appearance of the book in 1859 that aroused a storm of controversy inside Hungary.

What had Liszt said? A basic miscalculation was his confusion of Hungarian music with Gypsy music. By regarding them as one and the same, Liszt unwittingly made a gift to the *Zigeuner* of a remarkable treasury of music that really belonged to the Magyars. In fact, the problem is more complex still. The music that Liszt heard the Gypsies play came from two quite different sources. It contained genuine Magyar folk-melodies, picked up by the Gypsies on their travels across Hungary and Transylvania and then fashioned by them after their own image.[42] But it also contained popular melodies of the day by a number of Hungarian composers (largely dilettante gentlemen of the middle class), whose identities have long been known to us; they included József Kossovits, Márk Rózsavölgyi, and Béni Egressy. Under their hands a new national form emerged in the 1840s—the csárdás, which soon captured Europe, was played everywhere by the Gypsy bands, and which the Hungarians themselves (with their growing sense of national identity) were happy to call "Hungarian." Lurking behind this newer instrumental music was the *verbunkos,* the old recruiting dance of the imperial wars of the eighteenth century, with its slow introduction and fast finale. The *verbunkos* had long since inspired the Gypsy bands to divide their own improvisations into the familiar *lassan* and *friss* while the omnipresent "Hungarian cadence" was perhaps the most familiar part of the *verbunkos* legacy:

---

41. ACLA, vol. 2, p. 389.
42. Nobody denies today that Liszt's Hungarian Rhapsodies contain authentic Magyar folk-songs. The reader who wants to pursue this matter should turn to the following Rhapsodies:

> No. 7: bars 56ff. and 105ff.
> 9: bars 242ff.
> 13: bars 100ff. and 124ff.

These five folk-songs were part of the Magyar heritage and are still sung by Hungarian schoolchildren today. A comprehensive list of such material has been drawn up by Zoltán Gárdonyi in GP, pp. 197–225. See also Ervin Major (MLMR), and Volume One, pp. 335–36.

Through their improvised performances the Gypsies obscured these vital cultural distinctions and made the music one. Liszt, like many other musicians of the day, was deceived by this blending of new and old, and he concluded that the music played by the Gypsies with such conviction must have been created by them, must be a part of their own cultural heritage. A typical example from the rhapsodies, and one that can stand for all the others, shows the nature of the problem. In the Eighth Rhapsody the first theme runs:

We now know this to be an elaboration of the old Magyar song "In the Rushes, That's the Duck's Home":[43]

43. In the rushes, that's the duck's home
    In good ground, that's where the wheat grows
    But as to where a faithful girl grows
    That's a place I do not know, not anywhere.

It is perfectly possible to follow a performance of the rhapsody while looking at the song, to hear the one as the inspirational source of the other. Moreover, Liszt has been extraordinarily successful in capturing the "sonic surface" of the Gypsy band—the repeated notes of the cimbalom, the chalumeau register of the clarinet, and the will-o'-the-wisp ornamentation of the violin. But this rhapsody holds yet more surprises for us. Its second theme is by the contemporary Hungarian composer Márk Rózsavölgyi, and it comes straight out of his "Gay Caprice" csárdás:

From this second theme Liszt moves straight into a third, from the "Tolna Wedding" collection, a popular anthology of Hungarian tunes, which was published around 1840:

Liszt switches back and forth between these last two ideas, creating the illusion that they belong to one another, flow out of one another. The rhapsody, then, is a potpourri of cultural sources, worked up into a brilliant mixture and made to sound like the improvisation that it originally was. In this connection it is important to remember that Gypsy bands always played by ear, and Liszt had to reconstruct the music's notation for himself. This task caused him endless problems, and he went to a great deal of trouble to get it right.[44] If we require

44. Liszt's total immersion in Hungarian Gypsy music in the early 1850s appears to have left its mark on his playing. According to William Mason (who studied with him at the very time he was involved in the topic, 1853–54), he was "unconsciously disposed to colour and mark the music of all composers with Hungarian peculiarities" (MMML, p. 94). Mason reports that this habit gave rise to a story that

further evidence of that fact, we need look no further than his correspondence with Hans von Bülow. In March 1853, when the twenty-two-year-old Bülow was about to make his first concert-tour of Hungary, under Liszt's auspices, the master gave his pupil a number of letters of introduction to Hungarian friends, together with a very special task. He instructed Bülow to contact Count István Fáy, who lived not far from Oedenburg, and who, so he went on to tell his protégé, "owns a large collection of Hungarian Gypsy melodies of the best quality."[45] Apparently Liszt had learned a short time earlier that Count Fáy (who was in debt) might be prepared to sell him the collection under certain conditions; although Liszt had asked Fáy to send the material to Weimar by parcel post, he had received no reply. Liszt now urged Bülow to inquire further about the sale of the collection; and should the reply be affirmative, he was instructed by Liszt to go to Oedenburg in person.

> You will go through the collection in two days, and will bring back a big parcel of them, judiciously chosen in accordance with my interests, which you know. . . . I particularly recommend that you do not hand over the 120 florins until after you have wrapped, sealed, and packed up the parcel of music, because in such matters it is necessary to foresee distractions which are sometimes irreparable . . . In short, I give you full authority to negotiate with Count Fáy in my name, with 120 florins in your pocket, and I am counting on your diplomatic talents to come to a conclusion which will be as satisfactory for me as for him—Amen.[46]

We gather from the Liszt-Bülow correspondence that the sale did not go smoothly. At his first attempt, Bülow found himself prevented from reaching Fáy's château by a heavy fall of snow. Then, having announced his visit, he received an evasive reply from the count, who pretended to be too distracted by business matters to see the young man personally and requested that the 120 florins be sent through the post. This Bülow wisely refused to do, bearing Liszt's firm injunction in mind. Eventually a sale of sorts was arranged, although it was hardly satisfactory to Liszt, who, having finally parted with 150 florins for

---

Liszt once forgot the ending of the theme of the *Kreutzer* Sonata's slow movement and absent-mindedly substituted the *verbunkos* cadence, thus:

45. LBLB, p. 8. Fáy (1809–62) was an accomplished pianist and an avid collector of old Hungarian music. Liszt had first made his acquaintance in 1840, during his triumphal visit to Pest.
46. LBLB, p. 9.

the entire Hungarian collection, received only a third of the material in exchange. Fáy's promise to forward to Bülow the remaining two-thirds "in a fortnight" remained unfulfilled.[47]

Why was Liszt so anxious at this particular juncture to possess such material? He was on the point of publishing a set of thirteen of the Hungarian Rhapsodies (with dedications to Leo Festetics, Casimir Esterházy, Antal Augusz, and others), and he wanted to check the texts against whatever "sources" he could lay hands on. The point is not so much the value of the material, which would hardly have met the requirements of modern scholarship; the point is that Liszt did his best to find some corroboration of his own notation.[48] As it was, no ethno-musicological claims were ever made on behalf of the rhapsodies. They fell into disrepute only when Liszt's book itself was published, in 1859.

VII

The first hint that Liszt was going to have trouble came in September 1859, when Kálmán von Simonffy[49] wrote him the following letter and sent a copy to the Pest newpaper *Pesti Napló:*

> Sir:
> What are you doing? What have you written in your pamphlet, which I myself have not yet read, but from which the entire Hungarian press quotes the following: "Hungarian music does not belong to the Hungarians but to the Gypsies." My goodness, what a deception! Public opinion is against you, and I inform you herewith that I have to refute you with all the severity you deserve.
> I am sorry to have to write against you, who were so good to me. But I cannot ignore my patriotic duties either.
> From this moment our roads will part. [When this letter was reprinted in *Hölgyfutár* on September 15, the editor inserted this

---

47. LBLB, p. 14.
48. Liszt further enjoined Bülow: "Go to hear the *Zigeuner* band known as Die Pariser and greet their leader cordially from me—that is, the violinist Bihari, who is, I believe, a grandson of the great [János] Bihari" (LBLB, p. 20). And a bit later: "Study the *Zigeuner,* and borrow their energetic accentuation of rhythm. Do not forget the long pedal-points either, and let yourself follow all the impulses of the wild passages according to the bitterness or the exuberance of your feelings." (LBLB, p. 21)
49. Simonffy (1832–89) was a Hungarian composer of popular songs who doubtless resented the fact that Liszt had made a gift of some of it to the Gypsies. It is clear that Simonffy, like other Hungarians who took part in the debate, had not read *Des Bohémiens,* since it was not published in Hungary until the end of 1859. In fact, the argument was fuelled by the extracts from the book that had appeared in *La France Musicale* in July and August 1859 and filtered through the Hungarian press during the weeks that followed.

reproof: "A remarkable expression! We never knew until now that Simonffy had been moving along the same path as Liszt."]

Farewell, forever!

Your servant, etc.
KÁLMÁN SIMONFFY[50]

With all the audacity of his twenty-eight years, Simonffy also proceeded to publish Liszt's private reply to him:

Weimar, August 27, 1859

Sir:

Your letter would have surprised me, did I not know through experience how often the best-intentioned men let themselves be taken in by the most obvious lies the moment a sensitive nerve is irritated.

You tell me that you have not read my book, which in any case has not yet been published; but relying on an ill-intentioned rumour spread by a few newspapers, which have not based their story on facts, you declare that you will deal with me "with all the severity I deserve"—and you will do it because they say (without having read me) that I have done harm to Hungarian music and consequently to my sense of patriotism.

Rest assured, sir, that this is not the case, and it is really I who have been completely wronged in this matter. As far as patriotism is concerned, no one can reasonably bring me to task for that, and if you will read my book sometime, you will see that it was prompted by the feeling of devotion which I have particularly nurtured towards my native land.

The pleasure I had when I heard several of your delightful Hungarian compositions prompts me to answer your letter; but I shall not feel obligated to do the same for everybody who might have the whim to inform me of the so-called storm my book has raised. I ask you, sir, not to view these lines in any way as a *captatio benevolentiae* [attempt to win goodwill] because I have absolutely no desire to protect myself from being judged with all the severity I deserve, convinced as I am that, in this instance, as in others, I can only gain by it—provided that those who place themselves in the role of my judges can justify themselves at the bar of conscience.

Believe me to be, sir, yours truly,

F. LISZT[51]

---

50. *Pesti Napló,* September 6, 1859.
51. Ibid.

If Liszt thought that this settled the matter, he was mistaken. The issue raged in the Hungarian press for weeks. The following year August Ritter von Adelburg and Sámuel Brassai both published highly aggressive tracts in which Liszt was pilloried.[52] Brassai's piece was by far the most penetrating criticism of the book ever to appear, and Liszt did not reply. But something of his hurt feelings came out in a letter to Antal Augusz, in which he wrote: "The fuss made about my book on the Gypsies has made me feel that I was much more truly Hungarian than the *Magyarmaniacs,* my antagonists. . . ."[53] Even those letters and articles which were published in support of Liszt, from such notables as Reményi[54] and Mosonyi,[55] could not undo the damage, and Liszt's reputation suffered for years. It was left to Hungary's greatest authority on this matter to put things into perspective. Béla Bartók knew better than anyone else how unreasonable it was of the Hungarians to adopt a holier-than-thou attitude towards Liszt, since they themselves were partly to blame for his error. They invariably referred to the music that the Gypsies played as "Gypsy music"; why should Liszt not do the same? Here is how Bartók expressed it in 1931:

> It is futile to look for logic in the use of language. The living tongue puts out the most peculiar off-shoots, which we simply have to

52. AE and BMC. Sámuel Brassai (1800–97), like other critics, was incensed at Liszt's confusion of Gypsy music with Magyar folk-song, and he even printed some music examples of the latter to help him build his case against Liszt. What made *Des Bohémiens* such a dangerous book for Brassai was its lack of scientific rigour, and he likened its smoke-screen prose to the stinkweed with which Hungarian fishermen traditionally drugged their fish in order to catch them more easily (p. 12). Brassai prints a number of Liszt's assertions about the Gypsy and invites his readers to believe the opposite. He is particularly indignant about Liszt's statement that the Gypsy is incapable of becoming civilized, and he refers to documentation going back to the fifteenth century which proves the contrary: namely, that the Gypsies were a constructive part of the social system in Hungary. Liszt's example of the untamed Gypsy boy "Josi," who was sponsored by Count Sándor Teleki and brought up by Liszt in Paris only to rebel against its "civilizing influences" and run back to his tribe in Hungary, is a poor one according to Brassai, since the boy adapted well enough to his new environment to become a "French dandy" (p. 20; see also Volume One of the present study, pp. 339–40).
    Brassai's fulminations against Liszt are made all the more effective by the literary structure of his own piece, in which he alternates between addressing first the reader and then Liszt himself—the latter as in an open letter. "Lo, behold the privilege of genius!" Brassai declares to his audience. "He creates facts that eyes have not yet observed and ears have not yet heard" (p. 5). Then, turning to Liszt, he remarks: "Of the language of your country you did not please to learn a single word" (p. 14). Brassai's tract, in fact, is spoiled by these occasional forays into *argumentum ad hominem,* and he allows himself a particularly hostile remark when he makes a thinly veiled reference to Liszt as "some fellow, of who knows what nationality, disguised as a Hungarian and spreading an inclination for bad taste" (p. 56).
53. CLBA, p. 89. One criticism to which Liszt did reply, albeit privately, was that of Eduard Hanslick, whose piece on *Des Bohémiens* was published in the Vienna *Presse* in September 1859. See LLB, vol. 2, pp. 407–09.
54. See Reményi's *feuilleton* "Of Hungarian Music," published in *Hölgyfutár,* October 1859.
55. *Zenészeti Lapok,* August 17 and October 17, 1861.

accept as the consequence of a natural growth, even though they are illogical. Thus, if we take the phrase 'gypsy music' as an example of incorrect usage we should long since have acquiesced in its acceptance were it not for the continued ill-effects of this false terminology. When Franz Liszt's well-known book on gypsy music appeared it created strong indignation at home. But why? Simply because Liszt dared to affirm in his book that what the Hungarians call gypsy music *is really gypsy music!* [56]

. . . The courage and conviction with which Liszt stated his opinions, wrong as they were, demands our admiration, for he must have known that by doing so he would rouse considerable hostility towards himself among his own people. It is rather ourselves we must blame for not being able to, or not wanting to, or at best failing to, set him on the road to truth, though that road was there before us in our own villages. [57]

VIII

The ill-fated history of *Des Bohémiens* is not quite finished. In the late 1870s a revised edition of the work was planned. Liszt was by now an old man, and he was somewhat alienated from this youthful work. Once more he approached Carolyne for help, this time in correcting the proofs. (In the light of what had happened to the second edition of *Chopin,* we may ask why he would do anything so reckless. It has to be remembered, however, that the new version of *Chopin* was as yet unpublished and did not appear until 1879.) Without Liszt's knowledge Carolyne had *Des Bohémiens* taken away from the printers, and she proceeded to lengthen it. [58] She inserted gaseous paragraphs full of Hegelian prose, parts of which are incomprehensible. The early section on the Israelites, which was already a simmering cauldron, was now worked up into a poisonous brew. Her comparison of the Gypsy with the Wandering Jew was unfavourable to the latter, whom she described as avaricious, cruel, and servile. It never occurred to her that Liszt would have objected to her views; and once she had taken over the operation, he never saw the proofs. When this edition

---

56. BES, p. 206.
57. BES, p. 508.
58. *Akadémiai Értesítő,* op. cit. Liszt must nonetheless have quickly learned what she had done, for as early as mid-June 1881 the princess wrote to him in order to reassure him that the new edition of *Des Bohémiens* would be sent to him once her revisions were finished (KFL, pp. 401–02). As a result of Carolyne's "proof checking," the book had already acquired a further fifty pages by this stage and was soon to acquire more. Carolyne's letter provides us with a direct admission from her that she was actively engaged in the preparation of the second edition of *Des Bohémiens.*

was published in 1881, a tempest blew up in the Jewish press. Liszt was accused of anti-Semitism; it was a false charge, but he could not publicly deny it without exposing Carolyne.[59] This must have cost him much anguish, since he had to endure a great deal at the hands of the critics. Leading the pack was Sagittarius, whose pamphlet *Franz Liszt über die Juden* depicts Liszt as a racist.[60] One of the few people Liszt was able to confide in was Princess Marie Hohenlohe, and her published comments on the dilemma in which Liszt found himself are worth recalling: "Of course he brushed aside every criticism and correction, and he avoided talking about it with my mother. I believe that she, in her cloistered world, never knew what a wicked trick she had played on him!"[61]

In 1911, the Liszt centennial year, Breitkopf & Härtel decided to publish a popular edition of the composer's prose writings. It is a little-known fact that Princess Marie herself undertook to revise the text of this book and to remove what she called the "ballast." The only two people who knew of her silent editorial work at the time were La Mara and Oskar von Hase, the head of Härtel's. "Do not betray me!" she begged Géza Zichy many years later, "for I would not like to be identified."[62]

Modern scholars are wise to treat *Des Bohémiens* with caution. The book has been twice cursed: first by the Magyars and then by the Jews. Moreover, its various translations and competing editions have turned the text into a mare's nest in which more than one writer has become hopelessly ensnared. Yet this cannot be the final word. At its best *Des Bohémiens* offers irreplaceable insights into music and musicians. For Liszt, the Gypsy musician was a noble savage in whom nature itself had placed the wonderful gift of music. Without any formal training whatever, and without even the ability to read notation, music

---

59. As early as 1859 it was already evident to those in Liszt's circle that the princess herself was responsible for the chapter on the Israelites. One need look no further than the letter Bülow wrote to Bronsart on August 20, 1859 (that is, at the very time that the book was appearing by instalments in the French press) to realize that the hand of Carolyne had already been detected. Indeed, it was Bülow's opinion (erroneous, as it happens) that Carolyne was the author of the entire book (BB, vol. 3, p. 254). But in any case, the 1859 version, with its milder description of the Jews, caused little comment. It was the second edition that did the damage. When Wagner read it, in November 1881, he exclaimed to Cosima: "Really—your father a Jew-baiter!" (WT, vol. 2, p. 756). The author of *Das Judenthum in der Musik* must have had his tongue in his cheek at that moment. This chapter on the Israelites also caused Lina Ramann, Liszt's first biographer, many problems. In her biography she felt impelled to ask the question: "Was Liszt anti-Semitic?"—to which she provided a resounding "no" (RLKM, vol. 3, p. 121). We now know that Ramann was trapped in a terrible dilemma. Ever since the posthumous publication of her book *Lisztiana* (1983), it has been clear that she knew from the start that the princess herself was the author of the Israelite chapter (RL, pp. 183–84). Since Liszt himself had kept silent on that point, however, Ramann felt bound by the same constraint. For a fuller discussion of this complex topic, see LLFM, pp. 157–64.
60. SFLJ. "Sagittarius" was the pen-name of Miksa Schütz (1852–88), a music critic on the staff of the newspaper *Pesther Lloyd*.
61. *Akadémiai Értesítő,* op. cit.
62. Ibid.

gushed forth from him like a fountain. How could such a thing happen? How could the Gypsy violinist become a virtuoso, a sovereign master of his instrument, without a teacher? It was one more proof for Liszt that music was God-given, part of a divine plan. He was so impressed by that central idea that he wanted to enshrine it in a book. This is the true message of *Des Bohémiens,* and we shall fail to understand it if we continue to look at it only as a flawed exercise in ethno-musicology. In fact, the text raises a topic of fundamental importance to all Lisztians, one which is rarely touched on, and one which we have a duty to illumine.

IX

Liszt's theoretical picture of music emerges with striking clarity from his writings. There is a golden thread running through his thoughts which binds them together and makes them shine as one. Music, for Liszt, was the voice of God. He often behaved as if music possessed healing properties. Because of its divine origin, he seemed to say, mere exposure to it was a spiritual balm. It followed from this that the musician himself was a specially chosen vessel through which divine revelation flowed. Moreover, the musician must be worthy of this noble task. That is the real meaning of Liszt's comment "For the formation of the artist, the first pre-requisite is the improvement of the human being."[63] More than once he used the metaphor of the priest or acolyte. He called the artist "the Bearer of the Beautiful,"[64] an intermediary between God and man. One of his happiest descriptions is that of artists as "the legitimate children of one family," and he contrasted them with those thousands of charlatans interested only in cheap success, whom he condemned as "intruders" into the family circle. For Liszt, there could be no nobler calling than this "attachment to art, *for which* (and not merely *by which*) one is to live. . . ."[65]

To conclude from this that Liszt regarded art as a calling hardly does justice to his views. He talked of a "sacred predestination which marks [the artist] at birth."[66] The artist does not choose his calling; his calling chooses him. That is the essential difference between a musician on the one hand and a grocer or a tailor on the other. The latter are free to exchange trades with one another but not with the former, who has no free will in the matter. This view of the artist as someone who is in the grip of forces he does not understand but has no alternative but to obey runs like a leitmotif through Liszt's writings. And when the artist happens to be a genius, his responsibility is heavy indeed. "Is

63. RGS, vol. 5, p. 195.
64. LLB, vol. 1, p. 263.
65. END, p. 187.
66. RGS, vol. 2, p. 135.

not genius the same as the sacerdotal power which reveals God to the human soul?"[67]

Since Liszt's views on art sprang from his innermost being, it was inevitable that they should inform his daily life. That simple connection explains why, after 1835, he never taught for money and why he gave so many concerts for charity. Since art was God-given, it must be given back again, unsullied by contact with Mammon. Herein lies the true meaning of Liszt's motto *Génie oblige!* Much more than *Noblesse oblige!,* the possession of genius puts one under an obligation to serve the rest of humanity not so fortunately endowed. Liszt's championship of individual artists in need falls into the same category. They were "members of one family" and therefore had to be helped.

Liszt's habit of walking onto the concert platform wearing his decorations provoked a good deal of attention, not all of it flattering. In Germany it aroused bewilderment; in France, mirth. His biographers, almost to a man, have dismissed it as a form of vanity. We shall come to understand Liszt's conduct only if we see in it a further symptom of his deep-seated view of the artist as someone who is predestined. A decoration, for Liszt, merely ennobled from without someone whom nature had already ennobled from within. Moreover, by wearing his decorations in public, he elevated the status of musicians everywhere, who in his day were all too often treated like servants. Liszt was generally contemptuous of decorations which merely gratified personal vanity. Whenever he received them, he did so in the name of artists everywhere, thereby bringing the decoration itself into repute. When he pressed Carl Alexander to bestow on both Berlioz and Wagner the Order of the White Falcon, there was nothing in it for him. His motives were disinterested; he simply wished to draw the world's attention to artistic genius, irrespective of where it was found or in whom it resided.

x

So consistent were the links between Liszt's art and his life that they also governed his relations with the critics. Whenever art came under attack, he was prompted to pick up his pen and defend it. And when individual artists were made to suffer for no other reason than that they had created something, Liszt suffered with them, and struck back. That fact never ceases to astonish those who do not know Liszt's character well; it seems undignified for a man of his stature to become involved in the rough-and-tumble of critical debate. Yet it is consistent with his view of art as a moral force. He once wrote, and always believed: "Art is a Heaven on earth, to which one never appeals in vain when

---

67. RGS, vol. 2, p. 109.

faced with the oppressions of this world."[68] Was not this view of art as a paradise worth fighting for? Those who entered the temple of art merely to defile it had to be chastised. And chastise them he did. He witheringly described the critics as the men of the "yet" and the "but," who would crush to death every living endeavour.[69] From his earliest years the criticism of criticism was a constant theme. That he actually regarded some critics as a menace to art is borne out by his view that nobody should be allowed to function as one who had not passed a test and received a certificate.[70] He regarded many of them as incompetents who, motivated by envy, wanted to increase their own reputations at the expense of their betters. Would it not be preferable, he asked, for such people to remain silent?[71] In his youth he had sometimes attempted to expose them by changing the order of pieces in his programmes in order to see if they even noticed. Pixis was passed off as Beethoven, Beethoven as Pixis. Liszt took pleasure in the fact that the "connoisseurs" were loud in their praise of Pixis, taking him to be Beethoven, and equally loud in their condemnation of Beethoven, taking him to be Pixis.[72] His contempt for critics never changed, as was borne out by his oft-repeated saying "Critics! If one would be a critic, one should begin with self-criticism!"[73] As an example of how ill-informed they were, he once quoted with glee a statement printed in the *Allgemeine Zeitung* that Wagner himself had never conducted *Lohengrin* better than Franz Lachner had recently done. Liszt called the assumption "droll" and pointed out that "it is well known that Wagner [who had been in exile for nine years at this point] has *never heard* the work, let alone conducted it!"[74] With the increase in the number of journals and newspapers during the 1840s and '50s, press coverage of music increased dramatically. Liszt never ceased to be astonished at the numbers of people who were actually paid to express their views about it:

> Twenty years ago there were hardly a couple of musical papers in Europe, and the political papers referred only in the rarest cases, and then briefly, to musical matters. Now all this is quite different, and with my *Préludes,* for instance (which, by the way, are only the *prelude* to my path of composition), several dozen critics *by profession* have already pounced on them, in order to ruin me through and through as a composer.[75]

---

68. An entry in Varnhagen von Ense's unpublished *Tagebuch* (WA).
69. LLB, vol. 1, p. 245.
70. RGS, vol. 2, p. 47.
71. RGS, vol. 2, p. 234.
72. RGS, vol. 2, pp. 139–40; CPR, pp. 118–19.
73. WFL(I), p. 120.
74. LLB, vol. 1, p. 301.
75. LLB, vol. 1, pp. 271–72.

The phrase "critics *by profession*" tells it all. Such trenchant views were not calculated to win friends among the men of the press, and Liszt paid dearly. By 1854 his reputation in the newspapers was at a low ebb. They could not attack him as a pianist, but they could punish him for wanting to be taken seriously as a composer. The "strong rain" that he had correctly forecast would fall on his compositions had within two years turned into a veritable deluge. At first Liszt dealt with the problem tongue-in-cheek, telling his friends with a wink and a nod that criticism of him must be true because it was in the newspapers. He jokingly referred to himself as "that notorious *non-composer* Franz Liszt."[76] But with the passing of time Liszt concluded that the only way to protect himself from the critical "deluge" was not to venture out of doors at all. When the psychopathology of music criticism comes to be written, Liszt's battles with the critics (among the least-documented aspects of his career) will emerge as historically important.[77] More than Wagner or Berlioz, Liszt bore the brunt of the aggression that was unleashed by the nineteenth century against its own avant-garde. For one thing, he had a much higher profile than most and therefore offered a better target. For another, he ruled over a clique in Weimar that seemed bent on taking over some of the conservative strongholds. First, Bülow had started to conduct the music of Liszt in Berlin; Tausig then followed suit in Vienna; finally Damrosch broke into Breslau. The man had to be stopped. With an almost uncanny instinct the press perceived his weakness: his love of his pupils. The critics could not break him, but they might be able to break them. Liszt shrank from the prospect of seeing those closest to him suffer for his sake, and he began to dissuade his acolytes from featuring his music in their concerts lest it harm their careers.[78]

It would be difficult to find a better example of Liszt's irony, apropos of the critics, than the letter he wrote to Alfred Jaëll on March 31, 1857. Jaëll had sought his permission to play the E-flat-major Piano Concerto, to which idea the composer responded in mock amazement:

> What is the matter? Cannot you hear the ever-increasing rumblings of the Goliaths of learned criticisms, the yappings and croaks, the protests and invectives from newspapers of all sizes . . . which declare in unison a truth which is truer than true: that LISZT has never been

---

76. LLB, vol. 1, pp. 343–44.

77. LLB, vol. 1, p. 272.

78. For somewhat similar reasons Liszt now began to refuse to give out testimonials to up-and-coming musicians. It is interesting to read the remarks he made on this topic to his pupil Draeseke. "Fischer (the organist) wrote to me recently, to ask me for a testimonial to his musical ability, as he wants to have one to show in Chemnitz. Please make my friendly excuses to him for not fulfilling his wish—possibly, in view of the enmity that I have to bear on all sides, such a document would do him more harm than good, apart from the fact that I very unwillingly set about drawing up such testimonials." (LLB, vol. 1, p. 295)

and never will be capable of writing four bars . . . that he is sentenced without remission to drag around the ball and chain of transcription in perpetuity.[79]

Similar irony was meted out to Liszt's protégé Alexander Ritter. Not long after Ritter had secured the post of music director at Stettin, he was moved by a desire to perform Liszt's symphonic poems and wrote to Weimar for the orchestral parts. That was the only cue Liszt needed. He picked up his pen and replied in his best schoolmasterly vein:

> You desire *Orpheus, Tasso,* and *Festklänge* from me, dear friend! *But* have you considered that *Orpheus* has no proper *working-out section,* and hovers quite simply between bliss and woe, breathing out reconciliation in art? And pray, do not forget that *Tasso* celebrates no *psychic* triumph, which an ingenious critic has already denounced (probably mindful of the *"inner camel"* [i.e. the "blockhead within"] which Heine designates as an indispensable necessity of German aestheticism!), and the *Festklänge* sounded too confusedly noisy even to our friend Pohl! And then, what has all this *canaille* of percussion instruments—cymbals, triangle, and drums—to do with the sacred domain of the symphony? It is, believe me, not only confusion and derangement of ideas but also a prostitution of the species itself![80]

Ritter could not be deflected so easily, however, and his concerts proved to be so unpopular with the Stettin critics that it hastened his departure from that city after only two seasons. This was not the only occasion when Liszt showed that he was in closer touch with reality than his admirers. But it is in his letters to leading conductors, such as Johann von Herbeck, the director of the Vienna Philharmonic concerts, that Liszt's desire to protect his students comes out most strongly:

> In case Bülow should make his appearance at the Philharmonic concert he will, on my advice, not play my A-major Concerto (nor any other composition of *mine*) but just simply one of the Bach or Beethoven concertos. My close friends know perfectly well that it is not my desire to push myself into any concert programme whatever.[81]

---

79. *La Revue Musicale,* no. 4, 1904.
80. LLB, vol. 1, p. 245.
81. LLB, vol. 1, pp. 333–34; see Liszt's letter to Bülow on the same topic, LBLB, p. 277.

Liszt had already urged Herbeck not to feature any of his orchestral works in the Vienna concerts:

> As regards the choruses to *Prometheus,* I confess to you candidly that, much as I thank you for thinking about them, I believe it is wiser to wait a little bit. I am not in the slightest hurry to force myself on to the public, and can quietly let a little more of the nonsense about my *failure in attempts at composition* be spread abroad.[82]

X I

The question that absorbed Liszt all his life was: "Whence does the critic derive his authority?" It is a good question, and it is still asked today. He had no difficulty in providing an answer when it was asked of artists. When he told his pupil Dionys Pruckner that the artist was "the Bearer of the Beautiful," he went on to point out that it was the artist's "inviolable consciousness" of his role that "alone assures his authority."[83] Once again we see the model of predestination lurking just below the surface. But that will not work for critics. No one is predestined to criticize in the same way that he can be said to be predestined to create. Is art, then, above criticism? It was at this point that Liszt introduced a telling conclusion. The real critic must himself be an artist. He must compose, play, conduct, teach, just like the people he wishes to judge. His authority, in brief, will flow from the same source as theirs. Art cannot be improved from without; it can only be improved from within, by the divine revelation imparted to the members of its inner circle. Liszt was the first musician in history to promulgate the idea of peer criticism, and it flowed from his theoretical picture of music. That is why he reacted so swiftly to criticism of his work by journalists, and why he constantly urged his pupils to take up the cudgels in behalf of their own. "War is too important to be left to generals," declared Clemenceau. For Liszt, criticism was too important to be left to critics. He once told Rubinstein that if artists were not prepared to take up the pen in defence of art, "they will have to bear the consequences and pay *their* damages."[84]

---

82. LLB, vol. 1, p. 313. The letter is dated "November 22, 1858, St. Cecilia's Day"—the feast day of the patron saint of music. The irony would not have been lost on Herbeck.
83. LLB, vol. 1, p. 263.
84. LLB, vol. 1, pp. 196–97. Liszt once wrote:

> The critics are puffed up with their own importance, very real in the outside world, often venial and concerned with quite different questions than those of art and artists. Musicians and musical people, editors, stockbrokers, antique dealers, etc., are full of impertinence,

Liszt certainly overestimated the power of music criticism in the newspapers. In his day, however, the activity was still relatively new, and it was starting to look dangerous. In one sense, though, his insight into the ultimate source of the authority of criticism has been borne out by posterity. By far the most interesting and useful critiques in the history of criticism to date have been left by musicians themselves. Schumann, Berlioz, Wagner, Wolf, Debussy, Stravinsky, Schoenberg, Bartók, Busoni, and many others have turned their hands to writing about music, and it is their position as artists which continues to lend their prose its timeless attraction. To this distinguished company we add the name of Liszt. His prose deserves a better fate than to fall victim to the stratagems and spoils of a conspiracy. When we read it without prejudice, it contains the ring of artistic truth. What more do we require?

---

jealousy, and stupidity. That is the picture offered to impartial judgement, more or less the same everywhere with mild variations. How can one create art in this wasteland? Yet it must be done, and we shall create it for them willy-nilly. (LLB, vol. 4, p. 425)

Vienna, Gran, and Aachen, 1856–1857

As our emblem and coat of arms, I suggest a tree
swaying violently in the storm, which reveals its
ripe fruit on every branch withal. Underneath, the
inscription: Dum convellor mitescunt ("While
I am uprooted the fruit ripens") or else: Conquas-
satus sed ferax ("Shaken but fruitful").

FRANZ LISZT[1]

I

Towards the end of January 1856 Liszt set out for Vienna in response to an invitation from Dr. Johann Ritter von Seiler, the mayor of the city, to direct the Mozart Centenary Festival. Seiler, a music-lover who had selected the programme himself, had hoped to persuade Liszt to appear as soloist in Mozart's Piano Concerto in C minor, K. 491. In his letter of acceptance Liszt requested that this work "be given to some other pianist of note. . . . For more than eight years I have not appeared anywhere in public as a pianist."[2] Clara Schumann was approached but declined to stand in, so the concerto was finally given to the Viennese pianist Josef Dachs. Hanslick's hostility towards the idea of Liszt conducting Mozart in Vienna has already been remarked. An even sharper attack was launched in the columns of the Vienna *Fremder Blatt* by a pseudonymous group of people signing themselves "Some Friends of Music." Their protest was published on January 23, less than a week before Liszt conducted the festival, and it was an attempt to poison the atmosphere before he walked onto the stage.

The opening concert took place on January 27, Mozart's birthday, and consisted of the following programme:

---

1. LLB, vol. 1, p. 272. These sentences occur in a letter written to Eduard Liszt, dated March 26, 1857. Although Liszt does not say so, he has taken them verbatim from Schopenhauer's *Parerga und Paralipomena* (SPP [2], vol. 2, p. 75).
2. LLB, vol. 1, p. 213.

Overture to *Die Zauberflöte*
Chorus "O Isis und Osiris" from *Die Zauberflöte*
Piano Concerto in C minor, K. 491 (soloist: Josef Dachs)
Dies irae (Requiem)

Interval

Symphony No. 40 in G minor, K. 550
Aria from *Don Giovanni*
Finale from Act One, *Don Giovanni*

More than five hundred players and singers were massed on the platform of the newly decorated great hall of the Redoute, which was specially illuminated for the occasion. Emperor Franz Joseph and Empress Elisabeth were present. The entire concert, which contained more than three hours of music, was repeated the following evening, and Liszt evidently acquitted himself with honours. Afterwards the mayor and the festival committee presented him with an inscribed baton which read, "From the City of Vienna to the conductor of the Mozart Festival."[3] On January 30, however, the "Friends of Music" were back again. Liszt, they said, understood nothing about conducting, and they added that the public had received him coldly, which was untrue. It was the sort of rebuff that Liszt was by now used to receiving. Under the circumstances his letter of thanks to Seiler, in which he expressed his gratitude "for the very great kindness shown to me during my stay in Vienna, the remembrance of which will not fade from my grateful thoughts," was a piece of diplomacy worthy of a Metternich.[4]

---

3. LLB, vol. 3, p. 60.
4. LLB, vol. 1, p. 216. Not everyone in Vienna was hostile towards Liszt. See the flattering toasts written after his Mozart concerts by Salomon Mosenthal and Eduard von Bauernfeld (LBZL, vol. 3, pp. 27–30).
    It was from this time that Liszt's interest in the idea of a complete edition of Mozart's works and the foundation of a Mozart-Verein in Vienna first emerged. (See his extremely detailed letter on the topic, dated February 9, 1856, to Eduard Liszt.) Its editorial principles, he argued, ought to be based on those used in the ongoing Bach *Gesellschaft* edition. "It will be easy to make out an analogous document for the publication of Mozart's complete works," he wrote:

> According to my ideas, the Friends of Music in Austria should constitute and set the matter going, and the Royal State Press should be employed for it, especially as one can foresee that special favours might be obtained from the ministry. Probably the whole *Festival Committee of the Mozart Celebration* will also consent to this undertaking, in the sense that, by an edition of Mozart's works, critically explained, equally beautifully printed, and revised by a committee appointed for it, a universally useful, lasting, and living *monument* to the glorious master will be formed, which will bring honour and even material gain to all Austrian lovers of music and to the city of Vienna itself.

Liszt goes on to suggest that the entire project might be completed in twelve years, and he proposes that Spohr, Meyerbeer, Fétis, Otto Jahn, Oulibicheff, and Härtel be brought in as consultants. "Haslinger, Spina, and Glöggl, being Viennese publishers, ought especially to be considered, and

Liszt returned to Weimar by train, breaking his journey at Prague and Dresden. He travelled at night in order to utilize his days more efficiently. In Prague he just had time to hear the first act of *Don Giovanni* before boarding the night train, which got him to Dresden at four o'clock in the morning. He arrived back at the Altenburg on February 5 suffering from "extreme mental and emotional weariness," to which was added "a lassitude in all my limbs."[5] His exhaustion was hardly surprising since he had spent two consecutive nights on the train without proper sleep.

Scarcely had Liszt got back to Weimar than Berlioz arrived to conduct a complete performance of his *Damnation of Faust*. Liszt had already rehearsed the chorus and orchestra by the time Berlioz got to the city on February 8,[6] and he also conducted yet another performance of *Benvenuto Cellini* for Maria Pawlowna on February 16 (it was an opera he now admired so much that he had taken to calling it "a second *Fidelio*").[7] Since the customary visit to the duke of Gotha was also included in the itinerary (parts of *Damnation* were played to the duke in the castle theatre), we cannot help observing that this visit demanded more of Liszt than it demanded of Berlioz, for it almost amounted to a third "Berlioz week." Berlioz also renewed his acquaintance with Princess Carolyne (whose admiration for him waxed as her tolerance of Wagner waned), and they had some lively discussions about Virgil and the *Aeneid*. It was Carolyne who aroused, and then sustained, his enthusiasm for the gigantic *Trojans* project—that "big dramatic machine," as he ruefully called it, and of which he was soon writing in terms of "the sorrows that this work cannot fail to cause me."[8] After spending three weeks in Weimar, Berlioz finally mounted the podium of the Court Theatre on March 1 and directed a performance of *The Damnation of Faust* for the benefit of the musicians' pension fund. The performance was notable for the fact that Liszt stood in the orchestra and played the bass drum.[9]

Among the highlights of the 1856 opera season was the appearance on the Weimar stage of Johanna Wagner. Liszt had been powerfully impressed by her rendering of Elisabeth in the Berlin production of *Tannhäuser* in January 1856 and resolved to bring her to Weimar. She arrived at the end of April and stayed with her sister Franziska, the wife of Alexander Ritter, whom Liszt had appointed to the violin section of the orchestra two years

---

would be the best to direct the distribution and regular sending out of the volume, which is to appear on the 27th of January *every year.*" (LLB, vol. 1, pp. 213–16)

5. LLB, vol. 3, p. 63.
6. LBZL, vol. 2, p. 57.
7. RGS, vol. 3, part 1, p. 14.
8. LBZL, vol. 2, p. 69. For more background on this sparsely documented visit of Berlioz to Weimar, see Liszt's letter to Franz Brendel, LLB, vol. 1, pp. 217–18.
9. SNW, vol. 2, p. 63.

earlier.[10] During the first week of May Fräulein Wagner appeared in Gluck's *Orpheus* and *Iphigenia in Aulis*. Such stage presence, coupled with the poise and classical dignity she brought to these operas, had rarely been observed, and her success, as Liszt remarked, went far beyond what they were used to locally. Liszt was fascinated with Johanna Wagner's musical personality and gave an interesting account of her vocal gifts to Agnès Street-Klindworth.[11] At the last of her performances in the title role of Donizetti's *Lucrezia Borgia* she received that rarest of accolades, a standing ovation from the orchestra. Later, at a reception at the royal castle, Carl Alexander himself asked her to extend her stay in order to repeat the performance of *Iphigenia,* and he telegraphed Herr von Hülsen, the intendant of the Berlin opera house (where Johanna had a contract), to secure the necessary permission. "The people here have gone simply mad," she wrote, "and I am being thoroughly spoilt."[12] The singer herself gave a reception for her Weimar friends in the home of Franziska Ritter, and she was not above donning an apron and giving her sister a helping hand in the kitchen.[13] Liszt, who was among the guests, good-naturedly acceded to her request to play. Hitherto Johanna had only seen him conduct (an activity in which she privately confessed that he was "absent-minded"), but the moment he sat down at the keyboard she was won over. Liszt tried to persuade her to join him on a visit to her uncle Richard in Zürich later in the year, but the plan fell through because of her secret engagement to Alfred Jachmann, which she temporarily wished to keep from the Wagners.[14]

If Liszt appeared to be "absent-minded," in Johanna Wagner's words, there were compelling reasons for it. On May 2, while La Wagner was still in residence, Liszt had hurried to Merseburg in order to be present for the first performance of his organ Prelude and Fugue on the name B-A-C-H, played on the cathedral organ by Alexander Winterberger. We know that he returned to Weimar almost at once, for on May 6 he conducted *Lucrezia Borgia* with Johanna Wagner in the title role. He then went back to Merseburg, where on the evening of May 11 he was joined by Hans von Bülow, who had travelled from Berlin in order to request Cosima's hand in marriage.[15] Master and pupil travelled back to Weimar, where Hans stayed on as Liszt's guest at the Alten-

---

10. KJ, p. 194; LLB, vol. 3, p. 70.
11. LLB, vol. 3, p. 71.
12. KJ, p. 171.
13. KJ, p. 194.
14. Johanna had become secretly engaged to Jachmann, a lawyer, about a month before her Weimar appearance. Her father, Albert Wagner, opposed the match, fearing that it would spell the end of her operatic career. Jachmann reports that when he was finally introduced to Johanna's mother, the latter scrutinized him and then remarked: "It is you, then, who wishes to rob me of my child!" (KJ, p. 192) Johanna was at this time a woman of thirty. The marriage finally took place in 1859.
15. LLB, vol. 3, p. 71.

burg for a week. Cosima was still only eighteen years old, and this marriage proposal, while not entirely unexpected, gave Liszt pause for thought.[16]

One of the visitors who arrived at the Altenburg in June 1856 deserves more than passing mention. Marie Lipsius was nineteen years old when she first visited Weimar and was introduced to Liszt at one of his Altenburg matinées. He was at his most chivalrous, sweeping the young woman off her feet with his charm and the many little attentions he paid her. Marie, the daughter of the rector of the Thomasschule in Leipzig, was already deeply interested in music; but like that of many another starry-eyed nineteen-year-old, her life lacked direction. This encounter with Liszt was to change all that. The next day she accompanied him and his entourage to Erfurt to hear a performance of Mozart's Requiem; but it was not the strains of this masterwork which lingered in the girl's memory. Rather, it was the animated conversation between Liszt and his companions, which seemed to her as if "spun with threads of gold."[17] It was dark when they all got back to Weimar, but when Liszt promised that he would try to visit her the next day, she felt (in words that she was to write sixty years later) as if she were walking with destiny. Her premonition did not mislead her. Today the world of music knows her as La Mara, the famous editor of thirteen volumes of Liszt's correspondence, a tribute to his memory without which Liszt scholarship as we presently know it could not exist. The following day Liszt joined the circle of friends gathered at the home of the Pohls, where La Mara was staying, and after the meal (during which she was tongue-tied) there was some music-making. Liszt ushered his fifteen-year-old pupil Theodor Ratzenberger to the piano and put Chopin's A-flat-major Polonaise on the music stand. But the young boy gave up after the first page, saying "I cannot play today."[18] It was a well-calculated ruse. Liszt, who could never bear to leave a piece unfinished, pushed the student off the stool and picked up the performance where Ratzenberger had left it. "Then began," wrote La Mara, "that unique playing whose power to uplift could be guessed at by no one who did not hear it for himself, or did not experience it resounding within his own soul."[19] The Hungarian Storm March came next, simply because the music happened to be lying on the piano. Liszt picked it up and remarked: "I haven't played this for a long time." The keyboard was suddenly transformed into flame and fire, and "the music flowed over us like stormy waves." Soon it was all over. "Come to the Altenburg tomorrow if you want to hear some more," Liszt said. With that he shook hands with everyone, bade them "Auf Wiedersehen!" and departed. When La Mara got to the Altenburg the next morning, she heard a flood of music pouring from the music-room. A servant showed her in, and

16. The long engagement and subsequent marriage of Cosima and Bülow is discussed on pp. 456–60.
17. LDML, vol. I, p. 27.
18. LDML, vol. I, p. 28. Shades of Tausig! (see pp. 179–80).
19. Ibid.

she observed Liszt and the fifteen-year-old Carl Tausig sitting at two pianos playing Liszt's arrangement of his symphonic poem *Hungaria*. Tausig was reading the manuscript at sight and doing it very well. By the time they had finished, more guests had arrived. Liszt got up and greeted everybody, and a general conversation ensued. It was La Mara's first real glimpse of the interior of the Altenburg. Richard Pohl drew her aside and pointed out various objects of interest in the large music-room, and she recalled seeing the three-manual Alexandre piano-organ, Beethoven's Broadwood grand, and Mozart's spinet, on which she had inadvertently placed her cape as she had entered the room. Liszt then gave her his arm, introduced her to some of the other guests, and took his seat at the piano. Turning to La Mara, he said: "I would like to play something just for you. Choose!" La Mara happened to be holding a copy of the "Swiss" volume of the *Années de pèlerinage,* which had recently appeared in a new edition. It was open at *Au Lac de Wallenstadt.* "You will not hear it played better anywhere," Liszt joked, "not even at the Leipzig Gewandhaus. You see, we provincials are conceited people!" Then began a recital that La Mara never forgot, as Liszt transported the company with his rendering of this little piece. He was in a relaxed mood and wanted to go on. The lake piece was followed in swift succession by *Pastorale* and *Au Bord d'une source.* When Liszt had finished, La Mara could only stammer her thanks to the Incomparable One, as she called Liszt. As the matinée drew to a close, she took a fleeting look inside Liszt's work-room, and with all the naiveté of her youth she picked up two little souvenirs of her visit: one of Liszt's pencils and a concert-flier containing the titles of some of his recently published symphonic poems. As the doors of the old house closed behind her, she tells us, she glanced up for the last time at the vine-covered windows behind which "the Magician of the Altenburg" cast his potions.[20]

I I

Not all Liszt's outside conducting engagements aroused the sort of controversy that had occurred in Vienna earlier in the year. Two that took place in the summer of 1856 deserve special mention. Liszt travelled to Magdeburg in order to participate in the music festival held between June 12 and 15. He was engaged to bring the festival to a conclusion with a performance of Beethoven's Ninth Symphony—a work of which he was now widely acknowledged to be the world's greatest living exponent. Players were brought in from as far afield as Brunswick and Berlin to swell the ranks of the local musicians, and the Weimar

---

20. LDML, vol. I, p. 32.

theatre "loaned" the festival Rosa Milde and the members of the Weimar String Quartet. An orchestra of a hundred players and a choir of 350 singers were assembled to perform the work under his baton. The critics Rellstab and Brendel were lavish in their praise and declared the rendering to be exceptional. Afterwards, the festival committee wrote a letter of appreciation to Liszt in which they described his interpretation of the Ninth as the "high-point" of the festival.[21]

Back in Weimar, Liszt began gathering himself for one of the most important events of his career. After countless delays the great basilica at Gran, in Hungary, was almost finished, and the Hungarians announced that they intended to consecrate their greatest cathedral on August 31. Liszt had already responded to a personal appeal from Cardinal János Scitovszky, the primate of Hungary, to compose a work for this national celebration: in fact, the "Gran" Mass had been in Liszt's portfolio for at least a year, awaiting its first performance,[22] and Liszt had already written to a number of close friends about it. On June 2, 1855, for instance, he had told Antal Augusz that he had "composed the mass in nine weeks, full of enthusiasm and love."[23] To his friend Carl Gille he wrote:

> You may be sure, dear friend, that I did not compose my work as one might put on a church vestment instead of an overcoat, but that it sprang from the truly fervent faith of my heart, such as I have felt since my childhood. *Genitum non factum.* ["Begotten, not made"] I can truly say that my mass has been more *prayed* than composed.[24]

Liszt put the best of himself into the "Gran" Mass. By common accord it is one of his masterpieces. Moreover, it provided the *raison d'être* to return to his native land after an absence of eight years. Since the war of independence, Hungary had come to resemble a graveyard, its national life crushed, and it was with mixed emotions that Liszt prepared himself for the long journey. He set

---

21. This unpublished letter, which is dated June 25, 1856, is preserved in the Goethe- und Schiller-Archiv, WA, Kasten 23, no. 1. See also LLB, vol. 4, pp. 306–08, where Liszt gives Princess Carolyne many details of the Magdeburg festival.

22. The piano reduction of the "Gran" Mass had been sent by Liszt to Scitovszky as early as July 1855 (CLBA, p. 52), at a time when Liszt had daily expected news of the completion of the basilica and a summons to Hungary. The work had its origins in Liszt's first encounter with Bishop Scitovszky (as he then was) ten years earlier, in 1846, during a visit to Fünfkirchen. Briefly, Scitovszky had asked for a Mass to celebrate the completion of the restoration of the cathedral there. Scitovszky was later transferred to Gran and elevated to the rank of cardinal; but he forgot neither Liszt nor the commission, and the "Gran" Mass was the result.

23. CBLA, p. 49.

24. LLB, vol. 1, p. 241. Eighteen months earlier Liszt had used a nearly identical phrase in a letter to Wagner: "I *prayed* it rather than *composed* it." (BWL, vol. 2, p. 69)

out from Weimar on August 7, in the company of Eduard Grosse, the trombonist and orchestral librarian,[25] and arrived in Prague the following day. He was met at the railway station by the pianist Dreyschock, and they were later joined by Jan Kittl and August Ambros, friends he had not seen since his last visit to Prague ten years earlier. During their subsequent dinner-party, there was talk of a "Wagner week" in Prague, similar to the ones mounted in Weimar, so Liszt promised to return through Prague on his way back to Germany. By August 9 he was in Vienna. He got there at five o'clock in the morning, after a gruelling thirteen-hour journey, stayed just long enough to catch a glimpse of his cousin Eduard, and then set out at six o'clock the following morning for Gran. He reached the old city in the afternoon of August 10 and had an audience with Cardinal Scitovszky, who well recalled their meeting a decade earlier. "His Eminence treats me graciously," Liszt told Carolyne.[26] After inspecting the new basilica and making sure that all was in readiness for the dress-rehearsals two weeks later ("The acoustics of the cathedral seem excellent to me, and the organ is perfect"), Liszt continued on his way to Pest. He arrived in the city of the Magyars on August 11, a homecoming that was filled with nostalgia for him. Liszt had last stepped on Hungarian soil in the summer of 1848, just before the war of independence. Although he knew that a welcoming party had been arranged for him, he wanted to savour the first moments alone, and so he deliberately caught an early train, which got to the Pest railway station at 5:00 a.m. For fifteen minutes he walked along the banks of the Danube, lost in his memories of Hungary.[27] He arrived at his hotel (the Queen of England) on foot and occupied the same bedroom in which he had stayed in 1846, with a huge balcony and a panoramic view of the river.

Within hours of his arrival in Pest, word had spread like wildfire that Liszt

---

25. Grosse was with Liszt throughout his Hungarian trip and was employed by him as a copyist and factotum (LLB, vol. 4, p. 313). He also played the trombone solo in the first performance of the "Gran" Mass. Edmund Singer, the Hungarian violinist, whom Liszt had appointed as his concertmaster the previous year, also travelled to Hungary at Liszt's request in order to act as his leader at all the rehearsals and public performances of the mass.

26. LLB, vol. 4, p. 313.

27. He wrote to Carolyne in detail about his revived impression of the Magyars, their dress, their clothes, and their food, and he claimed again his own identity with them. "Nothing elsewhere can replace these things, and the physiognomy of the race, when they are linked to childhood memories and when one has kept intact that tonality of the heart which is a feeling for one's fatherland. . . . So my heart began to weep as soon as we passed the frontier when I saw one of those simple tableaux of a shepherd squatting nonchalantly 'under the protection' of his sheep and oxen—because he was the one who seemed to be guarded by his animals." (LLB, vol. 4, p. 314) It is instructive to compare this letter with the well-known passages from the *Bachelor of Music* letter, written in 1840, in which the seductive power of Liszt's childhood memories is described in somewhat similar language (see Volume One, pp. 254–55). Such outpourings of feeling for Hungary demonstrate yet again that the country of his birth (as opposed to any of the countries in which he resided) was the only one with which he ever identified.

was back in Hungary. A stream of visitors descended on him—Augusz, Feste-tics, and Edmund Singer—the last of whom arrived at the hotel in a fluster because the welcoming committee he had so laboriously assembled in Liszt's honour was now in disarray. Everywhere Liszt went he was treated like royalty. People applauded him in restaurants and greeted him in the theatre with cries of "Éljen!" The main reason he was in Pest, of course, was to supervise the preliminary rehearsals of the mass. In the absence of a suitable concert audito-rium, the Ceremonial Hall of the National Museum was used, and the rehearsals were opened to the general public for an admission fee. "They applauded a great deal after each piece," wrote Liszt, "and at the end I was recalled three times."[28] Meanwhile, Alexander Winterberger had arrived in Pest in order to play the organ at the first performance of the mass. They journeyed to Gran a number of times in order to try out the organ and meet the local musicians who were to strengthen the main contingent from Pest. The last of these trips took place on August 28. Liszt could not help reflecting on the importance of this date in his life—the death of his father, Goethe's birthday, the first performance of *Lohengrin* in Weimar, the feast day of St. Augustine. And now, as chance would have it, he met his cousin Alois Hennig, who was a Jesuit priest, and heard him celebrate low mass in a small church in Gran.[29] This tiny incident seemed to foretell something of his own future.

On Friday, August 29, Liszt embarked on the steamboat *Marianna* with about a hundred musicians and set off along the Danube for Gran. There was a final dress-rehearsal that evening, after which Gran started to fill up with hundreds of dignitaries from across the Austro-Hungarian empire. In the early evening of August 30 a 101-gun salute boomed out across the old city to announce the arrival of Emperor Franz Joseph with an entourage of generals; they were greeted by Cardinal Scitovszky and his bishops in full regalia. Such a conclave had not been seen in Hungary since before the '48 revolution. Liszt was not wrong to see himself, in the midst of such a glittering assembly, as part of Hungary's national pride.[30] The following day was Sunday, August 31. At 7:30 a.m. the roar of gunfire announced that the ceremonials had begun. People streamed into the new basilica, and Cardinal Scitovszky led the consecration service. Liszt's "Gran" Mass was not performed until 1:30 p.m. By then, more than four thousand people were packed into the vast cathedral.[31] All eyes were fixed on Liszt as he guided his choir and orchestra through the complexities of his music. Such was the combination of visual and acoustical splendour that many were moved to tears. (One of Liszt's compatriots would later remark:

28. LLB, vol. 4, p. 325.
29. LLB, vol. 4, p. 326.
30. LLB, vol. 3, p. 77.
31. LLB, vol. 4, p. 329.

"This music is religious to the point of converting Satan himself!")[32] On Monday, September 1, Liszt returned to Pest by boat, and that evening he attended a dinner hosted by Cardinal Scitovszky. About sixty people sat down at the banquet table, including several archbishops. Liszt was placed between Bishop Lajos Haynald and Count István Károlyi. During the dinner the archbishop of Udine called Liszt "la gloria della Hungaria," and Scitovszky himself toasted the composer in Latin.[33] This visit to Hungary, in fact, gave Liszt the opportunity to become well acquainted with those Roman Catholic clerics who exercised power and influence in the religious life of the nation. His close friendship with Bishop (later Cardinal) Haynald, for example, dated from this time. And it was in the company of two bishops and several lesser ecclesiastics that he visited the church at Fôt, an architectural wonder, towards whose

---

32. LLB, vol. 3, p. 105. Liszt reported that the performance lasted about forty-five minutes, "watch in hand" (LLB, vol. 4, p. 328)—the usual duration, incidentally, for the "Gran" Mass. Behind Liszt's seemingly innocent observation lies the story of an intrigue. A month before he set out for Hungary, the Viennese press published some damaging reports about the "Gran" Mass—for example, that it lasted more than three hours, that it required seven hundred singers, that it was a cacophonous example of the Music of the Future, and that it would in consequence be difficult to rehearse and exorbitantly expensive to mount. The finger of guilt points to Liszt's former friend Count Leo Festetics, who, for reasons which remain obscure, favoured the performance of a specially composed mass by the Gran Kapellmeister, Carl Seiler, and had tried in vain to persuade Cardinal Scitovszky to drop Liszt's work from the ceremony. (The three-way correspondence between Liszt and Scitovszky on the one hand, and Scitovszky and Festetics on the other, has been ably summarized by Margit Prahács in PBUS, pp. 318–21.) When Festetics realized that the game was lost, he readily made it up with Liszt, who went out of his way to be friendly with his old compatriot and even wined and dined him tête-à-tête (LLB, vol. 4, p. 316). But the harm was already done. The Viennese press (including Fremdenblatt and the Oesterreichische Zeitung) accused Liszt of smuggling the Music of the Future and even the Venusberg into the Church—which Liszt described as "a low blow" (LLB, vol. 4, p. 331). This was by no means the worst of it, however. When it became known in Vienna that Liszt had said of his work, "My mass has been more prayed than composed," Monsignor Prela, the apostolic nuncio, responded sarcastically: "Thank God that Liszt still prays!" (LLB, vol. 4, p. 318).

It is an indication of the ultimate insignificance of the "opposition party" in Hungary that their favourite composer was Kálmán von Simonffy, a musician of severely limited talent. Nonetheless, such was the esteem in which Simonffy was held at that time that Count István Fáy spoke of him in front of Liszt as "the Hungarian Schubert." Liszt reflected on the implications of that lofty observation and replied jokingly: "In that case, the Germans can say that Schubert is their German Simonffy" (ÁMZSz, p. 241). The anecdote spread quickly and was taken up by the newspapers. Simonffy enjoyed his revenge some three years later, when he reviewed Liszt's book Des Bohémiens et de leur musique en Hongrie. (See pp. 385–86.)

A refreshing exception to these dismal views is to be found in the articles on the "Gran" Mass by Leopold Alexander Zellner, the Viennese composer and writer, which were published by instalments in the magazine he edited, Blätter für Musik, Theater und Kunst. Full of perceptive historical insights and illuminating analytical observations, these articles gave Liszt immense pleasure, and he was not slow to express his thanks. ("Your articles on the Mass delighted me, and I do hope that they will appear in collected form.") Two years later Liszt's hope was realized when Zellner published his occasional pieces in the form of a brochure, Über Franz Liszts Graner Festmesse (ZF). For an interesting run of letters from Liszt to Zellner on the subject of "Gran" Mass, see Schnapp, "New Documents on Franz Liszt," MMR, pp. 74–75; also LLB, vol. 1, pp. 297–98 and 304–06.

33. LLB, vol. 4, pp. 329–30.

construction Count Károlyi had already set aside one million francs from his personal fortune. Above all, Liszt renewed his links with the Franciscans. "Yesterday," he told Carolyne, "I dined with them at the very table where I had sat in 1823, '40, and '46. My former attachment to this monastery has not diminished with the years, and the Franciscans welcomed me as one of themselves." He added that he would shortly be admitted to their order as a "confrater."[34] It especially pleased him to note that he was already being called by the clergy "the regenerator of Church music."[35]

A further performance of the "Gran" Mass had been fixed for September 4 in the Pest parish church. The building was packed to capacity for the event. By now the singers and players were thoroughly acquainted with the score, and they gave the best performance that Liszt had so far heard. As he himself put it: "[They] raised themselves body and soul into my contemplation of the sacred mysteries of the mass. . . ."[36] Liszt's sojourn in Pest reached its climax on Monday, September 8, when he conducted a concert in the Hungarian National Theatre. This building was filled with memories, for it was the site of his spectacular triumph in January 1840, when the Hungarian nation had presented him with the famous "Sword of Honour."[37] The programme included the first performance of his symphonic poem *Hungaria,* a musical tribute to his native land. "There was better than applause," wrote Liszt afterwards. "All wept, both men and women!"[38] And he was reminded of the old proverb that "tears are the joy of Hungarians." So complete was his pleasure at the reception of *Hungaria* that he "did not wish to hear it again"[39] lest it spoil the memory of that perfect evening.

Although Liszt was under pressure to stay on in Hungary, he wanted to remain true to his promise to return to Prague. Despite the fact that plans for a "Wagner week" in Prague had fallen through, a performance of the "Gran" Mass had been arranged there for September 28, the Feast of St. Wenceslas. He spent his last few days in Hungary taking leave of his friends; he dined with Ferenc Erkel and then travelled to Szekszárd to visit Antal Augusz and his family—personal connections that were to become increasingly important to him as the years rolled by. As Liszt himself put it, his stay in Hungary could not have accomplished more. Everything he had set out to do had been achieved; his links with his native land were secure.

Liszt left Pest on September 14 and lingered in Vienna for almost a week.

---

34. LLB, vol. 4, p. 334. See Volume One, pp. 40–41, for the wider background to Liszt's connections with the Franciscans. See also pp. 490–91 of the present volume for a description of the ceremony at which the title "confrater" was bestowed on Liszt.

35. HLSW, p. 83.

36. LLB, vol. 1, p. 238.

37. See Volume One, pp. 323–32, for a full account of those earlier ceremonials.

38. HLSW, p. 82.

39. HLSW, p. 83.

It was his hope to rest there after the hectic round of the past few weeks, but he was besieged with visitors and with requests to appear in public. His fleeting itinerary need not detain the modern reader, with the exception of one remarkable detail. In the Vienna Volksgarten Johann Strauss the younger and his orchestra were already beguiling the ears of their audiences with those waltzes, marches, quadrilles, and polkas which for three generations symbolized Vienna to the rest of Europe. Hearing that Liszt was there, Strauss put on a programme at the Volksgarten that included the march from *Mazeppa* and two or three numbers from *Lohengrin,* a work that the whole world knew Liszt had rescued from possible oblivion. The printed programme bore the inscription "zu Ehren der Anwesenheit des Herrn Dr. Liszt."[40] Strauss and his band performed *Mazeppa* with such verve that it had to be encored. It was a remarkable tribute from the "Waltz King," and one that put most other Kapellmeisters of the day to shame. The only cloud to darken this stay in Vienna occurred when Eduard Grosse (who was still accompanying Liszt on his travels) heard that his young son had died in Weimar. Grosse was inconsolable; Liszt reported that he wept all day. He wrote to Carolyne and asked her to offer a few words of consolation to Grosse's wife—a token of the affection in which they held the Grosse family.[41]

Liszt got to Prague on September 20 and put up at the Black Horse hostelry. The following day he went over to St. Vitus's Cathedral to test the acoustics for the performance of his "Gran" Mass on Sunday, September 28. He told Carolyne: "In Prague things augur well, and I think I can tell you in advance that you have nothing to fear as regards next Sunday."[42] For much of the week he busied himself revising sections of the mass in the light of his practical experience conducting it in Gran and Pest; it was in Prague, for instance, that he wrote a new fugal ending for the Gloria. When he was not rehearsing, he spent time in the company of Kittl, Dreyschock, Ambros, and Jan Škroup (the cathedral's Kapellmeister). He also visited the theatre and saw, among other things, Verdi's *Ernani* and Donizetti's *Lucia di Lammermoor.* After the final dress-rehearsal he was dined by Cardinal Friedrich Schwarzenberg, who showed a keen interest in Liszt's work. The actual performance of the "Gran" Mass, in Liszt's words, "was satisfactory overall, although less harmonious than the one in Gran, and especially the one in Pest."[43] Liszt was amusing on the topic of his colleagues' reactions to the unfamiliar score. "Dreyschock kissed my hands with the expression of a man who knew what he was doing. . . . Škroup himself played the two notes on the snare-drum in the *Crucifixus.* As for Kittl,

40. "In honour of the presence of Herr Dr. Liszt" (LLB, vol. 4, p. 338). The date of the concert—Monday evening, September 15, 1856—deserves to be enshrined in the history books.
41. LLB, vol. 4, pp. 340–41.
42. LLB, vol. 4, p. 342.
43. LLB, vol. 4, p. 345.

he never varies from the remark 'highly interesting.' "[44] That same evening, September 28, Dreyschock arranged a great banquet in Liszt's honour in the dining-hall of the Black Horse. All the leading representatives of Prague's musical life were present, including the organist Karel Pitsch (who had taught Dvořák), the pianist Julius Schulhoff, Josef Krejči, Jan and František Škroup, Ambros, Kittl, and, most noteworthy of all, Bedřich Smetana. After praising Liszt's artistic merit, Dreyschock presented him with a silver baton in the name of all those present, which bore the inscription: "In friendly remembrance of September 28, 1856, in Prague."[45] Liszt finally got back to Weimar, via Dresden, on October 2, after an absence of seven weeks. What he ironically called "my little summer campaign" was over.[46]

III

Liszt's peregrinations through Vienna, Prague, and Pest, in fact, had exhausted him. He stood in need of a holiday but knew from experience that Weimar was the last place to provide it. His thoughts now turned to Switzerland and a long-postponed visit to Wagner. Wagner had actually been expecting to see Liszt since early September, but the celebrations in Gran had intervened. Liszt remained barely a week in Weimar before setting out for Zürich. Carolyne and Marie, who looked for any opportunity to get away from Weimar, for however brief a period, readily agreed to join him. Liszt went on ahead of them and arrived in Zürich alone on October 13. He put up at the Hotel Bauer au Lac. Wagner was overjoyed to see his old companion again and left a euphoric account of the visit in *Mein Leben.*[47] He tells us that his house, normally so peaceful, at once became a centre of musical activity. Liszt had brought with him the scores of his recently completed *Faust* and *Dante* symphonies, and he gave incomparable performances of them on the piano. A lively discussion broke out about the vigorous ending of the *Dante* Symphony (dedicated to Wagner), which Wagner thought inappropriate as a depiction of Paradise. "No, not that!" exclaimed Wagner. "Away with it! No majestic Deity! Leave us the fine soft shimmer!" "You are right," replied Liszt. "I said so too; it was the princess who persuaded me differently. But it shall be as you wish."[48] This

44. LLB, vol. 4, pp. 345–46.
45. BLB, p. 112. Smetana spent nearly every day in Liszt's company. In March 1848 the impoverished Czech musician had appealed to Liszt for money, and had enclosed the manuscript of his "Six Characteristic Pieces" for piano, which he had dedicated to Liszt. Better than financial help, Liszt had used his influence to get the pieces published, and Smetana was eternally grateful (LBZL, vol. 1, pp. 95–98).
46. LLB, vol. 4, p. 346.
47. WML, pp. 648–56.
48. WML, p. 649. Liszt, as we now know, kept both endings. It used to be thought that he regarded them as optional alternatives. An inspection of the holograph score in Weimar (ms. A13) points to

exchange set the tone for much of the rest of the visit. A few days later Princess Carolyne and her daughter arrived and joined Liszt at the Hotel Bauer. Wagner was astonished at the way in which Carolyne drew everyone into her orbit. It was as if Zürich had suddenly become a metropolis, he wrote. Carriages drove back and forth, footmen ushered visitors in and out, dinner parties erupted in all directions, and droves of interesting local people suddenly turned up, of whose existence Wagner had hitherto known nothing. Carolyne coaxed some of the University of Zürich professors out of their ivory towers in order to harangue them about art, politics, and life. Winterberger then turned up, and shortly after him, Theodor Kirchner. Soon it had become a festival in miniature, filled with the sort of intellectual hubbub that always seemed to grow up around Liszt and Carolyne, and which was as necessary to them as meat and drink. The festivities reached their climax on October 22, Liszt's forty-fifth birthday. Carolyne put on a great party for him, and the whole of Zürich seemed to turn out. As a birthday surprise she arranged for an ode by Hoffmann von Fallersleben to be telegraphed from Weimar and read aloud by the poet Georg Herwegh. Wagner then rendered parts of *Die Walküre,* with Liszt accompanying from the manuscript score. To round things off, Liszt and Winterberger played one or two of the recently published symphonic poems at two pianos. During the party a dispute arose about the merits of Heinrich Heine, who had recently died. Mathilde Wesendonck turned to Liszt and asked him if he did not think that Heine's name would be inscribed in the temple of immortality. "Yes, but in mud," was Liszt's celebrated reply.

Liszt was detained at Zürich by the recurrence of a painful illness, an outbreak of boils across the lower part of his body, which would lay him low for several weeks. By mid-November, however, he was sufficiently recovered to journey with Wagner and a small circle of their friends to St. Gallen, where the two musicians had agreed to support the local orchestral society. The party stayed at the Hecht Inn, where despite Liszt's infirmity the daily life was soon so active that, in Wagner's words, it yielded nothing to the hustle and bustle of life in the Hotel Bauer. On November 23 Liszt and Wagner shared the direction of an orchestral concert at St. Gallen: Liszt conducted *Les Préludes* and *Orpheus,* and Wagner followed with Beethoven's *Eroica* Symphony. *Orpheus* made a profound impression on Wagner. In fact, it is from this Swiss sojourn that students of the Liszt-Wagner connection can trace the subtle influence of Liszt's advanced harmonic language on Wagner's music. The

---

a different conclusion: namely, that he intended the loud ending to be a *second coda,* added to the first—the only option being not to play it at all. By washing his hands of the decision, as it were, Liszt avoided the necessity of offending either Wagner or Carolyne. One other matter requires attention here. Wagner's story, as told in *Mein Leben,* lent credence to the idea that Carolyne influenced Liszt "in the choice of his notes." Carolyne had no technical knowledge of music, however, and we know of no evidence to suggest that she could even read staff-notation.

following day everyone assembled in the home of Herr Bourit, a rich merchant of St. Gallen, and Liszt played Beethoven's *Hammerklavier* Sonata. At the conclusion of his overpowering performance Kirchner remarked: "Now we can truly say we have witnessed the impossible, for I shall always regard what I have just heard as an impossibility."[49] The impression made on Wagner was all the more durable because November 24 happened to be his twentieth wedding anniversary. The wedding music from *Lohengrin* was played, and the company formed a stately procession *à la polonaise,* in high good humour, which took them through the various rooms of Herr Bourit's mansion.

Towards the end of November Carolyne fell ill. Marie sat up with her mother at night, reading aloud to her, to while away the time.[50] Liszt, who was himself physically exhausted, was undecided what to do. Wagner urged him to take Carolyne back to Weimar, where they could both recuperate. He escorted them to Rorschach on November 27 and took his leave of them on board the steamer. Wagner was astonished to hear, a few days later, that they were in Munich, "attended by much noisy festivity." From this he concluded that "it was foolish to recommend to people with such constitutions either to do a thing or to abstain from doing it."[51]

The six weeks that Liszt and Wagner spent together in Zürich and St. Gallen were an important watershed in their artistic relationship. Never before had the two friends enjoyed such a sustained opportunity to submerge themselves in one another's music. In fact, Wagner had been engaged on a sustained study of the symphonic poems throughout the summer of 1856, long before Liszt arrived in Zürich. On July 20, while he was in the middle of a "hydrotherapy" cure at Mornex, on Mont Salève, not far from Geneva, Wagner had confessed to Liszt:

> With your symphonic poems I am now quite familiar. They are the only music with which I have anything to do at present, since I cannot think of doing any of my own work while I am undergoing my cure. Every day I read one or another of your scores, just as I would read a poem, easily and without hindrance. Then I feel every time as if I had dived into a crystalline flood, there to be quite by

---

49. WML, p. 655.

50. Wagner reports that he and his wife, Minna, occupied the adjoining bedroom, and the sound of Marie's voice ("raised a good deal above its normal pitch") drove him to distraction. At two o'clock in the morning he leaped out of bed, rang his bell in a fury, and insisted that the hotel staff move him into a room in the remotest part of the inn. The next morning, when he went down to breakfast and perceived the calm demeanour of Princess Marie, he learned that nocturnal disturbances of this kind were quite usual with Carolyne, who thought nothing of them. When we reflect on this scene of the daughter reading aloud to her insomniac mother, are we not reminded of another, one from Carolyne's own youth, in which she in turn had read throughout the night with her insomniac father?

51. WML, p. 656.

myself, having left all the world behind, to live for an hour my own proper life. Refreshed and invigorated, I then come to the surface again, full of longing for your personal presence. Yes, my friend, *you can do it! You can do it!* [52]

   Not long after Liszt's departure from Zürich, Wagner paid him a supreme compliment. "I think that I have discovered that you are the greatest musician of all time!" he told him.[53] It was a revelatory phrase, and we do well to note it. Whatever Wagner's later attitude of reserve towards Liszt, in Zürich he talked about the historical significance of the music quite openly, and particularly to Princess Marie. One of the fruits of their many conversations, as we have seen, took the form of an "Open Letter on Liszt's Symphonic Poems," which he sent to Marie on February 15, 1857. It was an attempt on Wagner's part to grant her oft-expressed wish to hear Wagner's "candid, definite estimate of Liszt," and it contains some memorable tributes to his old friend. "Do you know a musician who is more musical than Liszt? Who holds within his breast the powers of music in richer, deeper store than he?" And it ends with this urgent imperative to Marie: "Above all, greet my Franz for me, and tell him the old, old story, that I love him!"[54]

                                    I V

The illness which had plagued Liszt in Zürich persisted throughout the winter. On January 1, 1857, not long after returning to Weimar, Liszt told Wagner: "I am in bed once more, covered with the whole *flora* of my Zürich ills."[55] The weeks passed and Liszt got no better. His feet were covered with abscesses, and he could get about only with the aid of crutches. The princess, too, fell ill again, and the two patients passed notes to one another from their respective sickrooms in the Altenburg, via the ever-faithful "Scotchy" Anderson, in an attempt to cheer one another up during this depressing period.[56] Goullon, the Weimar doctor, was an almost daily visitor, but his ministrations (which in Liszt's case included homeopathy and the painful application of saltpetre)

---

52. BWL, vol. 2, p. 135; KWL, vol. 2, p. 130. Needless to add, there is not a word of any of this in Wagner's *Mein Leben.* He tells us a great deal about his "cure," about his encounter with the novels of Sir Walter Scott, and about the negotiations with Härtel for the sale of his *Nibelungen,* but there is not a syllable to do with Liszt and the symphonic poems. It was only after the publication of the Liszt-Wagner correspondence, in 1887, that the full extent of Wagner's absorption in Liszt's music became apparent to the world at large.

53. BWL, vol. 2, p. 143; KWL, vol. 2, p. 138.

54. This open letter was sent on almost at once to Brendel, who published it in the columns of the *Neue Zeitschrift,* on April 10, 1857.

55. BWL, vol. 2, p. 150; KWL, vol. 2, p. 145.

56. LLB, vol. 4, pp. 351–55.

brought little relief. Liszt wrote to Wagner on April 19: "After having been in bed for six weeks I am just able to hobble about the theatre and the castle."[57] The remarkable thing is that he continued to function at all. He dealt with a mass of correspondence from his sickbed,[58] received visitors, and issued a stream of directives to his orchestral staff. Somehow he dragged himself to the theatre on January 7 to conduct a concert, which included the first performance of his Piano Concerto in A major, with Bronsart as soloist. And on April 19 he even directed a performance of *Lohengrin,* but he sweated so profusely throughout the evening that he took to his bed, exhausted. Goullon forbade all further exertions, so Liszt had to content himself with attending rehearsals, sitting in the director's box with his feet in a footbag, resting on a footstool. He consulted a second doctor, one Professor Wedel from Jena University, who put a milk plaster on the whole length of his leg, which immobilized him still further.

Adelheid von Schorn observed him during these difficult days. In January 1857 she and her mother, Henriette, were invited to a soirée at the Altenburg in honour of Marie Seebach, the actress, who was making her first appearance at the Weimar theatre.[59] Liszt looked pale and fatigued, she wrote, and had been ill. Nonetheless, his face became radiant as he sat at the piano and accompanied Seebach in a melodrama by Hebbel, *Die Heideknaben.* So moved was the audience that scarcely anyone noticed that he played with only one hand: the other was so painful that he was unable to use it.[60]

Liszt's illness was serious enough to keep him away from the official première of the Sonata in B minor, given in Berlin on January 22, 1857, by Bülow. He was in bed, bearing his physical burdens with his usual stoicism, but we may be sure that his thoughts did not stray far from Bülow and the sonata. Aside from Liszt himself, no one was better qualified to introduce this pianistic masterwork to the public. It was not simply that Bülow's superb musicianship, coupled with his formidable command of the keyboard, gave him the means to do the work justice: he had also played the sonata to Liszt and had received his master's sanction.[61] The occasion was noteworthy for another reason too.

---

57. BWL, vol. 2, p. 159; KWL, vol. 2, p. 155.

58. Including two very long and extremely detailed letters: one written to Wasielewski about his years of association with Schumann (LLB, vol. 2, pp. 253–59), the other to Prince Wilhelm of Prussia, asking for a pardon for the fugitive Wagner (see p. 241, n.54).

59. Seebach appeared there in Goethe's *Faust* (January 2), Shakespeare's *Romeo and Juliet* (January 4), and Schiller's *Mary Stuart* (January 6). BCWH, p. 117.

60. SZM, p. 87. Schorn does not identify the nature of the injury to Liszt's hand or, for that matter, which hand was affected.

61. Bülow had known the sonata since 1854, when Liszt sent him a newly printed copy of the work (LBLB, p. 75). On July 21, 1855, he had heard Liszt play it to a group of friends at the Altenburg, among whom were Tausig and his father (HLSW, p. 68). It is evident that Bülow had by then already embarked on a serious conquest of the piece, since he himself gave it a preliminary run-through to Niels Gade in Berlin in August 1855 (LBLB, p. 141). However, he does not appear to have felt secure enough to play the sonata to Liszt until August 1, 1856. We know that Liszt was pleased with the

Carl Bechstein, a new and untested name in the field of piano manufacture, had placed one of his fledgling grand pianos at Bülow's disposal, and so began one of the most fruitful partnerships in the annals of the keyboard. When Bülow walked onto the concert platform, he probably had little idea of the epoch-making significance of the work he was about to deliver, whose structural originality and harmonic boldness were left for later generations to uncover. Although he gave a performance which came up to his own exacting standards, the newspaper critics condemned the work. Otto Gumprecht of the *National-zeitung* called it "an invitation to hissing and stamping,"[62] while Gustav Engel of the *Spener'schen Zeitung* wrote that not only had it nothing to do with beauty, but it conflicted with nature and logic—"it is scarcely possible to be further removed from lawful principles."[63] Bülow was livid with rage, and without telling Liszt he began a skirmish with Engel. When news of this dog-fight reached Liszt, he advised Bülow to desist and urged him not to take the press so seriously. For his part, he told Bülow, "I can only adopt a certain degree of passive curiosity, continuing along my path of creating new works, without being troubled by either the barking or the biting."[64] Not the least extraordinary thing about the scandal was that the sonata had had to wait for nearly five years for its première. Although it had been in print since 1854, hardly anybody outside Liszt's circle of intimates seemed to know of its existence. Even the *Neue Zeitschrift,* after noting in passing that "a new sonata by Liszt" had been performed, erroneously described the work as being "in manuscript."[65] The sonata was born neglected, so to speak, and critical opinion was not to change much for half a century or more. When, as late as 1881, Bülow played the work in Vienna, Eduard Hanslick wrote that he was at first "bewildered, then shocked, and finally overcome with irresistible hilarity. ... Who has heard *that,* and finds it beautiful, is beyond help."[66] As Peter Raabe was later to observe, such judgements make one ashamed for Liszt's contempo-

---

performance, because the following day he wrote to Pohl: "Bülow played several pieces for me quite wonderfully, among other things both of my polonaises and the sonata" (WLP, p. 197). Incidentally, the première on January 22, 1857, took place within the context of one of three so-called *Trio-soiréen* (given by Bülow, Laub, and Wohlers) whose main purpose was to introduce new chamber works to the conservative Berlin public, including the first performances there of trios by César Franck and Robert Volkmann. Bülow, in fact, was in bad odour with the Berlin press throughout this period for his championship of music by the avant-garde.

62. LLB, vol. 1, p. 323.

63. BB, vol. 3, pp. 65–66.

64. LBLB, p. 192.

65. NZfM, January 30, 1857. This brief mention occurs under the column "Tagesgeschichte." The fact that Brendel thought the sonata to be "in manuscript" is curious, since the *Neue Zeitschrift* had published a highly laudatory review of the piece in July 1854, shortly after it was printed. The reviewer was Louis Köhler, who made a number of perspicacious discoveries about the sonata's internal structure which delighted Liszt. See the composer's letter of thanks in LLB, vol. 1, pp. 156–57.

66. SLM, p. 116.

raries, that they allowed themselves to be led for so long by a man who was both blind and deaf to the beauties of the new music.[67]

With the memory of the Berlin scandal still fresh in everyone's mind, it was probably a mistake for Liszt to leave his sickbed in order to conduct the Leipzig Gewandhaus Orchestra at a concert for the benefit of its pension fund on February 26. This city, and this hall, had witnessed Liszt's first defeat as a pianist, seventeen years earlier. Leipzig had meanwhile become a seat of opposition to the Weimar School, and there were many in the audience who wanted to bring about a second failure. Moreover, this was a Liszt-Wagner evening, consisting of works never before heard in the city, and one can only assume that it was a deliberate act of defiance—Daniel walking into the lions' den.

LISZT	Symphonic Poem *Les Préludes*
WAGNER	Duet from *Der fliegende Holländer*
LISZT	Piano Concerto No. 1 in E-flat major
	(soloist: Bülow)
	Symphonic Poem *Mazeppa*

Liszt was unwise to end the programme with *Mazeppa*. It was one thing to do this piece in Weimar with a well-drilled orchestra, quite another to present it in unfriendly Leipzig with an orchestra unused to his ways. At the opening cymbal-crash a section of the audience burst into laughter, and hissing and whistling accompanied Mazeppa's headlong flight across the steppes.[68]

Away!   Away!

We shall probably never be certain about what actually happened in the hall that night; but shortly before going to bed, Liszt wrote a letter of appreciation to Ferdinand David, the orchestra's leader, in which he thanked him for his help earlier in the evening and called him a "gentleman." The letter contains the quotation from the beginning of *Mazeppa* which is cited above, and the words "Away! Away!" from Byron's poem are written by Liszt in English. The communication represents an "in joke" which Liszt knew that David would

---

67. RLS, vol. 2, p. 62.
68. It is a noteworthy coincidence that Liszt's second defeat in Leipzig, like his first in that city, in 1840, occurred while he was laid low with a debilitating illness (see Volume One, p. 349). The abscesses on his feet obliged him to conduct sitting down for much of this period (LLB, vol. 4, p. 356).

be the first to appreciate.[69] The moment Liszt got back to Weimar, he succumbed to renewed bouts of fever. As late as March 24, 1857, he wrote to Lenz: "For the present I am still pinned to my bed by a lot of boils on my legs, which I consider as the doors of exodus for the illness which has been troubling me rather violently since the end of October."[70]

V

In the spring of 1857 Liszt accepted the directorship of the thirty-fifth Lower Rhine Festival, which this year was to be held in Aachen. He had twice refused this prestigious invitation; but when a deputation of the organizing committee arrived in Weimar in mid-February to plead with him in person, he felt obliged to yield.[71] Liszt's initial reservations about going to Aachen were two-fold: he objected to the conservative programmes he was at first asked to conduct, and he objected to the idea of planning the festival around a "star attraction"—in this case, Jenny Lind. The "Swedish Nightingale" was arguably the most popular virtuoso appearing before the public, and Liszt yielded to no one in his admiration of her vocal skills. But, as he pointed out to Carl von Turányi, the resident Kapellmeister in Aachen, such was Lind's magnetic effect on the crowd that whatever she did, however slight, had the capacity to render superfluous everything else going on around her. "What is the use of orchestra and singers, rehearsals and preparations, pieces and programmes, when the public want to hear only La Lind—or, more correctly speaking, when they *must* be able to say that *they have heard her* in order to be able to wallow at ease in their enthusiasm for Art?"[72] In the end Liszt got his way on both counts: he was allowed to feature modern composers in his programmes, and Jenny Lind did not come to the festival. He was to pay a high price for these "victories," however, as we shall see.

The programmes Liszt agreed to conduct at Aachen covered a wide repertory. Let us note once more in passing the emphasis on the avant-garde: Berlioz,

---

69. LLB, vol. 1, p. 266.
70. LLB, vol. 1, p. 269.
71. Ibid., p. 265.
72. Ibid., p. 251. Was there perhaps a guilty recollection of Liszt's own past in such an utterance? One of the criticisms levelled against him in his younger years had been precisely the one that he was now levelling against "the Queen of Song," as he playfully called Lind: namely, that her vast popularity with the crowd might actually harm the appreciation of serious art, because the success or failure of the entire festival would be measured simply by the degree of astonishment aroused in the audience at the singer's "tricks of the trade." Liszt's letter to Turányi on this topic is worth reading in full because it indicates the distance that Liszt had meanwhile placed between himself and the demands of the great public in the decade that had elapsed since his heyday as a travelling performer. It also reveals him to have an uncommonly shrewd grasp of the perils of festival administration.

Wagner, and Liszt himself were all *enfants terribles* as far as the general public were concerned.

May 31	BEETHOVEN	Overture *Consecration of the House*
	HANDEL	*Messiah*
June 1	BACH	Cantata No. 7, "Christ der Herr zum Jordan kam"
	SCHUBERT	Symphony No. 9 in C major ("The Great")
	SCHUMANN	"Des Sängers Fluch" (Ballade nach Uhland)
	LISZT	*Festklänge*
	BERLIOZ	*L'Enfance du Christ,* Part Two: "La Fuite en Egypte"
June 2	MENDELSSOHN	Overture *Ruy Blas*
	BEETHOVEN	Violin Concerto in D-major (soloist: Edmund Singer)
	WAGNER	Overture to *Tannhäuser*
	LISZT	Piano Concerto No. 1 in E-flat major (soloist: Bülow)

Liszt arrived in Aachen on May 20 and stayed as a guest in the sumptuous home of the banker Barthold Suermondt.[73] As usual, Liszt's every move in Aachen became the object of notice by the local press. Bookshops advertized his music; photographers offered his latest portrait for sale.[74] A crop of smaller, supporting concerts had also been arranged for his students and colleagues who had followed him to Aachen. During the festival, Rosa von Milde gave a recital of his songs, Bülow and Bronsart played his two-piano arrangement of *Les Préludes,* and the Weimar String Quartet gave a chamber concert in the Kurhaus. An outsider could be forgiven for assuming that the Lower Rhine Festival had been transformed into the Weimar-by-the-Ilm Festival. Inevitably the old charge that Liszt ran a one-man show was revived. But it had even less substance in Aachen than it had at the time of the Beethoven Festival in Bonn, in 1845, where it had first been articulated. The sheer number of other musicians in Aachen disproved it.

Over the next few days Liszt made a number of fresh acquaintances. He saw

---

73. Suermondt, who lived at Adalbertstrasse 55, was renowned for his art collection. Liszt reported that his room was "lined on three sides by beautiful paintings" (LLB, vol. 4, p. 363).

74. The Aachen newspapers also advertized five volumes of contemporary piano music under the general editorship of Liszt. They contained works by Köhler, Benedict, Kittl, Ehlert, Kalliwoda, and Smetana. It is a pity that all traces of this edition have vanished. The volume might help to throw further light on Liszt as an editor—an activity about which we still know too little.

Carl von Turányi almost daily; on Sunday, May 24, they attended mass together at Aachen Cathedral and heard the boys' choir singing hymns and psalms. "A modulation from the psalmody which hurt Turányi's ears seemed beautiful to me," wrote Liszt,[75] a subtle indication of the distance that separated the two musicians. He also encountered Father Peter Roh, the famous Jesuit preacher, with whom he had a long discussion on theology. Somehow he also found time to read Vischer's *Ästhetik,* whose criticism of Hanslick pleased him.[76] On Wednesday, May 27, the Suermondts gave an official reception for all the notables attending the Lower Rhine Festival, at the conclusion of which the local regimental band serenaded the assembly with numbers from *Lohengrin* and *Tannhäuser.* Such social contacts were useful to Liszt. He met a number of members of the organizing committee, some of whom were nervous about his "modern" programmes, and was able to reassure them that all would be well. The day after his arrival in Aachen, in fact, he had already embarked on a series of daily sectional rehearsals, which was not his usual practice at such festivals. A combined ensemble of more than 550 players and singers had been amassed for the occasion—one of the largest bodies of musicians Liszt ever conducted. The orchestra contained 52 violins, 16 violas, 19 cellos, and 13 double-basses; there were also 38 wind and brass instruments. "It is enough to delight Berlioz himself," wrote Liszt.[77]

For the opening concert the festival committee had insisted that Liszt conduct Handel's *Messiah;* it was his only concession to their taste. He considered the work hackneyed; it had been performed not only in dozens of German cities but also at previous Lower Rhine Festivals. Liszt argued that his chief value as a conductor was to champion the new and unfamiliar. But May 31 was Whitsunday, and even Liszt admitted that there was hardly a more appropriate date on which to perform Handel's masterpiece. In the event, the work was not without its problems. During the rehearsals the bass, Dalle Aste, developed a cold, and at the performance he lost his voice and had to leave the hall.[78] On the second night the chief work was Berlioz's treacherous "La Fuite en Egypte," and Liszt experienced difficulty in holding that vast canvas together. (One wonders what lies behind his casual remark to Carolyne: "As for Berlioz, it

---

75. LLB, vol. 4, p. 364.

76. Ibid., p. 361.

77. LLB, vol. 4, p. 362. These statistics come from Richard Pohl, who was in Aachen as part of Liszt's entourage. The large ensemble was, in Pohl's phrase, "an imposing army whose collective might under General Franz Liszt promised a shining victory." From Pohl we also learn that the hall held about thirteen hundred people (PGS, vol. 2, pp. 188–89). According to one of the few copies of the festival brochure to have survived the years (WA, Kasten 241), Liszt had brought with him several of his own musicians to help swell the ranks of the orchestra. They included Singer and Stör (violins), Walbrül (viola), Cossmann (cello), Grosse (trombone), and Jeanne Pohl (harp).

78. LLB, vol. 4, p. 370. On one day's notice, Carl Reinthaler stood in for him.

was impossible to save him, despite all my efforts."[79] Liszt's own works, *Festklänge* and the E-flat-major Piano Concerto (for which Erard sent Bülow a new concert grand from Paris), went without a hitch, much to his surprise. The festival concluded with the traditional performance of the "Hallelujah" Chorus. At the final "Amen," thousands of multi-coloured leaflets showered down on the audience, bearing a poem extolling the virtues of the festival. The burgermeister's daughter, Fräulein Dahmen, mounted the platform and crowned Liszt with a laurel wreath, to the applause of the whole hall.[80]

These were by far the most demanding programmes yet mounted by the Lower Rhine Festival in its long and distinguished history, and it was generally agreed that Liszt had acquitted himself well. But the conservative opposition to his presence in Aachen had some old scores to settle, and they gleefully used his difficulties with *Messiah* as a rod with which to beat him. In fact, the festival was the occasion of some disgraceful scenes created by Ferdinand Hiller and his claque. Hiller, Liszt's erstwhile friend, was now the director of the Cologne Conservatory, and he had earlier directed the Lower Rhine Festival himself. He was piqued at being passed over in favour of Liszt, and while he promised to be present, we know that he was among those who objected to Liszt's choice of modern works.[81] Hiller had long since moved away from Liszt's ideals and had allied himself with the Schumann-Mendelssohn circle in Leipzig; he had even directed the Gewandhaus concerts during the 1843–44 season. Inspired, perhaps, by the Gewandhaus débâcle a few weeks earlier, Hiller now sought Liszt's downfall. At the conclusion of the E-flat-major Piano Concerto, Hiller began to whistle on his latch-key, and at this pre-arranged signal his group of rowdies began to bang their seats in protest, drowning out the applause. A majority of the audience objected to this behaviour, and the organizers of the festival presented Liszt with a gold medal to mark their appreciation, but the protest marred an important occasion. It has been suggested that Hiller's involvement in the demonstration was minimal, that he was incapable of stooping to such low conduct. But his polemical "Briefe über das Aachener Musikfest," published in the *Kölnische Zeitung*, are almost paranoiac, and his astonishing letter to Liszt written at Aachen on June 3, while the festival was still in progress, reveals that he was opposed to his former friend in almost every way. Even so, he could muster the gall to write: "From my heart I do not wish these little fights to endanger our old friendship," although there was now no friendship to lose.[82] It has been remarked elsewhere in this narrative that Hiller's

79. LLB, vol. 4, p. 370.
80. LLB, vol. 4, p. 372.
81. LBZL, vol. 2, p. 128.
82. LBZL, vol. 2, p. 129. Hiller's devastating criticism of Liszt's performance of *Messiah* went beyond the bounds of public comment and seems to have been designed to humiliate him. (*Kölnische Zeitung,*

relationship to Liszt was ambivalent. Masking his actions with a thin veneer of collegiality, Hiller did his best to damage Liszt's work in Germany until his dying day. He was quietly supported by many who had a vested interest in seeing Liszt fail. Typical of the detractors was Marie d'Agoult, with whom Hiller kept up a regular correspondence. She was in Italy, re-living her past,[83] when word of Hiller's diatribes reached her, and she registered her approval.

Florence, October 17, 1857

> Tell me about yourself, your compositions, and your campaign against the *Music of the Future*. I would really have liked to have read one of your articles on a festival directed against Liszt, about which I have heard a lot. Tell me a few details about it. Are you on bad terms?[84]

Nélida's interest is not hard to fathom. She could not bear the thought that Guermann might one day prove her wrong by painting his bare walls, and Hiller's criticisms of Liszt came as balm to her troubled soul.

After the final concert of the Lower Rhine Festival a special supper-party was given for Liszt in the Hotel Nuellens, at which a small but telling incident occurred. Hiller and a section of the *Liedertafel* from Cologne were dining in an anteroom through which Liszt had to pass in order to reach his own table. "We did not even greet each other," Liszt remarked. Afterwards Liszt had to

---

June 7, 1857: "Liszt conducted the *Messiah* with the expression of a stoic who bravely stares death or, what is worse, boredom in the face.") The story of Hiller whistling on his latch-key derives ultimately from the Weimar trombonist Eduard Grosse, who had travelled to Aachen with Liszt (RLKM, vol. 3, p. 98). Hans von Bronsart was also in the audience and later published a reproof of Hiller in the columns of the Berlin journal *Das Echo* (no. 27, 1857). The immediate cause of Hiller's bad humour is easy to find. A few days before his vitriolic criticisms appeared, he had been ejected from a rehearsal for his unseemly conduct. Liszt later wrote about this astonishing incident to Otto Lessmann: "Somebody told me that Hiller did not leave . . . the rehearsal of his own free will. Since I was busy at the conductor's desk, I was unable to observe the reason for his departure. . . . Unfortunately musical history is full to overflowing with unresolved dissonances." (LLB, vol. 2, pp. 333–34) See also Volume One, p. 188, of the present work for a further assessment of Hiller's attitude towards Liszt.

And what of Liszt's attitude towards Hiller? Two years earlier he had delivered himself of a withering verdict on Hiller's lacklustre performance on the rostrum after seeing him wield the baton during the Düsseldorf festival in May 1855. "Hiller's conducting is like his whole personality: accommodating, rounded, correct, even distinguished, but without tension and energy, and consequently without authority or communicative electricity. He might well be reproached with having no faults, and thus with giving criticism no foothold." (LLB, vol. 4, p. 217) In short, when Hiller conducted it was as if the podium were empty. Anonymity on the rostrum was, for Liszt, a worse crime than anonymity at the piano keyboard. In the latter case, one was responsible merely for oneself; in the former, one was responsible for the artistic direction of other musicians, and this demanded "communicative electricity."

83. See pp. 462–63.
84. *Revue Bleue,* November 9, 1913, p. 619.

cross the same room in order to leave the hotel. "I veered a little to the left," he wrote, "in order to avoid passing too near the large person of my former friend!"[85] It was the last time that Liszt and Hiller ever saw one another.

VI

During his stay in Aachen, Liszt consulted a local medical expert, Dr. Joseph Rodenburg, about the sores on his legs, which had plagued him for the past six months. Rodenburg urged him to take Aachen's six-week water-cure and so rid himself of the complaint for good. Liszt knew that he ought not to postpone his convalescence, and he resolved to begin his cure later that summer. When he got back to Weimar, on June 8, he found Carolyne critically ill. She was so weak that she could barely remain out of bed for half an hour, and her condition so alarmed Liszt that he "hardly knew how to bear it."[86] Dr. Goullon visited Carolyne every day, but he told Liszt that he could hold out no hope of an early recovery. For a month Liszt remained Carolyne's constant companion in the Altenburg, and she eventually rallied. By mid-July his own symptoms were no better, so he decided to place himself under the supervision of Dr. Rodenburg without delay; he returned to Aachen on July 22 and took up residence in the Hotel Nuellens, opposite the famous Rose Baths. His daily regime consisted of swallowing two glasses of sulphurated water and taking a hot mineral bath. "In three or four days," he told Carolyne, "we'll see if my sores will decide to heal for good. At the moment they've re-opened because the baths have taken off the scabs."[87] Rodenburg then applied some poultices "of a different colour to the ones prescribed by Goullon," which seemed to bring about some improvement. Altogether Liszt had twenty-one baths, and by mid-August he felt so much better that he terminated the cure on August 13, much against Rodenburg's advice, and returned to Weimar.

---

85. LLB, vol. 4, p. 373.

86. BWL, vol. 2, p. 170; KWL, vol. 2, p. 167.

87. LLB, vol. 4, p. 381. Liszt's name figured in the weekly bulletin *Aachener Kur- und Bade-Liste* for May 24 and 31 and June 4, 1857. An advertisement in this same journal for May 24 praised the therapeutic qualities of the Aachen waters in lurid prose:

> These chalybeate waters are of vast use in chlorosis; from poverty of the blood (anaemia); in general debility from loss of blood; in all cases of fluor albus and exhaustion from fevers; in great irritability of the nervous system and in all conditions consequent on it, especially cramp in the stomach (gastrodynia); in incipient paralysis; and in excessive sensibility of the skin, having a tendency to profuse perspiration; they are also highly efficacious in chronic catarrhs as well as scrofulous and tubercular affections.

It is difficult to imagine Liszt walking around the marbled terraces of the Bains de la rose, clad in bathrobe and slippers, or sitting in a deck-chair in the Kurhaus drinking sulphuric water and listening to a Palm Court orchestra. But this is the life he endured while his convalescence lasted.

We may be sure that another, more compelling reason prompted Liszt to curtail his ongoing treatment and hurry home. It was nothing less than the wedding of his nineteen-year-old daughter, Cosima, to Hans von Bülow, which was planned to take place in Berlin on August 18, in Liszt's presence. The story of Hans and Cosima's first meeting, their difficult courtship, and their betrothal has been told many times. As we shall discover, that story can only be understood through its connection to a greater one, that of Liszt and his three children, which forms a saga unto itself.

BOOK FOUR

Gathering Storms
1857 · 1861

Liszt and His Children

Sowing is not so difficult as reaping.

GOETHE[1]

I

When Liszt said farewell to his three children—Blandine, Cosima, and Dan-iel—in April 1844 in Paris, he had no idea that nine years would elapse before he set eyes on them again. The reader will recall that this was the month of his final rupture with their mother, Countess Marie d'Agoult. At first, Liszt had been content to let her make whatever arrangements she thought best for their children; as he himself put it, he knew of no one better qualified to direct their education. But not long after his departure from Paris, the pair had exchanged some bitter recriminations which had led in turn to a desperate custody battle. It is unnecessary to recapitulate the events that produced this unfortunate situation. Only one fact needs to be recalled: under French law Marie had no rights; these children were all born outside France, and they were all born illegitimate. Since Liszt had openly acknowledged paternity and had always borne the expenses of their upbringing, he had become at once their natural father and their legal guardian. During his subsequent concert tours of Europe he was constantly preoccupied with their welfare, and he corresponded with them from their earliest years.[2] By the time he retired from the concert platform

---

1. GMR, no. 57, p. 29.
2. Several hundred holographs of Liszt's letters to his children, and theirs to him and to one another, are preserved in the Bibliothèque Nationale in Paris and in the Richard Wagner archives in Bayreuth. Most of them remain unpublished, but a careful perusal of their contents reveals much new and hitherto unsuspected information about Liszt's complex relationship with his offspring. The Bayreuth collection, incidentally, arrived at that unlikely destination simply because Cosima took them there

in September 1847 he had amassed a capital sum of 220,000 francs, which was invested at Rothschild's bank in Paris, the interest from which was intended to secure their future.[3] In accordance with Liszt's wishes the children were brought up in Paris, in the home of their grandmother Anna. As soon as the two girls were old enough, they were placed in a fashionable boarding-school run by Madame Louise Bernard and her daughter Laure on the rue Montparnasse, Blandine in 1844 and Cosima a year later. Daniel was in despair at being separated from his sisters, to whom he was devoted, and it took Anna all her time to explain to him that small boys were not permitted to attend girls' schools. "Well, then," was the seven-year-old's forthright reply, "put one of Cosima's dresses and hats on me and I'll be a girl too . . . !"[4] For the next year or two his education was entrusted to a private tutor, Monsieur Harlez, who prepared him for the entrance examinations of the prestigious Lycée Bonaparte.

From the start, Anna encouraged the children to venerate their father—albeit from afar. His pictures, busts, medals, and books adorned the walls of her house, at any rate until the collection was transferred to Weimar; this way the children absorbed his spiritual presence. They also followed his career through the newspapers and cut out every scrap of information about him that they could find—their childlike way of drawing closer to him. The idea that they were the offspring of a great man whose name they must bear proudly, and never dishonour, was inculcated into them every day of their young lives. They longed to be re-united with this father whom they could barely remember; but as the months and then the years passed by without Liszt returning to Paris, the idea became an impossible dream. Whenever Liszt announced his intention to visit France, something occurred to prevent it. He was, in fact, always deterred for the same reason: his relations with Marie d'Agoult were so poor that he feared a violent confrontation of the type that had become commonplace during the final, unhappy years of their liaison. And so he kept in touch with his children through correspondence. It was always a day of rejoicing when they received a letter bearing a Weimar postmark. "Blandine and Cosima

---

in the 1870s after her marriage to Richard Wagner. She in turn had acquired them following the untimely deaths of Daniel and Blandine, and she guarded them as sacred relics until she herself passed away in 1930.

Incidentally, there remains a question mark over the exact date of Liszt's previous encounter with his three children. The best evidence that we have indicates that it took place in April 1844. But we know that Liszt passed through Paris in January 1846, and then spent a couple of weeks in the north of France. The purpose of this visit was to cash some shares to enable him to buy land and a house in Montparnasse which he proposed to share with Princess Belgiojoso (OAAL, pp. 192–93). Nothing came of this intriguing plan, but Liszt's fleeting presence in Paris gave rise to the idea that he may have visited his children at that time, although there are no documents to support it.

3. LLB, vol. 5, p. 54.
4. MCW, vol. 1, p. 35.

were beside themselves with joy when they received your letter," Anna wrote
to her son:

> Even Daniel is beginning to take a lively interest when you write
> to me. The next time add a few lines especially for him. The poor
> little love! Some time last summer I told you that I thought he was
> insensitive, because he was so little moved by happenings that often
> cause his sisters to cry—either a story I read them or a letter from
> you. I withdraw this judgement. He is not insensitive. He really
> demonstrated this when his sisters left for boarding-school. I was
> afraid he would fall ill. He asked for them endlessly.[5]

This letter furnishes yet another proof, if one were needed, of the abiding love
and concern that Anna Liszt felt for her young charges. Anniversaries such as
birthdays, name-days, Easter, and Christmas were often the occasion for letters
from the children, as were communions. On May 3, 1847, Cosima told her
father: "I want to announce to you the greatest event in my life. I will celebrate
my first communion on June 21. I really hope that you will be able to be
present, and I expect you impatiently at this time . . . our hopes have been
dashed for so long."[6] Of course, Liszt was not present (he was at that time
giving concerts in Turkey), and the disappointment of the nine-year-old child
was reflected in her next letter:

> I am writing to you to inform you of a solemn event which was
> nothing less than my first communion. I was confirmed a week after
> I took Jesus Christ into my heart. I was very happy on that lovely
> day which seemed only too short to me. Only you were lacking for
> my complete happiness. Grandmother came every time, and that
> gave me great pleasure.[7]

Although Liszt did not return to Paris, he nonetheless took an active interest
in the education of his children. He himself selected some of their teachers, and
he continually exhorted his daughters to improve their handwriting and to
stock their minds with sound ideas. He wrote to Blandine on October 22, 1849,
his thirty-eighth birthday:

> . . . May the blessing of God enter your heart through my prayer.
> May you, as well as your sister, always be a consolation, because to

---

5. MCW, vol. 1, pp. 34–35.
6. BLE, p. 28.
7. BLE, p. 28.

be sweet and kind to those who love you would be the best part of your happiness on earth. And who could love you as deeply as I do?

Your progress in your education and intelligence gives me great satisfaction. I note with pleasure that your handwriting continues to improve. Try to write more and more legibly and elegantly if possible, and be careful not to copy me in this area. The classes in literature and history, with analysis of Homer and Greek tragedies, which you tell me about, must have had a good influence on the development of your mind, which henceforth we must not neglect to supply with substantial and healthy nourishment. Would you not like to give me pleasure by sending me via Grandma, who is supposed to come and see me in Weimar at the end of December, a few of your analyses (for example, those of the *Iliad* and of *Antigone*) copied neatly and bound?

Add to that two or three of your drawings which I'll honour by framing and which I'll hang over my writing table. . . .

Good-bye, dear child; write to me soon and often. Keep me up to date with your studies, and do not fail to send me some samples (the most praiseworthy possible) of your knowledge and handiwork, which could not find a more sympathetic audience than your father, who will be so happy to become a little proud of you, and for you.[8]

Blandine replied at once. The thirteen-year-old girl told her father that his letters filled her with both joy and sadness—joy at each fresh proof of his love for them, and sadness that they must still wait for the happiness of embracing him. She assured him that she would return to her studies with renewed zeal, "since my progress interests you so much," and she did not despair of reaching his high standards because "I am surrounded by all the means of completing my education." On the question of her drawings, she was more modest and told him that she still had not done anything really good. "My masterpieces would show up really badly in a frame. Until now, music has taken up more of my time."[9]

Since the name of Liszt was synonymous with the piano, it was natural that the children should be put to the keyboard at an early age. Even before they had enrolled at the school of Madame Bernard, the girls had begun to receive piano lessons, and they had showed a genuine aptitude for the instrument. When they arrived at the rue Montparnasse, the headmistress faced a crisis. Music was taught in the school by a certain Mademoiselle Chazarin. She was generally held to be an exceptional teacher, but she shied away from the

8. OCLF, pp. 38–39.
9. OCLF, p. 39.

responsibility of instructing the daughters of Liszt. Matters were eventually smoothed over by Liszt himself, who wrote: "Tell Mlle Chazarin that I have no doubts about her excellent piano teaching. I want Cosima to work on sight-reading and to get used slowly to playing from memory."[10] Occasionally Liszt even sent his daughters a parcel of music that he wanted them to learn, which made them very happy.

II

At the beginning of 1850 Anna Liszt went to Weimar for an extended visit. For the first time since the girls had been enrolled at Madame Bernard's, they spent the weekends without direct supervision. There now unfolded a sequence of events which was to have profound consequences on the lives of the entire family. On New Year's Day, 1850, Blandine had happened to overhear someone mention the address of Marie d'Agoult, information that had always been withheld from her. Overwhelmed by curiosity, she and Cosima had set out the following day to find Marie's house for themselves. They arrived at the rue Neuve des Mathurins, rang the front door-bell, and were taken in to see Marie, who was astonished to see her daughters before her. They flung their arms around her neck and kissed her. Marie was overcome by emotion. This visit was a clear violation of her agreement with Liszt: she was supposed to see the girls only at their boarding-school, and then only by prior arrangement, but she had chosen not to visit them for five years. After chatting with them briefly, she hurried them home. Neither Blandine nor Cosima breathed a word of this escapade to Anna Liszt, who set off for Weimar a few days later, on or about January 7,[11] but the damage was done. Other clandestine visits followed during Anna's absence, and on one occasion Marie called at the house in order to pick up Daniel and take him out for a treat. It was only a matter of time before Liszt heard about it, and about a month later Blandine plucked up the courage to tell him.

February 1850

I am writing, dear Papa, to tell you how happy we are at the moment, and to confide in you how we attained this happiness which had been denied to us for a long time. We have seen Mama again, and this great joy has made us forget the sadness of our long separation from her. Every day I felt more and more the pain of not seeing her, and I tried to get news of her from time to time. I was never

10. BLE, p. 26.
11. VFL, p. 97.

so happy as when I heard her name pronounced. During the New Year's holiday someone mentioned her address in our presence. The next day, when I went out with Cosima, completely preoccupied by what we had heard the day before, we were suddenly inspired along the way with the idea of going to find her ourselves, and that is how we saw her again. We only stayed a moment at her house. She was really moved and really surprised to see us again, and she was especially happy to find that our feelings for her were just as strong and affectionate as ever.

When we returned to Grandma's we did not tell her what we had done. We were afraid that she would be vexed that we had acted without her knowledge. But I hope now that she will not bear us a grudge, and that she will share in our happiness, as she has always done. Mama has come to see us several times. She has inquired about our studies and seems pleased; we always try to prolong her visits, and we are extremely sorry to leave each other. The ladies have been kind enough to take Daniel out several times, because they always use the occasion to give us pleasure; he will come again on Monday and Mama will also come to see us, the three of us together, and enjoy the happiness of having all her children together. All that joy I feel near Mama, I will feel just the same near you and Grandma. Do not think that your absence is not felt deeply by me in these happy days. My happiness will be complete only when I see you and when I can share my embraces with both you and Mama. I hope, dear Papa, that you will not remain for long without seeing your children who have been deprived of seeing you for so long. . . .[12]

The arrival of this letter caused consternation at the Altenburg. Liszt was incensed at what he considered to be an act of deception on the part of his daughters. He showed the letter to Anna Liszt, who burst into tears when she realized that the girls had broken their trust. The fourteen-year-old Blandine could have had no idea of the dark emotions her letter stirred. Liszt was convinced that it was dictated by Marie d'Agoult herself; only this can explain the violence of his response.

Weimar, February 28, 1850

You were wrong, my daughter, to let yourself be secretly tempted into an act of which your inexperience could not allow you to foresee the consequences. You were wrong; and you have wronged me by supposing that, without serious reasons, I would have refused

---

12. OCLF, pp. 42–43.

to allow you and your mother to establish the natural relations which should exist between you—which it is not for some romantic incident or other to overrule. You will learn the reasons soon, all three of you, dear children; but until I give you the serious and precise explanation, the first and most important of your duties, the one to which all others must remain subordinated, is a respectful and absolute obedience to your father. . . .

However painful it may be for me to oppose the happiness which you naively tell me you are enjoying at the moment, my reason and conscience do not allow me to hesitate. I not only have to scold you but must reprimand you severely. You must be aware that your grandmother, by not taking you to your mother's house, was acting on my orders, and that to deceive her was to deceive me. The bitter tears she shed here about your behaviour are on your conscience. . . . As it seems probable to me that your last letter was dictated for you, I will not bother to point out what is improper about young girls "attaining happiness" for themselves, unknown and contrary to their father's wishes. When you have thought even a little bit that from your birth up to the present I have had to provide continually and exclusively for the costs of your upkeep and education, while your mother has only judged it proper to give you the benefit of her fine phrases, you will understand that I can neither think myself flattered by the promptness with which you offer me half your affection nor even accept the expression of your shared affection.

However precious to me your love may be, I tell you in all sincerity that I value it only insofar as you are daughters after my own heart, whose upright will, healthy reason, cultivated talents, noble and firm character, are capable of bringing honour to my name and assuring me of some consolation in my declining years.[13]

Confused and humiliated, Blandine could only stammer a few words of apology, promise to obey her father without question in the future, and undertake never to see her mother again.[14] Further retribution was to follow,

---

13. OCLF, pp. 43–45.

14. Liszt's critics, with Ernest Newman and Charlotte Haldane at their head, have called this letter "cruel" and "disgusting." In her blistering analysis of its contents Haldane remarks that it ranks with the harshest ever written by a Victorian father to an innocent daughter, likening it to "the worst tyrannies of a Mr. Barrett of Wimpole Street." We cannot allow this judgement to pass without comment. It is evident from Blandine's letter that a very long time had elapsed since Marie d'Agoult had last seen her children. Blandine complains of "a long separation" from her mother. In fact, Marie had not visited the children for nearly five years, and that places her in a questionable light when we recall that their school was less than two miles from her house. We surmise that this self-imposed separation began in June 1845, at the climax of Marie's violent quarrel with Liszt, when she had told

however. The children were withdrawn from Madame Bernard's school and ordered by Liszt to return to their grandmother's house until further notice. He told them not to leave the premises unaccompanied. Anna Liszt was despatched home post-haste in order to enforce this arrangement. The children wept and pleaded to remain at the *Pension,* where they had been especially attached to their teacher Mademoiselle Laure Bernard, but Liszt was unyielding.

That spring the main topic of conversation at the Altenburg must have been the future of the children, and how best to secure it against the disruptive influence of Marie d'Agoult.[15] It was Princess Carolyne who came forward with the solution. Madame Patersi de Fossombroni, the French governess who had educated Carolyne before her marriage to Prince Nicholas, was now in her seventies and still lived in Russia;[16] and Carolyne appealed to her to take on the task of educating Liszt's daughters. Despite her advanced years Madame Patersi heeded the call and came out of retirement. "The Great Instructress," as Du Moulin Eckart dubbed her, boarded a train at St. Petersburg, wearing a black dress with a whalebone collar; she sat bolt upright for the entire journey, refusing to relax against the cushion provided for her comfort. It was symbolic of her implacable character that she would not allow herself to sacrifice her "correct" posture even for a moment. When she arrived in Weimar, she was

---

him: "Be good enough to give your orders directly to Madame Bernard. Tomorrow I will go to say good-bye to Blandine, praying God to leave the impression on her forehead of her last kiss from her mother. One day, perhaps, your daughters will ask you: where is our mother? You will reply: it did not suit me for you to have one." (VFL, pp. 154–55. See Volume One of the present work, pp. 406–7, where this letter is reproduced in full.) And the cause of the quarrel? In 1845 Marie had wanted to remove Blandine from boarding-school before the end of term, in order to keep her at home during the summer holidays. Liszt's chief objection to this otherwise harmless arrangement had been that he could not allow Blandine to live under her mother's roof while Marie was spreading slander about him among his colleagues in Paris, for he feared that she would turn the child against him. When Blandine and Cosima turned up on Marie's doorstep in 1850, then, it was for him as if the clock had been turned back five years. Anna Liszt was at that moment in Weimar—the first time that she had been out of Paris for years. Blandine disclosed that her mother had "come to see us several times." We do not know whether these visits took place at Madame Bernard's school or in Anna's home—and neither did Liszt. But he obviously suspected a plot. And who wrote the "confession" that Blandine sent to her father? Liszt detected the hand of Marie d'Agoult, in which case his "cruel" reply was intended in part for her consumption. Incidentally, despite her naive promise never to see her mother again, Blandine wrote to Marie d'Agoult in the summer of 1850 and arranged a further meeting. She waited at the pre-arranged spot, but her mother failed to turn up (BA; unpublished letter from Blandine to Liszt, dated November 1, 1850).

15. These deliberations prompted Anna Liszt to make a second, unheralded visit to the Altenburg in March 1850. She remained there until after March 20, as a letter of Liszt's to Pierre Erard indicates (TLMF, vol. 2, p. 364).

16. When Madame Patersi first became Princess Carolyne's governess, she was already forty-eight years old and commanded a formidable reputation. Some years earlier Patersi, who was a widow, had lost her only son, the apple of her eye, when he was twenty-five years old, and thereafter she transferred all her maternal instincts onto her young students. "Unflagging zeal," "rigid adherence to principle," "a demanding disciplinarian" were just some of the epithets attached to her by her greatest pupil (S-WDL, pp. 2–3).

as stiff as a ramrod and had to take to her sickbed. For two months Carolyne nursed the old lady at the Altenburg before she was fit enough to resume the thousand-mile journey to Paris, where an apartment had been furnished for her in the home of her elderly sister, Madame de Saint-Mars, at no. 6, rue Casimir-Périer. By the time Madame Patersi arrived there, it was already November. Meanwhile, the most painful part of the arrangement had taken place two weeks earlier, when Liszt had instructed his mother to hand over his two daughters to Madame de Saint-Mars.

Weimar, October 5, 1850

I would have preferred to have this letter delivered by Madame Patersi herself. I ask you to hand over my two daughters to her care. Henceforth she is to supervise their education. I thank you with all my heart for the love which you have offered my daughters in the last months and I am sure that they as well will remain grateful for the care you have bestowed on their early youth.

Unfortunately Madame Patersi fell ill when she arrived here and she cannot come to Paris for another two weeks. Since you will be moving, her sister Madame de Saint-Mars has kindly consented to call for the children and take them to rue Casimir-Périer, no. 6, Faubourg St.-Germain, where they will be living from now on, remaining with her until Madame Patersi arrives. Would you therefore please, on receipt of this letter, deliver Blandine and Cosima at once to Madame de Saint-Mars. I hope that you will often give my daughters the pleasure of joining them at their meals, and I wish Daniel, too, to visit Madame Patersi frequently. . . . Would you also be so kind, dear Mother, as to arrange to send to the above-mentioned place all the furniture which you think you can spare, as well as other household necessities. . . . They will need six silver sets of cutlery, glasses, dishes, table- and bed-linen, etc. I should have to buy all that new, and therefore I would be much obliged if you could let them have whatever you yourself are not using. I have asked Madame Patersi to visit you often with my daughters. However, she is to accompany them everywhere. . . .[17]

---

17. LLBM, pp. 87–88. This letter was not the only one that Liszt wrote to his mother dealing with the delicate matter of his children. In this connection see the correspondence published in VFL, pp. 97–102, which not only provides many more details about the affair but makes it clear that Anna knew of Liszt's decision as early as March 1850. During Madame Patersi's convalescence at Weimar there were many discussions about the welfare of the children. On October 5, 1850, Liszt wrote to Blandine and gave her the first intimation of her fate.

> . . . I have been lucky enough to meet someone who, in the course of a very sorrowful and a very eventful life, has shown proof of such an exceptional character and such an

In vain did Anna Liszt protest to her son that this was an unreasonable decision. Liszt's view was that his mother was too indulgent towards the children and that as they grew older they would require stricter supervision than she alone could provide. They had not lived with Anna for the four years that they had both boarded with Madame Bernard, of course; so their transfer to Madame de Saint-Mars was simply a return to the status quo. In any case, Anna would continue to see them whenever she liked, a point worth observing in view of the fact that Liszt has sometimes been accused of heartlessly wrenching his daughters from her care.

Deeper motives were also at work. In 1850 Carolyne was still optimistic that her marriage to Nicholas would be annulled and that she would soon be free to legalize her union with Liszt. Madame Patersi's mission, then, was not merely to educate Liszt's children; it was also to prepare them to accept Carolyne as their new mother. To this end Madame Patersi made Carolyne a part of their curriculum, so to speak, by using every opportunity to praise the virtues of her former star pupil. She also censored all their correspondence and removed any remarks likely to displease Liszt and the princess. In short, Madame Patersi gave every appearance of being a martinet who ruled the girls with a rod of iron. "Satan finds mischief for idle hands to do" was a favourite saying. And if the girls sobbed over their daily chores, which happened a lot at first, Patersi would dismiss it all with the phrase "Tears are only water." On the other hand, she seems to have been an excellent teacher, who emphasized the study of languages and the humanities. Liszt had had most of his books moved from Anna's house to the rue Casimir-Périer, so the children and their governess had access to a small library. Both girls were soon able to write acceptable letters in German and English as well as in their native French. Patersi also took them to museums and to the porcelain factory in Sèvres; occasionally they would even attend a debate in the National Assembly.

Music played an increasingly important role in their lives. Their piano lessons were now supervised by François Seghers, an old acquaintance of Liszt, to

---

upright mind that she will be able to teach you the best way to become an elegant and respectable woman. She will teach you what solid piety consists of—that essential foundation of honour and dignity—judgement, prudence, and common sense, more necessary in your position than in others. Obey her, I command you; give her your trust. You will have reason to be proud of it. (OCLF, pp. 48–49)

The engagement of Madame Patersi as his daughters' governess was an expensive proposition for Liszt. It has been generally assumed that the princess must have taken on this financial burden, but a search of the Rothschild archives in Paris reveals that Liszt, too, paid a substantial share. On March 15, 1851, Rothschild's wrote to Liszt and confirmed that the capital that he had earlier invested with them was yielding 7,913 francs annually, and they undertook to pay Madame Patersi 1,000 francs every quarter (AN 132AQ 1794). The rest of the interest was to be paid to Anna Liszt, who was still submitting receipts for her share as late as June 1857, not long before both girls were married. Documents in the Daniel Ollivier Archives also support these figures (BN NAF 25193).

whom Cosima in particular became devoted. And since they were the daughters of a famous father, it was necessary for them, according to Madame Patersi, to associate with famous people. She took them to society functions, notably to the Erard family's villa, La Muette, where they mingled with several artists of repute, including Léon Fauché and his wife, the Gutmanns, and Krieger. Everybody made music on such occasions, and it was naturally expected that the daughters of Liszt would join in. At first they were reluctant to do so, but Madame Patersi insisted. She took the sensible view that since they were not aspiring to become professional performers it did not matter if their playing lacked polish. "You may perhaps play badly, but play!" she commanded. "We played," recalled Cosima. Blandine rendered a Czerny study and a Russian hymn (the only pieces that she could play from memory), while Cosima played Liszt's "Third Hungarian Melody" and his arrangement of Schubert's song "Lob der Thränen." Even Daniel was persuaded to take his turn at the keyboard; he played Moscheles's *Alexander* March, without the variations. Afterwards the company applauded vigourously.[18]

Marie d'Agoult knew perfectly well that Madame Patersi was in Paris for one reason only: to place distance between the children and her. Years later Marie wrote of this period: "My studies, my work, [were] interrupted by appalling upheavals, my children snatched from me. . . . One is not permitted to choose a mother for one's own children. The one they were given was a woman of Jewish origin, who is ending her life in the corridors of the Vatican."[19] Four years elapsed before Marie saw the children again. Then, in the spring of 1854, at a concert of music by Berlioz, the two girls happened to spot their mother sitting in the audience. At the conclusion there was an emotional reunion, and Marie invited them to visit her within the next few days. She had meanwhile come into possession of a considerable inheritance from her mother, Viscountess Marie-Elisabeth de Flavigny.[20] In December 1851 she had invested

18. MCW, vol. 1, p. 63. Cosima evinced a pronounced pianistic talent, a rarely observed aspect of her personality. She became so proficient in her teens, in fact, that she could play the standard Beethoven sonatas with aplomb. She also made a special study of Weber and Hummel, and she once took pleasure in telling her father that she had begun work on the latter composer's Concerto in B minor, a composition in which she knew that Liszt himself had at one time specialized. Later on, encouraged by Seghers, she began playing some of her father's own compositions, including the operatic fantasias on *Lucia di Lammermoor, Robert le diable,* and *Les Huguenots.* Marie d'Agoult saw in Cosima a second Clara Schumann and wanted her to concertize, but Liszt resisted the idea. We do well to remember that Cosima became a pupil of Hans von Bülow before she became his wife. After hearing her play for the first time Hans told Liszt that he was "affected and deeply moved at recognizing in Fräulein Cosima's playing the *ipsissimum Lisztum* ['the essence of Liszt']." Even allowing for some slight exaggeration on the part of Bülow in order to please his master, Cosima must have possessed an exceptionally musical nature.
19. AM, p. 217. Carolyne was not of Jewish origin, as Marie wrongly alleges.
20. Viscountess de Flavigny had died in 1847, but the execution of her will had been delayed by litigation brought by Marie's elder brother, Maurice. By 1851, Marie had inherited some, but by no means all, of the money she was entitled to receive.

much of the money in the purchase of a magnificent home, La Maison Rose, which stood on the Champs Elysées, not far from the Arc de Triomphe. Here Marie ran one of the most fashionable salons in Paris and gathered around her the cream of the city's intelligentsia. She was now universally admired as "Daniel Stern," the author of the definitive, three-volume history of the 1848 revolution.[21] The three children were overwhelmed by their visits to La Maison Rose. This house seemed like a fairy palace, with its luxurious furniture, its magnificent library, its stimulating guests, and above all its regal hostess, who had the bearing of a queen. The first thing they observed was a bronze medallion of Liszt by Bovy, prominently displayed over a bookcase; on the opposite wall was a portrait of Liszt drawn by Ingres.[22] At La Maison Rose the children were introduced to a galaxy of prominent lawyers, politicians, scientists, and writers of every hue. Among the foreign exiles were the Polish poet Adam Mickiewicz, the Venetian writer Daniele Manin, and the Hungarian patriot László Teleki; even the American philosopher Ralph Waldo Emerson paid a visit. It was in this same salon that Marie d'Agoult was one day to introduce Blandine to her future husband, a rising young politician named Emile Ollivier. More than twenty years later Cosima reminisced: "I cannot describe the impressions those Sundays always made on me. I can still see myself devouring with my eyes my mother's wonderful library; and even when we returned to our narrow, strict, suppressed life with two seventy-year-old gover-nesses, the impression remained with us of having returned from the realms of the blessed."[23] It was at this time, too, that the children first became acquainted with Claire d'Agoult, Marie's eldest daughter and their half-sister. Claire's marriage to Guy de Charnacé in 1849 had proved unhappy, and after the birth of her second child in 1851, she had left Croissy, the family seat, and had sought refuge in her mother's home. Later Claire attempted to emulate her mother, pursuing a modest career as a writer under the *nom de plume* Claire de Sault. She published her first article in October 1856 for Emile Girardin's *La Presse,* the newspaper in which Marie d'Agoult had made her own début as a journalist

---

21. *Histoire de la révolution de 1848* (1850–53).
22. This drawing is reproduced in Volume One, p. 268. Marie herself left a description of La Maison Rose. "It was situated in an avenue closed by iron gates at both ends, and planted with acacias, surrounded by land where animals grazed." The staircase and reception hall were "decorated in blue, red, and gold on an ebony background, lit by a beautiful heraldic stained-glass window, and covered with an orange carpet with black edges. It was so soft to the feet . . . and received such pleasant light . . . that we often spent our conversation time here, or our morning reading hours." (AM, pp. 220–21) See also the description of La Maison Rose in Louis de Ronchaud's introduction to Marie d'Agoult's *Esquisses morales.* He was not wrong to call it "a true house of Socrates." Ronchaud tells us that Marie received there "all the shipwrecked people of the Republic, and all the friends of liberty in these early years of Empire."
23. MCW, vol. 1, p. 760.

fifteen years earlier. Cosima, especially, retained a lifelong affection for Claire, as their correspondence shows.[24]

III

Meanwhile, the children had experienced the unspeakable joy of seeing their father again. One golden day, early in October 1853, they heard that he was about to visit them in Paris. Excitement mounted daily at the little apartment in rue Casimir-Périer in anticipation of his arrival. After conducting concerts at the Karlsruhe festival, Liszt had journeyed to Basel, where he was joined by Princess Carolyne and her daughter, in order to spend a few days with Richard Wagner, who was still languishing in Swiss exile. There Wagner began reading aloud portions of his *Nibelungen* poem, a work in which the little party became thoroughly engrossed. The original idea had been for Liszt and Wagner to go on to Paris by themselves, but the sixteen-year-old Princess Marie was so captivated by the *Nibelungen* saga that she begged to be allowed to hear the rest of it in Paris. And so it was that posterity acquired one of the best descriptions of the reunion between Liszt and his children.[25]

Nine years had elapsed since Liszt had bade farewell to his small family. On October 10, 1853, they were all assembled in the drawing-room of Madame Patersi. Liszt entered in the company of Wagner, Berlioz, Carolyne, Princess Marie, and Anna Liszt. The first moments were confused and awkward. Liszt was astonished to see that his daughters had grown so tall. (Cosima had already

---

24. The archives of Claire de Charnacé, which were deposited in the Versailles Municipal Library after her death in 1912, contain some remarkable disclosures. Claire, according to her own admission, was spared all knowledge of her mother's liaison with Liszt, and of the three children of that liaison, until the year 1853—that is, until she was twenty-three years old. In her unpublished reminiscences she tells us that she knew only that there was something abnormal in her mother's past, and it came as a considerable shock to learn the truth (VMA, F 859, carton 11). Madame d'Agoult must have gone to unimaginable lengths to conceal her chequered background from her eldest daughter for so long a time. Claire had been placed in a convent while still an infant and had remained cloistered there until she was seventeen. Her marriage to Guy de Charnacé, when she was only nineteen years old, had been arranged in Marie's salon. It brought much tragedy into Claire's life. Her first son, Henri, died not long after his birth in 1850; her second son, Daniel, was born in 1851 at about the time that Guy de Charnacé started losing huge sums of money (most of it Claire's wedding dowry) in a reckless business venture involving the purchase of livestock from England. When Claire fled Croissy, there followed bitter litigation as the lawyers tried to disentangle the complex property settlement drawn up between Guy and Claire at the time of their marriage. Throughout this period, 1847–53, Marie d'Agoult and Claire were drawn closer together by all these difficult circumstances, but not once did Marie reveal that there were two stepsisters and a stepbrother in the neighbourhood. The source is unassailable and tells us all that we need to know about Marie's self-proclaimed "interest" in Blandine and Cosima during their childhood years.
25. HERW, pp. 12–14.

been nicknamed "the Stork" by her sister.) They in turn were spellbound to find themselves in the presence of their genius-father, whom they recognized at once through his portraits, and they were overcome by shyness. It was Carolyne who dispersed their embarrassment by embracing them all, complimenting them on their good looks, and giving each of them a small gold watch. Wagner later wrote: "It was quite a novelty for me to see Liszt with these young girls, and to watch him in his relations with his growing son. Liszt himself seemed to feel strange in his fatherly position, which for several years had only brought him cares without any of the attendant pleasures."[26] Wagner, of course, had no idea that the occasion would turn, in retrospect, into a historic one for him too: it was the first time that he set eyes on Cosima, his future wife. His only comment about her at that time was that she seemed excessively reserved. Princess Marie tells us that after a plain meal in the small salon of the rue Casimir-Périer, Wagner read them the closing scene of the *Nibelungen*. After he had finished, everyone was overcome by emotion. Princess Marie crossed the room and took down from the wall one of the laurel-wreaths that Daniel had won at school and placed it on Wagner's head. "I can still see Cosima's rapturous expression with the tears running down her sharp nose," she wrote.[27] As for Cosima, she left her own poignant recollection of that day. "I did nothing but look at the floor; my weak eyes and shy disposition made me unable to do anything but snatch at everything by stealth, as it were, though I knew that, strictly speaking, it did not exist for me."[28]

A hectic week of activity followed. The three children were taken out for a family dinner at the Palais Royal, and they also heard their father play at Erard's—a legend become reality for Cosima, who for years had yearned to hear his piano playing and was held in thrall by his magical fingers. And then it was all over. After only eight days Liszt and his entourage left as abruptly as they had come, and the children were left to resume their cloistered existence. What this glimpse of "the high life" meant to the children can scarcely be imagined. They had basked every day in the reflected glory of their famous father, who had now vanished; it was as if the sun had gone out. Cosima was especially hurt by the brevity of Liszt's visit; twenty-five years later she still felt the heartache of his going.[29]

For much of 1854 and 1855 the children continued to make a regular

---

26. WML, p. 608.
27. HERW, p. 14.
28. MCW, vol. I, pp. 748–49.
29. "My whole youth was a staying at home! For example, when after eight years my father saw us again for eight days, we were taken nowhere with him and we found it quite natural that he went out with Carolyne and Marie" (WCWB, p. 233). By now Cosima had come to resent the strict childhood imposed on her by her father. Her well-known ambivalence towards Liszt in later life can be understood only in this context.

pilgrimage to La Maison Rose. Liszt was intelligent enough to know that he could not control the lives of his teen-age daughters indefinitely, and he bowed to the inevitable. He would approve of their visits, he informed Marie, providing that they observed a few basic rules: the visits must not conflict with their educational curriculum; the times must be arranged by agreement with Madame Patersi; Madame d'Agoult must treat Madame Patersi with due deference and not patronize her as if she were a common servant; and so forth.[30] He then instructed the girls to wait until Marie d'Agoult herself had come to pay her respects to Madame Patersi at rue Casimir-Périer, which would be a sure proof that she had accepted his terms.[31] It was a futile arrangement, an attempt to save face. Liszt was powerless to prevent the visits from taking place, and he must have known it. The situation was complicated for him by Marie's decision to endow each of her daughters with 100,000 francs as a wedding-dowry. Liszt could not afford to jeopardize their future by not acknowledging such a generous gift, yet he was determined that it be made without preconditions. "If you wish to augment Blandine's and Cosima's dowry, I can neither prescribe the method for you nor forbid it. It goes without saying that my daughters would never connect their pleasure in seeing you again with the thought of personal gain. . . ."[32] As for Liszt's own contribution to the dowry, he had long since told Marie that each daughter would receive 60,000 francs at the time of her marriage, or the interest therefrom, to be followed by a further payment of 40,000 francs to each of them. Marie's commitment, then, was simply a "reply" to his: if Liszt had said that he could afford only 50,000 francs, we may be sure that that is all Marie could have afforded as well.[33] Later events proved that Liszt was right to treat Marie's offer with reserve, for when the time came, she was at first unwilling to find the money and had to be pressed for it.[34] By now Blandine was eighteen years old and marriageable. Nor was there a shortage of suitors. She had already turned down three, decisions of which Liszt entirely approved. He had told her that he wanted her to marry only when she

---

30. These conditions were set out in a letter dated September 4, 1854 (ACLA, vol. 2, pp. 404–06).

31. OCLF, pp. 111–12.

32. ACLA, vol. 2, p. 409.

33. From the start Anna Liszt had been sceptical about Marie d'Agoult's intention to settle money on the children. Already in the summer of 1850 Anna had written to Liszt to tell him of Marie's vacillations. "She also told Belloni that she will provide for these children, each of them receiving a sum of 20,000 francs after her death. But I do not believe a word of it. Five months ago she spoke of 20,000 francs which each of them was to receive after her death. First it was 10,000, now it is 20,000. Eight years ago it was 100,000. Adieu, dear child!" (MCW, vol. 1, p. 48)

34. As late as 1867 we find Liszt writing to Emile Ollivier: "I wrote a short note to Madame d'Agoult to remind her about Cosima. It is time that the author of 'my conscience and my life' became more conscious of life by settling her *arrears* without any more fine phrases." (BN NAF 25180, ff. 112–13) Cosima by then had been married for ten years. Blandine's dowry, too, was subjected to delay by Madame d'Agoult (see pp. 466–67). Liszt's own undertaking with regard to his daughter's dowries is set out in ACLA, vol. 2, p. 403 (letter of August 8, 1854).

fell in love. She for her part was thankful that she would not become the victim of an arranged marriage—still a common fate for young women in those days—and she replied after rejecting the third suitor: "I have decided not to stop bearing your name for that of a man who would not please you in every way."[35]

IV

In July 1854, while all these matters were being negotiated, Liszt unexpectedly invited his daughters to meet him in Brussels. The girls could hardly believe their good fortune, for a mere nine months separated this meeting from the last one. Both Blandine and Cosima had recently fallen ill with fever, and this trip to Belgium was really something of a convalescence for them. Liszt travelled from Rotterdam, where he had been a special guest of the music festival committee, and was waiting for them when they arrived in the company of the indomitable Patersi and his old factotum, Belloni. Blandine and Cosima had never seen their father looking so relaxed. They all stayed at the Hotel Bellevue, where Liszt placed himself entirely at his daughters' disposal. "They look well and have kind hearts," Liszt observed.[36] He wined and dined them and genuinely enjoyed playing father. Once they all travelled to Antwerp, where they visited the famous zoological gardens and "passed in review lions, tigers, vultures, and ostriches."[37] For weeks afterwards the girls could not stop talking about their trip. Blandine sent her father an account of their return journey to Paris, from which we learn that Belloni suffered intensely from the heat on the train. The little party also brought back a white parrot for Anna Liszt, which she received with mixed emotions. "He is not much a Knight of the Bath," joked Blandine, "and Grandma has already received three or four bites in single combat with him about that."[38]

Throughout their long years of servitude under Madame Patersi, Blandine

---

35. OCLF, pp. 101–02. These "marriage interviews" were stiff and formal occasions, conducted in the presence of her confessor, Father Bucquet. Liszt's views on marriage were advanced. To regard matrimony as an extension of business, as did so many middle- and upper-class families of the nineteenth century, was anathema to him. He tried to reassure Blandine by telling her that those who went about attempting to arrange marriages were pursuing "the most foolish and immoral of occupations. Thus, I have never been able to develop a taste for certain ways of doing things which could not be undone later, and under which burden one stays dejected and broken all one's life. If you believe me, then, my dear daughter, you will not make haste to settle down to marriage. I have no desire at all for you to change your name before a proposal comes along that is absolutely suitable." (OCLF, p. 101)
36. LLB, vol. 4, p. 206.
37. LLB, vol. 4, p. 206.
38. OCLF, p. 103.

and Cosima never lost their sense of humour. Highly articulate and possessed of a penetrating intelligence, they had quickly learned to be tactful and circumspect in the presence of "the Great Instructress." They would present themselves for inspection each morning, starched and pressed ("Cleanliness is next to godliness") and ready to begin the day's work. Patersi ran a tight ship, and the girls were shrewd enough not to do anything to impede its magisterial progress. Cosima recalled that they had no domestic help whatsoever; they had to make their own beds, clean their own rooms, and do their own personal laundry.[39] Once the lessons were over, however, and the household chores were completed, the two girls would bubble over with mirth at the quaint mannerisms of the old ladies. Cosima became a splendid mimic, and her impressions of Madame Patersi had Blandine in fits of laughter. It was not for nothing that Marie d'Agoult had once dubbed Cosima "the Electric Girl."[40] Blandine's humour came out in a more subtle way. She wrote a two-act play called *Scenes from Private Life,* which reveals in exquisite detail what the daily routine at 6, rue Casimir-Périer might have been like.[41]

ACT ONE: TWO HOURS IN A CARRIAGE

(A nice, cheerful drawing-room, furnished with old, red furniture and a mahogany grand piano; two windows, two doors, a mantelpiece with a clock, two vases, two candelabra, and two shells. MADAME PATERSI *is in the centre of the stage writing,* COSIMA *at the piano,* BLANDINE *by the window reading.)*

MME PATERSI: I was writing to that dear Carolyne, to whom I tell everything and who is a woman of such intelligence, how people who are merely intelligent are only stupid.

COSIMA [*exchanging a meaningful look with* BLANDINE *and whispering to her from afar*]: "I would give anything to prove to her that people who are merely intelligent are not such blockheads.

BLANDINE: Hush! Such opportunities occur daily, perhaps right now.

MME PATERSI: In your boarding-school, dear children, did they show you what high-level reasoning is, and what use it is, and all the petty nuisances of everyday life it helps one to avoid?

COSIMA [*forcefully*]: No, Madame, they weren't as stupid as that!

MME PATERSI: Insolent girl, go to your room!

---

39. WCWB, p. 39.
40. Marie d'Agoult ("Daniel Stern"), *Lettres républicaines,* p. 22.
41. The holograph may be found in the BN (NAF 25191, vol. 17). Only fragments of the text are reproduced here.

[COSIMA *laughs and goes off.*]

BLANDINE [*very seriously*]: They didn't tell us about it, Madame, and if you would be kind enough to explain it to me, I would listen attentively. [*She laughs, because* COSIMA *has come to sit beside her without* MME PATERSI *having noticed.*]

MME PATERSI: Well, my dear child, high-level reasoning, or high-level judgement, or if you prefer, high-level understanding of all those things that are imperceptible to the mind that is merely intelligent, lead at once to everything that is noble and practical—

COSIMA [*aside to* BLANDINE]: Let's get to the end!

MME PATERSI [*continuing*]:—is that thing which prevents one from falling into a moral mire, which is worse than poverty: it is destitution!!!

BLANDINE [*with great aplomb*]: I thank you, Madame; that definition is quite precise and clear in my mind.

MME PATERSI: Wait a minute, I haven't finished.

COSIMA [*aside to* BLANDINE]: Heavens! It was long enough.

MME PATERSI: With mere intelligence one is robbed not only in moral matters but in private matters too. Now you can judge whether we should esteem high-level reason [*laughing*]. I don't know, my dear Blandine, how we'll finish the term.

[*The door-bell rings.*]

BLANDINE: Now judge whether or not we need our intelligence at the door [*aside to* COSIMA], and watch out for its enemy, high-level judgement.

COSIMA: May the unknown caller, whoever he is, be blessed a thousand times.

The caller is a disreputable coachman who claims that Madame Patersi and the children had dismissed him a few days earlier without paying their fare. Actually the journey never took place, but this charlatan (having been primed by one of the servants) presses his demand that Madame Patersi now hand over seven francs.

MME PATERSI: What day did this journey take place, my dear man?

COACHMAN: Shrove Tuesday.

BLANDINE: But we didn't go out on Shrove Tuesday.

MME PATERSI: Be quiet, my dear! Let me deal with this good fellow.

COSIMA [*aside to* BLANDINE]: Here's a vindication of high-level reason if you like. The man's a robber!

MME PATERSI: Well, my dear man, I don't remember anything about it; generally I pay at once, because I don't like having debts in the neighbourhood. It's not part of my character and it casts a murky light on the reputation of an honest woman. Let's see, there, how much is it, my dear man? Because my sister is about to return, she would scold me if she knew that I was paying for carriages.

COSIMA [*to* BLANDINE]: How intelligent that is!

COACHMAN: Seven francs, Madame, for two and a half hours. I remember because I saw these young ladies very clearly.

COSIMA [*sharply*]: That's not true—you're lying!

MME PATERSI: Goodness, what manners, my dear! Here, my good fellow, I'll give you four francs extra for the insolence of this ill-informed girl.

COSIMA: You should be taken to the police-station!

MME PATERSI: What are you saying to this good man, my dear? [*giving him fifteen francs*]. Give us your number and we'll hire your carriage when we go out. That will recompense you a little.

[*The* COACHMAN *leaves.*]

BLANDINE AND COSIMA [*together*]: Human wretch!

MME PATERSI [*to the girls*] That man was within his rights. It was high-level judgement to pay him, and not to have the petty vanity that consists of never admitting a mistake.

COSIMA: Freely translated: "One should let oneself be duped by people."

According to a note in Blandine's hand, the above scene took place at 6, rue Casimir-Périer "on the Wednesday following Ash Wednesday, February 28, 1855." It seems to be based on a real-life incident, then, and the text is in many respects more revealing than a diary-entry. The characterization of Madame Patersi is so sure, and her dialogue with Cosima so sharp, we can well believe that the daily lives of this extraordinary quartet—two old ladies and two adolescent girls—regularly turned on the morality of such trivial issues as the one dramatized here.[42] Less than a month later, on March 20, 1855, Blandine wrote a second instalment.

42. Blandine's real-life correspondence offers proof of this. In a letter to Princess Marie von Sayn-Wittgenstein, dated November 13, 1853, she draws a portrait of Madame Patersi that matches the one in her play and might even have provided some basic characterization for it. Apparently, when Liszt visited his children in Paris in October 1853, he left with Madame Patersi a banker's draft to cover the household expenses. Patersi worked herself into a panic, as she always did whenever she

ACT TWO: A WET RAG

[*It is nine o'clock in the morning, and everyone is in dressing-gowns. The door-bell rings. It is the* PORTIÈRE.]

PORTIÈRE: Madame, a policeman has sent me up. You're going to be given a fine.

MME DE SAINT-MARS: What's that? Now that would be something to see. And why, may I ask?

PORTIÈRE: He saw a wet rag fall from the window on the fourth floor. I didn't want to come up at all, but he forced me to.

MME DE SAINT-MARS: Oh, how amusing it is that honourable women are supposed to throw wet rags on the heads of passers-by! It's abominable! Let the stupid fellow come up if it amuses him!

[*Bedroom of the two sisters.*
COSIMA *and* BLANDINE *are getting dressed.*]

BLANDINE: It's really farcical. What do they want from us?

COSIMA: I'm not surprised. I'll even bet that it's Madame Patersi who threw the rag. Hurry up. I want to see the end of the comedy.

BLANDINE: Hold on, it takes time to get up four floors. It's really comical. Those ladies take it as seriously as if it were a question of murder.

COSIMA: But it *is* a murder—a moral one—to hear Madame Patersi tell it.

BLANDINE: We've got to see how it all ends.

COSIMA: My God, it will all end by itself!

[*Someone knocks at the door.*]

BLANDINE: How tiresome. Who is it?

[*Another knock on the door.*]
COSIMA: Good God, come in and don't break the door down!

[MME PATERSI *enters with a gloomy and foreboding air.*]

MME PATERSI: Children, we are being accused. I don't understand. As for me, I've no doubt that it fell from your room.

---

was in charge of money. She went to a bank in order to cash the draft and was mortified when the teller was joined by a man, presumably the manager ("who seemed foreign to her on account of his wild looks"), who questioned the value of the sum indicated. It was in a sort of terror, Blandine went on, that Patersi continued to Rothschilds; she even suspected that she was being followed. She arrived home ill, convinced that it was the result of her cloak-and-dagger experience. No such thing, Blandine declared flatly; Patersi was suffering from nothing more serious than an overdose of the Paris fog (BLE, pp. 49–50).

BLANDINE [*sharply*]: That's impossible, Madame, since we haven't opened the window all morning.

MME PATERSI: What! You haven't opened your window? But that's despicable, horribly unclean. Only porters' daughters do that!

COSIMA: But it was a question of a rag. It's got no connection to the dirtiness of a closed window.

MME PATERSI: Hold your tongue. I'm not speaking to you. You are an insolent liar. I predict for you . . . [*Her words are lost in a mumble.*]

COSIMA: Boring prophecies. They make you lose your mind.

BLANDINE: We were talking of the rag. It wasn't us.

MME PATERSI: I wasn't talking about that at all. Look how you change the topic. Really, there's no way for us to understand each other. As for me, I'll throw the helve after the hatchet.

COSIMA [*quietly to* BLANDINE]: The helve is poetically represented by the wet rag, and the hatchet by the passers-by.

[*The bell rings.*]

Oh, happy interruption!

[*Enter the* POLICEMAN (and MME DE SAINT-MARS)]

MME DE SAINT-MARS: What a devil of an idea to come and visit us in the morning!

POLICEMAN [*calmly*]: I've come because a wet rag fell from the fourth floor.

MME DE SAINT-MARS: You're mistaken. Who do you suppose let it fall? The maid has gone out, and these young ladies are in their room, getting dressed.

POLICEMAN: All I know is that I saw a wet rag fall from this room.

MME PATERSI [*disturbed*]: From my room, sir? It's impossible! I was in the process of ironing ribbons.

POLICEMAN: When one is ironing ribbons, one can easily throw a rag which is getting in one's way through the window.

MME DE SAINT-MARS: It was certainly from the fifth . . .

POLICEMAN: It was from the fourth.

MME DE SAINT-MARS: Firstly, we live on the third floor above the mezzanine.

POLICEMAN: No, no, it was from this room. I glanced up at the same time that the rag was leaving the room, and it's impossible that it had floated from higher up onto your window, since it was a wet rag.

MME PATERSI: Sir, I never have a wet rag because I use a sponge for washing myself.

POLICEMAN [*very calmly*]: I don't know to what use the rag was put; all I know is that it fell.

MME PATERSI: I swear to you before the Gospel, sir, before everything most holy, sir, that I didn't let the rag fall.

POLICEMAN: You can swear by whatever you like.

MME PATERSI: We are honest women. We are religious, and we haven't been picked up in the street, sir!

POLICEMAN: I'm well aware that you haven't been picked up in the street, but the rag was certainly picked up there.

There follows an altercation between the policeman and Mme de Saint-Mars— the one pressing his case, the other protesting her virtue.

MME PATERSI: Sir, you're the first to have suspected our morals. Go and ask the whole neighborhood who we are, and whether I have such bad taste as to throw wet rags through the window. Never, sir. My reputation is established. I have educated the most distinguished women of France and Poland, and neither I nor my pupils have ever been accused of such a thing. As sure as these spectacles are here, sir, I swear it on the memory of my forefathers.

POLICEMAN: I don't know about that. I know only that a rag fell. I'll let it go this time.

MME DE SAINT-MARS: Be careful what you say! We have never lied and we will not begin for a rag. That would be a fine example to set these young ladies.

The bell rings, a guest is announced, and the policeman goes away laughing up his sleeve. Blandine returns to Cosima's room and tells her what has happened. The two old ladies follow.

MME DE SAINT-MARS [*to the girls*]: Come along now—as many shot as wounded, nobody died.

MME PATERSI: Except the policeman, whose conscience is so lax that the death of his morals is inevitable.

COSIMA [*quietly to* BLANDINE]: I understand nothing if not that Patersi threw the rag and that the policeman is right.

We may be sure that neither Madame Patersi nor Madame de Saint-Mars ever saw this lampoon: the humiliating parody to which Blandine here subjects them would have led to a swift punishment. But the text of this comedy proves that Blandine understood the prudish character of her mentors through and through.

She was wise to hide it away among her papers and personal documents, where it lay forgotten for more than a hundred and thirty years.

V

After January 1855 the bonds between Marie and the children developed rapidly. The Sunday luncheons at La Maison Rose had by now become an institution, the high point of the week, which everybody anticipated with unabated pleasure. Marie often took her family to the Louvre and impressed them with her detailed knowledge of the modern French masters. She also revealed to them the beauties of Gothic architecture, and they all went to admire the contours of the Sainte-Chapelle together. Visits to the Comédie-Française were arranged, to see productions of Molière's *L'Avare* and *Les Précieuses ridicules.* For all these outings the children were expected to prepare themselves with background reading. On one occasion they went to the Opéra to hear Verdi's *Il trovatore.* In her paraphrase of the plot, Blandine wittily observed that Leonora threw herself into the arms of the count, thinking him to be the troubadour, simply because it was night-time. "From this we draw the moral that ... people ought to provide themselves with lanterns." Wagner was a constant topic of conversation, and in response to Marie's wish to learn more about his operas, the children lent her their own copies of the scores of *Lohengrin* and *Der fliegende Holländer.* She had to wait for *Tannhäuser,* since Daniel kept the score at school. When she finally read it, she was full of enthusiasm and asked Cosima to play for her the song "O, du mein holder Abendstern."[43] Liszt's pioneering work in Wagner's behalf aroused her interest, and she asked the children to procure Liszt's articles about the composer, and in particular the pamphlet on *Der fliegende Holländer*—an essay that was partly written by Princess Carolyne. We may be sure that Marie knew this and experienced more than a passing curiosity about a literary activity in which she herself had at one time collaborated. That Carolyne took a perverse pleasure in arousing that curiosity cannot be doubted. Not long after putting in a request for the *Holländer* pamphlet, Cosima received a sharp rebuff from Weimar; she was told that Marie must contact the Altenburg directly about such matters and not raise them through the children. In fact, both Blandine and Cosima were careful to send Liszt the fullest accounts of their activities with their mother.

43. Patersi (doubtless at the prompting of the princess) attempted to offset this new-found interest in Wagner by giving the girls periodic doses of Berlioz. On April 30, 1855, she took them to the church of St. Eustache to hear a performance of his Te Deum, rendered by nine hundred performers—an experience about which she afterwards waxed indignant. She wrote to Liszt in a highly emotional state and told him that henceforth she would include in her prayers the invocation "Preserve us, O Lord, from plague, war, famine—and Berlioz's Te Deums"! (LLB, vol. 3, p. 14)

They knew that Madame Patersi was in constant touch with Weimar, and they wanted to dispel whatever illusions her letters might create about a shift in their filial loyalties. In one of her rare communications to the princess, Blandine tactfully re-assures her that "we have never been able to regard our mother's return to us as . . . an attempt to alienate us from our father." Cosima expressed the same idea more forcefully when she told the princess that they had convinced their mother of the "eternal and unchangeable love and gratitude which we bear our father, and we hope that we have never in any way shown that we have forgotten what he is to us." Such words fell upon deaf ears, however. Liszt and Carolyne looked on with mounting concern as Marie's influence gained dominion. The princess became convinced that Marie was poisoning the minds of Liszt's children against him. It was not true, but by now the prolonged trauma of her thwarted marriage to Liszt had created in Carolyne a condition amounting to paranoia, and she was incapable of viewing the situation with detachment.

In July 1855 Liszt, with Carolyne's support and approval, decided to remove his daughters from Paris and bring them permanently to Germany. The move was to be accomplished by stealth. Under the guise of an invitation to Weimar for a short holiday, they were to be transferred to Berlin and placed in the care of Franziska von Bülow, the mother of Hans. It has always been widely assumed that this plot was hatched by Princess Carolyne, and that her chief motive was to crush the woman in La Maison Rose. Cosima, for whose life this move to Berlin was to have the most profound consequences, certainly believed it; and it is from her that the official account stems. A reading of the expurgated portions of Liszt's *Briefe an eine Freundin* seems to support her. On July 21, 1855, Liszt wrote to Agnès Street-Klindworth: "My daughters will definitely be lodged in Berlin at Madame de B[ülow]'s home this autumn— [but I will not inform them of this until they are settled there]."[44] The full story is somewhat more complex than this, however, and it is worth pursuing because it indicates some of the pressures Liszt was enduring. In May 1855 there were fears that Madame Patersi (who was now seventy-seven years old) might die. She was actually so ill that Madame de Saint-Mars, who was herself very frail, spent most of her time looking after her. By June, Liszt was writing that he did not have much hope of keeping Madame Patersi and must make alternative arrangements for his growing daughters.[45] He was, in fact, at his

44. DA, letter of July 21, 1855. The last part of the sentence was censored.
45. LLB, vol. 3, p. 27. Throughout May 1855 Blandine had sent a series of pessimistic reports on Patersi's sickness to Princess Carolyne, which must have thoroughly alarmed Carolyne and Liszt. On May 28, for instance: "Madame Patersi is still in bed with her abscess. It is drained every day by Dr. Crodart, which causes her a great deal of pain. She did not sleep last night and is very weak. The doctor says that her abscess will be cured within a week. He does not seem concerned about her condition. As for me, dear one, I am very worried and ask for hope. Let us pray for her!" Since

wits' end. He mentions Dresden as a possibility, with Frau Ritter as guardian (Dresden was only eighty miles from Weimar). Liszt even journeyed to the city on July 5, and he returned to Weimar in the belief that Frau Ritter would "take my daughters into her home for a year or two,"[46] but the idea fell through for lack of suitable accommodation. Liszt stated that he was unable to have his daughters live with him at the Altenburg, the undeclared but obvious reason being that his liaison with the princess was causing him difficulties enough with the Weimar Court without complicating matters still further by having his children by an earlier illicit union living there too. It is clear from the correspondence that had it not been for Madame Patersi's failing health, the immediate impulse to remove Liszt's children from Paris would have been lacking.[47]

And so it was that Princess Carolyne set out for Berlin in order to meet Frau Franziska von Bülow, reassure herself that she was indeed a worthy successor to the great Patersi, and confide in her the details of Liszt's plan. Urged on, perhaps, by a letter from her son, Hans (who had arrived at the Altenburg on July 21, just in time to learn about these intricate manoeuvres, and saw in the situation a way of helping his revered teacher in a moment of personal stress), Frau von Bülow agreed to carry out Liszt's bidding. The plan now went into motion. A letter of invitation left the Altenburg, beckoning all three children to Weimar for the summer, and telling them that Frau von Bülow would shortly arrive in Paris to escort them there by train. Liszt disclosed this part of the arrangement to Anna Liszt, whose suspicions were thoroughly aroused. "It is quite a rare thing for me to receive a few lines from your own hand," she wrote. "I was quite astonished—for once or twice while I was in Weimar I heard you say: 'I cannot let Cosima and Blandine

---

Madame de Saint-Mars was almost as old and frail as her sister, the two girls, according to Blandine, spent "part of our time in her room helping Madame de Saint-Mars as much as we can. This has preoccupied and worried us a great deal, and as I know how many sorrows you have I did not want to add this one." (Hitherto unpublished, BN NAF 25191, ff. 125–28) Even a casual look at these documents suggests that life at the rue Casimir-Périer had come to a standstill.

46. LLB, vol. 3, p. 31.

47. This much was already known to Du Moulin Eckart, who, however, continued to look at the picture through the tinted spectacles provided for him by Cosima, seventy years later, and saw only a beautiful mother being deprived once more of her children. Marie d'Agoult, however, had already declined to have the girls live with her at La Maison Rose. On June 2, 1855, Liszt had invited her to come to Weimar in order to discuss the future of their children. He told her that if she thought a personal discussion to be absolutely necessary, then she could easily come to Weimar for forty-eight hours or longer. "In effect your time is much more flexible than mine, since I have obligations of service and other duties to perform. Your stay here would not be a problem for anyone, still less for you, and the weather is now fine enough so that this thirty-hour journey might even be pleasurable for you." (ACLA, vol. 2, p. 410.) This meeting never took place. There was instead an acrimonious exchange of correspondence which culminated in a missive mentioned by Liszt on July 15, "an extremely imperious letter, *à la Nélida,*" to which he did not reply (DA, censored fragment). As Liszt put it, he no longer felt up to starting a new tug-of-war with Madame d'Agoult, so he proceeded with the removal of the girls from Paris without further consultation.

come to Weimar.' It is true that two years have gone by since then, and time changes many things."[48] As for the children, they were ecstatic at the thought of staying in the Altenburg and of seeing their father again—this time in his own element, surrounded by his coterie of pupils, friends, and disciples.

On August 21 the children arrived in Weimar in the company of Frau von Bülow. Two days earlier the princess and her daughter had departed on a trip to Paris, via Brussels. The two trains almost passed one another en route.[49] For the first time Liszt had them to himself, and he found them to be delightful companions. The Altenburg rang with laughter from dawn until dusk. "My daughters monopolize two-thirds of my day. They are pleasant young people, intelligent, lively, and even a little condescending," he wrote.[50] They upset his game of whist, engrossed him in conversation until after midnight, and disturbed him in his bedroom. He finally declared that he would not have breakfast with "the clan," and he stipulated that for the rest of their stay, whatever happened, the mornings were reserved for his work. Blandine continued to receive offers of marriage while she was in Weimar, which she turned down. Liszt mused that what the girls really required in a husband was a combination of a Beethoven or a Raphael with a nabob.[51]

The princess had meanwhile seen Anna Liszt in Paris, who was shocked to learn the full extent of the deception practised on her granddaughters. She wrote to Liszt on September 3:

> I can wait no longer, but must write to you. I am so upset since hearing the latest decision about Blandine and Cosima ten days ago. The princess told me about it with the greatest indifference, that they were to be sent to Berlin under the charge of Frau von Bülow, who

---

48. MCW, vol. 1, p. 90.

49. Why was Princess Carolyne in Paris? The usual view is that since Carolyne was Liszt's second mistress, it simply would not do to have the children of his first mistress become a part of the *ménage* at the Altenburg, for however brief a period. Therefore, she obligingly wandered off—to Paris. This explanation will no longer do. The chief reason that Carolyne went to Paris was the same reason that the children had left it: Patersi's sickness. Carolyne wanted to ascertain for herself the true nature of the elderly governess's illness and to pay her last respects to her former mentor. Already in May 1855, Carolyne had expressed the fear that "Patersi's last days are drawing near" (WA, Kasten 34, u. 4). Patersi was to linger on for seven years more, however. In October 1859 Carolyne saw her in Paris for the last time. By now Patersi was senile and hardly recognized the princess. "Poor Patersi has regressed into childhood," she told Liszt (WA, Kasten 35, u. 53). Carolyne clearly held herself to be responsible for the plight in which Madame Patersi and her sister now found themselves, and she made provisions for their future. As Anna Liszt expressed it: "These two ladies require rest. They know that the princess will never abandon them" (MCW, vol. 1, p. 95). Nor did she. Patersi was still receiving money orders from Carolyne in March 1862, through the good offices of Eduard Liszt in Vienna (unpublished letter from Blandine to Eduard, dated March 13, 1862; BN NAF 25191, f. 3).

50. LLB, vol. 3, p. 42.

51. LLB, vol. 3, p. 43.

is to be with them always and *gouverner* them. I could find nothing to say except that the children are too big to make another change. The princess replied that otherwise there would never be an end to Madame d'Agoult's scribbling, as she had been very impertinent in her letters to you for some time past. But consider, dear child, to hand these children over to strangers in a strange land, where they do not know a soul, is certainly no indifferent matter to them, and I am afraid that if this happens, one or the other of them will fall ill. . . .[52]

Anna's anguish can be read in every line of this letter. She faced the cruel prospect of never seeing her granddaughters again. With characteristic directness she went on to tell Liszt that it would have been better if Madame Patersi had never left Russia. The woman was already too old and tired when she took charge of the children. And she reminded Liszt that when she had said as much to the princess in Weimar in 1850, Carolyne's rejoinder had been that Patersi was "still full of vigour." And now Patersi was bed-ridden, and the girls were to be subjected to yet another upheaval. Worst of all, Anna continued, she was embarrassed to write to her granddaughters because they had not yet been informed of the fate that lay in store for them. This last charge was perfectly true. Liszt delayed telling his daughters for an unconscionable period of time. It is difficult for the impartial observer to find a single redeeming cause for his silence, except the all-too-human one that he hated "scenes" and hesitated to destroy the girls' evident pleasure at their stay in the Altenburg. When he was in their presence he melted easily beneath their charms; and so in the absence of the princess he simply vacillated. When Blandine and Cosima finally learned that they were not to be allowed to return to Paris, they were at first stunned, then very agitated. They beseeched Liszt to change his mind, and they brought all manner of arguments, both intellectual and emotional, to bear against his decision. Liszt would not even allow them to return to Paris in order to collect their personal belongings—a fact that resulted in an unfortunate discovery at rue Casimir-Périer, which will be related shortly. In the end, of course, they had to accept defeat. On September 4 they set out for Berlin, Liszt himself accompanying them as far as Merseburg, where he was supposed to hand them over to Frau von Bülow. He could not resist the temptation to show everyone round the cathedral and let them see the great new organ, which his pupil Alexander Winterberger had recently inaugurated. Blandine, seeing the high good humour in which her father found himself, pleaded to be allowed to spend a few more days in the Altenburg. Liszt relented and took both girls back to Weimar with him. They did not set out for Berlin again until September 8.

---

52. MCW, vol. 1, pp. 94–95.

Hardly had they settled into Frau von Bülow's apartment than they received a further, terrible setback. It seems that they had not tidied their rooms before leaving the rue Casimir-Périer and had left some personal belongings scattered around, including three letters from Marie d'Agoult addressed to Blandine. These letters were discovered by Madame Patersi and were immediately forwarded to Liszt. The last one sent him into a paroxysm of fury. Marie d'Agoult had been in Holland when her daughters had departed from Paris, and she was outraged that Liszt should have chosen that moment to remove the girls. Dated "The Hague, August 15," this letter is filled with invective against Liszt and the princess. Marie warned Blandine that she would meet a dishonourable fate at the Altenburg, where she would be "eating the bread of a stranger."[53] The holograph of her missive has not survived, but we know about the contents because Liszt made a copy in which he rebutted Marie's charges one by one, and then sent it to Blandine.[54]

> *"I have just received your letter,"* [wrote Madame d'Agoult]. *I remain so astounded that I cannot do anything. They waited until I was not there, my children, to have you do something dishonourable."*

COMMENT: No one had the idea of waiting until Madame d'Agoult was not there before asking you to come to Weimar. This trip, unless I am very much mistaken, was for a long time as much your wish as mine, and I simply waited for Daniel's vacation, without troubling myself in the slightest to find out where Madame d'Agoult was, or was not, in order to re-unite the three of you under the roof of the house in which I live. Since this house is, as you know, extremely spacious, possesses several stories and about thirty rooms, Madame the Princess Wittgenstein lives with her daughter on the first floor, and up to now the most honourable people have constantly been honoured to be admitted, without in the least suspecting that it could be dishonourable for anyone to come here. . . .

> *"They waited until I was no longer there . . ."*

COMMENT: Who are *they?* Me, of course, for not only did I write and ask you to come and see me, but I also asked Frau von Bülow

---

53. This evocative phrase comes from Dante's *Paradiso,* canto 17, and is typical of Marie's rhetorical tone. See the letter she wrote to Liszt some fifteen years earlier (ACLA, vol. 1, p. 292) where she quotes this same canto in an attempt to rouse his conscience.

54. Daniel Ollivier published this letter in mutilated form in OCLF, pp. 138–40. The full text was printed by Robert Bory in BLE, pp. 104–10. Marie's defenders have wrongly assumed that she opened the sluice-gates of her venom only after she discovered that the girls were to be sent to Berlin. A glance at the dates shows that this was not the case. On August 15, Marie did not even know that Berlin was a possibility, for Blandine herself had not yet been informed. Marie was enraged simply because the girls were visiting the Altenburg.

to be kind enough to go and fetch you from Paris and bring you to Weimar. So I am fairly and squarely accused of having you do "dishonourable" things. . . .

"I am not making an appeal to your affection. I am sure of it, I have never doubted it. But your youth, your inexperience, your blindness, horrify me. . . ."

COMMENT: How should we translate your *youth,* your *inexperience,* your *blindness* in such a situation? Quite simply by the good feeling that you still have for your father . . . and by the trust, which is quite legitimate, that he would not try to damage your honour. There is in that doubtless something that should horrify! But let us go on. . . .

"Conduct yourselves in such a way that whoever is deceiving you and oppressing you, and dishonouring you, will be happy to see you leave. . . ."

COMMENT: I would be much obliged to you if you could explain to me, with the help of your mother's insights, in *what way* this person has ever deceived you, how they have acted to oppress you, and in what way they are dishonouring you. For me this is much more than a matter of simple curiosity, and I await your explanation, in order to explain in turn to you, perhaps, what it is all about. . . .

At this point in his rebuttal, Liszt betrays the true source of his agitation: the denunciation of Carolyne by Madame d'Agoult. He leaps to Carolyne's defence, as he always did whenever she came under attack (and particularly from such a quarter), because the topic of their relationship had become to him like a raw nerve which his adversaries touched at their peril. Marie's next charge, and Liszt's reply to it, form the climax of the letter.

"You are eating the bread of a stranger, who is not your father's wife and never will be. I would rather see you work for a living, or beg, than this last affront. . . ."

COMMENT: From the day of your birth until this very day, your mother did not worry in the slightest over the *bread* you ate, the *place* you lived in, etc. Though she enjoys a considerable income, she prefers to spend it on her own personal enjoyment. For nineteen years, I and I alone have exclusively shouldered the task of caring for your personal needs and paying for your education. If a "stranger" were to appear to share this responsibility (which is not the case), then in my opinion she would be less of a stranger than your mother. . . . The violent outbursts of Madame d'Agoult merely prove that she concocts large phrases in order to quiet a bad conscience . . .

"I'll do my part. In Heaven or Hell, I am yours and you are mine. . . ."

COMMENT: Allow me, dear children, not to accept that alternative for you. My conscience must oppose it, as long as I am unconvinced by the sublime theories that Cosima gets from her mother about the charms and perfections of Satan. . . .

Regarding the rights of ownership that Madame d'Agoult claims and affirms over you . . . I will not undertake to dispute for the hearts and affection of any of my children. That task would be repugnant to me and beyond my capacity. If, in the final analysis, you think that the share should be equal between the one who does his duty faithfully and conscientiously, and the one who forgets it, I will not object at all. When you reach your majority, you will have to make the choice which suits you. . . .

"Oh! my proud children, always remain proud!"

COMMENT: This is a singularly imprudent apostrophe. If you were only proud, you would have to blush at your mother's outbursts and ill feelings. Since she wishes me evil at all costs and on all occasions, and since she can strike at neither my position nor my conscience, she takes pleasure in injuring me in your affection, and in the respect and deep love that I hold for a woman who, as the purest flame of my life, ought also to be *sacred* to you on account of the devotion she has so nobly shown me in the afflictions, sacrifices, and incessantly renewed griefs of the past nine years. . . .

Much has been made of this letter by Liszt's critics. The best that can be said for it is that his comments against Marie d'Agoult are outshone by hers against him. He ended with this blunt postscript: "If you feel like sending a copy of this letter to your mother, I authorize you to do so. In any case, I ask you not to keep it a secret from Frau von Bülow and to read it to her, for it is a good thing that she should know its contents." Blandine was so distraught when she read her father's commentaries on her mother's letter that she wrote to Daniel (who had remained behind at the Altenburg) and told him that Madame Patersi's action in forwarding the letter to Weimar was "vile and base." She added that she would refuse to write to Patersi anymore and so avoid the necessity of insulting her. That merely brought down more retribution on the poor girl's head. Liszt reminded her that Patersi was only carrying out his instructions. "What gives you the right," he asked, "to show such contempt for your father, and to describe as *vile* and *base* what he judges to be good and healthy?" Distressing though these exchanges between Liszt and his daughter were, we would not be without them. The Berlin episode offers a unique insight into the background of smouldering discontent against which Liszt's family life had for years unfolded.[55]

V I

Life in Berlin carried one great advantage for the two girls: Frau von Bülow loved to entertain, and her home on the Wilhelmstrasse became a regular meeting-place for the leading musicians of the city. Soon the girls had met Adolf Marx, Julius Stern, Ludwig Ehlert, Groll, and Bronsart. Within a week or two of their arrival they were taken to the theatre to see *Egmont* and *William Tell.* Berlin in those days stood on the brink of artistic greatness, and Hans von Bülow was already moving to the forefront of its musical life. He gave frequent piano recitals, conducted orchestral concerts in which he introduced new works, and generally helped to raise standards of music-making in the Prussian capital. He was also a respected teacher and had recently been appointed to the faculty of the Stern Conservatory. Naturally, the girls attended all his public appearances. They held him in awe, and were on tenterhooks whenever he entered the lists to do battle for their father's music. Berlin gave them their first intimation that Liszt was a controversial figure and that his newer works, which were even then being greeted by abuse, required persuasive advocacy.

---

55. At this point, the passages that La Mara censored from her edition of Liszt's letters to Agnès Street-Klindworth (LLB, vol. 3) become crucial to our understanding of Liszt's family problems. On July 15, 1855, in one such passage, he told Agnès: "It is my duty to arrange what will be useful and profitable for my daughters, who will have better marriage prospects in Germany than in France, where my contacts are too tenuous for me to be able to exert a favorable influence on their future lot in life." And Liszt continued: "Just recently [Madame d'Agoult] wrote an extremely peremptory letter *à la Nélida* to which I made no reply, because I loathe quarrels with women in general, and have completely abandoned the impossible task of straightening out her ideas or changing her feelings for the better, because: 'Old habits die hard'; 'The cloth has acquired the crease,' etc." These restored texts prove that the idea of transferring his daughters to Berlin was Liszt's and not the princess's. As these letters to Agnès progress, Liszt's relationship with his children stands revealed as a tragedy of classical proportions. In a moment of black despair, he confessed to Agnès that Cosima and Blandine had become like "a branch lopped off from my being and will. I pray God to make it flower and bear fruit, but *my sap* can no longer flow through it." (January 8, 1856) That Madame d'Agoult had soured the joys of fatherhood for him cannot be doubted. "As for the mother," he wrote, "I hope that after great efforts I can manage never to hear of her again—except through booksellers' advertisements."

The holographs of these letters may be consulted at the Hessische Landes- und Hochschulbibliothek in Darmstadt.

It was Hans von Bülow who took their musical education in hand. Ehlert was engaged to teach them harmony, while Bülow himself gave them regular piano lessons. Since Hans liked to practise every day, a second piano was moved into the Bülows' apartment for the girls' own use. Bülow was swept away by the "Erl King's daughters," as he called them. He wrote glowing letters to Liszt in which he praised their talents to the skies. Liszt, who was not used to receiving such positive accounts of his daughters, was at first taken aback. He told Bülow to "make them work seriously," and he abjured him to turn them into splendid propagandists of the Music of the Future, "as it is their duty to be."[56]

During these first few weeks the attitude of Bülow towards Cosima underwent a profound shift. Drawn to her initially only by her youthful exuberance and bright intelligence, he soon found her to be sympathetic and understanding beyond her years; he was gratified to discover that she empathized with his high artistic aims. While Bülow may have presented an imposing figure to the world outside, the man inside was shy and insecure, and there were days when he returned to Wilhelmstrasse frustrated and depressed. He began to turn to Cosima for solace and comfort; and she, for her part, was ready and able to provide it. Before long they were in love, but neither dared utter a word of their feelings to the other.

The dramatic circumstances in which they declared themselves have meanwhile passed into legend. On October 19, 1855, about six weeks after his first meeting with Cosima, Bülow conducted an orchestral concert that included the first performance in Berlin of the Overture and Venusberg Music from *Tannhäuser*. The entire household turned out to support him—Franziska, Cosima, Blandine—and Liszt himself journeyed from Weimar to attend the event. At the conclusion of the piece hissing and booing broke out in the audience. Bülow stalked off the rostrum, livid with rage. In the artists' room his feelings overcame him, and he fainted dead away. Liszt was with him, and he and a small group of Bülow's local supporters stayed in the empty theatre until the young man had recovered. The three ladies meanwhile returned to Wilhelmstrasse. Cosima insisted that it was their duty to stay up until Hans got back, in order to sustain him in his hour of need. It was after midnight when Blandine and Franziska finally went to bed, leaving Cosima to stand watch alone. At two o'clock in the morning Liszt pushed Hans through the front door and went back to his hotel. Hans entered the living-room and found Cosima waiting for him. The atmosphere was emotion-laden and proved too difficult to withstand. They sat up all night talking. Hans told her that she had become indispensable to him. Her simple reply showed that she already loved him. From that fateful night their long betrothal really began.[57]

---

56. LBLB, p. 143.
57. MCW, vol. 1, p. 107.

Liszt's first response to the idea of a marriage was not entirely favourable. Cosima was too young, he thought. Also, the couple barely knew one another. He had other reservations, too, concerning Hans's complex personality. Whatever praise he constantly heaped on his pupil's shoulders regarding his artistic talents, he was the first to recognize the manic-depressive qualities of Bülow's character, and he knew that Cosima would find them hard to bear. Hans persisted, however, and Liszt gradually dropped his objections, asking only that the young couple wait for at least a year before entering matrimony. The turning-point came in a letter which Bülow wrote to his master on April 20, 1856:

> I feel for her more than love. The thought of moving nearer to you encloses all my dream of whatever may be vouchsafed to me on this earth, you whom I regard as the principal architect and shaper of my present and future life. For me, Cosima is greater than all women, not only because she bears your name but because she resembles you so closely, being in many of her characteristics a true mirror of your personality. . . .[58]

If we did not already understand something of Bülow's total subjugation to Liszt, we might almost suspect him, on the basis of this letter, of attempting to win Cosima's hand through the most outrageous flattering of her father. In fact, Bülow spoke truer than he knew. Did Cosima realize then that she was not loved entirely for herself alone but partly because she reminded him of her father? The relationship was already flawed, and in time it helped to undo their marriage.[59] Liszt invited Hans to meet him at Merseburg on May 11 in order to discuss everything at leisure. They must have talked about Hans's poverty, of which the young man later revealed that he was deeply ashamed.[60] Master and pupil then went on to Weimar, where Bülow stayed at the Altenburg for a week. Since Liszt had always maintained that he wanted his daughters to marry only when they fell in love, he was prepared to give his blessing once he had reassured himself of the depth of Bülow's feelings. Bülow returned to Berlin to break the good news to Cosima. In order to keep up appearances he had already moved out of his mother's home and taken bachelor quarters at no. 10 Eichhornstrasse.

---

58. BBLW, p. 67.
59. There was a remarkable sequel to all this. When Luise von Bülow (Hans's stepmother, who had clairvoyant gifts) first met the young couple, she received the uncanny impression that a figure other than Hans was standing by Cosima's side. So certain was she of this presentiment that she recorded it at the time, and she lived to see it become reality (MCW, vol. 1, p. 120).
60. In a letter to Cosima written in 1869, shortly after they parted, Bülow confessed: "As for your own fortune which you brought to our disastrous marriage, was it not the first stumbling-block, the first trouble for me, ashamed as I was of my poverty . . . ?" (June 17, 1869)

Events now took a predictable turn. Madame d'Agoult heard of the betrothal and attempted to stop it. She sent her daughter Claire to Berlin with instructions to persuade Cosima to postpone the marriage indefinitely. In her unpublished memoirs Claire tells us that she stayed in the Hôtel de Rome in April 1856 and had several private conversations there with both girls. But Cosima remained adamant, and Claire returned to Paris, her mission a failure. Madame d'Agoult was convinced that Cosima was the victim of a plot concocted by Princess Carolyne, aided and abetted by Frau von Bülow, "her creature."[61] The Altenburg was kept in ignorance of this visit, of course; the slightest hint would have been sufficient to send Liszt rushing to Berlin to put a stop to it.

The attitude of Frau von Bülow towards Cosima now became highly ambivalent. Franziska was about to lose her gifted son to a young girl whom she barely knew and did not really like, and she found the prospect trying. From the moment that she and Cosima had first met, in 1855, a mutual coldness had prevailed. Cosima found Franziska hard and abrasive; she called her "Lady Perhaps" because whenever Cosima wanted to do something, Franziska vacillated. For her part, Franziska thought Cosima too callow for such a sensitive soul as her son. The relationship festered slowly throughout 1856. It came as a relief to both of them when Liszt agreed that Blandine and Cosima should return to Paris in October to see their grandmother. More than a year had elapsed since they had been parted from Anna Liszt, and they were overjoyed to be re-united with her again. Marie d'Agoult lost no time in contacting her daughters. She even took Cosima away with her on a four-day holiday into the country in an attempt to shake the girl's resolve to marry Hans, but to no avail. From that moment Marie knew that she had lost Cosima, and it is interesting to observe how she abruptly switched her attentions to Blandine, who, since she had gained nothing from the Berlin episode and was in any case nearing her majority, had become all the more vulnerable to whatever suggestions Marie cared to put to her. Cosima's impending marriage to Hans meant that she and her sister would be separated for the first time in their lives. This painful prospect caused heartache on both sides. Unable to bear the thought of returning to Berlin, Blandine stayed on in Paris with her grandmother (much against Liszt's wishes), while Cosima travelled

---

61. Claire de Charnacé archives, F 859, carton 9. During her conversation with Blandine and Cosima, Claire apparently learned many intimate details about Hans and his mother. It transpires that Hans was so frightened at the prospect of breaking the news to Liszt that he prevailed upon his mother to do it for him, who then claimed that "it was Cosima's idea." From the same source we learn that Cosima told Claire: "I am determined to marry Hans; I am well aware that it is a bad match, that it does not please mother." And Blandine added: "She loves him. What can be done about that?" Claire's reply was worthy of her mother. Turning to Blandine she remarked: "They [Hans and Cosima] are dupes of the crudest machinations," meaning Princess Carolyne and Franziska von Bülow.

back to the Prussian capital in the company of Frau von Bülow. Hans was at the station to meet them.[62]

V I I

Two further obstacles remained to be surmounted before the marriage date could be announced. Bülow was not yet a naturalized Prussian subject, and many months were to elapse before the necessary legal formalities could be completed. More serious was the question of the religious service. Cosima was a Catholic, while Bülow (insofar as he had any religious beliefs at all) was a Protestant. Liszt desired a Catholic wedding for his daughter, and Bülow bowed to his master's wishes. "I think more highly of a church that regards marriage as a sacrament," he told Liszt. "I could feel no personal satisfaction in the blessings of a Lutheran pastor."[63] By now the engagement had lasted for nearly two years, and Liszt was satisfied that the feelings of the young pair had been put to the test for long enough. The marriage accordingly took place in the Hedwigskirche on the morning of August 18, 1857. This date was chosen to allow Liszt time to complete his water-cure at Aachen (which he had refused to postpone) and then to travel to Berlin. Liszt was the only member of Cosima's family to be present. Because Bülow's relations with the press were

---

62. These train journeys in the company of the dour Franziska von Bülow must have taxed Cosima's patience to the limit. She left a comical account of one such trip from Leipzig to Berlin, a journey that lasted about eight hours. For much of the time "Lady Perhaps" fussed and fretted over a caricature that had appeared in the satirical journal *Kladderadatsch,* in which Liszt was depicted as Don Quixote and Bülow as Sancho Panza. "Oh, my God! Poo-or Henns. He will be ill. That article and that fire-sprouter will kill him. What a dishonour for him to appear in *Kladderadatsch!* With his name and his talent! I will never console myself!" "But, Madame," Cosima replied, "my father is there too!" "Oh, your father, that is something else." There followed a series of monologues in this style, and Cosima prayed that God would shorten the trip. At last the engine whistled, the train stopped, and they got off. Cosima continued:

> "Lady Perhaps" approaches a cab and cries to the coachman that since her son is at death's door, she has the right to the first carriage. But coachmen are heartless beings who do not stop for inner feelings; they take care of first arrivals without considering name, rank, illness, or motherhood. Having run about for five minutes like a poisoned rat, she suddenly saw her son and almost fell over backwards with surprise. "Good evening, Mama," said Hans. "My son, my dear son"—all this before embracing him, of course—"so you are not ill? I thought you would be in bed. Oh, that Wagner!! . . ." "Why should I be ill?" "But that article . . . everyone in Leipzig is laughing about it. . . . Ah! Your poor Aunt and Livie. . . . Ah! My God! My God!" Then, remembering that she has not seen him for ten days, she engulfs him in an embrace, coiling her little self like a serpent around him. Hans, already completely morose from this sympathetic reception, turns to us and welcomes us to Berlin (BLE, pp. 133–34).

63. MCW, vol. I, pp. 120–21.

so poor, he feared that his father-in-law's presence in Berlin might generate unwelcome publicity, and so no formal announcement was made until after the service. Liszt then sent round the following terse notice.

I have the honour to announce herewith
the marriage which took place today at the
CHURCH OF ST. HEDWIG, BERLIN,
between my daughter

COSIMA LISZT
and
HERR VON BÜLOW

Berlin, August 18, 1857   FRANZ LISZT[64]

That same day the young couple accompanied Liszt as far as Weimar and then continued their honeymoon journey to Baden-Baden, where they were guests of Richard and Jeanne Pohl.

Their ultimate destination was Lake Geneva, which held romantic allusions for Cosima. Liszt and Marie d'Agoult had eloped there as young lovers, twenty years earlier, and Cosima doubtless wanted to re-live those passionate days. She had already arranged to meet her mother, who at that moment was herself on a nostalgic tour of the Swiss lakes with Blandine. By the time the Bülows arrived, however, Marie and Blandine had left for Italy. When Liszt heard that they had missed one another, he was not displeased. In nearby Lausanne Bülow met his old school-friend Karl Ritter. Ritter, too, had just married, and like Bülow he was a convinced Wagnerian. The four young honeymooners decided that it was too good an opportunity not to visit the exiled master at his retreat in Zürich; accordingly they all set out at the beginning of September. The journey was not without incident. On the way there Bülow lost the trunk in which he kept all their money. Cosima insisted that it would be better to return to Berlin rather than to arrive in Zürich as beggars. Fortunately the trunk was recovered, but the attendant frustrations so upset Hans that when they got to their Zürich hotel, the Zum Raben, he had to take to his bed with a crippling bout of rheumatism. Wagner lived at that time with his wife, Minna, in a house called the Asyl ("Refuge") on the estate of his wealthy benefactor Otto Wesendonck. The story of his secret love-affair with Frau Mathilde Wesendonck, which even then was being conducted behind the backs of their respective spouses, is so well-known that it need not be related here. The point is that Wagner's genius was in full flood, either because of Mathilde or despite her. He had already completed the first two acts of *Siegfried* and was now embarked

---

64. MCW, vol. 1, p. 121.

on *Tristan.* Wagner lost no time in harnessing his young friend's pianistic powers to his latest music. As soon as Bülow had recovered, he and Cosima moved into the Asyl as Wagner's house-guests. *Das Rheingold* and *Die Walküre* were both brought to life under Bülow's fingers in Klindworth's arrangements. Bülow amazed Wagner by sight-reading the first two acts of *Siegfried* from the composer's pencil-sketches.[65] Wagner peered over his shoulder while Bülow, his eyes glued to the page, kept exclaiming "Colossal!" "Unique!" "Fit for the next century!" While all this was going on, Minna hovered around the admiring company, serving Wagner champagne and Bülow beer. Wagner was in his element; he was surrounded by Wagnerians. Every day the small group was treated to a reading by the composer of the recently completed *Tristan* poem. Bülow made a separate copy of it for Cosima, who would take it up to her room and re-read it late into the night. It made a deep impression on her, and she occasionally appeared with a tear-stained face. Did she see in the epoch-making poem a portent of her own future? Wagner observed that she seemed "strangely troubled" and "reserved," and he attempted to cheer her up with banter. He later told Ritter's mother, Julie, that this visit of the Bülows was by far the most pleasant event for him that summer.[66]

Hans and Cosima stayed at the Asyl for three weeks. On September 28 they bade farewell to Wagner and set out for Berlin. After brief stops at St. Gallen, Ötlishausen, and Munich (where they visited a number of exhibitions and galleries), they went back to Weimar as Liszt's guests. Hans found the atmosphere of the Altenburg so congenial, and he had in any case so much news to impart to Liszt about the exiled Wagner, that he lingered in Weimar for two or three weeks. Cosima took the opportunity to journey back to Berlin alone in order to set up their new home on the Anhalterstrasse, and all was in readiness by the time her husband joined her.

VIII

From the moment that Blandine decided to stay in Paris, her world had changed from night into day. Liszt announced that he would not even object to her staying there, providing she lived with Madame d'Agoult; but the latter, in a fit of intransigence, announced in turn that she was unwilling to take in her daughter. And so Blandine moved in with her grandmother, an arrangement of which Liszt disapproved but which was to last until her marriage a few months later.[67] In the early spring of 1857 she was introduced to one of Madame

---

65. WML, p. 669.
66. MCW, vol. 1, pp. 123–24.
67. Liszt would have preferred Blandine to return to Berlin and to servitude under Frau von Bülow, there to await further offers of marriage. He refused to sanction his daughter's unexpected display

d'Agoult's protégés, Emile Ollivier, a brilliant lawyer with a promising future in politics.[68] Ollivier had come to prominence during the revolution of 1848, in which he had been given the difficult task of subduing the riots in his native Marseille. After the *coup d'état* he and four of his parliamentary colleagues had formed a radical group called Les Cinq, which succeeded in gaining some important concessions from Napoleon III. Marie admired Ollivier's intelligence and was at one with his liberal political outlook. She encouraged him to stand for public office in Paris, and in July 1857 he was returned to the Chamber of Deputies. He was thirty-two years old. Ollivier was too shrewd not to realize that "Daniel Stern" and her influential circle of friends could be of inestimable value to him in his career, and he gladly allowed himself to be cultivated. Did Madame d'Agoult already see in him a future son-in-law? It seems so, for the following month he was invited to join her and Blandine on an extended trip through Switzerland and Italy. He arrived in Geneva on August 18 and found that Louis de Ronchaud and Claire de Charnacé had also joined the party. They crossed Lake Geneva, journeyed down the Rhône valley, crossed Lake Maggiore, and went on through Lombardy. The tour contained emotional echoes of the one taken by Marie and Liszt in 1837; no imagination is required to understand that Marie wanted to provide a similar romantic setting for Emile

---

of independence, and he made his displeasure known to Anna Liszt, who asked him for money on Blandine's behalf. His reply was unequivocal:

February 13, 1857

Dear Mother:

Certainly there is nothing that I would refuse you, and you may on every occasion dispose of the little that I own, when it is a *question of yourself*. But in the present circumstances it is scarcely a question of you but in fact of Blandine, who is using your intervention to make me give the money that I had refused her, and with good reason. Do not think it bad, dear Mother, that as a result of what I have said, I keep up my economical methods and wait until Blandine has moved out of your house until I put my purse at your disposal. At present it is Blandine who would put her hands on it, and that does not suit me at all. As soon as Blandine is housed according to my wishes you have only to write to me what I should send; but as long as the present arrangement continues, which she made against my formally expressed wishes, I am obliged to be totally negative. (BN, NAF 25179, ff. 15)

This letter is interesting because it reveals a basic character-trait of Liszt's: namely, his almost fanatical attachment to binding arrangements and legal understandings, especially where members of his own family were concerned. The lives of many people were affected by Blandine's recalcitrance, or so Liszt may have thought: Frau von Bülow, Anna Liszt (whose crippled condition was now so serious that she had to be carried from one room to another), and most of all Cosima, who had to return to Berlin without her sister. Liszt was often willing enough to change formal arrangements, especially if he was convinced that they did not work, but he invariably resisted such changes whenever they were brought about by others.

68. According to Ollivier's *Journal,* he first met Blandine on March 6, 1857. "A new personality has joined the mistress of the house and Madame de Charnacé," he reported. "It is Liszt's daughter." (OJ, vol. 1, p. 265)

and Blandine. Emile's *Journal* suggests that the magic of the warm Mediterranean nights began to cast its spell. In the evenings, tired of the day's conversation, they would read poetry to one another. If there was a piano in the lodging where they happened to be staying, Blandine would seek it out and play Beethoven sonatas to her companion. By August 28 they were in Pisa. Emile noted: "This young girl and I sit outside in the garden and give ourselves up to day-dreaming. What are her dreams? Mine are pleasant, full of hope and love."[69] The following day the party arrived in Florence, where Emile was re-united with his father, Démosthène, himself a lawyer, who, like so many of his generation, was languishing in a temporary exile for some minor infractions committed during the revolution. By now, Emile and Blandine were in love. On September 12 Emile declared himself. He waited all next day for an answer, but it did not arrive. On September 14, unable to bear the suspense, he passed the time wandering round an art-gallery. When he got back to his lodgings he found a short note waiting for him: "I am too moved now to reply to you. Come about one o'clock if you can."[70] After a brief conversation it was all settled, and their betrothal was announced the following day. They had known one another for less than six months.[71]

Although Liszt had not yet met Ollivier, and was not to do so until after the marriage,[72] Blandine begged her father for his blessing. She told him that he knew better than anyone else how ordinary marriage, as it was commonly understood, was repugnant to her; that she had almost given up hope of finding someone whom she could love in body, mind, and soul. In a letter dated October 1, 1857, Blandine provided Liszt with many details of Emile's career and of his family background. Emile also wrote to Liszt and told him simply: "I feel that in uniting her with me, I am completing myself, not weakening myself."[73] Liszt's eagerly awaited telegram arrived from Weimar on October 8: "I give my full consent to the marriage of my daughter with M. Emile Ollivier."[74] A week later Liszt wrote a letter to Blandine in which he told her: "Along with my consent I send you my most affectionate blessing." He enclosed

---

69. OJ, vol. 1, p. 298.

70. OJ, vol. 1, p. 302.

71. In a letter to Eduard Manet's mother, dated October 7, 1857, Ollivier confessed: "I am marrying her not because her father is a lawyer, nor because her mother has influence with such and such a judge, nor because this or that social consideration urges me, but uniquely for this mad reason that after having spent twelve days with her I saw that I loved her, that having spent thirty I was convinced that I adored her, and that after a month and a half I know that I can no longer live without her." (ZEO, pp. 47–48)

72. Not until Blandine and Ollivier travelled to Weimar on January 1, 1858, did Liszt meet his new son-in-law for the first time (LLB, vol. 3, p. 103).

73. OJ, vol. 1, pp. 307–08.

74. OJ, vol. 1, p. 309.

with his letter a banker's draft for 5,000 francs to cover Blandine's immediate expenses, and he reminded her: "With regard to your dowry, you have known for several years what I can do and desire to do for you."[75]

The wedding took place in Florence under the dome of the cathedral of Santa Maria del Fiore, at nine o'clock on the evening of October 22, Liszt's forty-sixth birthday. Only Marie d'Agoult, Emile's father, and a few friends of the Ollivier family were present in the church.[76] The following day, the newly-weds set out for Pisa; from there, they proceeded to Lucca. They returned to Paris in easy stages, moving up the coast through Genoa, Turin, and Chambéry, and arrived back in the French capital on November 4.

Madame d'Agoult had at first drawn justified pleasure from the fact that she alone had brought about the union between Blandine and Emile. Nonetheless, the wedding itself was marred for everybody by a series of petty quarrels that she provoked with Emile during the days leading up to the nuptials. She objected to the ceremony taking place on Liszt's birthday, and she tried unsuc-cessfully to make Emile change the date. We know from his *Journal* that their disagreement was acute, for he observed: "How I pity Liszt for having given his youth to such a woman." Marie d'Agoult attended the ceremony "cold and frosty." It cut Emile to the quick when she let him and Blandine leave on the honeymoon without even saying good-bye. "And I am taking her daughter away!"[77]

---

75. OCLF, p. 194.

76. Both Emile and Blandine left accounts of the ceremony. See OJ, vol. 1, pp. 313–14, and OCLF (October 26, 1857). Incidentally, the wedding had been arranged so swiftly that even Anna Liszt, who probably knew her granddaughter as well as anybody, learned of it only a day or two beforehand, and it was November before she met Ollivier for the first time.

77. OJ, vol. 1, p. 314. The friction that arose between Ollivier and Marie d'Agoult, which declared itself even before the marriage, has rarely been remarked. Ollivier's journal-entry for October 1 contains a candid assessment of her character. "Madame d'Agoult's behaviour is becoming incompre-hensible. She envisaged my marriage with pleasure, as long as she believed that I would be an instrument for her, a means of domination. Since she has concluded that that could not happen, she has become cold, constrained, almost an enemy." Ollivier leaves no doubt that it was his wish to secure Liszt's permission for the marriage that lay at the root of the problem. "Her duplicity has been outrageous for several days. One might say that she was trying to cause a rift between [Blandine and me]." Then comes this blunt conclusion: "She has not the least heart. She pretended to be a mother when convention demanded it, but she does not love her children any more today than she loved them when she stayed for ten years without seeing them." (OJ, vol. 1, pp. 302–03) These comments are unbelievably frank. Ollivier had not known Madame d'Agoult for long, and he had never been embroiled in the Liszt family quarrels until now. Given all the circumstances, one would have thought that if he were to take sides at all, it would have been with Marie d'Agoult against Liszt. Just the opposite happened.

On the basis of what the Ollivier *Journals* have to tell us, we conclude that Marie, having tried and failed to prevent Cosima's marriage to Bülow earlier in the year, would have been more than happy to see Blandine's marriage to Ollivier cancelled. In both cases, Liszt was at the heart of her jaundiced outlook: if her sons-in-law were for him, she seemed to argue, then they must be against her—even if some slight encouragement was required on her part to bring this last state of affairs into being.

I X

Settled in Paris, Blandine brought all her skills to bear on the task of providing a comfortable home for Emile. The newlyweds moved into his cramped bachelor apartments at 29, rue Saint-Guillaume (which were shortly to be expanded by the acquisition of additional rooms next door), where Blandine found herself doing a great deal of entertaining. Anton Rubinstein and Wagner were dinner-guests during these first few weeks; so, too, were Léon Gambetta and Jules Ferry, political friends of Emile, both of whom were destined to become prime ministers. Liszt had often told his daughters that a woman's destiny was to make life soft and smooth for those around her, and it pleased him to see Blandine play this part to perfection. Alfred Darimon left an interesting eye-witness description of the Olliviers' salon, which, he claimed, was modelled after that of Marie d'Agoult:

> There are neither chairs nor armchairs: a long divan in red velvet runs the length of the walls. In front of the window stands a magnificent Erard piano. On the mantelpiece, a bronze. On the wall, a portrait of Ollivier by Ricard. . . . I think that Madame Ollivier effaces herself a little too much in front of her husband. No longer can I see the Blandine of the avenue Sainte-Marie, so gay and pert; she is becoming almost solemn. She listens a lot, and when Emile speaks she seems to drink his words. The piano is silent, which is a pity, because that charming young woman is a natural virtuoso. With what style she renders the beautiful inspirations of Mozart and Beethoven![78]

Emile's legal fees brought in seven or eight thousand francs a year; added to that was his salary of eight thousand a year as a deputy. The couple were comfortably off, then, but they were far from wealthy.[79] When the Olliviers

---

In Volume One of this biography we had occasion to observe that the present-day picture of Marie d'Agoult as a rejected mistress and long-suffering mother called out for correction. Ollivier's observations (first published in 1961, long after that picture had become established) simply reinforce our earlier conclusions.

78. DHP, p. 108.

79. OJ, vol. 1, p. 307. In this very year of 1857–58, however, Ollivier was propelled to fame by the sensational de Guerry case, which he handled in such an exemplary fashion that his future in the legal profession was secured. Briefly: several nuns of the Picpus convent in Paris had released themselves from their vows, following certain disputes, and they sued for the restoration of their property (given to the convent when they entered it, in much the same way that a dowry was given by a bride to her husband). One of the nuns, Mme de Guerry, hired Ollivier as her lawyer; he fought and won

paid their first visit to Weimar as a married couple, in January 1858, financial discussions loomed large, and the matter of Blandine's dowry was settled at that time. A marriage-contract was drawn up among the three parties on January 4, 1858.[80] It was with this wedding dowry that the Olliviers managed to buy their country château, La Moutte, near Saint-Tropez. The property stands on a rugged stretch of the Provence coastline and possesses magnificent views of the Mediterranean Sea. Emile had loved that part of France since his boyhood. Even though La Moutte was dilapidated and the surrounding land overgrown, he and Blandine saw in it a perfect retreat from the political hurly-burly of Paris. Emile donned a peasant's smock and cleared the fifteen acres of land himself. He planted trees to shield the house against the *mistral,* the wind that continually swept in from the Rhône valley. He also drew up plans to enclose the house within a walled courtyard, with a fountain in the middle and cloisters all round. Blandine likened it to a monastery and called Liszt "the Great Prior," anticipating that he might one day join them in their cloistered retreat.

> This region is exquisite [she wrote to Liszt]. The Mediterranean is fretted into little bays, which gives it multiple views. Rounded hills, woods of cone pines, the open sea with its big waves . . . everything lit by a dazzling sun. This morning I got up at its rising. It surged out of the sea, the pines exuded their scent of resin, the birds began to sing.
>
> Emile is out of doors from dawn to dusk, using a pick, digging. . . . The trees will be magnificent when they have grown.[81]

The Olliviers' new purchase strained their modest resources, Liszt's help notwithstanding, so they now looked to Marie d'Agoult for assistance.[82] A few days before their wedding, the countess had assured Blandine that she could expect a payment of 40,000 francs on her dowry, but Marie now reneged on

---

the case against Pierre Antoine Berryer, one of the top legal brains of the day. De Guerry walked out of court with 500,000 francs, although her "dowry" to the convent had actually been in excess of one million francs.

Ollivier also began to build up an enviable reputation as an orator. During his first big speech in the French legislature, he held the house spellbound. Afterwards a Napoleonist remarked: "If only he would pocket his opinions and come over to our side!" Thereafter, Ollivier was one of the few politicians heard by the assembly in respectful silence. Blandine gave Liszt a full account of the speech, and of the dramatic impression it created, in a letter dated February 21, 1858 (OCLF, pp. 206–09). It was these triumphs, in the early years of his marriage to Blandine, that laid the foundations of Ollivier's personal prestige, which eventually carried him to the office of prime minister of France.

80. BN NAF 16440, ff. 1–3.

81. OCLF, pp. 255–56.

82. Emile paid 19,000 francs for La Moutte, all the money that he possessed at the time.

this promise. Ollivier anxiously reminded her of her undertaking and was shocked when she came back with the excuse that the legal formalities under which her fortune was administered made it impossible to transfer money without the consent of her estranged husband, Count Charles d'Agoult, and that such consent would be impossible to obtain. Ollivier knew this to be untrue, since he himself had carefully examined this "obstacle" and had found it to have no validity in law. To Emile's protest Blandine added her own. "I think it is my duty to make a last effort with you to arrange this business," she wrote. After reminding her mother that Emile had married her before he knew whether or not her parents would give her "a centime," she said that it was intolerable for him now to be treated as a man without honour. (Another of Madame d'Agoult's delaying tactics had been to agree to hand over the dowry only on condition that 5,000 francs of it be spent in creating an elaborate legal framework to secure the money against possible exploitation by Emile.) Blandine ended by saying: "Do not impose on me the misfortune of having to decide between my mother and my husband." In the end Madame d'Agoult paid up; but it caused Blandine, who found herself trapped once more in the middle of a family quarrel, many months of needless frustration. Relations between Marie and the Olliviers, in fact, were irreparably damaged because of the quarrel.[83]

---

83. Démosthène Ollivier, Emile's lawyer-father, had also entered the fray. In a letter to Liszt (dated April 21, 1859) he confirmed that Marie d'Agoult had given him a verbal undertaking, a year and a half earlier, to pay 40,000 francs within six months of the marriage. He denounced Marie's procrastinations and said that she was "taking pleasure in playing with everything which is most respectable . . . in this world, even her role as a mother. . . . I hope to persuade Emile to bring a suit against her—whatever image that may create before the court." (These letters from Marie, Emile, Blandine, and Démosthène are in the private possession of Roch Serra in St.-Germain-en-Laye and have not so far been published.) In his reply to Démosthène (dated May 5, 1859) Liszt expressed regret that he was unable to break the deadlock, and he added: "Since Madame d'Agoult always thought it proper never to contribute in any way towards either the upkeep or the education of our three children, I in turn always thought it proper to consider them my children, and more than once she obliged me to tell her so; I assured her that it would never be me who would be the one to remind her that she is their mother." (This letter is in the private possession of Elyse Mach and also remains unpublished.) In fairness to Madame d'Agoult we should point out that in 1857 she had suffered some material losses of her own, the worst of which had been the demolition of La Maison Rose by the Paris authorities, who wanted to clear a path for a new boulevard. She went to live in an apartment on the rue de l'Impératrice, but this temporary upheaval hardly explains her recalcitrance over the question of Blandine's dowry, which she seemed to regard not as a matter affecting her daughter's future security but rather as if it were some unpaid bill presented by the butcher, the baker, or the candlestick-maker—there to be disputed. We are probably correct in assuming that Ollivier's unexpected display of independence from her was responsible for her difficult attitude.

If further proof were required of the low relations between Marie d'Agoult and the Olliviers at the time of the marriage, it is to be found in the unpublished fragments of Ollivier's journal for 1857. In the entry for October 28, only six days after the wedding, Ollivier tells us that the negotiations with Marie on the question of the dowry were deadlocked, and he accuses her of deception and deceit. Apparently Démosthène went round to her hotel in Florence and left with the promise of a legal document. When he returned a few days later in order to pick it up, Marie "began to be evasive, and had the door barred against him." When the document was finally handed over, it was found

x

And what of Liszt's remaining child, Daniel? If he figures less frequently in the literature than his two sisters, that is because Liszt and Marie d'Agoult showed less inclination to dispute with one another about his upbringing. Indeed, Marie d'Agoult left Liszt to direct the education of their son as best he might. Daniel's story is worth telling, nevertheless, and we can add some worthwhile new facts to those already known.

In 1847, not long after Blandine and Cosima had been transferred to the school of Mademoiselle Bernard, Daniel acquired a private tutor, Monsieur Harlez. Harlez, a Latinist of exceptional merit, liked to ground his young charges in the classics. He awakened a love of Roman history in Daniel and gave the eight-year-old boy his first lessons in Latin and Greek. Since Daniel continued to live with Anna Liszt, he was frequently taken round to Mademoiselle Bernard's to see his sisters. His boyish clowning made them laugh, and they dubbed him "Choca," a nickname he constantly used in his letters to them.[84]

After the arrival in Paris of Madame Patersi in the late autumn of 1850, everything changed. Many curbs were placed on the girls' freedom, as we have seen, and Daniel saw less of his sisters. In the autumn of 1850 he was enrolled in the Lycée Bonaparte. At first, he pined for his family and fell behind with his studies. He received a severe reprimand from his father, who told him that he must work harder if he was ever to achieve anything in life and become worthy of the name Liszt. These words had a salutary effect on the boy, who became obsessed with the goal of attracting his father's pride. But Liszt's irritation at his son's initial lack of scholarly aptitude was hardly abated by the series of classroom confessions that Daniel was obliged to send to Weimar. In one such admission of guilt the eleven-year-old shamefacedly told his father: "Once I was punished for eating in class, another time for talking, another time for throwing pellets." The young miscreant then went on to admit to grand forgery: "I deceived the class teacher unworthily. The assistant head of the boarding-school had noted on my homework 'not done,' and I substituted 'done.' Afterwards they proved the full extent of my misdemeanor."[85] In letter

---

to contain things that were invalid. "Blandine, for her part, tells me about innumerable little dirty tricks about money [Marie] has played on her." (These unpublished journal entries are today preserved in the archives of La Moutte, Ollivier's former home, and were communicated by Mme Troisier de Diaz.)

84. Daniel's nickname was a contraction of *choco* late and *ca* fé, a mixture of drinks that became modish in the Paris of the late 1840s. The two girls thought it an ideal tag for Daniel, partly because he liked the drink, and partly because it symbolized the contrary elements in his character.

85. BA, unpublished letter dated Sunday, December 8, 1850.

after letter Daniel assured his father that he would try harder. That he was marked out by the staff as the son of a distinguished father, and that this was hard for him to bear, goes without saying. He was once approached by the curious headmaster and asked what had become of his father. "I replied that you were still in Weimar." Daniel, then, spent most of his early school years trying to live up to other people's high expectations of him. Perhaps the most revealing statement he ever made to Liszt, an unconscious disclosure of his psychological plight, was: "When I wear anything at all that has belonged to you, it seems that I am revolutionized."[86]

After only a year or two at the Lycée, Daniel's hard work bore fruit and he moved to the top of the class. In 1852 he won the school prize in history, and it was from this time that his brilliant academic career began.[87] In 1855 he was entered as a candidate in the national competition in Latin and walked off with the first prize. His classical studies came to their brilliant climax the following year when he graduated from the Lycée and won the national *prix d'honneur* and a special prize in rhetoric. The prize-giving ceremony was held on August 11, 1856, before the entire school and a large audience of distinguished guests.[88] Anna Liszt, Blandine, and Monsieur Harlez were present to

---

86. BA, unpublished letter dated Christmas Day, 1854.

87. "The news of your first prize in history made me extremely pleased and satisfied," wrote Liszt in 1852. "I am most grateful to you, my dear Daniel, for having responded like this to . . . my expectations of you. . . . Prepare yourself to win two prizes next year. You will be twice as pleased about it, and you will be well prepared to distinguish yourself in the career you choose." (HSD, p. 136)

88. A report of this ceremony, and of Daniel's success, was published in the *Journal des Débats* on August 11, 1856. Liszt had just left Weimar for Hungary, and Princess Carolyne wrote to him post-haste.

> Weimar,
> August 14, 1856
>
> Good news! Daniel has received one of the three honour awards newly created by the emperor, namely the one for Latin discourse in the arts section. We found it yesterday in the newspaper. . . . What he has won is impressive, since the honour award is even more important than a *first prize*. The dear child is still shilly-shallying, but I am convinced that in time he will settle down properly. (WA, Kasten 191)

Daniel's prize-winning essay has been preserved in the public education section of the Archives Nationales, AJ 726. He chose as his topic a free composition on a historical theme, the appeal of Pope Adrian to Charlemagne to help him repel the Lombard invasion of A.D. 722.

Until the long series of letters between Daniel and his father is published (it began in 1845, when Daniel was only six years old, and lasted until the young man's premature death in 1859) the world will remain in ignorance of the full extent of Liszt's interest in the education of his son. Typical of the correspondence is the essay Daniel sent to his father (February 28, 1850) on Alexander the Great. At that time Liszt was under immense strain, commuting back and forth between Weimar and Bad Eilsen, where Carolyne lay seriously ill. He was also burdened with problems in the Court Theatre. Nonetheless, he took the trouble to return Daniel's essay to him with detailed corrections (Pierpont Morgan Library, Heineman Collection, *M.S.* 134a). Two or three years later, when reports of Daniel's outstanding academic achievements had begun to reach Liszt, he sent his son a revealing letter about his own youth in which he expressed regret that he had not enjoyed the benefits of a more rigorous

see Daniel's triumph. It is from Blandine's eye-witness observations that the following account is derived. The prizes were handed out from the platform by Marshal Pélissier, on behalf of the emperor, Napoleon III. When he came to the rhetoric prize he called out in a stentorian voice: "The pupil Liszt!" Daniel jumped up from his seat, rushed precipitously to the dais, embraced Pélissier, received his prize, and rushed back to his place once again. He had hardly recovered his breath when it was announced that the emperor had offered a special prize to the most outstanding scholar in the school, and Daniel's name was called again. Amidst bravos and cheers Daniel returned to the platform to receive thirty volumes of Cicero, bound in leather and bearing the emperor's coat-of-arms. He was told that the books were too heavy to carry. "No, no," he cried, and to everyone's amusement he struggled back to his seat with all thirty volumes tucked under his arms. "Daniel did not seem to realize his good fortune," wrote Blandine. "All the students mobbed round him to congratulate him and tell him of the advantages of such a prize." (Those advantages were not to be despised. Daniel was spared the prospect of military conscription and received automatic entry into the Ecole Normale.) Later in the day a deputation arrived from the National Guard, beat the drums in his honour, and gave him an ovation. In the evening Daniel dined with the war minister, Marshal Vaillant; afterwards Monsieur Harlez took him to the Opéra-Comique.[89]

XI

Until the summer of 1854 Daniel could hardly claim to know his father at all. It was the boy's academic success that first told Liszt that he was blessed with a son of unusual distinction. As a reward for Daniel's efforts during the 1853–54 school year, Liszt invited him to the Altenburg for an extended holiday. For the first time Daniel was able to observe his father's career at first hand. He mingled with Liszt's students, attended the chamber concerts in the Altenburg, and saw Shakespeare's plays in the Weimar theatre. He also became well acquainted with Princess "Magne," whom he had met briefly in Paris a year earlier. (Their subsequent correspondence illuminates many of the obscure details of Liszt's family life in the Altenburg.) It was during this first visit to Weimar that a telling incident occurred. One afternoon Liszt took Daniel on

education. "More than once I have found myself regretting having neglected those subjects which, at a pinch, I might have been able to take after my father's death. But on the one hand I knew nobody who could advise me . . . and on the other, I was obliged to earn my living from the time I was twelve. . . . In your case, my dear Daniel, since you are placed in better circumstances, it is only right that you should learn more than your father was able to do at your age." (HSD, p. 137)
89. Unpublished letter from Blandine to Cosima, dated August 13, 1856 (BN NAF 25179).

a social visit, and the conversation turned on the delicate subject of the sons of men of genius. Unable to bear what he heard, the fifteen-year-old boy rushed out of the house in displeasure. An acquaintance stopped him and asked him what was the matter. "They began to go through the list of what the sons of such-and-such men of genius had become," replied Daniel angrily. "This one was nothing much, that one nothing at all, and so on. You can understand that I could not listen calmly to such an enumeration!"[90] The following year, 1855, Daniel again spent his summer holidays at the Altenburg. This time he met the young Tausig, with whom he became good friends. In late July his sisters turned up in Weimar, en route to Berlin. The happiness of that reunion was shattered, as we have seen, by Patersi's disclosure to Liszt of Madame d'Agoult's compromising correspondence with Blandine, a betrayal that Daniel called "despicable." Father and son exchanged some frank words about Patersi's action, an episode from which Daniel decided to profit. Thereafter his highly informative letters to his sisters contained pseudonyms, meant to protect the three of them in case his own communications, in turn, were intercepted.[91]

About Christmas 1856, a few days after he had received his baccalaureate from the Lycée, Daniel returned to the Altenburg and remained there for nearly four months—until April 1857. Liszt wanted to give his son uninterrupted leisure to consider his future career; he also wanted him to become more proficient in spoken German. We know from Daniel's correspondence that these months at the Altenburg were among the happiest of his life. "I miss Paris very little," he told Blandine. "Paris holds different memories for me than it does for you."[92] He had the run of his father's library (which did not contain a copy of Madame d'Agoult's *Esquisses morales,* so he had one smuggled onto the shelves); he read Schiller's *Wallenstein* and *Mary Stuart;* and he even began

---

90. S-WDL, p. 6.

91. As early as January 7, 1856, Daniel had written to Blandine instructing her to write to him in code. "If you have prohibited things to say, write to me ironically all the time, in case the letter should be read here. But so that I understand its equivocal nature, you will place beneath your signature 'Mioumi, *abracadabra,* which will mean that your letter has a cabalistic meaning of no concern to the masses." (BN NAF 25179) The diplomat in Daniel came out clearly in a letter to Cosima written from Weimar on January 9, 1857. What is the perplexed reader to make of the following?

> As for Mioumi, he is not in very good odour at the moment, but the game is far from lost. If he settles at the Campbells, as I advised him, Papa's relationship with him will become the same as before. Here we are, between Papa and Mimi, receiving all the blows they give each other, and our best policy is never to speak to Papa of Mimi, to Mimi of Papa. . . . (BN NAF 25179 9, 1/2)

"Mimi" and "Mioumi" are pseudonyms for Madame d'Agoult and Blandine respectively. The latter's gender has also been changed for good measure. The passage relates to the tussle going on between Blandine and her father over the all-important question of where in Paris she was going to live (see pp. 461–62, n.67).

92. NAF 25179 83/1. Unpublished letter from Daniel to Blandine, dated March 1857.

the serious study of harmony and counterpoint. He never missed an opportunity of seeing his father conduct opera in the Weimar theatre, and he mentions having seen Gluck's *Armide* and *Orpheus*. These halcyon days were crowned for Daniel when Liszt had a medal struck of him. All who saw it remarked on its likeness to the seventeen-year-old youth, and Daniel himself treasured it.[93] Daniel's friendship with Princess Marie also ripened during this period. The two young people saw one another almost daily. She nicknamed him "Birch Tree" because his slender frame reminded her of the birch trees around the Altenburg, so "Birch Tree" was how he invariably signed his letters to her.[94] Liszt, for his part, was pleased with Daniel's serious-minded approach to life, and he told Anna Liszt: "Daniel is marvellously well and kisses your hands. He is reading, skating, goes to shows, studies harmony, and behaves like a very good son with whom I am pleased."[95] Liszt and Daniel had many discussions about the choice of suitable profession—higher classical studies at a German university, jurisprudence, even the priesthood.[96] With Daniel's concurrence, Liszt finally arranged to send his son to Vienna to study law under the

---

93. The medal, which shows Daniel in left profile, was struck by the artist Adolf von Dondorff, a young pupil of Ernst Rietschel. It is reproduced in BVL, p. 151. Adelheid von Schorn recalled the first time that she set eyes on Daniel, in early January 1857, at a soirée in the Altenburg in honour of the singer Marie Seebach. She noticed with astonishment a tall, thin young man with long, blond hair—"He appeared to me like a Liszt rejuvenated"—and the mystery was resolved only when Princess Marie introduced him to Fräulein von Schorn as "Daniel, Liszt's son." (SZM, pp. 87–88) 94. See the run of Daniel's letters to "Magnolette" published in BLE, pp. 182–225. 95. BN NAF 25179. Unpublished letter dated February 13, 1857.

Daniel's entire situation at the Altenburg is set out in an unpublished letter to Cosima (BN NAF 25179) dated January 9, 1857. He wrote:

My dear Stork:
     You know, or you should know, that I am staying in Weimar for an indefinite time.
     . . . A completely new horizon has opened for me. I thought that Papa was a sort of meteor destined to pass before me without being able to be studied, understood, approached. And now this same Papa offers me a stay of three months or more with him.

Daniel goes on to describe his new-found interest in Romantic music in general and his father's music in particular. "I am beginning to get acquainted with Romantic music. A long initiation is required, but once initiated one understands something. It would be worth all the trouble if there were no other works than *Ce qu'on entend sur la montagne* and the Second Piano Concerto, which I think I can say I understand and which made a great impact on me yesterday." Then, in a candid comment about his father, Daniel continues: "The child from Raiding, Mimi's lover, the one who sang: 'What a pleasure to be Choco the Clown' and who wanted to become a priest, has portrayed himself perfectly in this piece [the Second Piano Concerto]." The reference to "Mimi's lover" is, of course, to Liszt's affair with Marie d'Agoult, a topic with which the children were constantly preoccupied. 96. A few weeks after Daniel's death Liszt disclosed to Antal Augusz that his son had once thought of taking holy orders (CLBA, pp. 87–88). In several of his letters Daniel evinced a natural leaning towards theology and Catholic dogma. His mystical leanings, so reminiscent of his father's, and at a somewhat similar age, led him to the discovery of Pascal's *Pensées,* which became his inseparable companion. Incidentally, in the Wagner Archives, Bayreuth, there exists a series of five "religious analyses" (including one called "On the Mystery of the Incarnation") which Daniel wrote for Monsieur Harlez while he was still a boy (BA, uncatalogued).

benevolent protection of Eduard Liszt, his "uncle-cousin" who was now the assistant imperial public prosecutor to the Habsburgs.

Daniel's future had never looked brighter, yet he already stood on the threshold of death. As the train pulled away from Weimar's tiny railway station, he gazed on the receding city of Goethe and Schiller for the last time.

The Death of Daniel Liszt

Were I to live for a thousand years, the work I
have in mind would still not be finished.
DANIEL LISZT[1]

By the middle of May 1857 Daniel was installed in Vienna.[2] For the first two or three days he stayed in a small hotel while Eduard Liszt helped him to find permanent accommodation. Soon he was the proud occupant of a spacious, quiet room in the Schottenhof, which, in his own words, was large enough for him to pace up and down, and peaceful enough for him to work without interruption.[3] There he installed himself with his law books, musical scores, and an old upright piano on which he intended to work during the summer. Since the university courses did not begin until October, Daniel spent a lot of time simply enjoying the city—attending plays and concerts, visiting museums and, of course, that great pleasure ground the Prater. He saw all the buildings associated with his father's early career, including the Redoutensaal and the Marienkirche; and he walked down the Krugerstrasse, where the Liszts had lived during the period of the lessons with Czerny. Not long after Daniel arrived in Vienna, in fact, Czerny died. Daniel was so moved by this event that he decided to represent his father and followed the funeral cortège to the Vienna cemetery. At the graveside he offered his own few words of silent tribute to his father's great teacher.[4]

Vienna had not changed much since Liszt's triumphant re-appearances there

---

1. Unpublished letter to his sister Blandine, dated January 18, 1859 (BN NAF. 25179 87/1).
2. Daniel's first letter to his father after his departure from Weimar is dated Vienna, May 23, 1857 (BA).
3. BA, letter dated June 30, 1857. Daniel never lived with Uncle Eduard, as some sources wrongly maintain. From the start, he pursued a fairly independent life in Vienna.
4. S-WDL, p. 9.

during the 1840s. There were many well-to-do families who retained a lively remembrance of the great virtuoso—the Schwarzenhübers, the Meyerhofers, the Löwys. In time they opened their doors to Daniel, who secretly enjoyed his minor celebrity. These social temptations could not deflect him from his studies, however. He read law incessantly, he began his own translation of the *Iliad,* and he even studied Hungarian for an hour each day in fulfilment of a promise that he had earlier made to his father.[5] He also spent twenty florins a month on private lessons in canon law, an expense that he could ill afford. His father gave him an allowance sufficient for his needs, but the luxury of these lessons left him short of money. He got into debt, and Liszt was obliged to come to his rescue. The frugal life-style that Daniel subsequently imposed on himself in Vienna did nothing to strengthen his delicate health. Nor did the "forced marches" (as he called them) that he made into the surrounding countryside whenever he wanted to escape from his work. For much of the year, in fact, the Vienna climate was far too raw for his weak lungs. Daniel was evidently aware that a large Liszt clan lived in Vienna and its environs, and he was naturally curious about his relatives. Not long after his arrival in the city he sought out Anton Liszt, the clock-maker. He decided not to tell his father about this visit, from which he seems to have derived some merriment. "The idea that he was my father's uncle amused me for a whole evening."[6]

One of his greatest joys was to be reunited with Tausig and Winterberger, both of whom arrived in Vienna during the period 1857–58. A highlight came in March 1858 when Liszt himself travelled to Vienna in order to conduct performances of his "Gran" Mass. Daniel and Tausig were at the railway station to meet him and transport him back to his hotel. Shortly afterwards the singers arrived from Pest, and Liszt arranged a banquet for them which, in Daniel's words, "must have cost a fortune." For the three weeks that Liszt stayed in Vienna, Daniel moved in with Tausig at the Empress Elisabeth Hotel, so that the two young men could rush over at short notice to be with Liszt whenever his rehearsal schedule allowed. Liszt, in turn, sometimes visited them in the company of "Uncle Eduard." Daniel wrote:

> [My father] often came up to see Tausig and me (for we were sharing a room), and then he was so gentle and affectionate that I am moved just thinking about it. One day he still had half an hour

---

5. BA, letter dated April 1858. Daniel appears to have found Hungarian difficult. He worked mainly from Rémélé's grammar and told his father: "I can say 'Papa,' 'Mama,' 'soul,' 'peach,' 'table,' etc., which gives me hope for later." He practiced spoken Hungarian with one of his father's Vienna colleagues, Tilsch.

6. BLE, p. 185. Liszt himself had had little to do with his father's kith and kin (with the exception of Eduard) ever since he had left Hungary as a child. See Volume One, p. 35, n. 19.

to spare before going out into society. Only I, Tausig, and my uncle were there. He told us to sit down. "Jetzt plaudern wir ein wenig. Ich bin so müde."[7] His behaviour was the same with the orchestra. He was very agreeable. It was beautiful watching him conduct his work. You know what an inspired expression he has when he conducts. So I will spare you all pathos. He is still as handsome as ever. His straight shoulders and his elegant figure, which is recognized from one end of the town to the other, have stayed the same. Oh! I become hard on Mimi[8] when I think of what abnegation and beauty lies in him. That he had a period of intoxication, what does that prove against him? Nothing, absolutely nothing.[9]

Occasionally there were other welcome visitors from Weimar. In December 1858, for instance, Alexander Ritter turned up and spent a whole day chatting about Liszt. A few days later Bernhard Cossmann arrived in the city and brought news of the *Barber of Bagdad* fiasco, the details of which we shall shortly consider. Such links were important to Daniel, who longed to feel part of the Weimar circle. When he learned that Hans von Bülow was to conduct a concert of Liszt's works in Prague, he wrote to the Altenburg and told his father that he wanted desperately to make the journey but lacked the funds. Princess Carolyne replied by return post with the money. Daniel rushed off to Prague and attended three rehearsals and the concert, which contained the *Ce qu'on entend sur la montagne, Mazeppa,* and *Festklänge.* It was the first time that Daniel had seen Bülow conduct, and he was impressed with the swiftness with which the latter imposed his authority on an indifferent orchestra. Afterwards he wrote to his father: "Bülow confirmed once again Philippe's witticism: 'Better a lion at the head of fifty stags than a stag at the head of fifty lions.' "[10]

In August 1859 Daniel arrived in Berlin in order to spend his summer holidays with Cosima and Hans. He came via Dresden, where he had begun to feel vaguely unwell. When Cosima saw him, she was struck by the change in his appearance. He looked undernourished, and he complained of dizziness. Cosima made it her task to spoil him with all the home comforts that he lacked in Vienna. By the autumn, despite her ministrations, Daniel lay seriously ill and was unable to return to his university. One morning he suffered a violent expectoration of blood, and Dr. Bücking, the family physician, was summoned.[11] In fact, the young man was already doomed; he had brought the seeds

7. "Now let us chat for a bit. I am so tired."
8. Madame d'Agoult. See p. 471, n.91, and p. 472, n.95.
9. Hitherto unpublished letter to Blandine, dated April 29, 1858 (BN NAF 25179).
10. BA, letter dated April 1, 1859.
11. This account of Daniel's last days, of his death, and of his funeral is based partly on the obituary notice written by Princess Carolyne and intended by her for private circulation (S-WDL, pp. 13–16)

of his fatal sickness from Vienna and had only a few more weeks to live. In November Hans was obliged to move out of the apartment on Anhalterstrasse so that he could practice without disturbing the patient, whose delicate lungs had already succumbed to galloping consumption. Since Daniel was unable to sleep at night, Cosima regularly sat up with him, either to read to him or simply to hold his hand. The strain gradually told, and she began to wear herself out. Soon news of Daniel's deteriorating condition so alarmed Liszt that he travelled to Berlin, arriving on December 11 at ten o'clock in the evening. He put up at the Brandenburg Hotel. At eight-thirty the following morning he went round to see Daniel for himself. He was let in by the chambermaid; Cosima had sat up until 6:00 a.m. and had retired to her bedroom in order to snatch a few moments' rest. After a few minutes Daniel was pushed into the living-room on a sofa. The first impression he made on Liszt was dreadful, although the young man was happy to see his father. Hans and Cosima came into the room, and the three of them had a quiet breakfast next to Daniel. He complained that he had no appetite, so they served him some milk to keep up his strength. His breathing was laboured and his speech broken. Despite his physical distress Daniel told his father that he intended to resume his law studies when he got better. At 10:00 a.m. Dr. Bücking arrived, conducted a medical examination, and prescribed a few mouthfuls of Tokay wine to revive him. Liszt then took Bücking aside and asked him for a prognosis, adding that he was prepared for the worst. Bücking could not give Liszt any firm assurances. At this point, Liszt made a conscious decision not to have the last rites imposed on his son for fear of alarming him—an action for which he was criticized by Princess Carolyne, but which he defended on the grounds that he did not wish to rob Daniel of hope. "It is dangerous to force [the last rites] on a nature so sensitive as Daniel's."[12] For the rest of the day Daniel lay in a darkened room. At 2:00 p.m. he was given a cup of broth, but he sank back into a fitful sleep. Later he was carried into his bedroom, which he was not to leave alive. About 11:00 p.m. Cosima accompanied Liszt back to his hotel and then returned to her vigil.

The next morning, Tuesday, December 13, Hans arrived at the hotel in tears to say that all hope was lost. For nearly twelve hours Liszt took turns with Cosima and Hans to sit by Daniel's side.

> His face was very pale [wrote Liszt], but not sunken. Right up to the moment when his coffin was closed, his features kept their gentle, harmonious expression. Cosima said that he looked like a Christ by Correggio—the colour of his beard and hair were slightly tinged

---

and partly on the extremely detailed letter written by Liszt on December 15, 1859 (LLB, vol. 4, pp. 500–07), two or three hours after the burial service.

12. LLB, vol. 4, p. 502.

with red. In one of his bouts of dozing, he distinctly pronounced these words: "I go to prepare your places!"[13]

At 10:00 p.m. Liszt withdrew and lay down on the bed in the adjoining music-room. Just over an hour later he spontaneously walked across to Daniel's room and observed Cosima kneeling by her brother's side. Several minutes slipped by; then Liszt said: "He is not breathing anymore." Cosima placed her hand on Daniel's heart. It was still. There had been no death-struggle; both Cosima and Liszt were amazed that anyone could pass away so peacefully. The next day Cosima washed Daniel's body herself and dressed it in a burial shroud. In his coffin she placed a portrait of his beloved Pascal, whose ideas had preoccupied his thoughts during the last weeks of his life.

The funeral took place on the morning of Thursday, December 15. A small party of mourners—Liszt, Cosima, Hans, and a group of pallbearers—followed the hearse to the Catholic cemetery, which lay beyond the Oranienburg Gate, a great distance from Anhalterstrasse. There they were joined by Frau von Bülow and her daughter, Isidora. Although it was cold, the sky was clear, and the cemetery was bathed in winter sunshine. The coffin was suspended over the open grave while three sacristans, dressed in white, swung their incense-lamps back and forth and the priest chanted prayers. At that moment Liszt looked upwards and perceived a flight of doves circling almost perpendicularly over the grave. Then the coffin was lowered into the ground, and Liszt and the others threw last shovelfuls of earth over Daniel's mortal remains.[14]

By early afternoon it was all over. The funeral party got back to Anhalterstrasse by 1:30 p.m. and began the sad task of writing letters to absent relatives. Cosima wrote to Blandine and Marie d'Agoult, while Liszt wrote to Carolyne and, the following day, to his mother.

December 16, 1859

Dearest Mother:

. . . Our dear son, Daniel, will no longer be the joy of our lives here below. He has ceased to breathe; his heart no longer beats. No more will we gaze upon him with weeping eyes! Do not let yourself be too overwhelmed by grief, dearest mother. You still have a son whose tenderness will try to replace the one we have both lost. . . .[15]

---

13. LLB, vol. 4, p. 503.
14. As this ceremony was unfolding in Berlin, a requiem mass was simultaneously celebrated for Daniel in the Catholic church in Weimar. This was arranged by Princess Carolyne, who had received a telegramme from Liszt on the morning after Daniel's death. She was ravaged by toothache and was unable to attend either ceremony (WA, Kasten 35, no. 64).
15. VFL, p. 103.

The Liszt family were shattered by Daniel's death, and for years their letters to one another were haunted by his memory. Cosima, who had borne the brunt of his final illness, came close to suffering a nervous breakdown, and for the rest of her life she carried an inexplicable sense of guilt about the tragedy.[16] Within four weeks of Daniel's passing she became pregnant, after two and a half years of marriage to Hans. She gave birth to a daughter on October 12, 1860, and named her Daniela, after her dead brother.

As for Liszt, he sublimated his grief in the only way that he could. The first of his Three Funeral Odes, for orchestra and male voices, was directly inspired by these mournful events. It bears the title *Les Morts,* after a poem by Lammenais which Liszt distributes through the score.[17] At the end of the manuscript Liszt expressed the wish that the ode be performed at his own funeral, but this was not done.

Not long after Daniel was interred, a large white cross of stone was erected over the tomb, which bears the simple inscription:

DANIEL LISZT

BORN IN ROME, MAY 9, 1839

DIED IN BERLIN, DECEMBER 13, 1859

---

16. See, for example, her diary-entry for September 23, 1870: "I blame myself now for not having saved him by going with him to Cairo; also I fear that I did not consult the right doctor when he was lying ill in my house. All this occupies my mind, and now chance will have it that at the first appearance of a ghost in Hoffmann's tale [*Das Majorat,* which was at that moment being read aloud to her by Richard Wagner, her soon-to-be husband] the name *Daniel* should twice be called out. As R. spoke the name in that meaningful, penetrating tone so peculiar to him, I shivered—not in fear, but in unutterable pain." (WT, vol. 1, p. 274)

17. "They too have lived on this earth; they have passed down the river of time; their voices were heard on its banks, and then were heard no more. Where are they now? Who shall tell? But blessed are they who die in the Lord." To which Liszt has added, as a benediction, part of the well-known verse from Revelation (14:13): "Tunc audivi vocem e caelo dicentem mihi, Scribe, Beati ab hoc tempore mortui ii, qui Domini causa moriuntur" ("And I heard a voice from heaven saying unto me, Write, Blessed are the dead which die in the Lord from henceforth.") Liszt actually misquotes this Latin text, an indication that he jotted it down from memory. (Consult his score: Collected Edition, part 1, vol. 12.) Incidentally, it was never Liszt's intention to have Lamennais' words declaimed during the performance; their original purpose was simply to give some idea of his musical thoughts. The practice of intoning the text has arisen in modern times, and it is very effective.

Of Triumph and Tragedy,
1857–1859

Art is a heaven on earth, to which one never appeals in vain when faced with the oppressions of this world.

FRANZ LISZT[1]

I

We must now return to the year 1857 in order to pick up the threads of our main narrative. Liszt had barely got back from his Aachen water-cure when he was caught up once more in the hurly-burly of musical life in Weimar. The autumn was fast approaching, and the city was beginning to take on a festive appearance. It was the one hundredth anniversary of the birth of Carl August, the man who had brought Goethe and Schiller to Weimar and first turned the small town into a centre of artistic activity. Carl Alexander wanted to honour the memory of his illustrious grandfather with due pomp and ceremony. Historic buildings were refurbished, new monuments were commissioned, concerts and plays were put into rehearsal; Goethe's house, which had remained shuttered since the poet's death in 1832, was opened to the public, furnished exactly as it was twenty-five years earlier. Weimar, which had been the home of many festivals in the past, would see nothing to compare with the Goethe-Schiller celebrations of 1857. Liszt was heavily involved in them from the start.

The festivities began at six o'clock on the morning of September 3, Carl August's birthday, with a service in the royal vault. Pastor Dittenberger offered prayers, and the tomb of the old grand duke was decked with flowers. At nine o'clock a thanksgiving service was held in the Herder Church. Afterwards a festival procession assembled in the square outside and wended its way to the Fürstenplatz, where Carl Alexander laid the foundation-stone for a statue to

---

1. From an entry in Varnhagen von Ense's autograph book, dated Weimar, May 1858.

his grandfather. Dr. von Watzdorf offered a eulogy to Carl August,[2] and the ceremony concluded with a performance of the "Weimars Volkslied," a new national anthem especially composed for the house of Sachsen-Weimar by Liszt.[3] An evening of entertainment in the Court Theatre brought the first day's festivities to an end. Fragments from Goethe's *Paleophron und Neoterpe* and from Schiller's *Don Carlos* were enacted, together with a festival play by Dingelstedt, *Der Erntekranz,* with the dramatist himself in attendance.

September 4 was the highlight of the festival. At half-past one in the afternoon, as a preliminary to the main event, a statue was unveiled to the poet Wieland, followed by another performance of the "Weimars Volkslied." Then came the occasion for which everyone had been waiting. In the square outside the theatre, a platform had been constructed in front of the draped statues of Goethe and Schiller. A vast throng jammed the concourse in order to see Carl Alexander and the royal family take their places on the podium. (Among the many guests who witnessed the ceremonials were descendants of Goethe, Schiller, Wieland, and Herder. Such a gathering of the progeny of Weimar's greatest sons had never before been assembled.) At a pre-arranged signal, Carl Alexander advanced towards the statues and cut the cords holding the veil, which fell back to reveal the shining bronze figures of Germany's greatest poets. The crowd burst into spontaneous cheers. "I never heard the like of it again," wrote Adelheid von Schorn, an eye-witness to this memorable day. The grand duke then beckoned to Ernst Rietschel, the creator of the monument, who mounted the platform and received the royal embrace.[4] That night fragments of Goethe and Schiller were again performed in the theatre—Act Two of *Tasso,* Act Three of *Egmont,* and Act Four of *Faust.*

A blight was cast over this otherwise happy day for Liszt, however. Henriette von Schorn (the mother of Adelheid, and a former lady-in-waiting to Maria

---

2. The eulogy is reprinted in full in SNW, vol. 2, pp. 68–69.

3. Carl Alexander had commissioned this anthem in July 1857. His request was born of an old complaint that every time the house of Sachsen-Weimar mounted a ceremonial, it had to fall back on the eternal "God Save the Queen." The anthem, wrote Carl Alexander, "should be somewhere between a prayer and a folk-song, more serious than merry, not too long and not too short—it should be perfection. You alone can create it." (LBLCA, pp. 58–59) The words were written by Peter Cornelius, and the first stanza runs:

Möge Segen dir entsprossen	May blessings ascend to you
Aus vereinten Sarkophagen,	From the gathered sarcophagi
Wo unsterbliche Genossen	Where immortal companions
Diadem und Lorbeer tragen	Wear diadem and laurel;
Aus geweihter Gräber Spalten	From the crevices of consecrated tombs
Brechen Lebensblumen aus:	Flowers of life break forth:
Möge Gott dich stets erhalten,	May God protect you forever,
Weimars edles Fürstenhaus!	Weimar's noble princely house!

4. SNW, vol. 2, p. 71. A few days later Rietschel was admitted to the degree of doctor of philosophy, *honoris causa,* at Jena University.

Pawlowna) had invited a number of her aristocratic friends, including Princess Carolyne and Marie, to view the unveiling ceremony from a house whose windows overlooked the square. Carolyne, who had been confined to her sickroom in the Altenburg for months, was barely well enough to attend but made the effort for Liszt's sake. The moment she entered the room all the ladies of the court got up and left. This was a pointed snub of the sort that Carolyne was by now well used to receiving, yet it distressed her hostess. Liszt came to the rescue by advancing towards Henriette and kissing her hand in silent acknowledgement of her support and friendship. He then led Carolyne and Marie towards prominent seats in the square outside, where they viewed the ceremony in full glare of the court officials positioned there.[5]

The following day, September 5, Liszt directed a large concert including a number of his works that possessed Goethe or Schiller connections. He called it a "dogmatic display of *Zukunftsmusik.*"[6] This occasion is famous in the annals of Liszt scholarship, since it saw the first complete performance of the *Faust* Symphony, with its newly composed ending, a setting for male voices of the Chorus Mysticus. The orchestra was doubled in size for the occasion by players recruited from Berlin, Leipzig, Meiningen, and Sondershausen.[7] In view of the fact that Liszt was so often disappointed with first performances of his own works, it is worth recording that he pronounced himself well pleased with this one.

The Goethe-Schiller festivities were concluded on Sunday, September 6, with a performance of *Tannhäuser* conducted by Liszt. Two days later Carl Alexander issued a proclamation in the columns of the *Weimarische Zeitung,* in which he extended his thanks to all who had participated in the festival.[8]

I I

One of the things that gave Liszt pleasure about the time of the Goethe-Schiller festival was to appoint Leopold Damrosch to the violin section of the Weimar orchestra. Damrosch had pursued a medical career out of respect for the wishes of his family; but after graduating in medicine from Berlin University in 1854, he had returned to his first love, the violin, and within three years had launched himself on a concert career. It was in Weimar that Damrosch married Helene

5. SZM, pp. 92–93.
6. LLB, vol. 3, p. 97.
7. The players included Ferdinand David, Friedrich Grützmacher, Hermann, and Röntgen from Leipzig, Kapellmeister Joseph Bott from Kassel, and the Müller String Quartet from Meiningen. There was also a male chorus of one hundred voices (LLB, vol. 3, p. 97). Despite a personal plea from Liszt, Joachim declined to attend. See his letter of refusal, pp. 346–47.
8. *Weimarische Zeitung,* September 8, 1857.

WEIMAR.

Sonnabend den 5. September 1857.

Großes

Vokal- und Instrumental-Conzert

(mit verstärktem Chor und Orchester)

im

Grossherzoglichen Hof-Theater

unter Leitung des Herrn Kapellmeister

Dr. F. LISZT.

Erster Theil.

1) „An die Künstler". Gedicht von Schiller. Männer=Chor, Solis und Orchester.
   Solis: Herr Caspari, Knopp, Milde und Roth.
2) „Die Ideale". Symphonische Dichtung nach Schiller.
3) Gruppe aus dem Tartarus. (Schiller.) Männer=Chor.
4) „Ueber allen Gipfeln ist Ruh". (Goethe.)
   Solo=Quartett, vorgetragen von den Herren Caspari, Knopp, Milde
   und Roth.
5) „Schwager Kronos". (Goethe.) Männer=Chor.

Zweiter Theil.

6) Eine Faust=Symphonie in drei Charakter=Bildern:
   1. Faust,
   2. Gretchen,
   3. Mephistopheles,
   und den Schluß Chorus mysticus des Faust zweiter Theil.
7) „Weimars Volkslied" für Männer=Chor.

Sämmtliche Compositionen, mit Ausnahme der Nummern 3 und 5, von J. Schubert
als Lieder componirt, und für Orchester und Männer=Chor eingerichtet von Carl Stör,
sind vom Herrn Kapellmeister Dr. F. Liszt.

Textbücher sind an der Kasse für 2½ Sgr. zu haben.

Preise der Plätze:

Fremden-Loge	1 Thlr. — Sgr.	Parterre-Loge	— Thlr. 15 Sgr.
Balkon	— , 20 ,	Parterre	— , 10 ,
Sperrsitze	— , 20 ,	Gallerie-Loge	— , 7½ ,
Parket	— , 15 ,	Gallerie	— , 5 ,

Anfang um 7 Uhr.   **Ende halb 10 Uhr.**

Das Theater wird um 6 Uhr geöffnet.

Druck der Hof-Buchdruckerei.

Liszt conducts the first complete performance of the Faust Symphony
during the Carl August centennial concert, September 5, 1857.

von Heimburg, who sang Ortrud in the Weimar production of *Lohengrin*.[9] It is an indication of the zeal with which Damrosch embraced the ideals of the New German School that he christened their first son Richard, after Wagner (the child died in infancy), and their second Franz, after Liszt.[10]

Another appointment made at this time brought Liszt far less satisfaction. It was entirely at his instigation that Franz Dingelstedt attended the Goethe-Schiller festival for the production of his play *Der Erntekranz*. Dingelstedt had been the theatre intendant at the Munich Court Theatre since 1850, and Liszt admired his work. For months Liszt had tried to persuade Carl Alexander to entice Dingelstedt away from Munich and offer him the still vacant position of theatre intendant at Weimar.[11] *Der Erntekranz* pleased Carl Alexander so much that he acceded to Liszt's request. Dingelstedt began his duties on October 1, 1857, at an annual salary of 1,400 thalers and with the elevated title of "general intendant." Almost at once a series of disputes arose between him and Liszt about the use to which the limited resources of the theatre should be put. There had scarcely been a time in the recent history of the Weimar theatre when opera and drama had not clashed. These two art-forms, with their essentially different requirements, had always vied with one another for the same stage. Liszt's close personal relationship with Ziegesar and then with Beaulieu-Marconnay had ensured that compromises would always be found. But these men were dilettantes; they ran the theatre for a hobby. Dingelstedt was a professional whose perfectly legitimate ambition was to mould the Weimar theatre to his will and restore it to national prominence. Typical was the little disagreement about how best to celebrate Maria Pawlowna's birthday on February 16. Liszt proposed a production of Wagner's *Rienzi,* whose third act, he observed ironically, might have to be shortened, since "the Weimar theatre, like the Weimar Court, is little adapted to revolutions."[12] The idea was rejected by

---

9. According to Walter Damrosch (the youngest son), his parents became engaged in the home of the Weimar painter Friedrich Preller (DMML, p. 4).

10. After the family moved to America in 1871, Franz became known as "Frank." The Damrosch family formed one of the most important artistic dynasties of the New World, dominating the musical life of New York for over half a century. Although it goes well beyond the confines of the present volume, it is worth observing that Leopold Damrosch did pioneering work in behalf of the New German School in America, giving the first performances there of a number of works by Liszt, Raff, and others. Only five years after he had settled in the States, Liszt acknowledged his debt to Damrosch: "How shall I thank you for the edifying goodwill which you manifest towards my compositions? Your intelligent, enthusiastic conducting of my scores prevents anyone noticing the defects of the composition. A hearty greeting to your wife, and with warmest esteem, Ever yours, F. Liszt." (LLB, vol. 2, p. 239)

11. Dingelstedt paid a preliminary visit to Weimar in April 1857, in order to hold some discussions with Liszt, who sent a message to the grand duke: "Dingelstedt has just arrived. I chatted with him for quite a long time yesterday evening. It seems to me that there would be an advantage in harnessing him to the chariot of Thespis for the [Goethe-Schiller] festivities on September 3." (LBLCA, pp. 57–58)

12. BWL, vol. 2, p. 181; KWL, vol. 2, p. 180.

Dingelstedt on grounds of expense, and he mounted instead an inconsequential play by Gustav Schmidt, *Weibertreue, oder Kaiser Konrad von Weinsburg.* [13] It is a fact that between January and June 1858 Liszt conducted only one opera and two concerts in the Court Theatre. Nothing else could be expected from a colleague such as Dingelstedt, who once told Liszt: "The theatre is a necessary evil; the concert is a superfluous one." [14] Thus were the seeds of crisis sown.

Within weeks of arriving in Weimar, Dingelstedt had joined the Neu-Weimar-Verein and had begun to stir up controversy within the organization. Weissheimer describes an occasion when the Verein met in its usual quarters in the Town Hall, and Liszt and Dingelstedt got into a violent argument. In his frustration Liszt consumed too much alcohol and left the building "tipsy." It was a small but telltale symptom of his inability to dominate the strong personality of the new general intendant, although this particular incident ended in comedy. Weissheimer tramped with Liszt through the streets of Weimar half the night until he had been revived by the fresh air. The pair got to the Altenburg at least twice, but each time Liszt insisted that it was now *his* turn to accompany Weissheimer home. They passed Goethe's house several times on their nocturnal ramble, and on the last circuit Liszt stopped and asked: "What would the old man say if he could see us now?" " 'Once more you approach, you tottering shapes,' " laughed Weissheimer. [15] With that they

---

13. Liszt kept insisting on *Rienzi,* however. Thanks entirely to his efforts, the first performance in Weimar was mounted on December 26, 1860. Liszt conducted the preliminary rehearsals, but he handed over the baton to Carl Stör for the performance itself.

14. LLB, vol. 2, p. 251. Liszt closed the year 1857 with a performance of *Fidelio* on December 30. The symbolic gesture is subtle, but it is there: *Fidelio* is, above all, about the triumph of individual freedom over tyrannical authority. Liszt's relations with Dingelstedt went back at least seven years and were at first cordial. In his earliest letters to the dramatist he could pen such phrases as "You are the most delightful of friends, dear Dingelstedt" (LLB, vol. 8, p. 63) and "Come straight to the Altenburg, where you will be welcomed with open arms" (LLB, vol. 8, p. 68). It was Liszt who arranged to have Dingelstedt's prologue in praise of Goethe read aloud before the first performance of *Lohengrin,* on August 28, 1850; who introduced him at that time to Carl Alexander; and who thereafter worked ceaselessly to involve him in the literary life of Weimar. Whatever gratitude Dingelstedt may have felt towards Liszt, he did not allow it to compromise him in the carrying out of his duties—as he perceived them to be. Liszt was not the first administrator to find himself in the quixotic position of having helped to appoint his own executioner.

15. WEW, pp. 52–53. Weissheimer's witty response comes from the opening of Goethe's *Faust* (Part One). Liszt's dependency on alcohol has already been remarked in Volume One (pp. 428-29). During the Weimar years alcohol remained a constant adjunct to his hectic lifestyle, and was a routine expression of conviviality. Edmund Singer recollected one occasion in the mid 1850s when Liszt and his companions were playing whist in the Erbprinz Hotel. Liszt suddenly got the idea that Bavarian beer and Russian schnapps would go well together. He mixed this poisonous brew in a glass and offered it to his colleagues. Only Lassen, Stör, and Liszt himself had the courage to sample the fiery beverage. "The consequences," wrote Singer, "were frightful." At midnight the inebriated trio were taken to their respective homes "with great difficulty." Stör, who was the most powerfully affected by the fatal mixture, could not get beyond the steps outside his apartment, and lay there all night. The next morning, word reached Singer that Liszt, Lassen and Stör were all ill, and that he would have to conduct a previously scheduled rehearsal of *Tannhäuser* himself (SAMK, p. 389).

retraced their steps, scrambled through the bushes skirting the Altenburg, embraced one another at the front door, and, much to Weissheimer's relief, finally took their leave.

October 22, Liszt's forty-sixth birthday, was a day of mixed emotions. The failure of the B-minor Sonata in Berlin and of *Mazeppa* in Leipzig, the criticism of his direction of the Aachen festival, and his ongoing troubles with Dingel-stedt all weighed heavily upon him. No better birthday present could have been given to him during this difficult year than the one conceived by Gustav Steinacker: the melodrama *Des Meisters Bannerschaft,* which paid tribute to Liszt and his circle at the Altenburg. It revived his flagging spirits to see so many of his friends and colleagues come to the old house and pay their respects—Pohl, Fallersleben, Cornelius, Brendel, Zellner, Singer, Stör, Walbrül, Coss-mann. As Liszt and his birthday guests listened to Heinrich Grans unfold the eulogy, his thoughts must more than once have drifted towards distant Flor-ence, where at that very moment Blandine and Emile Ollivier were celebrating their nuptials.

III

After his return from Aachen in the summer of 1857, Liszt had spent much time putting the finishing touches to his *Dante* Symphony, a difficult work that made many new technical demands on the orchestra. Anxious to secure an early performance, Liszt rashly decided to conduct the première in Dresden, a city with which he had hitherto enjoyed good relations. Bülow foresaw the danger and begged Liszt to substitute an easier work, but to no avail. In the event, Bülow's worst fears were realized. The concert took place in the Royal Theatre on November 7, after only one rehearsal, and it was an unmitigated disaster. Bülow was sitting in the audience with his young bride, Cosima, and the pair squirmed with embarrassment as they witnessed the man that they both adored preside over a shambles. "A fiasco," wrote Bülow, "which can only be com-pared with that of Wagner's *Tannhäuser* in Paris."[16] Liszt had failed to follow his own advice, published the previous year in the preface to his symphonic poems, not to allow his music to be played unless it was adequately prepared. Moreover, the *Dante* Symphony is particularly treacherous. Its last movement calls for a female "choir of angels" to be placed in a high gallery above the orchestra, which can easily become detached from the instrumental ensemble and float away into the void if the conductor's sight-lines are not well planned. "Very unsuccessful from lack of rehearsal" was Liszt's laconic way of putting

---

16. NZfM, September 22, 1865.

it.[17] The Dresden press was hostile almost to a man. There was one notable exception: in the *Dresdener Nachrichten* there appeared a spirited defence of Liszt and his music by the twenty-two-year-old Felix Draeseke, who from that moment became one of Liszt's ardent supporters. At Liszt's invitation Draeseke moved to Weimar, where his name began to figure with increasing frequency in the activities of the Altenburg circle.

The main event of the Weimar concert season in 1857 was undoubtedly the appearance of the virtuoso violinist Camillo Sivori, the only pupil of Paganini.[18] Sivori was now forty-seven years old, the sole representative of his master's "diabolical" art, and his arrival in the small town aroused a flurry of interest. At the concert he gave in the Court Theatre on December 29, under Liszt's direction, he played three technically demanding works in a manner calculated to evoke memories of his master, and he galvanized orchestra and audience alike. The evening was rounded off with the first performance of Liszt's symphonic poem *Hunnenschlacht*.

BRONSART	*Frühlingsfantasie* for Orchestra
PAGANINI	Adagio and Rondo from Violin Concerto No. 2 in B minor *("La campanella")* (soloist: Sivori)
SCHUBERT	Die Allmacht (soloist: Helene von Heimburg)
SIVORI	Fantasy on Themes from *Lucia di Lammermoor* (soloist: Sivori)

Interval

LASSEN	Lied
SCHUBERT	"Widmung" (soloist: Heimburg)
SIVORI	*Carnaval* (Hommage à Paganini) (soloist: Sivori)
LISZT	Symphonic Poem *Hunnenschlacht*

Sivori's operatic fantasies are completely unknown, even to violinists, yet they are the logical descendants of Paganini's contributions to the genre. Given the resurgence of interest in the Romantic age, their revival cannot be much longer postponed. We learn from Liszt's correspondence that Sivori stayed in Weimar

---

17. SLBG, p. 23.
18. There were those in the audience who still remembered Paganini's appearance in Weimar on October 30, 1829, when he scored a spectacular triumph with a rendering of his unaccompanied "Military" Sonata on the G-string.

for several days, and it is unthinkable that the pair did not reminisce about Paganini. Before he left, Sivori asked Liszt to compose a violin concerto for him, but despite repeated requests over the years nothing came of this interesting idea.[19]

I V

With the arrival of the New Year, 1858, Liszt's conducting career in Weimar came to a temporary halt. Apart from the Mozart Commemoration Concert he directed on January 27 (Mozart's birthday) Liszt was not to appear on the Weimar podium for nearly six months. This was the first and most obvious manifestation of his growing estrangement from Dingelstedt, whose drama productions were not only keeping the resources of the small theatre fully stretched but were doing so at the expense of the musical ones. Liszt now turned his gaze abroad and accepted conducting engagements in Prague, Vienna, and Pest.[20] His itinerary at this time has scarcely been chronicled, and it will bear scrutiny.

Liszt set out for Prague in early March. He travelled via Leipzig and Dresden, where he was briefly re-united with three of his pupils, Draeseke, Bronsart, and Reubke. Reubke was already mortally ill, and Liszt knew that this talented musician had only a few weeks left to live.[21] By March 5 Liszt was in Prague, where he plunged into a busy round of rehearsals and social calls. Two concerts of his works were planned. The first, which took place on March 11, contained the *Dante* Symphony and the A-major Piano Concerto, with the seventeen-

---

19. LLB, vol. 2, pp. 113–14.
20. Liszt was absent from Weimar for nearly seven weeks. His letters to Princess Carolyne contain several passing references to Dingelstedt and make it clear that the problems of the Court Theatre were never far from his thoughts. On April 6 he wrote from Pest: "Give me news of Dingelstedt and the Weimar theatre," and added, "without omitting the drama." And two days later he urged Carolyne "to try to preserve good relations with Dingelstedt—because I still have the idea that we shall be able to travel a certain distance together" (LLB, vol. 4, p. 426). Later in this same letter there is a tongue-in-cheek request to Carolyne to "place another bouquet on Dingelstedt, so that he leaves me [Eduard] Grosse, whom I could not do without"—a phrase that implies that Dingelstedt may well have been firing orchestral players behind Liszt's back. Morale among the players was certainly low, and it is no accident that Leopold Damrosch left Weimar in mid-April, during Liszt's absence, in order to take up a conducting appointment in Breslau. Liszt did not hear about Damrosch's impending departure until April 25 or 26. He wrote to the princess: "I enclose a few lines for Damrosch, whose decision to leave Weimar I approve of totally. I shall endeavour to be useful to him in Breslau too." (LLB, vol. 4, p. 438)
21. Reubke died of tuberculosis three months after this meeting. He was nursed with devotion by the two sisters of Alexander Ritter. Liszt wrote to Carolyne: "This excellent and charming young man does not have long to live, I fear . . . Chest ailments which have reached this stage rarely get better; usually the patients delude themselves until the last minute, and die peacefully." (LLB, vol. 4, p. 404) The words have a particular poignancy when we recall that Daniel Liszt was to die in exactly the same manner less than eighteen months later.

year-old Carl Tausig as soloist. We learn from Liszt's correspondence that Carolyne had prepared a literary "programme" for this particular performance of the *Dante* Symphony, so that the audience would better understand the source of his inspiration.[22] The débâcle of the Dresden première a few months earlier was still a painful memory. Three days later, on March 14, the second concert was given. It consisted of two works: the symphonic poem *Tasso* and the E-flat-major Piano Concerto, in which the soloist was Liszt's pupil Robert Pflughaupt. During the rehearsal of *Tasso,* a dog started to howl between the two adagios. "Another critic," Liszt muttered beneath his breath,[23] and continued to conduct. The performance itself went well, however, or rather (in Liszt's sardonic phrase) the work "was *acquitted* by the big-wigs here." Robert Pflughaupt had journeyed from Weimar to Prague at Liszt's request and had brought with him his twenty-one-year-old bride, Sophie, who was herself a pianist. The young couple planned to put on one or two joint concerts of their own in order to help defray their expenses, but they got into difficulties. When Liszt discovered that they were in penury and could not even pay their hotel bill, he himself settled their account and saw them safely back to Weimar.[24]

From Prague Liszt travelled to Vienna, where he conducted two performances of his "Gran" Mass on March 22 and 23. It was a special pleasure to meet Daniel, who, as we have learned, had moved in with Tausig for the duration of Liszt's stay in order to attend the daily rehearsals, take occasional breakfasts with his father, and generally feel part of the Liszt circle. While in Vienna, Liszt received an invitation to take part in a court concert and play before Emperor Franz Joseph. He declined this royal summons on the grounds that he no longer classed himself as a *Kammervirtuos* and did not wish others to do so either.[25] Behind this little rebuke lurked the desire to be taken seriously as a composer, especially in Vienna. Liszt knew that the moment he sat down at the piano the press would talk of little else but his playing; it was ever thus. A number of journals carried favourable notices about the "Gran" Mass, including the *Oesterreichische Zeitung,* Saphir's *Humorist,* and the *Vorstadt-Zeitung,* and Liszt was not displeased at this unexpected turn in his critical fortunes.[26] Even so, he was not prepared to risk the performances of two of the symphonic

---

22. LLB, vol. 4, p. 405. "The concert here will be on Thursday, March 11," Liszt told Carolyne. "If it were possible for me to receive the *Dante* programme on Monday morning I should be pleased." It arrived two days later, and Liszt wrote: "Your programme of the *Dante* is a masterpiece. . . . I scarcely found three or four words to change." (LLB, vol. 4, p. 406) The material was later used by Richard Pohl as the basis for his substantial essay on the *Dante* Symphony in PGS, vol. 2, p. 238.

23. HLSW, p. 95.

24. LLB, vol. 4, p. 422. Robert (1833–71) and Sophie (1837–67) Pflughaupt had both been pupils of Henselt in St. Petersburg. They lived in Weimar from 1857 to 1862.

25. LLB, vol. 4, p. 419.

26. These performances of the "Gran" Mass took place in the large hall of the Redoutensaal. Liszt had under his command a combined ensemble of 250 singers and orchestral players, many of them

poems in Vienna at this time, and he turned down the opportunity with the wry comment "The hare prefers to wait to be skinned [until next year]."[27]

The major disappointment for Liszt in Vienna, in fact, had nothing to do with his own reception but rather with that of his protégé Tausig. Liszt was angered at the hostility with which the Viennese critics reacted towards Tausig's well-prepared début; the youth had been thrown into despair by his press-reviews and was reluctant to leave his hotel-room. "Tausig made a little mistake by making his début in [Ferdinand] Laub's concert in Vienna," observed Liszt ruefully. "I have advised him to remain absolutely quiet for now."[28] Since Tausig had recently finished the piano arrangements of Liszt's *Faust* and *Dante* symphonies, the composer felt especially solicitous towards his young charge. "I feel a serious duty to be useful to him," wrote Liszt. "For now there is no way of establishing him . . . but I shall probably manage to make a nest for him next autumn when the concerts begin again."[29]

Pest still lay ahead. On Wednesday, March 30, at six o'clock in the morning,[30] Liszt boarded a steamboat and set out for the city of the Magyars. We know from his correspondence with Carolyne that he at first intended this visit to Hungary to be a private one, with no concerts. It was due entirely to public demand that he agreed to conduct two performances of the "Gran" Mass, one of them for charity. As he himself put it:

> Although my current trip to Pest had no other purpose than a cordial gesture to my four singers from the Hungarian theatre, who put themselves to the trouble of singing my mass in Vienna, and to their leader, Count Ráday, I was not able to refuse the wish expressed on all sides to hear again the "Gran" Festival Mass. This work will be performed next Friday in the Museum Hall, for the benefit of the conservatory, and on Sunday in the big parish church of Pest.[31]

These two concerts involved Liszt in at least five rehearsals; on the other hand, the Pest singers knew their parts so well that there was little for him to do except give the mass a single run-through, with predictable success.

It was during this visit to Pest that Liszt was admitted to the order of St.

---

from Hungary. The four soloists, in fact, were from the Hungarian National Theatre: Josephine Ernst-Kaiser, Therese Ellinger-Engst, Albert von Jékelfalussy, and Károly Kősseghy. The organ part was played by Alexander Winterberger, as on the occasion of the work's première performance at Gran.

27. LLB, vol. 4, p. 419.
28. LLB, vol. 4, p. 425.
29. LLB, vol. 4, p. 440.
30. LLB, vol. 4, p. 422.
31. LLB, vol. 4, p. 424. In fact, the first performance was delayed for one day and did not take place until Saturday, April 10. The second one followed on Sunday, April 11.

Francis as a "confrater." Liszt himself described the ceremony in detail.[32] It was held on Sunday, April 11, in the Franciscan monastery he had known since his earliest years. He was accompanied to the monastery by Antal Augusz and Count Guido Karátsonyi, who were also admitted to the order on that day. After a short mass, the three companions joined about a dozen monks in the refectory for lunch. Liszt's bust and portrait had been placed in the refectory to mark the occasion. During the meal the father superior toasted Liszt and the others in Latin, and after a simple ceremony they were admitted to the order. Since Liszt had to leave Pest that evening, the preparation of his illuminated diploma was expedited and delivered to him before his departure.[33]

Liszt travelled back to Weimar via Vienna and Prague. In Vienna he attended a large banquet given by Countess Bánffy at which Tausig and Laub played. When he heard that the minister of the interior, Count Lanckorónsky, had refused permission to allow some Italian singers to take part in the concert on political grounds, Liszt stepped in and favoured the audience with two works of his own. The gesture was misinterpreted by the press, which accused him of meddling in politics. "If things go on like this," he remarked drily, "I shall be forced to go and join our friend Wagner in Zürich."[34] A day or two later he had a personal encounter with Hanslick, who turned up at a supper-party Liszt gave for Ferdinand Laub. The highlight of the music-making came when Liszt and Hanslick sat down together and performed the third of Schubert's Hungarian Divertissements for four hands. "If only this little incident could become a symbol . . . for the happy alliance of Art and Criticism," commented

---

32. LLB, vol. 4, pp. 430–31.

33. This ceremony, which had been postponed for nearly two years, had its origins in Liszt's encounters with the Franciscans during his previous visit to Pest, in 1856. The certificate admitting him as a "confrater" of the Order of St. Francis is actually dated June 23, 1857 (see BVL, p. 160). Liszt himself was confused about the date, which he reported wrongly to Carolyne before having seen the documents.

From the start Liszt was nervous about what the newspapers might make of this open declaration of his connections with the Franciscans, which, as we now know, went back to his childhood. "I do not know whether the newspapers will concern themselves with this event, but that is of no interest at all to me," he wrote, with feigned indifference (LLB, vol. 4, p. 428). In fact, after his 1856 visit to these same cloisters, word had quickly got back to Protestant Weimar that Liszt was about to become a "confrater." The local newspaper *Deutschland* had come out with a sarcastic editorial on its front page, for home consumption. "You will be astonished or amused, as you wish, at the following article taken from a religious newspaper in Hungary called *Religio*. It goes without saying that I cannot vouch for the truth of *Réligio*." (February 3, 1857) The necessary note of scepticism having been struck, the editor (Karl Panse) then re-printed the account in *Religio*, which told of the preliminary moves to make Liszt a "confrater." This was more than simple reporting on *Deutschland*'s part; it was an attempt to weaken Liszt's credibility among his Protestant colleagues in Weimar, most of whom had not the faintest idea as to the meaning of "confratership," even though it was bestowed on thousands of lay Catholics across the world and was, in fact, a universal brotherhood of individuals who accepted the precepts of St. Francis as a proper foundation for their everyday lives.

For a further account of the ceremony see the *Pressburger Zeitung*, April 16, 1858.

34. LLB, vol. 4, p. 437.

Liszt.[35] By April 23 Liszt had arrived in Löwenberg, in Silesia, where he joined Bülow and Tausig as guests of Prince Hohenzollern-Hechingen. This music-loving aristocrat maintained a small private orchestra, and he regaled Liszt with performances of *Tasso, Les Préludes,* and *Festklänge.* While in Löwenberg Liszt received some assurances from the princess of Prussia that she would offer her protection to Bülow until he had become properly established in Berlin. As he was leaving Löwenberg, the prince handed Bülow a valuable turquoise bracelet for Cosima as a gesture of friendship. The last leg of his journey took Liszt to Berlin, where he spent two days with Hans and Cosima, catching up on all the family news. He finally arrived back in Weimar by train on Sunday, May 2.[36] He had been on the road for seven weeks.

v

The 1857–58 season marked the tenth anniversary of Liszt's arrival in Weimar, and a series of great parties was arranged at the Altenburg to celebrate the event. Mention has already been made of the melodrama *Des Meisters Bannerschaft* by Steinacker, which was mounted at the Altenburg on October 22 in honour of Liszt's forty-sixth birthday. Since the "production" involved not only actors but incidental music as well, to say nothing of the sizeable contingent of guests who saw it, we assume that at least sixty people gathered in the old house to pay tribute to Liszt. And this was but a portent of things to come. On February 8 Princess Carolyne celebrated her birthday, which also happened to be the tenth anniversary of her union with Liszt. A large banquet was laid on in her honour. Among the first guests to arrive were the Fallerslebens, whose tiny son Franz (named after Liszt) advanced towards Carolyne and handed her a poem and a bouquet of flowers. The Prellers, Bronsart, and the poet Alfred Meissner were also present. During the dinner Fallersleben got to his feet and delivered an ode in honour of Carolyne.[37] Meissner then followed suit with a poem about the chain-like bracelet that Liszt had given Carolyne to mark their ten-year liaison, whose texts unfold some symbolic variations on chains broken, melted down, and forged afresh.[38] For Meissner the Altenburg was "a modern Monsalvat," and he would have settled in Weimar if Liszt had been able to procure for him a long-sought appointment at the Court Theatre. His admiration of Liszt came out when he dedicated to the composer his four-

---

35. HLSW, p. 98.
36. LLB, vol. 4, p. 441.
37. HML, vol. 6, pp. 240–41.
38. LAG, p. 254.

Liszt in Munich, a photograph by Franz Hanfstaengl (1858).

volume novel *Sansara,* completed during this very season of 1857–58.[39] On February 18 the Altenburg filled up with visitors yet again, this time to celebrate the birthday of Princess Marie, whom Meissner extolled in poetry as "an ideal woman."[40] No one could have guessed from such joyous occasions that Liszt's tenure at Weimar would shortly come to an end. Yet during this very year of 1858, a complex web of intrigue was woven around him, from which it became impossible to disentangle himself, and which led to his resignation.

V I

The story of how that came about really begins in the spring of 1858. After an absence of several months, Peter Cornelius returned to the Altenburg with the newly completed score of his comic opera *The Barber of Bagdad,* a work dedicated to Liszt and full of portent for him. When *The Barber* had first begun to occupy Cornelius's mind, he had withdrawn from the hurly-burly of Weimar and retired to his brother-in-law's cottage in the Thuringian woods in order to work on the music without interruption. The opera was ready in all its essential details by the spring of 1858, for Liszt wanted to stage it at that time. In the execution of this plan he was hampered at every touch and turn by Dingelstedt, who refused to make room for it in the theatre calendar. More than that, he provoked a quarrel with Liszt over who would sing the role of the Caliph: Dingelstedt wanted Heinrich Grans, while Liszt (whose view prevailed) insisted on Feodor von Milde.[41] By May 1858 the preliminary rehearsals were under way. Cornelius was perturbed that Liszt did not at first like the libretto, although he was quickly won over by the music and told the princess (who in turn told Cornelius) that "Berlioz himself might envy [Cornelius] this work."[42] Cornelius's descriptions of the piano rehearsals in the Altenburg are filled with perspicacious detail. He reported:

> It is strange how Liszt understands these things; e.g., he took the overture at once exactly as I meant it to be taken, and called it very happily invented. The further we got, the more interested he became, and after the second rehearsal he expressed himself entirely convinced and delighted. . . . The "Shaving Minuet" created a furore at Liszt's. At first he was astonished; then he grew annoyed because he could

39. HFLW, p. 83.
40. LAG, pp. 256–57.
41. CSB, pp. 239–40.
42. CLW, vol. 1, p. 276.

not play it right away at sight. Afterwards he was greatly amused; several times he broke out into such fits of laughter that I could scarcely continue my singing.[43]

The Barber was finally scheduled for performance on December 15, much against Dingelstedt's wishes. It later transpired that Dingelstedt was so convinced that the opera would not get beyond the first act that he told Carl Alexander that he had actually prepared a comedy to take over after the intermission.[44]

When Liszt walked onto the podium, he had no idea of the fiasco that lay in wait for him. With the staging of *The Barber*, in Gyula Hollitzer's telling phrase, "Dingelstedt exploded the mines that he had set for Liszt a long time ago."[45] Although the main outlines of the affair have become part of the mythology of opera, they will bear repetition. The theatre was sold out, we are told, and the performance was excellent; even so, there was a clumsy attempt on the part of a section of the audience to interrupt the first act with whistling. Liszt kept on conducting. At the end, however, the opposition unleashed a clamour that lasted for ten minutes.[46] It was the duty of Dingelstedt, as the theatre intendant, to intervene and stop the rowdy behaviour, but he did nothing. Liszt than returned to the conductor's desk, brought the orchestra to its feet, faced the hostile audience, and began to applaud the opera. The players joined in but were drowned out by the booing and hissing. Eventually Frau von Milde (who sang the role of Margiana in the opera) led Cornelius onto the stage, but this only served to increase the volume of noisy protest. Liszt then laid down his baton and walked out of the auditorium, white with anger. Afterwards he and a group of frustrated colleagues gathered at the Erbprinz Hotel to drown their sorrows. Felix Draeseke reports that Cornelius appeared to be the calmest person in the room, despite his ordeal,[47] but he added that he would never forget the look on Liszt's face. Liszt felt deeply wounded and announced to his friends that he intended to resign his office: he understood very well that the protest he had just witnessed was not directed against *The Barber*

---

43. CSB, p. 224.

44. CSB, p. 239.

45. HFLW, p. 53.

46. Cornelius described the commotion as "unprecedented in the annals of the Weimar opera" (CSB, p. 236).

47. Draeseke's eye-witness account of the demonstration was published posthumously in the *Karlsruher Tagblatt*, April 25, 1925, under the title: *"Der Barbier von Bagdad:* Die Uraufführung nach dem Bericht eines Augenzeigen." It is an indication of the confusion that prevailed in the theatre that night that Draeseke, from his coign of vantage in the auditorium, hurled a large wreath of flowers onto the stage, but in his zeal he missed the target and hit a horn-player on the head. The innocent recipient of this missile was so outraged that he rounded on a nearby demonstrator and "reduced him to silence"—by methods not reported (RDL, p. 93).

but against him. Cornelius, too, saw the struggle in its real light, and expressed it succinctly: "Liszt wants—art. Dingelstedt wants only—himself."[48]

The morning after the débâcle Liszt wrote a letter to Carl Alexander in which he extolled the virtues of *The Barber* and its young composer.[49] It was entirely typical of Liszt to do this, since he felt that no blame should attach to Cornelius for the disastrous première of his opera. That same day the grand duke had Liszt bring Cornelius to the palace so that he might get to know him better. Cornelius described the occasion to his sister: "In the course of the conversation Liszt remarked: 'Your Royal Highness, Cornelius is a noble fellow.' The grand duke shook hands with me at parting as with a friend."[50]

Liszt had one more concert engagement to fulfil before stepping down from the Weimar podium. On December 17 he conducted an all-Beethoven concert in honour of the master's birthday, which consisted of the following works:

> Overture   *Consecration of the House*
> Cantata   *Calm Sea and Prosperous Voyage*
> Romance in F major for violin and orchestra
>   (soloist: Edmund Singer)
> Piano Concerto No. 5 in E-flat major ("Emperor")
>   (soloist: Martha von Sabinin)
>
> *Interval*
>
> Symphony No. 7 in A major

After the performance of the overture, Feodor von Milde advanced from behind the curtain and delivered a "prologue" in praise of Beethoven, written by Cornelius, which was crowned by a storm of applause. Cornelius tells us that he was sitting in the stalls, expecting Milde to reappear, when he was suddenly propelled from his seat towards the stage. Throwing aside his hat and gloves, he took Milde's hand and acknowledged his triumph.[51] It was a belated gesture on the part of the audience to compensate for the shoddy treatment meted out in that same theatre two nights earlier, and it confirms the generally held view that Cornelius was not the real target of their hostility. The concert that followed was, according to Cornelius, one of the most memorable that Liszt ever directed. At the conclusion of the Seventh Symphony he received a standing ovation. Twelve years would elapse before he mounted that podium again.

---

48. CSB, p. 239.
49. LBLCA, p. 65.
50. CSB, p. 237.
51. CSB, pp. 237–38.

Word spread quickly through Weimar of Liszt's impending resignation. A month elapsed, and still no official announcement was made. On Sunday, February 6, 1859, the *Weimarische Zeitung* published an unfriendly article about Liszt.[52] It insisted that the general public was entirely within its right to demonstrate against Cornelius's opera if it chose to do so. "Can one really say that Liszt was thereby insulted and had to step down in order to preserve his honour? Why would that be necessary? Because he conducted the opera? In that case, the general intendant would have to abdicate every time he brought a play to the stage that was badly received!" It went on to ask, somewhat condescendingly, what would be lost by allowing Liszt to go on making a few isolated experiments and conducting two or three Wagner operas. "Very little. But much more would be gained if he did the opposite!" The article was published anonymously and provoked outrage among Liszt's supporters. The hand of Dingelstedt was detected, and the editor (Karl Biedermann) was compelled to reveal the writer's identity. It turned out to be Alexander Rost, a Weimar poet and supporter of Dingelstedt, who confessed to writing it "of my own free will and without Dingelstedt's knowledge."[53] This was the context in which Liszt wrote his letter of resignation to Carl Alexander, dated February 14, 1859. It is a long, uneasy epistle, and Liszt appears to have had some trouble in writing it. He refers only obliquely to the *Barber* scandal and to the confrontations with Dingelstedt (". . . If recent events have with their last drops made the urn overflow, it was already full to overflowing"). But he becomes ironic when he refers to his ten wasted years in Weimar and the small-minded minions who were fearful that he might "cause the boards of the entire theatre to collapse" were he allowed to mount his extravagant productions. After reviewing the shortcomings of the Weimar theatre, and his role in the artistic life of the city, Liszt went on:

> People have told you, sire, with a sort of disdain, of the *experiments* with which I have overloaded . . . your stage. Let me point out once more that the importance of a theatre is measured by its initiative, which necessarily entails those first performances which people try to denigrate with the term "experiment." By virtue of this principle, I have come to the conclusion that Wagner's operas, already estab-

52. "Liszt's Rücktritt und das Publikum," *Weimarische Zeitung,* February 6, 1859.
53. *Weimarische Zeitung,* February 8, 1859. By this time, many other newspapers had picked up the scent of a good story and had published their own accounts of Liszt's resignation. Perhaps the first to talk of a "theatre scandal" was the Hamburg newspaper *Die Reform* (January 12, 1859).

lished in the repertory . . . which it will always be an honour to conduct—together with other masterpieces—no longer require my services. Those with the ambition to walk along the path of glory do not linger at gates that have already been conquered. . . . I am not unaware how much not only the artist but art itself can appear to be a useless luxury, [and] that in several respects I am superfluous in Weimar.[54]

The grand duke's reply has not been preserved. Perhaps he assumed that this crisis, like all the others, would blow away, that Liszt would continue to accept the unacceptable. If so, he was sadly mistaken. Whatever passed between the pair was sufficient to convince Liszt that his days in Weimar were numbered. His duties at the theatre were taken over by Eduard Lassen, who had already been appointed music director on January 1, 1858, in succession to the ailing Chélard.[55] Two and a half years were to elapse before Liszt left "the Athens of the North," and during this painful period he gradually withdrew from the musical life of the city.

　　Carl Alexander was still not convinced that Liszt planned to leave Weimar for good. He made several attempts during the winter of 1859–60 to entice his erstwhile Kapellmeister back to the podium, but Liszt refused to be drawn. In a letter dated February 6, 1860, Liszt told him that while he would be flattered to be invited to participate in court concerts (generally held in the castle), "I resign totally the title of Kapellmeister, as of now." Liszt went on to review his years at Weimar and uttered some veiled reproaches to the grand duke. "In ten years I founded *eine Weimar'sche Schule* without any support. . . . I defy anyone else to do what I did with so few means." He reminded his royal

---

54. LBLCA, p. 70. This last phrase, of course, was a cynical echo of Dingelstedt's aphorism that a theatre was a necessary evil but that opera was a superfluous one.

　　Liszt's letter to the grand duke brings to light a wealth of detail about his grievances with the Weimar theatre. He insists that if he is to carry on he must be granted five basic rights:

　　1. to perform twelve operas annually, some of them new;
　　2. to issue (or withhold) players' contracts;
　　3. to grant leaves-of-absence;
　　4. to engage one foreign artist each season;
　　5. to recommend promotions and awards for merit.

These powers, he admits, were never entirely withheld from him, but since they were never put into writing either, they are now given grudgingly. They would amount to no more, he goes on, than an acknowledgement that he is a man of common sense who could be trusted to make judicious decisions. It is clear that the rights Liszt wanted to keep must have been the very ones that Dingelstedt was now busily engaged in appropriating for himself. Robbed of initiative, Liszt must have felt that he was rapidly becoming a guest-conductor of his own orchestra, a visitor to his own theatre.

55. Chélard was now sixty-nine years old. Although he was long past the age of retirement, he had been kept on the grand duke's payroll throughout Liszt's years of tenure. He died in Weimar in February 1861.

benefactor that if he could only count on his support Weimar would become in reality what it remained only in name: the seat of the New German School. "My stay in Weimar has identified the name of this town with that of this school. If I spent ten years in Lübeck they would speak of *die Lübeck'sche Schule!* And they would say it for more than ten years, I assure you, for the victory and the future are ours."[56] Liszt was, of course, absolutely correct in this assessment of his place in the history of nineteenth-century music, and the grand duke knew it. All the more lamentable, then, that he failed to take any practical steps that would secure Liszt for Weimar. He granted Liszt an audience on February 10, from which, despite some fine words spoken on both sides, Liszt concluded that the divisions between himself and the theatre administration would remain as deep as ever.

In the midst of this crisis with the Weimar Court, Wagner (who was on a visit to Venice) sent Liszt some impossible demands for money, including one for an annual pension of "two or three thousand thalers." The timing of these letters was almost as clumsy as the language in which they were couched. "I do not blush in naming such a sum. . . . My experience of what I want . . . teaches me that I cannot do with less."[57] Wagner, in blissful ignorance of what was happening in Weimar, went on to harangue Liszt. "Have you *nothing at all* to say to me? What is to become of me if *everyone* ignores me?"[58] Liszt's angry reply was one of the sharpest he ever sent to Wagner. He told him that he no longer saw any point in sending Wagner copies of the *Dante* Symphony or the "Gran" Mass (which he had earlier promised to do) since, as he sarcastically put it, "they cannot be treated as bank stock." And he added that it would be equally superfluous to receive any further telegraphic despatches from Venice appealing for money, or letters which "cannot but wound me."[59] Wagner

---

56. LBLCA, p. 90.
57. BWL, vol. 2, p. 231; KWL, vol. 2, p. 243.
58. BWL, vol. 2, p. 232; KWL, vol. 2, p. 244.
59. This letter of January 4, 1859, was omitted from BWL but was published by Erich Kloss in KWL, vol. 2, p. 245.

The reason for Liszt's unexpected outburst against Wagner becomes clear when we place it within the context of their correspondence. On December 26, 1858, Liszt had received from Härtel the proofs of Act One of *Tristan* and was overwhelmed by it. In his letter of thanks, which is filled with the most fulsome praise of this masterpiece, Liszt promised to send Wagner in return copies of his *Dante* Symphony and his "Gran" Mass. He added the news that Duke Ernst of Gotha was about to dedicate to Wagner his new opera *Diana von Solange,* to which Wagner ought to send a gracious acknowledgement. (Duke Ernst was a firm ally in the ongoing fight for Wagner's amnesty.) Wagner had been expecting yet another banker's draft from Liszt, and when it did not arrive he hurled insult after insult at his old friend and at the theatrical establishment of Weimar generally, which was just then placing obstacles in the way of a production of *Rienzi.* "What in God's name am I supposed to do with *Diana von Solange*? Why should I put up with such open contempt on your part? Not a word? No money? . . . I can see you simply do not *know* what hardship is—you lucky man! . . . Send *Dante* and the mass. But first send me—money! A fee for God knows what! Tell Dingelstedt he is a fool as long as he lives! And tell the grand duke that his snuff-box has been pawned—it's

tried to mollify his friend in a long letter of self-justification, written on January 7, 1859, and Liszt finally sent him a measured response on February 17, just three days after writing his fateful letter to the grand duke. It was impossible, he told Wagner, to grant his request for a pension; with patience, however, Wagner might reasonably expect a small sum of money to tide him over his present difficulties. "Anything more cannot be hoped for."[60] The first disaffection between Liszt and Wagner had set in. It was an unexpected development in their relationship, and one which Liszt might well have been spared at this time.

VIII

Beleaguered as he was inside Weimar, Liszt could do little more for now than hope that the Music of the Future would not quickly become the music of the past but might in fact prosper in centres beyond Thuringia's conservative borders. He could console himself with the thought that several of his disciples had meanwhile taken up the baton—Ritter in Stettin, Damrosch in Breslau, Tausig in Vienna, and Bülow in Berlin—in whose concerts his music was regularly featured and in whose hands his reputation would surely remain secure. But within a short time Tausig had to withdraw his *Zukunftskonzerte* because of financial considerations, while Damrosch (having delivered the first performance of Liszt's *Héroïde funèbre*) decided to emigrate to America. As for Ritter, he was forced to resign his position after he made enemies through his championship of Liszt's *Tasso*. Only the faithful Bülow remained at his post, and he now found himself struggling for life in a sea of troubles. On January 14, 1859, Bülow conducted Liszt's *Die Ideale* in the Berlin Singakademie. As the closing chords died away, a section of the audience started to hiss, and Bülow left the platform. Moments later he came back to the podium and delivered a stinging rebuke: "I request that the hissers leave the hall, since it is not customary to hiss here."[61] Bülow stood there, baton in hand, glaring at the audience. In the long and distinguished history of the Singakademie many artists had come under critical fire, but this was the first time that one of their number had struck back. Everybody expected an explosion, but a painful silence

true! It's up to him to redeem it for me. Never again write to me in such a serious and emotional tone! God! I told you last time that you all bore me. Was it to no avail?" (Letter dated December 31, 1858, omitted from BWL and published in KWL, vol. 2, pp. 237–38)

  Wagner's boorish reply cut Liszt to the quick, and he retaliated: "I am sending the first act of *Tristan* back to Härtel, and would ask you not to acquaint me with the remaining ones until they appear in print." (KWL, vol. 2, p. 245)

60. BWL, vol. 2, p. 237; KWL, vol. 2, p. 251.

61. BB, vol. 3, p. 203.

descended on the hall. The princess of Prussia disappeared from the royal box in search of a cup of tea, while her husband, Prince Friedrich, sank back into the shadows. Having thoroughly cowed the audience, which smarted beneath the knowledge that it was the object of Bülow's scorn, the maestro deigned to continue the concert.

The rest of the programme was devoted to works by Raff, Berlioz, and Liszt himself ("Die Loreley," sung by Emilie Genast); and since it passed off without further incident, Bülow had every reason to suppose that he had struck a blow for *Zukunftsmusik* and won a moral victory for himself. Within a few days, however, a storm of newspaper criticism broke over him, he became the recipient of anonymous letters containing personal abuse, and friend and foe alike urged him to resign.[62] But Bülow stood his ground. At his next concert, on February 10, the whistling and stamping against which he had been fore-warned failed to materialize; but the newspaper reviews were more hostile than ever. When Liszt heard what was happening to his erstwhile pupil, he proffered him one of Goethe's aphorisms: "Dass die Hunde bellen, beweist nur, dass wir reiten,"[63] which was hardly the sort of comfort that the embattled Bülow could put to practical use at this stage of his career. So Liszt came to the rescue and agreed to share the podium with him on February 27, conducting a repeat performance of *Die Ideale.* Liszt, who was himself no stranger to the hostility of audiences, had no idea what to expect from Berlin; he simply felt that the best reply to the critics was to give them an even more powerful dose of the medicine that had so upset their delicate constitutions in the first place. To everyone's surprise, not least his own, his rendering of *Die Ideale* was regarded as something of a triumph. It was the same hall, the same work, the same orchestra, and the same audience. The conductor alone was different. There can be no better illustration of a point touched on several times in the course of this narrative: namely, that the "experimental" nature of Liszt's music was such that even those interpreters who claimed to be close to it (and Bülow certainly falls into that category) did not always find its secret pulse, and so gave the impression that the work itself was still-born. Liszt remained his own best interpreter.

This trip to Berlin was notable for another reason. The day before Bülow's concert Liszt was invited to a gala reception in the palace of the prince regent, with about four hundred guests in attendance. Among the people he met was Prince Viktor Hohenlohe, duke of Ratibor. The duke invited Liszt to dine with him and his family a day or two later, and it was on this occasion that he was introduced to Monsignor Gustav Hohenlohe, one of Prince Viktor's younger brothers. Did the parties understand what a fateful encounter this was? Prince

---

62. The reader will find a useful summary of the affair in BB, vol. 3, pp. 202–06.
63. LBLB, p. 250. "That the dogs are barking only proves that we are in the saddle."

Viktor asked Liszt whether he had yet met Konstantin Hohenlohe, the youngest member of the clan, who resided in Vienna. It was a pointed question. Before the year was out Konstantin had taken Marie Wittgenstein as his bride, while Cardinal Gustav Hohenlohe (as he later became) proved to be one of Liszt's most powerful benefactors during his later years in Rome.[64] During this sojourn in the Prussian capital Cosima put on a buffet supper for her father in the Bülows' apartment in the Anhalterstrasse. There he met Lassalle, Otto Roquette, Weitzmann, and about twenty other notables. Afterwards Emilie Genast sang a group of Liszt's songs, Liszt himself played his D-flat-major Concert Study, and the evening was rounded off when Weitzmann joined Liszt at the keyboard for a rendering of the latter's "puzzle canons."[65] He finally got back to Weimar on Thursday, March 3, at about 10:00 p.m., and was picked up at the railway station by the carriage from the Altenburg.[66] Brief though it was, this trip to Berlin was well worthwhile. It had raised Bülow's sagging spirits and perhaps even his own. He was now "a quarter of a gentleman,"[67] —his ironical way of saying that, poor as this was, it was still an improvement on the way he had been regarded in Berlin a little earlier.

I X

Liszt's correspondence at this time reveals a growing attachment to his Lieder, a branch of his output that has received scant attention from posterity. This is perplexing when we consider that the best of them ("Mignon's Lied," "Die Loreley," "Freudvoll und leidvoll," "Vergiftet sind meine Lieder") form the "missing link" between Schumann and Hugo Wolf. The sheer size of the output is impressive. Altogether Liszt composed more than seventy songs—settings of texts in six languages[68] by such diverse poets as Goethe, Herwegh, Schiller, Heine, Rellstab, Hugo, Petrarch, Uhland, Rückert, and Lenau. Liszt had composed his first songs, "Angiolin dal biondo crin" and the "Tre sonetti di Petrarca," as a direct result of his sojourn in Italy during the years 1838–39.[69] By the time he got to Weimar he had at least twenty songs in his portfolio.

---

64. LLB, vol. 4, pp. 447, 448 and 450; LBZL, vol. 2, pp. 250–51. See also pp. 515–16 and p. 518 of the present volume.

65. LLB, vol. 4, p. 453.

66. LLB, vol. 4, p. 454.

67. LLB, vol. 4, p. 447.

68. French, German, Italian, English, Hungarian, and Russian.

69. The date of composition of Liszt's first songs still seems to be a matter of debate. In reply to one of Lina Ramann's questionnaires, he told her that "Angiolin dal biondo crin" was composed during the summer of 1839 for his infant daughter Blandine. Elsewhere, however, he told Ramann that the first songs he ever wrote were "Die Loreley" and "Mignon" (WA, Kasten 351, no. 1; RL, pp. 387 and 389). All three songs were published in 1843.

He now began to revise these early efforts and to add to them. His letters to Brendel, and especially to the publisher Kahnt, show how anxious he was to bring these scattered efforts together into one collection.[70]

It is no accident that Liszt was beguiled by this art-form during his Weimar years. Two conditions helped to bring this about. First, he had at his disposal four outstanding singers who were ready and able to do these pieces justice: Rosa and Feodor von Milde, Emilie Genast, and above all Franz Götze. Secondly, the Altenburg "matinées" provided a perfect setting for the performance of the songs, within a charmed circle of Liszt's own admirers, and often with Liszt himself presiding at the keyboard. Historically, these "matinées" may be regarded as natural successors to the "Schubertiads" that had taken place in Vienna some thirty years earlier.

Liszt himself recognized in Franz Götze one of the leading exponents of his songs. Götze, who was one of the best lyric tenors of the day, had formerly played in the first violin section of the Weimar orchestra and was now a teacher of singing in Leipzig. He had developed a passion for Liszt's songs in the mid-1850s which he communicated to his pupils, chief among whom was his daughter Auguste, whose career Liszt helped to promote.[71] When the *Gesammelte Lieder* appeared, in 1860, Liszt asked Brendel (their editor) to be sure to send a copy to Götze because his pioneer work in earlier years gave him "a special claim to them."[72] Two songs that Liszt associated with Götze's renderings were "Kling leise, mein Lied" (Nordmann) and "Angiolin dal biondo crin" (Bocella). Emilie Genast likewise aroused Liszt's admiration for the way in which she handled his songs, particularly "Mignon's Lied" (Goethe) and "Die Loreley" (Heine), and it was for her that he provided orchestral accompaniments for both songs.[73] As for the merits of Rosa and Feodor von Milde, they have been extolled elsewhere in this volume. It remains only to add that these faithful artists frequently included Liszt's songs in their programmes in such places as Karlsruhe, Aachen, and Berlin. All four singers had this supreme advantage: they were coached and accompanied by Liszt himself and may therefore be said to have sung his songs with authority. But Liszt was fortunate, too, since it is evident that all four singers were possessed of highly musical ears, which allowed him to make correspondingly unusual demands on them.

---

70. In a letter to Brendel dated December 6, 1859, Liszt wrote: "It is of great consequence to me not to delay any longer the publication of my *Gesammelte Lieder.* Forgive me, therefore, if today I am somewhat troublesome to your friendship." (LLB, vol. 1, p. 343) Compare also letters 232, 247, and 249 in the same collection.

71. It was for Auguste Götze that Liszt composed his recitation "Lenore," which she performed in Jena in November 1860 (LLB, vol. 1, p. 376).

72. LLB, vol. 1, p. 351.

73. In 1860, Liszt formed a deep attachment to Emilie Genast. Their letters to one another remain unpublished (WA, Kasten 63 and 64).

In general, the songs are characterized by an unparalleled freedom of the vocal line, often coupled with an advanced harmonic texture from the piano. Moreover, Liszt's penchant for plunging from one extreme key to another ensures that these pieces remain a challenge to the singer even today. At the dramatic close of "Vergiftet sind meine Lieder" (Heine) the singer is required to remain secure throughout the following "enharmonic" change (*):

Similar challenges face the singer in "Freudvoll und leidvoll" (Goethe), where the vocal line is fraught with enharmonic subtleties. Measures 2–4 and 6–8 are almost identical in pitch, but their notation is quite different. The technique is typical of Liszt; but it is one thing to give it to a pianist (where the player simply manipulates a keyboard), quite another to give it to the human voice, where these pitches actually have to be created by throat and larynx.

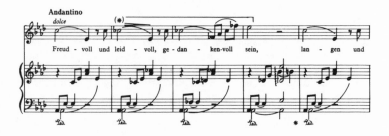

Liszt was not the first composer to discover that strict adherence to the strophic form (i.e., the same music set to different verses) sometimes led to artistic contradictions. Both Beethoven and Schubert had occasionally employed what the Germans call the *durchkomponiertes Lied,* or "through-composed song," in which the several verses of the poem unfold against an ever-changing musical landscape.[74] Liszt carried this method forward with impressive results. His songs tend to be highly developmental, and they are usually devoid of literal repetition. He will seize upon the dramatic essence of the poem—some colourful image or pronounced mood—and turn it into a leading feature of the accompaniment. In the song "Wie singt die Lerche schön" (Hoffmann von Fallersleben), it is clearly the idea of the ascending lark that has inspired the basic keyboard configuration, which forms the unifying element of the entire piece.

74. Schubert's "Erlkönig" and "Gretchen am Spinnrade" are two outstanding examples of the form. Liszt's youthful piano transcriptions of both songs gave him an insider's knowledge of the genre. Incidentally, Liszt was delighted when he learned from a friend that a group of his songs had recently been passed off as posthumous Lieder by Schubert and had been encored! Liszt begged the unidentified singer to continue with the joke. This was possibly Götze in Leipzig, since Liszt tells us that the event took place "in salons that are very much set against me" (LLB, vol. 1, p. 344).

Liszt frequently demanded of his singers that they "colour" their voices where the text demanded it, and scattered throughout the songs are injunctions such as "fast gesprochen," "mit halber Stimme," "geheimnisvoll," "phlegmatisch," and "hinträumend."[75] He was also uncompromising in his use of the full range of the voice. In "Der alte Vagabund" (Rehbaum) Liszt calls for a bass with an unusually wide compass:

practically all of which is used in the space of a few notes:

Not surprisingly, "the King of Pianists" will sometimes call upon the accompanist to forsake his role as a mere provider of background harmony and assume a leading role in the proceedings. "Die drei Zigeuner" (Lenau), for example, requires a pianist who can at least do justice to the Hungarian Rhapsodies and can emulate the sound of the Gypsy cimbalom. An even more difficult task awaits the "accompanist" in "Der Fischerknabe" (Schiller), which may be well described as a piano concerto with vocal obbligato.

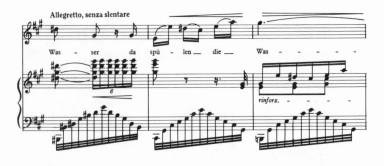

---

75. "Almost spoken," "with a half-voice," "mysterious," "phlegmatic" (i.e., dull or heavy), and "day-dreaming."

Not the least remarkable thing about the songs is the speed with which some of them were composed. Thus "Freudvoll und leidvoll" bears the inscription "composed March 30, 1848"; "Es muss ein Wunderbares sein," "composed July 13, 1852"; and "Ich scheide," "composed May 27, 1860." Liszt tended to work quickly as a matter of course. But there are few better examples of him moving with the somnambulistic certainty of a sleepwalker towards his artistic goals.

Mention should also be made here of Liszt's interest in a closely related genre known as the melodrama—a poem declaimed to music. Such "recitations" were becoming fashionable in the drawing-rooms of the mid–nineteenth century, and a number of Liszt's contemporaries tried their hands at them, including Schumann and Mendelssohn. Liszt composed three such pieces during his final years in Weimar: "Lenore" (Gottfried Bürger), "Vor hundert Jahren" (Friedrich Halm), and "Der traurige Mönch" (Nikolaus Lenau).[76] By far the most intriguing work in the group is "Der traurige Mönch," which was composed for Franziska Ritter, Wagner's niece. The poem unfolds a Gothic tale of horror and the supernatural. An ancient grey tower, whipped by rain, lightning, and wind, is haunted by the ghost of a sorrowful old monk. Legend has it that such is the sadness that emanates from this spectre that whoever looks it in the face will himself succumb to unutterable gloom and will want to die. Into this haunted tower wander a knight and his steed, in search of shelter from the

---

76. Two other melodramas followed in later years: "Des toten Dichters Liebe" (Mór Jókai), and "Der blinde Sänger" (Alexei Tolstoy).

howling storm outside. They sleep, and as the midnight hour strikes, the tower is surrounded by light. Awakened by his startled horse, "its teeth bared in fright," the knight sees before him the ghost of the grieving monk. Even as he stares into the face of the apparition, he is overcome by a great and secret sorrow. On the morrow, the warrior resumes his journey, but now both horse and rider are oppressed by feelings of mourning and lamentation from which they are unable to escape. "Every leaf laments, and the very air is aching and sore." As the sun sets, the curse is fulfilled, and the afflicted horse carries its rider into a lake, where they sink to their watery tomb. This ghostly tale evoked from Liszt music that aptly symbolizes the supernatural. The remarkable thing about the accompaniment, in fact, is that for much of the time it is based on the consistent use of the whole-tone scale, from which all its melody and harmony are derived. Freed from the usual tonal constraints, this atonal background creates a world unknown to mid-nineteenth-century ears. It is, perhaps, the first composition in musical history to apply the whole-tone scale with such rigour; after all, keyless music such as this did not make its official debut until fifty years later, in the works of Debussy, Schoenberg, and others.[77]

Liszt feared that the melodrama's "keyless discords" would prove impossible of performance, and he was quite prepared for it not to be taken up, "so indescribably wild and monstrous do these bleak dissonances sound."[78] In fact, the work was not published until 1871, and there is no record of it ever having been performed during Liszt's lifetime. The strange combination of declaimed voice and keyless accompaniment reminds one forcibly of Schoenbergian *Sprechstimme*. It is hardly an accident that this futuristic work has come to enjoy something of a cult status among today's dodecaphonic composers.

When we stand back and regard the songs as a whole, what lingers in the mind's ear is their economy of means. Not a note is wasted; some of the pieces, in fact, are painfully brief. Songs like "Einst," "Vergiftet sind meine Lieder," and "Was Liebe sei" last for barely one minute and reveal Liszt in the unusual guise of miniaturist. Liszt poured the best of himself into his songs, and he knew

---

77. The history books commonly assert that Alexander Dargomijsky (1813–69) invented the whole-tone scale. In fact, it was known to theorists considerably earlier and even appears in Mozart's "A Musical Joke" (1787). Liszt's serious use of the scale seems to make him a rare exception.

78. Letter to Emilie Genast, dated October 10, 1860 (JLB, pp. 190–91). From this same source we learn that Liszt had completed the piece the previous day, October 9.

it. It was particularly galling to him that they made their way so slowly, and he correctly perceived this to be due to the prejudice attached to his name. By now he was known as "that notorious *non-composer* Franz Liszt," and everything he did was suspect.[79] Such judgements simply spurred him to greater efforts, however, and his Lieder have meanwhile become a standing indictment against his critics. Whenever they sound, in fact, criticism is silenced.

x

One of the rare satisfactions Liszt received during these bleak months was that of his elevation to the Austrian nobility. In April 1859, after years of prevarication, Emperor Franz Joseph finally bestowed on Liszt the Order of the Iron Crown. It is unnecessary to dwell in detail on this topic, whose background has already been unfolded in Volume One.[80] Nonetheless, one or two points can usefully be clarified here, since they generally escape attention. It will be recalled that the question of Liszt's "nobility" had first been raised twenty years earlier, at the time of his triumphal return to Hungary in the winter of 1839. His aristocratic friends and supporters had failed at that time to secure for him a title from Vienna, but the idea was never entirely abandoned. Eduard Liszt had meanwhile been in intermittent touch about the matter with a number of authorities, including Alexander von Bach, the Austrian minister of the interior, and his persistence had its reward: Liszt was inducted into the Order of the Iron Crown (third class) on April 10, 1859. The decoration itself was delivered to the Altenburg later that same month.[81] Liszt now had an automatic right to petition the emperor for a knighthood, and he lost no time in despatching this request to Vienna. He was particularly anxious that the title be declared hereditary, for he wanted it to pass to Daniel. Meanwhile, he gave much thought to the design of his coat-of-arms and especially to the title by which he ought to be addressed. In a letter to Carolyne he asked: "What do you think of the idea of adding to my name that of *von Raiding?* I would not be afraid of looking as if I came from my village."[82] A few days later he asked her again: "What do you think of my village whimsy? . . . It would be a match for Hoffmann von Fallersleben!"[83] The idea of Liszt styling himself "Ritter Liszt von Raiding" may strike the modern reader as amusing, although it is by no means incongruous when set beside the titles of numbers of latter-day English baronets who originated in the sooty towns and villages of industrial England,

79. LLB, vol. 1, pp. 343–44.
80. See Volume One, pp. 30–33.
81. HLSW, p. 107.
82. LLB, vol. 4, p. 467.
83. LLB, vol. 4, p. 474.

the names of which are duly hyphenated to their owners' royal crests and seals. It was Carolyne who saw the dangers to Liszt in such a title; she rightly feared that his critics would lampoon him, and she came back with the following thoughts: "The 'von' and the 'de,' in their deepest meaning, are designations of property conquered by the sword, and whose hereditary possession transmits the 'von' and the 'de' to succeeding generations. I do not see the point of adopting the word 'von,' quite outside its original meaning. . . . I would only see in it a question of vanity which is unworthy of you."[84] Liszt eventually compromised, and when he was at last admitted to the Austrian nobility on October 30, 1859, he settled for the straightforward title of "Franz, Ritter von Liszt," which is indicated on the proclamation itself.[85]

XI

The year 1859 marked the hundredth anniversary of the death of Handel. Despite the difficulties Liszt now faced in Weimar, he was determined not to let the occasion pass unnoticed: Handel was one of Thuringia's greatest sons. All Liszt's old players and singers rallied to the cause, and on May 20 he stepped before the altar of the Herder Church in Weimar and conducted Handel's *Judas Maccabeus,* the first time that oratorio had been heard there. The following day Liszt and his forces travelled to Erfurt, where they performed *Messiah.* During the festivities Liszt invited a number of distinguished colleagues to Weimar, including Moscheles, with whom he played the latter's *Hommage à Handel* for two pianos. Moscheles tells us of the pleasure both men took in this reunion. He recalled one occasion when

> Liszt sat down at the piano, and I heard, to my no small astonishment, my old variations, op. 42, on the pretty Austrian melody

> which I had consigned to oblivion for the last forty years. He played them by heart and introduced startling effects. He then gave us his own organ Fantasia on the letters B-A-C-H, a piece full of extraordinary combinations and stupendously played.[86]

---

84. WA, Kasten 35, no. 29. Unpublished letter dated May 5, 1859, Munich.

85. It is reproduced in BVL, p. 161. Liszt never used the title, and before he could arrange for it to pass to Daniel the latter died. In 1867 it was assumed by Eduard Liszt and remained in his family until modern times (see Volume One, p. 32).

86. MAML, vol. 2, p. 292. Moscheles's observation that Liszt played a piano arrangement of the organ

XII

During the Handel festival there was much talk of the forthcoming Tonkünst-ler-Versammlung ("Congress of Musical Artists") to be held in Leipzig be-tween June 1 and 4. The moving spirit behind this gathering of musicians from across Germany was Franz Brendel, and its immediate impulse was the celebra-tions surrounding the twenty-fifth anniversary of the *Neue Zeitschrift für Musik*. Even Brendel could hardly have foreseen where such an idea might lead. The Versammlung quickly grew into the influential Allgemeiner Deutscher Musik-verein, one of the most powerful musical organizations in Germany, whose declared purpose was "to promote the welfare of musicians and improve musical conditions through the union of all groups and parties." Liszt was appointed its first president, and he remained in this elevated office for twenty-five years. (Later on, the presidency was held by Richard Strauss.) By far the best account of this first, historic meeting of the Tonkünstler-Versammlung was written by Richard Pohl, whose 180-page brochure[87] provides us with irre-placeable descriptions of the congress—its concerts, its personnel, and its guid-ing philosophy. In an appendix to the brochure Pohl lists well over three hundred musicians who travelled to Leipzig (from such diverse places as Berlin, Schwerin, Breslau, Dresden, Merseburg, Prague, St. Petersburg, Stockholm, and even New York) in order to take part in the celebrations. Liszt himself arrived towards the end of May and took rooms at the Hotel de Pologne. There he was joined by Princess Carolyne and Marie, who travelled from Munich in order to be with him.[88] It was entirely appropriate that the day before the congress began, there was a full-scale production of the opera *Genoveva* in honour of Robert Schumann, the founder of the *Neue Zeitschrift für Musik*. In his keynote address to the congress Brendel paid tribute to Schumann (who had died three years earlier) and adopted a conciliatory tone towards the opponents of *Zukunftsmusik* in general. He admitted that the term had done the cause of modern music great harm, and he proposed that the phrase "New German School" be used henceforth. And this historic name was the one by which Liszt and the Weimar circle came to be known to posterity.[89]

Prelude and Fugue on B-A-C-H as early as 1859 arouses interest. All the main work catalogues tell us that this piece dates from 1871, but Liszt obviously had a solo piano version in his fingers twelve years earlier which he went on elaborating. Tausig also played this early arrangement to Wagner in May 1860 (WML, p. 780; see p. 543 of the present volume), so it is evident that a manuscript copy was already in circulation among Liszt's acolytes. It was recently published in NLE 1:5.

87. PT-VL.
88. SNW, vol. 2, p. 98.
89. PT-VL, pp. 75–95. Poor Brendel, whose sole purpose was to hold out an olive-branch to the enemies of *Zukunftsmusik*, could not have foreseen the consequences of this proposal when he

The congress opened on June 1 with a concert in the Stadttheater, at which Liszt shared the podium with the resident Kapellmeister, August Riccius. Liszt's chief contribution was to conduct his symphonic poem *Tasso* and Wagner's newly completed Prelude to *Tristan,* billed as "played from the manuscript."[90] The following day Liszt conducted a performance of his "Gran" Mass in St. Thomas's Church, with the Gewandhaus Orchestra and a choir of 250 voices. According to Pohl, about 3,000 people attended the event[91]—perhaps the largest audience before which Liszt ever appeared as a conductor. During the festival Moscheles (who now taught at the Leipzig Conservatory) put on a large dinner-party for Liszt. After dinner, Liszt, puffing on his cigar, rummaged amongst Moscheles's music and found the latter's *Tanz* and the Humoristischen Variationen. Moscheles reported that Liszt made him sit down at the piano and play them with him. "It was a genuine treat to draw sparks from the piano as we dashed along together."[92] A day or two later they played again. "When we are harnessed together in a duet we make a very good pair; Apollo drives us without a whip."[93] On Friday, June 3, there was a full-scale performance of Bach's Mass in B minor in the St. Thomas Church, under the direction of Carl Riedel. The festival concluded the following day in a chamber concert, which included a performance of Schubert's Piano Trio in B-flat major, played by Ferdinand David (violin), Friedrich Grützmacher (cello), and Bülow. For those visitors who were willing to stay on for an extra day, Sunday, June 5,

---

published his speech in the columns of the NZfM (June 10, 1859). It was that issue in particular which inflamed the passions of Joachim and Brahms and led them to publish their "Manifesto" in the columns of the *Berliner Musik-Zeitung Echo* the following March. Their attack was specifically directed against the movement calling itself the New German School (see p. 349)—the old enemy under a different name.

90. For the complete programme see NZfM, May 27, 1859. The background to this performance of the Prelude to *Tristan* is not without interest. Wagner had not yet finished Act Three of *Tristan;* even so, the prelude was already well-known to his admirers. Liszt himself had been familiar with Act One since December 26, 1858, the date on which he received the sheets direct from the printers, and he had enthused to Wagner over his "divine Christmas present" (BWL, vol. 2, p. 225). Liszt harboured a desire to give the first performance of the prelude, but that honour went to Bülow, who directed the première at a *Zukunftskonzert* in Prague on March 12, 1859. Since the Prelude to *Tristan* flows without interruption into Act One, it had been necessary for Bülow to compose a concert ending for the first performance. Wagner had told him: "If you want to perform the *Tristan* Prelude in Prague I have nothing against it: only you yourself must compose an ending for it. You cannot demand that of me." (WBB, p. 118) Liszt used Bülow's ending for the second performance, in Leipzig, not realizing that Wagner was critical of it. In fact, Liszt never sought Wagner's permission to put the unpublished prelude into his programme at all; and when he asked Bülow to send him the score, the latter was understandably cautious. Bülow refused to despatch the score to Leipzig ("a city unworthy of the piece"; LBLB, p. 266) and sent it instead to Weimar. By the time the manuscript reached Weimar, Liszt himself was already in Leipzig, and the parcel had to be sent on to him. This means that Liszt had three days at most in which to rehearse the work.

91. PT-VL, p. 20.

92. MAML, vol. 2, p. 292.

93. MAML, vol. 2, p. 292.

a special outing to Merseburg had been arranged ("on the Thuringian railway"), and an organ recital in the cathedral brought the congress to a rousing finale.

X I I I

Scarcely two weeks after Liszt got back to Weimar, the city was plunged into mourning. On June 23 Grand Duchess Maria Pawlowna died at Belvedere Castle, and for the next three months all court functions came to a standstill. Liszt felt her loss keenly and hastened to send his condolences to Carl Alexander.[94] He knew full well that the true source of whatever benefaction he had enjoyed in Weimar flowed from Maria Pawlowna, without whose money the artistic life of the city would long since have foundered. On the day of her interment, June 27, Liszt convened a special meeting of the Neu-Weimar-Verein and delivered a eulogy to her memory. "Today is Old Weimar buried with that coffin," he observed.[95] Later events bore out that judgement. Left to steer the ship of state alone, Carl Alexander in the 1860s and '70s was unable to produce a single artistic advance over the achievements of the '50s. Liszt knew that a turning-point had been reached. His departure from Weimar could not be delayed much longer.

Typical of the low profile Liszt now desired to keep in Weimar and its immediate environs was his absence from the Schiller centenary celebrations, which fell on November 9 and 10, 1859. He attended neither the first performance of his music to Friedrich Halm's festival-play *Vor hundert Jahren*[96] nor the performances of his festival chorus "An die Künstler," which was mounted both in Jena and in Berlin. It would have been easy for him to involve himself in the celebrations, but he resolutely refused to pick up the baton. As he put it: "I have resolved to keep at a distance all the delights of conductorship, and to give the baton a rest, just like the piano."[97] And just a week before the festival: "I, for my part, shall not stir from the Altenburg, where I plan to finish my *Elisabeth* and to live more and more as a recluse. . . ."[98]

---

94. Carl Alexander's acknowledgement may be found in LBLCA, p. 73.
95. HML, vol. 6, p. 290.
96. The score of *Vor hundert Jahren* remains unpublished. "Friedrich Halm" was the pseudonym of Baron Eligius Münch-Bellinghausen, who later became the intendant of the Vienna Court Opera.
97. LLB, vol. 1, p. 334.
98. LLB, vol. 1, p. 339.

Of Marriage and Divorce

*You know that in this union with the princess lies
all the honour and all the happiness to which I
aspire and hope in this world.*

FRANZ LISZT TO CARL ALEXANDER[1]

I

When we stand back and take stock of Liszt's varied activities during the year
1859, one question keeps recurring: why did Liszt and the princess stay on in
Weimar now that he no longer held an official appointment there? After all,
the city retained few charms for either of them. Liszt's future was bleak, and
since he was resolute in his determination not to conduct in the Court Theatre
again, his career there was now at a standstill. As for the recent Handel festival
and the concerts of the Tonkünstler-Versammlung in Leipzig, Liszt could have
played just as significant a role in them, or in any such gatherings, irrespective
of his domicile. Moreover, as attached as he was to the local musicians, there
were obstacles to engaging them outside Weimar. He actually had had to plead
with Dingelstedt for the release of some of the soloists for the Leipzig concerts,
an indignity he could hardly have relished. Weimar, in short, had become not
only unnecessary for the fulfilment of his artistic plans, but was now an
impediment to them. So why did Liszt and Carolyne stay on?

One thing kept the pair tied to the Altenburg: the ongoing marriage negotiations for Princess Marie, which had occupied Carolyne for more than four years
and which had now reached a delicate stage. Intimately woven into the fabric
of these negotiations was the matter of Carolyne's divorce. We shall have to
disentangle many threads in this complex story in order to understand how two
quite separate issues could ever have come to be regarded as one.

---

1. LBLCA, p. 95.

Princess Marie was now twenty-two years old, fair and slender, well-educated, and immensely rich. It should not have been difficult to select a suitable husband for her, and in fact she was not short of suitors. But no candidate had found equal favour in the eyes of both Carolyne and Nicholas Wittgenstein. The problem was always the same: the Iwanowsky fortune. On February 18, 1858, her twenty-first birthday, Princess Marie had inherited the Iwanowsky estates which until then had been sequestered by Tsar Alexander II. On that date, too, she had ceased to be a ward of Grand Duchess Maria Pawlowna and was therefore free to dispose of her wealth as she thought fit. Carolyne was now in the paradoxical position of being dependent on her daughter for money. As for the Wittgensteins, they worked ceaselessly behind the scenes to bring about a marriage that would protect their own interests. The poor girl, in short, had become a pawn in the hands of her warring parents.

When Marie was still only eighteen years old, Baron Talleyrand, a diplomat attached to the French consulate in Weimar, had asked for her hand in marriage. Carolyne thoroughly approved of this match and hastened to inform the tsar, who alone could lift the sequestration order imposed on her properties and hand them over to Marie. When Nicholas Wittgenstein heard of this development he intervened on the grounds that he was reluctant to give his daughter to a Frenchman. It was the time of the Crimean War, passions were running high, and Nicholas's voice was heeded.[2] The marriage, planned for July 1855, was abruptly cancelled.[3]

In 1859 a new suitor appeared on the horizon. He was Prince Konstantin Hohenlohe-Schillingsfürst, the thirty-one-year-old scion of one of the most powerful dynasties in Germany. Konstantin was an aide-de-camp to Emperor Franz Joseph and was based in Vienna; an elder brother, Prince Chlodwig, later rose to become chancellor of Germany. By coincidence Liszt had already met some of the family when he paid a brief visit to the home of Prince Viktor Hohenlohe, duke of Ratibor, at Rauden in February 1859.[4] On that occasion he had also made the acquaintance of Monsignor Gustav Hohenlohe, from whom he was later to receive the tonsure. In fact, during that same visit to Rauden Liszt had arranged to have two specially bound copies of his "Gran"

---

2. The diary of Frédéric Soret observed the many obstacles which were strewn across Talleyrand's path. "The saddest part of the story is that the young princess is promised to M. Talleyrand, who, I think, is waiting for the regularization of the mother's situation before he can marry the daughter. The poor man will wait a long time!" (SG, p. 71) After the cancellation of the marriage, Talleyrand took up a diplomatic posting in Brussels.

3. Tucked away in a fairly long paragraph which La Mara censored from a letter Liszt wrote to Agnès Street-Klindworth on April 11, 1855 (the mutilated version is in LLB, vol. 3, pp. 3–5) is a confirmation of the actual marriage date: "It will take place very probably before I leave for Hungary in July; T[alleyrand] arrived here last Thursday and stayed until Monday" (DA).

4. LLB, vol. 4, pp. 447. Prince Viktor was the head of the Hohenlohe clan; he had succeeded to the dukedom of Ratibor on the death of his father in 1841. See the Family Tree, pp. xviii–xix.

Mass presented to Pope Pius IX and Cardinal Antonelli through the good offices of Gustav (who had apartments inside the Vatican), for it was his hope to have the work performed within the Basilica of St. Peter itself. Liszt, we know, approved of Marie's marriage into this august family. From Carolyne's point of view, however, it was not an ideal match, and at first she prevaricated. She knew that the Hohenlohe and Wittgenstein families were distantly related, and that left the Iwanowsky legacy exposed to Nicholas's influence.[5] So why did she submit to their wishes?

In the summer of 1859 the drama had taken an unexpected turn with the arrival in Weimar of one of Carolyne's land tenants from Ukraine. His name was Ladislaw Okraszewsky, a lawyer by profession, and he brought with him a tantalizing proposition. He informed Carolyne, in confidence, that the bishops

---

5. The marriage negotiations were begun in Munich in April 1859; it was there that the young couple met for the first time (Princess Marie had gone to the Bavarian capital, accompanied by her mother, to have her portrait painted by Kaulbach). By the end of the month the terms of the contract appear to have been worked out, and by mid-May a wedding was agreed upon. On September 3 Konstantin sent a ring to Weimar for Princess Marie, enclosed with a letter (LLB, vol. 4, p. 490). It was clearly the arrival of this ring that prompted Liszt to write to Monsignor Hohenlohe, who had meanwhile returned to Rome, that same day. In his reply, dated the Vatican, September 28, 1859, Monsignor Hohenlohe communicated to Liszt some flattering words from Pius IX: "Tell M. Liszt that I send him my blessing, and that I have handed his celebrated mass to the Chapter of St. Peter. Tell him also that it will be sung in the month of November at St. Peter's in Die Dedicationis Basilicae S.S. Apostolorum Petri et Pauli and that I shall be present. This mass may not be able to produce the immense effect that it has elsewhere, because we do not have instruments at St. Peter's, but without doubt it will still be really beautiful, and I am very much looking forward to hearing it." (LBZL, vol. 2, pp. 250–51) Hohenlohe also issued an invitation to Liszt to visit Rome and stay with him in the Vatican.

This letter is notable because it became the starting point of the famous "conspiracy theory" favoured by a number of latter-day Liszt scholars, led by Emile Haraszti (HFL, pp. 181–82). According to this theory, the Hohenlohes conspired to prevent Liszt's marriage to Carolyne by playing on his vanity. They held out before him the prospect of one day taking charge of music at the Vatican; in this position his old dream of reforming church music could literally come true. In order to do this, however, Liszt would have to remain single and he would have to take holy orders. Carolyne, in brief, was to be sacrificed on the altar of Liszt's ambition. And what interest did the Hohenlohes have in playing such a deceitful game? They were already connected to the Wittgenstein family through the tie of marriage: Prince Chlodwig was married to Marie's cousin—a daughter of her uncle Ludwig Wittgenstein—and both families therefore had a vested interest in keeping the Iwanowsky fortune within their orbits. Marie herself tells us that it was Chlodwig, her cousin-in-law, who actually arranged her marriage to Konstantin (MH-S, vol. 1, p. 141), a clear proof that the Hohenlohes were willing tools of the Wittgensteins.

There is only one thing wrong with this theory. It requires the participation of Liszt, and there is no evidence that he went along with it. On the contrary, the letters he exchanged with Carolyne between May 1860 and October 20, 1861, the longest period for which they had ever been separated, indicate a deep commitment to their marriage plans. We do not accept that Liszt, aided and abetted by the Hohenlohes, secretly intended to abandon Carolyne at the altar. That the Hohenlohes and the Wittgensteins connived to prevent her marriage (not just to Liszt but to anyone) we do not doubt at all, and they had weapons enough at their disposal, as we shall see. But that is quite another matter. The essential point to bear in mind here is that whatever they did, they could not count on Liszt as an ally.

of Vilnius and Kamenez both believed that an annulment of her marriage could be obtained through the sacrifice of money. Okraszewsky offered to act as an intermediary in this complex affair and made Carolyne an offer she found impossible to refuse. If the negotiations failed, he would ask for nothing; but if they succeeded, he would require a payment of 70,000 silver roubles. This was an enormous sum, and as the princess's case unfolded, there arose a suspicion that Okraszewsky used some of it to bribe the Russian clerics. Why should Carolyne cooperate in such a risky venture? In 1855 the inflexible metropolitan of St. Petersburg, Archbishop Ignaz Holowinsky, had died; his successor, Archbishop Wenceslas Zyliński, had shown himself to be more tolerant on matters concerning canonical divorce. But there was a difficulty, and once more Okraszewsky proposed the solution. Since the princess could no longer dispose of her fortune, this debt would have to be assumed by Princess Marie. On July 15, Marie wrote to Baron von Maltitz affirming her decision to help her mother.

> Your Excellency,
>   According to your wish, and in reply to your objection, I convey to you here afresh my firm and invariable resolution to conclude a contract with M. Okraszewsky, by which I agree to pay him the sum of 70,000 silver roubles if he obtains the canonical divorce of my mother, Princess Carolyne von Sayn-Wittgenstein. I thereby obey my filial duty and use in this the rights conferred on me by law.[6]

Okraszewsky departed for St. Petersburg in September 1859. Six months later he would return to Weimar in triumph, an annulment in hand.

This was the Machiavellian background against which the nuptials of Princess Marie and Prince Konstantin unfolded. Carolyne dared not risk jeopardizing Okraszewsky's delicate mission. Had she voiced her inner fears about this marriage, she knew that the Wittgensteins could easily retaliate by embarking on a fresh round of litigation which might postpone her annulment indefinitely. The role of Prince Nicholas in all this was truly extraordinary. In 1855 he had secured a Protestant divorce and had remarried in January 1856; his second wife was Marie Michaïloff, a twenty-six-year-old nurse to the children of Prince Souvaroff, governor of Riga. There was one daughter of this union, born in February 1857, whom Nicholas, with exquisite tactlessness, named Marie.[7] Carolyne was well aware of all this,[8] but she knew that it could make little

---

6. HL, p. 180.
7. There were now four Marie Sayn-Wittgensteins: Nicholas's two daughters, his new wife, and his brother Ludwig's daughter.
8. This is borne out by a letter which Liszt drafted (on June 25, 1858) for Carl Alexander to send on to Tsar Alexander when the question of Carolyne's annulment had become crucial. In it he specifically points out that Carolyne's annulment would be "all the more legitimate in that Prince

difference to her own plight. Only the Catholic Church could loosen her bonds.
That is why Okraszewsky's mission was crucial.

11

The marriage of Princess Marie and Prince Konstantin took place on October
15, 1859, at eleven o'clock in the morning, in the small Catholic church of St.
John the Baptist, which stood on Marienstrasse. The local priest, Anton Hohmann, officiated. According to Eduard Lassen it was a melancholy occasion.
Very few people were in attendance, and Carolyne and "Scotchy" Anderson
sobbed loudly throughout the ceremony.[9] It was particularly hard on Miss
Anderson, who had been Marie's governess for most of the girl's life and was
now about to be parted from her young charge. After a small reception at the
Altenburg, the newlyweds left for Vienna, where they took up permanent
residence.

The departure of Princess Marie threw the Altenburg into gloom and despair.
She was not only a daughter to Carolyne but her inseparable companion. Four
days after the wedding Carolyne, in an effort to shake off her depression, set
out for Paris in the company of her maid, Augusta. During the week she spent
there she saw Anna Liszt and also encountered Berlioz, whose appearance
shocked her. "I have never seen such thinness," she told Liszt. "He is no longer
a body, he is scarcely anything like a human being . . . I no longer know
how much longer he has to live." After regaling Carolyne with a catalogue of
aches and pains, Berlioz cried out: "It's absurd, it's terrible to die, horrible,
horrible!"[10]

Liszt celebrated his forty-eighth birthday at the Altenburg in almost total
seclusion. He dined with "Scotchy" Anderson and Cosima, who had unexpect-

---

Wittgenstein . . . contracted a second marriage three years ago" (HL, p. 179). The commonly held
view that Carolyne knew nothing of Nicholas's divorce until she read about it in the *Almanach de
Gotha* for 1861 cannot be sustained (LLB, vol. 5, p. 96). There is a strong suspicion that Carolyne
herself may have published that information in the *Almanach* in order to lend greater piquancy to
her own divorce action, which at that point had reached a critical stage in Rome.

9. SNW, vol. 2, p. 51. The details of Princess Marie's wedding are preserved in the Catholic church's
marriage register in Weimar (vol. 32, p. 20). From this source we learn that Konstantin was attended
by his brother Prince Viktor and that the bride was led to the altar by her cousin Prince Emil von
Sayn-Wittgenstein. Her father, Prince Nicholas, was not present and may thus have avoided the
charge of perjury—in Protestant eyes, at any rate. For not only does the marriage declaration make
no mention of the divorce that he had obtained four years earlier, but it describes Princess Marie
as his "only legitimate daughter"—despite the birth of his second daughter two and a half years
earlier. Both Nicholas and Carolyne were saved from further embarrassment in this matter by Carl
Alexander, who on October 12, 1859, "most graciously consented to grant dispensation [to the
parents] from submitting the required marriage certificate."

10. WA, Kasten 35, no. 53. Unpublished letter dated October 20, 1859.

edly come down from Berlin to spend the day with him. They talked of Daniel (who was now a patient in her home) and of the seriousness of his illness. Even so, Liszt appears to have had no idea that his son's life was threatened. Later in the evening he went across to the Erbprinz Hotel, where a small supper-party had been arranged by the Neu-Weimar-Verein.[11] Gone were the days of ostentation and brilliant parties. The year 1859 drew to a close with the stunning blow of Daniel's death and its mournful aftermath.

During the weeks that followed it was as if time stood still at the Altenburg while Carolyne and Liszt awaited word from Okraszewsky. Then, in March 1860, there was an outbreak of jubilation. Carolyne learned that her annulment had been granted on February 24 (Old Style) by the Catholic consistories of Russia and countersigned by the metropolitan of St. Petersburg, and that Okraszewsky himself would return to Weimar with the relevant documents.[12] Some impression of the excitement that prevailed can be gained from Liszt's letter to Princess Marie dated April 7, 1860, in which he writes: "You may well imagine that for the past three weeks all we have done is to await Okra's arrival. Minette can neither eat nor drink nor sleep."[13] We shall probably never know exactly what transpired at the Altenburg when Okraszewsky finally got there, but the outcome was clear enough. The Russian annulment, so painstakingly negotiated by Okraszewsky, was not recognized by the bishop of Fulda, who immediately suspended it on the authority of Monsignor Antonino De Luca, the papal nuncio in Vienna.[14] Carolyne knew that she would have to look to Rome to have that suspension lifted. A decision was taken—either by Carolyne or Liszt, or more likely by them both—that she herself would have to accompany Okraszewsky to the Eternal City and press her case in person.

III

Carolyne set out for Rome on May 17 in the company of Okraszewsky and her maid, Augusta. The details of their journey are preserved in Carolyne's

---

11. LLB, vol. 4, p. 494.
12. The decree of annulment is published as Appendix II to the present volume, p. 567.
13. HLSW, p. 122.
14. From the time of the Reformation, Fulda had been the centre of the Roman Catholic administration in Thuringia. Since Carolyne and Liszt were both domiciled in the diocese of Fulda, they were bound by the bishop's suspension. Incidentally, Liszt himself confirms the granting of Carolyne's annulment in two letters to Agnès Street-Klindworth. The first, dated May 28, 1860, was published by La Mara in LLB, vol. 3, pp. 122–23; the second, dated November 8, 1860, contains details that were hostile to the Hohenlohes and the Wittgensteins and was heavily censored by her. The holograph of the latter document may be consulted in DA.

unpublished letters to Liszt.[15] It is clear that she expected her stay in Rome to last no more than a few weeks, after which she would return to Weimar. In the event, she and Liszt were to be parted for sixteen months, until he himself joined her in Rome. Carolyne was never to see Weimar again.

The little party travelled first to Frankfurt, then journeyed through France to Marseille, where they took ship for Rome. The crossing was rough, and the princess provides a vivid description of the ship at sea. "I was not afraid for an instant," she wrote, "even at the time of the most violent tossing about, when we were thrown left and right like so many parcels."[16] After brief stopovers in Genoa, Livorno, and Pisa (whose leaning tower was scaled by Okraszewsky—"just as in Genoa and the south of France he scaled everything that had steps"[17]), the party arrived in Rome on May 24, Pentecost Sunday.

One of the first people she consulted was Monsignor Gustav Hohenlohe. This was a natural thing for her to do, since Gustav had quarters in the Vatican, knew several cardinals intimately, and was well versed in canon law. Moreover, since he was now a member of her family, she doubtless thought that he could be trusted with the details of her case. Within days of her arrival in Rome, in fact, Gustav had invited Carolyne to his private chapel in the Vatican, where she observed him celebrate early-morning mass. Afterwards Gustav took her to have breakfast with two key members of the Holy Congregation which had been convened to consider her case, Monsignors Salva and Ferrari, with whom she had a brief conference. She and Gustav then returned to his apartments, where she admired his impressive library and where they engaged in a two-hour conversation during which Gustav groomed her for her forthcoming audience with Pope Pius IX. She noticed that Gustav's mitre, while studded with precious stones, was lacking in emeralds, so she later presented him with two such jewels from her own collection.[18] Thereafter they met almost daily; he took her on various sight-seeing tours of the museums and chapels inside the Vatican and generally played the part of an attentive host. Occasionally they even travelled outside Rome. This was Carolyne's first experience of Italy, and she enthused over Hadrian's villa and Tivoli. It is strange to think of her visiting the Villa d'Este and admiring the fountains in the company of Gustav Hohenlohe long before

---

15. WA, Kasten 36 and 37. Carolyne's itinerary, which was followed by Liszt with great interest, ran:

May 17	Frankfurt	19	Dijon	21	Nîmes	23	Livorno
18	Strasbourg	20	Lyon	22	Marseille	24	Rome

She sent letters to Liszt from each of these locations.

16. Letter dated May 24, 1860. The name of the ship on which the princess travelled was the *Quirinal,* which she took to be a happy omen. The Quirinal Palace, situated on one of the seven hills of Rome, was a summer residence of the popes.

17. Ibid.

18. Letter dated June 1, 1860.

Liszt himself took up residence there.[19] Although Carolyne did not at first know it, every conversation she had with Gustav was reported back to his brother Konstantin in Vienna. Gustav, in fact, soon proved himself to be a master of duplicity who, in the matter of the Iwanowsky fortune, was determined to place the interests of his brother first.

I V

What was the basis of Konstantin's hostility towards Carolyne? He wanted at all costs to prevent the annulment of her marriage to Prince Nicholas, but still more her nuptials with Liszt. From the moment that "Magnolette" became his bride, Konstantin exercised complete control over her fortune. He feared that if Carolyne succeeded in gaining an annulment, Marie could be declared illegitimate, and the marriage-contract so laboriously drawn up might come to be regarded as null and void.[20] More serious still were the possible consequences of a marriage between Liszt and Carolyne. In 1860 Carolyne was still only forty-two years old and was therefore theoretically capable of bearing Liszt a child. This offspring would certainly be regarded by the church as legitimate and would therefore be a strong claimant to the Iwanowsky fortune, the possession of which the newly illegitimate Marie might be forced to relinquish. Such were the dark thoughts that turned Konstantin into Carolyne's adversary within weeks of becoming her son-in-law. That same fortune which had made Carolyne a hostage of the Wittgensteins was about to bind her to the Hohenlohes, who would prove to be far more implacable foes.

There can be no better illustration of the nightmare in which Carolyne found herself entangled than the little matter of Okraszewsky's fee of 70,000 silver roubles. This debt, incurred by Princess Marie on her mother's behalf, had become the responsibility of Konstantin at the moment of his marriage, and he refused point-blank to discharge it. In desperation Carolyne withdrew 55,000 florins from money invested with Eduard Liszt in Vienna and paid Okraszewsky herself.[21] Konstantin never refunded this money. His intransigence soured Carolyne's relations with her daughter, who, she thought, should have stood up to her husband and compelled him to settle this "debt of honour." Carolyne even toyed with the idea of having Okraszewsky sue Konstantin

---

19. WA, Kasten 37, letter dated July 5, 1860.
20. WA, Kasten 37, letter dated August 30, 1860. The fear that Marie could be declared illegitimate on the dissolution of her mother's marriage was a real one. We are dealing here with the concept of annulment, not of divorce. Divorce acknowledges that a marriage once existed but is now ended. Annulment is a retrospective admission that the marriage had never existed in the first place, since the ceremony itself was based on some grave impropriety, offensive both to God and to the Church. The offspring of such unions often had to protect their inheritance rights by means of legally binding contracts drawn up at the time of dissolution.
21. WA, Kasten 37, letter dated September 30, 1860.

through the courts, but she was deterred by the expense. "Once hostilities begin between [Konstantin] and Okraszewsky, it will always be the *millionaire prince* who will win over a farmer in a court case."[22]

Within three months of her arrival in Rome, Carolyne knew exactly where she stood. We need look no further than Carolyne's letter to Liszt dated August 30, 1860, in which she speaks of Gustav's "unbelievable treason" and goes on to accuse him of having broken her confidences and of having "exercised an influence on the pope that was disastrous for me." Gustav, she claimed, had represented her to the pope as a fool, a ridiculous old woman who, by wishing to re-marry at her age, was exposing her daughter to the charge of illegitimacy. At least one member of the Holy Congregation, the papal nuncio of Vienna, Monsignor De Luca, saw her as a bigamist, an image that was duly relayed to Konstantin and found its way back to Carolyne in one of the rare letters she received from Princess Marie.[23] From September 1860 she was under no illusions that she had a minor theological war on her hands and that if it was to be won, she would require the assistance of some powerful friends. She cultivated Monsignor Angelo Quaglia (the secretary of the Holy Congregation) and also the vicar general of the Society of Jesus, who called on her one day to discuss theological matters.[24] Her greatest supporter was Cardinal Giacomo Antonelli, the secretary of state at the Vatican and one of the most powerful figures in Rome. Antonelli gave Carolyne a great deal of inside information on the progress of her case and helped to guide her efforts through the complex machinery of the Vatican bureaucracy.

V

Before we follow the progress of Carolyne's petition through the corridors of the Vatican itself, we would do well to take stock of the legal position in which she now found herself. Some recently discovered documents in the Vatican archives allow us to reconstruct the tortured history of her case with more detail than has hitherto been possible.[25] Her plea for an annulment was twelve years old when she finally brought it to Rome, and during the next few months it would exercise some of the best theological brains within the Church hierarchy.

---

22. Ibid.
23. WA, Kasten 37, letter dated August 30, 1860. Carolyne, who was normally so shrewd in her dealings with others, seems to have lost her bearings with Gustav Hohenlohe. Yet there was one clue that might have suggested an intrigue to Carolyne had she thought about it a little longer. This was the near-total silence of her daughter, Marie. Since her marriage to Konstantin, "Magnolette" had had scarcely any contact with her mother. Carolyne was distraught at the silence and was convinced that her mail to Marie was being intercepted.
24. WA, Kasten 37, letter dated September 30, 1860.
25. ASVR.

Carolyne's original plea had been submitted to the consistory of Mohilow in St. Petersburg on May 4, 1848, one month after she had fled Russia. This ecclesiastical court of three judges had appointed one Deacon Mierzwinsky to be the Defender of the Marriage Bond,[26] and the case was tried on May 12. Drama and confrontation must have characterized the occasion: ten family witnesses were called for Prince Nicholas and five for Princess Carolyne, including her mother. One of the witnesses, a servant named Julianna Stolavczuk, claimed that fustigation had been used against Carolyne, and that she had listened to it through the door. The case for the princess was nonetheless flimsy, Mierwinsky argued. Carolyne had been married for twelve years before filing her petition, which alleged *vis et metus*. Why had she not begun these proceedings at once? Moreover, there was a child of the union, which further strengthened the matrimonial bond. Carolyne, for her part, made it clear through written documentation that she was only seventeen at the time of her marriage, that it was her father (not Prince Wittgenstein) who had coerced her; and there were family witnesses to testify to that fact. Mierwinsky, for all his eloquence, failed to convince the court; Carolyne's case was upheld, and it was then referred to her own diocese of Luk-Zhitomir, where the evidence (which included a written protest from Mierwinsky) was re-examined. More than three years elapsed before the Luk-Zhitomir court brought forth its decision: "that the matrimonial bond between Prince Wittgenstein and Carolyne Iwanowska be declared valid."[27] Carolyne now had two court decisions, one in her favour and one against. A year later her case was referred once more to the consistory of Mohilow, which, after reviewing the case ruled again in Carolyne's favour. It was at this point that Archbishop Ignaz Holowinsky stepped in with his veto and halted Carolyne's motion in its tracks.[28] This was indeed devastating news for the princess. Four years of legal activity had come to nought. The case had been tried in Mohilow (1848), reviewed in Luk-Zhitomir (1851), appealed in Mohilow (1852), and finally ruled against by St. Petersburg (1852). And there the matter might have rested.

But in 1855 two very important developments occurred. Holowinsky died and was succeeded by Archbishop Wenceslas Zyliński, who knew the details of this case very well. That same year, too, Prince Nicholas secured his Protestant divorce, and in 1856 he re-married. Carolyne's legal advisers informed her

---

26. The role of *Defensor Vincali Matrimoni* was more than a hundred years old at this time, having been introduced by Benedict XIV in his papal bull *Dei miseratione* of 1741. There was no more powerful symbol of the profound importance attached to the annulment proceedings than the presence in court of "God's advocate," whose holy task it was to defend the sanctity of the marriage bond by all legal means. It was also his ecclesiastical duty to appeal all decisions affecting the bond to a higher court.

27. ASVR, fol. 143.

28. ASVR, fol. 83.

that the complexion of her case now looked somewhat different; in 1857 they brought it once more before the lower consistory of Luk-Zhitomir, the court that had originally denied her petition. That court, however, upheld its earlier decision and, by implication, Holowinsky's veto.

This was the dismal history of the legal wrangle when Okraszewsky arrived at the Altenburg in the spring of 1859 and persuaded Carolyne to appeal to the new archbishop, Zyliński, the consequences of which have already been related. A legal technicality arose at this juncture, however. It was argued that since Carolyne's petition had already been heard by the Mohilow consistories on two occasions, it could not be heard by them a third time. Accordingly, Zyliński sought a dispensation from Rome to allow him to reconsider the case; this was granted on August 8, 1859.[29] The Mohilow court was re-convened towards the end of the year, with Deacon Basil Zottek as Defender of the Marriage Bond. As we know, Zyliński issued a decree on February 24, 1860, which declared Carolyne's marriage to be null and void. At this point Basil Zottek appealed to Rome, and charges of bribery and corruption began to emerge. Pius IX, deeply concerned at such allegations (which Archbishop Zyliński strenuously denied), instructed Monsignor De Luca in Vienna not to sanction the annulment until Zottek had presented the facts of the matter to the Vatican.[30]

---

29. ASVR, fol. 90. The three-month delay in issuing this dispensation was caused by the fact that Archbishop Zyliński was obliged to direct his request through the Imperial cabinet in St. Petersburg. Russian prelates were not permitted to communicate directly with the Holy See.

30. Pius IX's consternation was reflected in the communication his secretary Angelo Quaglia sent to De Luca on May 3. Quaglia reported that the Holy Father had learned that Carolyne had taken 80,000 scudi from her daughter's wedding dowry for the fraudulent purpose of corrupting the Russian consistories (ASVR, fol. 90). There could be no question of her re-marriage until these charges were answered.

The active interest that Cardinal Antonelli showed in the case at this time is borne out by his request to De Luca for a full account of the reason behind the suspension of the St. Petersburg annulment. As secretary of state to the Vatican, Antonelli did not normally meddle in matrimonial disputes; but he seems to have been impressed by the personality of the princess and the dogged determination with which she pursued her case against impossible odds. On July 14, 1860, four or five weeks after Carolyne first met him, Cardinal Antonelli received this deferential reply from De Luca (ASVR, SS. 1860, rub. 247, prot. no. 12754).

No. 1057
Re: Marriage Case Wittgenstein-Iwanowska

To   His Most Reverend Eminence Cardinal Antonelli
      Secretary of State to His Holiness
      Rome
      (With Enclosure)

Most Reverend Eminence:
    In accordance with the request I received from Monsignor the Secretary to the Sacred Congregation of the Council in his letter of May 3, I immediately forwarded, on behalf of the Holy See, to Monsignor the Bishop of Fulda and Monsignor the Archbishop of Mohilow in St. Petersburg, a formal injunction not to proceed with the implementation of the sentence pronounced by the latter prelate by special pontifical proxy. The sentence

When Carolyne arrived in Rome in May 1860, she found herself already caught up in a tangled web of disputation and intrigue. Her case was not only famous; it had now become notorious. Indeed, from any rational point of view, the case had acquired so many facets, both sacred and secular, that it appeared to be insoluble. Carolyne knew that only the pope himself had the authority to cut through the jungle of arguments that bound her with malevolent tentacles to the past. That is why she spared no effort to confront the pontiff with the facts of the matter, although it was to take three months before he agreed to receive her.

VI

On September 9, 1860, Carolyne's long-awaited audience with Pope Pius IX took place in the Vatican. She begged the Holy Father for his blessing, told him that her marriage was the result of parental constraint, and pleaded with him for his intervention. "Mia cara figlia, non ti dimenticherò!"[31] he reassured her, and undertook to convene a Council of Cardinals to examine the question. This audience with Pius IX was an important turning-point in the disposition of Carolyne's case. On September 22, the Council of Cardinals assembled and recommended in favour of the princess; the Russian annulment would be upheld. Two days later Pius IX gave his formal assent. The decision was transmitted to the bishop of Fulda through De Luca's office in Vienna. Unfortu-

---

declared the marriage between Prince Nicholas Wittgenstein (Calvinist) and his putative wife, Princess Wittgenstein (Catholic), to be null and void. I gave, moreover, the afore-mentioned Archbishop instructions to suggest to the Defender of the Marriage Bond in his Bishopric that he lodge an appeal to the Holy See against that sentence, and to forward the records of the case.

Monsignor the Bishop of Fulda acted in strict conformity with the injunction; moreover, he informed me that Princess Iwanowska was undertaking a voyage to Rome.

As for Monsignor the Archbishop of Mohilow, I received from the Russian Legation in Vienna an official note, dated July 6, forwarding to me this prelate's answer. I have the honour of enclosing in this brief a copy of this latter document in order that Your Most Reverend Eminence be acquainted with its contents and be fully and specifically informed of a situation which the Imperial Cabinet in St. Petersburg thought it should deal with in order to uphold the principle that it is not permitted to bishops and other members of our Faith in that vast Empire to communicate directly with the Holy See.

With a sense of the deepest respect, I bow to kiss the holy purple you wear, while I have the honour of confirming myself the most humble, devout, and obliging servant of Your Most Reverend Eminence.

Ant. Archbishop of Tarso, Apostolic Nuncius
Vienna, July 14, 1860

This letter does not tell us anything about the case that we do not already know, of course. Its interest for us lies in the fact that it offers proof that Antonelli was briefed with documents from both Vienna and St. Petersburg, and we may be sure that he advised Carolyne of their contents.
31. "My dear daughter, I shall not forget you!" (LAG, p. 425)

*Princess Carolyne in Rome, in the clothes she wore at her
audience with Pope Pius IX on September 9, 1860.*

nately, Carolyne had some old scores to settle, and she proceeded to complicate her case by insisting that Okraszewsky take the instruments of annulment to De Luca and the bishop of Fulda in person and then return to Rome with written confirmations from both clerics that they were in receipt of those documents. It is indicative of Carolyne's combative attitude that she believed it to be "important that our marriage take place *precisely in Fulda itself,* in order to give it greater validity."[32] The result was predictable. Neither the nuncio nor the bishop was about to become a tool of the princess, and they raised further objections, which were relayed to Rome. They argued that the conclusion of the College of Cardinals was merely a recommendation, not a decision, and that it was therefore not binding. What was the basis of this display of intransigence? Gustav Hohenlohe had meanwhile acquired some new and potentially devastating information which suggested that the Russian annulment, issued on February 24, had been obtained through perjury. Quite by chance, Carolyne had met in Rome one of her Polish cousins, Denise Poniatowska (the daughter of her father's brother, Dionys Iwanowsky), and her husband. It seems to have dawned on her but slowly that the chief purpose of Denise's visit to the Eternal City was to inform Gustav Hohenlohe that her cousin's wedding to Nicholas Wittgenstein was not forced, as Carolyne claimed, but was entered into quite freely. The Poniatowsky family, in fact, were witnesses to the wedding service, which had taken place at her father's estate in Starosteine, and denied all knowledge of coercion. It will be recalled that the Poniatowskys had in earlier years tried to wrest Carolyne's inheritance from her by fraud. Were they now paying her back for having frustrated their efforts?[33] We shall

---

32. WA, Kasten 37, letter of September 28, 1860.
33. See Carolyne' letters to Liszt dated May 24 and June 1, 1860 (WA, Kasten 36).
   How had Gustav Hohenlohe acquired knowledge of Denise Poniatowska and her family? Carolyne implies that Denise was in Rome by chance, but another interpretation is possible. In December 1859 Prince Konstantin and his new bride, Marie, had journeyed to St. Petersburg to meet her relations (CLW, vol. I, p. 436). It is inconceivable that the question of Carolyne's annulment was not discussed, since the case was just then in full swing; indeed, within two months that annulment had been approved by the archbishop of St. Petersburg, to the consternation of the Hohenlohes. Was Denise despatched to Rome as a hostile witness at Konstantin's suggestion, in order to block its further progress through the Vatican? It is certainly strange that this witness should travel there in the early summer of 1860—that is, at the very time that Carolyne herself took up residence in the city.
   The memoirs of Marie von Hohenlohe provide us with many details of her mother's struggle to procure an annulment. According to Marie, the Poniatowskys were motivated by a purely spiritual desire not to see Carolyne commit a mortal sin by gaining her annulment through perjury (LSJ, p. 42). Carolyne herself did not believe such pious sentiments for a moment. Nevertheless, she reported to Liszt a revealing conversation she had had with Denise Poniatowska shortly before the latter's departure from Rome in June 1860. Carolyne observed that "since my salvation was more important to her heart than my happiness, she was incapable of wishing for the result I was trying to obtain, but [she said] that if the Holy Father gave his approval she would be very happy and would receive you as a brother with open arms" (WA, Kasten 36, letter dated June 1, 1860). Such a sentiment must have sent a shudder down Carolyne's spine. Everyone knew that perjury in matrimonial affairs was punishable by imprisonment. Coming from a member of her own family, such a charge was

probably never be in a position to disentangle the canonical dispute that such powerful testimony engendered, but the outcome was plain enough. On January 8, 1861, the College of Cardinals was once more convened to review the case, and it upheld its earlier decision: the annulment granted by Mohilow in 1852 would stand.[34] Carolyne could not contain her elation and wrote to Liszt:

> A triumph, a complete triumph . . . Through his resistance, Monsignor Luca has only earned a letter, infinitely more peremptory than the first, which enjoins him to obey [the College of Cardinals] and does so in such a way that he is left with no possibility of a refusal. His Holiness has had added, as a peroration, that if scandal were talked of, "Monsignor Fulda has a duty to dissipate it by pointing out that those of whom it is said are scandalized in turn, since the matter has been dealt with and judged twice in Rome . . . with regard to all the circumstances, personal and local, and therefore no one has any grounds to oppose it."[35]

There was now no legal impediment whatsoever standing in the way of a marriage between Carolyne and Liszt. The only matter to be decided was where to hold the ceremony itself. If, at that moment, the couple had decided to be married by a local priest in some small town or village well away from Rome, the débâcle which occurred at the church of San Carlo al Corso on October 21 might have been avoided. But they vacillated, and with the passing of time they were delivered into the hands of their enemies.

---

the last thing that she had expected to encounter. In the event, the entire case was to turn on this question: was her marriage forced or was it entered into freely?

34. It is interesting to note that it was the decision of 1852 that was upheld by Pius IX, not the more recent one approved by the consistory in February 1860. The pope thus circumvented all the charges of bribery and corruption which had meanwhile attached themselves to the later proceedings as a result of Okraszewsky's "fees and disbursements."

35. WA, Kasten 37, unpublished letter dated January 11, 1861.

Liszt Makes a Testament and Leaves Weimar, 1860–1861

> *At a certain period (about ten years ago) I had visions of a new epoch for Weimar, similar to that of Carl August, in which Wagner and I should have been the leading spirits, as Goethe and Schiller were formerly. The meanness, not to say villainy, of certain local circumstances, all kinds of jealousies, ineptitudes, both external and internal, have prevented the realization of this dream. . . .*
>
> FRANZ LISZT[1]

I

We must now go back and look at the situation through Liszt's eyes. That he willingly supported Carolyne's efforts to resolve her problems directly with Rome cannot be doubted. To maintain, as the older biographies did, that Liszt was reluctant to see his years with Carolyne culminate in matrimony flies in the face of the evidence. Within days of Okraszewsky's arrival in Weimar in the summer of 1859, in fact, Liszt had petitioned Carl Alexander, asking him to intercede with the Vatican on Okraszewsky's behalf. On July 8 Liszt wrote to the grand duke:

Sire,
   You have been kind enough to tell me more than once that you would not refuse to lend me your support in Rome. A situation has arisen in which I must now seek this promised protection. Monsieur Okraszewsky, of whom Your Royal Highness perhaps has heard, has just brought Princess Sayn-Wittgenstein a resolution from the Archbishop Metropolitan of Saint Petersburg concerning her divorce,

---

1. From his testament, September 14, 1860 (LLB, vol. 5, p. 56).

according to which Monsieur Okraszewsky must go to Rome to obtain the order whereby this case might be reconsidered, reviewed in Russia, and judged afresh by his Grace the Metropolitan. This would not involve the court in Rome in any liability, and it is to be hoped that this order could be issued without difficulty. Nonetheless, Monsieur Okraszewsky could not go to a foreign country with any chance of success in a matter of this importance unless he is furnished with a high recommendation. The petition he will present in the name of the princess will be addressed to the Commission for Requests, presided over by Cardinal Antonelli.

If your Royal Highness would be so kind as to promise to look at it [i.e., the petition] tomorrow or later, I would be be able to explain verbally why it is urgent that Monsieur Okraszewsky leave as soon as possible, without a minute's delay.

F. Liszt

To this letter Liszt attached an aide-memoire meant to remind the grand duke that Liszt's many charitable services to the Catholic Church across the years might not be without interest to officials in the Vatican.

As claim on a particularly sympathetic audience from His Holiness on behalf of M. Liszt, one might point out the numerous donations made by Liszt to Catholic churches and religious foundations in all countries. The concerts given in Berlin and Cologne for the benefit of Cologne Cathedral, in Pest for the construction of the Leopold Church, in Brussels for the re-construction of the Mount-Carmel Church, etc. produced a sum of more than 8,000 écus, not counting an equally large amount distributed by him to various charitable institutions, hospitals, orphanages, and other benevolent work. M. Liszt was elected in 1841 an honorary member of the steering committee of Cologne Cathedral, an exceptional honour at that time, when the committee consisted of only a few members; and in 1857, the Franciscan monastery in Pest admitted him as a confrater, to which the enclosed document attests.[2]

It is unusual to see Liszt parading his charitable works like so many worldly triumphs, and it is indicative of the urgency he attached to the matter. Ten days after the departure of Okraszewsky and Carolyne for Rome, and with the St. Petersburg annulment now in her possession, Liszt wrote another letter, to

---

2. HFL, pp. 182–83.

Agnès Street-Klindworth, which further strengthens our view that marriage with the princess was his dearest wish:

May 28, 1860

. . . The princess left for Rome about ten days ago. The great event of her life and her heart has finally found a favourable and lawful solution, which would have been obtained *ten years* earlier had it not been for the despicable intrigues [of a family whose cupidity and relentless persistence are equally ignominious]. Two months have passed since the *annulment* of her marriage to Prince N[icholas] W[ittgenstein] was pronounced by the Catholic consistories of Russia who are responsible for this matter and countersigned by the metropolitan archbishop of [St.] Petersburg. All is then perfectly in order in this respect, just as she wanted it. What ensues depends on certain conventions which there is no reason to go against now.[3]

Under the circumstances, Liszt's use of the phrase "certain conventions" to explain the delay in getting the annulment recognized in Rome was a masterpiece of understatement.

Time passes and the princess does not return to Weimar. It becomes clear to Liszt that Carolyne is locked in a complex struggle from which she may not easily extricate herself. He urges caution, for he knows how stubborn she can be when confronted by overwhelming odds. By August 1860 the mood of heady optimism which had prevailed at the Altenburg at the time of Carolyne's departure has all but dispersed. Liszt realizes for the first time that her adversaries in Rome have the advantage of remaining largely unseen, that she is fighting her battles in the dark. Once more Liszt turns to Carl Alexander for support:

Weimar, August 19, 1860

Save me, sire—you can do it! Wherever the obstacle might be, you are in a position to remove it. My gratitude is of such little use that I forbear to mention it at this moment. But the feeling of having done a good and noble thing will bear a reward worthy of you, and God who rules our conscience will bless you.

Do not abandon me, then. You know that in this union with the

---

3. LLB, vol. 3, pp. 122–23. When La Mara published this letter, she censored Liszt's criticism of the Wittgenstein family. The holograph is in the Széchényi Library, Budapest. Ep. Mus. 798.

princess lies all the honour and all the happiness to which [I] aspire and hope in this world.

Your very respectfully devoted and grateful servant,

F. LISZT[4]

The full extent of the grand duke's involvement in Carolyne's annulment has gone largely undocumented. He not only interceded with Cardinal Antonelli[5] but also wrote letters to the Russian ambassador to Rome, Count Kisseleff, and to other officials there. The unpublished correspondence of Liszt and Carl Alexander reveals that in August and September 1860 there was a five-way exchange between Carolyne, Liszt, the grand duke, Count Kisseleff, and Cardinal Antonelli, much of which was regarded as so urgent that it was conducted by telegramme.[6] Liszt very early identified the Russian legation in Rome as a hotbed of intrigue, determined to prevent his nuptials with the princess. "As long as the Russian legation follows its former instructions," he told the grand duke, "I will always have a *noose* around my neck."[7] So convinced was Liszt that the Russian diplomats were working against him that he petitioned Carl Alexander to intercede directly with Tsar Alexander II when the two rulers met in Warsaw later that year. "The effect of the tsar's words on the Russian embassy in Rome . . . would have a sovereign impact," Liszt wrote.[8] We may be sure that such words were never uttered. Tsar Alexander was no friend of either Liszt or the princess; indeed, since the latter had been exiled by him in 1855, she was effectively removed from his protection. It was part of the Russian diplomats' case against her, in fact, that Carolyne was stripped of her citizenship and therefore did not exist as far as they were concerned; her Russian annulment was at best an anomaly. On September 15, six days after Carolyne's audience with Pope Pius IX (during which, we recall, the pontiff had promised to help her), Liszt received an urgent letter from her, part of which he transmitted to Carl Alexander. Carolyne wrote:

> The trick that they [i.e., the Russian embassy] could play on me now would be to send for papers from Russia, under the pretext that they are judging the matter anew, unknown to me. I still hope that neither the metropolitan of St. Petersburg nor the Russian government will allow the illegal extradition of documents which the court of Rome does not have the right to demand nor the church of Russia the duty to communicate. . . . It is a wasps' nest from which pettifoggery

4. LBLCA, p. 95.
5. LBLCA, pp. 95–97.
6. WA, Kasten 457. Unpublished letters dated August 25 and September 3, 1860.
7. WA, Kasten 457. Unpublished letter dated September 3, 1860.
8. LBLCA, p. 97.

would never let me escape, were I ever unfortunate enough to enter it.[9]

The Hohenlohes continued to play the Russian card for all it was worth. They mired Carolyne in bureaucracy, slandered her cause, and began a whispering campaign against her character in which, as we have seen, words like "perjury" and "bigamy" played a devastating role. Despite all the odds, however, her cause prevailed, and she and Liszt were legally entitled to marry at any time after January 1861.

II

In Weimar itself there was much speculation about the princess's departure. The whole city thought that it was only a matter of weeks before she would return. But when she did not get back in time for Liszt's birthday, on October 22, Liszt's circle feared that he himself would soon leave Weimar. According to Adelheid von Schorn, who saw much of Liszt during the year 1860–61, no one in Weimar would have believed it had they been told that Carolyne would never return to Weimar, and that she would remain in Rome as a recluse for the next twenty-six years.[10] That Carolyne herself thought her trip would be a brief one is borne out by the fact that she asked "Scotchy" Anderson to stay on at the Altenburg until her return.[11] As for Liszt, he remained totally silent and refused to confide his fears and hopes to anyone save the grand duke. He became introspective, and his closest friends remarked how sad and drawn he looked. On October 26, in a belated act of recognition, the city of Weimar honoured him with the freedom of the city.[12] While he appreciated the gesture, it did little to lift his spirits and nothing at all to change his mind about the straitlaced burghers who ran the place. It was as if he were weighed down by an invisible force, lightened only occasionally by friends in whose company he could relax. Few people knew it at the time, but one of the reasons for his

---

9. WA, Kasten 457. Unpublished letter dated September 15, 1860.
10. Schorn's account of this period will be found in SNW, vol. 2, pp. 52–57.
11. SNW, vol. 2, p. 52.
12. The document is reproduced in BFL, p. 215. Four days earlier, on October 22 (his forty-ninth birthday), the city had honoured him with a traditional *Fackelzug,* a torch-light procession which wended its way across the river Ilm and assembled outside the Altenburg to pay him homage. Was this delayed honour touched off by another that Liszt had received earlier in the year? On August 25, 1860, Napoleon III had made Liszt an officer of the Legion of Honour. When news of the award was transmitted to Weimar, according to Liszt, "some oaf asked Count Mulinen (chargé d'affaires for France here) for what reason this mark of favour on the part of His Majesty had been shown to me." Count Mulinen thought for a moment and then replied: "Just because Herr Dr. Liszt is *Liszt*" (LLB, vol. 3, p. 131). The Weimarers, it seems, had only now woken up to the fact that their erstwhile Kapellmeister was—*Liszt!*

subdued mood was the fact that he and Carolyne had begun to draw up their wills.[13] His is a particularly complex document which reveals him in a disturbed frame of mind. In it he reviews his years of struggle in Weimar, speaks bitterly of the tribulations he has endured, and declares his love for Carolyne. He also makes a number of important bequests to family and friends. The act of writing this will involved Liszt in long hours of reflection, forcing him to re-live painful moments he would have preferred to forget. Music was his only consolation, and during these stressful months he returned once more to the piano and composed some of his most effective works for the instrument. These included:

> Three concert paraphrases on Verdi operas
>   *Ernani*
>   "Miserere" from *Il trovatore*
>   *Rigoletto*
> Two Wagner transcriptions
>   Spinning Chorus from *Der fliegende Holländer*
>   Pilgrims' Chorus from *Tannhäuser*
> Waltz from Gounod's *Faust*
> *Venezia e Napoli*
>   (supplement to the Italian book of *Années de pèlerinage*)
>   Gondoliera
>   Canzone
>   Tarantella
> *Mephisto* Waltz No. 1

We are not wrong to regard the six operatic arrangements as a nostalgic coda to his Weimar years, as performances by proxy. He may have been deprived of a podium, but there was nothing to prevent him from offering the world some matchless transcriptions of operas that, by now, he must have known backwards.

He often went across to the Schorns' for his evening meals, after which he might wander down to the Erbprinz Hotel to meet old colleagues. Sometimes he even gave small dinner-parties at the Altenburg, and on these occasions "Scotchy" Anderson would act as hostess. Henriette and Adelheid von Schorn spent an evening there in the winter of 1860 and had the pleasure of hearing Liszt play to his friends. Henriette had heard him many times, but this must have been an exceptional experience. "Liszt was—one cannot find words to express it. He played as no one [else] ever has played, does play, or ever will

---

13. Both documents are reproduced in full in Appendix I of this volume.

play. I struggled to keep back my tears."[14] On such evenings Liszt was so solicitous towards his guests that, irrespective of the weather, he would often accompany them out of the house without hat or coat and lead them through the copse at the end of the garden and down the steps leading towards the bridge over the Ilm. Then he would disappear into the darkness as he climbed the steps back to the Altenburg.

The winter of 1860–61 brought further worries. On October 12, 1860, Cosima had given birth to her first child, Liszt's first grandchild, who had been named Daniela Senta, after Cosima's dead brother and the heroine of *Der fliegende Holländer*. Unfortunately, Cosima had recuperated very slowly; by January she was in need of medical attention.[15] At Liszt's insistence she came to Weimar and stayed with him in the Altenburg for about ten days. Everyone who saw her knew that she was desperately ill. She had a dry, hacking cough which allowed her no sleep, and Eduard Lassen observed that Liszt feared Cosima might succumb to the same illness that had carried off Daniel a year or so earlier. Liszt begged her to seek a cure and took her to see a local specialist. Part of Cosima's trouble was the irascible Bülow, who was given to moods of black depression followed by outbursts of verbal violence. Cosima knew that they did not represent Bülow's innermost nature and bore them in silence. He had once described himself as a sort of Hamlet, someone destined to drown in a sea of troubles. As long as Cosima tried to protect him from the outside world, which it was her natural inclination to do, she did it at the expense of her own health. It was Blandine who alerted Liszt to Cosima's plight, and she told her father bluntly that the Bülow household was the last place in the world for Cosima to convalesce.

> Bülow is ill himself, and although he may worry for a moment, Cosima will answer him that she is fine and he will be re-assured. As for Mme von Bülow, the mother, you know as well as I do that she is *pour la phrase*. Cosima could die in six months if she has only these people about to persuade her to take care of herself. You are the only one who can save her.[16]

Liszt finally persuaded Cosima to enter a sanitorium at Reichenhall, in the Bavarian Alps, where she spent much of the summer. The clear mountain air

---

14. December 8, 1860. SZM, p. 103.
15. Liszt travelled to Berlin for Daniela's baptism, which because of the poor condition of Cosima's health did not take place until Saturday, December 1, 1860. The ceremony, conducted by the local Catholic priest, took place in the same room in which Daniel had died almost a year earlier (LLB, vol. 3, pp. 138–39).
16. OCLF, p. 271.

and the long country walks each day gradually restored her to health. To Bülow, Liszt had already written a letter in which he begged his old pupil not to give in to his "migraine moods." He re-assured Bülow that he was someone, with something to do in the world. As hard and unbearable as our existence sometimes is, he told him, it is a question of using life well. "Continue to go on as before, and live with what you are. It is good and beautiful to do so—believe me."[17] This was sound advice, but Bülow did not, or could not, accept it. He suffered accordingly and brought much unhappiness into his life and into the lives of those around him.

III

The payment to Okraszewsky of his 70,000 silver roubles caused Liszt almost as much worry as it did Carolyne. This was a huge sum to withdraw from what was to become their joint capital. In October 1860 Liszt was obliged to travel to Vienna in order to arrange the transfer of this payment through Eduard Liszt, who administered Carolyne's funds. He spent "three or four extremely unpleasant days" there, as he put it, from October 16 to 20. It says something about the strained relations with Konstantin Hohenlohe that for the whole of this period Liszt did not attempt to contact either him or Princess Marie. There was a painful interview with Gustav Hohenlohe, however, who was on a visit to Vienna from Rome. The Hohenlohes, it will be recalled, were at that moment on the defensive, having lost the first round in the battle to have Carolyne's annulment quashed when the College of Cardinals ruled in her favour on September 22. "[Gustav] put forward certain theological scruples, not wishing to tell me quite simply what I am as well aware of as he: namely, that the Wittgensteins have conferred power of attorney with regards to their *underhand manoeuvres* on the Hohenlohes, and they are determined to prevent by every means the marriage of the princess to a person of my ilk."[18] Liszt then presented himself at Monsignor De Luca's, who, in Liszt's words, "rode on his high horse" and claimed that there was a contradiction between the decision of Rome and certain articles in the Concordat of Vienna. Since Liszt was an Austrian citizen, the nuncio argued, it was precisely those articles which should govern this case. Liszt reported this conversation with irony and listened with all the mock conviction necessary "when one knows in advance that white must be black, and that the moon is indisputably made of green cheese."[19]

---

17. LBLB, p. 291.
18. DA, unpublished fragment of a letter written to Agnès Street-Klindworth dated November 8, 1860. La Mara censored two-thirds of this letter when she published it in LLB, vol. 3, p. 134.
19. Ibid.

I V

From the moment Carolyne left Weimar, in May 1860, and moved to Rome, she began to sign her letters "ta fiancée." This reflected her growing confidence in the validity of the Russian annulment and her certainty that it would be upheld by the Vatican. On January 1, 1861, she even allowed herself to write to Liszt: "Is it really true that this year will *finally* consecrate my title of fiancée by that of wife? The augury seems promising."[20] After the College of Cardinals had held its second convocation, on January 8, 1861, and ruled in her favour, she began drawing up her wedding plans in earnest. Fulda, the centre of Roman Catholicism in Germany, had already been thought of as a possible location for the ceremony; but Pope Pius IX's reprimand to the bishop of Fulda now made that city a sensitive choice. Carolyne even toyed with the idea of Florence and Loreto—the latter place for no other reason than the fact that it had been consecrated by the Pontiff on one of his pilgrimages there.[21] The important thing for Carolyne was that she and Liszt should be married, take up their winter quarters in Rome, and then decide at leisure where they would have their permanent residence. So why did they delay?

Two sets of circumstances conspired to keep Liszt in Weimar until the late summer of 1861. The first was the upcoming meeting of the Tonkünstler-Versammlung, which had already been advertised to take place in Weimar during the first week of August, under the aegis of Liszt and the grand ducal court. Many of his friends, pupils, and colleagues were preparing to converge on the city, and his presence was indispensable for the success of the festival. It is evident from the correspondence that Carolyne agreed with him.[22] The other problem had to do with the Altenburg. Someone had to take responsibility for closing down the building, putting the furniture and precious objects into storage, and letting the servants go. These tasks fell on Liszt's shoulders and caused him much concern. Meanwhile, various trips outside Weimar stood in the way of an early departure for Rome, the main one being to Paris, a journey to which we must now turn.

---

20. WA, Kasten 38. Unpublished letter.
21. WA, Kasten 38. Unpublished letter dated June 11, 1861.
22. LLB, vol. 5, p. 164. The first advertisements for the Tonkünstler-Versammlung had appeared as early as December 1860. As Liszt put it: "Once this hare was started, I couldn't change its course, but I could very easily abstain from chasing it!" (LLB, vol. 5, p. 163) Carolyne herself refused to accept this sacrifice.

V

Liszt spent a whole month in Paris, from May 10 to June 8, 1861. It was his
first visit to the French capital in more than seven years. Two reasons compelled
him to go there. The first had to do with his securities in Rothschild's bank,
against which he proposed to negotiate a loan of 23,000 francs in order to help
Carolyne with her ongoing Roman expenses.[23] The second reason had to do
with his family. Anna Liszt, who was now crippled in both legs and practically
immobile, had gone to live with Blandine and Emile Ollivier in their Paris
apartment, which Liszt had not yet seen.[24] He set out from Weimar on April
30 in the company of Count Mulinen, the chargé d'affaires at the French
legation, and arrived in Frankfurt a day or two later. From there he travelled
to Brussels, where he was briefly re-united with Agnès Street-Klindworth. He
finally arrived in Paris on May 10.

It was inevitable that the moment Liszt set foot in Paris he would be caught
up in a social whirl. He visited Berlioz, Meyerbeer, Halévy, Rossini, Delacroix,
Lamartine, and his old secretary, Gaëtano Belloni. Like Carolyne during her
trip to Paris eighteen months earlier, Liszt was shocked to see the change that
had come over Berlioz. "Our poor friend Berlioz is really low and full of
bitterness," he told Carolyne. "His family life weighs on him like a nightmare,
and outside he meets nothing but opposition and disasters. . . . The tone of
Berlioz's voice has faded. He usually speaks in a low voice, and his whole being
seems to lean towards the grave!"[25] His encounter with Rossini, on the other
hand, was almost a branch of low comedy. The two composers had last met
in Italy in 1838, and Rossini could not get over the fact that Liszt was still
well-preserved while he, Rossini, was almost decrepit. He touched Liszt's hair
to make sure that it was genuine. Then, pointing to his own sparse crown, he
remarked: "See, there's nothing left there now—and I have hardly any teeth
or legs."[26]

---

23. Baron de Rothschild was out of town when Liszt got there, and he had to wait until May 22
before he could see his itinerant banker. Liszt and Rothschild also dined together on May 25 (LLB,
vol. 5, p. 176). The famous financier advanced the full loan of 23,000 francs against Liszt's signature,
free of all interest. The signature was later bought back by Eduard Liszt from Carolyne's investment
holdings in Vienna (EKFL, pp. 32 and 37).
24. In July 1860 Anna had sustained a deep fracture at the head of the femur, and the bones had been
slow to knit. Because of the position of the fracture the doctors had been unable to put the leg into
splints, and the old lady had been obliged to remain immobile in bed. About mid-November she
was placed on a litter and carried through the streets from her apartment on rue Penthièvre to the
Olliviers' on rue Saint-Guillaume. For the remaining five years of her life she was bed-ridden in the
Olliviers' guest-room (LLB, vol. 3, p. 138).
25. LLB, vol. 5, p. 171.
26. LLB, vol. 5, p. 173.

In view of all the dining out that he found himself doing, Liszt had himself measured for two suits by Chevreuil, the most celebrated tailor in Paris, which cost him 500 francs (he took Blandine along with him to advise on the fittings, so as to meet the requirements of current fashion). He also hired a coach and horses to take him on his various social calls.[27] These were expenses that he could ill afford, but, as he told Carolyne, they were necessary if he was to be seen in society. He was, in fact, taken up by Princess Metternich and Count Walewski among others, and he was entertained by his old friend Lamartine. At the home of the Metternichs Liszt dined with Gounod, who had brought along with him the score of his latest opera, *Faust,* a work which was already the talk of the town. Liszt wrote: "I presented him with his waltz for dessert— to the great entertainment of those listening."[28]

Liszt's arrival in Paris after so long an absence touched off much speculation about his *ménage* with Princess Carolyne. At a dinner-party given by the Rothschilds, Liszt found himself seated near Countess Delphine Potocka, whose name had once been linked with that of Chopin. The countess, who was never one to stand on ceremony, came right out with the question that was burning on everyone's lips, and inquired after Princess Carolyne. Liszt's non-committal reply induced her to make another effort. "And her daughter, where is she?" Liszt nipped the conversation in the bud. "I am not obliged, madame, to serve as your information bureau—but if you are curious, you will find out from the *Almanach de Gotha.*"[29] It was an uncharacteristically brusque retort, which shows that Liszt's determination not to discuss Carolyne's family situation with anyone, least of all with Paris society, remained as firm as ever. His private life he kept to himself. We know from Ollivier's *Journal,* however, that Liszt spent a good deal of time in Blandine's apartment and even had some of his meals served at his mother's bedside.[30] The day after he arrived in Paris, Blandine took him to see the ailing Madame Patersi, who was still receiving a pension of 1,000 francs a year from Carolyne. Not long after this visit, the old lady's pension was increased by 200 francs.[31]

His invitation to dine with the Lamartines in their home on rue Ville l'Evêque was the occasion of a famous gaffe which typified the improvisatory nature of Liszt's social life in Paris. Wishing to entertain his old friend, Lamartine secured Liszt's permission to arrange a small "family dinner" in his honour. Lamartine was no exception to all the other hosts in that he secretly

---

27. LLB, vol. 5, p. 169.
28. LLB, vol. 3, p. 151.
29. LLB, vol. 5, p. 178.
30. OJ, vol. 2, pp. 21–22. That was during the first week or two of Liszt's visit. Ollivier became somewhat critical of Liszt towards the end of his stay for spending less time with his family as his social life took hold.
31. EKFL, p. 32. Madame Patersi lingered for three more years and finally died on June 22, 1864.

hoped that Liszt might be persuaded to play the piano at some point during the evening. He sent out a few hurried invitations, including one to the editor of *Le Siècle,* which, by some error, found its way into the compositor's room instead. The next morning the whole of Paris was electrified to read the following notice.

> My dear Havin:
>   Liszt, who does me the inappreciable honour of dining with me on Thursday next, consents to allow my humble parlour to hear those wonderful sounds so long unheard in Paris, and to witness the renewal of the old prodigy of Orpheus who animated wood and metal at his pleasure! *He that hath ears to hear,* etc.
> Yours ever,
>
>   LAMARTINE[32]

Lamartine, thoroughly alarmed, addressed a second letter to M. Havin, this time intended for publication, in which he implored the public to stay away. His "humble parlour," he explained, was not nearly large enough to contain his official guests, let alone the vast readership of *Le Siècle.* This did not prevent many music-lovers from converging on Lamartine's house, which was packed to overflowing that night. Liszt was too gracious not to come to the rescue of his host, and he gallantly consented to play at the "family dinner." As he ironically put it, it was at least better than the old invitation cards which Princess Belgiojoso used to send out, in which she wrote in her own hand: "M. Liszt will play."[33]

These several encounters were all faithfully reported back to Carolyne in Rome, who, as always, could share in Liszt's social life only at a distance.[34] He had already informed her: "The Sphinx will probably do me the honour of seeing me soon."[35] This was a veiled reference to the Emperor Napoleon III, who had expressed a desire (through the Metternichs) to meet the great pianist.

---

32. *Le Siècle,* June 3, 1861.
33. LLB, vol. 5, pp. 179–80.
34. While Carolyne rejoiced at Liszt's easy acceptance into Paris society after so many years away from it, she knew that it was possible only so long as she herself was absent. Her forlorn comment on all this is worth reporting. She knew full well, she told him, that she was "an obstacle against which society stumbled during the past years—but from now on it will no longer be like that. Magne's departure, the regularization of our position, and, if God and you wish it, our establishment in Rome, are going to place me in a position . . . which will free you of the embarrassment you suffered with such admirable dignity." (WA, Kasten 40; unpublished letter dated June 20, 1861)
35. LLB, vol. 5, p. 173. Protocol demanded that Liszt himself write to the emperor for an invitation. His note was delivered by Metternich.

VI

Liszt's visit to Paris was, in fact, crowned by an invitation to dine with Napoleon III at the Tuileries on May 22. This famous encounter between Liszt and the French emperor has been much reported. After dinner the conversation turned on politics, and Napoleon III expressed his thanks to Liszt for the goodwill he had always shown towards France. He then became sombre as he spoke of the heavy burdens he had to bear. "There are days when I feel as if I had lived for a century," he remarked wearily. Liszt's reply has gone down to posterity. "Sire, you *are* the century."[36] The response made a visible impression on the emperor, who now asked Liszt to play something. Liszt sat down at the piano and began with his recently composed *Trovatore* paraphrase. After he had finished, the empress asked him to play the Funeral March from Chopin's B-flat-minor Piano Sonata. As he was playing, she began to weep and was forced to withdraw into an adjoining room. Liszt finished the mournful dirge, and there was an embarrassed silence while the emperor went to inquire after his wife. Apparently the music had aroused in her some powerful memories of her dead sister, and she was unable to contain her emotions. In order to revive their flagging spirits, Liszt plunged into one of his Hungarian Rhapsodies. At the triumphal conclusion everybody gathered round the keyboard to congratulate him. As they chatted, one of the ladies began to experiment with a glissando she had heard Liszt play. Whereupon Liszt remarked: "You should not tackle it like that, madame," and proceeded to execute a marvellous glissando in thirds. The emperor, stupefied, approached the keyboard and tried the effect for himself. There followed some good-humoured repartee about Napoleon being a good skater. Then Liszt said: "I will play a piece in which this particular hand movement is applied," and went straight into the "Patineurs" Waltz from Meyerbeer's *Le Prophète,* which created a furore. Everybody wanted him to play it again, but the hour was late, Liszt was tired, and he finally took his leave of the Tuileries at about 11:15 p.m. A week later, Napoleon III made Liszt a commander of the Legion of Honour.[37]

---

36. See, for example, LLB, vol. 5, pp. 177–78; OJ, vol. 2, p. 22; and Dwight's *Journal of Music,* July 13 and August 3, 1861. By far the most interesting description of Liszt's encounter with the emperor, however, will be found in a hitherto unpublished letter from Blandine to Princess Carolyne, dated May 27, 1861 (Daniel Ollivier Archives, NAF 25191). Liszt was accompanied to the Tuileries by the Olliviers, and it is on Blandine's eye-witness account that the above description is based.

37. This was less than a year after he had made Liszt an officer of the Legion of Honour (See Volume One, p. 147). A number of commentators have claimed that the only reason Liszt went to Paris in the first place was to receive this honour directly from Napoleon himself. The fact is that Liszt had no idea that he would be elevated to the level of commander until well after his arrival in the city. Even as late as May 28 he noted: "There is talk of promoting me at once to the rank of commander

VII

This visit to Paris was also notable for a meeting with Marie d'Agoult, the first time that he had seen his former lover since their rupture nearly seventeen years earlier. It appears the Marie herself took the initiative by inviting him to a small luncheon party at her home, together with some literary people, including Edmond Texier of Le Siècle. Marie greeted him at the door. "It is a very long time since you were in Paris," were her opening words.[38] The subsequent conversation was somewhat formal, but Marie invited Liszt back again to dine with her in a few days' time, and he accepted. It was clear that his presence had shaken her, for a day or two later she wrote in her journal: "Ever since his appearance I have been preoccupied with him. On the first night I had difficulty in sleeping."[39] All the bitterness and recrimination that had echoed between them across the years seemed to vanish. For Marie, it was as if the clock had gone back to 1833 and she was glimpsing the "young enchanter," as she had then called Liszt, crossing the threshold of Marquise Le Vayer's drawing-room for the first time. On that earlier occasion, too, Liszt had caused her a sleepless night. He returned to dine with her on May 31, and both Liszt and Marie have left detailed descriptions of the occasion.[40] They talked of his work at Weimar, his championship of Wagner, and the question of the Music of the Future. There were also some passing references to their two daughters. He told Marie that he had a particular passion for Cosima, who closely resembled her mother. As Liszt talked, he noticed that Marie's face was bathed in tears. When the time came to say good-bye, she spontaneously got up and embraced him.[41] Liszt kissed her on the forehead and said: "Come, Marie, let me speak to you in the language of the peasants: 'God bless you, and may you wish me no harm.'" At that her tears flowed still more copiously. Liszt then told her that during her recent travels in Italy, Ollivier had often seen her weeping at their youthful haunts, and that this reminiscence had touched him deeply. She replied

---

of the Legion of Honour. I have already been complimented about this—although up to now I have received no official notification." (LLB, vol. 5, p. 177)

38. OJ, vol. 2, p. 22.

39. These fragments from Marie d'Agoult's Mémoires were left unpublished when that book went to press in 1927. They might have escaped the attention of Liszt scholars had it not been for the perspicacity of Madame Anne Troisier de Diaz, who printed them in her edition of Emile Ollivier's Journal (OJ, vol. 2, pp. 454–56). "He has aged a lot," wrote Marie after this first reunion, "but he has remained handsome. His face has become tanned, his eyes no longer have their sparkle, but his manner is young. His beautiful hair falls in long straight tresses on both sides of his noble, saddened face."

40. Liszt's will be found in LLB, vol. 5, pp. 195–99. Marie's is in OJ, vol. 2, pp. 454-56.

41. OJ, vol. 2, p. 456.

stammeringly: "I shall always remain faithful to Italy—and to Hungary!" As they were descending the stairs, the image of poor Daniel arose before Liszt's mind. "Nothing at all had been said about him during the three or four hours spent chatting with his mother."[42] After he had gone, Marie, deeply moved, poured out her heart to her journal: "Inexpressible charm! It is still him and him alone who makes me feel the divine mystery of life. With him gone, I sense the emptiness around me and weep."[43]

V I I I

Shortly before Liszt left Paris he had a couple of chance encounters with Wagner. At first it had looked as if the two old friends might not be able to meet. Wagner had left Paris a month before Liszt got there, in the wake of the disastrous performances of *Tannhäuser* at the Opéra, and he did not get back until the end of May.[44] Liszt went to have dinner with Wagner and Minna and found Tausig there as well, whom he had not seen for many months.[45] To round off the evening Liszt played his Prelude and Fugue on B-A-C-H, which by a curious coincidence Tausig had played to Wagner only the previous day. As Liszt thundered and lightninged his way across the keyboard Tausig collapsed in amazement "before this wonderful prodigy of a man."[46] Even a cursory reading of *Mein Leben* is sufficient to inform us that Wagner was piqued with Liszt for not having come to Paris in March to save him from the débâcle of *Tannhäuser*. Liszt's mere presence in the opera house, Wagner thought, would have had a moderating effect on his persecutors. But in response to various inquiries as to the cause of Liszt's delay, all Wagner could elicit from him was "an epistolary shrug of the shoulders."[47] It did not occur to Wagner to suppose that Liszt's personal affairs in Paris could not be timed to coincide

---

42. LLB, vol. 5, p. 199. Liszt's account of this meeting with Marie d'Agoult was written from Weimar on June 29—that is, about a month after it took place, and three weeks after Liszt had left Paris. Why the delay? Liszt evidently wanted to spare Carolyne these details until she knew that he was safely back in the Altenburg. It is not true that Liszt hoped to conceal from her the fact that he and Marie had socialized in the latter's home. He himself told her about it on May 28, the day after their first luncheon, and he passed along to Carolyne the note of invitation he had earlier received from Marie (LLB, vol. 5, p. 177).

43. OJ, vol. 2, p. 456.

44. The performances took place on March 13, 18, and 24. The noisy disruption of *Tannhäuser* by members of the Jockey Club had reaped for Wagner a far greater notoriety in Paris than a mere performance of that work could have procured for him, and had turned him once again into a *cause célèbre*. Wagner himself has reported the affair in some detail in WML, pp. 760–69.

45. Tausig was now based in Vienna, where he had caused something of a stir by conducting a series of Liszt concerts.

46. WML, p. 780.

47. WML, p. 775.

with a production of *Tannhäuser,* and that if anyone had a right to absent himself from a performance of that work it was Liszt, who had done more than anyone else in Germany to promote it.[48]

Although the *Tannhäuser* episode rankled with Wagner, it was but the outward and most obvious symptom of an inner discord between him and Liszt. The reader with the time and patience to go through the long correspondence they exchanged with one another, and more importantly *about* one another with such mutual friends as Bülow, Pohl, and Brendel, will have no difficulty in identifying those elements which had threatened their relationship almost from the start. Wagner's constant cry for money and the unrelenting pressure he put on Liszt to help him secure his amnesty were but small fragments of a complex picture. Even Wagner's colossal egotism, his assumption that the world existed primarily to serve his own artistic ends, was tolerated by Liszt because he knew that those ends were of epoch-making significance. Of greater concern to Liszt were their radically different views on religion. Wagner the agnostic had no time for Liszt the Catholic. Even in their early letters Wagner had made no secret of his contempt for the God of Christians and for Liszt's concept of the artist-priest—a part of the latter's belief in the divine origin of music. Liszt had once told Wagner: "Everything is transitory except the Word of God, which is eternal—and the Word of God reveals itself in the creations of Genius."[49] To these and similar evangelical interjections all that Wagner could reply was: "Of your Christianity I do not think much; the Saviour of the world should not desire to conquer the world. There is a hopeless contradiction in this in which you are deeply involved."[50]

It is not impossible for an agnostic and a theist to remain the best of friends, of course, even though the ethical foundations on which they build their lives may lead them in opposite directions. But at the time Liszt encountered Wagner

---

48. Wagner, in *Mein Leben,* fails to make it clear that Liszt intended all along to be present at the Paris performance of *Tannhäuser.* This is evident from letters he wrote to Carolyne, starting as early as December 28, 1860. His difficulties were compounded by the fact that the opera kept getting postponed. Liszt first planned to get to Paris in time for the performance projected for the end of January (LLB, vol. 5, pp. 114 and 117). Then he learned that the production had been put off until mid-February (LLB, vol. 5, p. 121). On March 6, he heard that *Tannhäuser* had been postponed yet again (LLB, vol. 5, p. 136). Wagner evidently expected Liszt to sit in the Altenburg, bags packed, ready to dash to the railway-station on an instant summons from Paris. By March 14 Liszt knew that he had missed the first performance, but he was then so immersed in a fresh crop of problems at Weimar that it was impossible for him to detach himself, and he decided to abandon the trip for the time being (LLB, vol. 5, p. 138). These problems included: (a) the gathering of a dossier of legal documents to send to Rome in support of his marriage plans; (b) a visit to Weimar by the ailing Cosima, who, Liszt feared, might have contracted tuberculosis from nursing her dead brother; (c) a burst of creative activity which included the transcription of the Pilgrims' Chorus from *Tannhäuser* itself. This is the background to be borne in mind when we read of that "epistolatory shrug of the shoulders" which Liszt is supposed to have offered Wagner at this time.
49. BWL, vol. 1, p. 204; KWL, vol. 1, p. 194.
50. BWL, vol. 2, p. 109; KWL, vol. 2, p. 104.

in Paris in June 1861, something had happened which cast a shadow over the artistic side of their relationship as well. In 1859, in the wake of the first performances of the *Tristan* Prelude, Richard Pohl had come out with a panegyric in which he traced the new harmonic world inhabited by this piece directly to the influence of Liszt.[51] Wagner's response to Pohl's revelation has often been quoted, for it was one of deep consternation. On October 7, 1859, he made his feelings known to Bülow: "There are many matters on which we are quite frank among ourselves—for instance, that since my acquaintance with Liszt's compositions my treatment of harmony has become very different from what it was formerly. But when friend Pohl blurts out this secret before the whole world, at the very head of a short notice of the *Tristan* Prelude, this is, to say the least, indiscreet; or am I not to assume that he was authorized to commit such an indiscretion?"[52] Wagner's letter to Bülow can only be understood in the context of one that Bülow himself had written to Brendel (a part of which the latter had promptly published in the *Neue Zeitschrift*) in which Bülow had declared Wagner's new opera to be the most important work yet to emerge from the New German School, but added: *"Tristan und Isolde* can hardly become popular." Wagner was fearful lest such comments harm his chances of getting the work published, for he knew that Breitkopf was by no means enthusiastic. As Wagner saw it, Pohl had questioned its originality, and Bülow had questioned its comprehensibility. The fact that both men were among the work's most ardent champions mattered not one jot to him. The burden of Wagner's reply was: "Keep silent and let my music speak for itself!" No one could quarrel with so eminently sensible a view. Yet the fact remains that both Bülow and Pohl were perfectly correct. The early rehearsals of *Tristan* were fraught with problems, as Bülow well knew that they would be.[53] As for Pohl, if he had not drawn public attention to the influence of Liszt on Wagner's harmonic style, someone else would have done so, since the influence is there. This was the simple, inescapable truth which Wagner had not yet absorbed when he and Liszt met in Paris. From his point of view things looked quite different. Had not Liszt called Wagner his "guide and master"? And had not Liszt inscribed on Wagner's copy of the *Dante* Symphony the following words?

As Virgil guided Dante, so have you guided me through the mysterious regions of the life-imbued worlds of tone. From the depths

---

51. Pohl's article appeared in the *Neue Zeitschrift für Musik* in four instalments: June 17, June 24, August 5, and August 19.

52. WBB, pp. 125–26.

53. Proof of Bülow's prediction was quickly forthcoming. The projected first performance of *Tristan*, at Karlsruhe in 1860, was set aside, and the work pronounced "unproduceable" (*Neue-Berliner Musik-Zeitung*, December 28, 1860). When Vienna then attempted to mount the opera, it had to withdraw the work after seventy-seven rehearsals!

of his heart calls to you *"Tu sei lo mio maestro, e il mio autore!"* and
dedicates this work to you in unchangeably faithful love,

Your

F. LISZT[54]

Shortly after receiving this inscription Wagner had told Liszt: "We had better
keep the dedication, written in my copy, to ourselves. I, at least, shall not
mention it to a soul."[55] Perhaps this, too, had meanwhile turned into a source
of distress for Wagner. For while he had been careful to keep the little matter
of his influence on Liszt "to ourselves," Liszt's influence on him was "blurted
out to the whole world" by Pohl. Wagner, in brief, felt betrayed, although
no dispassionate observer could possibly agree with him. But something deeper
still, and potentially far more malevolent, had entered their relationship. It
emerges from this same letter of Wagner's to Bülow (October 7, 1859) that
Wagner was convinced he had detected the fine hand of Princess Carolyne in
Pohl's article.[56] There is no evidence that Carolyne had anything whatever to
do with Pohl's perception of the harmonic origins of *Tristan;* it is sufficient to
understand only that Wagner believed that she had. And Wagner rightly
guessed that Carolyne would be pleased by Pohl's comments. His growing
ambivalence towards her did the rest. Wagner went on to express to Bülow
his reservations about the forthcoming marriage of Liszt and Carolyne, a
woman whose domineering influence, so he felt, could only be harmful to his
friend. This was a major indiscretion, and it placed Bülow in a quandary. He
worshipped Wagner and his music, but he loved Liszt still more; as Liszt's
son-in-law, moreover, it raised for him some ethical questions of disclosure. In
the end he disclosed everything, and he passed Wagner's letter along to Liszt.
Liszt, it is evident, was distressed by what he read, for on October 20, 1859,
he wrote to Carolyne: "It emerges from this letter that [Wagner] wants to
separate those whom God has joined—that is to say, you and me."[57] After
telling her that Wagner had complained about a number of things in his
(Liszt's) recent conduct towards him, and about Pohl's article in particular, Liszt
added: "In short, he seems determined to suggest to Hans that you exert an
unfortunate influence on me which is contrary to my real nature."[58] This was

---

54. BWL, vol. 2, p. 248; KWL, vol. 2, p. 264. Liszt quotes the words that Dante uttered to Virgil:
"You are my master and my author." (*Inferno,* canto 1, line 85)

55. BWL, vol. 2, p. 250; KWL, vol. 2, p. 266.

56. Wagner went on to tell Bülow: "Herr Pohl might be recommended by both of us [i.e., Liszt
and Wagner] to exercise more discretion, since I believe he is compromising Liszt, even though he
gratifies the princess."

57. LLB, vol. 4, p. 492.

58. Ibid. The psychology of all this will hardly be lost on the modern reader. Wagner, revealed by
Pohl to show Liszt's influence, feels impelled to defend himself and strikes back in two ways: (a)
he discloses that Liszt himself has admitted to *Wagner's* influence in the private dedication copy of

the background against which Liszt and Wagner were re-united in Paris in June 1861. When Liszt sat down to dine with Wagner that evening in the latter's apartment on the rue d'Aumale, the air was heavy with portent. Among all their unspoken thoughts, one must have reigned supreme, but it was so cynical that neither would have dared to utter it to the other. Wagner had seen in Liszt a champion; Liszt had seen in Wagner a cause. But Wagner now stood on the brink of an unparalleled European reputation, and he no longer needed Liszt; as for Liszt, he had lost control of the Weimar theatre and could no longer help Wagner anyway. Thus the *raison d'être* for their old relationship had vanished. They were left simply with their utterly dissimilar personalities, and neither man seemed to know what to do about it.

Liszt left Paris on June 8 in the company of Tausig. They went first to Brussels, where Liszt had another meeting with Agnès Street-Klindworth, and then made their way back to Weimar. In less than six weeks' time Liszt was to host the Tonkünstler-Versammlung, and he had to make sure that all was in readiness for that landmark event.

IX

At the beginning of August the Altenburg started to fill up with guests for the second festival of the Tonkünstler-Versammlung. All the old guard were there—Cornelius, Bülow, Tausig, Bronsart, Brendel, Damrosch, and Draeseke—together with Eduard Liszt and the Olliviers, and Liszt somehow found the space to distribute most of these guests throughout the old house. A special guest-of-honour was Wagner, who had been granted amnesty the previous year and was now making his first visit to Weimar since 1849. The Olliviers arrived from Paris on August 4, and Liszt was at the railway-station to meet them. The first person they encountered at the Altenburg was Wagner, elated to be back in Germany among all his friends and supporters.[59] Although none of Wagner's music was being played, he was serenaded by the students of Jena University, and there were several dinner-parties in his honour at which the old revolutionary was formally welcomed back to the fatherland. Liszt had tried hard to

---

the *Dante* Symphony; (b) he then goes on to accuse Liszt of succumbing to influence of a general and potentially more damaging kind—that of Princess Carolyne. By a neat twist of logic it is now Liszt who stands in the dock. One requires no special psychoanalytical insights to observe the mechanism of "projection" at work in Wagner—that is, the process of defending oneself by attacking one's assailants with their own weapons.

59. OJ, vol. 2, pp. 28–29. Further details of the Tonkünstler-Versammlung will be found in WML, pp. 787–90, and SNW, vol. 2, pp. 54–56. During the course of the festival a committee was struck and the name Allgemeiner Deutscher Musikverein was formally adopted to describe the organization, with Liszt as its first president (see p. 511). As so often before on such occasions, Liszt bore the brunt of the festival expenses, and ended up 900 thalers out of pocket (LLB, vol. 5, p. 219).

persuade Carl Alexander to bestow on Wagner the Order of the White Falcon, but that was something which the grand duke refused to sanction, since Wagner was still barred from his native Saxony.[60]

The festival opened on August 6 with a performance of Beethoven's Missa Solemnis in the Herder Church. Then followed a banquet for three hundred people in the Town Hall, during which toasts were drunk to Liszt and Wagner. The main event of the festival was Liszt's *Faust* Symphony, which Bülow conducted from memory in the Court Theatre on August 7. He shared the podium with Carl Stör, who conducted Liszt's *Prometheus* Choruses. The following day, August 8, Carl Tausig played Liszt's A-major Piano Concerto to general acclaim.

Throughout the festival Liszt was determined to keep a low profile. He not only refused to conduct any of his own works, but declined to come forward and acknowledge the applause of the audience. That he was showing his contempt for the Weimar public goes without saying, and it was nicely illustrated by a minor scandal that broke out on the last night. Liszt's pupil Felix Draeseke had composed a German March which was receiving its first performance, under Bülow. Practically everyone agreed that this march was an inferior composition. According to Wagner the work was a caricature, while Ollivier, who was sitting next to him, thought it "completely absurd." The Weimar public evidently agreed and showed its displeasure by rejecting the work with ill humour. At that, Liszt, who had not been seen by the general audience throughout the festival, jumped to his feet, his face red with anger, entered the stage-box, and began to applaud frantically, crying "Bravo!" all the time. Tausig and other supporters joined in, and a shouting match ensued. Wagner could not understand why there was such a fuss over so trivial a piece. There was little to be got out of Liszt, he observed, who kept referring furiously to the Weimar audience, "for whom the march was far and away too good."[61] Memories of *The Barber of Bagdad* were not far below the surface, however, and Wagner concluded that Liszt was still trying to avenge Cornelius.

Despite the bustle of the festival and the general merry-making of the guests, an air of melancholy hung over the Altenburg itself. Ollivier could not help remarking that the house seemed sad and abandoned. "Everything shows the

---

60. DA, censored paragraph from Liszt's letter to Agnès Street-Klindworth, dated March 21, 1861. "My gracious master the grand duke has just caused me some distress. I suggested to him, three or four months ago, that he should give Wagner a decoration. . . . At first he seemed inclined to do it; but in the end, the deference that M. de Watzdorf insists on showing to the court at Dresden prevailed." (Saxony was not to grant Wagner an amnesty until 1862.) Nothing daunted, Liszt tried to secure the grand duke's help in mounting the as-yet-unplayed *Tristan* at Weimar during the 1861–62 season, under Wagner's direction (LLB, vol. 3, p. 148). "I brought up the matter with His Grace, and he seemed quite inclined to do it." This idea, too, foundered on the shoals of poverty, like the *Ring* project before it.
61. WML, pp. 788–89.

absence of a mistress of the house, and also preparations for packing up. Four years ago, when I came here for the first time, there was life everywhere—although it was winter."[62] Ollivier knew that Liszt was labouring under immense strain, that even as the festival was in full swing his thoughts were preoccupied with the imminent closure of the Altenburg and his departure from Weimar. Matters were not made easier by the fact that Wagner and the Olliviers stayed on after the Tonkünstler festival and did not disperse until August 10. As they took their leave of Liszt at the railway-station they were full of compliments for the absent Bülow (he had started out the previous day), who had distinguished himself throughout the festival. After listening to this paean of praise Wagner added jestingly: "There was no need for him to marry Cosima." The remark sounded cruel: it implied that Bülow had married Cosima in order to advance his career. Liszt rose to the occasion, bowed slightly, and remarked: "That was a luxury."[63] Nobody realized it at the time, but the exchange contained an ominous glimpse of the future, in which the break-up of the Bülows' marriage would shake all their lives.

Wagner and the Olliviers travelled as far as Reichenhall together, where Cosima herself awaited them. She had been a patient at the Reichenhall sanatorium since June, we recall, having entered it at Liszt's insistence in pursuit of its famous "whey cure," and she had consequently missed the Tonkünstler festival. While they were in Reichenhall, Ollivier had occasion to observe Wagner's egotistical nature at its worst, "a boundless pre-occupation with himself."[64] Ollivier was upset that Wagner, without any scruples, took over a bedroom with two beds while the ailing Cosima had to sleep on a sofa. Another point of contention with Ollivier was that Wagner had travelled to Reichenhall first-class, while the Olliviers themselves had had to make do with a second-class carriage on the same train. After announcing that the food in Germany affected his stomach, Wagner continued his journey alone to Vienna, his ultimate destination. As Wagner's carriage approached the Austrian border, with its usual customs inspection, Wagner removed from their box the costly cigars which Liszt had given him in Weimar, and hid them among his dirty linen in order to avoid detection. To his indignation the deception was revealed by an old border-guard, who, after accepting a bribe from Wagner, promptly reported him to a superior officer. Wagner was made to pay a heavy fine, and since he refused to pay the duty on the cigars, he was forced to leave them at the border. It was a poor consolation that the old guard had the decency to return to him the Prussian thaler with which Wagner had tried to bribe him; the scene must have been re-enacted many times daily. As his carriage pulled

---

62. OJ, vol. 2, p. 27.
63. WML, p. 790.
64. OJ, vol. 2, p. 30.

away, Wagner observed the guard sitting on a bench, contentedly eating his bread and cheese, the model of integrity. In retrospect, he struck Wagner as being a particularly faithful servant, "in which capacity I should have liked to engage him myself . . ."[65]

X

The unpublished letters of Princess Carolyne throw a flood of light on Liszt's behind-the-scenes activities at this time. We have observed that one of Liszt's house-guests during the Tonkünstler-Versammlung was Eduard Liszt, who had arrived in Weimar towards the end of July for the express purpose of making an inventory of the contents of the Altenburg before the house was closed. As early as June 11, 1861, Carolyne had advised Liszt to seal up the Altenburg and formally hand back the building to the Weimar Court. She herself had written a letter to Count Friedrich Beust, the marshal of the court, charging him with "the integrity of the house" and the care of their belongings.[66] Liszt was entirely in agreement with this plan, but its execution weighed heavily on his mind, and the arrival of Eduard had a calming effect on him. The Altenburg was the only real home that Liszt had ever known; moreover, it was filled with priceless memorabilia of his remarkable career—souvenirs, honours, medals, gifts from potentates, manuscripts, paintings, musical instruments—as well as all the furnishings that the princess herself had bought across the years. Carolyne was well aware of the material value of these objects, for she told Liszt: "In the end, our furnishings are a form of capital, without taking into account the sentimental value I attach to some of them."[67] The comment carried some ominous overtones which were not lost on Liszt. Carolyne's capital had dwindled to the point where she feared that it would no longer be sufficient to guarantee a secure future for them. In a revealing sequence of letters to Eduard Liszt, her financial adviser, Carolyne goes into the question of her assets and concludes that if she and Liszt lived frugally, there might be enough money to last for ten years. After that, she fears, they would have to consider turning to the Church, whose charity would at least "give us . . . a roof and a food allowance."[68] The mind boggles at the thought of Liszt, who had come to the rescue of so many charitable causes in the past, becoming in turn a cause for charity. But that is how Carolyne viewed their plight in 1861. She was doubtless reflecting on the fact that her wealth had brought her little but unhappiness when she told Eduard:

---

65. WML, p. 792.
66. WA, Kasten 40. Unpublished letter dated June 11, 1861. See also EKFL, p. 38.
67. WA, Kasten 40. Unpublished letter dated June 11, 1861.
68. EKFL, p. 40.

"It would have a certain pleasantness for me, who was destined for millions, and who possessed them, to live as a burden on the Church."[69]

XI

Liszt finally closed the Altenburg on August 12. Eduard Liszt was with him until the last moment and witnessed the seals affixed to the doors.[70] As Liszt walked away from the house for the last time, a flood of emotion overcame him. He told Carolyne:

> It is impossible for me to re-assemble on a single threshold all the emotions of my last hours at the Altenburg. Each room, each piece of furniture, down even to the steps of the staircase and to the green lawns of the gardens, all were illuminated by your love, without which I would feel myself annihilated. . . . I could not keep back my tears. But, after a last prayer at your prie-dieu, where we used to kneel side by side before I set off on one of my journeys, I felt a feeling of liberation that comforted me again. . . . In bidding [the Altenburg] farewell, I feel I am coming nearer to you, and I breathe more freely.[71]

The faithful "Scotchy" Anderson set out for England on August 15. She returned to live with her brother, the Reverend Andrew Anderson, a rector in Somerset, in whose house she spent her declining years. Just before she left, Konstantin Hohenlohe informed her that she was to be given an annual pension

---

69. EKFL, p. 40. The princess's new-found caution over money matters explains why Liszt had gone out of his way, while in Paris earlier this summer, to apologize to Carolyne for the bills that he was running up. It is clear that if he had known how serious was their plight, he would never have stayed on alone at the Altenburg. In retrospect he considered it stupid of him not to have put a stop to the enormous expenses of their household in Weimar the moment Carolyne had left for Rome, by moving into other quarters, "which would have cost me half as much money, and, in addition, have given me the chance to work without interruption" (LLB, vol. 5, p. 169).

70. The princess was nervous to the point of paranoia about having the Altenburg "hermetically sealed," as she put it. She was particularly concerned about a cupboard set in the wall between Liszt's Blue Room and her own bedroom (EKFL, p. 34). The lock was poor, and it was in this cupboard that Carolyne had stored a lot of her business papers and personal correspondence that she wished to keep from prying eyes. In a letter written by Carolyne to cousin Eduard on September 6, a week or two later, she thanked him "for the consolation *your* presence gave Liszt at the time he was leaving the Altenburg, certainly heart-broken. . . . No one [else] could understand and sympathize as well as you with the feelings aroused by the closure of this house, where we had lived for twelve years with so much love and unity." (EKFL, p. 31) In this same letter she also thanked Eduard for paying a number of local bills out of her Vienna account, including the cost of tidying up the front garden and paying certain local citizens to guard the exterior of the Altenburg while it stood empty.

71. LLB, vol. 5, pp. 209–10.

of three hundred silver roubles in recognition of the years of loyal service she had devoted to Princess Marie.[72]

The subsequent history of the Altenburg is not without interest, even though it takes us a little ahead of our story. The old house remained sealed, together with all its contents, until Liszt could make up his mind what to do about it. The years rolled by, and still no decision was made. In the summer of 1867 Liszt was notified by the Weimar Court that the house was required as a home for the family of Colonel von Bessel, the new commander of the Ninety-fourth Infantry Regiment.[73] One part of the furniture was sold at auction that same year; the other part was stored privately, in the home of Frau Rosina Walther. In August 1868 Eduard Liszt despatched his son Franz to draw up a detailed inventory of the extant items.[74] Many objects were brought to Eduard's Vienna apartment in the Schottenhof and formed the basis of the so-called Blue Room, where Liszt stayed in future years whenever he passed through the city. In 1977 the contents of the Blue Room were transferred to Eisenstadt, where they are now exhibited in the Burgenländisches Landesmuseum.

And so Liszt turned his face towards Rome. He was nearly fifty years old. As he surveyed his turbulent years in Weimar and the destruction of his Camelot, he must have thought that his life was almost over. Although he did not know it, a new and far more fruitful life was about to begin.

---

72. LLB, vol. 5, p. 213. The Reverend Mr. Anderson was the rector of Culbone and Oare. He lived in Worthy Manor, a large house in the parish of Porlock, Somerset. According to the census records for Porlock, assembled in 1871 (schedule no. 42), "Scotchy's" real name was Janet, and she was born in 1816 at Berwick-on-Tweed. She was fifty-five years old at the time of her retirement, and there were two other unmarried sisters living at Worthy Manor, Margaret and Annie.

73. HA, p. 189. Liszt actually stayed in his old rooms at the Altenburg in September 1864, and again during the early part of August 1867—this latter visit while preparing for the performance of his oratorio *St. Elisabeth,* which he conducted in the Wartburg on August 28 at the command of Carl Alexander, as part of the celebrations surrounding the eight hundredth anniversary of the castle (LLB, vol. 3, p. 195).

74. This inventory may be consulted in the Burgenländisches Landesmuseum under the catalogue number 50538. See EKFL, pp. 58–61, where the inventory is reproduced in full.

Appendixes
Sources
Index

Appendix I:
The Wills of Liszt and Carolyne von Sayn-Wittgenstein

I. LISZT'S TESTAMENT

Liszt himself tells us that he wrote his last will and testament, a complex document of sixteen pages, in a single day—September 14, 1860.[1] Written in French, it reveals that his main asset was 220,000 francs invested with Rothschild's bank in Paris. The primary purpose of this money, raised during his years as a travelling virtuoso, was to establish a trust for his mother and children. Liszt wanted to be sure that in the event of his death, the capital would be divided according to his instructions. He also possessed a great many valuable objects—pictures, medals, watches, precious stones, autographed manuscripts—whose proper disposition was also a matter of concern to him. The will falls into two parts. In the first he makes major bequests to those family members who were closest to him: Carolyne, Anna Liszt, his two daughters, Blandine and Cosima (Daniel had died the previous year), and his cousin Eduard. In the second he dwells at length on his twelve years at Weimar, on his friendship with Wagner, on the work of the New German School—to some of whose members he leaves small tokens of remembrance.

The document was left behind in Weimar when Liszt moved to Rome. Two paraphrases were made in a German translation by Eduard Lassen.[2] Although they are not dated, it can be inferred that they were made immediately after Liszt's death, in response to urgent appeals from Bayreuth (where he had expired on July 31, 1886), to ensure that his last wishes were respected. Because the will was more than twenty-five years old when Liszt died, it is hardly surprising that his body was already interred before the document could be found. In the event, his wish "to be buried simply, without pomp, and if possible at night" was not observed. Many Liszt admirers were later

---

1. LLB, vol. 5, p. 65.
2. WA, Kasten 216.

put out by what they considered to be a mark of disrespect. But since the will was not available at the time of Liszt's funeral, such criticism lacks substance.

Eduard Lassen provided a brief explanation of why he had confined himself to translating only a portion of the will instead of the whole document. The testament, he said, had been found among some private papers of Princess Sayn-Wittgenstein and contained much of a personal nature which it was not possible to publish. The other parts, however, "will be of interest to all the friends of the departed master." By setting himself up as a censor, Lassen introduced a note of confusion into what was already a difficult situation. One can sympathize with Lassen's position, of course. The testament refers to the petty intrigues with which Liszt was surrounded during his Weimar years, as well as to the vindictiveness extended towards the princess—"whom I have so dearly wished to call by the sweet name of wife." It is difficult to imagine the effect that this last disclosure would have had on the châtelaine of Bayreuth, who had always insisted that her father looked forward to his marriage with Carolyne "as to a burial service." Many interests were served when Lassen's mutilated version was published in the *Neue Zeitschrift für Musik,* May 4, 1887, less than three months after Carolyne's death, and from which version her name has been completely excluded. The text was taken over by La Mara and published in the first volume of her *Briefe* (1893); and it was in this truncated form that the will was reproduced by Ramann in her Liszt biography (RLKM, vol. 3, pp. 427–29). Seven years elapsed before La Mara was able to rectify the injustice done to Carolyne, and she published the complete will in its original French in volume 5 of the ongoing *Briefe* (1900).[3] The entire will is given here in English for the first time.

Liszt registered a copy of the testament with the Weimar city notary on April 21, 1861, one week before his departure for Paris. During his month-long sojourn in the French capital he met a certain Mother Élodie, to whom Carolyne had entrusted some letters for Liszt, and to whom Liszt in his turn was now to entrust the will.[4] This nun delivered the document to Carolyne in Rome, on June 10, 1861. Although Carolyne had known of the existence of the will since September 1860,[5] we know that she saw it for the first time on June 10, because her unpublished letter to Liszt on that same date tells us that her "tears flowed for eight consecutive hours" after she had read it.[6] Evidently the testament was sent back to Liszt for some minor corrections, since he withdrew it from the Weimar notary on August 15, just two days before

---

3. LLB, vol. 5, pp. 52–63.
4. LLB, vol. 5, pp. 181 and 185.
5. LLB, vol. 5, p. 65.
6. WA, Kasten 39.

he left the city en route for Rome.[7] It must have been Liszt's intention to replace it with a second will, perhaps in the light of Princess Carolyne's own will (dated October 23, 1861, and reproduced on pp. 564–65). Although there has been much speculation about the existence of a second will, no such document has ever come to light.

THIS IS MY LAST WILL

Weimar, September 14, 1860

I am writing this on September 14, the day on which the Church celebrates the Festival of the Holy Cross. The name of this festival is also that of the glowing and mysterious feeling that has pierced my entire life, as with a sacred wound.

Yes, "Jesus Christ crucified," "the foolishness and the exaltation of the Cross," this was ever my true vocation. . . .

I have felt it in my innermost heart ever since I was seventeen years old, when I implored with tears and supplications that I might be permitted to enter the Paris seminary, and when I hoped that it would be granted to me to live the life of the saints and perhaps to die the death of the martyrs. This has not happened, alas! Yet, in spite of the numerous transgressions and errors which I have committed, and for which I feel sincere repentance and contrition, the divine light of the Cross has never been entirely withdrawn from me. At times, indeed, it has overflowed my entire soul with its glory. I give thanks to God for this, and I shall die with my soul fixed to the Cross, our redemption, our highest bliss; and in acknowledgement of my belief, I wish before my death to receive the holy sacraments of the Catholic, Apostolic, and Roman Church, and thereby to obtain the forgiveness and remission of all my sins. Amen.

My best thoughts and actions over the past twelve years I owe to her whom I have so dearly wished to call by the sweet name of wife, a wish that human malignity and the most deplorable chicanery have so far obstinately prevented—

To Jeanne-Elisabeth-Carolyne, *née* Iwanowska.

I cannot write her name without an ineffable thrill. All my joys are from her, and all my sufferings go to her to be appeased. Not only has she become associated and completely identified with my existence, my work, my worries, my career, helping me with her advice, sustaining me with her encouragement, reviving me with her enthusiasm and with her unimaginable prodigality of attentions, anticipations, wise and gentle words, ingenious and persistent efforts; more than that, she has often renounced herself, abdicating whatever there is of a legitimate imperative in her nature, the better to bear my own burden, which she has made her wealth and her only luxury!!

I kneel before her in thought in order to bless her and render thanks to her as my guardian angel and my intercessor with God; she who is my glory and my honour, my forgiveness and my rehabilitation, the sister and the bride of my soul! What words can I use to tell of the wonders of her devotion, the courage of her sacrifices, the greatness, the heroism, and the infinite tenderness of her love? I should have liked to possess an immense genius to sing in sublime harmonies of that sublime soul. Alas! I have but scarcely succeeded in stammering a few scattered notes borne away by the wind. If, however, there were to

---

7. In reporting the dates of the testament's deposition and its withdrawal, La Mara misattributed the year to 1860, thus sowing yet more uncertainty. See Friedrich Schnapp, *Liszt's Testament: Aus dem Französischen ins Deutsche übertragen und herausgegeben* (Weimar, 1931).

survive something of my musical toil (to which I have applied myself with an overriding passion for the last ten years), let it be the pages in which Carolyne has the greatest share because of the inspiration of her heart! I beg her to forgive me for the inadequacy of my artistic legacy, as well as the still more distressing insufficiency of my good intentions intermingled with so many shortcomings and disparities. She knows that the most poignant grief of my life is to feel myself unworthy of her and not to have been able to elevate myself to that holy and pure region which is the abode of her spirit and her virtue. If I continue to remain on this earth for some time, I vow to strive to become better, to diminish my failings, make amends, to acquire more moral stability, and to neglect nothing in order to leave behind a reputation of some good example.

Lord have pity on me; have mercy on me, and may Thy grace and blessing be upon her in time and in eternity!

Just as I owe to Carolyne the little good that is in me, I also owe her the small share of material possessions that I possess—in a phrase, the little I am and the little I have. It is she who has seen to the conservation, the growth, and the regular investment of the funds that constitute my heritage, amounting to about 220,000 (two hundred and twenty thousand) francs, the certificates of which are deposited with Rothschild in Paris, and, for a small sum (invested by my father with Prince Esterházy) with my cousin Dr. Eduard Liszt, state prosecutor in Vienna.

I beg Carolyne to see that this estate that I leave is divided as simply as possible in equal shares to my two daughters, Blandine and Cosima Liszt, the former married to M. Emile Ollivier, Paris deputy in the Legislative Assembly and barrister; the latter (Cosima) married to M. le Baron Hans Guido de Bülow in Berlin.

It goes without saying that the modest pension that my very dear mother, Madame Anna Liszt in Paris, has been receiving for some years from the interest on my funds must be kept wholly for her. After her death, this sum will be divided similarly (in equal shares) between my two daughters, who are my legitimate heiresses.

The good and sweet harmony of upright and pious sentiment that has always existed between my mother and my children is a great consolation to me. May God keep them unchangeably united after my death!

I thank my mother with veneration and tenderness for her constant show of kindness and love. In my youth it was said of me that I was a good son; there was certainly no merit in that, for how could I not be a good son with a mother so exemplarily devoted! If I die before her, her blessing will follow me to the grave.

I bless my two daughters, Blandine and Cosima, and thank them warmly for the sweet joys and satisfactions that they have caused me through their noble hearts and their uprightness. May they walk in the path of God and adhere to the Cross of Jesus Christ, indissolubly, without asking from the world, its vanities and its passions, what these things cannot give!

They are worthy of conceiving and practicing the passion for Good. I ask them to make the moral heritage that I pass on to them bear fruit, the heritage of high aspirations, of scorn for what is false and trifling, of simple faithfulness and simple good deeds.

I commend them to honour my memory, especially through their feelings of affection, respect, gratitude, and filial piety towards Princess Carolyne Wittgenstein, who for so many years, and in the most distressing and difficult circumstances, has always been truly in thought, and words, and deeds, a mother to them after my own heart.

This commendation must appear superfluous, for Blandine and Cosima will certainly feel the need to show in every way possible those just and proper feelings to her who has shown me nothing but sacrifice and devotion without end.

Cosima intends to have a modest monument erected on the grave of my son Daniel, buried in the Catholic cemetery of Berlin. I ask her to arrange with Carolyne for the execution of this monument, which M. Dondorff (a pupil of Rietschel) would perhaps model—already having made a medallion of Daniel—and which will have to be unassuming, the imprint of life having failed the fine qualities of my dear child.

My cousin Eduard Liszt (doctor [of law] and royal and imperial prosecutor in Vienna) has the right to be assured here of my sincere and grateful affection, and I thank him for all his loyal and steadfast friendship. By his merit, his competence and character, he does honour to the name I bear, and I pray God to grant him his blessing, and also his wife and children.

In the world of contemporary art there is one name that has already become glorious, and which will become ever more so—Richard Wagner. His genius has been to me a flaming torch; I have followed it, and my friendship for Wagner has always been of the character of a noble passion.

At a certain period (about ten years ago) I had visions of a new epoch for Weimar, similar to that of Carl August, in which Wagner and I should have been the leading spirits, as Goethe and Schiller were formerly. The meanness, not to say villainy, of certain local circumstances, all kinds of jealousies, ineptitudes, both external and internal, have prevented the realization of this dream, which would have brought honour to the present grand duke. Nevertheless, I remain of the same feeling, still having the same conviction, which it was only too easy to make obvious to all! . . . and I beg Carolyne to be willing to accommodate it by continuing with Wagner our affectionate relationship after my death. Who better than she could understand the high impulse so resolutely given by Wagner to art, his divine feeling for love and poetry?

For the few objects that belong to me and are at the Altenburg (they are few in number, for all the furniture in the Altenburg, the library, books and music, pictures and works of art, are the property of the Princess Carolyne Wittgenstein), I beg Carolyne to keep them in memory of me as long as she lives—in particular the ones that follow:

1. (a) The little diamond seal with the Spanish device "Pundonoroso" ["Worthy of Honour"]
   (b) A platinum ink-well with a large talisman
   (c) A baton of solid gold with emeralds and pearls
   (d) A bar of solid gold on which is engraved the instructive story of King Midas
   These four objects were given to me by Carolyne before her journey to Germany in 1848.
2. (a) A Sword of Honour from Pest (presented in January 1840)
   (b) A gold crown of laurel leaves (presented at Temesvár in 1846)
   (c) The little prayer-book, bound in ivory, that I received from Cardinal Scytowski [*sic*], archbishop of Gran and primate of Hungary, signed by him. He gave it to me on the occasion of the first performance of my mass at Gran.
   (d) A small gold goblet engraved with the names of Countesses Batthyány, Karoly, Szécheny [*sic*], Princess Odescalchi, etc., etc. (it was given to me on my first stay in Pressburg in 1840)
   (e) A silver jar from Warsaw, presented to me in 1843
3. (a) The solid silver desk with the busts of Beethoven, Weber, and Schubert with the inscription of a mass of names at the base
   (b) The Medal of Prussia for Arts and Sciences, for which His Majesty King Friedrich

Wilhelm IV (whom I remember with gratitude) graciously had a small frame made for me

(c) The gold medal bearing my portrait and a flattering inscription in German, which was presented to me, at a banquet given in my honour in 1842 in Berlin, by Meyerbeer, Mendelssohn, and the rector of the University

(d) The medal struck for me in Vienna in 1846, bearing my effigy (on payment of a subscription in which M. le Baron de Prokosch, now the Austrian internuncio for Constantinople, had taken a particular interest) with a beautiful Latin inscription

(e) The three Mozart medals (gold, silver, bronze) presented to me by the mayor of Vienna, Herr von Seiler, on the occasion of the Mozart festival which I directed

4. (a) The autographed manuscript of Frederick the Great of a flute concerto (in a violet, velvet casket), given to me by Her Royal Highness Princess Auguste of Prussia, *née* Princess of Sachsen-Weimar

(b) The *Mappe* in red velvet, with Goethe's autograph, which I received from the grand duke

(c) Preller's picture of the Sirens—a gracious present from H.R.H. the reigning Grand Duchess Sophie of Sachsen-Weimar

5. The original death-mask of Beethoven and the Broadwood piano that belonged to Beethoven. The former was given to me by a painter of great talent, M. Danhauser (in Vienna), the latter by the late M. Spina (senior) in Vienna.

6. The manuscript scores by Wagner of *Lohengrin* and *Der fliegende Holländer,* with the autographed score of *Tannhäuser* which is in the same box. A present from Wagner.

7. My two watches: one with a portrait of Pius IX which Carolyne gave me in 1848 in Vienna; the other (with my coat-of-arms inlaid) which was given to me by her daughter, Princess Konstantin Hohenlohe-Schillingsfürst (*née* Marie Wittgenstein), in Vienna.

I ask Carolyne to be good enough to keep the above-named objects with her until her death. If her daughter, Princess Hohenlohe, would accept one or two of her own choice, she would fulfil one of my wishes, for I should like something always to remind her of her years at the Altenburg! Later, when Carolyne comes to join me, I ask her to share the legacy of these objects, as she wills, between my two daughters, Blandine and Cosima. I also ask her to send directly to Cosima the drawing by Steinle representing my patron saint, St. Francis of Paule, standing on the waves of the sea, with his cloak spread beneath his feet, calmly holding in one hand a burning ember, the other hand raised either to bid the storm cease or to bless the mariners in distress, and with his eyes raised towards heaven, where in glory shines the redeeming word "Caritas." This drawing, which was given to me by Carolyne, has always stood on my desk. Nearby stands an old clock of carved wood, made from four hour-glasses, which I intend also for my daughter Cosima.

Among several other objects I have, I ask Carolyne to choose two that she thinks most suitable for my cousin Eduard Liszt and my very dear, gallant son-in-law Hans von Bülow. I ask her also to send to several members of our brotherhood of the New German School, to whom I remain attached—Hans von Bronsart (Leipzig), Peter Cornelius (Vienna), Eduard Lassen (Weimar), Dr. Franz Brendel (Leipzig), Richard Pohl (Weimar), Tausig (from Warsaw), and a few others whom Carolyne will decide upon—perhaps one or other of my objects, or a ring with my monogram on it, or my portrait, or my coat-of-arms, in memory of me. May they continue the work we have begun! This cause cannot be lost, were it only to have rare defenders!

I am indicating on a separate sheet attached to this will the arrangements I have made concerning the publication of several of my works which are in manuscript. I ask Carolyne to charge my son-in-law H. von Bülow to have them published after carefully reviewing the proofs.

I also wish that the few lines of dedication that I wrote for my twelve symphonic poems (*Symphonische Dichtungen,* published by Härtel at Leipzig) be printed at the top of the edition. [They are] dated 8 February 1855, [and] I transcribe them here (the original has remained since then in a little brown wooden box on a shelf above Carolyne's writing-desk in this room):

> To her who perfected her faith through love—
> Exalted her hope through suffering—
> Edified her happiness in sacrifice—
> To her who is forever my life's partner,
> The firmament of my thoughts, the loving prayer
> And the heaven of my soul—
> To Jeanne Elisabeth Carolyne.
>
> F. Liszt
> 8 February 1855.

Lastly, I also ask Carolyne to send to Madame Caroline d'Artigaux, *née* Countess de St. Cricq (at Pau in France), one of my talismans mounted in a ring; and to Princess Konstantin Hohenlohe, *née* Princess Marie Wittgenstein, her daughter, the ivory crucifix—"cinq cento"—which was given to me by my kind patron Prince Hohenzollern-Hechingen—and also a pair of buttons with five different stones which show the five different letters of my name.

The crucifix with the motif of my "Gran" Mass is to remain with Carolyne.

And now I kneel once more with Carolyne to pray (as we have often done together) that the reign of our Father Who is in Heaven may come, that His Will be done on earth as it is in Heaven. Forgive us our trespasses as we forgive them that trespass against us and deliver us from evil. Amen!

F. Liszt

Written on September 14, the Festival of the Exaltation of the Holy Cross (in the absence of Carolyne, who left here for Rome on May 17 last).

See the supplementary sheet which contains the list of my manuscripts to be published, and two other dispositions relative to my former secretary and friend M. Gaëtano Belloni in Paris and M. Grosse, member of the grand ducal orchestra at Weimar.

September 14, 1860

SUPPLEMENT

Supplementary sheet to my will, containing the list of a few manuscripts which I ask Carolyne to have printed if I die before their publication, and to charge my son-in-law H. von Bülow to see to it that the edition conforms in every respect to the best publications of this kind.

1. Psalm 18, "Coeli enarrant"—Latin and German text for chorus of men's voices with accompaniment of large orchestra, organ, etc.—to be printed

according to the score copied by Carl Götze. I wrote this psalm for Carolyne (as well as the "Beatitudes") in August 1860, during her stay in Rome.

2. Psalm 13, "Lord, how long wilt Thou forget me?"—tenor solo, choir, and orchestra—dedicated to my friend P. Cornelius. To be published in score with the piano arrangement at the bottom of each page.

3. Two Psalms:

    23, "The Lord is my shepherd"

    137, "By the waters of Babylon"

    for bass voice accompanied by harp, organ, etc.

4. The "Franciscus Lied" (for male voices). N.B.: On the title-page I wish the drawing of St. Francis by Steinle to be reproduced—the one I mentioned in my will.

5. "Les Morts" prayer—with score (the text of M. de Lamennais as I have written it at the bottom of each page), and also the arrangements for piano and for 2 and 4 hands—(written for my younger daughter, Cosima von Bülow) and for the organ.

6. Hungarian Rhapsodies for large orchestra, orchestrated by F. Doppler— revised by F. Liszt. N.B.: The name Doppler must not be omitted from the title-page, for he has done the work marvellously.

7. Four Marches of F. Schubert—orchestrated by F. Liszt. The manuscript is with Herbeck in Vienna.

8. Six songs by F. Schubert—orchestrated by F. Liszt.

9. A Mass (in C minor) for men's voices with accompaniment of wind and brass by Herbeck—performed for the first time at the celebration of the festival of the president of the French Republic, Louis Napoleon, on August 15, 1852, in the Catholic Church in Weimar, and published since (but with organ accompaniment only) at Härtel's in Leipzig.

Herr Grosse, a member of the grand ducal orchestra (as trombonist and double-bass player), who for many years has been copying out my works and looking after the mass of orchestral and vocal parts that that necessitated, knows in which compartment of the music library and the Altenburg (the whole of which belongs to Princess Carolyne Wittgenstein) the above-mentioned works may be found. I have told him that he had to give them to the princess, and I ask her to make a gift to Herr Grosse of 100 thalers (minimum) in recognition of the good and affectionate service he has rendered.

To the names of my friends of the New German School that I mentioned on p. 10 [see p. 560] of my will, I have to add—or rather I ought to have put in the forefront—that of M. Gaëtano Belloni (in Paris). He was my secretary during the period of my concerts in Europe from 1841 to 1847 and remained my faithful and devoted servant and friend. Carolyne already showed him much kindness at Woronince and Odessa, where he had accompanied me. . . . I ask her not to forget him. Moreover, whether he would or not, he is part of the New German School through his great attachment to me—as also through his more recent participation in the concerts of Berlioz and Wagner.

I wish to be buried simply, without any pomp whatsoever, and if possible at night. May eternal light shine on my soul. My last breath will be a blessing for Carolyne.

F. LISZT

On August 15, 1861, Liszt added to his will the following codicil, which has never before been published. Its main purpose was to appoint Princess Carolyne as his "residual legatee" and invest her with the authority to carry out certain tasks which, during the eleven months that had meanwhile elapsed, had begun to assume a different perspective for both of them. In short, Carolyne was now the will's executrix, and she did indeed lay claim to this title within days of Liszt's death nearly twenty-five years later. (Carolyne's own will, incidentally, drawn up within weeks of Liszt's, reciprocates the arrangement by naming Liszt her "sole heir and executor"; see p. 564.) The document may be inspected among the Rothschild papers in the Archives Nationales de France, Box 3V47.

MY WILL

1. I appoint Princess Carolyne von Sayn-Wittgenstein, *née* Iwanowska, as the residuary legatee of the whole of my property and goods. Therefore, the publication of my manuscripts also falls within her jurisdiction.
2. Only the monies deposited in Paris with Messrs. de Rothschild, which I have promised in writing and assigned to my two daughters, Blandine (married name Ollivier) and Cosima (Baroness von Bülow) at the time of their marriages as a dowry and from which these two have drawn the interest annually, should become the property of my two above-mentioned daughters immediately after my death.
3. I also resolve that my dear mother, Mme Anna Liszt in Paris, should continue to draw annually the same amount she has received from me every year until today, in the same way, until the last day of her life, through the good offices of my residuary legatee.
4. I request that Princess Carolyne von Sayn-Wittgenstein, *née* Iwanowska, accept the responsibility of realizing my last wishes stated here, and of transmitting to my friends the legacies which I have already made known to her.

F. LISZT
Weimar, August 15, 1861

2. PRINCESS CAROLYNE'S TESTAMENT

Princess Carolyne appears to have drawn up her testament not long after reading Liszt's, and possibly in response to it. The document came to light only in modern times. Evidently it passed into the possession of Carolyne's daughter, Princess Marie Hohenlohe, after Carolyne's death in 1887, and it was preserved as a curiosity within the Hohenlohe family. The last owner was Countess Maria Lambart, the great-granddaughter of Carolyne, from whom the will was purchased by the Library of Congress in 1966.[8]

When the two wills are placed side by side, it is evident that they serve the common purpose of a pre-nuptial agreement: Carolyne and Liszt are one another's chief beneficiaries. This idea is strengthened when we look at the signature and date on Carolyne's will. She signs herself "Carolyne Liszt" and dates the document "Rome, October 23, 1861." Since the projected date of her wedding to Liszt was October 22, 1861, his fiftieth birthday, it has been

---

8. The full story of the discovery and purchase of the will is given in WPFL, which also presents Carolyne's original French text in full.

surmised that the will was finalized only after the marriage plans were in place, and then post-dated to October 23—that is, to the day after the wedding. Obviously the will could not have been dated and signed in this way *before* the wedding date was known. The most likely time for this to have happened would have been during the first week of October 1861, since on October 4 Liszt wrote to Carolyne from Berlin expressing his pleasure that she had arranged the ceremony for his fiftieth birthday.[9] In the event the will was never executed because the princess never became Carolyne Liszt. The document nevertheless throws light on her intentions at this time, and as a nostalgic relic of her dashed hopes and lost aspirations it is irreplaceable.

In the name of the Father, of the Son, and of the Holy Ghost, Amen.

Being today, thanks be to God, perfectly sound in mind and body, I want to record my last wishes in a will conforming in all respects with the laws of the Pontifical States, where I have been domiciled for a year and half; in pursuance thereof I write it, I sign it, I seal it with my own hand, and I shall deposit it myself with a notary in the presence of the number of witnesses required by law, desiring that nothing will be lacking for its complete validity.

Having commended my soul to the infinite mercy of God, to the intercession of the Immaculate Virgin Mary and of my patron saints, I begin by bequeathing to the *hôpital* of the Holy Spirit in Rome *ten* (10) Roman crowns, to the Propagation of the Faith *one thousand* (1,000) Roman crowns, and a like sum to Peter's Pence, if it is still being collected. Besides this, there will be established in St. Peter's Basilica a daily mass throughout the entire year for the repose of my soul and for those of my parents.

At the time of the marriage of my only daughter, Princess Marie Pauline Antonia von Sayn-Wittgenstein, to Prince Konstantin von Hohenlohe-Schillingsfürst, I gave her through her marriage contract, stipulated, drawn up, and signed by me, all the properties that constituted the inheritance I had received from my father and mother, the said properties all situated within Little Russia, now being fully and entirely in her possession, in virtue of both the aforementioned marriage contract and also the restitution made by His Majesty the Emperor of Russia, Alexander II, after the Russian government had confiscated them from me. Thus I am in the position of having already given within my lifetime all my patrimony to my sole legitimate heir. If, however, it should be necessary, I renew this same gift to my dearly beloved daughter, with the same love and the same maternal blessing for her, for her husband, and for her children in this will, wherein I intend to declare once again that I bequeath to her all the rich properties I possessed in Russia and of which she is already in perfect tenure.

I therefore dispose in full knowledge and legal freedom of the little that I now possess of personal chattels of whatever nature they may be, as well as whatever might be owing to me by whomsoever, and of whatsoever manner, except for my daughter, in favour of my husband, M. Franz Liszt, whom I appoint my sole heir and executor.

I ask him to receive and to keep in memory of me and of the long, deep, and grateful attachment which brought me to consecrate my whole life to him, the whole and absolute ownership of all that belongs to me at the hour of my death.

I add only the request to give:

---

9. LLB, vol. 5, p. 235.

A. To my above-mentioned daughter, Princess Hohenlohe:

   1. A painting by the celebrated French artist Ary Scheffer, representing the Wise Kings, which I bought from the estate of the late King Willem of Holland
   2. Her own portrait painted in Paris life-size by the same master, Ary Scheffer
   3. Her own bust in marble, worked in Weimar by the famous sculptor Ernst Rietschel
   4. All my jewels, matching-pieces, necklaces, bracelets, used for personal attire

   It would please me if my son-in-law, Prince Konstantin von Hohenlohe, in memory of the affectionate feelings with which I gave him my daughter, would choose from my jewels a fine stone for his personal use; if my grandson, Franz Joseph,[10] first-born of my daughter, would one day receive as a gift the above-mentioned portrait of his mother, in memory of me, his grandmother; and if the above-mentioned bust were given one day to the eldest daughter of my daughter, if God bestows one on her.

B. To His Eminence Cardinal Count Giacomo Antonelli, in witness of my admiration for services rendered by him to the Church in his capacity as secretary of state, with high esteem for his character as a private citizen and with respectful personal friendship, the biggest of all my turquoises, backed with Oriental enamel and carrying a beautiful Persian inscription.

As a faithful Catholic, devoted to the Church, I wish to be buried in Rome, if my husband concurs, forbidding that my body be dissected, embalmed, exhibited, or dressed; let it be simply wrapped and sewn in a shroud.

I pardon all who did me wrong, near or far, dead or alive; I thank all who helped and protected me in my cruel tribulations. I bless with a last, fervent benediction those who loved me: may God grant the last wishes of my tender affection for them.

I commend myself once more to divine goodness, through the power of the precious blood of Our Lord Jesus Christ, who died on the Cross for the remission of our sins, to the prayers of our Holy Mother the Church in the holy sacrifice of the mass, and to those people who will remember me, in the hope that the Lord, through their virtue, will deign to pardon me my sins and make me worthy of his Paradise.

CAROLYNE LISZT
Rome, October 23, 1861

---

10. Carolyne's first grandson, Franz Joseph, had been born a few weeks earlier in Vienna.

Appendix II:
The Vatican's Marriage-File on
Liszt and Carolyne Iwanowska

For more than one hundred and twenty-five years the whereabouts of the Vatican's file on the thwarted marriage of Liszt and Princess Carolyne von Sayn-Wittgenstein remained shrouded in mystery. Although the College of Cardinals was convened by Pope Pius IX on two separate occasions in order to review the case (on September 22, 1860, and December 22, 1860), no record of the convocation appeared to have been kept, and no document containing its judgement ever appeared to have been issued. That fact alone always aroused interest among Liszt scholars; after all, the question of Liszt's marriage to Carolyne was one of the central issues of his life, and the presence of documents in Rome would be of fundamental interest to his biographers. All inquiries made through the labyrinthine organization of the Vatican Library, however, invariably encountered a negative response. The suspicion soon arose in Lisztian circles that the Vatican was part of a conspiracy to suppress information. In which case, what were its motives?

The entire case turned on the question of perjury. Anyone who was knowingly about to bear false witness on a matter as grave as a second Catholic marriage-service had to be made aware of the legal and ethical consequences of such actions. And where the annulment of a previous marriage was an issue, as it was in this case, false testimony could lead to charges of bigamy. Bigamy was not only a mortal sin but a crime as well, and it was usually punished both by excommunication and a long term of imprisonment. Before Carolyne and Liszt could marry, therefore, they would both have been subjected to questioning by clerics charged with such tasks, and they would also have been obliged to provide various documents in order to protect their legal position. Their case was both complex and notorious; whatever the outcome, the Catholic Church was also on trial.

In the summer of 1985 I located the "missing" files in two quite separate archives. The Archivio Segreto Vaticano contains a cache of some forty documents drawn from the papers of Cardinal Antonino De Luca, papal nuncio to Vienna, and the Bishop of Fulda (1860–61). These papers bear the description "Special Annex: The Matrimonial Case of Wittgenstein versus Iwanowska," and they relate mainly to the long struggle leading up to the annulment of Carolyne's marriage and to the issuing of the decree itself. The other file is in the Vicariato di Roma in San Giovanni in Laterano, and it bears the shelf-mark N. 4477 L/41. The seven documents it contains relate specifically to the forthcoming nuptials between Liszt and Carolyne. Taken together, the documents from both archives allow us to review the tortured history of the case with some precision. *And they show conclusively that it was not the fault of the Catholic Church that Carolyne did not marry Liszt.*

When the Holy Congregation was convened on September 22, 1860, it had before it the Decree of Nullity issued by the consistories of Russia on February 24, 1860 (Old Style), which declared that Carolyne's marriage to Prince Nicholas was null and void. This was the decree that had been suspended by the bishop of Fulda, in whose diocese Carolyne lived; and her purpose in travelling to Rome in May 1860 was to have that suspension lifted. And the cardinals did indeed lift it, thereby declaring that the Russian annulment was valid. In many respects this Russian decree of February 24 is the most interesting of all the documents that came to light in Rome, because the consistories of St. Petersburg had reviewed the case from its very beginning, and they went over the old, familiar ground with care.

ABSTRACT

Wenceslas Zyliński, by the grace of God and the Apostolic See Archbishop of Mohilow, Metropolitan for all Roman Catholic churches in the Russian Empire, apostolic delegate as it pertains to what is written below.

To each and every one who will read the present letters, we make it known and testify that not long ago, the Office of the Minister for Internal Affairs of the Russian Empire brought to our attention a communication from the Holy Congregation of the Council, issued on the 8th day of August of the year 1859, in which the Holy Father, kindly condescending to the requests made by Carolyne Iwanowska, deigned to order that we be empowered, if there were no reasons to the contrary, to take up again the case of annulment of her marriage to Prince Nicholas Wittgenstein, review it, and, with the help of God, render judgement on it with a definitive sentence, according to the level of appeal, observing otherwise what needs to be observed and especially the dispositions of the late Pope Benedict XIV in the Bull "Dei miseratione."

Having received this communication with all due reverence, we proceeded to its execution and entrusted the most distinguished fathers Maximilian Haniewski, bishop of Plateen and our auxiliary; Andreas Dobszewicz, monsignor provost of Szydov and canon of Samogit; Dominic Moszezynski, prelate and dean of Minsk; we summoned also, after he made the usual oath, the Defender of the Matrimonial Bond, Basil Zottek, especially selected by us for this task; and we gave them the mandate of reviewing again the whole case from the beginning, examining carefully how it was dealt with by the consistory of Luk-Zhitomir and how it was examined by the consistory of Mohilow, and, finally, of voting freely and spontaneously on its merits after receiving a full summary of the evidence about and apropos of the validity or the invalidity of the said marriage.

At the conclusion of the proceedings, they found the following:

1. Carolyne Iwanowska, a Catholic young lady of noble birth, having reached the age of seventeen, was subjected to intimidation and grave threats by her father, as was proved by witnesses who have sworn to that effect, and was joined in matrimony, on the 26th of April 1836, with Prince Nicholas Wittgenstein, an adept of the sect of Calvin. She, moreover, after the death of her father, and no longer fearing that he could deprive her of the fruits of her inheritance, sent in 1848 a request to her own Ordinary Office of Lvov in order to obtain a declaration of annulment of the aforementioned marriage contract by cause of violence and threat. The case, then, was dealt with according to law and brought to judgement, in the first instance, before the consistory of Luk-Zhitomir.

2. The consistory of Luk-Zhitomir gathered to deliberate on the 6th of November 1851—given that the witnesses (the mother of the requesting party, a noble lady-in-waiting, and some of her servants of plebeian birth, who were brought forth for the purpose of proving that the requesting party had been compelled, with violence and intimidation, to contract marriage) caused the case to appear doubtful and provided insufficient evidence— declared, then, that the marriage was to be deemed valid on the strength of the ruling in Pichler's Code, Tome 1, Book 4: *"If, when everything has been considered, doubt persists as to whether or not the marriage has been contracted under such conditions of intimidation as to render it invalid, one must presume its validity, and presume, of course, in favour of the sacrament, of the offspring and the state."*

3. The same case being presented in the second instance, namely before the consistory of Mohilow, it being pertinent to the situation that the marriage was at first contracted through intimidation, though it is contemplated in common law that, later, through subsequent free and voluntary consummation it can be ratified and validated, nevertheless, at present, according to the new rules made by the Council of Trent, the initial contracting of an invalid marriage is not validated by the consequent consummation, no matter how freely performed, and a new consent before the Church is necessary as, in accordance with the declaration of the Holy Congregation, is confirmed by Fagnano in the formulary of Monacelli at Chapter VIII, Formula 10, No. 17—the judges, therefore, on November 13, 1852, pronounced the aforesaid marriage invalid, with only the vicar general dissenting. The archbishop of Mohilow, Ignaz Holowinski, our fatherly predecessor, ratified his opinion on the validity of the marriage which rested on the aforementioned declaration of the consistory of Luk-Zhitomir, thus showing his disapproval that a clear majority of the judges had voted in favour of the annulment.

4. Prince Nicholas Wittgenstein, a follower of the Calvinist sect, had already remarried, in the year 1857, a lady of the Russian Orthodox faith.

On the basis of these findings, the above-named unanimously decreed the marriage of Carolyne Iwanowska to be null and void.

Therefore, having studied the above proceedings and decrees, checked the laws that were brought to our attention, especially the chapter *Videtur nobis* which the petitioners for annulment placed at the end *("What we read is true, namely that, in criminal cases, the father is not to be a party in the case of the son, nor is the son in the case of the father. However, in the conjoining or disjoining pertaining to marriage, as a prerogative of marriage itself and because the thing is favourable, they are properly admitted")* and also the aforementioned declaration of the Holy Congregation reported in Monacelli *("Today, according to the new rules approved by the Council of Trent, a marriage contracted from the beginning in a situation of intimidation must be deemed invalid, and it cannot be validated by its consequent consummation, no matter how freely and willingly performed; a new consent is, therefore, required, etc.")* and all those other things according to which, in the act of contracting marriage, it is required that there be a true consent, not simulated but positive, reciprocal, given in total freedom from threats, violence, and intimidation, and with immunity, and, having consulted the Defender of the Matrimonial Bond—by the apostolic authority invested in us, we deliberated that the marriage of Carolyne Iwanowska with Prince Nicholas Wittgenstein, having been contracted through violence and intimidation, must be said, pronounced, and decreed definitively to be and have been, therefore, null, void, and without effect. Accordingly, through the present letters, in the absence of any other impediment which His Holiness thought might be an obstacle, we state, pronounce, declare, and, moreover, issue a definitive sentence attributing to the aforesaid Carolyne full faculty to contract a new marriage freely and legitimately.

In proof of the above etc.
Given in St. Petersburg on the 24th day of February of the year 1860.
†Wenceslas, Archbishop.

S.S. [Sequitur Sigillum]
I have seen this decree.
Basil Zottek, Defender
of the Matrimonial Bond in this case.

Otto Prosciewski,
Secretary for Spiritual Matters to His Excellency
The most Reverend and Illustrious Archbishop.

(original text)

EXTRACTUM

Venceslaus Zyliński Dei et Apostolicae Sedis gratia Archiepiscopus Mokyloviensis, Metropolitanus omnium Romano-Catholicorum in Imperio Rossiaco Ecclesiarum, ad infra scripta Delegatus Apostolicus.

Universis et singulis praesentes inspecturis, notum facimus, atque testamur, qualiter nuper exhibitum fuerit ex Ministerio Negotiorum Internorum Imperii Rossiaci Rescriptum S[anctae] Congregationis Concilii sub d[ie] 8 Augusti 1859 anni emanatum, quo Sanctissimus Dominus Noster praecibus Karolinae Iwanowska benigne annuens, mandare dignatus est, ut contrariis quibuscumque non obstantibus, Nos causam super nullitate matrimonii eius cum Principe Nicolao Wittgenstein reassumere, cognoscere ac per definitivam sententiam, in appellationis gradu, servatis ceteroquin servandis ac praesertim Constitutione sa[nctae] mem[oriae] Benedicti XIV, "Dei miseratione," diiudicare valeamus. Nos rescripto hoc cum omni, qua decuit, reverentia recepto, ad executionem eiusdem procedentes, Perillustribus DD. Maximiliano Haniewski Episcopo Plateensi, Suffraganeo Nostro, Andreae Dobszewicz Infulato Praeposito Szydoviensi, Canonico Samogitiensi et Dominico Moszezynski Praelato Decano Minscensi commisimus, ut Defensore Matrimoni R[everendo] D[omino] Basilio Zottek, specialiter a Nobis ad id destinato, post praestitum ab ipso consuetum iuramentum, citato, totam causam in Luceovio-Zytomirensi Consistorio tractatam, atque in Consistorio Mohyloviensi examinatam, denuo reassumptam cognoscant et diligenter examinent, ac summaria informatione de expositis capta, de et super validitate aut nullitate dicti matrimonii, libera ac spontanea suffragia sua proferant. Qui cum in processu constructo reperiissent, 1., Karolinam Iwanowska Catholicam, septemdecim annorum aetatis, nobilem virginem, metu et minis gravissimis a proprio genitore, prout a testibus, interposito iuramento, probatum sit, adactam et matrimonio 26 d[ie] Aprilis 1836 anni coniunctam fuisse cum Principe Nicolao Wittgenstein Calvinianae Sectae addicto, illamque post mortem patris sui 1848 anni non amplius metuentem, quin ab illo praediis bonisque haereditariis privaretur, supplicem dedisse libellum proprio Ordinariatui Looi, pro declaratione nullitatis praedicti matrimonii per vim et minas contracti. Causam inde ad tramites iuris confectam, Consistorio Luceovio Zytomirensi ex ordine ad diiudicandum oblatam fuisse. 2., Consistorium Luceovio-Zytomirense 6 d[ie] Novembris 1851 anni censendo, quod testes inducti, prout mater oratricis, famula nobilis et nonnulli ex domesticis eius de plebe, ad probandum, oratricem vi metuque adactam fuisse ad contrahendum matrimonium, dubium facerent iudicium, satisque non probarent, adductis verbis C[odicis] Pichleri Tom[i] I Libr[i] IV: "Si omnibus consideratis manet dubium, an matrimonium tali metu, quo illud redditur invalidum, contractum sit necne? praesumendum est pro valore, scilicet propter favorem sacramenti, prolis imo et rei publicae," declarasse matrimonium illud pro validum habendum. 3., Proposita eadem causa in secunda instantia, coram Consistorio Mohyloviensi nempe, Iudices, attento quod matrimonium a principio metu contractum, licet iure communi inspecto, per copulam postea libere et voluntarie subsecutam ratificeretur at convalidaretur, nihilominus hodie, iure novo Concilii Tridentini, matrimonium nulliter a principio contractum, non convalidetur per subsecutam copulam quantum vis libere habitam, sed requiratur novus consensus in facie Ecclesiae, prout ex declaratione S[anctae] Congregationis firmat Fagnanus apud Monacelli in Formulario Tit[ulum] VIII, for[mulam] X, N[umerum] 17 dictum matrimonium 13 d[ie] Novembris 1852 an invalidum pronuntiasse, uno vix dissentiente Vicario generali, cuius sententiam pro validitate matrimonii supradictae declarationi Consistorii Luceovio-Zytomirensis innixam, Archiepiscopus Mohyloviensis, p[ater] m[eus] Ignatius Holowinski, ratam habuerit, reprobato suffragio pro nullitate eius a maiori parte iudicum lato. 4., Principem Nicolaum Wittgenstein Calvinianae sectae asseclam iam anno 1857 ad alias nuptias cum virgine Graeco-Rossiacae religionis convolasse; unanimiter matrimonium Karolinae Iwanowska nullum ac invalidum edixerunt. Idcirco Nos visis actis et decretis suprascriptis ac attentis iuribus coram Nobis exhibitis praesertim cap[itulo] *Videtur Nobis* qui matr[imonii] accus[atores] pos[uerunt] in fine: "Quod vero legitur, Pater non recipiatur in causa filii nec filius in causa patris in criminalibus causis et contractibus verum est. In matrimonio vero coniungendo et disiungendo, ex ipsius coniugii praerogativa et quia favorabilis res est, *congrue* admittuntur." et supracitata declaratione S[anctae] Congregationis apud Monacelli: "Hodie iure novo Concilii Tridentini matrimonium nulliter a principio metu contractum, non convalidatur per subsecutam copulam, quantumvis libere habitam, sed requiritur novus consensus etc." ac omnibus, iuxta quae in contrahentibus matrimonium expostulatur consensus verus, non simulatus, positivus, reciprocus, libertas totalis a minis, vi et metu, immunitas, nec non audito Defensore matrimonii, Auctoritate Apostolica Nobis concessa, matrimonium Karolinae Iwanowska cum principe Nicolao Wittgenstein per vim et metum contractum adeoque nullum, irritum et invalidum fuisse et esse dicendum, pronunciandum ac definitive sententiandum esse duximus, prout per praesentes, contrariis quibuscumque non obstantibus, quae Sua Sanctitas non obstare voluit, dicimus, pronunciamus, declaramus ac per definitivam sententiam diiudicamus, plenam dictae Karolinae facultatem, ut ad alias nuptias libere ac licite transire valeat, concedendo.

In quorum fidem etc.
Datum Petropoli 1860 anni Mensis Februarii 24 die.
†Venceslaus Archiepiscopus:

S.S. [Sequitur Sigillum]

Hoc decretum legi.
Basilius Zottek Defensor
Matrimonii hac in causa

Otto Prosciewski
Secretarius in Spiritualibus
Suae Excell[entiae] R[everen]d[issi]mi
[&] Ill[ustrissi]mi Archiep[iscopi].

On the basis of this document alone, Carolyne was now free to contract another marriage inside the Catholic Church. It is at this point that the papers in the Vicariato di Roma are of interest. They reveal that both Liszt and Carolyne actively pursued their marriage plans throughout much of 1861 and assembled the necessary documents required for the ceremony. But first they had to fight a fresh appeal brought against the annulment by the Hohenlohes. That appeal was heard by the Holy Congregation on December 22, 1860, and once more the Russian annulment was upheld. Pope Pius IX confirmed the decision on January 7, 1861, and the final judgement was released by the cardinals on the following day, January 8. The document was eventually included in a dossier marked *"Interrogatoria Facienda,* October 20, 1861—Francesco Liszt e Carolina Iawanowska [*sic*]," which contains the following papers:

1. The final judgement of the Holy Congregation, issued on January 8, 1861, which upholds their earlier decision and the Russian annulment;
2. An instrument of interrogation, in which the penalties for bearing false witness are set forth;
3. A deposition from Father Anton Hohmann, the Roman Catholic priest in Weimar, dated July 18, 1861;
4. A deposition from Carolyne, dated September 18, 1861;
5. A communication from the Office of the Holy Congregation to Pope Pius IX, dated September 18, 1861;
6. A request to waive the reading of the marriage banns;
7. A joint deposition from Liszt and Carolyne, testifying to the fact that they are both single, dated October 20, 1861.

Since both the Hohenlohe and the Wittgenstein families were deeply implicated in the Church's formal resistance to Carolyne's case, it comes as no surprise to learn that the marriage-file was placed in the "secret archive" of the Vicariato di Roma. This restriction remained in force until recently because (as it was explained to us) "the descendants of the Hohenlohe and Wittgenstein families might still have a vested interest in maintaining the *status quo."* Happily, that turned out not to be the case. The file is published here for the first time with the permission of Cardinal Ugo Poletti, the head of the Vicariato.

I. THE FINAL JUDGEMENT OF THE HOLY CONGREGATION,
ISSUED ON JANUARY 8, 1861

On January 8, 1861, the Holy Congregation of the most eminent Cardinals of the Holy Roman Church, interpreters of the Council of Trent, by order of Pope Pius IX dated September 22, 1860, gathered in general assembly and conducted a review of the various and different decisions provided by the consistories of Luk-Zhitomir and Mohilow in the case of annulment of the marriage of Princess Carolyne Iwanowska, Catholic, and Prince Nicholas Wittgenstein, non-Catholic, because of alleged *vis et metus* [violence and fear] removing the impediment, particularly in order to establish whether there was anything preventing the carrying out of the last decision of the archbishop of Mohilow in favour of the annulment of the marriage, which was issued on February 24, 1860, on the strength of special faculties given him by a rescript of His Holiness on August 8, 1859. From a thorough examination of all things pertinent both to the propriety of the decision and the intrinsic merit of the case, the same Holy Congregation deliberated that there was nothing preventing the carrying out of the aforesaid decision of the archbishop of Mohilow, and it ordered that the bishop of Fulda be notified of this resolution. Earlier, because of peculiar circumstances, he had been given orders to deny Princess Carolyne, who lived in his diocese, permission to contract another marriage until the Holy See decided otherwise. Having reported on the above to the Holy Father at an audience on the 24th of the aforesaid month and year, His Holiness condescended to approve and confirm the decision of the Holy Congregation. Since the execution of the aforementioned sentence was left suspended because of unforeseen developments, His Holiness thought to expedite the matter and order the same Holy Congregation to conduct a new review of the whole situation. Therefore, in a general assembly on December 22 of the same year, the most eminent fathers, having debated all that was pertinent according to the law and according to the facts brought forth so far, and having considered all the other concomitant things added to the facts, deliberated that the judgement of the archbishop of Mohilow issued on February 24, 1860, was to be executed. Such a resolution His Holiness in his benevolence both approved and confirmed in the audience of January 7, 1861.

Signed: P. CARDINAL CATERINI, PRES.
ANGELO QUAGLIA, SECRETARY

The above conforms fully to the signed original with which it was compared.

BERNARDINO CARD. MAGGI, DEPUTATO.

(Original text)

Die 8 Januarii 1861 S[ancta] Congregatio Eminentissimorum S[anctae]R[omanae] E[cclesiae] Cardinalium Concilii Tridentini Interpretum de mandato S[anctissi]mü D[omi]ni Nostri Pii Papae IX die 22 Septembris 1860 in Generali habito Conventu examen instituit super variis iisque difformibus sententiis editis a Consistoriis Zitumiriense et Mokilowiense in causa nullitatis matrimonii inter Carolinam Iwanowska Principissam catholicam et Nicolaum Wittgenstein Principem Acatholicum ob assertum *vis et metus*

*A facsimile page of the judgement of the Holy Congregation,
issued on January 8, 1861, upholding Carolyne's annulment.*

dirimens impedimentum, praesertim vero ut decerneretur an aliquid obstaret quominus exequutioni esset committenda postrema sententia ab Archiepiscopo Mokilowiensis edita pro nullitate matrimonii die 24 mensis Februarii 1860 in vim specialium facultatum eidem tributarum rescripto S[anctissi]mi D[omi]ni Nostri diei 8 Augusti 1859. Ex rebus omnibus mature perpensis tum ad iudicii ordinem tum etiam ad intrinsecum causae meritum pertinentibus eadem S[ancta] Congregatio censuit rescribendum, nihil impedimento esse exequitioni praefatae sententiae Archiepiscopi Mokilowiensis; et hujusmodi resolutionem, ad effectum supradictae exequuitionis, notificari mandavit Episcopo Fulden [si], cui antea ob peculiares circumstantias litterae datae fuerant eum in finem, ut Principissae Carolinae, quae in eius Diocesi domicilium agebat, licentiam denegaret alias ineundi nuptias usquedum a S[ancta] Sede aliter non provideretur. Factaque de praemissis relatione S[anctissi]mo D[omi]no Nostro in audientia diei 24 praedicti mensis, et anni, Sanctitas Sua resolutionem S[anctae] Congregationis benigne approbare, ac confirmare dignata est. Cum vero ob nonnullas exortas difficultates exequutio praedictae resolutionis in suspenso relicta fuisset, expedire visum fuit S[anctissi]mo D[omi]no Nostro rem omnem ejusdem S[anctae] Congregationis examini iterum committere. Ideoque in Generalibus Comitiis diei 22 Decembris ejusdem anni, Emi [nentissimi] Patres ratione habita ad ea omnia quae in jure ac in facto hinc inde noviter deducta fuerunt aliisque omnibus concomitantibus rerum adjunctis maturiori consilio perpensis, rescribendum censuerunt sententiam Archiepiscopi Mokilowiensis diei 24 Februarii 1860 esse exequendam: quam resolutionem Sanctitas Sua in audientia diei 7 Januarii 1861 benigne pariter approbavit et confirmavit.

> P. Card. Caterini Praef[ectus]
> A[ngelo] Quaglia Secretarius
> Loco † Signi

Concordat cum originali subscripto exhibito.

> Bernardinus Can. Maggi deput[atus]

Now that all the legal and theological impediments had been formally removed, Carolyne began to plan her marriage to Liszt in earnest. She decided on Rome as the location, and she set the date for October 22, 1861, Liszt's fiftieth birthday—for reasons which have been elaborated elsewhere. Meanwhile, a variety of additional documents were accumulated. The ones which follow consist of depositions regarding the character and the status of the parties and a request to waive the marriage banns; they were submitted on October 20, 1861, on which day both Liszt and Carolyne were subjected to verbal interrogation.

2. INTERROGATORIA FACIENDA, OCTOBER 20, 1861

Questioning to be carried out in the examination of those witnesses who are convened in the chambers of the Most Reverend and Eminent Cardinal Vicar of the city, for the purpose of contracting marriage; witnesses have to be warned from the outset of the gravity of oaths, particularly terrifying in such a matter, since both the Divine and the human Majesties are offended, because of the importance and solemnity of what is involved, and because those who provide false testimony are sentenced to prison.

PERTAINING TO FRANCESCO LISZT

AND

CAROLINA IAWANOWSKA [*sic*]

(Original text)

Interrogatoria facienda pro examine illorum Testium, qui inducuntur pro contrahendis Matrimoni is in Curia E[minentissi]mi et R[everendissi]mi Domini Card[inalis]. Urbis Vicarii, et in primis monendi erunt Examinandi de gravitate juramenti in hoc praesertim negotio pertimescendi, in quo Divina simul, et humana Majestas laeditur, ob rei de qua tractatur, importantiam, et gravitatem, et quod imminent poena Triremium, deponenti falsum.

PRO FRANCESCO LISZT

E

CAROLINA IAWANOWSKA

[*sic*]

3. A DEPOSITION FROM FATHER ANTON HOHMANN, THE ROMAN CATHOLIC PRIEST IN WEIMAR, DATED JULY 18, 1861

I testify to the following: that the illustrious Mr. Franz Liszt, doctor of philosophy, born in Hungary, aged forty-nine years and nine months, from the year 1848, when he set up his residence in Weimar, to the present day, at which time he still resides in that same town and has lived there continually for thirteen years, has been always and is still single, is not bound in any way and is not held by any canonic impediment, as far as it is known, that may prevent him therefore from entering matrimony with an unattached woman. I testify, moreover, that the aforesaid Mr. Liszt, a Catholic, has always given evidence of piety and of a good Christian life and has not omitted to fulfil the duties that our Holy Mother Church prescribes to a male Catholic. Nothing contrary to the above has come to the attention of myself, the undersigned priest.

Weimar, July 18, 1861
A. HOHMANN
p.t. Catholic Priest in the City of Weimar

By apposing our seal, we hereby testify that the above was written and signed, in his own hand, by the priest of Weimar, A. Hohmann, and bore the seal of the parish.

Fulda, July 29, 1861
Chapter of the Cathedral of Fulda
F. Hohmann

(Original text)

Tenore praesentium testor, illustrissimum Dominum Franciscum Liszt, Doctorem philos [ophiae], natum in Hungaria, nunc in aetate annorum quadraginta novem novemque mensium constitutum, ab anno 1848, quo domicilium fixit in civitate Weimar usque ad presentem diem, qua adhuc in eadem moratur ibique continuo per tredecim annos permansit, in statu libero semper fuisse et esse, nulloque vinculo teneri vel impedimento canonico irretiri, quod sciatur, quominus matrimonium cum libera possit inire. Insuper testor, praefatum D[omi]num Liszt, catholicum religione, semper pietatis et vitae bene christianae praebuisse argumenta nec omisisse catholici viri officia, quae S[ancta] Mater Ecclesia praescribit, adimplere. De eo quid in contrarium nil mihi parocho infra scripto innotuit.

Weimar die 18 Julii 1861
A. Hohmann
p.t. Parochus catholicus civitatis Weimar

Quae supra leguntur, a parocho Weimariensi A. Hohmann manu propria scripta, subscripta, suoque sigillo parochiali munita esse, hisce testamur apposito nostro sigillo.

Fuldae, die 29 Julii 1861
Capitulum Eccl[esiae] Cathedr[alis] Fuldensis
F. Hohmann

4. A DEPOSITION FROM CAROLYNE, SEPTEMBER 18, 1861

I, the undersigned, testify on my honour and my conscience to the truth that Mr. Franz Liszt, son of the late Adam, born in Hungary in 1811, and brought to Paris in 1820 while still in his childhood, received there his confirmation in 1829 and resided there until 1838, when he went to Italy. Afterwards, having completed some voyages for the purpose of instruction to the main capitals of Europe, he established his residence in Weimar in 1848, attached to the court of the grand duke there, where he continued to reside and where he is still residing at present, living always as a true Christian Catholic. I can also testify with full and certain knowledge that, from his birth to the present, he has remained unattached, never having entered any bond or pledge that could prevent him from marrying according to the Catholic rite. This I can establish on the basis of the acquaintance I have had with him and his family. Faithfully, etc.

> Rome, this 18th of September 1861.
> Princess Carolyne von Sayn-Wittgenstein
> born Iwanowska[1]

(Original text)

Io sottoscritta attesto nel mio onore e coscienza per la verità che il Signor Francesco Liszt figlio del fu Adamo, nato in Ungheria nel 1811, sin dalla infanzia recato a Parigi nel 1820, ivi nel 1829 fu cresimato e vi rimase sino all' anno 1838, d'onde in questa epoca venne in Italia e poscia, fatti dei viaggi istruttivi nelle principali Capitali d'Europa, si ridusse nel 1848 a Weymar attaccato alla Corte di quel Granduca, ove è sempre rìmasto e vi rimane tuttora, vivendo sempre da vero cristiano cattolico. E posso anche attestare con piena e certa scienza che il medesimo si è sempre dalla sua nascita sino al giorno presente conservato libero, non avendo mai contratto alcun vincolo od impegno che possa impedirgli di

---

1. The factual errors in this sworn statement would have rendered it useless in law. Liszt was brought to Paris in 1823, not 1820; he resided there until 1835, not 1838; his "voyages" to the main capitals of Europe were hardly "for the purpose of instruction"; and in September 1861, Liszt no longer resided in Weimar, having closed down the Altenburg on Carolyne's own instructions the previous month. It remains only to observe that the princess appears to have been surprisingly ill-informed about the details of Liszt's earlier years.

contrarre matrimonio secondo il rito cattolico. E tuttociò mi costa dalle relazioni che ho avuto ed ho tuttora con esso e colla di lui famiglia. In fede etc.

Roma questo giorno 18 Settembre 1861.

Principessa Carolyna di Sayn-Wittgenstein
n[ata] Iwanowska

5. A COMMUNICATION FROM THE HOLY CONGREGATION TO POPE PIUS IX, SEPTEMBER 18, 1861

Most Blessed Father,

Franz, son of the late Adam Liszt, a Catholic from Hungary, aged fifty years, desiring to contract matrimony in Rome, presents a certificate of baptism and a certificate of single status from 1848 to the present, and for the previous period he is presenting a certificate from his future bride, from which it is desumed that he received confirmation in 1829. He requests Your Holiness to admit such documents and dispense with any other certificate.

Carolyne, daughter of the late Peter of the princes Iwanowski, a Catholic, aged forty-two, having been compelled to marry in 1836 Prince Nicholas Wittgenstein, a scismatic, in the metropolitan bishopric of Mohilow, legally introduced a case for the annulment of that marriage contracted *per vim et metum,* and the case was accordingly decided on February 24, 1860. The judgement declaring that marriage annulled, she obtained a document of single status. Having brought this resolution to the Holy Congregation of the Council, with pontifical approval she obtained the *exequatur* [authorization to proceed] on January 7, 1861, as it transpires from the authentic document which is exhibited with the intention to retrieve it and release a copy of it instead. She begs Your Holiness therefore to admit this authoritative certificate and to dispense her from exhibiting the certificates of baptism, confirmation, and single status from the time of that decision to the present in order to be able to marry the aforementioned Liszt.

On 18 September 1861, released
by the Holy Congregation of the Holy Office
on condition that there be no canonic impediment.

(Original text)

Beatissimo Padre,

Francesco del fu Adamo Liszt Cattolico di Ungheria di anni 50, volendo contrarre matrimonio in Roma esibisce la fede di Battesimo e stato libero dal 1848 fino al presente, e per l'epoca anteriore presenta l'attestato della sua futura sposa da cui si rileva che fu confermato nel 1829. Supplica V[ostra] S[antità] ad ammettere cotali documenti dispensandolo da ogni altra fede.

Carolina del fu Pietro de' Principi Iawanowska cattolica di anni 42 essendo stata costretta a sposare nel 1836 il Principe Nicolò Wittgenstein, scismatico, nella Curia Metropolitana di Mohylow, introdusse legalmente causa di nullità di quel matrimonio contratto *per vim et metum* e ne ebbe analoga sentenza a dì 24 Febraro 1860, nella quale dichiarato nullo quel matrimonio ottenne il documento di Libertà. Quindi portata questa risoluzione nella S[anta] C[ongregazione] del Concilio con approvazione pontificia ne ottene l'*exequatur* a dì 7 Gennaro 1861 come risulta dall' autentico documento che esibisce con animo di ritirarlo rilasciandone copia. Prega perciò V[ostra] S[antità] di ammetterle questo autorevole attestato dispensandola dall' esibire le fedi di Battesimo,

Cresima, e di stato libero da quella decisione fino al presente, onde potersi legittimamente congiungere col suddetto Liszt.

> Fer. IV. 18 Septembris 1861
> Sacra Congregatio S[ancti] Officii,
> dummodo nullum obstet canonicum
> impedimentum, remisit.

6. A REQUEST TO WAIVE THE READING OF THE MARRIAGE BANNS

To his Most Reverend Excellency, Mons. Vicar of Rome (October 20, 1861).

Most Reverend Excellency,

Commander Franz Liszt, son of the late Adam, having come to Rome *ad effectum nubendi* [for the purpose of entering into matrimony], and Lady Carolyne, Princess of Sayn-Wittgenstein, born Iwanowska, daughter of the late Peter from the parish of St. James in Avgustivka[2] . . . . wishing to join in holy matrimony in haste and secrecy on account of just and legitimate reasons presented verbally, beseech you to condescend to exempt them from the three customary publications.

C.E.

A sua Ec[cell] enza Rev[erendissim] a Mons[ignor] Vic[ari]o di Roma (20 Octobris, 1861).

Ec[cell]enza Rev[erendissi]ma

Il Commendatore Francesco Liszt, figlio della bo [na] me [moria] Adamo, venuto in Roma *ad effectum nubendi,* e Donna Carolina Principessa di S[ayn] Wittgenstein nata Iwanowska, figlia della bo[na] me[moria] Pietro della Cura di S[ancto] Giacomo in Augusta . . . . dell' A [ltezza] V [ostra] E [ccellentissima] bramando unirsi in S. Matrimonio con sollecitudine, e segretezza per giuste, e legittime cause esposte a voce, La pregano a degnarsi dispensarli, dalle tre consuete pubblicazioni.

C.E.

7. A JOINT DEPOSITION FROM LISZT AND CAROLYNE, TESTIFYING TO THE FACT THAT THEY WERE BOTH SINGLE, DATED OCTOBER 20, 1861

In the Name of God
Rome, October 20, 1861

In the personal presence of the Most Reverend Deputy in Charge of Marriages, the Most Illustrious Commander[3] Franz Liszt, chamberlain of the grand ducal court of Weimar, son of the late Adam, presently in Rome for the purpose of contracting marriage, and Her Highness Lady Carolyne Iwanowska, Princess of Sayn-Wittgenstein, daughter of the late Peter, spontaneously ratify the contents of the present document drawn on their request after the order of the Holy Office following the executive decree of His Excellency the Lord Cardinal Vicar, and swear, with their hand on the Holy Gospels, to be single, not to have taken respectively wife or husband, become a priest or a monk or a nun, contracted impediments, become wedded, or promised marriage to others to whom they may now

---

2. Present-day Ukrainian town in the region of Ternopir.
3. Liszt, it will be recalled, had been named Commander of the Legion of Honour six months earlier, on May 31, 1861.

Nel Nome di Dio

Roma 20 Ottobre 1861

[handwritten deposition in Italian]

F. Liszt

A joint deposition from Liszt and Carolyne, testifying to the fact that they are both single, dated October 20, 1861.

be bound, not even to relatives by blood in the first degree, from the unmarrying age to the present as far as the Most Illustrious Commander Liszt is concerned, and from the judgement declaring her first marriage null and void to the present as far as Her Highness Lady Carolyne is concerned. The aforementioned Illustrious Commander swears also to have received confirmation in Paris in the year 1829 in the Church of St. Vincent de Paul.

After receiving previous warning as to the force of oaths and as to the sentences meted out to those who are polygamous and perjurers, they have signed below

F. Liszt

Princess Carolyne von Sayn-Wittgenstein,
born Iwanowska

The above-named made their oath in the presence of myself, Canon Bernardino Maggi, Deputy

(Original text)

Nel Nome di Dio
Roma 20 Ottobre 1861

Avanti al Reverendissimo Sig[nor] Deputato a Matrimoni personalmente costituito l'Ill[us-trissi]mo Sig[nor] Commendatore Francesco Liszt, Ciamberlano della Corte Granducale de Waymar, figlio della bon[a] me[moria] Adamo, venuto in Roma *ad effectum nubendi,* e Sua Altezza Donna Carolina Iwanowska Principessa di S[ayn] Wittgenstein, figlia della bon[a] me[moria] Pietro, spontaneamente ratificando l'esposto nella presente memoria come che tutta a di loro istanza, in sequela del Rescritto del S[anto] O[ffizio] esusseguente Decreto esecutoriale di S[ua] Eccelenza Sig[nor] Card[inal] Vicario, giuzano toccando S[anto] Evangelo di esser liberi, non essersi ammogliato, o maritata, fatti prete o frate, Monaca, né aver contratto impedimenti, sponsali, o dato parola di matrimonio ad altri, cui ora siano tenuti, e nemmeno a Consanguinei rispettivi in primo grado dalla innubile età fino al presente in quanto all' Ill[ustrissi]mo Sig[nor] Commendatore Liszt, e dalla Sentenza che ha dichiarato nullo il primo Matrimonio fino al presente (in) rapporto a S[ua] A[ltezza] Donna Carolina. Giura inoltre il lodato Ill.mo Sig. Commendatore di esser stato confirmato in Parigi nell' anno 1829 nella Chiesa di S[an] Vincenzo di Paola.

Tutto ciò previa ammonizione sulla forza del giuramento e comminaz(ione) della pena contro i Poligami e Spergiuri e si sono sottoscritti.

F. Liszt

Pr[incipe] ssa Carolina di Sayn-Wittgenstein
nata Iwanowska
Supradicti jurarunt coram me
Bernardinus Can[onicus] Maggi deput[atus]

Appendix III:
Daniel Liszt's Birth Certificate

The birth certificates of Liszt's two daughters, Blandine and Cosima, have long been familiar to scholars of the composer. That of his son, Daniel, however, continued to elude detection. It was always known that Daniel was born in Rome on May 9, 1839, but the identity of the church in which he was baptized was not disclosed to posterity, and without that information the birth certificate could not be located. In 1984, while working in the Goethe- und Schiller-Archiv in Weimar, I came across a rare copy of the obituary notice of Daniel, written and published anonymously by Princess Carolyne von Sayn-Wittgenstein, in which she (or more likely Liszt himself) identified Daniel's baptismal church as San Luigi de' Francesi, in Rome. Inquiries at this church revealed that all records for the period in question had been transferred to the Vicariato di Roma, and it was in this latter archive that I traced Daniel's birth certificate in the baptismal records section of San Luigi de' Francesi (1835–66), vol. 101, p. 59.[1]

From the text of the certificate we observe that the name of the father was recorded as "the illustrious Franz Liszt" while that of the mother remained "unknown." The reason why it was necessary to hide Marie d'Agoult's identity was to protect her husband, Count Charles d'Agoult, from the rigours of French law, which would have regarded him as the legitimate father of any offspring his wife bore Liszt. That is why her identity was masked on the birth certificates of Liszt's two daughters as well.[2] The text of Daniel's certificate runs:

In the year of Our Lord 1839, on Saturday, May 11, I, the undersigned, baptized the child born on the ninth day of the month, at 6:00 p.m. of the illustrious Franciscus Liszt, son of the late Adam Liszt from the location of Raiding in Hungary; and of the mother N . . . N . . . of the parish of Saint Bernardus; to whom the names of Daniel, Henricus, Franciscus, Joseph were given. The godfather was Mr. Henri Lehmann, the son of Leo, of the city of Kiel in Holstein. The midwife was Laura Gogilla of the parish of Saint Laurentius in Lucina.

JOSEPH GRAZIANI (curate)

---

1. The facsimile of the birth certificate was published in my article "A Boy Named Daniel," *The New Hungarian Quarterly,* vol. 27, no. 102 (Autumn 1986), Budapest.
2. See Volume One of the present study, pp. 214–15 and pp. 248–49.

(Original text)

Anno Domini 1839 die Sabbati ll. mensis Maii, Ego subscriptus baptizavi infantem natum 9ª-ejusdem mensis hora 18ª ex Illmo [Illustrissimo] D° [Domino] Francisco Liszt fil. [filio] qm [quondam] Adami ex civitate vulgo nuncupate Raiding in Hungaria et ex Matre N . . . N . . . Parociae S. [Sancti] Bernardi cui nomen impositum fuit: Daniel, Henricus, Franciscus, Joseph: Patrinus fuit Donus [Dominus] Henricus Lehmann fil. [filius] Leonis ex civitate vulgo Kiel in Holstein [corrected into Helstein] Obstetrix Laura Gogilla Parociae S. [Sancti] Laurentii Lucian.

JOSEPH GRAZIANI
OECONˢ [OECONOMUS] CURATUS

Sources Consulted in the Preparation of Volume II

ACLA   Agoult Marie d'. *Correspondance de Liszt et de la Comtesse d'Agoult.* Edited by Daniel Ollivier. 2 vols. Paris, 1933, 1934.

Acta Mus.   *Acta Musicalia.* Esterházy Archive, National Széchényi Library, Budapest.

AD   Albach, Father Stanislaus. Unpublished diaries. 3 vols. Holograph in possession of Bratislava University Library, ms. 736.

ADGR   Auerbach, Dr. Leopold, ed. *Denkwürdigkeiten des Geheimen Regierungsrathes Dr. Steiber, aus seinen hinterlassenen Papieren bearbeitet.* Berlin, 1884.

AE   Adelburg, August Ritter von. *Entgegnung auf die von Franz Liszt in seinem Werke "Des Bohémiens et leur musique en Hongrie" aufgestellte Behauptung: Dass es keine ungarische Nationalmusik . . . gibt.* Vorwort von Alexander von Czeke. Pest, 1859.

ALC   *Aix-la-Chapelle (Aachen) as a Health Resort,* by Drs. Alexander, Beissel, Brandis, Goldstein, Mayer, Rademaker, Schumacher, and Thissen of Aix-la-Chapelle. Translated by James Donelan. London, 1892.

ALK   *Authentic Life of His Excellency Louis Kossuth, Governor of Hungary, with a Full Report of His Speeches Delivered in England.* London, 1851.

AM   Agoult, Marie d' ("Daniel Stern"). *Mémoires, 1833–54.* Edited by Daniel Ollivier. Paris, 1927.

ÁMZSz   Ábrányi, Kornél, Sr. *A magyar zene a 19-ik században* [Hungarian Music in the Nineteenth Century]. Budapest, 1900.

AN   Archives Nationales de France, Paris.

ASGB   *Arthur Schopenhauer: Gesammelte Briefe.* Herausgegeben von Arthur Hübscher. Bonn, 1978.

ASVR   Archivio Segreto Vaticano, Rome. Documents from the archives of Cardinal Antonino De Luca, papal nuncio to Vienna, and from the diocese of Fulda (1860–61). "Special annex: The Matrimonial Case of Wittgenstein versus Iwanowska." Cited by folio number.

AVR   Archivio Storico del Vicariato di Roma, St. John Lateran, Rome. Documents pertaining to the marriage of Liszt and Princess Carolyne von Sayn-Wittgenstein (1861). N. 4477, L/41.

BA   Bayreuth Archive. Nationalarchiv der Richard Wagner Stiftung, Bayreuth.

BB   Bülow, Hans von. *Briefe.* Herausgegeben von Marie von Bülow. 7 vols. Leipzig, 1899–1908.

BBLW   Bülow, Marie von. *Hans von Bülow in Leben und Wort.* Stuttgart, 1925.

BBRC   Barzun, Jacques. *Berlioz and the Romantic Century.* 2 vols. 3rd ed. New York, 1969.

BCWH   Bartels, Adolf. *Chronik des Weimarischen Hoftheaters, 1817–1907.* Festschrift zur Einweihung des neuen Hoftheater-Gebäudes, 11. Januar 1908. Weimar, 1908.

BDLL   Bory, Robert. "Diverses lettres inédites de Liszt." *Schweizerisches Jahrbuch für Musikwissenschaft* (Aarau) 3 (1928).

BECB   Bülow, Hans von. *The Early Correspondence of Hans von Bülow.* Edited by Marie von Bülow. Translated by Constance Bache. London, 1896.

BEM   Busoni, Ferruccio. *Von der Einheit der Musik.* Berlin, 1922. Translated by Rosamond Ley as *The Essence of Music.* London, 1957.

BES   Bartók, Béla. *Essays.* Selected and edited by Benjamin Suchoff. London, 1976.

BFA   Bowen, Catherine Drinker. *"Free Artist": The Story of Anton and Nicholas Rubinstein.* New York, 1939.

BFL   Burger, Ernst. *Franz Liszt: Eine Lebenschronik in Bildern und Dokumenten.* Munich, 1986.

BFM   Bettelheim, Anton, ed. *Fürstin Marie zu Hohenlohe und Ferdinand von Saar: Ein Briefwechsel.* Vienna, 1910.

BHCA   Bredsdorff, Elias. *Hans Christian Andersen: The Story of His Life and Work, 1805–75.* London, 1975.

BKMM   Beatty-Kingston, W. *Music and Manners: Personal Reminiscences and Sketches of Character.* 2 vols. London, 1887.

BLB   Buchner, Alexander. *Franz Liszt in Bohemia.* Prague, 1962.

BLD   Beale, Willert. *The Light of Other Days.* 2 vols. London, 1890.

BLE   Bory, Robert. *Liszt et ses enfants Blandine, Cosima et Daniel.* Paris, 1936.

BLTB   Bernhardi, Theodor von. *Aus dem Leben Theodor von Bernhardis.* 9 vols. Leipzig, 1893–96.

BM   Berlioz, Hector. *Mémoires.* Paris, 1870. Translated by David Cairns. London, 1969.

BMC   Brassai, Sámuel. *Magyar- vagy Czigány-Zene? Elmefuttatás Liszt Ferencz "Czigányokról" irt Könyve felett.* [Hungarian or Gypsy Music? Reflections on Franz Liszt's Book "On the Gypsies"]. Kolozsvár, 1860.

BMP   Boschet, Adolphe. *Musiciens, poètes.* Paris, 1937.

BN   Bibliothèque Nationale, Paris.

BSKP   Bas, Leontina. "Shlyakhamy kontsertnykh podorozhey" [By Way of Concert Tours] in the collection *Rozpovidi pro kompozytoriv* [Tales of Composers], pp. 133–45. Kiev, 1967.

BSSD   Bergfeld, J. *Die formale Struktur der symphonischen Dichtungen.* Eisenach, n.d.

BST   Barnum, P. T. *Struggles and Triumphs, or Forty Years' Recollections of P. T. Barnum, Written by Himself.* London, 1869.

BVL   Bory, Robert. *La Vie de Franz Liszt par l'image.* Geneva, 1936.

BWL   *Briefwechsel zwischen Wagner und Liszt.* 2 vols. Leipzig, 1887.

CE   The Breitkopf & Härtel Collected Edition of Liszt's works, in thirty-four volumes. Leipzig, 1901–36.

CJR   Chorzempa, Daniel. "Julius Reubke: Life and Works." University of Minnesota, Ph.D. thesis, 1971.

CLBA   Csapó, Wilhelm von, ed. *Franz Liszts Briefe an Baron Anton Augusz, 1846–78.* Budapest, 1911.

CLJ   Carse, Adam. *The Life of Jullien.* Cambridge, 1951.

CLW   Cornelius, Peter. *Literarische Werke.* 4 vols. Leipzig, 1904–05.

1–2: *Ausgewählte Briefe,* nebst Tagebuchblättern und Gelegenheits-gedichten, herausgegeben von seinem Sohne Carl Maria Cornelius. 2 vols. Leipzig, 1904–05.

3: *Aufsätze über Musik und Kunst,* zum erstenmal gesammelt und herausgegeben von Edgar Istel. Leipzig, 1904.

4: *Gedichte,* gesammelt und herausgegeben von Adolf Stern. Leipzig, 1905.

C-MCT   Charnin-Mueller, Rena. "Le Cahier d'esquisses du *Tasso* et la composition des *Harmonies poétiques et religieuses.*" Actes du Colloque internationale Franz Liszt. *La Revue Musicale,* pp. 11–28. Paris, 1987.

CMGM   Chorley, Henry F. *Modern German Music.* 2 vols. London, 1854.

CPC   Cornelius, Carl Maria. *Peter Cornelius, der Wort- und Tondichter.* 2 vols. Regensburg, 1925.

CPR   Chantavoine, Jean. *Pages romantiques.* Paris, 1912. Articles over Liszt's signature in the *Revue et Gazette Musicale,* 1835–40.

CSB   Cornelius, Peter. *Ausgewählte Schriften und Briefe,* eingeleitet und mit biographischen und kritischen Erläuterungen versehen von Dr. Paul Egert. Berlin, 1924.

DA   Darmstadt Archive. Originale der Briefe Liszts an eine Freundin. Hessische Landes- und Hochschulbibliothek, Darmstadt.

DEM   Dunkl, Johann Nepomuk. *Aus den Erinnerungen eines Musikers.* Vienna, 1876.

DGG   Dörffel, Alfred. *Geschichte der Gewandhausconcerte zu Leipzig vom 25. November 1791 bis 25. November 1881.* Leipzig, 1884.

DHP   Darimon, Alfred. *Histoire d'un parti: Les Cinq sous l'empire.* Paris, 1885.

DJE   Devrient, Theresa. *Jugenderinnerungen.* 3rd ed. Stuttgart, n.d.

DLR   Deák, István. *The Lawful Revolution: Louis Kossuth and the Hungarians, 1848–49.* New York, 1979.

DMML   Damrosch, Walter. *My Musical Life.* New York, 1923.

DPKG   De Puy, Henry Walter. *Kossuth and His Generals; with a Brief History of Hungary; Select Speeches of Kossuth, etc.* Buffalo, 1852.

EAML   Ernst, Duke of Sachsen-Coburg-Gotha. *Aus meinem Leben und aus meiner Zeit.* 4 vols. Berlin, 1889.

EDD   Eliot, George. *Daniel Deronda.* London, 1896.

EE   Eliot, George. *Essays.* Edited by Thomas Pinney. New York, 1963.

EG   Eliot, George. *The Works of George Eliot.* University Edition. 10 vols. New York, n.d.

EGEL   Eliot, George. *The George Eliot Letters.* Edited by Gordon S. Haight. 12 vols. New Haven, 1954.

EK   Ehrlich, Alfred Heinrich. *Wie übt man am Klavier? Betrachtungen und Rathschläge, nebst genauer Anweisung für den richtigen Gebrauch der Tausig-Ehrlich'schen "Täglichen Studien."* Berlin, 1879.

EKFL   Eckhardt, Mária P., and Knotik, Cornelia, eds. *Franz Liszt und sein Kreis in Briefen und Dokumenten aus den Beständen des Burgenländischen Landesmuseums.* Eisenstadt, 1983.

ELM   Eckhardt, Mária P. "Liszt à Marseille." *Studia Musicologica Academiae Scientiarum Hungaricae* no. 24. Budapest, 1982.

END   Eckhardt, Mária P. "New Documents on Liszt as Author." *New Hungarian Quarterly* 25, no. 95. Budapest, 1984.

EPL Eckhardt, Mária P. "Párizsi Liszt-dokumentum 1849-ből" [A Liszt document in Paris, from 1849] in *Zenetudomanyi Dolgozatok* 1978, pp. 79–93. Budapest, 1979.

ES Escudier, Léon. *Mes Souvenirs.* Paris, 1863. *Les Virtuoses.* Paris, 1868.

EV Ellis, Ashton, W. *1849, a Vindication.* London, 1892.

FBNS Fellinger, Imogen. "Brahms und die Neudeutsche Schule," in *Brahms und seine Zeit* (Symposium, Hamburg, 1983), pp. 159–69. Hamburg, 1984.

FLL Friedheim, Arthur. *Life and Liszt: The Recollections of a Concert Pianist.* Edited by Theodore L. Bullock. New York, 1961.

FMG Fay, Amy. *Music Study in Germany, from the Home Correspondence of Amy Fay.* Edited by Mrs. Fay Pierce. New York, 1880.

FPP Footman, David. *The Primrose Path: A Life of Ferdinand Lassalle.* London, 1956.

GAWZ Genast, Eduard. *Aus Weimars klassischer und nachklassischer Zeit: Erinnerungen eines alten Schauspielers.* Edited by Robert Kohlrausch. Stuttgart, 1903.

GB Geiringer, Karl. *Brahms: His Life and Work.* 2nd ed. London, 1948.

GCAF *Grossherzog Carl Alexander und Fanny Lewald-Stahr in ihren Briefen, 1848–1889,* eingeleitet und herausgegeben von Rudolf Göhler. 2 vols. Berlin, 1932.

GFL Goldhammer, Otto, ed. *Franz Liszt's "De la fondation-Goethe à Weimar."* Facsimile edition of Liszt's 28-page draft (dated September 1849) for his brochure of the same name. Weimar, 1961.

GFLF Gajdoš, Vševlad. *František Liszt a frantiskani* (Frantiskansky Obzor) [Ferenc Liszt and the Franciscans]. Bratislava, 1936.

GL Göllerich, August. *Franz Liszt.* Berlin, 1908.

GLEL Gut, Serge. *Franz Liszt: Les Éléments du langage musical.* Paris, 1975.

GLMM Gábry, György. "Liszt Ferenc emléktárgyai a Magyar Nemzeti Múzeumban" [Ferenc Liszt Relics in the Hungarian National Museum]. *Folia Historica* (Budapest) 5, 1977.

GLW Gottschalg, A. W. *Franz Liszt in Weimar, und seine letzten Lebensjahre: Erinnerungen und Tagebuchnotizen.* Berlin, 1910.

GMR Goethe, Johann Wolfgang von. *Maximen und Reflexionen.* Nach den Handschriften des Goethe- und Schiller-Archiv, herausgegeben von Max Hecker. Goethe-Gesellschaft, Weimar, 1907.

GRT Gregorovius, Ferdinand. *Römische Tagebücher (1852–74).* Stuttgart, 1892.

GSI Gardiner, William. *Sights in Italy, with Some Account of the Present State of Music and the Sister Arts in That Country.* London, 1847.

GSL Gutmansthal, M. de. *Souvenirs de F. Liszt.* Leipzig, 1913.

GVT Grans, Heinrich. *Vom Theater. Allerlei Aufzeichnungen. Fünfzehn Jahre in Weimar.* Leipzig, 1889.

GWLF Gadjoš, Vševlad. "War Franz Liszt Franziskaner?" *Studia Musicologica* 6, pp. 299–310. Budapest, 1964.

GWM Gutmann, Albert. *Aus dem Wiener Musikleben: Künstler-Erinnerungen, 1873–1908.* Vienna, 1914.

GWNZ Gerstenberg, H. *Aus Weimars nachklassischer Zeit.* Hamburg, 1901.

HA Hecker, Jutta. *Die Altenburg: Geschichte eines Hauses.* 2nd ed. Berlin, 1983.

HAR Hausegger, Siegmund von. *Alexander Ritter: Ein Bild seines Characters und Schaffens.* Berlin, 1908.

HBD	Herwegh, Marcel. *Au Banquet des dieux.* Paris, 1931.
HERW	Hohenlohe, Marie Fürstin zu. *Erinnerungen an Richard Wagner.* Weimar, 1938.
HFLA	Haraszti, Emile. "Franz Liszt: Author Despite Himself." *Musical Quarterly* 33, no. 4 (October 1947): pp. 490–516.
HFLW	Hollitzer, Gyula. *Liszt Ferenc és a weimari irodalmi élet* [Franz Liszt and the Literary Life in Weimar]. Budapest, 1913.
HGC	Hanslick, Eduard. *Geschichte des Concertwesens in Wien.* 2 vols. Vienna, 1869, 1870.
HGE	Haight, Gordon S. *George Eliot: A Biography.* Oxford, 1968.
HHB	Hiller, Ferdinand. *Aus Ferdinand Hillers Briefwechsel: Beiträge zu einer Biographie Ferdinand Hillers von Reinhold Sietz.* 5 vols. Cologne, 1958–66.
HK	Hiller, Ferdinand. *Künstlerleben.* Cologne, 1880.
HKM	Hoplit [Richard Pohl]. *Das Karlsruher Musikfest im Oktober 1853.* Leipzig, 1853.
HL	Haraszti, Emile. *Franz Liszt.* Paris, 1967.
HLLA	Heymann, Fritz. "Liszt, Lassalle und die schöne Agnes." *Vossische Zeitung* (Berlin) no. 104, May 5, 1929.
HLP	Haraszti, Emile. "Liszt à Paris." *La Revue Musicale,* April and July 1936.
HLSW	*The Letters of Franz Liszt to Marie zu Sayn-Wittgenstein.* Translated and edited by Howard E. Hugo. Cambridge, 1953.
HLW	Hoffmann von Fallersleben, August Heinrich. *Lieder aus Weimar.* Hanover, 1854.
HMBE	Hiller, Ferdinand. *Felix Mendelssohn-Bartholdy: Briefe und Erinnerungen von Ferdinand Hiller.* Cologne, 1875.
HML	Hoffmann von Fallersleben, August Heinrich. *Mein Leben: Aufzeichnungen und Erinnerungen.* 6 vols. Hanover, 1868.
HMS	Hanslick, Eduard. *Vom Musikalisch-Schönen.* Leipzig, 1854. 7th ed., 1885.
HMW	Huschke, Wolfram. *Musik im klassischen und nachklassichen Weimar, 1756–1861.* Weimar, 1982.
HPD	Herwegh, Marcel. *Au Printemps des dieux.* Paris, 1929.
HPL	Haraszti, Emile. "Le Problème Liszt." *Acta Musicologica,* December 1937.
HSD	Herwegh, Marcel. *Au Soir des dieux.* Paris, 1933.
HSW	Heine, Heinrich. *Sämtliche Werke.* Herausgegeben von Fritz Strich. 10 vols. Munich, 1925.
JLB	Jung, Hans Rudolf. *Franz Liszt in seinen Briefen.* Berlin, 1987.
JMBJ	Joachim, Johannes, and Moser, Andreas. *Briefe von und an Joseph Joachim.* 3 vols. Berlin, 1911–13.
JRS	Jansen, F. Gustav. *Robert Schumanns Briefe: Neue Folge.* Leipzig, 1904.
KAS	Kapp, Julius, ed. "Autobiographisches Skizze (1881)," *Die Musik* (Berlin), 1911.
KE	Kellermann, Berthold. *Erinnerungen, ein Künstlerleben,* herausgegeben von Sebastian Hausmann und Hellmut Kellermann. Zürich, 1932.
KFL	Kapp, Julius. *Franz Liszt.* Berlin, 1909.
KHC	Királyi, Béla K. *Hungary in the Late 18th Century.* New York, 1969.
KJ	Kapp, Julius, and Jachmann, Hans. *Richard Wagner und seine erste "Elisabeth," Johanna Jachmann-Wagner.* Berlin, 1927.
KJB	Kalbeck, Max. *Johannes Brahms.* 4 vols. Berlin, 1904–14.
KLB	Kapp, Julius. *Liszt-Brevier.* Leipzig, 1910.

KLF   Kapp, Julius. *Liszt und die Frauen*. Leipzig, 1911.

KLP   Keeling, Geraldine. "The Liszt Pianos: Some Aspects of Preference and Technology." *New Hungarian Quarterly* (Budapest) 27, no. 104 (1986).

KLV   Koch, Ludwig. *Franz Liszt: Ein bibliographischer Versuch*. Budapest, 1936.

KRW   Klebe, Friedrich Albrecht. *Historisch-statische Nachrichten von der berühmten Residenzstadt Weimar*. Leipzig, 1975.

KS   Kolb, Marthe. *Ary Scheffer et son temps (1795–1858)*. Paris, 1937.

KTYM   Klein, Hermann. *Thirty Years of Musical Life in London, 1870–1900*. New York, 1903.

KWL   Kloss, Erich, ed. *Briefwechsel zwischen Wagner und Liszt*. 2 vols. Leipzig, 1910.

LAG   La Mara [Marie Lipsius], ed. *Aus der Glanzzeit der Weimarer Altenburg*. Leipzig, 1906.

LBCW   La Mara, ed. *Briefe von Hector Berlioz an die Fürstin Carolyne von Sayn-Wittgenstein*. Leipzig, 1903.

LBD   *Letters from Benjamin Disraeli to Frances Anne, Marchioness of Londonderry, 1837–1861*. London, 1938.

LBLB   La Mara, ed. *Briefwechsel zwischen Franz Liszt und Hans von Bülow*. Leipzig, 1898.

LBLCA   La Mara, ed. *Briefwechsel zwischen Franz Liszt und Carl Alexander, Grossherzog von Sachsen*. Leipzig, 1909.

LBZL   La Mara, ed. *Briefe hervorragender Zeitgenossen an Franz Liszt*. 3 vols. Leipzig, 1895–1904.

LCD   Lobe, J. C. *Consonanzen und Dissonanzen*. Leipzig, 1869.

LCS   Litzmann, Berthold. *Clara Schumann: Ein Künstlerleben*. 3 vols. Leipzig, 1902–08.

LDML   La Mara. *Durch Musik und Leben im Dienste des Ideals*. 2 vols. Leipzig, 1917.

LEJ   Lewald, Fanny. *Erinnerungen aus dem Jahre 1848*. 2 vols. Braunschweig, 1850.

LEL   Léon-Bérard, Marguérite. "Une Élève de Liszt." *La Revue des Deux Mondes* (Paris), April 15, 1960, pp. 682–94.

LFLW   Legány, Dezső. *Franz Liszt: Unbekannte Presse und Briefe aus Wien, 1822–1886*. Budapest, 1984.

LKVL   Lepsha, Ivan. " 'Kolosky Voronynts' Ferentsa Lista." *Novi Dni,* January–February 1986, pp. 24–26.

LLB   La Mara, ed. *Franz Liszt's Briefe*. 8 vols. Leipzig, 1893–1905.
       1: *Von Paris bis Rom*
       2: *Von Rom bis ans Ende*
       3: *Briefe an eine Freundin*
       4, 5, 6, 7: *Briefe an die Fürstin Carolyne Sayn-Wittgenstein*
       8: *Neue Folge zu Band I und II*

LLBM   La Mara, ed. *Franz Liszts Briefe an seine Mutter*. Leipzig, 1918.

LLC   Legány, Dezső. *Liszt and His Country, 1869–1873*. Budapest, 1983.

LLF   La Mara. *Liszt und die Frauen*. Leipzig, 1911.

LLFM   Legány, Dezső. *Liszt Ferenc Magyarországon, 1874–1886*. Budapest, 1986.

LMM-K   La Mara, ed. *Marie von Mouchanoff-Kalergis (geb. Gräfin Nesselrode) in Briefen an ihre Tochter*. Leipzig, 1911.

LSJ   La Mara, ed. *An der Schwelle des Jenseits: Letzte Erinnerungen an die Fürstin Carolyne Sayn-Wittgenstein, die Freundin Liszts*. Leipzig, 1925.

LZBL	Lewald, Fanny. *Zwölf Bilder nach dem Leben.* Berlin, 1888.
MAL	Melegari, Dora. "Une Amie de Liszt, la Princesse de Sayn-Wittgenstein." *La Revue de Paris,* September 1, 1897.
MAML	Moscheles, Ignaz. *Aus Moscheles' Leben,* nach Briefen und Tagebüchern herausgegeben von seiner Frau. 2 vols. Leipzig, 1872–73.
MAR	McArthur, Alexander. *Anton Rubinstein, a Biographical Sketch.* Edinburgh, 1899.
MB	Mendelssohn-Bartholdy, Paul, and Dr. Carl, eds.. *Briefe aus den Jahren 1830 bis 1847 von Felix Mendelssohn Bartholdy.* 2 vols. Leipzig, 1863, 1864.
MBJ	Moser, Andreas, ed. *Johannes Brahms im Briefwechsel mit Joseph Joachim.* 2 vols. Berlin, 1908.
MCW	Moulin Eckart, Richard, Graf du. *Cosima Wagner, ein Lebens- und Charakterbild.* 2 vols. Munich, 1929.
MGMP	Milde, Natalie von. "Zum Gedächtnis der Maria Pawlowna." *Monatschrift für das gesamte Frauen Leben unserer Zeit* (Leipzig) no. 13 (1904), pp. 34–35.
MH-S	*Memoirs of Prince Chlodwig of Hohenlohe-Schillingsfürst.* Edited by Friedrich Curtius. 2 vols. London, 1906.
MJ	Moser, Andreas. *Joseph Joachim: A Biography (1831–1899).* Translated by Lilla Durham. London, 1901. [An expanded version of the German original, Berlin, 1898.]
MLB	Mayer, Gustav, ed.. *Ferdinand Lassalle: Nachgelassene Briefe und Schriften.* Vol. 4: *Lassalles Briefwechsel mit Gräfin Sophie von Hatzfeldt.* Stuttgart-Berlin, 1924.
MLMR	Major, Ervin. "Liszt Ferenc magyar rapszódiái." Muzsika (Budapest) 1 (1929), pp. 47–54.
MMLA	Mason, Lowell. *Musical Letters from Abroad.* New York, 1854.
MMML	Mason, William. *Memories of a Musical Life.* New York, 1901.
MQLN	*Musical Quarterly* (New York) 22, no. 3 (1936): Special Liszt Number.
MRL	Müller-Reuter, Theodor. *Lexicon der deutschen Konzertliteratur von Theodor Müller-Reuter,* vol. 1. Leipzig, 1909.
MRR	Merrick, Paul. *Revolution and Religion in the Music of Liszt.* London, 1987.
MS-W	Letters to Princess Marie von Sayn-Wittgenstein from her grandmother Pauline Iwanowska. Unpublished. Liszt: MNY Folder 10. New York Public Library, Lincoln Center.
NFL	Neumann, W. *Franz Liszt.* Cassel, 1855.
NLE	New Liszt Edition, Complete Works. Edited by Zoltán Gárdonyi, István Szélényi, Imre Sulyok, and Imre Mező. Budapest, 1970–
NLFL	Nerval, Gérard de. *Lettres à Franz Liszt.* Textes inédits présentés et publiés par Jean Guillaume et Claude Pichois. Paris, 1972.
NLRW	Newman, Ernest. *The Life of Richard Wagner.* 4 vols. London, 1933–47.
NML	Newman, Ernest. *The Man Liszt: A Study of the Tragi-comedy of a Soul Divided Against Itself.* London, 1934.
NO	Nerval, Gérard de. *Oeuvres.* Texte établi et annoté par Albert Beguin et Jean Richer. 2 vols. Paris, 1960.
NPM	Niecks, Frederick. *Programme Music in the Last Four Centuries: A Contribution to the History of Musical Expression.* London, 1906.
NRS	Niecks, Frederick. *Robert Schumann: A Supplementary and Corrective Biography.* London, 1925.

NSB   Newman, William S. *A History of the Sonata Idea.* 3 vols. Rev. ed. New York, 1972.

NZfM   *Neue Zeitschrift für Musik* (Leipzig), 1834–68. Edited by Robert Schumann (1834–44) and Franz Brendel (1845–68). Cited by issue.

OAAL   Ollivier, Daniel, ed. *Autour de Mme d'Agoult et de Liszt (Alfred de Vigny, Emile Ollivier, Princesse de Belgiojoso).* Lettres publiées avec introduction et notes. Paris, 1941.

OCLF   Ollivier, Daniel, ed. *Correspondance de Liszt et de sa fille Madame Emile Ollivier, 1842–1862.* Paris, 1936.

OIL   Ott, Bertrand. "An Interpretation of Liszt's Sonata in B minor." *Journal of the American Liszt Society* (Louisville, Ky.) 10 (December 1981), pp. 30–38.

OJ   Ollivier, Emile. *Journal, 1846–1869.* 2 vols. Text selected and edited by Theodore Zeldin and Anne Troisier de Diaz. Paris, 1961.

PA   Pohl, Richard. *Autobiographisches.* Leipzig, 1881.

PBUS   Prahács, Margit, ed. *Franz Liszt: Briefe aus ungarischen Sammlungen, 1835–86.* Budapest-Kassel, 1966.

PGS   Pohl, Richard. *Gesammelte Schriften über Musik und Musiker.* Leipzig, 1883–84.

    1: *Richard Wagner: Studien und Kritiken*
    2: *Franz Liszt: Studien und Erinnerungen*
    3: *Hektor Berlioz: Studien und Kritiken*

PHH   Pamlényi, Ervin, ed. *A History of Hungary.* By István Barta, Iván T. Berend, Péter Hanák, Miklós Lackó, László Makkai, Zsuzsa L. Nagy, and György Ránki. Budapest, 1973.

PHZ   Pukánszky, Béla. "Hohenlohe Mária hercegnő levele gróf Zichy Gézahoz" [A letter of Princess Marie Hohenlohe to Count Géza Zichy]. *Akadémiai Értesítő* 42 (October–November 1932), pp. 287–92.

PMG   Pohl, Richard. *Meiner theuren Gattin, Frau Jeanne Pohl (geb. Eyth) zum Gedächtniss.* Baden-Baden, 1870.

PMHL   Pulszky, Theresa. *Memoirs of a Hungarian Lady.* 2 vols. London, 1850.

PMPE   Pincherle, Marc. *Musiciens peints par eux-mêmes: Lettres de compositeurs écrites en français (1771–1910).* Paris, 1939.

PPSA   Probst, Franz. *Pater Stanislaus Albach (1795–1853).* Burgenländische Heimatblätter, Eisenstadt, 1948.

PT-VL Pohl, Richard. *Die Tonkünstler-Versammlung zu Leipzig, am 1. bis 4. Juni 1859: Mittheilungen nach authentischen Quellen.* Leipzig, 1859.

PW   Posse, Otto. *Die Wettiner: Genealogie des Gesammthauses Wettin, Ernestinischer und Albertinischer Linie.* Herausgegeben von Otto Posse. Leipzig, 1897.

PWC   Pretsch, Paul, ed. *Cosima Wagner und Houston Stewart Chamberlain im Briefwechsel, 1888–1908.* Leipzig, 1934.

RA   Royal Archives, Windsor Castle, England.
    (a) Queen Victoria's Journal
    (b) Correspondence between Queen Victoria and her relations in Germany.

RB   "La Comtesse d'Agoult: Lettres à Ferdinand Hiller, 1838–57." *Revue Bleue* (Paris), November 8 and 15, 1913.

RCAL   Raabe, Peter. *Grossherzog Carl Alexander und Liszt.* Leipzig, 1918.

RDL   Roeder, Dr. Erich. *Felix Draeseke: Der Lebens- und Leidensweg eines deutschen Meisters.* Dresden, 1925.

REOL   Raabe, Peter. *Die Entstehungsgeschichte der ersten Orchesterwerke Franz Liszts.* Inaugural-Dissertation zur Erlangung der philosophischen Doktorwürde der hohen philosophischen Fakultät der Grossherzoglich Herzoglich Sächsischen Gesamt-Universität Jena. Leipzig, 1916.

RFD   Rodenberg, Julius. *Franz Dingelstedt: Blätter aus seinem Nachlass.* 2 vols. Berlin, 1891.

RGS   Ramann, Lina, ed. *Franz Liszts gesammelte Schriften.* 6 vols. Leipzig, 1880–83.

        1: *Friedrich Chopin*
        2: *Essays und Reisebriefe eines Baccalaureus der Tonkunst*
        3: *Dramaturgische Blätter*
          (a) *Essays*
          (b) *Richard Wagner*
        4: *Aus den Annalen des Fortschritts*
        5: *Streifzüge; Kritische, polemische und zeithistorische Essays*
        6: *Die Zigeuner und ihre Musik in Ungarn*

RKU   *Edouard Reményi, Musician, Litterateur, and Man: An Appreciation, with Sketches of His Life and Artistic Career by Friends and Contemporaries.* Compiled by Gwendolyn Dunlevy Kelly and George P. Upton. Chicago, 1906.

RL   Ramann, Lina. *Lisztiana: Erinnerungen an Franz Liszt in Tagebuchblättern, Briefen und Dokumenten aus den Jahren 1873–1886/87.* Herausgegeben von Arthur Seidl. Textrevision von Friedrich Schnapp. Mainz, 1983.

RLKM   Ramann, Lina. *Franz Liszt als Künstler und Mensch.* 3 vols. Leipzig, 1880–94.

RLP   Ramann, Lina. *Liszt-Pädagogium: Klavier-Kompositionen Franz Liszts nebst noch unedirten Veränderungen, Zusätzen und Kadenzen nach des Meisters Lehren pädagogisch glossirt von Lina Ramann.* Leipzig, 1901.

RLR   Raff, Helene. *Franz Liszt und Joachim Raff im Spiegel ihrer Briefe.* Die Musik, vol. i (1902–03), vol. ii (1903).

RLS   Raabe, Peter. *Franz Liszt: Leben und Schaffen.* 2 vols. Stuttgart, 1931; rev. ed., 1968.

RM   *La Revue Musicale* (Paris), May, June, 1928: Special Liszt Numbers.

RR   Raff, Helene. *Joachim Raff: Ein Lebensbild.* Regensburg, 1925.

RW   Raff, Joachim. *Die Wagnerfrage.* Brunswick, 1854.

RWL   Raabe, Peter. *Wege zu Liszt.* Regensburg, 1943.

SAMK   Singer, Edmund. *Aus meiner Künstlerlaufbahn. Biographisches—Anekdotisches—Aphoristisches.* Neue Musik-Zeitung, 32. Jahrgang, Heft 1 (1911), Stuttgart.

SANZ   Schnaubert, Guido. "Aus Weimars nachklassische Zeit. Der 'Neu-Weimar-Verein' und die Stätte seines Wirkens: das Genelli-Zimmer im Goldenen Adler." *Neu Musik-Zeitung* (Stuttgart) 31, no. 1 (1910).

SBBI   Schultz, Georg von. *Briefe eines Baltischen Idealisten an Seine Mutter, 1833–1875.* Gestaltet von Johannes Werner. Leipzig, 1934.

SC   Sárosi, Bálint. *Cigányzene.* Budapest, 1971. Translated by Fred Macnicol as *Gypsy Music,* Budapest, 1978.

SCC   Sydow, B. E., ed. *Correspondance de Frédéric Chopin.* 3 vols. Paris, 1953–60.

SE   Stradal, August. *Erinnerungen an Franz Liszt*. Leipzig, 1929.

SFLJ   Sagittarius [Miksa Schütz]. *Franz Liszt über die Juden*. Budapest, 1881.

SG   Soret, Frédéric. *Un Genevois à la cour de Weimar: Journal inédit de Frédéric Soret, 1795–1865*. Préface de Paul Hazard. Paris, 1932.

SGK   Stern, Alfred. *Georg Klindworth: Ein politischer Geheimagent des neunzehnten Jahrhunderts*. Bibliographie zur deutschen Geschichte. Dresden, 1931.

SGKP   *Słownik Geograficzny Królestwa Polskiego I Innych Krajów Słowiańskich*. Wydany Pod Red. Filipa Sulimierskiego, Bronisława Chlebowskiego, Władysława Walewskiego. 15 vols. Warsaw, 1880–1904.

SGSW   "Staatshandbuch für das Grossherzogtum Sachsen-Weimar-Eisenach." Unpublished. Weimar, 1843, 1859.

SGWT   Schrickel, Leonhard. *Geschichte des Weimarer Theaters von seinen Anfängen bis heute*. Weimar, 1928.

SLBG   Stern, Adolf, ed. *Franz Liszt's Briefe an Carl Gille*. Leipzig, 1903.

SLE   Schorn, Karl. *Lebenserinnerungen: Ein Beitrag zur Geschichte des Rheinlands im neunzehnten Jahrhundert*. 2 vols. Bonn, 1898.

SLJ   Smart, Sir George. *Leaves from the Journals of Sir George Smart*. By H. Bertram Cox and C.L.E. Cox. London, 1907.

SLM   Slonimsky, Nicolas. *Lexicon of Musical Invective. Critical assaults on composers since Beethoven's time*. New York, 1952.

SLMI   Schirokauer, Arno. *Lassalle: Die Macht der Illusion, die Illusion der Macht*. Leipzig, 1928.

SLS   Szász, Tibor. "Liszt's Symbols for the Divine and Diabolical: Their Revelation of a Programme in the B-minor Sonata." *Journal of the American Liszt Society* (Louisville, Ky.) 15 (June 1984), pp. 39–95.

SLWT   Sayn-Wittgenstein, Carolyne von. Last will and testament. Unpublished manuscript. Library of Congress, Washington, D.C.

SMB   Steinacker, Gustav. *Des Meisters Bannerschaft*. Weimar, 1857.

SMRS   Slater, E., and Meyer, A. "Contribution to a Pathography of the Musicians 1: Robert Schumann." *Confinia Psychiatrica* (London) 2 (1957), pp. 65–94.

SMS   Liszt-Bartók Report of the Second International Musicological Conference, held in Budapest, 1961. *Studia Musicologica* Academiae Scientiarum Hungaricae (Budapest) 5 (1963).

SMW   Steinacker, Gustav. *Des Meisters Walten*. Weimar, 1855.

SNW   Schorn, Adelheid von. *Das nachklassische Weimar*. 2 vols.
            1: *Unter der Regierungszeit Karl Friedrichs und Maria Paulownas*. Weimar, 1911.
            2: *Unter der Regierungszeit von Karl Alexander und Sophie*. Weimar, 1912.

SPP (2)   Schopenhauer, Arthur. *Parerga und Parolipomena*. 2 vols. Berlin, 1851. Translated by E. F. J. Payne, Oxford, 1974.

SSI   Schoenberg, Arnold. *Style and Idea: Selected Writings of Arnold Schoenberg*. Edited by Leonard Stein, with translations by Leo Black. London, 1975.

SSPS   Saint-Saëns, Camille. *Portraits et souvenirs*. Paris, 1900.

SUW   Sawycky, Roman. " 'Hryts' theme and variations." *Ukrainian Weekly*, January 29, February 5 and 12, 1984.

SVKL   Schnapp, Friedrich. "Verschollene Kompositionen Franz Liszts." In *Von deutscher Tonkunst: Festschrift für Peter Raabe*. Leipzig, 1942.

S-WA   *Ludwig Adolf Peter, Fürst zu Sayn und Wittgenstein, Kaiserlich Russischer General-Feldmarschall, 1768/69–1843.* Aus seinem Leben von seinem Enkel Alexander Graf von Hachenburg, Prinz zu Sayn und Wittgenstein. Hanover, 1934.

S-WDL   [Sayn-Wittgenstein, Carolyne von] "Daniel Liszt." An anonymous obituary notice, in reality written by Carolyne and printed for her in a limited edition by Giesecke and Devrient. Leipzig, 1860.

SWJ   Stahr, Adolf. *Weimar und Jena.* 2 vols. Oldenburg, 1852.

SWWV   Schopenhauer, Arthur. *Die Welt als Wille und Vorstellung.* Leipzig (?), 1819; 3rd ed., 1859. Translated as *The World as Will and Representation,* by E. F. J. Payne. Oxford, 1958.

SZM   Schorn, Adelheid von. *Zwei Menschenalter: Erinnerungen und Briefe.* Berlin, 1901.

TBC   Tiersot, Julien, ed. *Hector Berlioz: Correspondance (1819–55).* 3 vols. Paris, 1904–30.

TE   Teleki, Sándor. *Emlékeim* [Memoirs]. 2 vols. Budapest, 1879.

TLMF   Tiersot, Julien. *Lettres de musiciens écrites en français du XVe au XXe siècle.* 2 vols. Paris, 1924.

TSA   Thuringian State Archives. Decrees of the Weimar Court Theatre. Unpublished. Staatsarchiv, Weimar.

UB   "Unbekannte Briefe von Wagner, Liszt, Berlioz, Robert und Clara Schumann, und H. Heine." Edited by Gerhard Tischler. *Rheinische Musik- und Theater-Zeitung* no. 11 (1910), pp. 455–65.

VAMA   Vier, Jacques. *Marie d'Agoult—son mari—ses amis: Documents inédits.* Paris, 1950.

VCA   Vier, Jacques. *La Comtesse d'Agoult et son temps, avec des documents inédits.* 6 vols. Paris, 1955–63.

VDS   Vier, Jacques. *Daniel Stern: Lettres républicaines du second empire. Documents inédits.* Paris, 1951.

VFL   Vier, Jacques. *Franz Liszt: L'artiste, le clerc—documents inédits.* Paris, 1951.

VHW   Vehse, Eduard. *Der Hof zu Weimar.* Leipzig, 1854.

VLC   Valkó, Arisztid. "A Liszt család a levéltári iratok tükrében" [The Liszt Family in the Mirror of Archival Documents]. An account of some holdings in the National Széchényi Library. *Magyar Zene* (Budapest), 1961.

VLKN   Végh, Gyula. "Liszt Ferenc kiadatlan naplója: Memento Journalier, 1861–1862." *Muzsika* (Budapest) nos. 1/2 and 3 (1930).

VM   Viereck, Peter. *Metapolitics: From the Romantics to Wagner.* New York, 1941.

VMA   Versailles Municipal Library Archive. The unpublished legacy of Claire de Charnacé (*née* d'Agoult), including her letters, notebooks, and memoirs. F. 859, cartons 1–19.

VT   Varnhagen von Ense, Karl August. *Tagebücher.* 2 vols. Berlin, 1863.

WA   Weimar Archives. Liszt Collection now held by the Nationale Forschungs- und Gedenkstätten der klassichen deutschen Literatur in Weimar. Das Goethe- und Schiller-Archiv, Weimar.

WBB   *Richard Wagners Briefe an Hans von Bülow.* Jena, 1916.

WCWB   Waldberg, Max Freiherr von, ed. *Cosima Wagners Briefe an ihre Tochter Daniela von Bülow, 1866–1885.* Stuttgart and Berlin, 1933.

WEW   Weissheimer, Wendelin. *Erlebnisse mit Wagner, Liszt und vielen anderen Zeitgenossen.* Stuttgart, 1898.

WFL(1)   Wagner, Cosima. *Franz Liszt: Ein Gedenkblatt von seiner Tochter.* 2nd ed. Munich, 1911.

WFL(2)   Walker, Alan. *Franz Liszt,* vol. 1: *The Virtuoso Years.* New York, 1983; rev. ed., Ithaca, 1988.

WFLR   Wohl, Janka. *François Liszt: Recollections of a Compatriot.* Translated by B. Peyton Ward. London, 1887.

WGC   Weitzmann, C. F. *Geschichte des Clavierspiels und der Clavierliteratur.* Stuttgart, 1879.

WGSD   Wagner, Richard. *Gesammelte Schriften und Dichtungen.* 3rd ed. 10 vols. Leipzig, 1897–98.

WJR   *Richard Wagners Briefe an Frau Julie Ritter.* Munich, 1920.

WL   Walker, Alan, ed. *Franz Liszt: The Man and His Music.* London, 1970.

WLE   Weingartner, Felix. *Lebens-Erinnerungen.* 2 vols. Zürich, Leipzig, 1928, 1929.

WLP   Waters, Edward N. "Franz Liszt to Richard Pohl." *Studies in Romanticism* (Boston) 6, no. 4 (Summer 1967).

WLS   Winklhofer, Sharon. *Liszt's Sonata in B minor: A Study of Autograph Sources and Documents.* Ann Arbor, 1980.

WLW   Weilguny, Hedwig. *Das Liszthaus in Weimar.* Weimar, 1973.

WLWP   Wallace, William. *Liszt, Wagner and the Princess.* London, 1927.

WML   Wagner, Richard. *Mein Leben.* Munich, 1911. Authorized English translation, London, 1912.

WMME   Walker, Bettina. *My Musical Experiences.* London, 1890.

WPFL   Waters, Edward N. "Presenting Mrs. Franz Liszt" [The Last Will and Testament of Princess Carolyne von Sayn-Wittgenstein]. *Journal of the American Liszt Society* (Louisville, Ky.) 7 (June 1980), pp. 6–16.

WSPM   Wallace, William. "The Scope of Programme Music." Proceedings of the [Royal] Musical Association (London), Session 25, 1898–89, pp. 139–56.

WT   Wagner, Cosima. *Die Tagebücher.* 2 vols. Ediert und kommentiert von Martin Gregor-Dellin und Dietrich Mack. Munich, 1976, 1977. Translated by Geoffrey Skelton as *Cosima Wagner's Diaries.* London and New York, 1978 and 1980.

WTS   Winterberger, A. *Technische Studien für Pianoforte von Franz Liszt, unter Redaktion von Alexander Winterberger.* Leipzig, 1887.

WZL   Wagner, Cosima. *Das zweite Leben: Briefe und Aufzeichnungen, 1883–1930.* Munich, 1980.

ZEO   Zeldin, Theodore. *Emile Ollivier and the Liberal Empire of Napoleon III.* Oxford, 1963.

ZF   Zellner, L. A. *Ueber Franz Liszt's Graner Festmesse und ihre Stellung zur geschichtlichen Entwicklung der Kirchenmusik: Ein Beitrag zum wesenhaften Verständnisse dieses Werkes.* Vienna, 1858.

Index

Page numbers in italic refer to main entries.

Aachen (Germany), 227, 258*n.*, 269, 283, 503
  Kur- und Bade-Liste 219*n.*
  Lower Rhine Music Festival (1857), 101, 122*n.*, 187, 218, 259, 279, 281*n.*, 296, *416–21*
  Rose Baths, 219, 421
Abdul-Medjid Khan (1823–1861), Sultan of Turkey (1839–1861), 67
Abend-Post (Berlin), 174*n.*
Abt, Franz (1819–1885), 125, 265
Adelburg, August Ritter von (1830–1873), 387
Adrian I, Pope (772–795), 469*n.*
Agoult, Count Charles Louis Constance d' (1790–1873), 581
Agoult, Countess Marie Catherine Sophie d' (1805–1876), 20, 25–26 and *n.*, 50–51, 85*n.*, 99*n.*, 217*n.*, 221, 235, 368, 370–72, 380*n.*, 420, 425, 426, 429–32, 431–32*n.*, 447–48, 451, 452–53, 458, 460, 464, 471, 581
  Claire (daughter, see Charnacé), 458 and *n.*
  Croissy château, 436, 437*n.*
  as "Daniel Stern," 51*n,* 436
  daughters' dowries, 439 and *n.*, 466–67*n.*
  "Diotyma," 245*n.*
  financial position of, 435*n.*
  as Liszt's literary "collaborator," *370–72,* 381
  the Maison Rose, 436 and *n.*, 447, 448, 449*n.*, 467*n.*
  meeting with Liszt (1861), *542–43n.*
  as "Nélida," 50 and *n.*, 420
  WRITINGS
  Esquisses morales, 471

  Histoire de la Révolution de 1848, 436 and *n.*
  Mémoires, 371–72, 542*n.*
  Nélida, 51*n,* 248, 449*n.*
"Agriffina," the Gypsy woman, 44
Agthe, Rosa, *see* Milde
Aiud (Nagyenyed) Kindergarten Fund, 6
Akadémiai Értesítő (Budapest), 376*n.*, 388*n.*
Albach, Father Stanislaus (1795–1853), 68 and *n.*, 84*n.*
  Botanik, 68*n.*
  diaries of, 69*n.*
Albert, Prince Consort of Victoria (1819–1861), 133
Alexander the Great (356–323 B.C.), 469*n.*
Alexander I (1777–1825), Tsar of Russia (1801–1825), 92
Alexander II (1818–1881), Tsar of Russia (1855–1881), 262*n.*, 515, 517*n.*–18*n.*, 532, 564
Alexander, C.F. (piano maker, Breslau), 4–5
Alexandra (maid at Altenburg), 56*n.*, 78
Alexandre et fils (harmonium makers, Paris), 77*n.*
  three-manual "piano-organ," 77 and *n.*, 333, 402
Allgemeiner Deutscher Musikverein, 242, 299, 335*n.*, 511, 547*n.*
Allgemeine Musikalische Zeitung (Leipzig), 284*n.*
Almanach de Gotha, 518*n.*, 539
Altenburg, the, 8, 9, 11, 33, 54, 74–87, 104, 130, 131, 139, 141, 142, 143*n,* 145, 170, 171 and *n.*, 179, 184, 188, 189, 191, 192 and *n.*, 194–95, 206, 213, 227, 229–30, 241, 243,

A NOTE ON THE TYPE

The text of this book was set via computer-driven cathode ray tube in Bembo, the well-known monotype face. The original cutting of Bembo was made by Francesco Griffo of Bologna only a few years after Columbus discovered America. It was named after Pietro Bembo, the celebrated Renaissance writer and humanist scholar who was made a cardinal and served as secretary to Pope Leo X. Sturdy, well-balanced, and finely proportioned, Bembo is a face of rare beauty. It is, at the same time, extremely legible in all of its sizes.